BRAINWASHED FOR WAR: PROGRAMMED TO KILL

MATTHIAS CHANG

BRAINWASHED FOR WAR: PROGRAMMED TO KILL

MATTHIAS CHANG'S
BRAINWASHED FOR WAR PROGRAMMED TO KILL

ISBN 967-69-0674-3
Copyright © 2005, Matthias Chang

Published in America by
AMERICAN FREE PRESS
645 Pennsylvania Avenue SE, Suite 100
Washington, D.C. 20003
United States
www.americanfreepress.net

For further information, please contact the author at
Suite 1001, 10th Floor, Plaza Permata,
No. 6, Jalan Kampar, off Jalan Tun Razak,
50400 Kuala Lumpur, Malaysia.
or E-mail: matthias@skzcchambers.com

The Author asserts his moral right
to be identified as the author of this work

First Malaysian Edition	December 2005	
Reprint Malaysian Edition	January 2006	
First American Edition	October 2006	3,000 copies
Second American Edition	February 2007	2,000 copies

Originally published in Malaysia by
THINKER'S LIBRARY SDN. BHD. (110008-D)
123, Jalan Jasa 3, Taman Jasa, Sungai Tua,
68100 Batu Caves, Selangor Darul Ehsan
Malaysia
E-mail: thinkers@tm.net.my

Dedication:

To my parents,
Paul and Katherine Chang,
for bringing me up in the way
they did: the shared values,
the discipline to excel
and the strength to overcome
prejudice and bigotry.
And for keeping the family together.
87 and still keeping the pace;
Long may you both run life's race.

And to Mr. Willis A. Carto,
America's most consistent and
outspoken voice against Zionism.

Table of Contents

❑ **ACKNOWLEDGEMENTS**   *ix*

❑ **PUBLISHER'S PREFACE**   *xii*

❑ **INTRODUCTION**   *xv*

❑ **PART 1 : A CENTURY OF WARS AND CONTINUING...**   1

Chapter 1   : The Economics of War Part 1: War is Big Business   3
Chapter 2   : The Economics of War Part 2: Paper Money and War   14
Chapter 3   : The War Constitution of the 20th Century   22
Chapter 4   : The Mindset of Warmongers   35
Chapter 5   : The National Security State—Military State Capitalism   45
Chapter 6   : The Megadeath Intellectuals and the War Constitution
              of the 21st Century   61

❑ **PART 2 : FUTURE WARS**   77

Chapter 7   : Perpetual Wars Part 1: Burgers and Bullets   79
Chapter 8   : Perpetual Wars Part 2: Back to Hot Wars Again   92
Chapter 9   : Act 2, Scene 1: The WMD Lies, Again   101
Chapter 10 : Another War Party: First Get the Sunnis, Next the Shiites! 115
Chapter 11 : Dirty Wars: The Brutality Business   126
Chapter 12 : Pain Merchants' Trail of Blood, Broken Bones and the
              Odor of Death   140

❑ **PART 3 : THE PSYCHOLOGY OF WAR:**
   THE MAKING OF WAR JUNKIES   155

Chapter 13 : Torture and Murder Inc.: The Brutality Business Revisited 157
Chapter 14 : The Brainwashed Mind Part 1:
              New Technologies for Political Control   172

Chapter 15 : The Brainwashed Mind Part 2:
          The Secrets of Mind Control   187
Chapter 16 : The Mind Rapists: Inside the Dark Labyrinth   204
Chapter 17 : War Propaganda Part 1: PsyOps in the 21st Century   217
Chapter 18 : War Propaganda Part 2: Half-Truths, Limited Truths and Lies 207

❑ **PART 4 : ENDGAME: THE MANCHURIAN CANDIDATE**
            VS THE AWAKENED MIND   **247**

Chapter 19 : Packaging War Part 1: The "Truth" Peddlers   249
Chapter 20 : Packaging War Part 2: The "Truth" Forgers   261
Chapter 21 : The War Criminals—They Hang Them, Don't They?   275
Chapter 22 : The Empire Mindset—The Geographical
          Combatant Commander   288

❑ **POSTSCRIPT**   **302**

❑ **APPENDICES**   **315**

Appendix 1   : George Kennan's Long Telegram   317
Appendix 2   : The Sources of Soviet Conduct by X (George Kennan) 332
Appendix 3   : NSC 68: US Objectives & Programs for National Security 349
Appendix 4   : Winston Churchill's Iron Curtain Speech   406
Appendix 5   : PNAC: Letter to President Clinton of January 26,1998 418
Appendix 6   : PNAC: Letter to President Bush of September 20,2001 421
Appendix 7   : PNAC: Letter to President Bush of April 3, 2002   424
Appendix 8   : Joint Chiefs of Staff Joint Vision 2010   428
Appendix 9   : Joint Chiefs of Staff Joint Vision 2020   449
Appendix 10 : Executive Summary:
             Doctrine for Joint Nuclear Operations   472
Appendix 11 : US Space Command Vision for 2020   479
Appendix 12 : Executive Summary:
             Doctrine for Joint Psychological Operations   485
Appendix 13 : Executive Summary:
             The World with Commanders' Areas of Responsibility   490
Appendix 14 : The National Intelligence Strategy of the
             United States of America   497

❑ **INDEX**   **513**

Acknowledgements

After completing my first book, *Future FastForward* in February 2005, I was exhausted but happy as the response was better than I had expected. I had no intention to write another book, though I had enough research materials for at least two more.

But the warmongers did not let up in their campaign to reconfigure the world, in particular the Middle East. One would have thought that after all the exposé regarding the lies that led to the illegal invasion of Iraq, people would wise up to the dirty tricks of the Bush-Blair war cabal. The same modus operandi was being employed in the preparation for the war against Iran and Syria, but the Malaysian mass media seem to be oblivious to the extension of the war to Syria and Iran. The Iraq war is no longer headline news.

The Malaysian mindset reflects a "brainwashed mind", brainwashed for war, to accept the inevitable slaughter of the innocents in the coming months and years. Reading the newspapers convinced me more than ever that we need to change our attitude. I have no pretensions as to the impact of this book on the Malaysian psyche, but I do want to make a difference, no matter how futile it may be to some of my critics.

By early October, I had the basic outline for the book and plunged head on into further research, augmenting what I had gathered thus far. The next five weeks were "turbo-charged weeks" of intense concentration and focused typing with my laptop. In such a mood and environment, anything can overturn the apple cart. But I was blessed by having a family that understood my intensity and the need for peace and quiet. Having a workaholic "messing up the place" is a real test of patience and tolerance, and there were an abundance of both. Therefore my thanks, love and gratitude go first to my family, for being there. They gave me the silence that I needed so desperately, never intruding nor demanding my attention and time. Thank you guys, I will always love you. They understood and in silence inspired me.

I must thank *American Free Press* for coming forward to publish my second book. They did a fantastic job on my first book, *Future Fast-Forward* and I am lost for words to express my heartfelt appreciation for their confidence in the project. Special mention goes to Mr. Willis Carto, the spiritual founder of *American Free Press*. He is a remarkable man, having persisted over 55 years, bringing truth to the American people in the groundbreaking newspaper *The Spotlight*. When it was destroyed, protegés of Mr. Carto launched the *American Free Press* to continue the struggle. Such a faith in one's vision and the resilience to see it through is rare in the annals of journalism and publishing. Long may he continue. In recognition of his contribution I would like to dedicate the American Edition of my book to this courageous American Patriot, as well as to my parents.

Michael Collins Piper is a very dear friend and it was during his visit to Malaysia in June that he brought up the idea to publish an American edition. And within months, it has become a reality. His dedication to his craft is an inspiration and it is my fervent hope that he will make time to come Malaysia again so that *American Free Press* will have a second home in Malaysia.

Last, but not least a very special thank you to Paul Angel for the hard work in bringing out the American edition and the brilliant cover design. You are truly an angel on my shoulders. Your support and dedication is much appreciated.

To my editor, Mustafa Zubair, a very special wordsmith and a gentleman, my special thanks for the support and many fine touches, and putting the hours even during the Raya holidays. May God continue to bless you and your family.

When my first book was published many Muslims and non-Muslims came up to me and asked, "How come you got a Muslim to edit your book?" I was infuriated by these questions. Faith or religion was never an issue; our endeavors were for a common goal and that was reason enough for sharing. But it certainly does reflect the brainwashed mind of our society, and how so many have succumbed to the venomous propaganda of the war cabal which can only survive on the politics of divide and rule. How we live by labels! It is pathetic! We have to overcome this impediment if we intend to be a family.

As in *Future FastForward*, let me once again reiterate that the views expressed in this book are entirely mine and do not in any way represent those of the organizations, institutions or governments that I may be acquainted with. Any reference to any individual or organization, directly or indirectly, is merely for the historical record.

Finally, I seek your indulgence and understanding for any errors that might have occurred during the printing process. Any error, if duly notified, shall be rectified in subsequent editions.

Matthias Chang
September 21, 2006
Kuala Lumpur

Publisher's Preface

Eight months has passed since the publication of *Future FastForward: The Zionist Anglo-American Empire Meltdown.* Although there were some criticisms levelled at us from some corners, these were notably few and far between. They were mostly from pro-western establishment sympathizers who would pour righteous indignation at the author's aggressive approach in summing up his conclusions and forwarding his opinions, but who could only mumble unintelligible ramblings as refutation against the irrefutable mountain of documented evidence presented in *Future Fast-Forward.*

This comes as no surprise to us, for these people have been fed no other information other than misinformation throughout their lives. They had formed the unfortunate habit of swallowing fictitious facts in popular dailies and the Zionist-controlled mass media[1] hook, line and sinker; who could not—or simply would not—recognize media propaganda for what it is; and thus to whom seemed the representation in *Future FastForward* a conspiracy theory of the first water!

However, we are more than glad that the book has been generally well received by the reading public. Indeed, many had expressed astonishment on what they had learnt from that tome of revelations. They are those who had the ability to differentiate between fact and fiction; who had the intellectual honesty to accept facts as facts.

And this brings us to this volume: *Brainwashed for War: Programmed to Kill.* Despite the unfolding of the numerous lies that led to the illegal invasion and criminal occupation of Iraq by the US,

---

1   Refer to the author's first book, *Future FastForward: The Zionist Anglo-American Empire Meltdown*, (2005, Thinker's Library), Ch. 8, pp. 111–126, for a detailed discussion of how the Zionists have completely usurped the control of the global mass media.

the Bush-Blair duo of Zionist front men continues to terrorize the legitimate regimes of the Middle East, in particular Iran, by using the same stale lies of possession and manufacture of the kind of weapons which only the US and its allies may own (and use). The terms have been simplified since the decimation of Iraq, but the *modi operandi* remain remarkably the same. And yet, surprisingly, no one had as much as breathed a sigh of discontent, much less voice their opposition to these oppressive tyrants. The world remains indifferent while the power elites prepare to continue their killing spree!

The reason for this nonchalance among the masses is quite simple: we have been utterly brainwashed! To many, the harebrained lies and unfounded accusations of the Dynamic Duo are no longer convincing, and the US and its allies are clearly seen as opinionated dictatorial aggressors. Yet, we feel no sympathy for our fellow humans because we have been brainwashed to be unable to empathize with these victims of tyranny.

It is happening to some other people far away, it doesn't concern me, is the thought **IMPLANTED** in our collective conscience. But by remaining silent, we are aiding and abetting the murderers! By our silence, we are already complicit in the coming genocide of innocent peoples being planned by Bush and his Knights in the Oval Office! In short, we are killing them with our silence!

> Human beings are so made that the ones who do the crushing feel nothing; it is the person crushed who feels what is happening. Unless one has placed oneself on the side of the oppressed, to feel with them, one cannot understand.

The above quotation of Simone Weil,[2] suffices to explain the reason for the publication of *Brainwashed for War Programmed to Kill*. It is truly an ardent attempt by the erudite author to deprogram our programmed minds so that we regain our ability to look upon other human beings as we gaze upon ourselves and to be able to empathize with their predicament.

We must all—each and every one of us—free ourselves from the mental enslavement of the power elites, and become one with

---

2   Simone Weil (1909-43), French social philosopher, mystic, and political activist, whose writings influenced French and English social thought. Although a Jewess, Weil abandoned her Jewish heritage to embrace Christianity, but refused to join an organized church.

humanity at large; to recognize all human beings as a part of the divine whole and not by class, race, or religious differences; and to remove all subconscious notions of the *GOYIM* [3] from our mindset and to become TRULY HUMAN. As the great Saadi Shirazi[4] said:

> All Adam's sons are limbs of one another,
> Each of the self-same substance as his brothers,
> So, while one member suffers ache and grief,
> The other members cannot win relief;
> Thou, who are heedless of thy brother's pain,
> It is not right at all to name thee MAN.

In the following pages, the secret mind-control operations carried out by the Mossad, the CIA, the MI6, and other colonialist intelligence agencies are unravelled. Appended to the text are 14 must-read appendices which are historical documents on public records, published reports and intelligence manuals.

It is the sincere hope of the author and publisher that this work would serve to liberate the mental subservience of all the "liberated peoples" of the world from the Zionist imperialist powers so that we may at last attain TRUE FREEDOM.

Amen.

---

3   The Hebrew term "goyim" (singular, "goy"), translated as "gentiles" in English, actually means "nation" or "people". That, however, is only the etymological meaning. In the article, "Are Goyim Human?" by Michael Samuel, it is explained from an exegesis of the **Jewish Talmud** that this term also means **non-human**, for it is the belief of the Jews that each Jew has 3 creators: God and his parents; and **each non-Jew has 4 creators: God, his parents, and the Serpent. So, when a Zionist Jew calls non-Jews "goyim", he is also calling them non-humans!** We urge all readers to read this article @ http://resistance.jeeran.com/judaism/articles/chabad2.htm. Or, if the link has expired, email thinkers@tm.net.my to request a PDF version of the article from Thinker's Library.

4   The great Iranian philosopher, poet and mystic Mosleh al-Din Saadi Shirazi (c. 1210–1290) is known as the Genius of Shiraz. His prose and poetry has greatly influenced not only those great philosophers of the past, but many philosophers and students of philosophy of our time as well.

Introduction

> And when war did come we told youth, who had to get us out of it, tall tales of what it really is and of the clover beds to which it leads.
>
> **— Sir James Mathew Barrie**[1]

> People do not believe lies because they have to, but because they want to.
>
> **— Malcolm Muggeridge**[2]

> Make the lie big, make it simple, keep saying it, and eventually they will believe it.
>
> **— Adolf Hitler**[3]

I had often asked myself the question, since my student days when demonstrating against the war in Vietnam, the death squads in Latin America, the apartheid regime in South Africa and now the fascist wars against the Muslims, what must we do to get ordinary folks to come out to demand that political leaders who wage wars of aggression and genocide—the supreme crime—be tried and when found guilty, executed for war crimes?

It has been forty years and still counting, yet we are staring at the same problem, with seemingly no solution in sight. But there is a reason for this seemingly insoluble difficulty.

The colonial powers exploited our people, plundered our economy and over the years, tortured and raped our men and women, massacred hundreds of thousands, and yet when we struggled and won our freedom, there was no accounting. As a people and as a

1   Cited by Arthur Ponsonby, *Falsehood in Wartime* (1929, George Allen and Unwin)
2   Source: www.thinkexist.com
3   Ibid.

nation, we were free and independent until we were enslaved by colonialism. When we broke the chains of enslavement, we were brainwashed to the extent that we were thankful and grateful to the British colonial masters for granting us "independence."

The granting of "independence" by the colonial powers to the "native rebels" throughout the British Empire, when staring at the face of defeat, must rank as the most brilliant imperialist propaganda ploy ever to be conceived and executed.

It was not for the colonial powers to grant us "independence" but our birthright to reclaim it back. We won the battle to oust the colonial powers from our shores, the majority by legitimate armed struggle. Yet as victors, we did not demand reparations for the loss and damage suffered by our peoples. Instead, we prostrated before the "White Queen" to express our gratitude. There were even those who were so proud of having been conferred the OBE or MBE.[4]

Herein is the strategic difference between the mindset of the imperial powers (the British, French, Dutch, Portuguese, Spanish and the Americans) and the liberated peoples. Even in defeat, the British colonialist through propaganda warfare was able to turn the tables on us and make us feel the lesser of the two. Brilliant! This propaganda strategy has been replicated by other colonialists post-World War II.

Countries which have "obtained independence" from Britain, on their anniversary date, celebrate "Independence Day." Even the United States of America, whose struggle against King George's colonial rule, called the American Revolution, still celebrates the fourth of July as "Independence Day." George Washington led the militias to a resounding victory over the British military might. A bloody armed struggle! A more fitting title to the historic document, *The Declaration of Independence*, would be *A Declaration of Freedom*.

Let us recap what was declared in the first two paragraphs of that historic document.

> When in the Course of human events, it becomes necessary for one people to dissolve the political bands which have connected them with another, and to assume among the Powers of the earth, the separate and equal station to which the Laws of Nature and of Nature's God entitle them, a decent respect

4   OBE = Order of the British Empire; MBE = Member of the British Empire

to the opinions of mankind requires that they should declare the causes which impel them to the separation.

We hold these truths to be self-evident, that all men are created equal, that they are endowed by their Creator with certain unalienable Rights, that among these are Life, Liberty, and the pursuit of Happiness. That to secure these rights, Governments are instituted among Men, deriving their just powers from the consent of the governed. That whenever any Form of Government becomes destructive of these ends, it is the Right of the People to alter or to abolish it, and to institute new Government, having its foundation on such principles and organizing its powers in such form, as to them shall seem most likely to effect their Safety and Happiness. Prudence, indeed, will dictate that Governments long established should not be changed for light and transient causes; and accordingly all experience hath shown that mankind are more disposed to suffer, while evils are sufferable, than to right themselves by abolishing the forms to which they are accustomed. But when a long train of abuses and usurpations pursuing invariably the same Object evinces a design to reduce them under absolute Despotism, it is their right, it is their duty, to throw off such Government, and to provide new Guards for their future security. Such has been the patient suffrance of these Colonies; and such is now the necessity which constrains them to alter their former Systems of Government. The history of the present King of Great Britain is a history of repeated injuries and usurpations, all having in direct object the establishment of an absolute Tyranny over these States. To prove this, let Facts be submitted to a candid world.

The American people rebelled against the tyranny of King George III and seized power by armed struggle. But the U.S. has forgotten their history and has assumed the role of the British imperialists. She is now the undisputed superpower and sole hyperpower.[5] Incredible!

Such is the power and legacy of British colonial rule and propaganda.

I can anticipate the reaction of my readers. Before you criticize me, have you ever asked yourselves the question, why should we be

5 Ziauddin Sardar and Merryl Wyn Davies, *Why Do People Hate America?* (2002, Icon Books). The term "hyperpower" was first used in their book to describe the U.S. as "a nation so powerful that it affects the lives of people everywhere."

grateful to the colonial powers?

Let me use this simple analogy. Suppose a group of hoodlums came to your neighborhood and stole the cars, wrecked the houses and injured several of your neighbors and members of your family, and they then demanded a monthly "protection money" in the form of a "local tax" which you paid over fearfully. And let's suppose that this went on for several years until one fine day, the neighborhood decided enough was enough and began to organize to counter the ruffians. The lot of you first went after the corrupt police force who failed to take any action against the hoodlums, and then went after the invading hoodlums. Faced with the overwhelming force of your entire neighborhood up in arms, the hoodlums surrendered. Now, would you and your family then **THANK THE HOODLUMS** for the end to the bullying, humiliation and plunder; or would you **DEMAND COMPENSATION** for the loss you had suffered at their hands over the years? And, bear in mind that it is a given that had you failed to subdue those hoodlums, they would have exacted a heavy price for your audacity in challenging their might and authority. There would have been hell to pay!

Propaganda warfare, mind control and brainwashing are the subject matter of this book and the aforesaid discussion on "independence" illustrates succinctly the effectiveness and consequences of a well executed propaganda strategy. History has shown us how the British retreated from "direct rule" to that of "indirect rule" to maintain her stranglehold on her colonies. And although "independent", nothing much have changed in the former colonies of the British Empire, as we are still trapped in the mental straightjacket left behind by the Brits! We still believe in their lies. This is almost obscene!

Mao Tse Tung said that "political power grows out of the barrel of a gun." But this trite point was not the ideological invention of the commies, but the age-old adage of the imperialists and colonialists. The spice trade was always conducted peacefully by traders coming as far away as the Middle East and China. No one thought of monopolizing the market by armed suppression to the detriment of the majority. No doubt there was economic competition, but it was conducted on a level playing field: **that was until the Europeans came with their gun boats.**

By military might and brutality they conquered, plundered and oppressed the people of the third world. Colonial political power came explosively out of the barrels of their then muskets, and now in the 21st century from depleted uranium munitions, cluster bombs, napalm bombs, missiles, M-16s, 50mm machine guns, etc.

Lawful resistance by armed struggle permitted under international law is demonized as terrorism, and the heroic resistance fighters labeled as "terrorists." And we echo uncritically these labels! We are taught from an early age that in such circumstances, the better way is to "negotiate" for freedom. But history has shown that the colonialists were compelled to negotiate only when they realized that armed rebellion would be inevitable and that they would not, in that event, be able to impose "indirect rule."

The British therefore brilliantly created the political theatre of the "independence musical." From the earliest times, nations and people have always **UNILATERALLY** declared their political authority without having the need to seek from another authority for legitimacy, until the creation of "independence" by the British, as an instrument for indirect rule. Take the history of Malaya. The Sultans wielded their own authority, and presided over their kingdoms. Such authority was conferred by traditions and customs of the people. Through alliances and treaties, they may have merged their kingdoms, but they did not seek external conferment of legitimacy.

Like the creation of paper fiat money by the Federal Reserve System (and other central banks), the British by a simple stroke of a pen arrogated to themselves the power and right to confer "independence" to us "lesser mortals."

Pause and think this over carefully, do not react emotionally. Is this not the perverse logic of the colonialists? How stupid could we have been at the material time in history? Having confronted and defeated the bully, we then implored the bully to leave us be!

I challenge any historian to rebut my contention that the single most effective strategic propaganda tool of the imperialists for the mental enslavement of the "liberated subjects" was the act of "granting independence" by the colonial powers. The historic struggle and sacrifice of the people against colonialism is slam-dunked into the memory hole: that part of history is wiped clean and any heroic figures consigned to obscure footnotes. What I wanted to highlight here was the so-called magnanimous granting of "independence" by the colonial powers and, as Neill Ferguson, the British historian puts it, the benign and benevolent empire and how we have been "civilized" and transformed from tribesmen to loyal subjects of the Commonwealth! When the "White Queen" summons our services, we volunteer our brave young men to serve her cause in Africa and vice versa.

We have been brainwashed from an early age to respect the British Raj and his military might, his standards of justice and equity and his values, which keep changing from time to time as his military might ebbs and flows. The "British Standard" as applied to engineering specifications, production quality, etc., has its equivalents in international relations, trade and warfare.

My point here is that we have been brought up through the British mandated system of education to believe in the "history" as laid down by the system. There are two realities: one for the conqueror and occupier; one for the victims. I want you to commit to memory and then transmit to all your children what Thomas Friedman, an icon of the Zionist mass media, has said about this reality:

> The hidden hand of the market will never work without a hidden fist – McDonalds cannot flourish without McDonnell Douglas, the builder of the F-15. And the hidden fist that keeps the world safe for Silicon Valley's technologies is called the United States Army, Air Force, Navy and Marine Corps.[6]

This is a very different perspective of world trade, globalization, etc., than the normal diet of clichés, headlines, and conventional wisdom which you find in your daily newspapers, business magazines and so-called research papers from think tanks which you so gladly consume with gusto. Thomas Friedman's reality is grounded on the security interests of the United States and her allies and what is needed to ensure their protection. The other reality projected to us by their propaganda machinery is grounded on lies, disinformation, limited truths and half-truths.

A simple exercise will illustrate my point.

Let us take the cue from Thomas Friedman's perspective. Name me a third world country or a third world multinational that sees the world in Friedman's context: that when we invest in another country or trade with our neighbors, their resources are consid-

---

6   Thomas Friedman, "A Manifesto for the Fast World", The New York Times magazine, March 28, 1999.

ered "our security interests" and our investments need to have a "hidden fist" for protection. Has any third world country ever dispatched her miniscule army, air force, navy or special forces (if any) to protect its economic outreach? Thus, when we send our delegations to negotiate treaties and conventions, we are approaching the issues from two different realities and perspectives. Absent this basic understanding, we will in no uncertain terms be screwed. I am not surprised at all that after all the trade talks, from one city to another (Singapore, Uruguay, Doha, Cancun, etc.) there is but an impasse. What else can we expect?

McDonalds goes hand-in-hand with the McDonnell Douglas. Our *roti canai* [7] has not even ventured abroad, what more to be followed by a local gunslinger!

The status quo remains to the imperialists' advantage. They have never stopped waging wars to further their economic agenda. But these wars, we are told, are for the cause of freedom, democracy and to defeat extremism and whatever "isms" they can invent. Right now the flavor is the "War on Terrorism" and "Militant Islam." And we sheepishly accept such gobbledegook as rationale for wars without more!

Brainwashed!

In the inside cover of the book *Bodyguard of Lies*,[8] there is the following passage:

> "In wartime" Winston Churchill told Joseph Stalin at Teheran in November 1943, "truth is so precious that she should always be attended by a bodyguard of lies." Churchill's remarks were more than a witticism. They were a description of another front in the war against the Axis, a clandestine war of deception and detection, a series of battles that may have had as much effect on the outcome of the war as the military battles they hid or discovered.

Let me assure you that the "truth" referred to by Churchill was far from the truth you understand to mean when this brutal war was waged. The "truths" that we were given, "to defeat fascism", "to fight for a free world", "to preserve civilization", etc., are in fact the "body-

---

7   A perennial favorite dish among Malaysians, and dubbed by some as the Malaysian pancake. "Roti" is "bread" in Malay, and "canai" is a corruption of Chennai from where it originated.

8   Anthony Cave Brown, *Bodyguard of Lies*, (1977, Star Book)

guard of lies" to hide the **REAL REASON** for war: to secure the Zionists' interests. Rabbi Felix Mendelssohn was very frank and direct when he said:

> The Second World War is being fought for the defense of the fundamentals of Judaism.[9]

Chaim Weizmann, the then President of the World Jewish Congress on December 3, 1942 in New York City admitted:

> We are not denying and we are not afraid to confess, this war is our war and it is waged for the liberation of Jewry ... stronger than all fronts together is our front, that of Jewry. We are not only giving this war our financial support on which the entire war production is based.... We are also providing our full propaganda power which is the moral energy that keeps this war going. The guarantee of victory is predominantly based on weakening the enemy forces, on destroying them in their own country, within the resistance. And we are the Trojan horse in the enemy's fortress. Thousands of Jews living in Europe constitute the principal factor in the destruction of our enemy. There, our front is a fact and the most valuable aid for victory.

To buttress this exposé, in my book, *Future FastForward,* I quoted in extenso the contrition of Sir Hartle Shawcross, who was the British Chief Prosecutor at the Nuremberg Trials and later Attorney-General. This is what he said:[10]

> Step by step, I have arrived at the conviction that the aims of Communism in Europe are sinister and fatal. At the Nuremberg trials I, together with my Russian Colleagues, condemned Nazi aggression and terror. I believe now that Hitler and the German people did not want war. But we [Britain] declared war on Germany, intent on destroying it, in accordance with our principle of the balance of power, and we were encouraged by the Americans [Jews] around Roosevelt.

> We ignored Hitler's pleading not to enter into war. Now we are forced to realize that Hitler was right. He offered us the co-operation of Germany: instead, since 1945, we have been facing the immense power of the Soviet Empire. I feel ashamed and humiliated to see that the aims we accused Hitler of are being relentlessly pursued now, only under a different label.

9 Reported in the Jewish Chronicles, October 8, 1942.

10 Page 170, *Future FastForward*, (2005, Thinker's Library) citing the speech entitled "Ashamed and Humiliated" given by him at Stourbridge in March 12, 1948 and reported by AP and the Times of London.

This is one version of history which I am sure you are not familiar with. And why are we kept in the dark of this confession, coming from a man who was the British Chief Prosecutor at the Nuremberg War Crimes Tribunal? Churchill's "bodyguard of lies" ensured that we will never know the **REAL TRUTH**:—that as the lackey of the Zionists—**he conned the entire British nation to wage a war for the Zionists and to facilitate the creation of Israel soon after the war in 1948.**

At the very centre of this very elaborate deception is the London Controlling Section (LCS), a secret bureau set up by Churchill himself and located near his command post under the pavement of Westminster. Anthony Cave Brown commented in his excellent book, *Bodyguard of Lies,* that British "special means" (covert warfare) have a long history, longer than any other power—

> for over five hundred years her statesmen and generals had used them to establish first a kingdom and then an empire, and to defend both against their enemies. They had outwitted the Spanish, the French and the Dutch in previous centuries; and once before in this century they had been forced to fight the aggrandizement of Germany....

For those who have not been schooled in the art of psychological warfare, the ensuing discussions will seem to be flights of fancy, a good yarn. But let me sum up the issues raised in this book by the following two quotations which will be your guide in understanding **THE OTHER REALITY**—that of the imperialist warmongers. Read, understand and memorize these words.

The Soldiers Handbook 1869:

> We are bred up to feel it a disgrace ever to succeed by falsehood... we will keep hammering along with the conviction that honesty is the best policy, and that truth always wins in the long run. These pretty little sentiments do well for a child's copy book, but a man who acts on them had better sheathe his sword forever.

Bodyguard of Lies:

> It was clear that Churchill and the LCS would stop at nothing to ensure secrecy and surprise for Neptune.[11] Even Churchill's choice of code name for the cover and deception operations that would attend Neptune revealed something of

---

11 A covert military operation to deceive Hitler, masterminded by Churchill.

their cunning, mercilessness and intent. Jael was the woman in the Song of Deborah of the Old Testament who committed one of the blackest acts of treachery in that long dark chronicle. For the Song tells how Deborah the Prophetess plotted with Barak, the commander of the Israelite army, to defeat Jabin, the King of Canaan, and Sisera, the Canaan commander who, with "nine hundred chariots of iron" had ruled the Israelites for twenty years. Their stratagem succeeded and Sisera was lured to battle at the foot of Mount Tabor.... "And the Lord discomfited Sisera, and all his chariots... and all the host of Sisera fell upon the edge of the sword; and there was not a man left." Sisera survived and fled the battlefield on foot and as he was trying to reach Canaan he happened upon the encampment of Heber, the Kenite, who was absent that day. But his wife Jael greeted him cordially and believing that a treaty of friendship existed between the Canaanites and the Kenites, Sisera asked for food and a place to rest. To this Jael agreed, and exhausted by battle and his flight, Sisera lay down upon her bed. When Sisera was deeply asleep, she took a hammer and a tent peg and smote the nail into his temples, and fastened it to the ground." Thus ended the Canaanites' rule of the Israelites. And thus, it was hoped, would Jael help the Allies end the rule of Hitler.

Therefore to dismiss the ensuing discussion as a "conspiracy theory", propaganda and/or a fiction of the imagination is to remain in mental enslavement and in time total subjugation by the Zionist Anglo-American war cabal. Keep an open mind. Read the entire book and then decide whether to believe or not to believe.

Part 1

A Century of Wars and Continuing ...

We have about 50% of the world's wealth, but only 6.3% of its population.... In this situation, we cannot fail to be the object of envy and resentment. Our real task in the coming period is to devise a pattern of relationships which will permit us to maintain this position of disparity.... To do so, we will have to dispense with all sentimentality and day-dreaming; and our attention will have to be concentrated everywhere on our immediate national objectives.... We should cease to talk about vague and... unreal objectives such as human rights, the raising of the living standards, and democratization. The day is not far off when we are going to have to deal in straight power concepts. The less we are then hampered by idealistic slogans, the better.

— **George Kennan, 1948**[1]

There is nothing new about terrorism. What is new since 9/11 is the chilling realization that the terrorist threat we thought we had contained within tolerable boundaries was not contained at all, menacing our well-being as a people, even our survival as a nation. This realization stems, first, from the scale of 9/11, and beyond that, from the apocalyptic vision of the terrorists themselves. The chill comes from knowing that there are... hundreds and perhaps thousands who are ready to die in order to kill. They cannot be deterred. They cannot be appeased. The terrorists kill and will accept death for a cause with which no accommodation is possible. That cause is militant Islam.

— **Richard Perle & David Frum, *An End to Evil***

1   Source: www.zmag.org/chomsky/sam/sam-1-2.html

1

The Economics of War Part 1:
War is Big Business

> War belongs to the province of business competition, which is
> also a conflict of human interest and activities.
>
> — **Karl von Clausevitz**

Empire Capitalism[1] and imperial mobilization can only be sustained by a war economy. And there must be wars to justify a war economy. Once we have grasped this essence of empire capitalism, we will be able to better appreciate why, when and how wars are started and who are the ultimate beneficiaries of wars.

Every day, in every hour and in every minute, we are being brainwashed for war and programmed to kill. First reaction: bullshit, another conspiracy theory; this is nuts! Think again. Read your daily newspapers and books on management and advertising and look out for terms related to warfare. Watch the movies and television programs and the underlying theme is unmistakable: to glorify war by showing that killing is fun and by promoting the macho man image, such as that personified by Sylvester Stallone in the *Rambo* trilogy and other hardcore action movies.

In their ground-breaking book, *Marketing Warfare*,[2] the authors, Al Ries and Jack Trout dedicated their book to Karl von Clausevitz, who they consider as one of the greatest marketing strategists the world has ever known. It was an international best-seller that changed the mindset of the marketing profession. The cover boasts that American corporations are using military strategies to outmaneuver,

---

1   The term "Empire Capitalism" was coined by the author and first employed in his book *Future FastForward: The Anglo-American Empire Meltdown* (2005, Thinker's Library).

2   Al Ries & Jack Trout, *Marketing Warfare*, (1986, McGraw-Hill Inc).

outflank and even ambush their competition. The authors gave a riveting account of the *Cola Wars, the Computer Wars, the Burger Wars and the Beer Wars.* But we are not talking about *Cola Wars* here, but real wars that kill and maim men, women and children; wars that destroy the very fabrics of our societies by even more sophisticated and hideous weapons invented by the leading scientific brains employed by the best universities throughout the world.

Major General Smedley Butler, USMC got it spot on when he wrote *War is a Racket.*[3] He warns us way back in 1933:

> War is just a racket. A racket is best described, I believe, as something that is not what it seems to the majority of the people. Only a small inside group knows what it is about. It is conducted for the benefit of the very few at the expense of the masses.

> I believe in adequate defense at the coastline and nothing else. If a nation comes over here to fight, then we'll fight. The trouble with America is that when the dollar only earns 6 percent over here, then it gets restless and goes overseas to get 100 percent. Then the flag follows the dollar and the soldiers follow the flag.

> I wouldn't go to war again as I have done to protect some lousy investment of the bankers. There are only two things we should fight for. One is the defense of our homes and the other is the Bill of Rights. War for any other reason is simply a racket.

> There isn't a trick in the racketeering bag that the military gang is blind to. It has its "finger men" to point out enemies, its "muscle men" to destroy enemies, its "brain men" to plan war preparations, and a "Big Boss" Super-Nationalistic-Capitalism.

This observation coming from a major-general should grab your attention. A soldier who has spent more than thirty-three years in military service has condemned war as a racket, but today, as in the past, we accept without question the warmongering of cowards, who during the Vietnam War sought refuge in the safety of the National Guards and academia, that wars are necessary to bring freedom and democracy to the third world, in particular the people in the Middle East. It is ironic that those who advocate wars, the members of the Neocon war cabal, have neither served in the military nor volunteered the services of their children to the frontlines.

War is big business. Retired U.S. Admiral Gene La Rocque remarked, "Military product is manufactured primarily not for the

3   Source: www.fas.org/man/semdley.htm

defense of the USA or of any other country but merely for profit."[4] A quick examination of some economic figures will substantiate the fact that war is indeed a racket that benefits essentially, the small elite of bankers and vested interests.

The Brookings Institution's *U.S. Nuclear Weapons Cost Study Project*[5] which was completed in 1998 has revealed some interesting data.

1. The cost of the Manhattan Project: U.S. $20 billion.

2. Total number of missiles built: 67,500.

3. Estimated constructions for more than 1,000 ICBM launch pads and silos, support facilities: U.S. $14 billion.

4. Total number of nuclear bombs built: 4,680.

5. Peak number of nuclear warheads and bombs in the stockpile/year: 32,193 in 1996.

6. Total number and types of nuclear warheads and bombs built—1945 till 1990—more than 70,000 and there were 65 different types.

7. Number of nuclear warheads requested by the Army in 1956/57: 151,000.

8. Number of designated targets for U.S. weapons in the Single Integrated Operational Plan (SIOP) in 1976: 25,000; 1986: 16,000 and 1995: 2,500.

9. Projected operational U.S. strategic warheads and bombs after full enactment of the Strategic Offensive Reduction Treaty in 2012: 1,700—2,200.

10. Additional strategic and non-strategic warheads not limited by the treaty that the U.S. military wants to retain as a "hedge" against unforeseen future threats: 4,900.

11. Fissile material produced: 104 metric tons of plutonium and 994 metric tons of highly enriched uranium.

---

4   Cited by Dr. Charles Mercieca in "When Peace Is The Enemy" @ www.informationclearinghouse. info/article9095.htm

5   Source: http://www.brook.edu/FP/PROJECTS/NUCWCOST/50.htm. This project was completed in August 1998 and resulted in a book, *Atomic Audit: The Costs and Consequences of U.S. Nuclear Weapons Since 1940*, edited by Stephen Schwartz.

12. Total known land area occupied by U.S. nuclear weapons bases and facilities: 15,654 square miles.

13. Number of secret Presidential Emergency Facilities built for use during and after a nuclear war: more than 75.

14. Volume of cubic meters of radioactive waste material resulting from weapons activities: 104,000,000.

15. Number of U.S. nuclear bombs lost in accidents and never recovered: 11.

16. Estimated 1998 spending on all U.S. nuclear weapons and weapons-related programs: U.S. $35.1 billion.

If war was good business way back then, it is generating super profits today for the defense industry big boys. The fiscal 2006 defense budget[6] of the United States is set to climb to U.S. $441 billion, a whopping increase of U.S. $21 billion over 2005. There is a provision of another U.S. $50 billion for the wars in Iraq and Afghanistan. The U.S. Congress plans to approve U.S. $79 billion for weapons procurement and U.S. $69 billion for military research and development. The leading beneficiaries for this war expenditure are: Lockheed-Martin, Boeing, Northrop-Grumman, Raytheon, General Dynamics, Honeywell and United Technologies.

Lockheed-Martin, the biggest U.S. defense contractor made U.S. $830 million in profits in the first six months of 2005, a massive jump of 41 percent as compared to the previous year. Projected sales for 2005 is up U.S. $38 billion and has orders worth another U.S. $73 billion. Lockheed produces the F-16 Fighting Falcon, the C-130J Super Hercules, the stealth fighter F-117 Nighthawk and F/A 22 Raptor.

Boeing saw sales up 8 percent to U.S. $27 billion and its military division posted an increase in profits of 16 percent to U.S. $1.7 billion. Boeing is also involved in the development of *Future Combat Systems (FCS)*, a U.S. $125 billion project that will allegedly enhance the effectiveness of U.S. soldiers in the battlefield with new very high-tech equipment and communications systems.

Northrop is responsible for developing advanced information technology systems which will enable weapons systems to be more efficient. It developed the *Kinetic Energy Interceptors Missile Defense*

6   Taipei Times, 8/21/05.

Battle Management Capabilities (KEI).[7] KEI is a mobile, land-based missile defense system that when deployed will be able to destroy an incoming hostile threat during its ascent phase of flight. Northrop has also been selected as the lead system integrator for unmanned ground vehicles under the U.S. Army's *Family of Integrated Rapid Response Equipment* (FIRRE) program. FIRRE is intended to provide a soldier with a variety of modular force protection equipment including unmanned air, ground and undersea platforms for sensors, weapons and support equipment.[8] The company is also developing the high-power chemical laser component of MDA's *Airborne Laser* (ABL) pro-gram and is the contractor for the *Mobile Tactical High-Energy Laser.* In 2004, earnings rose from U.S. $534 million to U.S. $776 million.

General Dynamics is another big player employing over 70,000 people worldwide and in 2004 had revenues exceeding U.S. $19 bil-lion. The company is responsible for rockets that can be fired from a variety of rotary and fixed platforms that include, among others, U.S. Apache and U.S. Marine Corps Cobra attack helicopters.[9]

Raytheon is a leader in missile defense systems, from surveil-lance to BMC3, to interceptors and kill vehicles. The company is the prime contractor for the *Patriot Weapon System* used in the Gulf Wars and the kinetic warhead for the sea-based *Aegis Ballistic Missile Defense* program.[10] In the first half of 2005, sales rose by 8 percent to U.S. $10.4 billion.

Special mention must be made of two U.S. companies, namely Bechtel and Halliburton. Defense experts have characterized Bechtel as "more powerful than the U.S. army." George Schultz, the former Secretary of State and CEO of Bechtel played a crucial role in pushing for the invasion of Iraq and was rewarded with an exclu-sive no-bid contract for the reconstruction of Iraq. Is it any wonder that the Bush war cabal was so determined to destroy the entire infrastructure of Iraq, as obviously there can be no reconstruction without destruction? Bechtel reported record profits for fiscal years 2003 and 2004, amounting to U.S. $17 billion and U.S. $17.4 billion respectively. It should be noted that Bechtel has close ties with the Saudi-based bin Laden family.

---

7   Source: www.primezone.com/newsroom/?d=77675
8   Ibid.
9   Ibid.
10 Source: www.globalsecurity.org/space/systems/kei.htm

Having Vice-President Dick Cheney as the former CEO certainly helps the rapacious Halliburton. War profits poured into its coffers in 2003 and 2004 amounting to U.S. $18 billion with revenues increasing by 80% between 2003 and 2004. It is the most corrupt U.S. company and in just one instance overbilled U.S. taxpayers U.S. $213 million for fuel transportation in war torn Iraq. CorpWatch did not mince their words when they said:

> "Halliburton's agenda is so merged with that of the Bush administration that questions raised by auditors, inspectors-general, and other independent agencies—not to mention corporate accountability groups—languish silently in Congress and the White House."[11]

It therefore comes as no surprise when Major General Smedley Butler courageously admitted that during his 33 years of military service he was a war racketeer.

> I spent most of my time being a high-class muscle man for Big Business, for Wall Street and for the bankers. In short, I was a racketeer, a gangster for capitalism. I helped make Mexico, especially Tampico, safe for American oil interests in 1914. I helped make Haiti and Cuba a decent place for the National City Bank boys to collect revenues in. I helped in raping a half a dozen Central American Republics for the benefit of Wall Street. The record of racketeering is long. I helped purify Nicaragua for the international banking house of Brown Brothers in 1909-1912. I brought light to the Dominican Republic for American sugar interest in 1916. In China I helped to see to it that Standard Oil went its way unmolested.

> During those years, I had, as the boys in the backroom would say, a swell racket. Looking back on it, I feel that I could have given Al Capone a few hints. The best he could do was to operate his racket in three districts. I operated on three continents.

It was reported by Reuters[12] that world military spending rose for a sixth year running in 2004, growing by 5 percent to a whopping U.S. $1.04 trillion. The U.S. accounted for almost half of the global figure with an expenditure of U.S. $455 billion, more than the combined total of the 32 next most powerful nations. In 2003, U.S. war expenditure amounted to U.S. $405 billion. The United Kingdom is also hot on the

---

11 Source: www.commondreams.org/views05/0517.-33.htm. See also www.information clearinghouse.info/articles8904.htm.
12 Source: Peter Starck, Reuters, June 8, 2005

heels of the U.S. as arms merchant. Arm sales to Africa have risen to record levels in the last four years reaching the £1 billion mark.[13] Yet Blair has the audacity to put on the G8 show at Gleneagles that he would be leading the G8 countries to abolish poverty in Africa. Blair preaches freedom and democracy for Iraq but British arm merchants are supplying 90 percent of conventional weapons delivered in 2004, following the lifting of the arms embargo by the United Nations.[14] Jane Defense Weekly reported that Britain has been supplying more military equipment to Iraq in the first six months of 2005.[15]

According to the *SIPRI Yearbook 2005*,[16] the value of the combined arms sales of the top 100 companies in the world, excluding China, rose 25% in 2003 to U.S. $236 billion (in current dollars). Of the 100 companies, 38 are U.S. companies and together with the one based in Canada accounted for 63.2% of arms sales while 42 European companies (excluding Russian companies) accounted for 30.5% of sales. Five countries dominate the arms trade, namely, the US, U.K., France, Germany and Russia.

UPI reported[17] that the war on terror, being fought in Iraq and Afghanistan, is the fourth-most expensive military operation in U.S. history, and is moving on to the No. 3 spot. In inflation-adjusted dollars, UPI said that the War on Terror ranks behind World War II, Vietnam and the Korean War. It was also reported that Yale University economist William Nordhaus told *The Christian Science Monitor* that by end of September 2005, the military cost of the War on Terror, which began shortly after 9/11, with the invasion of Afghanistan, will exceed U.S. $250 billion. Linda Bilmes, with the Kennedy School of government at Harvard University was quoted as saying that if the war lasts another five years, the total bill will be about U.S. $1.4 trillion.[18] War indeed is a racket!

In *Future FastForward: The Zionist Anglo-American Empire Meltdown*,[19] I had referred to the U.S. as a serial war criminal and as a nation nurtured in war. I take comfort that there are others who share my viewpoint. Recently, in an article published on May 22,

13 Source: Anthony Barnett, The Observer, June 12, 2005
14 Source: IRNA June 7, 2005 @ www.irna.ir
15 Source: Jane Defense Weekly, June 7, 2005
16 Stockholm International Peace Research Institute (SIPRI).
17 UPI, Aug.29, 2005—Terror War is 4th Most Expensive U.S. War.
18 Source: www.informationclearinghouse.info/article10032.htm.
19 (2005, Thinker's Library.)

2005,[20] Evan Augustine Peterson III of the American Center for International Law (ACIL) suggested that the U.S. is "addicted to war." He points out that unbeknownst to most Americans, the Department of Defense (DoD) currently lists 725 official military bases outside the country and another 969 inside, excluding the numerous secret bases. He added that:

> The American military-industrial complex is poised to monopolize the global armaments industry. And yet the War Party's leaders and the Pentagon's brass deem these astronomical expenditures so inadequate that they're requesting considerably larger expenditures to sustain or expand their Romanesque Pax Americana Imperium. Americans should be asking themselves why they're being advised that they cannot feel safe after they've made grossly disproportionate investments, by global standards, in what is by far the world's largest military? What do these exorbitantly expensive forces exist to do? Could it be that war's tangible rewards are so much greater for militarists than they are for the average citizen that the militarists are exaggerating the need for a 'Global War On Terror' merely to justify their empire?

Chalmers Johnson rightly observed[21] that the U.S. is a big bully that prefers to conduct its foreign policy through the use or the threat of force rather than negotiations.

More importantly—and this is hardly on the radar screens of most political analysts—the welfare of the American people has over the last sixty years been made dependent to a very large extent on the war economy. When the Pentagon's Base Realignment and Closure Commission (BRAC) made public its plans for base closures, it unleashed a vehement backlash. Senators were up in arms opposing any closure of bases in their states, as these bases provided employment and revenues for their supporters. The military, for example contributes as much as U.S. $42 billion annually to the Californian economy and U.S. $18 billion to San Diego's local economy. Senator Olympia Snowe, R-Maine called the recommendation to close military bases a "travesty and a strategic blunder of epic proportions on the part of the Defense Department." The Chairman of the House Armed Services Committee, Duncan Hunter, R-California

---

20 Evan Augustine Peterson III, J.D., www.informationclearinghouse.info/article8904.htm

21 Chalmers Johnson, *The Sorrows of Empire: Militarism, Secrecy and the End of the Republic*, (2004, Metropolitan Books).

also opposed the move, in particular the closure of the submarine base at New London, Connecticut.[22] In the result, BRAC had to scale back its base closure program.

Tom Engelhardt did not mince any words when he described the United States as a **"vast military camp."**

Put in historical terms, in the last decade and more, as the pace of our foreign wars picked up, we've left behind, after each one of them, a new set of bases like the droppings of some giant beast marking the scene with its scent. Bases were dropped into Saudi Arabia and the small Gulf emirates after our First Gulf War in 1991; into the former Yugoslavia after the Kosovo air war of 1999; into Pakistan, Afghanistan, and those former Central Asian SSRs after the Afghan War of 2001; and into Iraq after the invasion of 2003. War in Iraq, in turn, has spawned at least 106 bases of various sizes and shapes; while a low level but ongoing guerrilla conflict in Afghanistan has produced a plethora of fire bases, outposts, air bases, and detention centers of every sort. It's a matter of bases and prisons where there is opposition and just bases where there isn't. Most Americans, knowing next to nothing about our global bases or the Pentagon's basing policies, would undoubtedly be surprised to learn that ours is an empire of bases.[23]

President Bush and Tony Blair speak of peace and democracy. But the more they speak on peace, the more they prepare for war. Their favorite catchphrase "all options are on the table" should convince the doubting Thomases that when warmongers speak of peace, they are actually preparing for war.

One of the difficulties in writing a book such as this is to explain the mindset of the warmongers—how they camouflage their real intentions behind the rhetoric and sophistry. I began by reading the autobiographies and biographies of leaders who have engaged in wars to get right inside their minds, but I could not get the quotation that would settle the issue once and for all. One of the most effective propaganda techniques against truth seekers and their exposés on warmongers is to label them as "conspiracy theorists." I suffered my fair share of such labeling.

But my persistence paid off when I came across a quotation by

---

22 Source: www.cnn.com/2005/POLITICS/05/13base.closings

23 Tom Engelhardt, Bases, Bases Everywhere @ www.tomdispatch.com

President Ronald Reagan. Let me explain. Way back in the 50s and the 60s, the Communist Bloc (Soviet Union and China) was propagated as the threat and the enemy. The Domino Theory propounded by Secretary of State, John Foster Dulles was used to justify the Vietnam War and to halt the "communist invasion" of Southeast Asia. After all, Mr. Dulles did say that:

> The Chinese Communists' continuing lack of genuine goodwill for peace is being demonstrated in Indochina. As one of the United Nations members who must pass on representation, we must ask: 'Will it serve the interest of world order to bring into the United Nations a regime which is a convicted aggressor, which has not purged itself from aggression, and which continues to promote the use of force in violation of the principles of the United Nations?' I can find only the answer 'No.' I said at Berlin: 'It is one thing to recognize evil as a fact. It is another thing to take evil to one's breast and call it good.' That we shall not do.[24]

How then do we explain President Nixon's decision in 1972 to form a strategic alliance with China to counter-balance the Soviet Union? This is how President Ronald Reagan explained a few years later.

> Let me suggest something about Nixon's China visit that unfortunately, the President can't say, or for that matter, I can't say publicly without blowing the whole diplomatic game plan. It is true the President dressed this visit up in all the proper diplomatic, peaceful co-existence, forgive-and-forget trappings that are so much a part of the great international game. It is also true that this does confuse and disturb Republicans who have believed in his hard-headed knowledge of the communists, if nothing else. But let's look at it as a move in a very dangerous game where the stakes are freedom itself.
>
> **American public opinion will no longer tolerate wars of the Vietnam type**, because they no longer feel a threat, thanks to the liberal press, from communism, and they cannot interpret those wars as being really in the defense of freedom and our own country. (Emphasis added)

So the President, knowing of the disaffection between China and Russia, visits China, butters up the warlords, and let them be, because they have nothing to fear from us. Russia, therefore, has to

---

24 John Foster Dulles, speech before the Overseas Press Club, March 29, 1954, as reported in U.S. News & World Report, April 9, 1954.

keep its 140 divisions on the Chinese border; hostility between the two is increased; and we buy a little time and elbow room in a plain, simple strategic move, a million miles removed from the soft appeasement of previous Democratic administrations.[25]

It follows that a warmonger will never announce his true intentions, but will cover it up in nice diplomatic language and game plans. They know too well, that if the truth be spoken the people will never support wars of aggression. More importantly, these war profiteers would be lynched!

---

25 Cited by Howard S. Katz in *The Warmongers*, (1979 Books In Focus Inc), and as quoted by John Nordheimer in the New York Times, February 14, 1976.

2

The Economics of War Part 2: Paper Money and War

> There is no doubt the war made an enormous difference in the American Economy. Before the war, we had 15%, and maybe, sometime more, unemployed. A very stagnant, unhappy economy and the war—war production—production of munitions, production of armaments—put enormous sums of money into the economy ....
>
> **— Prof. J. K. Galbraith**[1]

It is not the purpose of this book to present a detailed analysis of the economics of war. However, to really appreciate war propaganda, we must try to understand the *real* economic reasons for war and the role of bankers in promoting wars throughout history. In my book, *Future FastForward*,[2] I devoted an entire chapter in explaining how the bankers finance wars. In this chapter I would like to correlate specifically the role of *Paper Money* and *War*.

Notwithstanding the fact that Henry Ford tried to warn us of the dangers of the warmongering bankers, when he said, *"it is well that the people of the nation do not understand our banking and monetary system, for if they did, I believe there would be a revolution before tomorrow morning"* nothing much has changed to warrant any optimism that the anti-war movements or peace organizations truly understand the *real* economic reasons for war.

War is big business, but it is not easy to rally the people in support of war. Every war must be paid for by the people, usually through

1 Interview given on Nov.28, 1995.

Source: www.gwu.edu/~nsarchiv/coldwar/interviews/episode-2/galbraith1.html.

2 *Future FastForward: The Zionist Anglo-American Empire Meltdown*, (2005, Thinker's Library).

taxation and this is always very unpopular. Therefore the warmongers must find a way to overcome this obstacle. The answer was the creation of Paper Money.

The origins of Paper Money date back to the time when people deposited gold with private goldsmiths who would issue receipts to the depositors acknowledging the amount of gold that was deposited. At first the receipts were issued in the name of the depositor. Later, these receipts were exchanged between traders in settlement of debts and/or commercial transactions, as it was more convenient than the exchange of physical gold. It was accepted because the people had faith in the receipts, which were essentially a promise to pay the equivalent of gold on the presentation of the receipts. In time the goldsmiths realized that at any one time, the depositors would only reclaim a small amount of the gold deposited. The goldsmiths hit on a brilliant idea. They could issue receipts in excess of the gold deposited to those who were in need for such receipts to facilitate mercantile transactions, but at a price—the goldsmiths would levy interest on such receipts issued. This was the rudiments of banking in the early days. "Money" was created by the mere issuance of "receipts" in excess of the amount of gold deposited. Money was created out of nothing, by a mere stroke of a pen.

As stated earlier, wars are expensive and governments need money to wage war. Taxation of the people to raise money for war was unpopular and on many occasions gave rise to revolts. History has it that it was one William Paterson who came up with the idea of a national bank or central bank to duplicate the *modus operandi* of the goldsmiths—to create Paper Money and lend it to the king to wage wars. Thus the Bank of England was created, the first Central Bank.

There is a sordid history of the Bank of England which British people are unaware save a few historians—the sinister role of the Bank of England under Montagu Norman in arming Hitler. Eric Butler, in *The Enemy Within the Empire*,[3] wrote:

> In 1933 there appeared in Holland a book, written by a certain Sidney Warburg which quickly disappeared from booksellers' windows. In it the author stated that in the preceding year, 1932, he had attended meetings in the United States of financial gentlemen who were seeking means of subsidizing Hitler. It

3   Eric Butler, *The Enemy Within the Empire—A Short History of the Bank of England* (1940, Melbourne) p.10.

appears that among those present were Sir Henry Deterding, representatives of the Morgan Bank, Montagu Norman (Governor of the Bank of England), and representatives of the Mendelssohn Bank.

Let us fast forward to the modern era. Let me explain the mechanics of creating money out of thin air, literally out of nothing. Let's take the following scenario.[4] The President of the United States has just launched a war against a foreign country and had initially esti-mated that it would cost a mere U.S. $50 billion.

As a result of complications, e.g. citizens of the target country rose en masse to resist the invasion, the cost of the war escalated tremendously. The occupation of the country and the efforts to sup-press the resistance now cost U.S. $100 billion, but the U.S. govern-ment has no money to pay for the additional costs. What the govern-ment does is to issue what is generally referred to as "government bonds" or "Bills" with a face value of U.S. $100 billion which is essen-tially an "IOU"—that is to say an acknowledgement by the government to the holder of the bond (the person/institution who has purchased the said bond) that the principal will be repaid within a certain period at a fixed interest. People will buy these bonds, because they trust that the government will honor the pledge of repayment.

Let's say that investors (both local and foreign) took up only U.S. $50 billion worth of bonds. There is therefore a shortfall of U.S. $50 bil-lion. What happens is this: the U.S. Government goes to the Fed and asks it to take up the shortfall. No problem. The Fed issues a check for U.S. $50 billion. Just like that, out of thin air, as authorized by the Federal Reserve Act. This was explained eloquently by the Boston Federal Reserve Bank:

> When you and I write a check there must be sufficient funds in our account to cover the check, but when the Federal Reserve writes a check there is no bank deposit on which that check is drawn. When the Federal Reserve writes a check, it is creating money.

What happens next is that the Treasury official deposits the check into the government's account which will indicate in the state-ment of accounts a deposit of U.S. $50 billion. Suddenly, the govern-ment now has U.S. $50 billion to spend. But the amount of money bor-

---

4   Adapted from Edward Griffin's *Creature from the Jekyll Island* and the author's book, *Future FastForward*.

rowed must be repaid to all bond holders. This the government does by taxing the people, as without taxation, the borrowed money cannot be repaid.

The next stage of the money creation takes place when the U.S. government pays Halliburton U.S. $10 billion for services rendered in the war effort. This U.S. $10 billion is deposited in Halliburton's bank account, say Citibank. Under the existing banking laws, banks need only to keep a certain amount in reserve of the moneys so deposited, say 10%—U.S. $1 billion. The other U.S. $9 billion can be used by Citibank to lend to its customers and charge interest thereon. So what we have here is a situation where in step one, the Fed creates money out of thin air and collects interests on it; in the second stage, that same money is routed to a commercial bank, and is then used by that bank to create loans that earn further interest. The money is not backed by any asset like gold or silver. It is just paper!

One need not be a rocket scientist to realize from the above simple outline of the history of banking that a most compelling motive for war has its roots in bank lending. No business is more lucrative than bank lending for wars. The banker creates money out of thin air, lends it to the Military-Industrial complex and profits from the enormous amount of interest earned. Since the establishment of the Bank of England, it is no exaggeration to say that banks, specifically Zionist controlled banks have been in forefront in promoting and financing wars. And when President Wilson in 1913 signed a law, for the creation of the Federal Reserve System (i.e., the U.S. Central Bank), world wars became inevitable. It is therefore no coincidence that soon after the establishment of the Federal Reserve System, the U.S. entered the First World War on the urgings of the bankers headed by the Morgans, et al.

When Paper Money is issued in abundance to finance wars, the true cost of the war is hidden from the people—the inevitable depreciation of the currency. Even though the people have to pay more for the same amount of goods which they have been purchasing before, many would not be able to see the correlation.

This is the old con and it has been brilliantly played by the present Bush administration in waging the heinous War on Terror in Afghanistan and Iraq. President Bush reduced taxes to lull the people and to seduce them into believing the good times are rolling. But with the massive injection of Paper Money by the Federal Reserve, as well as the issuance of treasury bonds, to finance the war, the U.S. dollar has depreciated substantially, as much as 30% over the last few years. The U.S. government is in debt to the tune of U.S. $7.8 trillion at the last count.

Thus Paper Money provides a motive for war in two ways: (1) the true cost of the war is hidden from the people so that they cannot make a rational decision whether or not to bear it; (2) through the operations of Paper Money, the bankers make huge profits. Since very large paper issues are only associated with war, then if the banker can foment a war, he can enjoy these profits.[5]

Very few appreciate the consequences to our society and the democratic institutions that have been put in place to protect our freedom and independence. Many lecturers in our universities, when teaching economics and/or political science have consciously or through ignorance glossed over this critical issue. So important is this issue that Dr. Ron Paul, the Republican member of Congress from Texas in a speech to Congress on September 8, 2003 reminded his colleagues of the danger facing the United States and the world's financial architecture. It is appropriate and incumbent on us to take heed of his warnings. This is what he said:[6]

> All great republics throughout history cherished sound money. This meant that the monetary unit was a commodity of honest weight and purity. When money was sound, civilizations were found to be more prosperous and freedom thrived. The less free a society becomes, the greater the likelihood its money is being debased and the economic well being of its citizens diminished.

Alan Greenspan, years before he became Federal Reserve Board Chairman in charge of flagrantly debasing the U.S. dollar, wrote about this connection between sound money, prosperity, and freedom. In his article "Gold and Economic Freedom" (The Objectivist, July 1966), Greenspan starts by saying: "An almost hysterical antagonism toward the gold standard is an issue that unites statists of all persuasions. They seem to sense ... that gold and economic freedom [are] inseparable." Further he states that: "Under the gold standard, a free banking system stands as the protector of an economy's stability and balanced growth."

5   Howard S. Katz, *The Warmongers*, (1981, Books in Focus Inc.)
6   Source: www.dailyreckoning.com/Writers/Paul/Articles/090803.html

Astoundingly, Mr. Greenspan's analysis of the 1929 market crash, and how the Fed precipitated the crisis, directly parallels current conditions we are experiencing under his management of the Fed. Greenspan explains: "The excess credit which the Fed pumped into the economy spilled over into the stock market triggering a fantastic speculative boom." And, "by 1929 the speculative imbalances had become overwhelming and unmanageable by the Fed." Greenspan concluded his article by stating: "In the absence of the gold standard, there is no way to protect savings from confiscation through inflation." He explains that the "shabby secret" of the proponents of big government and Paper Money is that deficit spending is simply nothing more than a "scheme for the hidden confiscation of wealth." Yet here we are today with a purely fiat monetary system, managed exclusively by Alan Greenspan, who once so correctly denounced the Fed's role in the Depression while recognizing the need for sound money.

It follows that if gold and economic freedom are inseparable then Paper Money must lead to tyranny. Dr. Ron Paul correctly pointed out that printing money, which is literally inflation, is nothing more than a sinister and evil form of hidden taxation. Additionally, a central bank and fiat money will enable a government to maintain an easy war policy that under strict monetary rules would not be achievable. His next observation about Paper Money is most perceptive:

> Countries with sound monetary policies would rarely go to war because they could not afford to, especially if they are not attacked. The people could not be taxed enough to support wars without destroying the economy. But by printing money, the cost can be delayed and hidden, sometimes for years if not decades. To be truly opposed to pre-emptive and unnecessary wars one must advocate sound money to prevent promoters of war from financing their imperialism. Look at how the military budget is exploding, deficits are exploding, and tax revenues are running down. No problem; the Fed is there and will print whatever is needed to meet our military commitments, whether it is wise to do so or not.

I hope by now you can see the correlation between Paper Money, debt and wars. The vicious cycle can be illustrated thus: the bankers promote wars so that governments will borrow money from them to wage their wars. To finance wars, all the bankers need to do is to create money out of thin air—via the printing presses and earn the exorbitant interests. To continue to earn such interests, more wars

19

need to be conducted and financed. The cycle repeats itself.

The world is awash with Paper Money, in particular the U.S. Paper Money. In principle, it can be said that the U.S. is a bankrupt state. Technically she has been a bankrupt state since 1971, when President Nixon decided that the U.S. would no longer allow the redemption of its currency for gold as was agreed under the Bretton Woods agreement. Until the early 1980s, the U.S. was a creditor nation. But today it is the largest debtor nation. Yet the U.S. is waging wars. President Bush has said that the war on terror will be a long war and in a speech on August 7, 2002 warned the American people that "there is no telling how many wars it will take to secure freedom in the homeland." How is it that the U.S. being a bankrupt country can find the money to wage wars in Afghanistan and Iraq? Part of the answer lies in the fact that the bulk of the world's trade is denominated in U.S. dollars in particular the trade in crude oil. This is why the U.S. dollar is the predominant reserve currency. The U.S. cannot allow anyone to challenge her stranglehold on the monetary system based on fiat money—"paper-ticket-token" or "funny money"[7] as some writers prefer to call it. Any major attempt to abandon the dollar in the oil trade alone would result in the total collapse of the U.S. economy. The dollar would literally be toilet paper!

In the circumstances, it is inevitable that the U.S. will use force or threat of force against any country, especially oil producing countries that dare to challenge the financial status quo. In a brilliant article entitled "A New American Century? Iraq and the Hidden Euro-Dollar Wars"[8], published in June 2003, William Engdahl was one of the very few who appreciated the strategic reasons for the war in Iraq. He wrote:

> The coalition of interests which converged on the war against Iraq as a strategic necessity for the United States, included not only the vocal and highly visible neo-conservative hawks around Defense Secretary Rumsfeld and his deputy, Paul Wolfowitz. It also included powerful permanent interests, on whose global role American economic influence depends, such as the influential energy sector around Halliburton, Exxon Mobil, Chevron Texaco and other giant multinationals. It also

---

7   Ferdinand Lips used this term in his essay "Why Gold Backed Currencies Help Prevent Wars." Source: www.fame.org/goldwars.htm. See also his book, *Gold Wars: The Battle Against Sound Money as Seen From a Swiss Perspective*, (2001, FAME).

8   Source: www.williambowles.info/guest/dollar_euro.html

included the huge American defense industry interests around Boeing, Lockheed-Martin, Raytheon, Northrop-Grumman and others. The issue for these giant defense and energy conglomerates is not a few fat contracts from the Pentagon to rebuild Iraqi oil facilities and line the pockets of Dick Cheney and others. It is a game for the very continuance of American power in the coming decades of the new century. That is not to say that profits are not made in the process, but it is purely a by-product of the global strategic issue.

In this power game, least understood is the role of preserving the dollar as the world reserve currency, as a major driving factor contributing to Washington's power calculus over Iraq in the past months. American domination in the world ultimately rest on two pillars—its overwhelming military superiority, especially on the seas; and its control of world economic flows through the role of the dollar as the world's reserve currency. More and more it is clear that the Iraq war was more about preserving the second pillar—the dollar role—than the first, the military.

Obviously, the above reason cannot be used as a reason for war. A pretext had to be found. It was simple! The Military-Industrial-Financial complex asked their highly paid intellectuals employed by the think tanks to come up with the justification for wars. The warmongers came up with the pretext for the need to eliminate WMDs from rogue states, such as Iraq which happens to be a major oil supplier. The War on Terror is but another pretext.

It is no exaggeration to say that the global wars of the 21st century will be waged to perpetuate the U.S. dollar hegemony and the Paper Money financial system.

3

The War Constitution of the 20th Century

> The United States has it in its power to increase enormously the strains under which Soviet policy must operate, to force upon the Kremlin a far greater degree of moderation and circumspection than it has had to observe in recent years, and in this way to promote tendencies which must eventually find their outlet in either the break-up or the gradual mellowing of Soviet power.
>
> **—George Kennan**

The writings of George Kennan, Paul Henry Nitze, Norman Podhoretz, William Kristol, Richard Perle and his co-author[1] David Frum reflect just how much the Zionist Anglo-American establishment has betrayed the Constitution of the United States of America and the Declaration of Independence of July 4, 1776.

The blueprint for world domination through wars of aggression is not contained in a specific document but rather a series of documents published over a period of 50 years linked together by a common thread and evolved from a single source. I have in this book referred to them collectively as the *War Constitution for the 20th Century.*

It is, in my opinion, beyond debate that the wellspring for the ideological basis for the War Constitution must be George Kennan's *Long Telegram* of February 22, 1946, and his companion article *The Sources of Soviet Conduct* published in the journal *Foreign Affairs* in 1947 under the pseudonym "X."[2] His writings gave rise to the Truman Doctrine and the economic rationale for the Marshall Plan. They

---

1   David Frum, Richard Perle, *An End to Evil: How To Win The War On Terror,* (2004, Ballantine Book)

2   See Appendix 1 and 2 for the entire document.

must be read in conjunction with what was once a top secret document called *United States Objectives and Programs for National Security* more commonly referred to as *NSC-68*,[3] the brain child of Paul Henry Nitze.

When the warmongers needed a rationale for war, George Kennan provided the ideological blueprint and Paul Henry Nitze the grand military strategy. In preparing the world and the U.S. in particular, for the *Cold War,* which has been referred to by some experts as the Third World War, the Military-Industrial-Finance complex must first and foremost convince the electorate that there is an imminent danger. Post World War II, the demon that needed to be vanquished was the Soviet Union.

George Kennan, who was born on February 16, 1904, was a remarkable man who played a critical role in formulating the U.S. post World War II foreign policies. He has been called the "Father of Containment" and a resolute Cold War warrior. Soon after his death on March 17, 2005, Richard Holbrook wrote:

> He had watched Joseph Stalin at close hand, and sent Washington an analysis of Russia that became the most famous telegram in U.S. diplomatic history. This was followed by the most influential article ever written on American foreign policy, the "X" article in Foreign Affairs, which offered an easily understood, single word description for a policy ("containment") that our nation was to pursue for 40 years—with ultimate success. He felt lonely, conflicted and even anguished over his famous works, which, in retrospect, he felt were simplistic and had been misused by people he deplored. Yet his work inspired the hardheaded power politics that shaped the Cold War. He was our greatest diplomat.[4]

George Kennan advised that the "main element of any United States policy toward the Soviet Union must be a long-term, patient but firm and vigilant *containment* of Russian expansive tendencies … Soviet pressure against free institutions of the Western world is something that can be constrained by the adroit and vigilant application of *counter-force* at a series of constantly shifting geographical and political points, corresponding to the shifts and maneuvers of

3   See Appendix 3. All the three appendixes should be read thoroughly, without which we would not be able to appreciate how we can be and have been brainwashed for war.
4   Richard Holbrook, "The Paradox of George F. Kennan," Washington Post, March 21, 2005

Soviet policy." He correctly predicted that the Soviet Union, under the intense pressure of containment would result in "either break-up or the gradual mellowing of Soviet power."

In his later years, George Kennan denied that containment was a military concept—"My thoughts about containment were of course distorted by the people who understood it and pursued it exclusively as a military concept; and I think that that, as much as any other cause, led to 40 years of unnecessary, fearfully expensive and disoriented process of the Cold War."[5] It seems rather late to lament the consequences of his policy. It was his concept of applying *counter-force* at every geographical point of contention that gave rise to the infamous covert operations and coups that toppled Mossadegh, Arbenz, Lumumba, Diem, Allende etc. And whatever may have been his intentions, his writings were relied upon by the warmongers to advance their agenda—the massive rearming of the U.S. and the military adventures in Korea, Vietnam, and elsewhere.

If as asserted by John Lewis Gaddis[6] no article in the history of foreign affairs has lent itself to more variant interpretations than that of George Kennan's *The Sources of Soviet Conduct,* the same cannot be said of Paul Henry Nitze's NSC-68, written in April of 1950.

Paul Henry Nitze was born in Amherst, Massachusetts on January 10, 1907. He studied at Harvard University and upon graduation worked as an investment banker with Dillon, Read & Company where he made his fortune. In 1940, he worked under Jim Forrestal (who was his boss at the Wall Street firm) the Under-secretary for the navy, responsible for procurement and production. In 1944, he was promoted to Vice-Chairman of the United States Strategic Bombing Survey and played a crucial role in the bombings of Hiroshima and Nagasaki. His contemporaries were George Kennan, friend and rival, Frank Wisner, Richard Bissell, Desmond FitzGerald, Eugene Rostow, Chip Bohlen, Clark Clifford, David Bruce, Katherine Graham, and Joseph Alsop and were collectively referred to as the "Georgetown Crowd."

In 1950, he was appointed the head of Policy Planning in the State Department and whilst there, played a major role and was in fact the principal author of the report now more commonly referred

---

5   George Kennan, *Memoirs: 1925-1950*, (1967) pp. 354–367

6   John Lewis Gaddis, Reconsiderations:Containment: A Reassessment, July 1997, Foreign Affairs

to as the *NSC-68*. During the Presidency of John F. Kennedy, he was appointed Secretary of the Navy and continued to serve in that position during the Presidency of Lyndon Johnson. In 1967, he was made Deputy Secretary of Defense, reporting to Robert McNamara. In 1969, he was appointed a member of the U.S. delegation to the Strategic Arms Limitation Talks (SALT). He also served under President Ronald Reagan as Chief Negotiator for the Intermediate Range Nuclear Forces (INF) Treaty and in 1984 was appointed as Special Adviser to the President and Secretary of State on Arms Control. He co-founded the John Hopkins School of Advanced International Studies and established his very own Paul H. Nitze School for Advanced International Studies (SAIS). He died on October 19, 2004.

It has been said that if there was one man who was responsible for America's emergence as a global military power in the 20th century, and the nuclear nightmares that the world suffered along the way, it must be Paul Henry Nitze and his brain child NSC-68.[7] How did the NSC-68 came to be written and accepted as official policy?

Two events which occurred between the end of World War II and the outbreak of the Korean War brought about a crucial strategic review of the U.S. national security policy. The first was the explosion of an atomic device by the Soviet Union in August 1949 and the second was the establishment of the People's Republic of China by Mao Zedong on October 1949. The warmongers need not look any further for a pretext for massive re-armament. The combination of a nuclear nightmare and communist domination was more than enough to scare the living daylights out of every American!

However, it should be noted that the warmongers had their plans laid out much earlier. In October 1948, the Secretary of the Air Force, Stuart Symington and the USAF Chief of Staff, General Hoyt S. Vandenberg had already decided to re-organize the Strategic Air Command and reconstitute it as a strategic pillar of U.S. foreign policy and as a deterrent against the Soviet Union. Symington was pushing for more defense spending, as he felt that Soviet Union advances in atomic weapons created a new equation, "an entirely new and revolutionary factor in strategic planning, which has never before faced U.S. military planners. The U.S. was no longer secure." But his ambi-

---

7   Fred Kaplan, Paul Nitze: The Man Who Brought Us the Cold War, Oct. 21, 2004. @ www.slate.msn.com

tion was thwarted by the doves in Truman's administration in particular by the Secretary of Defense Louis Johnson (who was derided as the "Secretary for Economy") who had assured President Truman that he would maintain defense budget at U.S. $13 billion.

The two events referred to earlier convinced President Truman of the urgent need to review U.S. national security policy. He established a policy review group comprising members from the State Department and the Defense Department. Paul Nitze headed the policy review group. The group submitted its report in April 1950 and it was approved in September 1950 as the new security policy of the United States.

It is imperative for anyone who is interested in war propaganda to embark on a detail study of this blueprint for war. I have therefore annexed it to this book as appendix 3. However, for the purpose of this chapter, I have highlighted the relevant passages with my commentaries, to give an overview of the strategic implications of NSC-68.

NSC-68

United States Objectives and Programs for National Security

Background of the Present Crisis

Within the past thirty-five years the world has experienced two global wars of tremendous violence. It has witnessed two revolutions—the Russian and the Chinese—of extreme scope and intensity. It has also seen the collapse of five empires—the Ottoman, the Austro-Hungarian, German, Italian, and Japanese, and the decline of two major imperial systems, the British and the French. During the span of one generation, the international distribution of power has been fundamentally altered. For several centuries it had proved impossible for any one nation to gain such preponderant strength that a coalition of other nations could not in time face it with greater strength. The international scene was marked by recurring periods of violence and war, but a system of sovereign and independent states was maintained, over which no state was able to achieve hegemony.

Commentary: After World War II, the U.S. by any measure

became the most powerful nation and achieved hegemony. By unleashing the atomic bombs in Hiroshima and Nagasaki, the U.S. signaled to all potential challengers, in particular the Soviet Union, that she intend to maintain the hegemony.

> Two complex sets of factors have now basically altered this historic distribution of power. First the defeat of Germany and Japan and the decline of the British and French Empires have interacted with the development of the United States and Soviet Union in such a way that power increasingly gravitated to these centers. Second, the Soviet Union, unlike previous aspirants to hegemony, is animated by a new fanatic faith, anti-thetical to our own, and seeks to impose its absolute authority over the rest of the world. Conflict has, therefore, become endemic and is waged on the part of the Soviet Union, by violent or non-violent methods in accordance with the dictates of expediency. With the development of increasingly terrifying weapons of mass destruction, every individual faces the ever-present possibility of annihilation should the conflict enter the phase of total war.

Commentary: Recall the propaganda for War on Terrorism and the justification for the invasion of Iraq and the demonization of President Saddam Hussein. Recall also the use of WMD to instill fear of annihilation. In the next chapter, we shall draw a comparison between NSC-68 and Bush's National Security Strategy. The "new fanatical faith" of Soviet Union communism is now being replaced by the new fanatical faith of "militant Islam" and the risk of WMDs getting into the hands of Islamic terrorists.

> On the one hand, the people of the world yearn for relief from the anxiety arising from the risk of atomic war. On the other hand, any substantial further extension of the area under the domination of the Kremlin would raise the possibility that no coalition adequate to confront the Kremlin with greater strength could be assembled. It is in this context that this Republic and its citizens in the ascendancy of their strength stand in their deepest peril.

Commentary: Again putting fear and anxiety into the hearts and minds of the people. The parallel is clear when Condoleezza Rice warned the world that the U.S. could not afford to have the "smoking gun turn into a mushroom cloud," as the justification for the invasion of Iraq.

Nature of the Conflict

The idea of freedom... is peculiarly and intolerably subversive

27

of the idea of slavery. But the converse is not true. The implacable purpose of the slave state to eliminate the challenge of freedom has placed the two great powers at opposite poles. It is this fact which gives the present polarization of power the quality of crisis. The idea of freedom is the most contagious idea in history, more contagious than the idea of submission to authority.

Commentary: During the Cold War, the battle was between freedom and slavery. Today the War on Islam and the War on Terrorism is couched in terms of a battle between forces of good against forces of evil. High ideals are used to justify wars of aggression.

Objective

In a shrinking world, which now faces the threat of atomic warfare, it is not an adequate objective merely to seek to check the Kremlin design, for the absence of order among nations is becoming less and less tolerable. This fact imposes on us, in our own interests, the responsibility of world leadership. It demands that we make the attempt, and accept the risks inherent in it, to bring about order and justice by means consistent with the principles of freedom and democracy.... But every consideration of devotion to our fundamental values and to our national security demands that we seek to achieve them by the *strategy of the Cold War.*

Commentary: This sounds strangely familiar. It is again in the name of freedom and democracy that the people in Iraq is suffering from the brutal and barbaric war unleashed by the U.S. and the Coalition of the Willing. Again, wars are waged allegedly to protect "our values" and "our national security" but the values and security of other peoples are irrelevant in the warmongers' scheme of things.

Means

Our free society, confronted by a threat to its basic values, naturally will take such action, including the use of military force, as may be required to protect those values. The integrity of our system will not be jeopardized by any measures, covert or overt, violent or non-violent, which serves the purposes of frustrating the Kremlin design, nor does the necessity for conducting ourselves so as to affirm our values in actions as well as words forbid such measures, provided only they are appropriately calculated to that end and are not excessive or misdirected as to make us enemies of the people instead of the evil men who have enslaved them.

Commentary: Again this refrain sounds familiar. To quote Bush, "All options are on the table" and every means must be taken to root out the evil. The U.S. soldiers are there to deliver freedom and democracy and would be welcome with flowers. The Christian soldiers are of exceptional morality and honor. But reality belies the fiction—the My Lai Massacre, the Honduras Death Squads, the Iran-Contras, military coups, Abu Ghraib and Guantanamo Bay tortures. 500,000 Iraqi children have died as a result of 12 years of sanctions against Iraq, but to the Zionist Madeline Albright, "the price was worth it."

The Military Solution

The United States now faces the contingency that, within the next four or five years, the Soviet Union will possess the military capability of delivering a surprise atomic attack of such weight that the United States must have substantially increased general air, ground, and sea strength, atomic capabilities, and air and civilian defenses to deter war and to provide reasonable assurance, in the event of war, that it could survive the initial blow and go on to the eventual attainment of its objectives.

The military advantages of landing the first blow become increasingly important with modern weapons, and this is a fact which requires us to be on the alert in order to strike with our full weight as soon as we are attacked and, if possible, before the Soviet blow is actually delivered.

The United States is currently devoting about 6% of its gross national product (U.S. $225 billion in 1949) to military expenditures. In an emergency the United States could devote upward of 50% of its gross national product to these purposes.

Commentary: Finally, we see the ultimate objective of the warmongers in stark terms. In Chapter 1 and 2, I said that war is big business and General Smedley Butler was equally blunt when he referred to war as a racket. If 6% of the GNP was in 1949 values, a whopping U.S. $255 billion, what a war bonanza to the warmongers when expenditure climbed to 50% of the GNP.

Military expenditure during the Cold War was at an all time high. The American people were hoodwinked into allowing such a massive re-arming of the military. There was no justification for it. The Soviet threat was hyped to justify the massive expenditures demanded by the military-Industrial-Financial complex.

A careful reading of the NSC-68 shows very clearly that the perceived threat of the Soviet Union was at most based on crude estimates, no different from the lies of the neo-cons in justifying the invasion of Iraq. The NSC-68 states:

> We do not know accurately what the Soviet atomic capability is but the CIA intelligence estimates, concurred in by State, Army, Navy, Air force and Atomic Energy Commission, assign to the Soviet Union a production capability giving it a fission bomb stockpile within the following ranges:
>
> By mid-1950 – 10–20
> By mid-1951 – 25–45
> By mid-1952 – 45–90
> By mid-1953 – 70–135
> By mid-1954 – 200
>
> This estimate is admittedly based on incomplete coverage of Soviet activities and represents the production capabilities of known or deducible Soviet plants.

Yet based on incomplete coverage, the United States went on a massive re-armament program unmatched in any historical period. There is also a socio-economic reason for the massive buildup in the 1950s. As admitted by the NSC-68, "industrial production declined by 10% between the first quarter of 1948 and the last quarter of 1949. In March 1950 there were approximately 4,750,000 unemployed, as compared to 1,070,000 in 1943 and 670,000 in 1944. The gross national product declined slowly in 1949 from the peak reached in 1948 (U.S. $262 billion in 1948 to an annual rate of U.S. $256 billion in the last six months of 1949), and in terms of constant prices declined about 20% between 1944 and 1948."

The NSC-68 went on to state that:

> With a high level of economic activity, the United States could soon attain a gross national product of U.S. $300 billion per year, as was pointed out in the President's Economic Report (January 1950). Progress in this direction would permit, and might itself be aided by, a buildup of the ***economic and military strength*** of the United States and the free world; furthermore, if a dynamic expansion of the economy were achieved, the necessary build-up could be accomplished without a decrease in the national standard of living because of the required resources could be obtained by ***siphoning off*** a part

of the annual increment in the gross national product. These are facts of fundamental importance in considering the courses of action open to the United States. (Emphasis added)

It goes without saying that you cannot have a war economy without wars. The *Cold War* enabled the warmongers to have the cake and eat it as well!

The foregoing discussion shows that the warmongers were able to persuade Congress as well as the American people the need to re-arm and to re-arm massively as a result of the menacing threat of the Soviet Union. But was the threat real or just sophisticated spin, bearing in mind that it was the U.S. who unleashed the atomic bombs on Hiroshima and Nagasaki?

It has been reported by two nuclear historians recently,[8] that the U.S. decision to drop the atomic bombs on Hiroshima and Nagasaki in 1945 was meant to kick start the Cold War rather than end the Second World War. Peter Kuznick, the Director of the Nuclear Studies Institute at the American University in Washington DC, is of the view that President Truman, "knew he was beginning the process of the annihilation of the species. It was not just a war crime; it was a crime against humanity." Mark Selden, a historian from Cornell University in Ithaca expressed similar views—"Impressing Russia was more important than ending the war in Japan."[9]

This is further corroborated by Walter Brown, assistant to then U.S. Secretary of State, James Byrnes who said that President Truman agreed at a meeting three days before the bomb was dropped on Hiroshima that Japan was "looking for peace." He was advised by his army generals Douglas MacArthur and Dwight Eisenhower, and his naval chief of staff, William Leahy, that there was no military need to use the bomb. The President was also worried that he would be accused of wasting money on the Manhattan Project to build the first nuclear bombs, if the bomb was not used.[10]

I am indebted to David R. Morgan for his meticulous research[11] in compiling the data in his article *The Sixteen Known Nuclear Crises of the Cold War, 1946-1985.* Mr. Morgan is the National

8   Rob Edwards, "Hiroshima Bomb may have carried Hidden Agenda," NewScientist.com news service.
9   Ibid.
10 Ibid.
11 Source: Victoria Peace Coalition @ www.vicpeace.ca

President, Veterans Against Nuclear Arms. From the said analysis it is clear that if ever there was a nuclear threat, that threat came from the United States. The propaganda that unless the U.S. re-armed massively, the Soviet Union would over-take the U.S. in nuclear weapons has been proven beyond all reasonable doubt to be a lie— a *Cold War Propaganda Hoax.* Judge for yourself the data below.

Sixteen Nuclear Crises of the Cold War: Dates and Weapons[12]

Crisis	Year	Length	Threat by	Nuc. Strategic Weapons	
				USA	USSR
1 Iran	1946	1 day	USA	40	0
2 Yugoslavia	1946	1 day	USA	40	0
3 Berlin	1948	15 mths	USA	120	0
4 Korea	1950	36 mths	USA	400	?
5 Vietnam	1954	3 mths	USA	1200	?
6 China	1954	8 mths	USA	1200	?
7 Suez	1956	7 days	USSR & USA	2100	60
8 China	1958	2 mths	USA	3000	110
9 Berlin	1959	4 mths	USA	3200	175
10 Berlin	1961	4 mths	USA	*3600	240
11 Cuba	1962	2 weeks	USSR & USA	*3900	300
12 Vietnam	1969	3 mths	USA	*4000	1400
13 Jordan	1970	2 weeks	USA	*4000	800
14 Israel	1973	19 days	USA	*6800	2200
15 Iran	1980	6 mths	USA	*10312	6846
16 First Strike	1983–85	24 mths	USA	*	*
Total Threat	1945–83	107 mths	of nuclear crisis	* Nuclear Winter threat	

From the table it is clear that in 1956, the Soviet Union had only 60 strategic nuclear weapons. Therefore, prior to 1956, the Soviet Union could not have more than 60 strategic nuclear weapons. Yet according to NSC-68, by mid-1954, the Soviet Union would have 200 strategic nuclear weapons. From the above table it is equally

12 Ibid.

obvious that the Soviet Union could not have been a real threat to the United States and Western Europe, because at all material times, the United States out-numbered the Soviet Union in strategic nuclear weapons. Even taking the worst case scenario painted by NSC-68,[13] it is clear that the Soviet Union could not by any measure win any nuclear wars. And it was only on two occasions, 1956 and 1962 that the U.S. and the Soviet Union threatened each other with nuclear weapons. In the other 14 occasions, the threat emanated from the United States.

This inevitable conclusion has been corroborated by Robert Manning, the former Assistant Secretary of State under President Kennedy who said[14]:

> During the Cuban Missile Crisis the Soviet Union possessed at that time as few as 75 and no more than 300 strategic missiles. The United States could target and deliver perhaps as many as 5,000 nuclear warheads. To some American theorists this passed for a "parity" of sorts, but surely it could not look like that to Moscow, even without factoring in Soviet paranoia. If Khrushchev were so lunatic as to launch a first strike and kill thousands of Americans, it would be a terrible prelude to having his country wiped off the face of the Earth. Khrushchev knows that we have substantial nuclear superiority. McGeorge Bundy was to write later, "but he also knows that we don't really live under fear of his nuclear weapons to the extent he has to live under fear of ours."

The Cold War generation was so easily duped by the propaganda of the warmongers that they overlooked the fact that the Soviet Union suffered massive devastation from World War II, having lost approximately 26 million people during the war, one out of every seven Russians. Russia had to rebuild the country, as 17,000 towns, 70,000 villages, 31,000 factories, 84,000 schools, 40,000 miles of railroad track were destroyed[15] whereas continental United States was spared the ravages of the war. The turning point of World War II was the defeat of Hitler's elite troops at the Battle of

---

13 The NSC-68 asserted that should a major war occur in the 1950s, The Soviet Union would have been able to overrun Western Europe, to launch strikes against the British Isles and lines of communication of the Western powers in the Atlantic and the Pacific, and to launch selected targets with atomic weapons against targets in Alaska, Canada and the United States.

14 Source: Newsweek, October 20, 1997, p. 18.

15 David R. Morgan, *16 Nuclear Known Crisis of the Cold War, 1946-1985*.

Stalingrad. The Americans and the British were content to watch as Germany and Soviet Union slugged it out, in the hope that when all was over and done with, either Germany or Soviet Union would be defeated, or both so devastated and exhausted, that they could stroll in and pick up the spoils of the war. It was only when Hitler was defeated in the Eastern Front and the Soviet Union army counter-attacked and was at the gates of Germany, that the Western Front was opened—the Normandy landings by the American and British forces. By then Hitler's army was already a spent force!

The "Iron Curtain"[16] that divided Europe was not the result of any grand design by Stalin, but the strategic calculation of Winston Churchill and President Roosevelt, and the ensuing Cold War was the inevitable consequence. The war economy had to be sustained. The Cold War was the pretext.

---

16 The term coined by the war criminal Winston Churchill in a speech given in Fulton, Missouri, USA to describe the division of eastern Europe after the war.

4

The Mindset of Warmongers

In his ability to apply strategic foresight in that regard, Paul Nitze was, indeed, as Strobe Talbot called him, 'the Master of the game.' His strategic foresight produced a plan for the post-war world characterized by creativity and boldness...[1]

— **Paul Wolfowitz**

Very few understand why propaganda for war is so intense and sustained, stretching over long periods, even decades. This is because it is not enough having laid the ideological basis for war, to stand pat and assume that the citizens would thereafter continue to support the war efforts of the Military-Industrial-Financial complex. The fear factor is a critical component for war propaganda. Absent the fear factor, a war economy cannot be maintained.

Notwithstanding the exposé that the rationale of the atomic bombing of Hiroshima and Nagasaki was not to end the war with Japan but rather to intimidate the Soviet Union, debates on this issue still abound. The same con was perpetrated by the Bush regime in support of his illegal invasion of Iraq, and the threats against Iran, Syria and North Korea. To understand the propaganda behind the War on Terrorism, which is essentially a war against Islam, we need to understand the *mindset* of the warmongers behind the *Cold War*. This is because the warmongers today are using the same propaganda strategies and tactics in mobilizing the world in support of the War on Terrorism, and thereby the perpetual war economy.

William Kristol and Robert Kagan have already sounded the call to their troopers:

---

1 Paul Wolfowitz, "Paul Nitze's Legacy: For a New World." Speech delivered to the Aspen Institute at the U.S. Chamber of Commerce, Washington DC, Thursday April 15, 2004. Source: www.defenselink.mil/

> When it is said and done, the conflict in Afghanistan will be to the War on Terrorism what the North African campaign was to World War II: an essential beginning on the path to victory. But compared to what looms over the horizon—a wide ranging war in locales from Central Asia to the Middle East and,unfortunately, back again to the United States—Afghanistan will prove but an opening battle… But this war will not end in Afghanistan. It is going to spread and engulf a number of countries in conflicts of varying intensity. It could well require the use of American military power in multiple places simultaneously. It is going to resemble the clash of civilization that everyone has hoped to avoid.[2]

Charles Kessler, editor of the *Claremont Review* has this to say about a long war:

> If democratization is to succeed in the regimes of the Islamic world, a necessary precondition is to beat these regimes into complete submission and then occupy them for decades—not just months or years but for decades. Even then our troops may have to stay and die indefinitely on behalf of a mission.

We have been forewarned. The great American patriot, historian and leader, Harry Elmer Barnes some 45 years ago had the foresight to teach us that the warmongers have only one objective—*"Perpetual War for Perpetual Peace."*[3] He also warned us that wars are not necessarily championed only by the right wing warmongers. In his *Intellectual and Cultural History of the Western World,*[4] he points out that liberals and socialists have also been enthusiastic war supporters: in the United States, World War I and II, and the Korean War were essentially liberal wars. I may add the Vietnam War as well.

The essence of the warmonger is the *"bully"* mindset. It is as simple as that. The mindset of a school bully is no different from that of a warmonger. The warmonger is just a bigger bully with more options available to intimidate and to extract compliance and submission from his victims. I have spent over 15 years researching on warmongers and believe me, in the layman's language, a warmonger is a bully. And we need only to study the bullies post World War

2   The Weekly Standard, October 29, 2002.

3   Harry Elmer Barnes, "Revisionism and the Historical Blackout," in Barnes, ed., *Perpetual War for Perpetual Peace* (1953, Caldwell, Id.: Caxton Printers)

4   Harry Elmer Barnes, *An Intellectual and Cultural History of the Western World*, (1965, Dover Pub., New York).

II to appreciate this fact.

When the United States dropped the atomic bombs on Hiroshima and Nagasaki, the Zionist Anglo-American warmongers gave notice to the lesser bullies and the world at large that they will not countenance any challenge whatsoever to their just acquired status as the No. 1 superpower, the biggest bully ever!

Behind this bully was a more sinister character, the British Zionist establishment's representative, Winston Churchill. He is an agent provocateur par excellence, first by laying the groundwork to ensnare the United States' entry into World War II and secondly, in 1946 in planting the seed for the *Cold War* by his *Sinews of Peace* speech (more commonly referred to as the *Iron Curtain Speech*) at Westminster College in Fulton, Missouri.[5] Although George Kennan's *Long Telegram*[6] preceded Churchill's speech, some historians take the view that it was the Iron Curtain speech that started the Cold War. It may be said that the Iron Curtain speech did for Europe, what the Long Telegram did for the United States in conditioning the people for a new war, one that would span a few decades.

Yet, at the conclusion of the Yalta conference, Churchill felt, "we are all standing on the crest of a hill with the glories of future possibilities before us." Churchill was also quoted as having said that "Poor Neville Chamberlain believed he could trust Hitler. He was wrong. But I don't think I am wrong with Stalin." Harry Hopkins, Roosevelt's close adviser said, "We really believed in our hearts that this was the dawn of the new day we had all been praying for and talking about for many years... We had won the first victory of the peace."[7] It was not misplaced optimism.

Arnold A. Offner, the historian has this to say of Stalin:

> To be sure, Stalin was a brutal dictator who directed a murderous regime. But there is no evidence that he intended to march his Red Army westward beyond its agreed-upon European occupation zones, and he put Soviet state interests ahead of desire to spread Communist ideology. He was also prepared to deal practically with the U.S. whose military and

5   The Speech was delivered on March 15, 1946.

Source: www.historyguide.org/europe/churchill.html. See Appendix 4 for the full speech.

6   Kennan's telegram was written on February 22, 1946.

7   Cited by Eric Alterman in "When Presidents Lie," from Robert E. Sherwood, Roosevelt and Hopkins, *An Intimate History* (1948, Harper Bros., New York).

economic power he respected.[8]

Many of the Cold War generation who have been brought up in a staple diet of anti-communism find it hard to accept that it was the Western powers that were responsible for the Cold War. What made war time allies bitter enemies within a year? Eric Alterman suggests:[9]

> Yalta. Few words have entered the popular political lexicon with such destructive force... It was there in early February 1945 that Stalin, perhaps the most effective mass murderer in human history, met with Franklin Roosevelt and Winston Churchill, to plan the final phase of World War II and map out the contours of the post-war world. When it was over, Stalin, history villain, went home and kept his word about their agreement, while Roosevelt and Churchill lied about theirs. Therein lies one of the great and, for American democracy, most painful ironies of the beginning of the Cold War. The vicious killer atop the Soviet evil empire honored the deal; the Americans and their British allies reneged. That's how the Cold War began.

This is but one view, but it reflects the mindset of those who felt that Roosevelt had deceived them regarding the deal made in Yalta. In essence, Roosevelt was accused of surrendering Eastern Europe, in particular Poland, to the Soviets, ignoring historical reality that it was the Soviet army that swept back Hitler's army from Eastern Europe. There was also a secret deal at Yalta unbeknownst to many. Roosevelt offered Stalin extensive territorial concessions in East Asia in exchange for the Soviet Union's agreement to invade Japan. The Joint Chiefs were of the view that Soviet Union's entry into the Pacific war was crucial to reduce U.S. casualties in the planned invasion of Japan.[10] When Truman became President, he was not apprised of the true import of the Yalta agreement. He had a simple world view, best reflected in his statement regarding the war in Europe: "If we see that Germany is winning, we ought to help Russia and if Russia is winning we ought to help Germany and that way kill as many as possible."[11] He was easily manipulated by the warmongers to adopt their agenda and his Cold War policies came

---

8   Arnold A. Offner, *Another Such Victory: President Truman and the Cold War, 1945-1953* (2002, Stanford University Press) p. 456.
9   Eric Alterman, *When Presidents Lie, a History of Official Deception and its Consequences*, (2004, Viking Penguin)
10 Ibid.
11 Ibid., citing Peter Grosse, *Operation Rollback: America's Secret War Behind the Iron Curtain* (2000, Houghton Mifflin, Boston).

to be known as the *Truman Doctrine.*

The Revisionist historian William Appleman Williams in *Tragedy of American Diplomacy*[12] takes the view that the American capitalist ideology was the driving force behind its foreign policy. Gar Alperovitz[13] opined that "there is a tendency among some politicians and military leaders, though not all, to think of nuclear weapons as essential to American security. Some keep pushing for more nuclear weapons, even though it means other people are going to get them. The notion of us having a threat is bound to create counter-threats."

It is also not too far-fetched to say that Winston Churchill had his own agenda when he realized that he would not be able to have his share of the spoils of war. He had every motive to renege on the Yalta agreement. In his memoirs, he wrote that in October, 1944, he attempted to share Europe with Stalin behind the back of the United States. Europe was to be carved up as follows: Rumania, Russia 90%, the others 10%; Greece, Great Britain 90%, Russia 10%; Yugoslavia 50% each; Hungary 50% each; Bulgaria, Russia 75%, others 25%. However, Stalin declined the offer.[14] Churchill could not accept that Eastern Europe belonged to the Soviets and that Britain had to play second fiddle! A number of British historians have come round to this view and have even suggested that the early Cold War was essentially an Anglo-Soviet conflict, stemming from the failure by Britain to forge an Anglo-Soviet alliance during the period 1944-1945. Thereafter, Britain coaxed the United States into taking a more hostile stand towards the Soviet Union and to assume leadership of the Western world, which Britain was incapable of fulfilling.[15]

It must be remembered that Churchill in his early years had his eyes on Russia. At the time of the Russian Revolution, he was Great Britain's Minister for War and Air and was responsible for directing the invasion of the Soviet Union by the "Allies." This is what he said about that episode:

Were they [the Allies] at war with Soviet Russia? Certainly not;

12 William Appleman Williams, *Tragedy of American Diplomacy*, (1959, Dell Publishing Co, New York)

13 He is the President of the National Center for Economic Alternatives and a Fellow of the Institute of Policy Studies in Washington DC. Interview in May 1995 by the Sojourners. Source: www.sojo.net

14 Winston Churchill, *The Second World War*, Vol. 6, p. 198

15 Richard Crockatt, *The United States and the Cold War 1941-53* (1989 BAAS Pamphlet No 18). Source: www.baas.a.uk/resources/pamphlets

but they shot Soviet Russians at sight. They stood as invaders on Russian soil. They armed the enemies of the Soviet government. They blockaded its ports, and sunk its battleships. They earnestly desired and schemed its downfall. But war—shocking! Interference—shame! It was they repeated, a matter of indifference to them how Russians settled their own internal affairs. They were impartial—Bang![16]

It is indeed ironic that a speech entitled "Sinews of Peace" is alleged to have started the Cold War. But there is a common thread running through this speech and the *Long Telegram* and *The Sources of Soviet Conduct* written by George Kennan, and *NSC-68* authored by Paul Henry Nitze—*in the name of peace, freedom, democracy and civilized values, we shall wage wars*.

Let's take a closer look at the "Sinews of Peace" speech. It is a long speech, so I shall only highlight the key passages.

The United States stands at this time at the pinnacle of power. It is a solemn moment for the American Democracy. For with primacy in power is also joined an awe-inspiring accountability to the future… Opportunity is here and now, clear and shining for both our countries. To reject it or ignore it or fritter it away will bring upon us all the long reproaches of after-time. It is necessary that the constancy of mind, persistency of purpose, and the grand simplicity of decision shall rule and guide the conduct of the English-speaking peoples in peace as they did in war. We must, and I believe we shall, prove ourselves equal to this severe requirement.

Commentary: To the colonialist, the world is divided between the English-speaking peoples and the non-English-speaking peoples, the latter need to be saved and civilized by the former's values. World War II was won not by the English-speaking peoples, but rather by the non-English-speaking peoples. Additionally, we should not forget that it was Churchill who said, "I am strongly in favor of using poison gas against uncivilized tribes."[17]

It would nevertheless be wrong and imprudent to entrust the secret knowledge or experience of the atomic bomb, which the United States, Great Britain, and Canada now share, to the world organization, while still in its infancy. It would be

---

16 Winston Churchill, *The War Crisis: The Aftermath*, (1929, London) p. 235.

17 Departmental Minutes, War Office May 12, 1919. Source Vol 4, Part 1, *Biography of Winston Churchill* by Martin Gilbert (1976, Heinemann, London).

criminal to cast it adrift in this still agitated and un-united world. No one country has slept less well in their beds because this knowledge and the method and the raw materials to apply it, are present largely retained in American hands. I do not believe we should all have slept so soundly had the positions been reversed and some communist or neo-fascist state monopolized for the time being these dreaded agencies. God has willed that this shall not be and we have at least a breathing space to set our world house in order before this peril has to be encountered: and even then, if no effort is spared, we should still possess so formidable a superiority as to impose effective deterrents upon its employment, or threat of employment, by others.

Commentary: It is clear that the United States and Great Britain are using their nuclear monopoly to intimidate. Only these countries are responsible enough to own and use such heinous weapons. Yet, history has shown that the U.S. is the only country that had dropped atomic bombs. But it is the will of God that they should have a monopoly of WMDs to bully the rest of the world. The Cold War, according to their own historians, was started by them. Today, we hear a similar refrain. It is God's urgings that President Bush launched a war of terror against the Afghan people; and it is God's will, that the U.S. unleashed the "Shock and Awe" campaign against the helpless Iraqi people! But the Muslims cannot invoke Allah in defense of their homes, their way of life and their values.

All this means that the people of any country have the right, and should have the power by constitutional action, by free unfettered elections, with secret ballot, to choose or change the character or form of government under which they dwell. Here is the message of the British and American peoples to mankind. Let us preach what we practice—let us practice what we preach.

Commentary: Noble words indeed! But history has shown that the British and the Americans do not practice what they preach. Military coups in South-East Asia, East Asia, Africa, the Middle-East and South America have denied the people their democratically elected leaders.

This special relationship between the British Commonwealth and Empire and the United States of America.... It should carry with it the continuance of the present facilities for mutual security by the joint use of all Naval and Air Force bases in the possession of either country all over the world. This would perhaps double the mobility of the American Navy and Air

Force. It would greatly expand that of the British Empire forces and it might well lead, if and as the world calms down, to important financial savings.

Commentary: What can be a clearer indication of the Empire's ambitions? Having declined militarily and economically after World War II, the British still longed for their empire and by such subtle propaganda, Britain was able, with the aid of the U.S. to pursue her colonial ambitions. Britain has to be content with the role of a small bully, relying on the U.S. as the big bully to get what she wants.

> From Stettin in the Baltic to Trieste in the Adriatic an *Iron Curtain* has descended across the Continent. Behind that line lie all the capitals of the ancient states of Central and Eastern Europe. Warsaw, Berlin, Prague, Vienna, Budapest, Belgrade, Bucharest and Sofia, all these famous cities and the populations around them lie in what I must call the Soviet sphere.

Commentary: The same can be said that all the capitals west of this imaginary divide fell under the Zionist Anglo-American sphere of influence. American troops still occupy Germany, even after the end of the Cold War and the collapse of the Soviet Union. Japan remains occupied. Why have we accepted this occupation and why the need to prolong the occupation? Herein lies the duplicity of the Zionist Anglo-American war propaganda.

> Let no man underrate the abiding power of the British Empire and Commonwealth…. Do not suppose that we shall not come through these dark years… or that half a century from now, you will not see 70 or 80 millions of Britons spread about the world and united in defense of our traditions, our way of life, and of the world causes which you and we espouse…. If all British moral and material forces and convictions are joined with your own in fraternal association, the high roads of the future will be clear, not only for us all, not only for our time, but for a century to come.

Commentary: Such is Churchill's lust for empire. But his ambitions can only be fulfilled with the aid of the big bully. Instead of a century of peace, we have instead a century of wars, most of which were the makings of the Zionist Anglo-American war cabal. It is only the British and the United States that can aspire to world domination; any challenge would be construed as an unacceptable opposition to their way of life, their traditions and noble causes.

Such is the language of warmongers. In the name of peace and other noble causes, they wage wars.

Let us now examine whether the Zionist Anglo-American estab-лishment practiced what they had preached. We should also ask whether the world slept peacefully in the knowledge that the Zionist Anglo-American establishment had the monopoly of atomic weapons or experienced continuous nuclear nightmares.

The first nuclear nightmare came within ten months after the end of World War II. This came about as a result of the dispute between the U.S. and the Soviet Union over oil concessions in Iran. Notwithstanding an agreement reached during World War II for the joint occupation of Iran and the sharing of the oil concessions, President Truman gave an ultimatum to the Soviet Union that unless Russian troops were removed from Iran, the U.S. would drop atomic bombs in Russia. Not having means to resist the threat, the Soviet Union removed its military forces from Iran. It came as no surprise that the Russians opposed the Baruch Plan for control of nuclear materials in the production of atomic energy.

Another example of nuclear bully tactics by the U.S. was when the heroic Vietnamese people were fighting the French at Dien Bien Phu, President Eisenhower was advised that should Vietnam fall to the Viet Minh, the rest of Asia would follow like dominoes. This was the *Domino Theory* and to prevent such an outcome, *Operation Vulture* was planned.　President Eisenhower threatened to use atomic bombs in Vietnam. And when Dien Bien Phu fell, the Americans threatened to use atomic bombs on China, if she intervened in Vietnam.[18] China did not intervene. Soon after, the U.S. entered Vietnam and for almost two decades, slaughtered over three million Vietnamese and laid waste to the country with chemical agents, in particular *Agent Orange.* Operation Phoenix, Tiger Force and the My Lai Massacre exposed the United States as a war criminal, but she need not account for those crimes.

Many have tried to justify the brutal interventions by the United States in Asia, Africa and Latin America as a necessary response to the global threat of Soviet Communism. Is this a valid argument? No better answer can be found than that provided by historian and author, William Blum when he wrote:

---

18 For other examples of U.S. nuclear blackmail, see Chapter 3 of *Sixteen Known Nuclear Crisis of the Cold War, 1946-1985* by David R. Morgan.

This argument breaks up on the rocks of a single question, which was all one had to ask back then: Why would the Soviets want to invade Western Europe or bomb the United States? They clearly had nothing to gain by such actions except the almost certain destruction of their country, which they were painstakingly rebuilding once again after the devastation of the war. By the 1980s, the question that still dared not be asked had given birth to a U.S. $300 billion military budget and Star Wars.

There are available, in fact, numerous internal documents from the State Department, the Defense Department, and the CIA... wherein one political analyst after another makes clear his serious skepticism of the "Soviet Threat"—revealing the Russians' critical military weaknesses and/or questioning their alleged aggressive intentions—while high officials, including the president, were publicly presenting a message explicitly the opposite.[19]

As pointed out by William Blum, we were inundated with "the Soviet threat," "the Chinese threat," "the Cuban threat" and other scare stories: in the 1950s there was the "Bomber Gap" between the U.S. and the Soviet Union, followed by the "Civil Defense Gap," the "Missile Gap," the "Anti-Ballistic Missile Gap," the "Spending Gap" and the need for Star Wars. They were all lies. They were all war propaganda. The warmongers' objective was simple enough—to "create a larger and meaner enemy, a bigger national security budget, and give security and meaning to the Cold War warriors' own job!"[20]

19 William Blum, *Killing Hope*, (2003, Zed Books Ltd).
20 Ibid, p. 20.

5

The National Security State— Military State Capitalism

> If we just let our own vision of the world go forth, and we embrace it entirely, and we don't try to be clever and piece together clever diplomatic solutions to this thing, but just wage a total war against these tyrants, I think we will do very well, and our children will sing great songs about us years from now.[1]
>
> **— Michael Ledeen**

It is fair to say that not many of the present generation have read and/or even heard of George Orwell's prophetic book, *Nineteen Eighty Four.* It may be that with the collapse of the Soviet Union and the end of the Cold War, people have forgotten about such dangers. After all, 1984 had come and gone. But if we read *1984* carefully we cannot but come to the conclusion that *we are part* of the *animal farm,* our society is in fact an animal farm. How did we get to this state of affairs?

Harry Elmer Barnes, the great American patriot gave a penetrating analysis:

> In his devastatingly prophetic book, *Nineteen Eighty-Four* George Orwell points out that one reason why it is possible for those in authority to maintain the barbarities of the police state is that nobody is able to recall the many blessings of the period which preceded. The great majority of Western people today have known only a world ravaged by war, depressions, international intrigues and meddling, vast debts and crushing taxation, the encroachments of the police state, and the control of public

---

1   Source: Village Voice, November 27, 2001, "This is Total War." Michael Ledeen is a neocon based at the American Enterprise Institute and was involved in the Iran-Contra scandal.

opinion by ruthless and irresponsible propaganda.

Military State Capitalism is engulfing both democracy and liberty in countries which have not succumbed to communism. During the years since 1937, the older pacific internationalism has been virtually extinguished, and internationalism has itself been conquered by militarism and aggressive globaloney. Militarism was, formerly, closely linked to national arrogance. Today, it stalks behind the semantic disguise of internationalism, which has become a cloak for national aggrandizement and imperialism. The obvious slogan of the internationalists of our day, who dominate the historical profession as well as the political scene, is "perpetual war for perpetual peace." This, it may be noted, is also the ideological core of "Nineteen Eighty-Four" society.

The security measures alleged to be necessary to promote and execute global crusades are rapidly bringing about the police state in hitherto free nations, including our own. Any amount of arbitrary control over political and economic life, the most expansive invasions of civil liberties, the most extreme witch-hunting, and the most lavish expenditures, can all be demanded and justified on the basis of alleged "defense" requirements. This is precisely the psychological attitude and procedural policy which dominate "Nineteen Eighty-Four" society.[2]

During the Cold War, it was convenient to look the other way and to excuse the encroaching police state as the necessary price for freedom and democracy. Countries all over the world were asked to make a choice—to march behind the American flag or face the wrath of the military state. Most succumbed to the political blackmail and followed meekly against better judgment in return for some semblance of economic prosperity. The price was heavy—we lost our soul. In saying this, I am not making any excuses for the Stalin regime. The Communist police state and the Capitalist police state are both sides of the same coin. And this critique applies as much to the Communist police state as the Capitalist police state.

The point I am making here is that we are the victims of the capitalist police state. The capitalist police state is harder to expose precisely because it hides under the facade of the "democratic state" and

---

2   Cited by Murray Rothbard, "Harry Elmer Barnes as Revisionist of the Cold War." Article first appeared in Arthur Goddard, ed., *Harry Elmer Barnes: Learned Crusader* (1968, Ralph Myles Publishers Inc. Colorado Springs)

that we have parliamentary and/or congressional elections. We have been blinded by the constant rhetoric that we represent the "Free World." It is on historical record that more people have been massacred and more countries plundered in the name of "Freedom" and "Democracy" in the 20th century than any other cause.

Prof. James K. Galbraith admitted as such when commenting on the Cold War economics—"for decades, the Western world tolerated the exorbitant privilege of a dollar reserve economy because the United States was the indispensable power, providing reliable security against communism and insurrection without intolerable violence and oppression, thus conditions under which many countries on this side of the Iron Curtain grew and prospered. Those rationales evaporated 15 years ago, and the "Global War on Terror" is not a persuasive replacement. Thus, what was once a grudging bargain with the world's stabilizing hegemonic country is now widely see as a lingering subsidy of a predator state."[3]

There are no free lunches even for a predator state. A price has to be paid for maintaining such an economy. The recent devastation of New Orleans by Hurricane Katrina has exposed the failings of the mighty police state. Dan La Botz[4] attributed the failure to the skewed priorities of the National Security State. The Bush regime's priorities have been foreign wars and globalization, the agenda of U.S. weapons and oil corporations. In the result the domestic economy was sacrificed to meet the demands of the warmongers. The once mighty empire is now a failed state! The Bush regime diverted all the state's resources to pursue the War on Terrorism so that when New Orleans was attacked, albeit by the forces of nature, it was impotent to provide the most basic needs for the people. The National Guard, instead of being deployed, as intended for such a situation, have been sent to kill the innocent victims of Bush's global agenda in Afghanistan and Iraq. Hurricane Katrina blew off the façade of the American society.

When New Orleans Mayor, Ray Nagin vented his frustration and desperation to the media that: "they're feeding the people a line of bull, and they are spinning and people are dying," and demanded that the Bush regime, "Get off your asses and let's do something," it is surely the ultimate indictment that the National Security State has degenerated into a failed state.

3   Cited in *Future FastForward*, Interview of Prof. James K. Galbraith by Tompaine.com.
4   Dan La Botz, "Failing at War, Peace and Dignity," Counterpunch, September 3, 2005.

If we are to overcome the injustice and barbarism of such a failed state, we must strive to know how, over the last fifty years or so, we so willingly gave up our collective authority and rights to the power elites of the National Security State.

In a word, we were *brainwashed!*

The success of this manipulation was the result of painstaking efforts over a long period of time. Control was exercised mainly by sophisticated social engineering programs, war propaganda and an educational system that encourages strict conformity in matters political and ideological. Our social order was then structured on the basis of a perpetual war economy and the National Security State.

I must at this juncture refer to a Report of a Special Study Group assembled in 1963, entitled *On the Possibility and Desirability of Peace* and to stand accused as being a conspiracy theorist. Whatever the debate as to its authenticity, Harry Barnes, the American patriot considered the Report as "by far the most impressive statement of the domination of our society by the military-scientific-technological-industrial-economic-political complex that has thus far reached print." The fact that renowned economist and author, Prof. John Kenneth Galbraith wrote: "I would put my personal repute behind the authenticity of this document, so I would testify to the validity of its conclusions. My reservations relate only to the wisdom of releasing it to an obviously unconditioned public," should dispel any lingering suspicions as to its value.

Colonel L. Fletcher Prouty (Ret), former Chief of the Special Operations for the Joint Chiefs of Staff has quoted the Report in his book, *The Secret Team*. It was also reported in *The New York Times*, that Arthur I. Waskow of the Institute of Policy Studies was surprised to see one of his privately circulated papers mentioned in the Report.[5] It matters not whether you agree with the conclusions of the Report, more commonly referred to as the *Report from Iron Mountain*,[6] but what is important is for us to understand how its findings have influ-

---

5   New York Times, November 1, 1967. Arthur I. Waskow was quoted as saying that only 60 people in Washington saw his private report mentioned in "Report from Iron Mountain," if it is a hoax, it must have involved somebody high up.

6   Iron Mountain is an underground nuclear hideout for American corporations, consisting of storage vaults for important documents. Corporations such as the then Standard Oil of New Jersey, Manufacturers Hanover Trust, Shell, et al maintain substitute corporate HQs where essential personnel could take refuge and safety in the event of a nuclear war.

enced and continue to influence the thinking of the Military-Industrial-Financial complex. Absent this understanding, we will not be able to resist and overcome the brainwashing programs of the National Security State. Please bear with me and take time to study its findings and conclusions.

What are the findings and conclusions of the *Report from Iron Mountain?* [7] They are not for the faint hearted. The scenario is frightening and one cannot help but feel impotent at the prospect that there is nothing much we can do. It is the result of a two-and-a-half-year study of the broad problems to be anticipated in the event of a general transformation of the American society to a condition lacking its most critical current characteristics: its capability and readiness to wage war when doing so is judged necessary or desirable by its political leadership.

Summary

Lasting peace, while not theoretically impossible, is probably unattainable. Even if it could be achieved it would almost certainly not in the best interest of a stable society to achieve it.

War fulfills certain functions essential to the stability of our society. Until other systems of filling them are developed, the war system must be maintained.

Poverty is necessary and desirable.

Standing armies are, among other things, social welfare institutions in exactly the same sense as are old-people's homes and mental hospitals.

The space program and the anti-missile and fallout shelter programs are understood to have the spending of vast sums as their principal goals, not the advancement of science or national defense.

Military draft policies are only remotely concerned with defense.

General Conclusions

It is surely no exaggeration to say that a condition of general world peace would lead to changes in the social structure of the nations of the world of unparalleled and revolutionary magnitude. The world is totally unprepared to meet the demands of such a situation.

7   Source: www.hermes-press.com

The war system cannot responsibly be allowed to disappear until 1) we know exactly what it is we plan to put in its place, and 2) we are certain beyond all reasonable doubt, that these substitute institutions will serve their purpose in terms of the survival and stability of society. It will be then time enough to develop methods of effectuating the transition; procedural programming must follow, not precede, substantive solutions.

Although no insuperable obstacles lies in the path of reaching general agreements, formidable short-term private—group and general—class interest in maintaining the war system is well established and widely recognized. The resistance to peace stemming from such interest is only tangential, in the long run, to the basic functions of war, but it will not be easily overcome, in this country or elsewhere. Some observers, in fact, believe that it cannot be overcome at all in our time, that the price of peace is simply, too high.

The war system, for all its subjective repugnance to important sections of the "public opinion" has demonstrated its effectiveness since the beginning of recorded history; it has provided the basis for the development of many impressively durable civilizations, including that which is dominant today. It has consistently provided unambiguous social priorities. It is on the whole, a known quantity. A viable peace system assuming that the great and complex questions of substitute institutions raised in this Report are both soluble and solved, would still constitute a venture into the unknown, with the inevitable risk attendant on the unforeseen, however small and however well hedged.

At our present state of knowledge and reasonable inference, it is the war system that must be identified with stability, the peace system with social speculation, however justifiable the speculation may appear, in terms of subjective, moral or emotional values.

The "World's War Industry" accounts for approximately a tenth of the output of the World's total economy.[8] A national economy can absorb almost any number of subsidiary re-organization within its total limits, providing there is no basic change in its own structure.

Given genuine agreement on intent among the great powers, the scheduling of arms control and elimination present no inherently insurmountable procedural problems. No major

---

8   This has risen since the time of the report in the 60s.

power can proceed with such a program, however, until it has developed an economic conversion plan fully integrated with each phase of disarmament. No such plan has yet been developed in the United States. Furthermore, disarmament scenarios, like proposals for economic conversion, make no allowance for the non-military functions of war in modern societies, and offer no surrogate for these necessary functions.

It is the incorrect assumption that war, as an institution, is subordinate to the social system it is believed to serve. This misconception, although profound and far reaching, is entirely comprehensible. Few social clichés are so unquestioningly accepted as the notion that war is an extension of diplomacy (or of politics, or the pursuit of economic objectives). The point is that the cliché is not true, and the problems of transition are indeed substantive rather than merely procedural. Although war is "used" as an instrument of national and social policy, the fact that a society is organized for many degrees of readiness for war supersedes its political and economic structures. War itself is a basic social system, within which other secondary modes of social organization conflict or conspire. It is the system which has governed most human societies of record, as it is today.

It must be emphasized that the precedence of a society's war-making potential over its other characteristics is not the result of the "threat" presumed to exist at any one time from other societies. This is the reverse of the basic situation; "threats against national interest" are usually created or accelerated to meet the changing needs of the war system. Only in comparatively recent times has it been considered politically expedient to euphemize war budgets as "defense" requirements. The necessity for governments to distinguish between "aggression" (bad) and "defense" (good) has been a by-product of rising literacy and rapid communication. The distinction is tactical only, a concession to the growing inadequacy of ancient war-organizing political rationales.

Wars are not "caused" by international conflicts of interest. Proper logical sequence would make it more often accurate to say that war-making societies require—and thus bring about—such conflicts. The capacity of a nation to make war expresses the greatest social power it can exercise; war-making, active or contemplated, is a matter of life and death on the greatest scale subject to social control. It should therefore hardly be surprising that the military institutions in each society claim its highest priorities.

51

The "wastefulness" of war production is exercised entirely out-side the framework of the economy of supply and demand. As such, it provides the only critically large segment of the total economy that is subject to complete and arbitrary central con-trol. If modern industrial societies can be defined as those which have developed the capacity to produce more than is required for their economic survival (regardless of the equities of distri-bution of goods within them), military spending can be said to furnish the only balance wheel with sufficient inertia to stabilize the advance of their economies. The fact that war is "wasteful" is what enables it to serve this function. And the faster the econ-omy advances, the heavier this balance wheel must be.

A nation's foreign policy can have no substance it if lacks the means of enforcing its attitude toward other nations. It can do this in a credible manner only if it implies the threat of political organ-ization for this purpose—which is to say that it is organized to some degree for war. War, then, as we have defined it to include all national activities that recognize the possibility of armed con-flict, is itself the defining element of any nation's existence vis-à-vis any other nation. Since it is traditionally axiomatic that the existence of any form of weaponry insures its use, we have used the word "peace" as virtually synonymous with disarmament. By the same token, "war" is virtually synonymous with nationhood. The elimination of war implies the inevitable elimination of nation-al sovereignty and the traditional nation-state.

The war system not only has been essential to the existence of nations as independent political entities, but has been equally indispensable to their stable internal political structure. Without it, no government has ever been able to obtain acquiescence in its "legitimacy," or right to rule its society. The possibility of war provides the sense of external necessity without which no gov-ernment can long remain in power. The historical record reveals one instance after another where failure of a regime to maintain credibility of a war threat led to its dissolution, by forces of pri-vate interest, of reactions to social injustice, or of other disinte-grative elements.

In advanced modern democratic societies, the war system has provided political leaders with another political-economic func-tion of increasing importance: it has served as a last great safe-guard against the elimination of necessary social classes. The most obvious of these [sociological] functions is the time-hon-ored use of military institutions to provide anti-social elements with an acceptable role in the social structure. The younger, and more dangerous, of these hostile social groupings have been kept under control by the Selective Service System. Informed persons in this country have never accepted the official rationale for a peace time draft—military necessity, preparedness, etc.—as worthy of serious consideration. The armed forces in every civilization have provided the principal state sponsored haven for what we now call the "unemployable."

In general, the war system provides the basic motivation for primary social organization. In so doing, it reflects on the social level the incentives of individual human behavior. The most important of these, for social purposes, is the individual psychological rationale for allegiance to a society and its values. Allegiance requires a cause; a cause requires an enemy. This much is obvious; the critical point is that the enemy that defines the cause must seem genuinely formidable. Roughly speaking, the presumed power of the "enemy" sufficient to warrant an individual sense of allegiance to a society must be proportionate to the size and complexity of the society. Today, of course, that power must be one of unprecedented magnitude and frightfulness.

War is an ideological clarifier. Except for secondary considerations, there cannot be, to put it simply as possible, more than two sides to a question because there cannot be more than two sides to a war.

Let's pause and consider the key elements of the Report. On the first reading, one cannot but be attracted to the powerful logic of the war system as defined. Why? The message in the Report appeals to our longing for security, for the known factors and for stability. As we had for a century not experienced global peace, *Peace* was portrayed as an unknown factor, even an unstabilizing factor. I am very confident that the authors of the Report have the benefit of experts well versed in psychological warfare. Reading the Report is itself a "brainwashing" exercise.

The Report is essentially a militarist's manifesto. It seeks to legitimize the demands and agendas of the Military-Industrial-Financial complex. We have been warned that special interests will ensure that the war system is maintained. The price of peace is just too high for the Military-Industrial-Financial complex. What is most chilling and disorienting (at least for those who have been brought up on the diet of keeping faith with the military establishment) is the matter-of-fact admission that "wars are *not* caused by international conflicts of interest. Proper logical sequence would make it more often accurate to say that war-making societies *require* and thus *bring about* such conflicts."

This is the essence of the National Security State, and we should not entertain any more illusions as to the nature of our society. The National Security State is the inevitable consequence of "Military State Capitalism." [9] Harry Barnes correctly pointed out way back in the 60s that it is futile to battle against the *by-products* of the war system, such as economic controls or depredations of civil liberties; instead the core of the system must be challenged. There are three essential features or trends of a National Security State:

1   A war economy, with the inevitable trend of transforming itself into the *perpetual war economy;*

2   Pervasive use of national defense against an "enemy" to justify military outlays, propaganda programs, intimidation, witch-hunting forays or oppression of the masses;

3   An identifiable "enemy" for each phase of the evolving war economy.

The final paragraph as quoted above should serve as the wake up call to break free from the militarist induced slumber. The battle of ideas as suggested can only be resolved through wars, not by the persuasion of a superior mind. Ideological and political differences must be resolved by wars! War as an ideological clarifier was given new meaning by Condoleezza Rice when she said:

> I think September 11 was one of those great earthquakes that clarify and sharpen. Events are in such sharper relief.... How do you capitalize on these opportunities to fundamentally change American doctrine and shape the world in the wake of September 11.[10]

The same sentiments were echoed by Zbigniew Brzezinski when he said:

> As America becomes an increasingly multicultural society, it may find it more difficult to fashion a consensus on foreign policy issues, except in the circumstances of a truly massive and widely perceived direct and external threat. The pursuit of power and especially the economic costs and human sacrifice that the exercise of such power often requires are not generally con-

9   Harry Elmer Barnes coined the term to describe the political economy of the United States during the Cold War. The term is still appropriate as Military State Capitalism has in fact grown to the monster we know it today.

10   Interview with Nicholas Lehmann, New York Times Magazine, April 1, 2002

genial to democratic instincts. Democracy is inimical to imperial mobilization.[11]

I have said earlier that the mindset of a warmonger is the *bully* mindset and I can find no better corroboration than this arrogant confession. The War System is but an instrument of the power elites to control us, and to do their bidding.

Enemies are created to justify the war economy. Recall and repeat over and over again these words:

> The presumed power of the enemy sufficient to warrant an individual sense of allegiance to a society must be proportionate to the size and complexity of the society. Today, of course, that power must be one of unprecedented magnitude and frightfulness.

> Threats against the national interest are usually created or accelerated to meet the changing needs of the war system.

I hope by now, you will understand why the Zionist Anglo-American war cabal must demonize their enemies and magnify the presumed power of the enemy. Recall the rationale for the illegal invasion of Iraq. It was part of the War on Terrorism. The smoking gun must not be allowed to turn into a mushroom cloud. The enemy is the Axis of Evil!

It is interesting to note that the Report was the effort of leading intellectuals recruited from the leading think tanks and universities in the United States. There is a reason for this. It was explained by Murray Rothbard[12] that the contemporary reversion to the savagery of a Genghis Khan—to a garrison state, to military conformity, to mass murder of civilians, to scorched earth and unconditional surrender, has been achieved through the quest for power and its perquisites by the ruling groups, the "power elites" of the various states. These consist of full time members and rulers of the state *apparatus,* as well as those groups in society (e.g. arms contractors) who benefit from the military and warfare systems. In particular, this reversion has been made possible by the reappearance on a large scale of the *"Court Intellectual"*— the intellectual who spins the apologia for the new dispensation in return for wealth, power, and prestige at the hands of the state and its allied "Establishment." There have been, after all, but two mutually

11 Zbigniew Brzezinski, *The Grand Chess Board: American Primacy and Its Geostrategic Imperatives,* (1997, Basic Books, New York)
12 Murray N. Rothbard, *Harry Elmer Barnes: Learned Crusader,* (Noontide Press)

exclusive roles that the intellectual can play and has played through history: either independent truth-seekers, or kept favorite of the court.

Marcus Raskin echoed similar views when commenting on the role of professional strategists of the Cold War military agencies. Calling them *"Megadeath Intellectuals"* [13] he considers that their most important function is to justify and extend the existence of their employers. In order to justify the continued large scale production of these thermonuclear bombs and missiles, military and industrial leaders need some kind of theory to rationalize their use. This became particularly urgent during the late 1950s when economy-minded members of the Eisenhower administration began to wonder why so much money, thought and resources were being spent on weapons if their use could not be justified. And so began a series of rationalizations by the defense intellectuals in and out of universities. Military procurements will continue to flourish, and they will continue to demonstrate why they must. In this respect they are no different from the great majority of modern specialists who accept the assumptions of the organizations which employ them because of the rewards in money, power and prestige. They know enough not to question their employers' right to exist.

Very few outside of America know the extent of collaboration between institutions of higher learning and the Military-Industrial-Financial complex. The War on Terrorism has provided the rationale for closer collaboration at a higher and more dangerous level between the leading universities and the Pentagon. More than 300 universities are developing weapons for the Pentagon's Future Combat Systems (FCS) program, many involving nanotechnologies.[14] M.I.T.'s Institute for Soldier Nanotechnologies was funded with U.S. $50 million from the Pentagon and together with U.S.C.'s Institute for Creative technologies are pioneering the development of FCS *Objective Force Warrior.*

The Department of Defense (DoD) hypes the achievements thus far in such glowing terms: "Arnold Schwarzenegger as the Terminator has nothing over the Objective Force Warrior." Even the sporting goods manufacturers got involved in the development of this high-tech warrior—they incorporated nanotechnology into the soldier's shoes

---

13 Marcus Raskin, former staff member of the NSC in the Kennedy Administration, "The Megadeath Intellectuals," The New York Review of Books, November 14, 1963.

14 Brian Bogart, "America Programmed for War: Causes and Solutions," Source: www.informationclearinghouse.info/article9831.htm

15 Ibid.

and this was done in 2001.[15] Nanotechnology is the ability to manipu-late materials on an atomic or molecular scale.

Let me assure you that this is not science fiction taken from the television series, "The X Files." The FCS Objective Force Warrior, by its very name reflects the extent of the domination by the National Security State's war system in the field of scientific research. It is mind boggling, what the scientists are paid to do.

The U.S. army's Objective Force Warrior (OFW) soldier ensem-ble is a lightweight, fully integrated individual combat system, includ-ing weapons, head-to-toe individual protection, netted communica-tions, soldier worn power sources, and enhanced human performance aids.[16] Such a soldier will have 20 times the capability of today's sol-diers. The army's vision for the OFW is of a highly lethal, survivable, networked soldier within a small combat team operating across a spectrum of future army and joint service operations.[17]

From the above brief discussion on weapons technologies we can see that in the last decade or so, the U.S. military has been transformed in more ways than one. The modern soldiers have been transformed into remote killing machines, no more the foot soldier with a high risk of a gory and painful death. Such a trans-formation serves a higher purpose—to condition society that wag-ing wars can be the first option and allegedly cost effective, with minimum casualties. Terms such as "surgical strikes," "precision bombings," "laser-guided munitions," "unmanned drones" etc. seem to convey that we can conduct "clean wars" as opposed the "dirty wars" of yester-years.

Paul Wolfowitz in the statement to the Senate Armed Services Committee Hearing on Military Transformation explains:[18]

> The agility that we need to continue meeting threats here and abroad depends on more than just technology, although that must be a fundamental part of our response. It is tied to changing our organizational designs and embracing new con-cepts. One of my key points today is that transformation is about changing the military culture into one that encourages, in Secretary Rumsfeld words, "innovation and intelligent risk taking."

16 Source: http://www.globalsecurity.org/military/systems/ground/ofw.htm
17 Ibid.
18 April 9, 2002. Source: www.defencelink.mil/speeches/2002/

September 11 brought home the fact that, while it is likely that few would seek to meet us head to head, they can still attack us. They can still threaten us. And when they did attack last September, using box cutters and jetliners, our response required much more than just box cutters and jetliners. Our response, as we seek to deny future terrorists avenues to similar attack, has been—and must be—disproportionately asymmetrical. And it does not come cheaply or without great effort at innovation.

Although we now face the enormous challenge of winning the global war on terrorism, we must also address the equally large challenge of preparing our forces for the future. We cannot wait for another Pearl Harbor or 9/11, either on the ground, in space or in cyberspace… That is why we must develop the transformational capabilities that will provide our crucial advantages a decade or more from now. Even as we take care today, we must invest in tomorrow—an investment we simply cannot postpone. It is a process of balancing the risks of today with those of tomorrow, one that should redefine how we go to war.

Our overall goal is to encourage a series of transformation that, in combination, can produce a revolutionary increase in our military capability and redefine how war is fought.

The six [transformation] identified are:

- First, to defend the U.S. homeland and other bases of operations, and defeat nuclear, biological and chemical weapons and their means of delivery;
- Second, to deny enemies sanctuary—depriving them of the ability to run or hide—anytime, anywhere;
- Third, to protect and sustain forces in distant theatres in the face of access denial threats;
- Fourth, to conduct effective operations in space;
- Fifth, to conduct effective information operations; and
- Sixth, to leverage information technology to give our joint forces a common operational picture.

While new technologies represent only a portion of the Department's overall transformation program, transformational investments account for 17% (about U.S. $21 billion) of all procurement and RDT & E in 2003, rising to 22% by 2007. Over the next five years, we plan to invest more than U.S. $136 billion in transformational technologies and systems. The total additional investment in systems to support transformation approaches U.S. $25 billion in FY2003 and U.S. $144 billion over the FYDP (Future Years Defense Plan).

I seek your indulgence in quoting extensively the speech of Paul Wolfowitz. My reason for doing so is to draw your attention to the similarities in the rationale for war preparation in his speech before the Senate Armed Services Committee and the Report from Iron Mountain.

Notwithstanding the above discussion, I still have the nagging question as to how the warmongers were able to transform the most advanced industrial economy into a perpetual war economy with so little resistance or objections from the people. Going over literally hundreds of books and monographs on modern economics did not help. I was baffled because the numbers just did not jibe! The technology required to transform the military even as outlined above would not need to embrace the industrial sector to such an extent as to change the fundamental character of the economy to that of a war economy. I was at a dead end. But Lady Luck was kind and generous to me. By chance I came across a brilliant article, entitled *Nuclear Weapons Stealth Takeover* by Leuren Moret[19] which indirectly provided the answer.

Leuren Moret mentioned in her article that in 1939, the Nobel Prize winning physicist Niels Bohr had argued that building an atomic bomb "can never be done unless you turn the United States into one huge factory." Years later, he told his colleague Edward Teller[20], "I told you it couldn't be done without turning the whole country into a factory. You have just done that," when the United States successfully developed the atomic bomb. This makes sense, if we just analyze the economics involved in the land, sea and air-borne delivery systems. The entire aerospace industry must be involved; the entire shipping industry will also need to be involved; and when we consider land based systems of delivery, the construction of such bases would involve one way or another the entire engineering and construction industry. And this is only for starters! The economic pyramid in support of the nuclear weapons program would invariably impact on every sector of the economy. It is safe to say that the transformation of the U.S. economy to a

19 Source: www.mindfully.org/Nucs/2004/Moret-Nuclear-Carlyle16sep04.htm

20 Edward Teller was also known as "Dr. Strangelove" who was responsible for the nuclear weapons program that went on for 61 years at the nuclear weapons labs: Berkeley, Livermore and Los Alamos.

war economy started with the development of the atomic bomb and by the 1950s the United States became for all intents and purposes a military capitalistic state. The farewell address by President Eisenhower on January 1961 to a large extent confirms my contention. He warned:

> In the counsels of government, we must guard against the acquisition of unwarranted influence, whether sought or unsought, by the Military-Industrial complex. The potential for the disastrous rise of misplaced power exists, and will persist. We must never let the weight of this combination endanger our liberties or democratic process.

However, this warning came rather late. President Eisenhower was responsible as much as his predecessors in the creation of the Military-Industrial complex.

On second and subsequent readings of the Report from Iron Mountain, one cannot but reluctantly agree with its authors that the vested interests of the warmongers are so pervasive, that it would be very difficult to mount an effective campaign to change the economic equation. We must nevertheless mount a challenge, for the prospect of bequeathing the future generations to a state of perpetual war for perpetual peace is plainly unacceptable, and if we truly desire peace.

6

The Megadeath Intellectuals and the War Constitution of the 21st Century

> Since 1947, America has been the chief and pioneering perpe-
> trator of 'pre-emptive' state terror, exclusively in the Third World
> and therefore widely dissembled. Besides the unexceptional
> subversion and overthrow of governments in competition with
> the Soviet Union during the Cold War, Washington has resorted
> to political assassinations, surrogate death squads and
> unseemly freedom fighters (e.g. Bin Laden)... and vetoes all
> efforts to rein in Israel's violations of international agreements...
> but also its practice of pre-emptive state terror.
>
> — **Arno J. Mayer**[1]

The War Constitution of the 21st Century, like the War Constitution of the 20th Century is not contained in a specific document but rather a series of documents written mostly in the last decade of the 20th century. After a long lull, the warmongers were itching for a major war, one that would engulf the entire world. Just as in the Cold War, the warmongers needed ideologues to lay the ideological basis for war. While George Kennan and Paul Henry Nitze were the masterminds for the Third World War (i.e. the Cold War), no one or two individuals could actually lay claim to such a leadership for the *War on Terrorism,* which initiated World War IV.[2] But it is safe to say that the leading representatives of the Neo-Conservatives led the way.

---

1 Cited by Gore Vidal, *Perpetual War for Perpetual Peace: How We Got To Be So Hated*, (2002, Thunder's Mouth Press/Nation Books, New York). The quote is taken from Le Monde

2 Norman Podhoretz's articles in the Commentary Magazine. They were: How to Win World War IV, World War IV: How It Started, What It Means, and Why We Have to Win, and The War Against World War IV.

3 See Note 13, Chapter 5. The term was coined by Marcus Raskin.

"Megadeath Intellectuals"[3] is indeed an apt and a better description than the general label, "neo-conservatives." They have so far laid waste to two countries, Afghanistan and Iraq, slaughtered hundreds of thousands and destroyed the lives of millions more and intend to replicate their experiences in other countries in the near future.

These Megadeath Intellectuals are masters of the ideological game and credit must be given to them for their brilliant strategy in positioning *Islam* as the ideological enemy. A mere prefix, one single word was enough to brainwash initially an entire nation, and soon after the rest of the world.

The word "militant" was prefixed to Islam. And a new enemy was created, the handiwork of the warmongers' spin doctors! Even Muslims, the very target of the War on Terrorism, were themselves brainwashed that *"Militant Islam"* was the ideological enemy. This has brought propaganda warfare to a new level, the best thus far. The earlier spin doctors of World War II and the Cold War did not achieve the same measure of success in their propaganda war against Nazism and Communism.

There is no such thing as "Militant Islam" except that created by the Megadeath Intellectuals. There is only *Islam,* the *Revelations from Allah to Prophet Muhammad* and none other. It is indeed revealing that throughout the ages, historians, philosophers, scholars etc. never ever referred to the ideology of those that have betrayed the teachings of Christ as *"Militant Christianity,"* or like terms and expressions. But these same historians, philosophers and scholars, the mouthpiece of the warmongers have always demonized their enemies and even religions are not spared. The end justifies the means!

It was and still is theatrical therefore, to see how the various Muslim political and religious leaders, with a few exceptions, prostrate themselves before Zionist controlled media to display their credentials that they are the "good Muslims" and that Islam is indeed a peaceful religion. It is as if the West was ignorant of the teachings of Islam. When the crusading armies, principally of the United States and Britain unleashed their barbaric weapons on the innocents of Afghanistan and Iraq, was there a parade of Christian political and religious leaders declaring that Christianity is a peaceful religion? Did they distance themselves from fascist Bush and Blair? Did they condemn them as the personification of evil and that their preaching and calls to arms are not a reflection of the fundamental tenets and precepts of Christianity? Did they implore for understanding and tolerance and/or that the members of their community should not be made targets of witch-hunts? Nothing of the sort!

In contrast, during the crusades, Saladin, the great leader never demonized Christianity, the religion, and he made a distinction between the believers and the non-believers, the latter referred to as *"Infidels."* He was honorable in war and in peace; upright in his Islamic faith and respectful of the Christian religion. He had no need to explain.

The Holy Qur'an is clear:[4]

Those who believe and those who follow the Jewish [scriptures], and Christians, and Sabians—any who believe in God and the Last Day and work righteousness, shall have their reward with their Lord; on them shall be no fear, nor shall they grieve.
— Surah Al Baqarah, 2 : 62

Behold! The angel said: "O Mary! God giveth thee glad tidings of a word from Him: his name will be Christ, Jesus, son of Mary, held in honor in this world and the Hereafter and of [the company of] those nearest to God."
— Surah Aali 'Imran, 3:45

She said: "O my Lord! How shall I have a son when no man has touched me?" He said: "Even so: God createth what he willeth: when He hath decreed a plan, He saith to it, 'Be' and it is."
— Surah Aali 'Imran, 3:47

When Jesus came with clear Signs, he said: "Now I have come unto you with Wisdom, and in order to make clear to you some of the [points] on which ye dispute: therefore fear God and obey me."
— Surah Al Zukhruf, 43:63

Behold! God said: "O Jesus: I will take thee and raise thee to Myself and clear thee (of the falsehoods) of those who blaspheme; I will make those who follow thee superior to those who reject faith, to the Day of Resurrection: then shall ye all return unto me, and I will judge between you of the matters wherein ye dispute."
— Surah Aali 'Imran 3: 55

Centuries of lies and propaganda have not been able to desecrate Islam, yet the Megadeath Intellectuals are hell bent to vilify Islam.

4   The Holy Quran, translated by Abdullah Yusuf Ali (Saba Islamic Media, Kuala Lumpur). I have chosen this translation, because the English employed is preferable over other translations.

So beware! The spin doctors have been working over-time to come out with a series of books demonizing Islam, but none is more vicious and effective in misleading the West about Islam than that of *An End to Evil: How to Win the War on Terror*.[5] And when *The New York Times* Book Review gives legitimacy to such trash by saying that it is, "intelligent and worthwhile... deserves special attention," we must take time to study and penetrate the fascist mindset of its authors, David Frum and Richard Perle. They wrote:

> In militant Islam, we face an **aggressive ideology of world domination**. Like Communism, this ideology perverts the language of justice and equality to justify oppression and murder. Like Nazism, it exploits the injured pride of once-mighty nations. Like both Communism and Nazism, militant Islam is opportunistic—it works willingly with all manner of unlikely allies, as the Communists and Nazis worked with each other against the democratic West. (Emphasis added)

> Since 1940, American democracy has faced three great ideological enemies: first Nazism, then Communism, and now militant Islam. And in each of these struggles, a certain number of Americans have found themselves out of sympathy with the nation's cause. During the Cold War, many Americans succumbed to the ideology of the enemy. Nazism was and militant Islam is much less attractive to Americans. But in both cases, many Americans wished to opt out of the fight—not because they loved the enemy, but because they so intensely hated one of the enemy's targets: Britain back in 1939 -1941; Israel today.

How history has been subverted. While Nazism holds no attraction for me, it must be pointed out that World War II was essentially a British Zionist instigated war. As pointed out in the preceding chapters, war is a racket and the Zionist bankers made enormous war profits from the killings and devastation. Rabbi Felix Mendelssohn knew what he was talking about when he said that "the Second World War is being fought for the defense of the fundamentals of Judaism."[6] Chaim Weizmann, President of the World Jewish Congress on December 3, 1942 in New York City said:

> We are not denying and we are not afraid to confess, this war is our war and that it is waged for the liberation of Jewry...

5   David Frum and Richard Perle, *An End to Evil*, (2004, Ballantine Books).
6   Source: The Jewish Chronicle, October 8, 1942.

64

> stronger than all fronts together is our front, that of Jewry. We
> are not only giving this war our financial support on which the
> entire war production is based. We are not only providing our full
> propaganda power which is the moral energy that keeps this
> war going....

Richard Perle and his co-author have declared that the War on Terrorism will not end in Iraq. They want more blood letting. It is going to be a long war. Posing to themselves the question, "Where does it all end?" they replied, "We cannot offer specific description of how the final defeat of extremist Islam will occur or even the most approximate guess of when this defeat may be looked for. But we know this: the sounds we hear coming from the angry extremists of the Muslim world are not sounds made by people who feel confident of their triumph. They are the sounds of fury and bafflement and despair. They sense as we do that their defeat is coming—and very possibly that it will arrive much sooner than we dare hope."[7] They want a perpetual war. The War on Terrorism, the initial pretext for a long war has now given way to the "War against Islam" and the official designated enemy of the warmongers—**"Militant Islam."**

The warmongers and their financial backers, the international bankers and the oil cartels knew that the war party would be over if a pretext for another war could not be found soon enough. The rationale for a war economy can only be maintained if there was an external threat—a power of unprecedented magnitude and frightful-ness. The Cold War was over and people began to think of the *Peace Dividend*—more resources for health care, education, hous-ing and social security.

If the idea caught on, it would have been a total disaster for the war cabal. They began to plan for the next global war. On this sordid story we shall now focus our attention.

The mindset of the warmongers and the Megadeath Intellectuals prior to the launching of the War on Terrorism is best reflected in the thinking of Paul Wolfowitz. He felt wasted as the West and the United States in particular was living in ambiguity, without any sense of direction. The Cold War brought issues into sharp focus, but the post Cold War era left a flat taste in the mouth. It was indeed difficult to be a warmonger when there is no enemy to shout at. Wolfowitz's initial strategy was to shift the focus to the need of the

---

7   David Frum and Richard Perle, op. cit., pp. 264.

National Security State to assert its hegemony and to prevent the emergence of a rival power. The Defense Planning Guidance, 1992 was the blueprint.[8] It stated:

> Our first objective is to prevent the re-emergence of a new rival. This is a dominant consideration underlying the new regional defense strategy and requires that we endeavor to prevent any hostile power from dominating a region whose resources, would, under consolidated control, be sufficient to generate global power. These regions include Western Europe, East Asia, the territory of the former Soviet Union, and Southwest Asia.
>
> There are three additional aspects of this objective: First the U.S. must show the leadership necessary to establish and protect a new order that holds the promise of convincing potential competitors that they need not aspire to a greater role or pursue a more aggressive posture to protect their legitimate interest. Second, in the non-defense areas, we must account sufficiently of the advanced industrial nations to discourage them from challenging our leadership or seeking to overturn the established political and economic order. Finally, we must maintain the mechanism for deterring potential competitors from even aspiring to a larger regional or global role.

In plain language, the Defense Planning Guidance is nothing but a "Big Bully's Charter." Another objective which it expounded was the promotion of American values, whatever that means and that to achieve those objectives, the U.S. must be prepared "to take unilateral action," and "should be postured to act independently when collective action cannot be orchestrated." In essence, we were served with the notice that should the members of the UN Security Council fail to comply with the dictates of the United States, she would pursue her agenda regardless of international consensus.

Dennis Ross[9] supported the new approach and said that it was the beginning of what was going to be a serious dialogue about trying to take a look at what were the new threats. It was an attempt to create a "new architecture of international politics and national security ... a coherent way to deal with the post Cold War world." There was a feeling, a consensus amongst the Megadeath Intellectuals that if there

---

8   Paul Wolfowitz was at the material time, the Under-Secretary of Defense for Policy, the 3rd ranking civilian in the Pentagon.

9   Interview with PBS Frontline on January 27, 2003. Source: www.pbs.org

were going to be new threats, new premises needed to be created to deal with those threats—it is not possible to use the same theories, premises and doctrines that have guided the world [i.e. the Cold War world] to the new equation that was evolving. It is clear from the discussion at the material time the warmongers have yet to identify an appropriate "enemy."

Recall the Report from Iron Mountain—"Threats against national interest are usually created or accelerated to meet the changing needs of the war system... Wars are not caused by international conflicts of interest. Proper logical sequence would make it more often than accurate to say that war-making societies require—and thus bring about—such conflicts."

In a parallel development, the ideas expressed by Wolfowitz were explored in Israel by the Institute for Advanced Strategic and Political Studies and the ensuing study was entitled: "A Clean Break: A New Strategy for Securing the Realm"; it was the blueprint to secure Israel's supremacy in the Middle East. The people behind this audacious document at the material time were:

Richard Perle — American Enterprise Institute;
James Colbert — Jewish Institute for National Security Affairs (JINSA);
Charles Fairbank Jr. — Johns Hopkins University;
Douglas Feith — Feith & Zell Associates;
Robert Loewenberg — Institute for Advance Strategic & Political Studies;
Jonathan Troop — Washington Institute of Near East Policy;
David Wurmser — Institute for Advanced Strategic & Political Studies; and
Meyrav Wurmser — Johns Hopkins University.

David Wurmser, is the author of the book, *Tyranny's Ally: America's Failure to Defeat Saddam Hussein,* and it is important to keep his ideas in full view at all times. He wrote that the 1991 Persian Gulf War was the greatest direct military investment the United States has ever made in the Middle East. Kuwait was never in the equation, but a mere pretext for the First Gulf War. It is interesting to note that at the material time, *Pan-Arabism* was identified as the ideological enemy and Saddam Hussein was targeted as its embodiment and the greatest threat to the security of Israel.

At this stage of the preparation for perpetual war, we can already discern an emerging trend and convergence—*the identification of Israel's security interests with that of the United States.* Brilliant! But we were in a slumber. The dagger has been taken out of its sheath and pointed at our jugulars, but we were complacent, especially the Muslims.

By the middle of the 1990s, the stage was set for the key players to come out openly to declare their agenda and prepare the public for the new War Constitution. It was a bold move, but they were prepared. The organization chosen to prepare the ideological war was the *Project for a New American Century.* It was headed by William Kristol, the editor of the right-wing publication *The Weekly Standard.* The first salvo was the letter addressed to President Bill Clinton in 1998:

> We are writing to you because we are convinced that current American policy towards Iraq is not succeeding, and that we may soon face a threat in the Middle East more serious than any we have known since the end of the Cold War. We urge you to enunciate a new strategy that would secure the interest of the U.S. and our friends and allies around the world. That strategy should aim, above all, at the removal of Saddam Hussein's regime from power.
>
> The only acceptable strategy is one that eliminates the possibility that Iraq will be able to use or threaten to use weapons of mass destruction. In the near term, this means a willingness to undertake military action as diplomacy is clearly failing. In the long term, it means removing Saddam Hussein and his regime from power. That now needs to become the aim of American foreign policy.[10]

Anyone reading this letter cannot but come to the conclusion, that the Megadeath Intellectuals and their Masters' war agenda would be best served by the convergence of Israel's and the United States' security interests. Weapons of mass destruction, for the first time were added to the equation, to add to the frightfulness of the threat. *Terrorism* was not even an issue then. This is because the *Global War Agenda* cannot be jump started. World War IV has to be preceded by a regional war. The global threat must be phased in *after* the war in Iraq. This was the important stepping stone. The mood for war was fast gaining momentum.

10 See Appendix 5.

68

In October 1998, President Bill Clinton signed into law the *Iraq Liberation Act*. The U.S. Congress was now primed for war. The test run began with *Operation Desert Fox* on December 16, 1998 when the combined U.S. and British air force conducted a devastating bombing campaign against 100 Iraqi military targets. It created hardly a ripple of protest, notwithstanding that the military action was a war crime.

Just as the *Long Telegram* and *The Source of Soviet Conduct* of George Kennan laid the foundation for the national security policy embodied in NSC-68 of the Truman Administration, the Megadeath Intellectuals' *Rebuilding America's Defenses: Strategy, Forces and Resources For a New Century*[11] was the defining ideological rationale for the *National Security Strategy* of the Bush Administration in 2002.[12] In the ensuing discussion, I will show that the events of September 11, 2001 *fast-forwarded the Global War Agenda* and the entrance of the *New Enemy—Militant Islam!*[13]

The ideological blueprint was authored principally by Thomas Donnelly[14] and provides the most militaristic vision in the history of the United States. The warmongers were compelled to come up with this blueprint because since the end of the Cold War, the United States has struggled to formulate a coherent national security or military strategy, one that accounts for the constants of American power and principles yet accommodates 21st century realities. Absent a strategic framework, U.S. defense planning has been an empty and increasingly self-referenced exercise, often dominated by bureaucratic and budgetary rather than strategic interests—hence, the need for a new blueprint. It states:

> The United States is the world's only superpower, combining pre-eminent military power, global technological leadership, and the world's largest economy. At present the United States faces no global rival. America's grand strategy should aim to preserve and extend this advantageous position as far into the future as possible.

11 September 2000, Project for a New American Century

12 In this book, the reference to the "Bush Administration" refers to that of President George W. Bush. Reference to President H.W. Bush Administration will be referred to as the "First Bush Administration."

13 This has been discussed at length in my book, *Future FastForward: The Zionist Anglo-American Meltdown*. The main arguments are reasserted here for completeness.

14 The Co-Chairmen for the project was Donald Kagan and Gary Schmitt. As stated earlier, William Kristol is the Chairman of PNAC with Robert Kagan, Devon Gaffney Cross, Bruce P. Jackson and John R. Bolton as directors. Gary Schmitt is the Executive Director.

In broad terms we saw the project building upon the defense strategy outlined by the Cheney Defense Department in the waning days of the Bush administration.[15] The Defense Policy Guidance (DPG) drafted in the early months of 1992 provided a blueprint for maintaining U.S. pre-eminence, pre-cluding the rise of a great power rival, and shaping the inter-national security order in line with American principles and interests.

In short, it was the vision for Pax Americana in the 21st Century. The Military-Industrial-Financial complex demanded four core missions for the U.S. military:

1. Defend the American Homeland;

2. Fight and decisively win multiple, simultaneous major theatre wars;

3. Perform the constabulary duties associated with shaping the security environment in critical regions;

4. Transform U.S. forces to exploit the "revolution in military affairs."

And in order to fulfill the above stated missions, the blueprint demanded that the United States must:

• Maintain nuclear strategic superiority, basing the U.S. nuclear deterrent upon a global, nuclear net assessment that weighs the full range of current and emerging threats, not merely the US-Russia balance.

• Restore the personnel strength of today's force to roughly the levels anticipated in the "Base Force" outlined by the Bush Administration.

• Reposition U.S. forces to respond to 21st century strategic realities by shifting permanently-based forces to Southeast Europe and Southeast Asia, and by changing naval deployment patterns to reflect growing U.S. strategic concerns in East Asia.

What is equally ominous is the stated aim of controlling the "international commons" of space and cyberspace and pave the way for the creation of a new military service—U.S. Space Force—with the mission of space control. Again it should be noted when reading the blue-

---

15 In this original quotation, this refers to the First Bush administration.

print, there is not one word on Militant Islam. The long-term enemy was China. It states:

> Raising U.S. military strength in East Asia is the key to coping with the rise of China to great-power-status. For this to proceed peacefully, U.S. armed forces must retained their pre-eminence and thereby re-assure our regional allies. In Northeast Asia, the United States must maintain and tighten its ties with the Republic of Korea and Japan. In Southeast Asia, only the United States can reach out to regional powers like Australia, Indonesia and Malaysia and others. For operational as well as political reasons, stationing rapidly mobile U.S. ground and air forces in the region will be required. A heightened U.S. military presence in Southeast Asia would be a strong spur to regional security cooperation, providing the core around which a de facto coalition could jell.

But from the propaganda point of view, the Megadeath Intellectuals were stumped. China is a huge market and providing very cheap and needed imports for the insatiable U.S. domestic consumers. American corporations were shifting their operations to China. There were rich pickings to be made. China had become a critical engine for global economic growth. Demonizing China was easier said than done. The momentum for war stalled.

Another Pearl Harbor was required to bring the war fever to a pitch. The attack on the World Trade Center and the Pentagon on September 11, 2001 was carefully war-gamed and executed by elements of the Zionist controlled intelligence services and financed by key Wall Street establishments. The ultimate pretext for war—a surprise attack on the United States—was laid before the American people. America responded by giving President Bush unlimited power to wage war indefinitely.

The Global War on Terrorism was seized as the opportunity to *fast-forward* the warmongers' global agenda. George W. Bush played the role and read the script. In his speech to the Joint Session of Congress on September 20, 2001, he said:

> We will pursue nations that provide aid or safe haven to terrorism. Every nation, in every region, now has a decision to make. Either you are with us, or you are with the terrorists. From this day forward, any nation that continues to harbor or support terrorism will be regarded by the United States as a hostile regime.

> Our nation—this generation—will lift a dark threat of violence from our people and our future. We will rally the world to this cause by our efforts, by our courage. We will not tire, we will not falter and we will not fail.

War drums were rolling. The smell of blood was in the air, it was time for bloodletting. The PNAC was quick to take advantage of the mood and by a letter dated September 20, 2001 to President Bush, the warmongers urged:

> Even if the evidence does not link Iraq directly to the attack, any strategy aiming at eradication of terrorism and its sponsors must include a determined effort to remove Saddam Hussein from power in Iraq. Failure to undertake such an effort will constitute an early and perhaps decisive surrender in the war on terrorism. We believe that the administration should demand that Iran and Syria immediately cease all military, financial, and political support for Hezbollah and its operations. Should Iran and Syria refuse to comply, the administration should consider appropriate measures of retaliation against these known state sponsors of terrorism.[16]

Thus we can see how 9/11 came to be exploited to advance the global war agenda. The cowboys must be sent out to get the scalps, starting with the Arabs. Again, notice that at this stage, militant Islam is not in the equation. The Zionists' priority is to secure Israel and its supremacy in the Middle East. This was evident in PNAC's letter of January 2002 to the President. The Zionist war agenda was merged with the U.S. war agenda. The letter states:[17]

> No one should doubt that the United States and Israel share a common enemy. We are both targets of what you have correctly called the "Axis of Evil." Israel is targeted in part because it is our friend, and in part because it is an island of liberal, democratic principles—American principles—in a sea of tyranny, intolerance, and hatred. As Secretary of Defense Rumsfeld pointed out, Iran, Iraq and Syria are all engaged in "inspiring and financing a culture of political murder and suicide bombing against Israel, just as they have aided campaigns of terrorism against the United States over the past two decades." You have declared war on international terrorism, Mr. President. Israel is fighting the same war.

> Israel's fight against terrorism is our fight. Israel's victory is an

16 See Appendix 6.
17 See Appendix 7.

important part of our victory. For reasons both moral and strategic, we need to stand with Israel in its fight against terrorism.

At this juncture, I would like to remind the reader that lurking behind this grand strategy is the British Zionists who are always in the shadows. Remember how they brought the United States into World War I, when Britain was on the verge of defeat; remember again how Roosevelt was seduced to go to war on the side of the British during World War II; remember also, following the *Sinews of Peace* (Iron Curtain) speech by Winston Churchill, America was re-armed for the Cold War.[18] Prime Minister Blair's role in the build-up to the war in Iraq must be seen in this context. He was to President Bush what Churchill was to Roosevelt. This is British Zionist diplomacy at its very best. Make no mistake about this.

The final step in transforming the Megadeath Intellectuals' ideas and concepts into official policy was taken when President Bush spoke to the next generation of warmongers at West Point on June 2002. The strategic linkage between the Defense Policy Guidance 1992 of Paul Wolfowitz and the War Constitution of the 21st Century was finally hooked up. President Bush said:

> Our security will require all Americans to be forward looking and resolute, to be ready for *pre-emptive actions* when necessary to defend our liberty and to defend our lives. America has, and intends to keep, military strengths beyond challenge.

On September 17, 2002, the National Security Strategy—the War Constitution of the 21st Century was published. Some called it the Bush Doctrine. According to John Lewis Gaddis in an interview with PBS[19] the *NSS* is an historic shift for American foreign policy as it is the first serious American grand strategy since containment in the early days of the Cold War. In looking back, he pointed out that "when the Cold War ended, we got into a new situation without a grand strategy; this was similar to the situation after World War I. But the shock of Pearl Harbor gave rise to a new strategy. Similarly the shock of 9/11 gave rise to the present grand strategy."

---

18 For more details, see Chapter 11 and 12 of *Future FastForward*.

19 Interview on January 16, 2003 with PBS Frontline. Source: www.pbs.org. John Lewis Gaddis is the Robert Lovett professor of military and naval history at Yale University and author of several books.

What was interesting coming out of the interview was the rationale for pre-emption. Mr. Gaddis explains:

> The doctrine of pre-emption really has emerged in response to this new kind of threat that was demonstrated to us on 9/11.... In order for pre-emption to work, you have to be in a lot of different places at the same time, with a lot of different capabilities. So pre-emption does, at least in the thinking of the administration, presume hegemony. The fact is the hegemony was there before they came up with the doctrine of pre-emption. But I think what they're arguing is that a condition for pre-emption is hegemonic authority. And indeed, I think they are even arguing this is one of the other things that the rest of the world should come to accept....

When pre-emption was first promoted, it drew an outcry, as if such a policy was inconsistent to American principles. In fact the policy of pre-emption has a long history in American foreign policy, lest we forget. It was the fundamental pillar of America's foreign policy in the 19th century.

Mr Gaddis was brutally frank when he said that "pre-emption was how we took Florida. Pre-emption is, in some way, how we took Texas. Pre-emption is how we took the Philippines, basically, in 1898. So to say that pre-emption is an un-American doctrine is not right historically.

President Bush promised a long war, fought on many fronts against an elusive enemy. He also promised a transformation of the military to ensure total dominance and to prevent any challenge to its hegemony. Donald Kagan[20] had no qualms in agreeing with the new vision and strategy, and the United States' right to act unilaterally. He was quoted as saying, "You saw the movie High Noon? We're Gary Cooper."[21]

It is interesting that even at this point in time *Militant Islam* was not targeted as *the* enemy. The War on Terrorism was marketed as necessary pre-emptive wars against rogue states from acquiring WMDs. The enemy, *Militant Islam* was reserved for Phase 2.

It is obvious why this was so. The Zionists were in control of the

---

20 Donald Kagan is a professor of classical Greek history and a key member of the PNAC.

21 Cited by Jay Bookman in, The President's Real Goal in Iraq, Atlantic Journal and Constitution, September 29, 2002.

National Security Strategy and as far as they were concerned, the priority was to bring the entire Middle East to its knees, and that the Arabs submit and bow to the supremacy of Zionist Israel. Phase 2 would come later. Weapons of mass destruction and the psychological and emotional trauma of an impending mushroom cloud was sufficient incentive to rally the Americans behind the war agenda. After all it is the U.S. soldiers who have to do the bulk of the fighting.

This is the brilliance of British Zionist diplomacy—when you are no longer a superpower or an empire, it best to get someone else to do the dirty work. Since the end of World War II, this has been the dominant foreign policy strategy of the British Zionist warmongers.

By now, I hope it is clear that in preparing for the War Constitution of the 21st Century, the Megadeath Intellectuals were shifting their positions as situation and events evolved. The initial justification for a perpetual war economy was the need to maintain the supremacy of the United States.

The idea of *Full Spectrum Dominance* was bandied about. But this was a hard sell, as the U.S. was the sole superpower and no country by any measure could really challenge the hegemonic status of the U.S. given her vast arsenal of weapons of mass destruction.

9/11 provided another pretext, the danger of WMDs falling into the hands of terrorists and rogue states. The War on Terrorism was the battle cry. However, Afghanistan could only absorb so many bombs and missiles; there were not too many targets, once the Taliban was removed from power.

Saddam Hussein was a better bet and it would also justify military forays into neighboring countries such as Iran and Syria. Wars would keep the U.S. military busy for years. But things did not go as planned and the Iraqi quagmire was the result. Saddam Hussein was captured but the resistance continues to gather strength and military engagements with U.S. forces have escalated. Disillusionment has set in and people are beginning to demand the return of the troops. A new and more frightening enemy was needed. *Militant Islam* was the chosen enemy. Why? The previous designated enemies were essentially military threats. However, *Militant Islam* according to Richard Perle, besides being a military threat is also an ideological threat, one that seeks world domination. He equates the new ideological enemy with Nazism and Communism.

This confirms the conclusions of *The Report from Iron Mountain* that wars are not caused by international conflicts of interest. It is more accurate to say that war making societies require—and thus bring about—such conflicts. Threats are usually created or accelerated to meet the changing needs of the war system.

Part 2

Future Wars

See in my line of work you got to keep repeating things over and over again for the truth to sink in, to kind of catapult the propaganda.

— President George W. Bush,[1] **May 24, 2005**

Naturally the common people don't want war; neither in Russia, nor in England, nor in America, nor in Germany. That is understood. But after all, it is the leaders of the country who determine policy, and it is always a simple matter to drag the people along, whether it is a democracy, or a fascist dictatorship, or a parliament, or a communist dictatorship. Voice or no voice, the people can always be brought to the bidding of the leaders. That is easy. All you have to do is to tell them they are being attacked, and denounce the pacifists for lack of patriotism and exposing the country to danger. It works the same in any country.

— Hermann Goering, Nuremberg Tribunal

It's fun to shoot people. You go to Afghanistan. You've got guys who slap women around for five years because they don't wear a veil. You know, guys like that ain't got no manhood anyway, so it's a hell of a lot of fun to shoot them.

— Lt. General James N. Mattis,[2] **U.S. Marines**

---

1 Cited by Tom Engelhardt, "Catapulting the Propaganda," August 29, 2005. Source: www.TomDispatch.com

2 Cited by the Author in his book, *Future FastForward*, p. 272

7

Perpetual Wars Part 1: Burgers and Bullets

> The chain reaction of evil wars producing more wars must be broken, or we shall be plunged into the dark abyss of annihilation.
>
> **— Dr. Martin Luther King, Jr.**

> The de facto role of the U.S. armed forces will be to keep the world safe for our economy and open to our cultural assault.
>
> **— Major Ralph Peters**

One of the major failings of the anti-war movement is the failure to pin point and track the warmongers and expose their war agenda before the Megadeath Intellectuals and spin doctors launch their propaganda offensive. In the preceding chapters, I have shown that wars require years of preparations, as people need to be conditioned for war. The armed forces need to be prepared as well.

When the U.S. Army War College Quarterly, *Parameters* published in the summer of 1997 the article by Major Ralph Peters,[1] entitled *Constant Conflict,* my radars were alerted and I began to devote more time to the developments in U.S. military affairs.[2] What the major wrote was remarkably prescient as recent events have confirmed. With the discipline and assuredness gleaned from years of military training, he wrote a chilling scenario:

1   Major Ralph Peters, at the material time, was assigned to the Office of Deputy Chief of Staff for Intelligence where he was responsible for Future Warfare. He is a graduate of the U.S. Army Command and General Staff College and holds a master's degree in international relations.

2   Obviously there were other warmongers, but I have highlighted this article because Major Ralph Peters was responsible for articulating U.S. Future Wars. It was an important, if not a critical pointer.

There will be no peace. At any given moment for the rest of our lifetimes, there will be multiple conflicts in mutating forms around the globe. Violent conflicts will dominate the headlines, but cultural and economic struggles will be steadier and ultimately more decisive. The de facto role of the U.S. armed forces will be to keep the world safe for our economy and open to our cultural assault. **To those ends, we will do a fair amount of killing. We are building an information-based army to do that killing.** (Emphasis added)

We have entered **an age of constant conflict.** We are entering a new American century, in which we will become still wealthier, culturally more lethal, and increasingly more powerful. We will excite hatreds without precedent... One of the defining bifurcations of the future will be the conflict between information masters and information victims. How can you counterattack the information others have turned upon you? There is no effective option other than competitive performance. For those individuals and cultures that cannot join or compete with our information empire there is only inevitable failure. (Emphasis added)

So when Paul Wolfowitz appeared before the Senate Armed Services Committee on April 9, 2002,[3] the concepts and ideas first propounded by the Major in 1997 had been transformed into policies. The warmongers were already prepared for war, while we were still shopping for goodies in the high streets. The writing was on the wall but we chose to ignore it.

But what really caught my attention and kept me awake the whole night were Major Peters's insights on cultural wars as being an integral part of the overall military game plan. When I told my colleagues that Big Mac and Coca Cola are an essential part of the U.S. imperial agenda, they would laugh at me and the label "conspiracy theorist" would inevitably be hurled at me! Read carefully what the Major has to say, he is having the last laugh:

Information, from the internet to rock videos, will not be contained, and fundamentalism cannot control its children. **Our victims volunteer. American culture is the most powerful in history and the most destructive of competitor cultures.** The genius, the secret weapon, of American culture is the essence that the elites despise: ours is the first genuine people's culture. It stresses comfort and convenience—ease—and

3   See the detailed discussion in Chapter 5.

it generates pleasures for the masses. We are Karl Marx's dream, and his nightmare. (Emphasis added)

It is time for a reality check. This is the deadliest propaganda warfare strategy at the cultural level by far that I have studied. The arrogance and confidence is not misplaced and I must grudgingly say, well earned. I have always contended that war, any war, starts at the propaganda level. If we lose this war, we will lose the "Hot War" even before a shot has been fired. We have been and continue to be brainwashed. And it looks like we can't do very much about it.

The Major continues:

Secular and religious revolutionaries in our century have made the identical mistake, imagining workers of the world or the faithful can't wait to go home at night to study Marx or the Koran. Well, Joe Sixpack, Ivan Tipichni, and Ali Quat would rather "Baywatch." America has figured it out, and we are brilliant at operationalizing our knowledge ... and our cultural empire has the addicted men and women everywhere clamoring for more. And they pay for the privilege of their disillusionment.

The films most despised by the intellectual elite those that feature extreme violence and to-the-victors-the-spoils-and-sex—are our most popular cultural weapon, bought or bootlegged nearly everywhere. American action films, often in dreadful copies, are available from the Upper Amazon to Mandalay. They are even more popular than our music, because they are easier to understand. The action films of Stallone or Schwarzenegger or Chuck Norris rely on visual narratives that do not require dialogue for a basic understanding. They feature a hero, a villain, a woman to be defended or won— and violence and sex. Complain until doomsday; it sells. The enduring popularity abroad of the shop-worn Rambo series tells us far more about humanity than does a library full of scholarly analysis. (Emphasis added)

If we are honest and desire to win the propaganda war, we must *i* first admit that the observations of the Major are not only correct, but that the American culture has become the dominant culture in our societies. And yes, we are even willing and silly enough to pay to be victims of this cultural assault. My reaction, when reading this article was how unprepared we are for the coming wars. I took a day off to think about the whole scenario and wrote down a list of Q & A the Why, Who, How and When questions. Then I went to my library and took out at random 50 of the so-called best sellers on wars, media etc., and critiques of the last three U.S. regimes.

I was stumped. Without exception all of them were focusing on the neo-conservatives and their agendas. There were some superficial references to the military, but not enough to make any sense. The perspectives were essentially from the "civilian warmongers." No doubt they were important but there were no serious and in-depth military inputs. I was so caught up with the Megadeath Intellectuals that I overlooked that they were all connected in one way or another to the Department of Defense, and surely the military think tanks, such as the Army War College and the Naval War College and other relevant agencies and units would have given their inputs. A chill ran down my spine. I missed some very critical intelligence in my on-going research. It would never happen again. That was how way back in the 1990s, I began tracking the mindset of the military establishment and that was how I came across the article by Major Ralph Peters.

The Major is a true warrior and a thinking one at that. And that is why he is so dangerous. When muscle and brain come together, what you get is one efficient killing machine. When you have a major within the enormous military hierarchy thinking in such terms and getting noticed, it is time for a wake up call. So let's get right back into his head and see what else he has in store for us. Study him as you would study for your graduation examinations. What he says next is truly an eye-opener:

> It remains difficult, of course, for military leaders to conceive of warfare, informational or otherwise, in such broad terms. **But Hollywood is "preparing the battlefield," and burgers precede bullets. The flag follows trade.** Despite our declaration of defeat in the face of battlefield victory in Mogadishu, the image of U.S. power and the U.S. military around the world is not only a deterrent, but a psychological warfare tool that is constantly at work in the minds of real and potential opponents… **Our unconscious alliance of culture with killing power is a combat multiplier no government, including our own, could design or afford.** We are magic. And we are going to keep it that way.
>
> Culture is fate. Countries, clans, military services, and individual soldiers are products of their respective cultures, and they are either empowered or imprisoned … The current chest-thumping of some Asian leaders about the degeneracy, weakness, and vulnerability of American culture is reminiscent of nothing so

much as of the ranting of Japanese militarists on the eve of the Pacific War. I do not suggest that any of those Asian leaders intend to attack us, only that they are wrong…. **Their failure is programmed.**

The next century will indeed be American, but it will also be troubled. We will find ourselves in constant conflict, much of it violent. The United States army is going to add a lot of battle streamers to its flag. We will wage information warfare, but we will fight with infantry. And we will always surprise those critics, domestic and foreign, who predict our decline. (Emphases added)

People like me must have been on his mind when he wrote the last sentence. But he got it wrong. I have always held that the Zionist Anglo-American war cabal is a paper tiger, but it would be foolish and reckless and highly irresponsible to dismiss the mighty war machine in the immediate and middle term when preparing a counter-strategy in defense of our independence and sovereignty as a nation and as a people. Let us have no illusions. The major's views are not those of a minority, but reflect the mindset of the entire Military-Industrial-Financial complex. And if corroboration is needed, recall what Thomas Friedman said in 1999, and I quote:

The hidden hand of the market will never work without a hidden fist. McDonald's cannot flourish without McDonnell Douglas, the designer of the F-15. And the hidden fist that keeps the world safe for Silicon Valley's technologies is called the United States Army, Air Force, Navy and Marine Corp.[4]

You can bet your bottom dollar that Mr. Friedman took his cue from Major Peters and/or warriors who share similar sentiments. So be serious, for when such warmongering has reached the main street, *Constant Conflict* is a given!

Query: Which Communist country in the last 40 years embarked on a similar cultural war as intense and far reaching as that described by Major Ralph Peters? If you got the answer, then you must agree that there is no difference between Cultural warfare under Communism and Militarist State Capitalism. But what has happened is that anti-communist warmongers have been so successful in demonizing its enemies that we overlooked that we are also victims of their brainwashing programs as well. Even after such frank and brutal admissions by Megadeath Intellectuals such

4   Source: New York Times Magazine, March 28, 1999.

as Major Peters, we refuse to confront the issue and choose to bury our heads in the sand. It makes no difference whether warmongers are Communist *red* or Capitalist *blue,* they are all the same murderers, plunderers and war criminals. A bullet from a M16 or an AK47 makes no distinction when it rips the guts of its victims. Victors always give their version of history. But we are no longer stupid and ignorant as before.

Simone Weil pointed out some time ago that the great error of nearly all studies of war has been to consider war an episode in foreign policies, when it is an act of internal politics. Major Ralph Peters and Thomas Friedman make it very clear that preserving America's interests is in fact the No. 1 priority and the primary rationale for the coming wars.

To meet the needs of *Constant Conflict,* the United States Joint Chiefs of Staff came up with their grand vision, entitled *Joint Vision 2010.*[5] The then Chairman of the Joint Chiefs of Staff, John M. Shalikashvili, explained how the United States would be fighting future wars. He said that, "The nature of modern warfare demands that we fight as a joint team. This was important yesterday, it is essential today and it will be even more imperative tomorrow. Joint Vision 2010 provides an operationally based template for the evolution of the Armed Forces for a challenging and uncertain future. It must become a benchmark for Service and Unified Command vision."

Joint Vision 2010 (JV2010) is the military blueprint for future wars: "Persuasive in Peace, Decisive in War and Pre-eminent in any Form of Conflict." It is the conceptual template for how America's Armed Forces will channel the vitality and innovation of its personnel and leverage technological opportunities to achieve new levels of effectiveness in joint war-fighting. It will be focused on achieving dominance across the range of military operations through the application of new operational concepts. JV2010 begins by addressing the expected continuities and changes in the strategic environment, including technology trends and their implications for the U.S. Armed Forces. It's a prescription for fighting in the early 21st century. This vision of future war-fighting embodies the improved intelligence and command and control available in the information age and goes on to develop four operational concepts: dominant manoeuvre, precision engagement, full dimensional protection and focused logistics to

5   See Appendix 8.

achieve *Full Spectrum Dominance.*

Notwithstanding the scope of JV 2010, the Joint Chiefs of Staff under Chairman, General Henry H. Shelton decided to extend and refine further JV 2010 and in May 30, 2000 released the expanded *Joint Vision 2020* (JV 2020).[6]

JV 2020 builds upon and extends the conceptual template established by the earlier JV 2010 and to provide the guidance for the continuing transformation of America's Armed Forces. The primary purpose of those forces has been and will be to fight and win the nation's wars. The overall objective is the creation of a force that is dominant across the full spectrum of military operations. Attaining the goals requires the steady infusion of new technology and modernization and replacement of equipment. The evolution of these elements over the next two decades will be strongly influenced by two factors. First, the continued development and proliferation of information technologies will substantially change the conduct of military operations. These changes will be a key enabler of the transformation of the operational capabilities of the joint force and the evolution of the joint command and control. Second, the Armed Forces will continue to rely on intellectual and technical innovation.[7]

In March 15, 2005, the Joint Chiefs of Staff published their *Doctrine for Joint Nuclear Operations.*[8] This document provides the guidelines for the joint deployment of forces in nuclear operations. The use of nuclear weapons in the coming wars is no longer a fiction. The Joint Chiefs have declared that it is essential for U.S. forces to be prepared to use nuclear weapons effectively to prevent and to retaliate against WMD use. What is significant is the role played by *Combatant Commanders* in the use of nuclear weapons. The new doctrine gives the responsibility to the geographic Combatant Commander the responsibility for defining theatre objectives, selecting specific targets and targeting objectives, and developing the plans required to support those objectives. It follows from this that nuclear weapons are no longer to be employed as strategic weapons, but would be used as tactical weapons as well.

Specifically, geographical Combatant Commanders may request Presidential approval for use of nuclear weapons in the

6   See Appendix 9.
7   Condensed from the "Introduction" to JV 2020.
8. See Appendix 10.

following scenario:

- To counter potentially overwhelming adversary conventional forces, including mobile and aerial targets (troop concentrations);
- For rapid and favorable war termination on U.S. terms;
- To ensure success of U.S. multinational operations;
- To demonstrate U.S. intent and capability to use nuclear weapons to deter adversary use of WMD.

The new paradigm in nuclear theatre warfare is best illustrated by the Diagram below.[9]

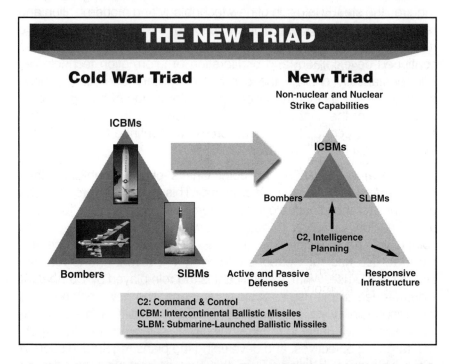

It is not possible for the purposes of this book to analyze in depth how the National Security State of America intends to wage wars in the 21st Century. The above discussion, I believe is sufficient to give an appropriate overview of the challenges we would face in engaging such a predator state. However, it would be remiss of me not to highlight the immense danger of the United States' intention to militarize *Space.* The United States Space Command's *Vision for 2020*[10] in com-

9   Source: Joint Chiefs of Staff, Doctrine for Joint Nuclear Operations

bination with the Joint Chiefs of Staff's *Doctrine for Joint Nuclear Operations* is a recipe for global disaster for humanity.

Anyone who is interested in world peace must oppose vehemently the militarization of space. The blueprint unequivocally declares:

> U.S. Space Command Dominating the space dimension of military operations to protect U.S. interests and investments Integrating Space Forces into war-fighting capabilities across the full spectrum of conflict.

General Howell M Estes III[11] made it very clear that "the increasing reliance of U.S. military forces upon space power combined with explosive proliferation of global space capabilities makes a space vision essential. As stewards for military space, we must be prepared to exploit advantages of the space medium. This vision serves as a bridge in the evolution of military space into the 21st century and is the standard by which United States Space Command and its components will measure progress in the future."

We had earlier mentioned that the "flag always follow trade," that is to say that the military will always be deployed to secure the economic interests of the National Security State. A very bright young boy once asked me, "How would Space Warfare secure economic interests?" A very interesting and relevant question, one which even adults would not contemplate.

It is therefore critical for the anti-war movement to understand the significance of the militarization of Space. The United States Space Command's *Vision for 2020* gives an explanation which should be committed to memory:

A Historical Perspective—Evolution of Space

> Historically, military forces have evolved **to protect national interests and investments—both military and economic.** During the rise of sea commerce, nations built navies to protect

10 See Appendix 11.

11 A Command pilot with more than 4,500 flying hours and his military assignments included Director of Operations (J-3), the Joint Staff at the Pentagon and before his retirement Commander-in-chief, North American Aerospace Defense Command (CINCNORAD) and United States Space Command (USCINCSPACE), and Commander, Air Force Space Command (COMAFSPC), headquartered at Peterson Air Force Base, Colo. He was elected to the Board of Directors of the Space Foundation in 2001 for a 3-year term.

and enhance their commercial interests. During the westward expansion of the Continental United States, military outpost and cavalry emerged to protect our wagon trains, settlements, and railroads. (Emphasis added.)

As Air power developed, its primary function was to support and enhance land and sea operations. However, over time, air power evolved into a separate and equal medium of warfare.

The emergence of Space power follows both these models. Over the past several decades, space power has primarily supported land, sea and air operations. During the early portion of the 21st century, Space power will also evolve into a separate and equal medium of warfare. Likewise, Space forces will emerge to protect military and commercial national interests and investments in the space medium due to their increasing importance.

The medium of space is the fourth medium of warfare—along with land, sea, and air. Space power (systems, capabilities, and forces) will be increasingly leveraged to close the ever-widening gap between diminishing resources and increasing military commitments.

The above is essentially a short history of Colonial and Imperialist economics, as history is also replete with accounts where trade and commerce were conducted in peace and harmony without the threat of war and/or the need to monopolize and/or dominate trade. Obviously, if a foreign power drives away the indigenous people from their land and commits genocide, the victims would retaliate and defend themselves, as in the case of the native Indians in America and elsewhere. The logic of a predator state is to rob and plunder and therefore the need to protect the spoils of war. If we gather in peace and trade in peace, there would be no need for military forces.

Soon after the publication of *Future FastForward,* I was invited to explain the various issues raised in my book, in particular the coming nuclear and space wars. Not many took my briefings seriously, and even those who did, there was a distinct annoyance and a matter-of-fact attitude that it would not occur in my part of the world. I am therefore extremely grateful to Dr. Helen Caldicott, author of *The New Nuclear Danger* [12] for so forcefully bringing to the world's attention this real and pressing danger. This is a *must read*

12 Dr. Helen Caldicott, *The New Nuclear Danger,* (2004, The New Press, New York)

book and the chapter, "Space: The Next American Empire" should convince even the most skeptical.

General Richard B. Meyers[13] was quoted as saying that, "The threat, I believe is real. It's a threat to our economic well-being. This is why we must work together to find common ground between commercial imperatives and the president's tasking me for space control and protection." Way back in 1996, another general was already advocating the need to control space. He said, "It's politically sensitive, but it's going to happen. Some people don't want to hear this, and it sure isn't in vogue, but absolutely we're going to fight in space. We're going to fight from space and we are going to fight into space. That's why the U.S. has developed programs in directed energy and hit-to-kill mechanisms. We will engage terrestrial targets someday— ships, airplanes, land-targets—from space. We will engage targets in space from space."[14]

Recent developments in the United States have alarmed many in the corridors of power throughout the world. The January 2001 *Report of the Commission to Assess United States National Security Space Management and Operation* states that the government should "vigorously pursue the capabilities called for in the National Space Policy to ensure that the President will have the option to deploy weapons in space to deter threats to, and if, necessary, defend against attacks on U.S. interests." The report went on to state that it is possible to project power through space and from space in response to events anywhere in the world. This capability would give the U.S. a much stronger deterrent and, in a conflict, an extraordinary military advantage.

In December 2001, the United States notified Russia of its intention to withdraw from the ABM Treaty[15] which in turn led to Russia's withdrawal from its obligations under START II Arms Reduction Treaty. In 2002, the Bush regime presented the Nuclear Posture Review to Congress which allows the President the option to use nuclear weapons against non-nuclear states. There were also contingency

---

13 He was the former Commander-in-Chief of the U.S. Space Command, 1999 and the current Chairman of the Joint Chiefs of Staff.

14 General Joseph Ashy was the former Commander-in-Chief of U.S. Space Command. Cited by Helen Caldicott. Source: Aviation Week & Space Technology (August 5, 1996) William Scott, "USSC Prepares for Future Combat Missions in Space."

15 The Anti-Ballistic Missile (ABM) Treaty was entered into between the U.S. and the then Soviet Union in 1972.

plans to nuke Russia, China, North Korea, Iraq, Iran, Syria and Libya. This is a direct violation of the obligations under the Nuclear Non-Proliferation Treaty (NPT) which the U.S. has ratified. Yet, the U.S. has the audacity to demand Iran forgo her rights under the NPT to use nuclear power for peaceful energy purposes.

In the First Gulf War and the recent illegal invasion of Iraq, the United States and Britain have unleashed tons of depleted uranium on the Iraqi people. The U.S. Nuclear Defense Agency has condemned the use of depleted uranium as it can cause cancer, leukemia, kidney failures and horrendous birth defects. Leuren Moret, an international expert on Depleted Uranium and who has worked in two U.S. nuclear weapons laboratories, including the Livermore Laboratory, has declared that they are WMD as they meet the definition of weapons of mass destruction in two out of three categories under U.S. Federal Code Title 50, Chapter 40, Section 2302.[16] Depleted uranium on the battlefield has three effects on living systems: it is a heavy metal "chemical" poison, a "radioactive" poison and has a "particulate" effect due to the very tiny size of the particles that are 0.1 microns and smaller.

I would like to end this chapter by discussing briefly another horrendous weapon of mass destruction—*weapons that trigger climate change.* According to Prof. Michel Chossudovsky, the United States and Russia have developed capabilities to manipulate climate.[17] The Prof. informs us that the U.S. has the technology which was developed under the *High-Frequency Active Auroral Research Program* (HAARP) as part of the Strategic Defense Initiative (SDI) more commonly referred to as "Star Wars." It is fully operational and has the ability to trigger floods, droughts, hurricanes and earthquakes. As an instrument of conquest, it is capable of destabilizing agricultural and ecological systems of an entire region.

The *Times* of London, in November 23, 2000 carried a story[18] that world renowned scientist, Dr. Rosalie Bertell had revealed that the "US military scientists are working on weather systems as a potential weapon. The methods include the enhancing of storms and

16 Leuren Moret, "Depleted Uranium is WMD," August 9, 2005, Battle Creek Enquirer. Source: www.commondreams.org

17 Michel Chossudovsky, "Weapons Have the Ability to Trigger Climate Change," January 4, 2002. Source: Center for Research on Globalization @ www.globalresearch.ca

18 Ibid.

the diverting of vapour rivers in the Earth's atmosphere to produce targeted droughts or floods."

Welcome to the "Weather Wars!"

This is the mad, mad world which the Megadeath Intellectuals have in store for us. The point is, "What are you doing about it?"

8

Perpetual Wars Part 2:
Back to Hot Wars Again

> America and the Western world are at war with 'fascist' Middle
> East governments and totalitarian Islamists. The freedoms we
> stand for are loathed and our vulnerable systems under attack.
> Liberty and security will be in conflict as we line up behind the
> new march of democracy.
>
> — **James Woolsey, Former CIA Director**[1]

> There has never been a just one, never an honorable one, on
> the part of the instigator of the war.
>
> — **Mark Twain**

Soon after the invasion of Iraq, James Woolsey in an address to a group of students informed them that World War IV has started and explained that the Cold War was the Third World War. He further warned that this Fourth World War would last considerably longer than either World War I or II but maybe not as long as the four decades of the Cold War.

Since then there has been debates within the anti-war movement whether the wars in Afghanistan and Iraq could be construed as the commencement of World War IV. This is intellectual masturbation and serves no purpose. As far as I am concerned, it matters not whether the Neo-conservatives are right in labeling the present conflict as World War IV. The anti-war movement should adopt the correct attitude toward this issue. When the warmongers have declared World War IV and are formulating their policies on that basis and executing military operations on a global scale, we should structure our

---

1   James Woolsey, "At War for Freedom," July 20, 2003.
     Source: www.defenddemocracy.org

response accordingly. It is common sense!

Sun Tzu, the great military strategist advises us to "know your enemy and know yourself." When they are conducting their operations on a global scale our counter-strategies must correspond to that reality. Failure to do so would ensure our defeat. Major Ralph Peters knows something that the anti-war movement doesn't and/or refuses to acknowledge, and that is why he is confident enough to declare that we are "programmed for failure." The debate should end here and now!

Let's get back to James Woolsey. He said that the new war is against three enemies: the religious rulers of Iran, the "fascists" of Iraq and Syria, and Islamic extremists like Al Qaeda. "As we move toward a new Middle East," Woolsey said, "over the years and, I think, over the decades to come, we will make a lot of people very nervous. It will be America's backing of democratic movements throughout the Middle East that will bring about this sense of unease. Our response should be, good!"

In July 2003, Mr. Woolsey elaborated further his thoughts about his enemies. It is important that we understand where he is coming from. Mr. Woolsey explains:

> We are loathed for our freedom of speech, freedom of religion, freedom of the press, open economies, equal or almost equal treatment of women, and so on. It is not what we have done wrong, that is creating the problem; it is what we do right.

> If that is true, then this is not a war that will end with an Al Qaeda Gorbachev; it will not end with arms control agreement. **It is war to the death, like the war with the Nazis, and we should understand that it will have to be fought that way.**
> (Emphasis added)

The Zionist Anglo-American war cabal is on a "new march for democracy" in the Middle East, another rationale for war. How convenient, just when the previous rationale "to rid Saddam Hussein of weapons of mass destruction" was exposed as a lie. They think we are stupid and/or have short memories. History has confirmed the wisdom of Mahatma Gandhi who taught us that "liberty and democracy become unholy when their hands are dyed red with innocent blood." The "Old March for Democracy" during the Cold War was also about weapons of mass destruction from the "Evil Empire" and the need to preserve democracy in the "Free World." Instead, we were left with a legacy of coups, murders, tortures and fascist dictatorships in countries from Latin America, Africa and Asia. Are we to forget Nicaragua, Honduras, El Salvador, Guatemala, the Apartheid regime of South Africa, Namibia, the Zionist occupation of Palestine, Vietnam, Laos, Cambodia, and East Timur? Senator Robert M. La Follette warned that every nation has its war party—it is not the party of democracy, it is the party of autocracy and it seeks to dominate.

The new march for democracy is an old tune, only this time performed by second rate artists. And the ideological enemy is Islam.

On September 29, 2004, Deputy Secretary of Defense Paul Wolfowitz, Senator Jon Kyle, Senator Joseph Lieberman, James Woolsey, Norman Podhoretz, Eliot Cohen and other warmongers were invited to attend a forum, sponsored by the Committee on Present Danger and the Foundation for the Defense of Democracies, titled: *World War IV: Why We Fight, Whom We Fight, How We Fight.* This gathering of warmongers would like us to believe that they are the praetorian guards for democracy and peace. But we are mindful that President James Madison has counselled that no nation could preserve its freedom in the midst of continual warfare. I find it hard to believe that our leaders, historians and political scientists are not aware that even the warmongers such as Zbigniew Brzezinski have said that democracy is inimical to imperial mobilization. So why are these leaders at the United Nations waving the flag of democracy in the midst of the global war unleashed by the Zionist war cabal? There is only one answer—they have all sold out to the war-profiteers.

Those who still insist on questioning my approach should seriously go for a brain scan to determine whether they can be "re-programmed" from being a war junkie back to a normal human being.

Just to ensure that we are still on the same wavelength, my writings are not *Anti-America* or *Anti-Britain* but it is undeniably and without apologies *anti-Zionist, anti-warmongers* and *anti-Megadeath Intellectuals.* We have been brainwashed for war and programmed to kill. And unless we make an attempt to understand and grapple with the issues relating to war, we will never succeed in our quest for peace. Let's get real. Being brainwashed for war and programmed to kill, means that we have been *programmed for failure.* This is what Major Peters has in store for us. He has unashamedly confessed to his crime. We become killers in their service and in the process ends up getting killed in some forsaken battlefield. The equation is simple and neat:

Brainwashed for War = Killing Machine = Death

There is a book written in 1999 called *Total War, 2006* by Simon Pearson[2] which was based on military theories propounded way, way back in 1993. The jacket cover describes Mr. Pearson's work as "a dazzling and terrifying future history of the next world conflict." The author even wrote about a Second Pearl Harbor, though not as played out in 9/11, as the trigger for the global conflict. Although the timing was a bit off, on the whole he got it right. There will be total war in the 21st Century. September 11 has been described as the "New Pearl Harbor" and exploited by the Bush and Blair regimes to launch the Global War on Terrorism. I wonder how many military strategists and political analysts on this side of the divide have read this incredible book. If so, why have they remained silent?

And yet, the truth-seekers are still labeled as "Conspiracy Theorists."

Dr. Earl Tilford, professor of history and a fellow at the right-wing *"Foundation for the Defense of Democracies"* wrote in June 24, 2004:

> **World War IV is a total war on a global scale.** World War IV seems complex but keep in mind during World War III (the Cold War) while American forces fought North Vietnamese regulars and National Liberation Front (Vietcong) guerrillas in South Vietnam, we also fought the Pathet Lao in Laos and Khmer Rouge in Cambodia. From Greece and Yugoslavia to Korea and Vietnam and the Caribbean and jungles of South America, the Cold War involved a large number of nations and groups. **Nevertheless, it all came together as part of a struggle between competing worldviews.**
>
> The **"War on Terror" is no less complicated and similarly encompassing.** Since it is an Information Age War in which knowledge is power. It is essential to understand who we fight and what they aim to achieve. Our enemies are more than savage barbarians with a penchant for decapitating the innocent. They are integral to a concerted effort to redefine the world order.
>
> **This is World War IV.** Forget the sleazy sickness of Abu

2   1999, Hodder and Stroughton, London

Ghraib. Stop mouthing meaningless slogans like, 'Bush Lied, Soldiers Died.' **Steel yourselves for a long bloody fight. This is a war we must not lose.** (Emphases added)

How do they intend to win this long bloody fight? They had it all figured out, so it seems as far back as 2002, before the invasion of Iraq. Norman Podhoretz in his article, "How to Win World War IV"[3], was confident enough to give the answer. He was contemptuous of the counsels of Colin Powell, the Secretary of State and former Chairman, Joint Chiefs of Staff, that unless the United States applied massive military force, she would be bogged down in a long war. He scoffed at the possibility that the United States would end up in a quagmire in the war against Iraq as was the case in Vietnam. His confidence was simple enough, the superior air power of the United States would be sufficient to destroy any enemy that dare confront the sole superpower. When the B-52s and the 15,000 pound "Daisy Cutters" were unleashed in Afghanistan, Mr. Podhoretz proclaimed in jubilation, "The ghost of Vietnam was exorcised!" The 15,000 pound Daisy Cutter exerted a huge and terrifying psychological impact as it exploded just above ground, destroying everything in its path. It was all part of the "Shock and Awe" strategy that would demoralize the enemy troops. Killing needn't be messy, just bomb the enemy to smithereens! The war in Iraq is only the beginning.

Norman Podhoretz advocates a bold vision, a war to transform the entire Middle East. He takes the view that all wars have consequences that may not always be foreseeable, but they invariably reshape the world. World War IV would enable the United States to reshape the world in accordance with her values. There is therefore the need to topple five or six or seven more tyrannies in the Islamic world. This war would deliver the death blow to "Militant Islam" which is the real enemy and not the abstraction "terrorism."

But that was before the fierce resistance against the U.S. occupation of Iraq. It would be wrong and naïve to believe that warmongers would give up the fight easily or that they would cut and run. In another article,[4] entitled *World War IV: How It Started, What It Means, and Why We Have to Win,* Mr. Podhoretz was not in the least perturbed by the battlefield setbacks in Iraq. He declared that "Iraq is only the second front... the second scene so to speak, of the first act of a five-act

3   Norman Podhoretz, "How To Win World War IV," February 2002, The Commentary Magazine.
4   The Commentary Magazine, September 2004.

play. In World War II and then in World War III, we persisted in spite of impatience, discouragement, and opposition for as long as it took to win, and this is exactly what we have been called to do today in World War IV." Norman Podhoretz assures his followers that victory is certain and promises that Islam would be eliminated as an ideological threat.

However, we have detected a sign of anxiety on his part in 2005. In the article *The War Against World War IV*,[5] the third in his trilogy on the Fourth World War, he surmised whether George W. Bush would be backing down from the ambitious strategy that was contained in the *Bush Doctrine* for fighting and winning World War IV. Recall that the 2004 Presidential election was waged and won on the basis of continuing the war in Iraq, that there will be no retreat and pre-emption would still be the first choice in dealing with the enemies of the United States. Why then, should the question now be raised?

There are two factors. Firstly, to the disappointment of the warmongers, the "bunker buster" mega bombs like the "Daisy Cutter" failed to do their job. When intelligence officers went to do damage assessments, they found the Taliban and Al Qaeda bunkers largely intact. Adding to this military setback is the fact that the United States and Britain having 150,000 troops and the largest intelligence network in the world have failed to infiltrate the ranks of the resistance in Iraq and to execute successful military operations against them.

There is also the growing dissatisfaction within the ranks of the warmongers that all is not well. In May 2005, the old Cold War warrior, Mr. Robert McNamara[6] wrote that the United States should cease its Cold War style reliance on nuclear weapons as a foreign policy tool. He castigated the current U.S. nuclear weapons policy as immoral, illegal, militarily unnecessary and dreadfully dangerous. Coming from the man who was the Defense Secretary during the Vietnam War this is a revelation. He further lamented that "the whole situation seems so bizarre as to be beyond belief. On any given day, as we go about our business, the president is prepared to make a decision within twenty minutes that could launch one of the most devastating weapons in the world. To declare war requires an act of congress, but to launch a nuclear holocaust requires twenty minutes' deliberation by the president and his advisors…"

5   The Commentary Magazine, February 2005.
6   Robert McNamara, "Apocalypse Soon" (Foreign Policy, May/June 2005 Issue). Source: www.truthout.org

Secondly, Fear! Fear in the knowledge that the hidden role of Israel would be exposed. Norman Podhoretz singled out Pat Buchanan for character assassination as he was one of the earliest to point out that the Neo-cons' sole purpose for waging wars was to make the Middle East safe for Israel. What Buchanan wrote shocked the Zionist establishment.

✳ *Cui Bono?* For whose benefit these endless wars in a region that holds nothing vital to America save oil, which the Arabs must sell to us to survive? Who would benefit from a war of civilizations between the West and Islam? Answer: one nation, one leader, one party. Israel, Sharon, Likud.

Betraying that fear, Podhoretz expressed the hope that should George Bush pass the test in Iraq, there will be fewer and fewer "ears to hear what will more and more, sound like a crackpot talk it always was." World War IV must continue to its logical end.

There we have it, the common thread—World War IV—linking the Megadeath Intellectuals James Woolsey, Simon Pearson, Major Ralph Peters, Eliot Cohen, Dr. Earl Tilford, and others too numerous to be referenced here. General W. Sherman has also taught us that there is another common thread amongst warmongers. It is that those who have neither fired a shot not heard the shrieks and groans of the wounded are the ones who cry loudest for blood. War is hell!

It literally sickens me to have to listen almost on a daily basis, to those myopic Muslim leaders, opinion makers, so called civil society advocates and do-gooders, and "brand consultants" pleading that we should "tone down," "we should not annoy America," "we need their trade," "we must be moderate" and so on and so forth!!! But sad to say, the former Prime Minister of Malaysia is the only exception.

The rest have sold their souls and are worshipping at the Altar of the War Profiteers, the Hedge Funds, Money Markets and Financial Investments Pimps! There is a popularity contest going on, to see who would be chosen as the "Most Acceptable Muslim Leader" by the Washington Consensus. The front-runner seems to be President Musharraf of Pakistan, but there are two or three others running hard to overtake him in this Islamic Leaders Relay. And the coveted reward for these stooges is to be seen with Blair at international summits, to be singled out for some miniscule role in international affairs and *the* invitation to be with the Cowboys and gunslinger at the Crawford Ranch!

Approbation by Blair and Bush, it seems, legitimizes their administrations. How pathetic can we get!

I am going to unmask all these hypocrites. Besides the above political prostitutes, there are other political opportunists. They do take part in some anti-war activities but purely to project a well-crafted image of a "progressive"—whatever that means. They are mere sound bites—a PR exercise. They are usually the first to throw insidious labels such as "conspiracy theorists," "extremists," "left-wing," "the minority," "fanatics" and the like at truth seekers. They live in comfort in suburbs reserved for the rich, and intellectualize every suffering and horror of war as being attributable to poverty, some disgruntled intellectuals, misguided individuals and terrorists. They are the Zionist warmongers' indispensable mouthpieces, albeit some of them are unconscious lapdogs.

They know that their wives would not likely be raped, molested or murdered; their children would not be orphaned; their wealth would not be confiscated or diminished and if it should happen that their fairy tale world is about to be destroyed, they have the means to fly to some safe haven abroad. They are the fifth column within the anti-war movement.

To get back to the matter at hand, I would like to draw your attention to a very courageous Jew, yes a Jew, Mr. Daniel Amit an Israeli physicist who refuses to correspond with any American scientific institution. This might seem odd and extreme to many. But his rationale and courage found wanting in so many scientists and academicians, is indeed worthy of emulation. If only our own intellectuals and scientists are as noble and honest. In response the Editor-in-Chief of the American Physical Society who wrote, "We regard science as an international enterprise and we do our best to put aside political disagreements..." The Jew replied:[7]

> Thank you for your letter of April 8. I would have liked to be able to share the honorable sentiments you express in your letter as well as your optimism in the future role of science and the scientific community. To be frank, and with much sadness and pain, after 40 years of activity and collaboration, I find very little reason for such optimism. What we are watching today, I believe, is a culmination of 10-15 years of **mounting barbarism of the American culture the world over, crowned by**

7   Source: www.informationclearinghouse.info/article10304.htm. Cited by James Rothenberg, "Rich Countries Problems: Too much military—Too little humanity."

the achievements of science and technology as a major weapon of mass destruction. (Emphasis added)

We are witnessing manhunt and wanton killing of the type and scale not seen since the raids on American Indian populations, by a superior technological power of inferior culture and values. We see no corrective force to restrain the insanity, the self-righteousness and the lack of respect for human life (civilian and military) of another race.

Science cannot stay neutral, especially after it has been so cynically used in the hands of the inspectors to disarm a country and prepare it for decimation by laser guided cluster bombs. No, science of the American variety has no recourse. I, personally, cannot see myself anymore sharing a common human community with American science. Unfortunately, I also belong to a culture of a similar spiritual deviation (Israel), and which seems to be equally incorrigible.

In desperation I cannot but turn my attention to other tragic periods in which major societies, some with claims to fundamental contributions to culture and science, have deviated so far as to be relegated to ostracism and quarantine. At this point I think American society should be considered in this category. I have no illusions of power, as to the scope and prospect of my attitude. But, the minor role of my act and statement is a simple way of affirming that in the face of a growing enormity which I consider intolerable, I will exercise my own tiny act of disobedience to be able to look straight into the eyes of my grandchildren and my students and say I did know.

I have read this statement, God knows how many times and I have always been inspired by its message, courage, honesty and humility. Each time, I felt discouraged and not wanting to continue writing, re-reading this eloquent statement urges me on. I, too, want to exercise a tiny act of disobedience and be able to look straight into my children's eyes and say that I did know and I tried to do something about it.

I have said in my book, *Future FastForward,* that the American people are not the enemy, the Jews are not the enemy, the Muslims are not the enemy, and the Christians are not the enemy. The Megadeath Intellectuals and scientists in the employ of the Zionist warmongers are the enemy and all of us must exercise our own tiny act of disobedience if we are to make a difference.

9

Act 2, Scene 1:
The WMD Lies, Again

> Iran aggressively pursues these weapons and exports terror,
> while an unelected few repress the Iranian people's hope for
> freedom… States like these, and their terrorist allies, constitute
> an Axis of Evil, arming to threaten peace of the world. By seek-
> ing weapons of mass destruction, these regimes pose a grave
> and growing danger. They could provide these arms to terrorists,
> giving them the means to match their hatred. They could attack
> our allies or attempt to blackmail the United States. In any of
> these cases, the price of indifference would be catastrophic.
>
> — **President George W. Bush**[1]

When I first read the State of the Union speech I could not help
but recall the venerable Vietnamese Buddhist monk, Thich Nhat
Hanh's wise words regarding warmongers—"In order to rally people,
government need enemies. They want us to be afraid, to hate, so we
will rally behind them." It was fear that drove the American people to
rally blindly behind Bush to invade Afghanistan and Iraq. The nuclear
weapons bogey is whipped up once again by the warmongers to justify a war against Iran.

In the previous chapters, I have shown that Iraq was merely Act
One, Scene Two of a five-act War Play.[2] The War Play envisages the
violent disposal of five, six or seven regimes in the Middle East following the invasion of Iraq. What is astonishing is the arrogance and
confidence of the warmongers that they can repeat the lies all over
again and no one, save a handful, would be the wiser. The response

---

1   State of the Union Address on January 29, 2002.

2   This was the description given by Norman Podhoretz to the War in Iraq in his "Trilogy on
    World War IV" published in the Commentary Magazine.

thus far from the member countries of NAM and OIC[3] currently under the chairmanship of Malaysia, to the bullying of Iran suggest that the warmongers may yet again get away with their lies.

This is the pathetic situation in spite of the fact that the UN watchdog, the International Atomic Energy Agency (IAEA) after two years of intensive investigations reported that it had found no evidence that Iran had a nuclear weapons program and that Iran's cooperation with the agency was very good.[4] The IAEA has found no evidence that NPT-proscribed materials have been stolen or diverted, or that Iran was engaged in any NPT prohibited activity. In particular, there is no evidence that Iran has been enriching uranium in the facilities it has constructed or is constructing.[5] On August 15, 2005, it was reported by the British daily, *The Independent* that the IAEA has rebutted claims that Iran is "trying to make A-bomb."[6]

The United States, notwithstanding the abovementioned reports, continues to threaten Iran with military action and economic sanctions. Once again the world turns a blind eye. The world is indeed a village and its reaction reflects that of a village mindset to the village bully. The UMMAH's silence is deafening as was the case of Iraq before the illegal invasion. To be sure, they do protest and demand justice but only after the fact, when bombs have been unleashed and hundreds of thousands have been slaughtered, and when others have come out to the streets to protest. Why take risks, when you can follow. That way, they can still proclaim that they are for justice and peace.

We do have short memories!

Recall, just before the Iraq invasion. The Director-General of the IAEA, Mohammed Elbaradei reported that "after three months of intensive inspections, we have to date found no evidence or plausible indication of the revival of a nuclear weapons program in Iraq." The United States then resorted to forgery to accuse Iraq of trying to import uranium from Niger, the "Yellow Cake" story. That was also exposed as a lie when Elbaradei reported:

---

3   NAM = the Nonaligned Movement; OIC = Organization of Islamic Conference.

4   IAEA Report on the November 15, 2004, as reported in the Washington Post on November 16, 2004.

5   Ibid.

6   Anne Penketh, "UN Nuclear Watchdog Rebuts Claims that Iran is Trying to Make A-bomb," August 15, 2005.

Iraq has provided a comprehensive explanation of its relation with Niger. The IAEA was able to review correspondence from the government of Niger and compare full format contents and signature of that correspondence with those of the alleged procurement related documentation. Based on thorough analysis, the IAEA has concluded with concurrence from outside experts, that these documents which formed the basis for the reports of recent uranium transactions between Iraq and Niger are, in fact, not authentic.[7]

No doubt in the near future, similar intelligence deceptions would be perpetrated by the warmongers, but this time round, they may not be so careless in employing obvious forgeries. And, if they are not exposed as such, are we to accept as Gospel truth, the war propaganda against Iran?

It is on record that Iran is a signatory to the *Additional Protocol* to the IAEA *Safeguard Agreement,* which is a qualitative system that enables the IAEA to establish a comprehensive picture of a state's nuclear and nuclear related activities, including all nuclear imports and exports. It also provides the IAEA the authority to visit any of the signatory's facilities to investigate questions about—or inconsistencies in—the signatory's nuclear intentions.[8]

But the spin for war against Iran has already started. The culprit is again the fascist militarist Colin Powell. Contrary to the well crafted image of a "moderate," he is playing the same old trick. He said, just before his retirement:

> I had seen some information that would suggest that they [Iranians] have been actively working on delivery systems. I'm not talking about uranium or fissile material or the warhead. I am talking about what one does with the warhead.[9]

Colin Powell must earn his retirement pension. What better way then to give Bush the excuse to go to war as he did in the United Nations in the 2nd Gulf War. This Afro-American is a disgrace to his race and people. The warmonger does not cite the source for his rabid warmongering stance and/or produce concrete evidence in support of his allegations. But through subtle nuance, he is suggesting that Iran

7   Source: Garland Favorito, "Our Nation Betrayed: The Iraq WMD Intelligence Deception" @ www.blackforest.com/cat_law_politics.htm

8   Gordon Prather, "Powell Singing Pre-War Tune on Iran?" @ www.lewrockwell.com. See also www.WorldNetDaily.com

9   Ibid.

can deliver nukes small and light enough by means of ballistic mis-siles. Are we to believe him, when upon his retirement, he belatedly confessed that he was wrong in delivering the speech at the UN–"it was painful then; it is painful now."[10] This man has no principles. Even his contrition is a fake.

This warmonger's con trick was followed up by John Bolton[11] in his address to the Hudson Institute on August 17, 2004:

> Today, I'd like to speak about Iran, which has concealed a large scale, covert nuclear weapons program for over eighteen years, and which therefore, is one of our most fundamental prolifera-tion challenges.
>
> All of Iran's WMD—chemical weapons, biological weapons, nuclear weapons, and ballistic missiles—pose grave threats to international security. Iran's pursuit of these deadly weapons, despite its signature on treaties that ban them, marks it a rogue state, and it will remain so until it completely, verifiably and irre-versibly dismantles its WMD-related programs.

But where is the evidence?

In contrast, we have the United States and President Bush declaring in the National Security Strategy and the Nuclear Posture Review that they reserve the right to use nuclear weapons against non-nuclear weapons states, as well as against Russia, China, North Korea, Iran, and Syria. The United States has also abrogated the ABM Treaty with Russia and is now developing "baby nukes," tactical nuclear weapons and bunker busters. So who is proliferating nuclear weapons?

There is a disconnection here. No one asks the crucial question, why is it right and proper for the United States and Britain to have WMDs and to threaten countries with annihilation? Third World coun-tries, in particular Muslim countries (with the exception of Pakistan, a stooge of the US) are not even allowed to have nuclear energy. There is an implied racism here. The white man can be trusted to behave responsibly when in possession of WMDs, but not the non-whites. But the historical record shows otherwise.

Let us for a moment assume that Iran is in fact pursuing a

---

10 Interview with ABC's Barbara Walters, and reported in the New York Times, September 17, 2005. See also www.gulfnews.com and www.rockymountainnews.com.

11 Jon Bolton is now the U.S. Ambassador to the UN.

nuclear weapons program. So what? In the circumstances of the war-mongers' threats of pre-emptive action, economic sanctions, being labeled as part of the "Axis of Evil," surely Iran and for that matter any country under threat of war should be entitled to defend itself by any means. But no, Iran is not even entitled to a legitimate nuclear fuel program allowed under the NPT because the United States and Israel say so! I would even go as far as saying that the NPT is a big con, set up to serve the interest of imperial powers and to ensure nuclear monopoly just so that they can continue to be the world's great bullies. It has not stopped proliferation at all in its entire history. It is a sham. It should be scrapped. Instead an international treaty aimed directly at the nuclear powers to *disarm as a pre-condition* for other states to agree to non-proliferation should be put in its place. The burden shifts and while critics argue that it will not work, at the minimum it exposes the hypocrisy of the entire NPT regime. We shall all be compelled to make a Hobbesian choice!

In the recent UN Summit of world leaders, allegedly a gathering to reform the UN, leaders from the OIC member states were conspic-uously slavish and submissive. Other than President Chávez of Venezuela who had the courage to expose the double standards of the United States and Britain, the rest merely recited the usual plati-tudes. This was how President Chávez castigated the warmongers and their cronies and I make no apologies in quoting him extensively.

> The original purpose of this meeting has been completely dis-torted. The imposed center of debate has been a so-called reform process that overshadows the most urgent issues, what the peoples of the world claim with urgency; the adop-tion of measures that deal with the real problems that block and sabotage the efforts made by our countries for real devel-opment and life.
>
> Five years after the Millennium Summit, the harsh reality is that the great majority of estimated goals—which were very modest indeed—will not be met. We pretended reducing by half the 842 million hungry people by the year 2015. At the current rate that goal will be achieved by the year 2215. Who in this audience will be there to celebrate it? That is only if the human race is able to survive the destruction that threatens our natural environment.
>
> At the Porto Alegre World Social Forum last January different personalities asked for the United Nations to move outside the

United States if the repeated violations to international rule of law continue. Today we know that there were never any weapons of mass destruction in Iraq. The people of the United States have always been very rigorous in demanding the truth to their leaders; the people of the world demand the same thing. There were never any weapons of mass destruction; however Iraq was bombed, occupied and is still occupied. All this happened over the United Nations. That is why we propose this Assembly that the United Nations should leave a country that does not respect the resolutions taken by this same Assembly.

Not too long ago the President of the United States went to an Organization of American States' meeting to propose Latin America and the Caribbean to increase market oriented policies, open market policies—that is neo-liberalism—when it is precisely the fundamental cause of the great evils and the great tragedies currently suffered by our people: the neo-liberal capitalism, the Washington Consensus. All these have generated a high degree of misery, inequality and infinite tragedy for all the peoples on his continent.

What we need now more than ever Mr. President is a new international order. Let us recall that the United Nations assembly in its sixth extraordinary session period in 1974, 31 years ago, where a new International Economic Order action plan was adopted, as well as the States Economic Rights and Duties Charter by an overwhelming majority, 120 votes for the motion, 6 against and 10 abstentions. This was the period when voting was possible at the United Nations. Now it is impossible to vote. Now they approve documents such as this one which I denounce on behalf of Venezuela as null, void and illegitimate. This document was approved violating the current laws of the United Nations. This document is invalid! This document should be discussed; the Venezuelan government will make it public. We cannot accept an open and shameless dictatorship in the United Nations. These matters should be discussed and that is why I petition my colleagues, heads of states and heads of government, to discuss it.... This document was approved by a dictatorial hammer which I am here denouncing as illegal, null, void and illegitimate.

The only country where a person is able to call for the assassination of a head of state is the United States. Such was the case of a Reverend called Pat Robertson, very close to the White House: He called for my assassination and he is a free person. This is international terrorism...

Let us not permit that a few countries try to reinterpret the principles of international law in order to impose new doctrines
such as "pre-emptive warfare." Oh do they threaten us with pre-
emptive war! And, what about the "Responsibility to Protect"
doctrine? We need to ask ourselves. Who is going to protect
us? How are they going to protect us?

Precisely, who is going to protect us from the warmongers?
The answer is not as complicated as we are led to believe. It is the
people. People the world over must come together to confront the
bullies. We must unite to disarm the bullies. Absent an international
concerted effort to disarm the bullies, *there can be no genuine
peace.* This is a given. When the entire village rises up against the
village bully, he will be isolated and he can bully no more. This is a
simple fact of life—tried and tested, and proven successful. All we
need to do is to extend it on a global scale. Remember Vietnam? A
small agricultural country by her own efforts, albeit with the moral
support of the world's people, defeated within a span of fifty years
two global bullies, *the French Colonialists* and the *American
Imperialists.*

I agree with James Woolsey, the former CIA Director that there
is a new march for democracy. But he got it wrong. It is *our* new
march for democracy against the dictatorship of warmongers that
will sweep the world in the 21st century. The likes of him should be
worried and feeling unease. It is good that they feel so. And, it is
about time.

I am getting ahead of myself. I do seek your indulgence. Let us
get back to the warmongers' lies and deceptions.

I am going to share some very interesting information about
Iran's nuclear program. It all started in the 1960s. And Uncle Sam
was right there providing the assistance and know-how. It was all
very proper as there was a bilateral agreement between the United
States and Iran. It was to enable Iran to tap nuclear power for civilian energy use. The Shah had signed and ratified the Nuclear Non-
Proliferation Treaty (NPT), so there was no risk of Tehran going off
on a tangent.

The United States supplied the first 5-megawatt nuclear
research reactor to the Tehran Nuclear Research Centre, operated by
the Atomic Energy Organization of Iran (AEOI). Back then, everyone
was very chummy.

How then do we square the stance taken by the United States at the present moment with their past practice? The answer is simple enough, the Shah was a stooge and there were big bucks to be made—U.S. $6 billion to be precise. What was really interesting was the role played by Henry Kissinger, who was then the Secretary of State under President Ford, and his underlings Dick Cheney and Paul Wolfowitz. In 1975, Kissinger signed the *National Security Decision Memorandum 292*[12] with copies to the Director of CIA and Secretary of Defense. It expressly permits U.S. materials to be fabricated into fuel in Iran for use in its own reactors and for pass-through to third countries with which the U.S. has agreements. Kissinger has recently confirmed that when approving the deal, the issue of proliferation never came up.[13] The Shah was a reliable and obedient stooge.

There was no debate why Iran needed nuclear energy when it was a major oil producer and was in fact pumping an estimated 6 million barrels of oil per day, much more than what she is producing today. As the saying goes, the devil is always in the details. In 1976, President Ford approved a directive to allow Iran to operate a reprocessing facility for *extracting plutonium from nuclear reactor fuel.* The deal was for a complete *Nuclear Fuel Cycle.* In simple layman terms, if a country is allowed to complete the nuclear fuel cycle, that country is in a position to develop nuclear weapons.

Following the Iranian revolution which overthrew the Shah, all work at the nuclear plant at Bushehr stopped. It was severely damaged during the Iraq/Iran war in the 1980s. Work resumed in 1995 when Iran entered into an agreement with Russia to complete the half-built Bushehr plant.

Let us now examine the accusations by the Bush warmongers against Iran and see how they stacked up with their previous stance. Dick Cheney recently said, "They're already sitting on an awful lot of oil and gas. Nobody can figure why they need nuclear as well to generate energy." It is strange that the same question did not occur to Dick Cheney when President Ford approved nuclear cooperation with Iran. Dick Cheney conveniently forgot what the President Ford administration said at the material time: "Tehran needed ... to prepare against the time—about 15 years in the future when Iranian oil production is

12 April 22, 1975, a copy is in the possession of the author. The document sets out the parameters for nuclear cooperation between the U.S. and Iran. Source: www.ford.utexas.edu/library/document/nsdmnssm/nsdm292a.htm

13 Interview, Washington Post, March 27, 2005.

expected to decline sharply."[14] Iran is now in the period of production decline. And in spite of the IAEA reports cited above, that there is no evidence of a nuclear weapons program, why is the U.S. so hell bent to deny Iran its rights for nuclear fuel which is expressly allowed for under the NPT? Why the flip-flop?

Kissinger replied that in the 70s, "they [Iranians] were an allied country, and this was a commercial transaction."[15] Today, Iran is no longer a stooge and Russia is having the commercial transaction.

In recent weeks, a new momentum has been gathering to demonize Iran and exaggerate the nuclear threat. As in the Iraq war, the Project for the New American Century (PNAC) fired the first salvo when its Executive Director, Gary Schmitt challenged the accuracy of the January 2005 National Intelligence Estimates that Iran is 10 years from having a nuclear bomb. Citing Israeli sources, he said that Iran could have a bomb as early as 2008. Adding fuel to the fire, the British International Institute for Strategic Studies came out with a report that Iran is five years or so from developing nuclear bombs.

Yet again a British intelligence dossier is relied upon to heighten the fear factor. This is the same outfit that proclaimed back in 2002 that Iraq could assemble nuclear weapons within months, if fissile material from foreign sources were obtained. We now know how that dossier was "sexed up" and then covered up by the infamous Hutton Inquiry.

I am sure there will be a repeat performance at the UN Security Council with another Afro-American taking the lead in the puppet show. Already moves are being made to refer Iran to the Security Council. And there will be another scare tactic by Condoleezza Rice that we cannot allow "the smoking gun to be a mushroom cloud."

Let us now get back to basics and expose the lies and pinpoint exactly who are the real proliferators. On this very important issue of non-proliferation, very few opinion makers have actually read the Nuclear Non-Proliferation Treaty (NPT) and related documents. Yet these political pundits jump on the bandwagon to denounce and demonize North Korea and Iran for alleged proliferation. The chorus was singing the same tune just before the illegal invasion of Iraq. I am therefore not surprised that the warmongers' scare tactics have been so effective. They prey on our collective ignorance.

14 Ibid. Cited by Dafna Linzer, "Past Arguments Don't Square with Current Iran Policy."
15 Ibid.

The treaty was the initiative of Ireland which became the first signatory when the treaty opened for signing in 1968. All the five "declared nuclear powers (the US, Soviet Union, China, France and United Kingdom) had signed the treaty by 1992. With the demise of the Soviet Union, Russia assumed the obligations and rights of NPT.

Many will be surprised to know that South Africa during the Apartheid regime had a nuclear weapons program aided by Israel but had since 1991 abandoned its nuclear program and signed the NPT. The former Soviet republics have also relinquished their nuclear arsenal and/or transferred them to Russia.

The NPT can be summarized into three components, more commonly referred as the *Three Pillars.*

First Pillar: The signatories have agreed that the five declared nuclear-weapon states (NWS), which are also the 5 permanent member states of the UN Security Council are permitted to own nuclear weapons and they are obligated not to transfer nuclear weapons technology to other states. The quid pro quo on the part of the non-NWS is that they agree not to seek and/or develop nuclear weapons.

Additionally, and this is very important, the 5 NWS signatories have undertaken *not to use* their nuclear weapons against a non-NWS party *except* in response to a nuclear attack, or a conventional attack in alliance with a Nuclear Weapons State. Although these undertakings have not been incorporated in the treaty, they have been an integral part of the non-proliferation regime. But the bullies have not kept to their word. More of this later.

Second Pillar: It is an express obligation under Article VI of the treaty and the preamble that the NWS parties reduce and liquidate their nuclear stockpiles. This is a sham promise, as it was never intended to be fulfilled. Article X provides that any state/signatory *can withdraw* from the treaty if they perceive that "extraordinary events" force them to do so, for example, if threatened with war by another country, in particular a NWS state and/or the threat of a preemptive war.

Third Pillar: The treaty expressly recognizes the right of all states to peacefully use nuclear technology, in particular energy generation. However, this right is subject to stringent conditions so as to prevent the development of nuclear weapons.

Many nuclear power stations are "light water reactor nuclear power stations." They use "enriched uranium." So it does not make sense to say that a country can install light water reactor nuclear power stations but cannot have access to enriched uranium. It is as ridiculous as saying that you can buy a car, but you cannot have the *fuel* that *drives* the car.

Theoretically, uranium enrichment is a small but one of many steps toward the development of a nuclear weapon. But under the terms of the NPT inspection regime, it is nigh impossible to do so. One need not be a rocket scientist to understand the basic principles which I shall now proceed to explain. It has all to do with *The Nuclear Fuel Cycle.* Once we grasp this issue, we can easily expose the lies and fabrications by the Bush regime's warmongers.

I shall now endeavor to give a brief explanation.

Uranium, contrary to popular myth is a relatively common element and like tin is found throughout the world. It is 500 times more abundant than gold and is found in most rocks and soils as well as in many rivers and sea water. Where there is high concentration of uranium, such concentration is called an ore. It must be processed before it can be used as fuel for a nuclear reactor.

The nuclear fuel cycle has the following key elements:[16]

1. **Mining:** Uranium ore can be mined by excavations and in situ techniques (In Situ Leaching, ISL).

2. **Milling:** Processing the ore to produce uranium concentrate, "Yellow Cake."

3. **Conversion:** The concentrate must be processed and this stage is called conversion—the uranium is converted into a gaseous form called uranium hexafluoride.

4. **Enrichment:** There are two enrichment processes in large scale commercial use, gaseous diffusion and gas centrifuge. The enriched uranium hexafluoride is reconverted to produce enriched uranium oxide—U235.

5. **Fuel Fabrication:** Uranium oxide is baked at very high temperatures (1400°) to form pellets which are then encased in

16 Source: www.worldnuclear.org

metal tubes to form fuel rods.

6. **Fission:** When the U-235 atom is split (when fission occurs) energy is released to heat water and turn it into steam to power electricity generating turbines.

7. **Spent Rods / Fuel:** These rods can be reprocessed to extract plutonium (Pu239) or (Pu241) which in turn can be used as fissile material. It is therefore a renewable source of energy.

Therefore, when the U.S. and the trio of European states, France, Germany and the United Kingdom demanded that Iran cease enriching uranium, they are denying the entrenched right of all signatories to the NPT to use nuclear energy for peaceful purposes. Surely the issue of non-proliferation should be directed more at the 5 NWS to disarm rather than preventing the use of nuclear energy for peaceful purposes.

The hypocrisy of the five nuclear weapons states, in particular the United States can be illustrated by their non-compliance with the provisions of the NPT. During the Cold War, the U.S. in agreement with NATO member states deployed nuclear weapons in Europe, and as of 2005 there are about 180 tactical B61 nuclear bombs in Belgium, Germany, Italy, the Netherlands and Turkey. This is certainly a contravention of Article I and II of the NPT. The Cold War argument, if that was the case is no longer applicable with the collapse of the Soviet Union and the demise of the Warsaw Pact.

This was in fact the rationale for reaffirming the principles of NPT at the NPT conference in 1995. The parties agreed inter alia:

Reaffirming the preamble and articles of the Treaty on Non-Proliferation of Nuclear Weapons,

Welcoming the end of the Cold War, the ensuing easing of international tension and the strengthening of trust between states,

Desiring a set of principles and objectives in accordance with which nuclear non-proliferation, nuclear disarmament and international cooperation in the peaceful uses of nuclear energy should be vigorously pursued and progress, achievements and shortcomings evaluated periodically within the review process provided for in article VIII(3) of the Treaty, the enhancement and strengthening is welcomed,

Reiterating the ultimate goals of the complete elimination of nuclear weapons and a treaty on general and complete disarmament under strict and effective control....

The parties agreed that the universal adherence to the NPT is an urgent priority and every effort should be made to prevent proliferation, and the NWS should commit to disarmament.

The review in May 2005 did not disclose any improvement in the state of affairs and attempts to move the agenda forward was scuttled by the United States. While the United States connives with Israel, Pakistan and India, non-signatories of the NPT and confirmed nuclear powers, the world's attention is diverted to the so called imminent threat of Iran and North Korea.

It is important that the member countries of NAM and OIC give the fullest support to Iran and expose the duplicity of France-Britain-Germany in conniving with the U.S. to refer Iran to the UN Security Council for breaching its obligations under the agreement made in 2003. There were never any obligations undertaken by Iran in the talks with the European trio. We must get our facts right.

To prove to the world its peaceful intentions in developing nuclear energy, Iran offered to sign an *Additional Protocol* which would set in place a more stringent regime of inspections and monitoring of her nuclear activities. And in a further measure of goodwill and confidence building, Iran *volunteered to temporarily suspend* all uranium enrichment and processing activities current or otherwise. The IAEA was even invited to verify the suspension of activities. Instead of responding positively to these gestures, the European trio and the U.S. demanded the total surrender of Iran's rights under the NPT.

What was most infuriating was the stance of the IAEA who having given a report that Iran had no nuclear weapons program, made veiled threats and imposed additional conditions not within the ambit of the NPT in the knowledge that Iran could not and/or would not comply as it would tantamount to relinquishing all her rights.

If the Malaysian media is deemed to be representative of the third world media, it is apparent that the United States has succeeded to a large extent in misrepresenting the facts and demonizing Iran as a rogue nation. The Malaysian media without exception was rehashing every headline and hype spun by CNN, Fox News, *The New York Times*, *The Washington Post*, etc., and not once (and this is not a typo), yes, not once did they give an impartial and accurate account of Iran's position on this issue.

Be it negligence or ignorance, the media have become the willing mouthpiece of the Zionist propaganda machine. We are indeed brainwashed for war!

10

Another War Party: First Get the Sunnis, Next the Shiites!

> We gave potential enemies a vivid and compelling demonstration of America's ability to win swift and total victory over significant enemy forces with minimal U.S. casualties. The overwhelming American victory in the battle of Baghdad surely stamped a powerful impression upon the minds of the rulers of Teheran and Pyongyang….
>
> We have learned valuable lessons about how to fight wars in the region….
>
> — **Richard Perle and David Frum**[1]

You will recall that in the war against Iraq, the Zionist warmongers' mouthpiece was the Project for the New American Century (PNAC) and their lackey, the Iraqi National Congress headed by Ahmed Chalabi. We saw how they laid the ideological groundwork, followed by a legal framework and then a full scale propaganda war. When public opinion was in their favor, they unleashed the "Shock and Awe" brutal war on the innocent Iraqi people.

The same blueprint is being followed in the next war in the Middle East and the most likely target will be the Shiites in Iran. However, if circumstances permit the warmongers will also go after Syria. I am more inclined to the view that Zionist Israel is more eager for Iranian blood.

As a consequence of the quagmire in Iraq, the warmongers in PNAC have lost their credibility and have tactically retreated to allow others to push their Middle East agenda forward. In the war against Iran, a new grouping has emerged, calling itself the "Iran Policy

---

1   Richard Perle and David Frum, *An End to Evil*

Committee" (IPC). The leading members of the IPC are as follows:

1. **Ambassador James Atkin (Ret.)**; he was the Ambassador to Saudi Arabia during the Nixon regime.

2. **Lt. General Thomas McInerney**, USAF (Ret.).

3. **Lt. General Edward Rowny**, USA (Ret.).

4. **Major General Paul E. Vallely**, USA (Ret.).

5. **Lt. Col. Bill Cowan**, USMC (Ret.).

6. **Captain Charles T. "Chuck" Nash**, USN (Ret.).

7. **Paul Leventhal**, Founder & President, Nuclear Control Institute.

8. **Dr. Neil Livingstone**, CEO Global Options Inc.

9. **R. Bruce McColm**, President, Institute for Democratic Strategies.

10. **Prof. Raymond Tanter**, former Senor Staff Member, NSC.

11. **Clare M. Lopez**, Executive Director, IPC, former CIA Intelligence Analyst.

The Committee had on February 10, 2005 published a report entitled *U.S. Policy Options for Iran,* which serves the same purpose as the PNAC's report, *Rebuilding America's Defenses*—to lay the ideological rationale for war. Before proceeding to analyze the report, I would like to draw your attention that in January 2005, the war cabal's representatives led by House International Relations Subcommittee Chair for the Middle East and Central Asia, Ileana Ros-Lehtinen (R-Fl) and five other prominent members of the U.S. Congress introduced the *Iran Freedom Support Act,* with more than 50 sponsors. Remember the *Iraq Liberation Act 1998* and the *Syria Accountability Act 2003?* Like I said, they are following the same modus operandi.

The IPC has the *Mujahideen-e Khalq* (MEK) as its collaborators and they are playing the same role as the INC in Iraq. Until early 2005, the State Department has always considered this crude outfit as a terrorist organization. But today, the MEK is Washington's indispensable ally against the Mullahs in Tehran. When the end justifies the means, using terrorists to do the dirty work is to be expected.

The next little bit of information about the MEK should explain to a large extent the mindset of the Muslims in the Middle East and why the Zionists are so confident of their superiority over their enemies. In the War in Iraq, the Bush regime had to consider the danger to their right flank when they had to push fast toward Baghdad from Kuwait. The danger Iran posed could not be discounted. Iran has legitimate grievances, to put it mildly, with America who had financed Iraq in the Iraq/Iran war in the 1980s. So in order to secure her flanks, the U.S. offered to get rid of the opposition's military bases along the Iraq/Iranian border. Iran was only too happy to see the rebels blasted away. But in the process, Iran sold its soul to the "Great Satan."

Yes, you got it right, the opposition was the MEK and their bases were destroyed by American bombs! The actors in Act Two, Scene Two have their roles reversed. But no sooner was the role reversed, then the authors of the War Play decided yet again to reverse the role. Having successfully invaded Iraq, the right flank was no longer a threat, but has in fact turned into the staging ground for the next phase in the Zionist Middle East Agenda.

This is how the Zionists are able to twist the Muslims around their little fingers and the Muslims are none the wiser! Iran is once again the enemy and the MEK the ally. Should we really be surprised? They did teach that *"the enemy of my enemy is my friend."*

The report "U.S. Options for Iran" makes interesting reading. We need only to consider two recommendations by the IPC to appreciate and anticipate the events that would unfold in the coming months. The first is *Destabilization,* a time tested strategy to subvert and overthrow any government.

The report says:

> The ... option would open a campaign of destabilization, whose aim would be to weaken the grip of the ruling regime over the Iranian people sufficiently that Iranian opposition groups inside the country and abroad are empowered to change the regime. To the extent that any or all of the.... Diplomatic measures, coercive or not, are deemed useful, their application should be sustained during a destabilization phase.

> The next stage of an American led campaign to compel conformity to international norms of behavior would be to encourage Iranian opposition groups. This is an option that has never actually been on the table and has not been explored sufficiently; this option relies on the Iranian opposition to take the lead role in coordinating a campaign for regime change and

establishing representative institutions. Secretary of State Condoleezza Rice told reporters on her February 2005 European
trip, "The Iranian people should be no different from the Palestinians or Iraqis or other peoples around the world." That is people of Iran are not immune to the wave of democracy in the
Middle East.

As stated earlier, the warmongers never ceased to use "Democracy" as the rationale for war, and incredibly, the Arab world still
dances to the tune. I hope that the next passage of the report will be
sufficient to wake up the Muslim world to the duplicity of the Zionist
Anglo-American war cabal. If not, and I am not sorry to say in spite of
repeated warnings, they deserve the bashing that is sure to come in
the near future.

> At this juncture in 2005, therefore, a review of U.S. policy con-
> cerning the MEK and the overall Iranian opposition is in order. The
> designation of the MEK as a foreign terrorist organization by the
> State Department **has served, since 1997, as an assurance to
> the Iranian regime that the United States has removed the
> regime change option from the table. Removing the terrorist
> designation from the MEK could serve as the most tangible
> signal to the Iranian regime, as well as to the Iranian people,
> that a new option is now on the table.** Removal might also have
> the effect of supporting President Bush's assertion that America
> stands with the people of Iran in their struggle to liberate them-
> selves. (Emphasis added)

Let's pause and read the above passage again and again. In the
Iraq/Iran war, Muslims were made to fight fellow Muslims. The historic
acrimony and mistrust between Sunnis and Shiites was exploited by
the Zionist war cabal in accordance with the "divide and rule" policy.
Muslims slaughtered Muslims by the hundreds of thousands contrary
to the teachings of the Holy Quran.

Further exploiting the need for revenge and to settle scores, the
Zionists, in order to secure the right flank in the war against Iraq, tactically placated the Iranians. Since the U.S. was doing the killing, the
Iranians should be more than happy. Misapplying the adage, "the
enemy of my enemy is my friend," the Mullahs were hoodwinked into
believing that the *Great Satan* has changed, become a friend, and
convinced that regime change was no longer an option on the table
by the cheap con-trick of bombing a few military bases of the MEK,
their immediate opposition and threat.

Mr. Corleone, the Mafia Godfather said, "hating your enemy clouds the mind." How very true. The warmongers would not have dared to launch the invasion of Iraq knowing the right flank was exposed and at risk to Iranian intervention or subversion. To secure the flank, the Zionist strategists played the oldest con trick in the book.

Now that Saddam Hussein is deposed, it is the Mullahs' turn to be clobbered.

The con-trick will be played once more in the war against Iran. Exploiting the animosity of the Arab world toward the Shiites, Saudi Arabia, Egypt and Jordan will be told to stay out of the fray as the U.S. is in fact doing them a favor by curtailing the Shiite's influence in the region. Typically, these spineless leaders in order to preserve their rule will obediently fall in line, forgetting that once Iran is destabilized, the U.S. will find some other reason to wage another war and that they will be next in line for regime change. Have they not read Oded Yinon's Plan in the 1980s, Benjamin Netanyahu's Clean Break in the 1990s, Ariel Sharon's Grand Vision for Israel—From Mauritania to Afghanistan in the early years of the 21st century, PNAC's blueprint for the Middle East and last but not least, Richard Perle's, *An End to Evil?*

Thus far, what I have quoted relates only to the first option. Let us continue reading.

> Iranian groups, whether domestic or internationally based, which seek to broadcast or publish pro-democracy messages inside the country might be provided with equipment, facilities, funding, and support. Relatively modest expenditures on such purposes can spell the difference between a capability for such groups to get their message out to international publics and in Iran.

> Should the United States reach a decision to support an explicit policy of regime change in Iran, a Presidential Finding would be a necessary first step, enabling many activities by U.S. entities that cannot take place without such a finding.

> The United States should ensure that Iran understands that **neither it nor the Iranian opposition will take any option off the table,** if Iran remains unwilling to address adequately international concerns about its nuclear programs in particular. The goal is to ensure that democracy, tolerance, and the rule of law are established in an Iran that abjures use of WMD, terrorism, and threats against its neighbors. Bringing Tehran's flagrant

non-compliance with the NPT before the UN Security Council would be an important first step. (Emphasis added)

What this means is that the IPC will prepare the initial ground work for a coup[2] and when the President gives the OK, the operation would go into full swing. This is the most blatant disregard for international law and the principles of sovereignty of a nation. This is the typical bully mindset.

Let us now examine the 2nd option of the IPC.

"We do not want American armies marching on Tehran," then Secretary of State Colin Powell said in November 2004. Despite the official position of the administration, there are some who suggest that given the failure of the engagement option over the past quarter century and the urgency to counter the Iranian threat, Washington should adopt a military option. Despite its risks and implications, they are willing to absorb the costs and consequences. Proponents of strikes believe that United States interests are better served by taking preventive military action in the present than facing the future nightmare of a nuclear Iran with extensive regional dominance armed with the ideology of hate.

Conventional force military options have a broad spectrum upon which to draw, which individually or collectively might evoke different results and/or responses from the Iranian regime.

On the one hand, Special Operations Forces options include low-end clandestine ground operations supported by air insertion/extraction to acquire target information, emplace sensors or precision guidance beacons, or preposition arms/equipment for local insurgents. On the other hand, high end options consist of direct action missions against pre-selected targets, link-up with indigenous forces to engage and attack government facilities, bases, and personnel. In the total context, combinations of the various minimal to maximum options provide a wide array of choices that can exert significant impact on Tehran and influence the regime economically, diplomatically, and politically.

Recall the nuclear time clock that is ticking down as Iran drives to reach nuclear weapons capability. If the regime continues to prove intransigent with respect to fulfilling its obligations under the NPT, the international community may not have the luxury of pursuing only a regime change policy. The theocratic leadership in Tehran must know that they will not be permitted to achieve a nuclear

2   In the author's book, Future FastForward, there is a detailed account as to how the CIA organized the coup against the democratically elected Mossadeq.

bomb status. A military option, which could include limited strikes against Iran's nuclear program infrastructure, clearly would be a last option but must clearly be understood to remain on the table.

Is this not an echo of the entire rationale for the war in Iraq? So intense is this propaganda, that many people have forgotten that it is merely the replay of an old song. Recall what George Bush has to say on propaganda:

"See in my line of work you got to keep repeating things over and over again for the truth to sink in, to kind of catapult the propaganda."

Soon after the publication of *Future FastForward,* I was invited to elaborate on the issues raised in my book to various groups of people and one question that was often asked was, "When will the war in Iran commence?" When I replied that the war had already started, the audience found it hard to accept. I based my assessment on other military campaigns in the past and the recent war in Iraq. I informed them that in the latter part of 2002, the United States and Britain conducted a massive air campaign to destroy and immobilize the Iraqi air defenses. This was necessary and a pre-condition to a successful land invasion earmarked for early 2003. Since then many experts have concurred with my conclusions that the war against Iraq started in 2002. It is not that I am an expert. It is just common sense.

Read the above report by IPC again, in particular the military options and reference to special operations and the air offensive options and you will have to agree that before any major land incursion, there must be a "softening" of the enemy's infrastructure and its military forces. This is standard operating procedures.

The softening of Iran's military infrastructure has already commenced with the emplacement of sensors, precision guidance beacons, and surveillance of potential targets, pre-positioning of equipment and arms for future insurgents and other Special Forces operations. This is a given. I take comfort that an expert has since confirmed my assessment. Scott Ritter, a former weapons inspector was reported by Aljazeera[3] as having said, "The reality is that the U.S. war with Iran has already begun. As we speak, American over-flights of Iranian soil are taking place, using pilotless drones and other, more sophisticated capabilities. The violation of a sovereign nation's airspace is an

---

3   Scott Ritter, "The U.S. War with Iran Has Already Begun," June 19, 2005, Aljazeera.

act of war in and of itself. But the war with Iran has gone far beyond the intelligence gathering phase. The CIA-backed MEK terror bombings in Iran are not the only action ongoing against Iran. To the north, in neighboring Azerbaijan, the U.S. military is preparing a base of operations for a massive military presence that will foretell a major land-based campaign design to capture Tehran."

This makes sense, as the punch from the north from Azerbaijan to Tehran is a much shorter route and the air force need not be stretched, if they had to punch in from the south. The marines will be deployed in the south to keep open the vital Straits of Hormuz, a classic pincer strategy.

It is imperative for the worldwide anti-war movement to expose the warmongers' military agenda for Iran over and above the current campaign to end the occupation of Iraq. The authors of the IPC report have stated that the warmongers are prepared, notwithstanding the setbacks in Iraq, to pay the costs and consequences for the war with Iran. Anyone who continues to entertain the illusion that the quagmire in Iraq will prevent any further military adventure by the Bush regime is utterly irresponsible.

Already, Zionist Israel has upped the ante by proclaiming contrary to all intelligence sources and estimates[4] that Iran can have a nuclear bomb in six months.[5] I would not be surprised if Blair in due course repeats his earlier scare tactic that Iran is able to attack Britain with WMD within minutes of the outbreak of hostilities. Additionally, Israel has also called for the development and deployment of space-based weapons to ensure a decisive victory in any future wars.[6] Yuval Steinitz, Chairman of Israel's Defense and Foreign Affairs Committee said that Israel must compensate for its lack of strategic depth on land by expanding the use of sea and space-based attacks. He went on to say that, "We can draw many lessons from the evolution of air warfare. Just as the airplane evolved from an intelligence gathering platform to a self-protected precision attack system, so should the satellite—in the years ahead—be maximized for all kinds of missions."[7]

---

4   The National Intelligence Estimate 2005 says that it would take some ten years for Iran to develop an A-Bomb. The fascist British International Institute for Strategic Studies gives an estimate of five to six years.

5   Source: The Independent, September 22, 2005.

6   Barbara Opall-Rome, "Israel Official Urges Space-Based Weapons."
    Source: www.DefenseNews.com

7   Ibid.

Yet again, the world remains generally silent regarding this Zionist warmongering. I am most disappointed with my country, Malaysia, the Chair of NAM and OIC for failing to rally the member countries to demand the total and complete disclosure by Israel of its WMDs and to impose sanctions against her outside the ambit of the UN Security Council. Any sanction regime need not go through the Security Council. Member countries of NAM and OIC can by their own resolutions impose sanctions on Israel and demand compliance by its members. It is cowardice and hypocrisy of the highest order to appeal to Iran to forego its rights under the NPT without demanding Israel's submission to the NPT.

In Iran, we see once again a convergence of Israel's interests with those of the United States and how skillfully Israel has exploited that convergence. The Zionists made no bones that the first threat to Israel's supremacy was Iraq, then Iran and once these intractable foes have been defeated, the rest of the Middle East would be ripe for the picking.

The former Deputy Defense Secretary and current President of the World Bank, Paul Wolfowitz had admitted as a matter of fact at the 2003 ASEAN Security Conference that the issue of WMD was merely a bureaucratic excuse to justify the war in Iraq:

> For reasons that have a lot to do with the U.S. government bureaucracy, we settled on the one issue that everyone could agree on: weapons of mass destruction ... Look, the primary difference—to put it a little simply—between North Korea and Iraq is that we have virtually no option with Iraq because the country floats on a sea of oil.

In the present circumstances, it is also obvious that for bureaucratic reasons, the issue of Iran's alleged nuclear weapons program is only a mere pretext to launch a war, as Iran like Iraq is also floating on a sea of oil. There is just no other option for Israel and the United States. For Israel, Iran must be destroyed in order that she may continue her unchallenged hegemony in the Middle East. For the United States, Iran, like Iraq before, is a threat to the petro-dollar hegemony and the economic well being of the U.S. war economy.

Those of you who have read *Future FastForward* will recall that Saddam Hussein decided to sell Iraq's oil in Euros instead of U.S. dollars. Wall Street and City of London panicked and this was the ultimate reason to remove Saddam. Recall also, that immediately after the invasion of Iraq, sale of Iraqi oil was redenominated in U.S. dollars. The danger to the dollar supremacy was averted and Wall Street breathed a sigh of relief, but not for long.

Iran has recently threatened that comfort when they announced that in early 2006, it will establish an "Oil Exchange" for trades in energy. This would challenge the monopoly of the oil trade by the New York Mercantile Exchange and the London International Petroleum Exchange (IPE). Wall Street and City of London immediately suffered a heart attack and double by-pass had to be performed!

❊ Let me explain. When oil is sold in U.S. dollars, every country that needs to purchase oil must accumulate dollars. They must use their national currency in exchange for dollars to buy the oil. The U.S. also buys oil. But for her, all she needs to do is to print the money. Therefore unlike the US, these countries must have a reserve of dollars, without which their economy would ultimately collapse, because then they would not have the money to buy the oil. In this sense, it can be said that the largest U.S. export is its fiat money—the U.S. dollar! I have in the preceding chapters in Part I of this book explained that the U.S. dollar would be worthless toilet paper at the most if not for the trade in oil being denominated in U.S. dollars. There would be no demand for that Paper Money if the case was not so.

For all intents and purposes, the U.S. is bankrupt, a banana republic[8] and that the rest of the world is still willing to accept dollars is because of the oil trade. With the Euro as an alternative trade and reserve currency, the U.S. economy would free fall! The U.S. cannot allow this to happen. I hope you can understand why the world's superpower (in a reality a paper tiger) is in such a panic. And notwithstanding the quagmire in Iraq, the U.S. has no real options but to attack Iran. The only question is, "when will a full scale war be launched?" Israel seizing the opportunity, conveniently whispered to the war cabal that action must be taken if they are to survive collectively in this "violent Islamic world." Therefore, the present campaign to demonize Iran and the need to eliminate this fabricated nuclear threat. This is all war propaganda! We are being brainwashed again.

Once again, Muslims will betray Muslims, and the main culprit will be Saudi Arabia. This is because, Saudi Arabia's survival and that

---

8   Pedro Nicolaci da Costa, Krugman: Economic Crisis a Question of When, Not If, Reuters November 22, 2004.

of her corrupt feudal rulers is tied with that of the United States. This was the agreement imposed by Henry Kissinger after the Oil Crisis in the 1970s. Henry Kissinger demanded that the surplus petro-dollars must be recycled into the U.S. economy in exchange for U.S. Imperial protection. Everyone should attempt to read William Endahl's excellent book, *A Century of War*,[9] which explains the duplicity of Henry Kissinger and the betrayal of the Saudis. Sheikh Zaki Yamani, the former Oil Minister of Saudi Arabia praised Mr. Engdahl's efforts as "This is the only accurate account I have seen of what really happened with the price of oil in 1973..."[10]

What infamy, the custodians of the Holy cities of Mecca and Medina are the intimate collaborators of the Zionist Anglo-American oil interests and lackeys. This indictment applies equally to the other Gulf States!

Islam is allowed to be demonized and abused in exchange for feudal survivorship and dollar lifestyle. There will be another brutal slaughter of the innocents but this time round the devastation will be astronomical for all sides. Israel hopes to survive this fiasco, but she will not.

9   For more details, read the excellent book by William Engdahl, *A Century of War: Anglo-American Oil Politics and the New World Order*, (Revised edition 2004, Pluto Press)

10 Ibid, cited on the back cover of the book.

11

Dirty Wars:
The Brutality Business

How is it in our nation's interest to have civilian contractors, rather than military personnel, performing vital national security functions in a war zone?

— **U.S. Senator Carl Levin**

The worst barbarity of war is that it forces men collectively to commit acts against which individually they would revolt with their whole being.

— **Ellen Key**

Frederick Gareau defines terrorism as "deliberate acts of a physical and/or psychological nature perpetrated on select groups of victims. Its intent is to mould the thinking and behavior not only of those targeted groups, but more importantly, of larger sections of society that identify or share the views and aspirations of the targeted groups or who might easily be led to do so. The intent of the terrorists is to intimidate or coerce both groups by causing them intense fear, anxiety, apprehension, panic, dread, and/or horror."[1]

This is a broad definition of terrorism for which I give my unqualified endorsement. The net is big enough to catch most if not all the big fishes in the sea of terrorism. Most important, it does not exempt state terrorism. The spotlight must be *focused on state terrorism*, in particular Zionist Anglo-American State Terrorism. This is because we tend to associate "terrorists" with fringe groups or extremists hell bent to destroy society because of some grievances, real or otherwise.

This is a brilliant diversion strategy to shift the attention away

---

1   Frederick Gareau, *State Terrorism and the United States*, (2004, Zed Books, London)

from "state terrorism" to that of fringe groups. Al Qaeda captures the headlines but not the fascist regimes of Bush and Blair. Soldiers that commit the most heinous crimes are never referred to as "terrorists" because they are "lawful combatants." This really sucks and shows how the law, in particular international law (notwithstanding the Geneva Conventions and Protocols) treats this issue differently from such acts committed by resistance movements to imperial occupation. In essence, international laws favor the state and its inherent power to wage wars. Any resistance to the abuse of power by a state, in particular the abuse of the power to wage wars, is always construed as illegal, unconstitutional and those who participate is demonized as "rebels" "the resistance" and "a rebellion" until the equation changes and the rebellion succeeds, and a new state is established. The previous demonized resistance, labeled as "terrorists" is now accepted as part of the club of "legitimate states."

Soldiers that commit atrocities such as the "My Lai Massacre," *the tortures at Guantanamo Bay and Abu Ghraib are considered as having committed crimes and they are tried before military courts. Even when they are found guilty of such crimes, they are seldom severely punished in times of war. However, a different standard is applied to national liberation movements—their acts (regardless whether it is an act of defense) are always labeled as "terrorism" and the perpetrators "terrorists." They are not subject to the provisions of the usual criminal laws. Once labeled a "terrorist," they are denied all rights and any retribution is justified on account that they are not "lawful combatants." Can you see this perverse logic? Only a state can sanction "lawful combatants." No matter how abusive and repressive a state is towards its citizens, resistance fighters can never be construed as "lawful combatants."

To avoid any misunderstanding, I am not for one moment advocating that any abuse of power by a state justifies armed rebellion. There must be proportionality in the response to the abuse and/or repression. This principle is grounded in criminal law. Killing a man in an act of self-defense must be proportional to the danger and risk to his life from the threat of the assailant. Obviously, if the assailant is armed with a weapon and intent to kill, the act of self-defense is both proper and lawful.

There is also an equivalent principle in international law. Faced with a threat of war and/or an invasion, a state is entitled to defend itself against the external threat. But this threat must be *an imminent threat.* However, in the last fifty years, this principle has been abused, especially by the Zionist Anglo-American regimes. Waging pre-emptive wars, on the mere suspicion of a threat, is now justified for an invasion of another country, as in the case of Iraq. The use of nuclear weapons to *pre-empt* the *possible acquisition* of such weapons by non-nuclear weapon states is now promoted as a legitimate option by the Bush and Blair regimes. Nuclear terror by superpowers cannot be questioned. They are not terrorists, but guardians of democracy and freedom.

In the following pages, I will share with you some of the horrors perpetrated by terrorists, in particular *State Terrorists* because they are the main source of terrorism throughout the ages. Intelligence Services—MI6, CIA, Mossad, KGB, etc., and Special Forces—SAS, U.S. Navy Seals, Delta Force etc., are the main organs of the fascist states[2] for terrorist operations.

Whenever I labeled the American and the British regimes as terrorist regimes, I always get a very stupid reaction—"How can you say such a silly thing? We must not be anti-America. How can you lump the U.S. and Britain with the Taliban?" This usual retort, coming from many Malaysian CEOs (who cringe at the very mention of the word "terrorist") reflects either their ignorance, stupidity or plain slavishness to the Anglo-American establishment. Plainly there is a distinction between the Zionist Anglo-American regimes and the people. My critics seem to wear blinkers, oblivious of the fact that millions of Americans and British people have demonstrated against their governments for the war crimes committed in Vietnam, Cambodia, Latin America, Afghanistan and Iraq.

More remarkable is the constant depiction and caricature in the mass media of the heroic Palestinian liberation fighters and the Iraqi Resistance as "militants," "Jihadists," "extremists," "terrorists," "fundamentalists" etc. Anyone who resists Imperial occupation is conveniently labeled as "terrorists" and such demonization is accepted without more! Horrors of wars are seldom depicted on the excuse that Malaysians have no stomach for such brutal reality. We cannot have blood splattered all over the pages. It won't sell newspapers. It is as if peace will be served on a silver platter.

The brave Palestinians and heroic Iraqi people have pleaded

2   The term is used in this book to mean both Capitalist and Communist fascist state.

that the truth be told and the horrors exposed, but we take the selfish and cowardly line that such exposé will inflame *"anti-American feelings."*

I am going to pose a question to my fellow Malaysians. Suppose Malaysia were a victim of an illegal invasion and as a result hundreds of thousands were killed and injured, and many more raped, molested and plundered. Would you my fellow Malaysians demand that the truth be told without any censorship and the horrors depicted in starkest terms so that the world's conscience be pricked sufficient enough to stop the massacre?

There is another strange phenomenon. Notwithstanding more than two hundred years of British colonialism and imperial occupation and the brutal slaughter of our people by the British forces, our politicians and historians have never referred to their actions as that of state terrorism and/or the crimes committed as war crimes. More Malaysians have been killed by the British colonialists than by the communists during the entire period of our "Emergency" but white men's crimes are whitewashed. Many historians have covered up these crimes of the colonialists, but far worse, they participated in the insidious propaganda campaign to distort our history.

At this juncture, I intend to give these "enlightened" CEOs, elite opinion makers and historians a reality check. I am sure they have heard of Paul Craig Roberts, a blue-chip establishment figure who has more integrity and honor than the whole bunch of these Zionist Anglo-American apologists. But just in case they are ignorant, Mr. Roberts served as Assistant Secretary of the Treasury for economic policy under President Reagan and was credited by Treasury Secretary Donald Regan[3] with a major role in the Economic Recovery Tax Act 1981. He is the John M. Olin fellow at the Institute for Political Economy, research fellow at the Independent Institute and senior research fellow at the Hoover Institution, Stanford University. He was a former editor and columnist for *The Wall Street Journal* and was distinguished fellow at the Cato Institute.[4]

This is what he said about his own government and President:[5]

3   Often confused with President Ronald Reagan. His name is Donald Regan, not Reagan!
4   His biodata is just too long and comprehensive to be given full credit here. More details can be obtained from the internet. Just do a Google search. There are others like him. But what he wrote recently is most appropriate in the context of the present discussion.
5   Paul Craig Roberts, "Washington is the Source of Terror."
    Source: www.informationclearinghouse.info/article9012.htm

> Aside from 9/11, an event of several years ago, the only ter-
> rorism the U.S. has experienced is the **terrorism Bush cre-
> ated by invading Iraq. Why are we worried about Osama
> bin Laden when the moronic Bush administration is so
> adept in creating terrorism?** (Emphasis added)

I wonder whether these CEOs, elite opinion-makers and historians will now bow in shame for their dishonesty and duplicity. Let us
read more of what Mr. Paul Craig Roberts has to say. What follows,
I hope, will shut up these hypocrites and left-over Cold War warriors
who are themselves the brainwashed victims of the Zionist Anglo-
American war cabal.

> The U.S. government **gave the slave trade a boost** by offer-
> ing money for Al Qaeda and Taliban fighters. Afghan and
> Pakistani warlords simply rounded up people who looked
> Arab or foreign and **sold them to the Americans as cap-
> tured fighters.** The "fighters" apparently included relief work-
> ers, refugees, and Arab businessmen. The tribunals looking
> into the classification of Guantanamo prisoners as "enemy
> combatants" have uncovered numerous examples of hapless
> victims of a naïve U.S. government too flush with money.

> The Bush administration, of course, denies that it bought the
> detainees, as it denies everything. However, on May 31, 2005,
> Michelle Faul of the Associated Press reported that in March
> 2002, leaflets and broadcasts from helicopters in Afghanistan
> enticed Afghans to **"hand over Arabs and feed your fami-
> lies for a lifetime."**

> More is going on here than merely unintended consequences
> of a harebrained policy. The Bush Administration has proven
> itself to be **utterly irresponsible in the use of power.** And it
> keeps demanding more power, including suspension of our
> civil liberties in order to better fight "terrorism."

> Notice the pattern. **Bush creates terrorism** and then sus-
> pends our civil liberties in the name of his war on terror. **The
> real terror Americans experience comes from their own
> government.**[6] (Emphases added)

In the case of the British, we can cite the fascist General Frank
Kitson, 'who first thought up the concept that was later used in the
formation of Al Qaeda. He called it the "pseudo-gang"—a state sponsored group used to advance an agenda, while discrediting the real

6   Ibid.

opposition."[7] The strategy was used in Kenya and Northern Ireland. In the case of the latter, most of the violence that was attributed to the "loyalists" and the IRA was not their handiwork, but the result of the activities of death squads established by British Intelligence and the Special Forces. Of all the countries in the world that practices state terrorism as an essential part of state policy, none can compare to Britain in terms of its historical experience, efficiency, brutality and scope. They are the Masters. The Zionist butchers have caught up in some key aspects after 50 continuous years of occupation in Palestine, but many of the techniques were conceived by the British intelligence services and the SAS.

Sound too incredible for your liking? I challenge anyone to prove me wrong on this issue, especially left-over Cold War warriors. But before anyone takes up my challenge, I suggest that they read the following narratives very carefully.

In 1996, by chance I stumbled upon a book, *The Nemesis File* written by a former SAS assassin.[8] It is an autobiographical account of his military service with the British Army. His mission was to execute *unarmed IRA suspects* in *cold blood.* The experience shattered his life and his family and it was only after prolonged treatment and rehabilitation at a center for alcoholics and drug addicts, that he was able to regain his life and sanity.

What drove him almost to insanity were the cold-blooded murders that his team committed in Northern Ireland. Initially, his mission was simple enough–to hunt down the "IRA terrorists" crossing over from the Republic of Ireland. He was able to rationalize his actions as killing enemy combatants in a vicious war. They would abduct suspected IRA activists, take them out for a drive to a designated spot in the countryside, put a couple of bullets in the back of their heads and have the "cleaners" (specialists in disposing of dead bodies) tidy up their dirty work.

When this ruthless policy failed, the British government and the military brass decided to pursue a more ruthless and barbaric policy. This is how Mr. Paul Bruce described it:

> The idea is this. The brass wants to encourage a no-holds-barred, real sectarian war between the Catholics and the

7   Kurt Nimmo, "General Frank Kitson: Trail Blazing Fake Terrorists," citing Ian Buckley. Source: www.propagandamatrix.com/articles/august2005/030805faketerrorism.htm
8   Paul Bruce, *The Nemesis File*, (1995, Blake Publishing Ltd, London)

Protestants so that the army can stand back and see the two sides tear each other apart. They reckon that within a matter of weeks both sides will want a truce and then the politicians can start to put the province back together again, in peace.

Our job is to make sure the war starts between the two sides and keeps going. We will be going to the Catholic areas of Belfast at night, shooting at anyone we see on the streets. The idea is to kill Catholics, to provoke an even greater backlash against the Protestants. (Emphasis added)

He gave horrifying details of the killings and executions to which he was an active participant—killing innocent people who just happened to be walking near where the team of assassins were stationed and/or patrolling along the streets of Belfast. He became a killing machine. He was programmed to kill. The executions were efficiently carried out. In plain simple language, he was a member of a death squad, just like his American counter-parts in Guatemala, Honduras, El Salvador, Chile and elsewhere. Their secret code sign was *NEMESIS*. They received their orders from the Intelligence Services based at the 39th Infantry Headquarters at Lisburn. It was this cold-blooded execution of innocent men and women randomly selected off the streets to serve the wider interests of the warmongers in Whitehall that drove him to alcohol and drugs, and near insanity.

Let me assure you that reading the detailed accounts of the killings and executions would make you sick and want to throw up. In July, 2005, Neil Mackay of *The Sunday Herald*[9] exposed that British double-agent Kevin Fulton was a member of the IRA's Omagh bomb team. The report states:

> Kevin Fulton is very clear about where the orders were coming from. "I was told that this was sanctioned right at the top. I was told there'll be no medals for this and no recognition, but this goes to the whole way to the Prime Minister... This was 1980, and if Margaret Thatcher knew about the activities of military intelligence agents such as Fulton, then she was also aware her own military officers were planning to infiltrate soldiers as "moles" into the IRA. **These moles were ordered by their handlers to carry out terrorist crimes** in order to keep their cover within the Provos so they could feed information on other leading Republicans back to security forces.

9   Source: www.sundayherald.com/25646

For almost two years *The Sunday Herald* has been investigating the activities of the FRU—the Force Research Unit, an ultra secret wing of the British Intelligence. Fulton worked for the FRU for much of his career as an IRA mole. This unit, which has been under investigation... **was involved in the murder of civilians in Northern Ireland.** (Emphasis added)

In another report, *The Sunday Herald* revealed[10] that the most feared IRA torturer was from the Royal Marines. He was a member of the Special Boat Squadron, the Marines' equivalent of the SAS. John Joe Magee was called the "Angel of Death." He was the head of the IRA's "Internal Security Unit" for more than a decade and executed all those he interrogated and tortured. He was a sadist without equal. Another killing machine, programmed to kill.

The White Rhodesians[11] under the leadership of Ian Smith adopted a similar policy in the suppression of the black people who were rebelling against the racist regime. Ian Smith and his security services employed the "pseudo-gang" strategy to destabilize the country and blame the ensuing violence on the guerrilla movement. The Rhodesian African Rifles was a ruthless unit in the suppression of the black people. They had gained valuable experience in the 50s and 60s when they were deployed in Malaya in the war against the Communists.

The former South Africa death squad commander, Colonel Eugene de Kock admitted that he was involved in *Stracom*[12] and confessed that its operations included attacks and bombings of white people which were falsely alleged to have been committed by the black people, thereby provoking a racial backlash by the white community.[13]

The mastermind of this strategy was none other than Frank Kitson, who wrote the terrorist manual, *Low Intensity Operations*. He polished his skills in Kenya, Malaya and Cyprus. He was the Commandant of the School of Infantry at Warminster in Wiltshire (a very prestigious appointment) in 1972, GOC 2nd Armored Division in 1976 and Commander-in-Chief of United Kingdom Land Forces in 1982 and was awarded a knighthood.

10　Source: www.sundayherald.com/29997

11　Rhodesia was the colonial name of the present independent state of Zimbabwe.

12　A strategic deception unit of the former Apartheid regime's police force.

13　Kurt Nimmo, op. cit.

Just some food for thought—when the British Intelligence Services were and are willing to kill their own in Northern Ireland, and they being Christians, don't you think that they would not bat an eyelid doing the same to the Muslims in Afghanistan, Iraq, Palestine and in the future, Iran, Syria and elsewhere? They have provoked sectarian violence between Catholics and Protestants in Northern Ireland by assassinations, car bombings, pub bombings and other PSYOPS. They engineered racial violence between the Malays and the Chinese in Malaya. They will provoke sectarian violence between the Sunnis and the Shiites in Iraq. This is a given!

For those who still insist on burying their heads in the sand, the recent news item coming out from Basra, Iraq may just convince them that the better view is above the ground. Two SAS under-cover soldiers dressed as Arabs were arrested by Iraqi police on September 19, 2005. What prompted their arrest was their suspicious behavior. The car they were using was packed with explosives and all sorts of weaponry. According to reports, the car was "booby-trapped."

Now instead of waiting for the usual procedure to take its course, i.e. police investigation and verification of their status, the British Army in Basra stormed the police station, in which the SAS soldiers were held captive, to "liberate" them from their Iraqi allies. The raid was led by a phalanx of 10 tanks, air-cover by helicopter gun-ships and backed by ground troops.

Questions! Questions! Questions!

Why were the SAS soldiers dressed as Arabs?

Why was the car they were travelling in, stashed with explosives and booby-trapped?

Why was the car parked in an area where there was a high concentration of civilians?

Why was there a need to "liberate" the soldiers from the Iraqi police, the allies of the British occupation forces?

Before we examine the "official" story churned out by the British authorities and the BBC, let us conduct a crime scene investigation. Let us examine some eye-witnesses' reports.

An Iraqi Interior Ministry official told Xinhua news the following:

> Two persons wearing Arab uniforms opened fire at a police station in Basra. A police patrol followed the attackers and

captured them to discover they were two British soldiers. The two soldiers were using a civilian car packed with explosives.

Sheik Hassan al- Zarqani, spokesman for the Mehdi Army said:

> What our police found in their car was very disturbing— weapons, explosives, and a remote control detonator. These are weapons of terrorists. We believe these soldiers were planning an attack on a market or other civilian targets.

Abdel al-Daraji told the U.K. *Telegraph*[14] "Britain was plotting to start an ethnic war by carrying out mass-casualty bombings targeting Shia civilians and then blaming the attacks on Sunni groups. Everyone knows the occupier's agenda. Their intention is to keep Iraq an unstable battlefield so they can exploit their interests in Iraq."

I hope I have got your attention now! Muslims, wake up! They are definitely coming for your blood.

Syrian correspondent Ziyad al-Munajjid reported:

> Many analysts and observers here had suspicions that the occupation was involved in some armed operations against civilians and places of worship and in the killing of scientists. But those were only suspicions that lacked proof. The proof came today through the arrest of the two British soldiers while they were planting explosives in one of the Basra streets. This proves, according to observers, that the occupation is not far from many operations that seek to sow sedition and maintain disorder, as this would give the occupation the justification to stay in Iraq for a longer period.

The British and American Intelligence Services and Special Forces can only be described as sadistic butchers who should be exposed as the real terrorists killing innocent civilians. When a booby-trapped car wired by the Special Forces blows up, it is so convenient to blame it on "suicide bombers." The identity of the alleged suicide bomber is a mystery and the media is given a field day to speculate and/or report the "official" story.

So on to the "official" story, which we shall now examine.

The initial broadcast from the BBC states that the two men wore Arab dress (September 19) but later reports mentioned that they were in "civilian dress." On the "release" of the two soldiers, con-

---

14 Source: cited by Mike Whitney, "A Policy of Absolute Barbarism? Basra, Another Milestone in a War on Terror," September 24, ICH.

flicting reports also emerged. BBC truthfully reported that the two soldiers were rescued after British tanks attacked the police station. But the British authorities (Ministry of Defense) denied the attack and claimed that "the release of the soldiers had been negotiated." A spokeswoman, Lisa Glover for the British Embassy in Baghdad said that three people have been wounded in the course of rescuing the soldiers.

CNN reported that the two were interrogated by an Iraqi Judge and not by insurgents. Obviously, it cannot be insurgents, as it has already been reported that they were captured by the police! Yet by another report, the British army after attacking the police station discovered that the two soldiers were no longer there but have been moved to another building.

Until this story of the SAS under-cover operation was exposed, the world was led to believe that Al Qaeda, and in particular, al-Zarqawi was responsible for all the so called "suicide bombings" in Iraq and that "foreign Jihadists" are leading the resistance. This campaign of disinformation was used to justify the political line that should the U.S. and British forces withdraw from Iraq, there would be chaos and civil war in Iraq, sparked by sectarian violence between the Sunnis and the Shiites! The terrorist activities of al-Zarqawi are lies. The Imam of Baghdad's al-Kazimeya mosque, Jawad al-Kalesi has said that "al-Zarqawi is dead but Washington continues to use him as a bogeyman to justify a prolonged military occupation.... He is simply an invention by the occupiers to divide the people.... His family in Jordan even held a ceremony after his death."[15]

If the above story has got you all worked up against the Brits in Iraq, the next story will drive you raving mad. And if this exposé does not get you off your butts to do something about the madness that has been inflicted on the Iraqi people, nothing will. Imad Khadduri tells the mind-boggling "suicide bombing" attempt by a patsy.

> A few days ago, an American manned check point confiscated the driver license of a driver and told him to report to an American military camp near Baghdad airport for interrogation and in order to retrieve his license. The next day, the driver did visit the camp and he was allowed in the camp with his car. He was admitted to a

15 Source: Cited by William Bowles, "British Undercover Operations in Basra Agents Provocateurs?," September 23, 2005 @ www.williambowles.info

room for an interrogation that lasted half an hour. At the end of the session, the American interrogator told him: "OK, there is nothing against you, but you do know that Iraq is now sovereign and is in charge of its own affairs. Hence we have forwarded your papers and license to al-Kadhimia police station for processing. Therefore, go there with this clearance to reclaim your license. At the police station, ask for Lt. Hussain Mohammed who is waiting for you now. Go there now quickly, before he leaves his shift work."

The driver did leave in a hurry, but was soon alarmed with a feeling that his car was driving as if carrying a heavy load, and he also became suspicious of a low flying helicopter that kept hovering overhead, as if trailing him. He stopped the car and inspected it carefully. He found nearly 100 kilograms of explosives hidden in the back seat and along the two back doors.

The only feasible explanation for this incidence is that the car was indeed booby-trapped by the Americans and intended for the al-Khadimiya Shiite district of Baghdad. The same scenario was repeated in Mosul, in the north of Iraq.[16]

Had the driver proceeded as instructed, he would be a "suicide bomber" without even knowing it and he would be held responsible for the "suicide attack" on the police station. His name would be flashed round the world as another suicide bomber who died for the cause of Islam and Al Qaeda.

This is a clear case where innocent men were selected at random at check points to be "designated suicide bombers." So the next time you read about a suicide bomber attacking a police station, please bear in mind this insidious attempt by the U.S. and British intelligence services to set up an innocent man as the patsy to terrorize the Iraqi people. So stop accusing the heroic Iraqi Resistance of suicide bombings, for such accusations give credence to the fascist propaganda against the Iraqi people.

The propaganda that Iraq is infested with foreign terrorists like al-Zarqawi serves the warmongers' overall objective of discrediting the heroic resistance of the Iraqi people, and to gain support for the continuing occupation of Iraq as an essential phase in the global war on terrorism. The war on terrorism is a bogus war, a pretext for colonial occupation in Iraq and in the near future other parts of the Middle East and South-East Asia. Jose Luis Zapatero, the Prime Minister of Spain was vigilant enough to see the *Madrid Bombing* as

16 Source: www.albasrah.net/maqalat/english/0505/Combat-terrorism_160505.htm

what it was—a Special Forces *False Flag* operation to get the Spanish people to support Bush's war on terror. On May 20, 2005, the Spanish Prime Minister said that "the colonial invasion of Iraq and the ugliest of lies of the lie machine that propagated and justified these barbarous acts will forever remain among the greatest and unpardonable crimes against humanity."

And that is why what is happening in Southern Thailand is so dangerous. There is a hidden hand in the exploitation of the Muslim unrest in that part of Thailand. Malaysian Muslims have fallen for the propaganda ploy hook, line and sinker and are agitating for action. Exploiting the sentiments of Muslims on both sides of the Thai/Malaysia border, the Zionist Anglo-American warmongers have to a certain extent succeeded in fomenting sectarian animosity between Muslims and Buddhists in that region.

Some Malay Muslims in Malaysia are entertaining the ridiculous idea that the southern provinces ought to revert to Malaysia as historically, they were part of the Malay Peninsula. Taking their argument to the extreme, every country in theory can claim that its national boundaries ought to be redrawn for some historical reason. After all, Malaya was never a "nation state" prior to colonialism. It was made up of several kingdoms. In theory, I suppose the Sultans can claim that they were hoodwinked into accepting the concept of Constitutional Monarchy within a Federation and demand their little kingdoms back.

These myopic sectarian Muslims are in fact giving credence to the Zionist political line and rationale for the creation of Israel— since, from biblical times Palestine belonged to them, and it is therefore right that the Palestinian Arabs be forced out of their lands. Yet, there are Jews who scoffed at such a ridiculous idea.

I had in *Future FastForward* warned in no uncertain terms that Malaysia, Thailand and other countries within ASEAN have been earmarked as "Seam States" and targeted for U.S. military intervention in the event that threats spilling over from "rogue" states within the "GAP" pose a security risk to the United States.

In *The Pentagon's New Map: War and Peace in the 21st Century,*[17] Professor Thomas P.M. Barnett said:

17 Thomas P.M. Barnett, (2004, G.P. Putnam & Sons, New York)

In the era of globalization, we draw the line between those parts of the world that are actively integrating their national economies into the global economy, or what I call globalization's Functioning Core, and those that are failing to integrate themselves into that larger economic community and the rule sets it generates or those states I identify as constituting the Non-Integrating Gap. **A country's potential to warrant a U.S. military response is inversely related to its globalization connectivity.**

But just as important as "getting them where they live" is stopping the ability of these terrorist networks to access the Core via the "seam states" that lie along the Gap's bloody boundaries. It is along this seam that the Core will seek to suppress bad things coming out of the Gap. Which are some of these classic seam states? Mexico, Brazil, South Africa, Morocco, Algeria, Greece, Turkey, Pakistan, **Thailand, Malaysia, the Philippines and Indonesia come to mind.** (Emphasis added)

Therefore, Muslims on both sides of the Thai/Malaysia border should stop their mischief unless they want to be the pawns and sacrificial lambs in the Zionist Anglo-American global agenda. The Zionist bogus war on terror will be extended to the region as the pretext to plunder the two strategically located nations.

Let me be blunt: Whatever fantasies Muslims may have for a "Muslim Patani state" will remain a fantasy because when the cowboys and their posse ride in, Malaysia as we know today will be carved up as is being done in Iraq. By all means stoke the fire, but be prepared to be burnt! You have been warned by Prof. Barnett.

12

Pain Merchants' Trail of Blood, Broken Bones and the Odor of Death

> We know more about war than we do about peace—more about killing than we do about living.
>
> — **General Omar Bradley**

> No historian would deny that the part played by crimes committed for personal motives is very small compared to the vast populations slaughtered in unselfish loyalty to a jealous God, king, country or political system … the ravages caused by individual self-assertion are quantitatively negligible compared to the number slain out of self-transcending devotion to a flag, a leader, a religious faith or political conviction… Man has always been prepared to die for good, bad, or completely harebrained causes.
>
> — **Arthur Koestler**

The next time you visit London, please find time to visit the *Dungeon,* the museum of torture, located approximately five minutes walk from the Tower of London where kings, nobles and common thieves were once beheaded. There you will find every conceivable contraption designed to extract a confession. The modern equivalent is no better. They are mere variations of a basic principle—how to inflict maximum pain at all the nerve centers of a human body. And if you have time, go to Vietnam, to the war museum in Saigon and see the torture villas set up by the U.S. army and the CIA. Even after all these years, the smell of blood and death lingers on, it could be my imagination, but it is a grim reminder that war turns good people into beasts. Even that may not be a fair comparison. Beasts only kill for food, and never indiscriminately. How does one describe such evil?

It is important that we understand and acknowledge that the tortures, murders and executions by *State-Sponsored Terrorists* far exceed the number of people killed by "non-state terrorists." The War on Terrorism is a bogus war precisely because the main perpetrators are states and not individuals or groups. It is nauseating to keep hearing from political leaders of all hues that "to stop terrorism we must identify the root cause of terrorism, and the root cause is the Palestinian issue." The implication being that the Palestinians' ongoing struggle against Zionist Israel is the root cause of all terrorism and it is manifested by "suicide bombers" killing Jewish settlers in the occupied Palestine.

We must debunk this political line, for terrorism is but a method of warfare and the *preferred instrument* of oppression by states against their own citizens as well as against weaker states. Zionist state terrorism is principally responsible for the bloodbaths that have taken place in Palestine in the last fifty years. The Zionist terrorists murdered and terrorized Arabs to drive them out of Palestine before setting up the Zionist state of Israel, with the connivance of Britain, the United States, France and Russia.

We do need to focus on the Middle East, but the spotlight must be pointed at Israel and Zionism. It is the Zionist war machine and its global terrorist network that is the source of terrorism.

Prime Ministers David Ben Gurion, Begin, Shamir, Sharon are all terrorists! They have the blood of thousands on their hands. Stop calling the Palestinians terrorists. Terrorism existed before the creation of Israel!

There is absolutely no correlation between the oppression in Palestine and the terrorist activities in various parts of South America and Asia save for the fact that state terrorism was and is still mainly responsible for disappearance and deaths of hundreds of thousands. Osama bin Laden is the creation of the CIA and the Pakistani intelligence services (ISI). In fact just before he died, Robin Cook, the former British Foreign Secretary wrote, "Al Qaeda, literally the 'data base' was originally the computer file of the thousands of mujahideen who were recruited and trained with help from the CIA to defeat the Russians."[1] Following this disclosure, fascist Tony Blair declared, "Al Qaeda is not an organization. Al Qaeda is a way of working." Fox News reported on Blair's comments and in turn

1   Source: www.guardian.co.uk/terrorism/story/0,12780,1523838,00.html

affirmed that Al Qaeda is not and never has been a so-called "terrorist organization."[2]

So why is Aljazeera repeating the previous propaganda and continuing to be the source of this disinformation? Why, whenever a video-tape or an audio-recording that purports to come from Al Qaeda or Osama bin Laden, is it first released through this news agency? Why is this news agency giving so much credibility to the fiction of al-Zarqawi? Are Muslims so blind as to not notice that whenever the fascist occupation forces wants to initiate a mass killing in Iraq, this fiction crops up time and time again as the pretext for the brutal massacre of innocent Iraqis? Prof. Michel Chossudovsky explains it well in his article, *Al Qaeda and the Iraqi Resistance Movement.*[3] The Prof. pointed out that while the media reports focus on the presence of "foreign fighters," most of the resistance fighters are Iraqis. There have been no reliable reports of mass arrest of foreign fighters. This has been corroborated by Col. Robert Brown in a statement issued by the State Department, States News Services on September 14, 2005.

However, Aljazeera works overtime to extol and glorify the fictional exploits of this "Jordanian terrorist," when in fact all the bombings are the handiwork of the CIA, Mossad and MI6 and the notorious SAS. This news agency has a dubious background. It is financed by the Qatar regime. The same regime that agreed to turn the entire country as the staging ground for the Iraq invasion and the headquarters of U.S. Central Command. Its so-called "objective" reportage of the Iraq war is but the time-tested method of MI6 and other intelligence services in establishing its "credentials" and the "legend" of an independent Arab news service. When such a media is used as a conduit for CIA assets to disseminate disinformation, it is a potent combination. The result can be seen in the propaganda for the brutal military assault on Fallujah and other cities in Iraq.

Intelligence assets such as Al Qaeda and Al Zarqawi are instruments of the occupying forces and are used to weaken the genuine resistance movement and to divide the occupied country, in this case, Iraqi society. The propaganda role of these CIA assets is to enable the Megadeath Intellectuals and spin doctors to portray

2 Ibid. See also www.foxnews.com/story/0,2933.162476,00.html
3 Michel Chossudovsky, Al Qaeda and the Iraqi Resistance Movement, September 18, 2005. Source: www.globalresearch.ca

the legitimate resistance as "terrorists." The demonization of the resistance can only be effective if there are such assets. The resistance must be represented as devoid of morals, inhuman and attacking civilians. No one bothers to ask, why would the resistance attack their own people?

The occupying forces know that the resistance will succeed if supported by the people. Therefore the entire strategy of the fascist regime is to put a divide between the resistance and the Iraqi people. What better way than to portray the heroic resistance killing innocent Iraqis. But the recent exposure of British SAS false flag operations in Basra has enlightened the Iraqis. They were caught dressed as Arabs in a car wired with explosives and other lethal weapons in a crowded area of Basra. Why would SAS undercover operatives be driving a car already booby-trapped with explosives? Surely they do not intend to blow themselves up as "suicide bombers"? Car bombs are the handiwork of the CIA, MI6, Mossad and the SAS.

But Muslims and Arabs remain gullible. They don't even know that they have been conned into believing that Aljazeera serves their interests. Aljazeera is the Arab mouthpiece for the Zionist Anglo-American war cabal. A common method of propaganda warfare is to insert in a legitimate news item, false information so that the latter is accepted as truth. Very few spend time analyzing news and features by well known columnists. The Megadeath Intellectuals and spin doctors know this for a fact and that is why it is so easy to brainwash the masses. This is the principal role of Aljazeera—to churn out news containing nine-tenths of genuine and truthful reports, sprinkled with one-tenth of lies and disinformation. But the lies are enough to sow confusion and division. When Ritz Khan of CNN fame is carefully selected to head its English channel, be prepared for more of the same bullshit!

I have observed at close hand, close enough to smell their cheap aftershave cologne, the so-called investigative journalists. It is not confined to the male species. The "liberated" ones are more deceptive. They have a common agenda and most have links with intelligence services, domestic and foreign. You can tell them apart a mile away and it is really comical how they try to portray themselves as something else. However, the majority of journalists, reporters and columnists are hardworking, decent folks and they do a good job. It is unfortunate, that ordinary people cannot tell the difference and thereby get conned.

Non-state entity use of terrorism as an instrument of warfare is inherently ineffective for the simple reason they do not and cannot control the mass media, and hence *the propaganda campaign* so crucial to the success and effectiveness of terrorism *as a means to intimidate and control* the masses. And terrorism is effective only if it is conducted on a massive scale—*full spectrum dominance*—and, only states and/or state-sponsored terrorists can have such capabilities.

To put the competing argument in its proper perspective[4], we need only to examine two cases on the opposite sides of the globe, Guatemala in Latin America and Vietnam in Asia.

In her gut-wrenching book, *Buried Secrets: Truth and Human Rights in Guatemala*[5] Victoria Sanford gave a statistical dimension to *"La Violencia,* the terror unleashed by the U.S. backed regimes of General Lucas Garcia and General Rios Montt in the years 1978 to 1983. She wrote:

> In any book or article about Guatemala, one is bound to come upon statistical data about *La Violencia*: 440 massacres in villages burned off the map by the Guatemalan army, one and a half million people were displaced, 150,000 fled into refuge, and 100,000—150,000 were dead or disappeared... The Report of the Commission for Historical Clarification identified 83 percent of the victims as Maya and attributed blame to the Guatemalan army for 93 percent of the human rights violations, violations that were so severe that the Commission determined that the army had committed acts of genocide against the Maya. The numbers are staggering for any country and especially for a country of only nine million citizens. But often times, when people become numbers, their stories can be lost.

I challenge any historian to provide statistical data of any *non-state terrorist organization* that has inflicted similar atrocities in the last 100 years in any part of the world. Yet, we are subjected to the daily bombardment in the mass media that every explosion is the handiwork of the "suicide bombers"; that they are the culprits. "Suicide bombers" are convenient scape-goats whenever civilians are killed. There is no need for any supporting evidence. A mere attribution by

4　Resistance Movements are not terrorist organizations, but rather state organs like CIA, MI6, etc., are terrorist organizations.

5　Victoria Sanford, *Buried Secrets: Truth and Human Rights in Guatemala*, (2003, Palgrave Macmillan)

"official" sources or a Zionist controlled international media that the bomb blast is the work of a suicide bomber is sufficient to be accepted as gospel truth and the pretext to demonize lawful resistance against imperial occupation.

We must ask, why at the height of the IRA's struggle in Northern Ireland, the Western mass media did not demonize the IRA, the PROVOS etc? Is it because they are Europeans and Christians?

In the Middle East, you will notice that the demonization of the Resistance and the Muslims is a common feature. The term "suicide bombers" has been most effective in demonizing the Arabs and the Palestinians. And the Arabs and Muslims have fallen for this propaganda trap hook, line and sinker!

In the previous chapter, we have shown conclusively that it is the intelligence services and Special Forces that are responsible for most of such bombings. Yet there are people who insist on wearing blinkers. Should some of you persist in this intellectual frolic, and when you guys get clobbered in the next round of bloodletting, don't expect any sympathies. God will only help those who help themselves. I challenge anyone who can show me an editorial from the mainstream media[6] in Malaysia, CNN, Fox News, *The New York Times* and *The Washington Post* of a reference to the U.S. and British regimes as terrorist regimes. I am willing to make this challenge a little easier—show me an editorial reference that the U.S. and British soldiers are even considered terrorists!

Let us now turn our attention to Asia, more particularly to Vietnam and the brutality and horrors inflicted on the heroic Vietnamese people. I trust your memory has not failed you with regard to the heinous slaughter of the innocents at the My Lai hamlet. There are many accounts, but I have chosen the one written by Doug Linder.[7] Reading his account sends a chill down the spine. I will quote certain portions of his account of the massacre.

> U.S. military officials suspected Quang Ngai Province, more than any other province in South Vietnam, as being a Viet Cong stronghold… Military officials declared the province a "free-fire zone" and subjected it to frequent bombing missions and

6   This challenge applies as at the date of the publication of this book. I am giving them some leeway so that after reading this book, they may have enough conscience to do what is right, but not before. But it is a big, if!

7   Source: www.umkc.edu/faculty/projects/ftrials/mylai/Myl_intro.html

artillery attacks. By the end of 1967, most of the dwellings in the province had been destroyed and nearly 140,000 civilian left homeless.

Two hours instructions on the rights of prisoners and a wallet-sized card "The Enemy is in Your Hands" seemed to have little impact on American soldiers fighting in Quang Ngai. Military leaders encouraged and rewarded kills in an effort to produce impressive body counts that could be reported to Saigon as an indication of progress. GIs joked that "anything that's dead and isn't white is a VC" for body count purposes. Angered by a local population that said nothing about the VC's whereabouts, soldiers took to calling natives "gooks."

My Lai had about 700 residents … Calley's platoon … entered the village. They encountered families cooking rice in front of their homes. Soon the killing began. The first victim was a man stabbed in the back with a bayonet. Then a middle- age man was picked up, thrown down a well, and a grenade lobbed in after him. A group of 15 to 20 mostly old women were gathered around a temple, kneeling and praying. They were all executed with shots in the back of their heads…By 11 am, when Medina called for a lunch break , the killing was nearly over. By noon, "My Lai was no more"; its buildings were destroyed and its people dead or dying. Soldiers later said that they didn't remember seeing "one military-age male in the entire place." By night, the VC returned to bury the dead… Twenty months later army investigators would discover three mass graves containing bodies of about 500 villagers.

They have brought Milosevic, the former President of Yugoslavia to the Hague to answer charges for alleged war crimes in the recent Balkan wars; they are now considering pressing charges against President Saddam Hussein for similar offenses. But what of President Johnson, President Nixon, President Reagan, President Bush Sr., President Clinton, President G.W. Bush, Defense Secretary Robert McNamara, Henry Kissinger, Dick Cheney, Donald Rumsfeld, General Westmoreland, General Ricardo Sanchez, General Tommy Franks, Prime Minister Margaret Thatcher, Prime Minister John Majors, Prime Minister Tony Blair etc., and their crimes in Vietnam, Laos, Cambodia, Falklands, Nicaragua, Panama, Afghanistan and Iraq? A convenient silence!

One more name needs to be added to the list.

What I would like to share with you next is the dastardly deed of an officer by the name of Colin Powell who subsequently became the Chairman, Joint Chiefs of Staff and Secretary of State. He covered-up the war crimes in Vietnam and lied to the UN to precipitate the invasion of Iraq. He dishonored the uniform. But before going into that episode of his sordid career, let me backtrack a bit.

In 1963, he was one of those gung-ho advisers with the rank of Captain, who advocated torching villages to discourage them from supporting the liberation fighters. He called the strategy the "drain-the-sea" approach and was unrepentant of his actions as he made it abundantly clear in his memoirs, *My American Journey.* Once programmed to kill, fascist soldiers are doomed to be mere killing machines. Additionally, I suppose being black, he knew what he needed to do to climb up the star-studded ladder. He knew where to put his tongue!

After his first one year tour of duty, he returned to the United States to be reprogrammed for more efficient killing. In 1968, he returned for his second tour as a Major and was appointed to the prestigious post of G-3, Chief of Operations for Division Commander, Maj. General Charles Gettys at Chu Lai, climbing over several senior officers. It was in that position that he received a report from a young soldier named Tom Glen who reported in detail the widespread massacre of civilians and the use of torture by soldiers in the Division. Although the report did not mention specifically the My Lai massacres, it showed the overall pattern of indiscriminant killings which had become routine in the division. Without even questioning Tom Glen or assigning an investigation, Major Colin Powell accepted without more Tom Glen's superiors' comments that Glen had no direct knowledge of the atrocities. Major Powell submitted a report to his superiors that there were no wrongdoings and that the soldiers were trained to treat Vietnamese with respect!

Colin Powell is a war criminal, if not, at the least an accomplice to the war crimes committed in Vietnam. Judge this for yourself. This is what he wrote in his memoirs, *My American Journey:*

> I recall a phrase we used in the field, MAM, for military-age-male. If a helo[8] spotted a peasant in black pajamas who looked remotely suspicious, a possible MAM, the pilot would circle and fire in front of him. If he moved, his movement was judged evidence of hostile intent and the next burst was not in front, but at

8　An abbreviated term for helicopter.

him. Brutal? Maybe so. But an able battalion commander with whom I had served at Gelnhausen (West Germany), Lt. Col. Walter Pritchard, was killed by enemy sniper fire while observing MAMs from a helicopter. And Pritchard was only one of many. The kill-or-be-killed nature of combat tends to dull fine perceptions of right and wrong.

It is so easy to justify the killing of innocent folks. It is perverse logic to expect a person, for that matter anyone, who had been shot at, to remain static and not attempt to seek cover. As they say, it is just killing "gooks," a statistic in the self-deluding "body-count" measure of success. The General has no remorse; he lacks the intellectual honesty to accept and admit that if he and his GIs were not in Vietnam, the choice of "kill or be killed" would not arise at all.

The atrocities of the infamous *Tiger Force* in the central highlands of Vietnam must now be mentioned.[9] Tiger Force atrocities began with the torture and execution of prisoners in the field, then escalated to the routine slaughter of unarmed farmers, elderly people, even small children. One former sergeant was reported as having said, "It didn't matter if they were civilians. If they weren't supposed to be in the area, we shot them. If they didn't understand fear, I taught it to them." The Tiger Force killed so many civilians that the soldiers lost count, but the numbers were in the hundreds.

Again, the murderers and butchers were not indicted for these heinous crimes. The standard explanation is simple enough. They are not terrorists but lawful combatants going about their jobs—to win the war by putting fear in the hearts and minds of the Vietnamese.

The trail of blood, broken bones and deaths is not just confined to the battlefields, for there is another side to wars—the hidden or dark side. In this dark labyrinth of brutality, *torture* is the favorite sport of the *Pain Merchants*. I will now share some of their secrets which have taken years to retrieve. Be prepared for mental anguish and disorientation. Read the following at least three times.[10]

> The Vietnamese did not conceive the PICs (Province Interrogation Centres); they were the stepchildren of Robert Thompson, whose aristocratic English ancestors perfected torture in

9   The account of the atrocities is cited by Mike Davies, "The Scalping Party," June 13, 2005 @ www.motherjones.com

10 Source: Taken from Douglas Valentine, "ABCs of American Interrogation Methods" @ www.DouglasValentine.com

dingy castle dungeons, on the rack and in the iron lady, with thumb screws and branding irons.[11]

As for the American role, according to Muldoon,[12] "you can't have an American there all the time watching these things."

"These things" included: rape, gang rape, rape using eels, snakes, or hard objects, and rape followed by murder; electrical shock ("the Bell Telephone Hour") rendered by attaching wires to the genitals and other sensitive parts of the body, like the tongue; the "water treatment"; "the Airplane" in which a prisoner's arms were tied behind the back and the rope looped over a hook on the ceiling, suspending the prisoner in mid-air, after which he or she was beaten; beatings with rubber hoses and whips; and the use of police dogs to maul prisoners. All this and more occurred in PICs, one of which was run by Congressman Rob Simmons (R-CT) while he was CIA officer running the PIC in Phu Yen Province in 1972.

Robert Thompson first experimented and perfected his torture techniques in Malaya. Thereafter, his skills were much sought after. He is the Godfather of the modern Pain Merchants.

Go and visit Vietnam, go to the war museum and see for yourself these labyrinths of depravity, brutality and darkness. I have visited these playgrounds of the Pain Merchants and I came away in many ways a different person, and I promised to myself and to the victims that the Pain Merchants, the Megadeath Intellectuals and the warmongers would all be exposed. They must ACCOUNT for their crimes.

Pursuing these Pain Merchants is not to seek vengeance, but to ensure that their war crimes are fully examined under the glare of public scrutiny and rigorous criminal procedures so that the indisputable evidence would be duly recorded for posterity. No one thereafter can ever claim that such atrocities are mere fiction and/or conspiracy theories. It is hoped that the public would be more vigilant and be able to prevent a repetition of such heinous crimes should the next generation of Pain Merchants emerge from the woodwork.

Unfortunately, we have failed and the Pain Merchants are at it

11 That is why at the beginning of the Chapter I requested that when you next visit London, go to the Dungeon, the Torture Museum.

12 John Patrick Muldoon, "Picadoon" to the people who knew him in Vietnam, was the first director of CIA's PIC program in Vietnam. He joined the CIA in 1958 and got his early training in the dark side in Korea in 1962.

again in Guantanamo Bay, Abu Ghraib and other dark places not yet uncovered, applying the same old torture techniques, plus some new ones and getting away with their crimes.

How did we allow it to happen?

September 11 gave the warmongers the pretext to declare a global War on Terrorism and the brutal bloodletting that followed. "Vengeance is mine" were the by-words and the masses were easily persuaded that to win such a war, all gloves must be off!

As in waging wars, the public must be conditioned to accept the "no-holds-barred" policy and so a very clever propaganda campaign was conducted to justify the use of torture—the handiwork of the Megadeath Intellectuals.

By a memo dated January 25, 2002, White House Counsel Alberto Gonzales[13] urged President Bush to reject the "obsolete" and "quaint" provisions of the Geneva Conventions. After the brutal devastation of Afghanistan, thousands were detained in prisons all over the country and those suspected of being involved, however remotely in 9/11 were dispatched to Guantanamo Bay, Cuba. To extract intelligence from the captives, barbaric tortures were inflicted with approval from the highest levels at the Pentagon and the White House. The United States had thereby committed war crimes in violation of the provisions of the Geneva Conventions, and is open to prosecution.

There was therefore an urgent need to circumvent this legal hurdle. The answer was simple enough as far as Alberto Gonzales was concerned—apply the times tested Imperialist perverse logic—*Might Is Right*. Just like the bankers who with a stroke of the pen can create money, the legal hound-dogs of the Dark Labyrinth by a stroke of the pen declared simply, *the Geneva Conventions and any laws relating to torture shall not apply to United States military or anyone remotely connected to the Global War on Terrorism, as the victims are not lawful combatants.*

The cocaine and crack traffickers in South Central, Los Angeles can be incarcerated for life with lesser crimes, but killing, raping, plundering, torture of innocents *IS ABSOLUTELY LEGAL* if so declared by the Zionist Anglo-American war cabal.

13 He is presently the Attorney General of the United States.

I know this is ridiculous to the average Joe in downtown L.A., New York, Chicago etc.; to the blokes in Fulham, Manchester, Birmingham, London having their daily pint and to the *Pak Chik and Mak Chik*[14] in Kota Bahru, Ipoh, Malacca, Kuala Lumpur in Malaysia. I can even visualize their first knee-jerk reaction—"Matthias has gone too far," "He has gone bonkers," "This confirms that he is a conspiracy theorist, period!"

If this is your immediate reaction on reading the above five paragraphs, it supports my contention that the majority of the people are brainwashed for war and just as easy to be programmed to kill, if the need arises. Why am I so confident? Let me share something with you. Lawyers are trained to think in a certain way, and in conducting cross-examination of witnesses in court, adopt a certain approach and techniques that will check-mate a lying son-of-a-bitch! I have been in this business for 30 years, so I know what I am talking about.

I started the discussion by specifically referring to a memo written by White House Counsel Alberto Gonzales in January 25, 2002. This was the iron-clad evidence, my foundation for exposing the Imperialist perverse logic—the smoking gun, if you like. This is enough to put all these warmongers in the slammer and have the key thrown away. The Nazi war criminals were executed for less. This memo is the key evidence, an irrefutable, incriminating declaration of criminal intent by none other than the White House Counsel of the fascist Bush regime. The fact that President Bush did make such a declaration,[15] there is therefore, a causal connection between the memo and the official declaration—*the criminal intent was put into operation.* Yet, with the ease of internet access and the incredible power of search engines like Google and Yahoo, readers generally would not even pause to verify this *horrifying truth,* that Imperial America and Britain can with a stroke of the pen declare the barbaric and brutal murder, rape, sodomizing and torture of innocent men, women and child in the bogus War on Terrorism is absolutely legal.

Alberto Gonzales advised President Bush that the torture and murder of the detainees can be justified by declaring the detainees

---

14 Malay for "uncle" and "aunt" respectively.

15 In February 2002, Bush determined that Al Qaeda terrorists were not prisoners of war under the Treaty known as the Third Geneva Convention.

arrested in the global War on Terrorism are exempt from the Geneva Conventions, the Torture Convention and the U.S. War Crimes Act. The trick was not to reject the Conventions *but to assert that resistance to imperial conquest is not covered by the Geneva Conventions, the Torture Convention or the U.S. War Crimes Act.*

Emboldened by this "legal precedent" the Pentagon under the watchful eyes of Donald Rumsfeld issued the *"Rules of Engagement Relative to Interrogation"* to the Pain Merchants to do their dirty work after the illegal invasion of Iraq. I need not go into the details, for the pictures of the tortures and murders at Abu Ghraib and Guantanamo Bay speak for themselves.

In the past nine months, we have seen and heard of reports that soldiers have been brought before tribunals for committing the various atrocities cited above by the U.S. and British military authorities. Some have been punished with custodial sentences while others, usually senior officers were merely reprimanded. It is obvious that the message intended by the military brass is that these crimes were committed by rank and file soldiers and it is not reflective of any official policies and/or a system of abuse. How very convenient, but evidence points to the contrary. And the law is equally clear, the buck stops at President Bush and all his senior appointees.

Article 12 of the 3rd Geneva Conventions provides:

> Prisoners of war are in the hands of the **enemy power,** but not of the individuals or military units who have captured them. Irrespective of the individual responsibilities that may exist, the Detaining Power is responsible for the treatment given them. (Emphasis added)

The Geneva Conventions, the Torture Convention and the U.S. War Crimes Act provide protection of prisoners of war and they are not to be subjected to torture. It is expressly provided by the Convention that "no physical or mental torture, nor any other form of coercion, may be inflicted on prisoners of war to secure from them information of any kind whatsoever. Prisoners of war who refuse to answer may not be threatened, insulted, or exposed to any unpleasant or disadvantage treatment of any kind."

The argument put forward that Al Qaeda, the Taliban and the Iraqi Resistance are "terrorists" and were responsible for 9/11 and, therefore not deserving of protection is spurious because the United

States and Britain have a long history of torturing and murdering any-one who challenges and resists their Imperial conquest and occupa-tion–Northern Ireland, South America, Vietnam, Cambodia, Laos and Malaya. They have never adhered to the Conventions in the past. This recent excuse for non-compliance is bullshit, horseshit and whatever shit you like to call it!

Additionally, Article 2 of the Convention governs the conduct of signatories regardless whether the "enemy" is or is not a signatory and Article 4 permits the people of a country to take up arms in self-defense and resist any invading force without the necessity of forming themselves into regular fighting units.

Finally, I would like to reiterate that it is extremely important that we recognize the Bush and Blair regimes as fascist regimes, and expose them widely as such. Some of you may take objections that this is mere name calling and unnecessary, and that it is not fair to compare Bush and Blair to Hitler and Mussolini.

I have a simple reply. Just as the "Allied Powers" and the Zionists never let up in their propaganda campaign till today, and especially on each and every anniversary of V-Day 1945, that Nazi Germany, Italy and Japan were fascist powers and their leaders, war criminals for committing the atrocities during World War II, we should do likewise to those countries and leaders who in the last forty years have been committing the very crimes for which the Nazis and the Japanese were convicted at Nuremberg and Tokyo War Crimes Tribunal.

Let us not have double standards. Call a spade a spade and move on. Don't talk of peace when we do not even have the courage to confront such barbarities. I cannot speak for other countries but we have our fair share of hypocrites and cronies who would sell their souls for a handful of U.S. toilet Paper Money. They are mainly Chairmen, CEOs of conglomerates and budding politicians who have grand visions to expand their slice of the American pie. Nothing must be done to upset their apple-cart.

It is these people who refuse to see the distinction between the people and the government of a particular country. These Malaysians insult the intelligence of those American patriots who have steadfastly opposed and continue to oppose the fascist policies of their governments.

In any colonial wars of aggression, they are the first recruits of the Colonial powers to undermine the independence and sovereignty of the nation. They are the equivalent of the "Chalabis" of Iraq and "Hamid Karzais" of Afghanistan. They are the scum of the Earth. Keep a watchful eye on them and *hunt them down* when the time comes, before they can betray our country for a fistful of U.S. toilet Paper Money.

Part 3

The Psychology of War:
The Making of War Junkies

In a world where evil is still very real, democratic principles must also be backed with power in all its forms: Political and economic, cultural and moral, and yes, sometimes military… Any champion of democracy who promotes principles without power can make no real difference….

— **Condoleezza Rice, U.S. Secretary of State**

Perpetual Peace is a dream and not even a beautiful dream, and war is an integral part of God's ordering of the universe. In war, man's noblest virtues come into play: courage and renunciation, fidelity to duty and a readiness for sacrifice that does not stop short of offering up life itself. Without war the world would become swamped in materialism.

— **Hellmuth von Moltke,**
Member, German General Staff, World War I

The men who planned bureaucratic homicide in Vietnam were among our best: They were Rhodes Scholars, university professors, business leaders, war heroes. All men who had succeeded brilliantly in their careers. They were models of respectability and achievement. They were superior by almost any accepted definition of society.

— **Richard J Barnet, *The Roots of War***

13

Torture & Murder, Inc.:
The Brutality Business Revisited

Nature keeps her orchard healthy by pruning, war is her pruning hook.

— **Sir Arthur Keith, Anthropologist**

Man aggresses not only out of frustration and fear but out of joy, plentitude, love of life. Men kill lavishly out of the sublime joy of heroic triumph over evil… I think it is time for social scientists to catch up with Hitler as a psychologist, and to realize that men will do anything for heroic belonging to a victorious cause if they are persuaded about the legitimacy of that cause.

— **Ernest Becker,[1] Escape from Evil**

In researching and writing this part of the book, I had deliberately quoted extensively comments from key thinkers and opinion makers about the "positive effects" of wars on society and the individual. We cannot simply dismiss such ideas. Take for example the following comments about war, which I am sure never occurred to you as coming from such illustrious thinkers and writers.

Shakespeare in *Coriolanus*, Act 4, scene 5 wrote, "Let me have war, say I: It exceeds peace as far as day does night; it's sprightly, waking, audible, full of vent. Peace is a very apoplexy, lethargy, mull'd, deaf, sleepy, insensible; a getter of more bastard children than war is a destroyer of men."

Freud takes the view (the psychological theory) that war stems from the basic nature of human beings. There is the group theory of

---

1 The above quotes were taken from the excellent book by Lawrence LeShan, *The Psychology of War: Comprehending its Mystique and Madness*, (2002, Helios Press, New York).

Le Bon which asserts that war is due to the way humans function in groups. This theory is supported by Arthur Koestler who in his book *Janus* postulates that men go to war for reasons of group identification and loyalty and having an external enemy enhances such emotions within a group. And for General Friedrich von Bernardi, war is a "biological necessity" as expounded in his book, *Germany and the Next War.*

Classical thinkers advanced three basic causes for war:

1) Human nature: men have a basic instinct to acquire power and the pursuit of power leads to war;

2) Wars are fought for economic power;

3) The herd instinct, i.e. man is essentially a group animal and the nature of groups inevitably leads to conflicts.

If there is one book we should read about war, it must be Lawrence LeShan's *The Psychology of War.*[2] He explains that "when we go to war, our perception of reality—of what we are and what is happening in the world around us—is quite different from that which we commonly used in peacetime. This shift when it occurs makes war much more difficult to prevent, or to stop once it started. But understanding how and why this shift comes about allows us to see signs that indicate a society is moving toward war, and to understand what has to be done to stop this movement."

There are many good people involved in the peace and anti-war movements who don't have the foggiest ideas about wars and how we are manipulated and brainwashed for wars. While I appreciate their naïve intentions, often times, their actions and rhetoric do more harm than good in that they confuse the issues that need to be confronted and debated head on.

In this, the third part of my book, I intend to be brutally frank, and I will not hold back any punches. Wars are nasty, brutal and very profitable business and the people we are dealing with are "men who planned bureaucratic homicide ... models of respectability and achievement,"[3] the very best in society. But *they are homicidal butchers* on a global scale. So, for God's sake and your sanity, be real for once. Stop the intellectual masturbation and walk the talk.

2   Ibid.

3   Richard J. Barnet, *Roots of War*, (1973, Viking Press).

Let me give you the first dose of reality. Doctors,[4] yes those squeaky clean men in white overalls, have a history of participating in tortures and even have an explanation why it is not in conflict with medical ethics. *Lancet,* the internationally renowned medical journal reported in August 21, 2004,[5] "Government documents show that the U.S. military medical system failed to protect detainees' human rights, sometimes collaborated with interrogators or abusive guards, and failed to properly report injuries or deaths caused by beatings."

This startling disclosure about the tortures at Abu Ghraib has been corroborated by other observers. This is what they found:

> Physicians and other medical professionals breached their professional ethics and the laws of war by participating in abusive interrogation practices. Not only did caregivers pass health information to military intelligence personnel; physicians assisted in the design of interrogation strategies, including sleep deprivation and other coercive methods tailored to detainees' medical condition. Medical personnel also coached interrogators on questioning techniques.

The doctors who gave the information did not see their conduct as unethical! The observers reported:

> On the contrary, a common understanding among those who helped to plan interrogation is that physicians serving in these roles do not act as physicians and are therefore not bound by patient-orientated ethics. In an interview, Dr. David Tornberg, Deputy Assistant Secretary of Defense in Health Affairs, endorsed this view. Physicians assigned to military intelligence, he contended, have no doctor-patient relationship with detainees and, in the absence of life-threatening emergency, have no obligation to offer medical aid.

The perverse logic is expressed as follows:

> Doctors, they argue, act as combatants, not physicians, when they put their knowledge to use for military ends. A medical degree, Tornberg said, is not a "sacramental vow"—it is a certificate of skill. When a doctor participates in interrogation, "he

---

4   I am not saying all doctors are evil and take part in tortures. My point is that even perceived good and upright citizens can be persuaded to do evil. If doctors can be so persuaded, what more of others if properly brainwashed for war!

5   Steven H. Miles, "Abu Ghraib: It's Legacy for Military Medicine," Lancet, 364, 2004.

6   Gregg Bloche, Jonathan Marks, "When Doctors Go to War," New England Journal of Medicine 352.1, January 6, 2005; "Doctor's Orders... Spill Your Guts," Los Angeles Times, January 9, 2005.

is not functioning as a physician" and the Hippocratic ethic of commitment to patient welfare does not apply.

This is the kind of degenerate values which President Bush and Tony Blair insist on pain of war we must emulate. He even asked the stupid question, "Why do they hate our values?"

The second dose of reality is that these respectable high achievers, the *Megadeath Intellectuals,* have no respect for laws and will twist the law to suit their purpose. I have in the previous chapter mentioned the memo from the White House Counsel, Alberto Gonzales that was instrumental in President Bush declaring that the Taliban and the Resistance in Iraq are exempt from the protection of the Geneva Conventions and the Torture Convention.

In August 2002, another memo was submitted at the request of Alberto Gonzales entitled, *Standards of Conduct for Interrogation under U.S.C. 2340—2340A.* This is damning evidence that will send the Bush cabal to the gallows for war crimes.

U.S.C. 2340—2340A defines "torture" and proscribes torture as defined therein. But that did not deter the Megadeath Intellectuals in applying their perverse logic to circumvent the law. The memo states:

> We conclude below that section 2340A proscribes acts inflicting, and that are specifically intended to inflict, severe pain or suffering whether mental or physical. Those acts must be extreme nature to rise to the level of torture within the meaning of Section 2340A and the Convention. **We further conclude that certain acts may be cruel, inhuman or degrading but still not produce pain and suffering of the requisite intensity to fall within 2340A's proscription against torture.** (Emphasis added)

To those sycophants of the United States and Britain who condemn my criticisms of the Zionist Anglo-American warmongers, do you know of any, and can you show me any equipment that *measures pain?* These sadists inflict the torture and subjectively decide whether the pain and suffering is of such nature as to contravene the law. Obviously and conveniently, the measurements of the pain and suffering inflicted always fall short of the legal requirement, whatever that may be. No crime committed—Q.E.D. So they hope, but the law is clear. Let me explain. U.S.C. 2340–2340A provides:

"Torture" means an act committed by a person acting under the color of law specifically intended to inflict severe physical or mental pain or suffering (other than pain or suffering incidental to lawful sanctions[7]) upon another person within his custody or physical control;

"Severe pain or suffering" means the prolonged mental harm caused by or resulting from:

a) the intentional infliction or threatened infliction of severe physical pain or suffering;

b) the administration or application, or threatened administration or application, of mind altering substances or other procedures calculated to disrupt profoundly the senses or the personality;

c) the threat of imminent death; or

d) the threat that another person will imminently be subjected to death, severe physical pain or suffering, or the administration or application of mind-altering substances or other procedures calculated to disrupt profoundly the senses or personality.

Offense: Whoever outside the United States commits or attempts to commit torture shall be fined under this title or imprisoned not more than 20 years, or both, and if death results to any person from conduct prohibited by this subsection, shall be punished by death or imprisoned for any terms of years or for life.

Jurisdiction: There is jurisdiction over the activity prohibited in subsection a) if:

1) the alleged offender is a national of the United States; or

2) the alleged offender is present in the United States, irrespective of the nationality of the victim or alleged offender.

There is no time-bar against war crimes. They may gloat now, but when the tide turns as surely it will, these war criminals will face a War Crimes Tribunal.

Alberto Gonzales contends that none of the photographs of tor-

---

7   As when a person is convicted and sentenced to death. The process of execution would surely cause pain and suffering to the convicted criminal, but it is done under lawful sanction of a court of law. This distinction is important.

ture that came out of the Abu Ghraib prison constitutes torture within the above-stated definition. Let us put the issue to the test of public opinion. The evidence:

1) The horrendous picture of a hooded man, arms spread out in the form of a cross, standing on a box, with electrodes attached to his penis and fingers and being told that he would be electrocuted to death if he falls off the box.

2) Naked men are attacked by a dog and subsequently had the injuries stitched up by their torturers instead of by qualified medical personnel.

3) A man with hands and legs spread out and tied to a bed, with a female panty covering his head and the body arched back-wards.

4) A hooded man tied up and placed over the protective railings along a corridor, two storeys high and the risk of plunging to his death.

5) Blunt instruments inserted into the anus of the detainees.

6) Men forced to masturbate in front of female American sol-diers.

7) Men forced to simulate oral and anal sex.

There were also cases of women and young children being raped and molested.

Surely the tortures inflicted under sub-paragraph (1) to (5) fall under sub-paragraphs (a) and (c) of the definition and the tortures inflicted under sub-paragraph (6) and (7) fall under sub-paragraphs (b) and (d) of the definition. Yet we have the perverse logic of the memo that such tortures are not sufficiently painful to be considered as "severe pain and suffering."

The stance taken by the White House goes against the *Taguba Report* on the treatment of Iraqi prisoners of war. Maj. General Antonio Taguba in his investigation of the 800th Military Police Brigade found that:

> Between October and December 2003, at the Abu Ghraib Confinement Facility (BCCF), numerous incidents of sadistic, blatant, and wanton criminal abuses were inflicted on several detainees. This systemic and illegal abuse of detainees was intentionally perpetrated by several members of the military police guard force (372nd Military Police Company, 320th

Military Police Battalion, 800th MP Brigade), in Tier (section) 1-A of the Abu Ghraib Prison (BCCF).

In addition, several detainees also described the following acts of abuse, which under the circumstances, I find credible based on the clarity of their statements and supporting evidence provided by other witnesses:

a. Breaking chemical lights and pouring the phosphoric liquid on detainees;

b. Threatening detainees with a charged 9mm pistol;

c. Pouring cold water on naked detainees;

d. Beating detainees with a broom handle and a chair;

e. Threatening male detainees with rape;

f. Sodomizing a detainee with a chemical light and perhaps a broom stick.

The intentional abuse of detainees by military police personnel included the following acts:

a. Punching, slapping, and kicking detainees; jumping on their naked feet;

b. Videotaping and photographing naked male and female detainees;

c. Forcibly arranging detainees in various sexually explicit positions for photographing;

d. Forcing detainees to remove their clothing and keeping them naked for several days at a time;

e. Forcing naked male detainees to wear women's underwear;

f. Forcing groups of male detainees to masturbate themselves while being photographed and videotaped;

g. Arranging naked male detainees in a pile and then jumping on them;

h. Positioning a naked detainee on a MRE Box, with a sandbag on his head, and attaching wires to his fingers, toes, and penis to simulate electric torture;

i. Using military working dogs (without muzzles) to intimidate and frighten detainees, and in at least one case biting and severely injuring a detainee;

These findings are amply supported by written confessions

provided by several of the suspects, written statements provided by detainees, and witness statements. The various detention facilities operated by the 800th MP Brigade have routinely held persons brought to them by Other Government Agencies (OGAs) without accounting for them, knowing their identities, or even the reason for their detention. The Joint Interrogation and Debriefing Center (JIDC) at Abu Ghraib called these detainees "ghost detainees." On at least one occasion, the 320th MP Battalion at Abu Ghraib held a handful of "ghost detainees" (6-8) for OGAs that they moved around within the facility to hide them from a visiting International Committee of the Red Cross (ICRC) survey team. This maneuver was deceptive, contrary to Army Doctrine, and in violation of international law.

The Human Rights Watch (HRW) has also come out with its own report which was based on soldiers' testimony. Tom Malikowski, the Washington Director of HRW revealed that a West-Point Officer criticized the military establishment and said that what happened was a result of leadership failures at the highest levels. Besides Abu Ghraib, there were tortures at the "Mercury Forward Operating Base" and at Camp Tiger near the border with Syria.

The soldiers have a special name for Iraqi POWs, "PUCs—Persons Under Control." The soldiers gave details of the tortures and abuse inflicted on detainees: "To fuck a PUC means beating him up. We would give them blows to the head, chest, legs, and stomach, pull them down, and kick dirt on them. This happened every day." And "to smoke someone is to put them down in stress positions until they get muscle fatigue and pass out. That happened every day." The beatings were so severe that they often resulted in broken bones.[8]

What was most revealing in the report was that the soldiers believed that what they were doing was legal and that the detainees were exempt from protection under the Geneva Conventions. The soldiers said: "We knew where the Geneva Conventions drew the line, but then you get that confusion when the Secretary of Defense and the President make that statement that Geneva did not apply to the detainees... Iraq was cast as a part of the War on Terrorism, not a separate entity in and of itself, but a part of a larger war.."

If that is not bad enough, the ICRC reported that the military

8   Source: Ghali Hassan, Enduring Torture, September 25, 2005, @ www.globalresearch.ca

intelligence revealed that between 70% and 90% of the 43,000 Iraqi detainees have been arrested by mistake and whatever information was collected was of no value. These innocent Iraqi civilians were usually arrested during random house raids and at check-points and road blocks. I will not mince my words, the entire Bush regime are war criminals and murderers. They must be tried and executed in the same manner as the Nazi and Japanese war criminals.

Since the exposé of the tortures at Abu Ghraib and Guantanamo Bay, the British military has kept a very low profile on this issue, as if they were never part of this policy and system. And they almost got away with their culpability. But the long arm of the law has caught up with them. In fact the British Pain Merchants are worse than the Americans.

Why? It was the Brits who taught the Americans the more effective methods of torture. David Leigh, in *The Guardian*, on May 8, 2004 reported:

> The sexual humiliation of Iraqi prisoners at Abu Ghraib prison was not an invention of maverick guards, but part of a system of ill-treatment and degradation used by Special Forces soldiers that is now being disseminated among ordinary troops and contractors who do not know what they are doing.
>
> The techniques devised in the system, called R2I—"Resistance To Interrogations" match the crude exploitation and abuse of prisoners at Abu Ghraib jail in Baghdad.
>
> There is a reservoir of knowledge about these interrogation techniques which is retained by former Special Forces soldiers who are being hired as private contractors in Iraq. Contractors are bringing in their old friends.

But these techniques are not of recent origin. They have been in use for a very long time. The CIA incorporated these techniques with their own inventions in two torture manuals entitled, *KUBARK Counter-intelligence Interrogation (1963)* and *Human Resource Exploitation Training Manual (1983).*[9]

The first manual, KUBARK—a CIA codename for itself, is a comprehensive guide for training interrogators in the dark art of extracting intelligence from "resistant sources." The manual states that "the threat of coercion usually weakens or destroys resistance more effec-

9   Source: National Security Archive Electronic Briefing Book No 122 @ www.gwu.edu/~nsarchiv

tively than coercion itself. The threat to inflict pain, for example, can trigger fears more damaging than the immediate sensation of pain." The manual also instructs that the simple method of forcing the detainee to stand at attention for long periods of time is very effective. Another method is to subject a detainee to long periods of sensory deprivation such as putting him/her in a room without any sensory stimuli of any kind, such as a cell without any light. More effective still is putting the subject in a water tank.

The second manual was compiled from sections of the KUBARK guidelines, and from U.S. Military Intelligence field manuals written in the mid 1960s as part of the army's "Foreign Intelligence Assistance Program" codenamed "Project X." This manual was relied on by the CIA and the Green Berets in their operations in Latin America in the 1980s. It was the textbook of choice of the Honduran military units. Thousands were tortured. The manual describes torture methods very similar to those practiced in the Abu Ghraib prison.

The most famous center for torture training must be the notorious School of the Americas (SOA) at Fort Benning, Georgia. The instructors used manuals advocating torture, assassination, and kidnapping as tactics to be used against dissidents in Latin America. In 2000, pressure on Congress to stop funding the SOA increased to the point where the Department of Defense decided to rename the school the Western Hemisphere Institute for Security Cooperation. But nothing has changed save the name. The United States is still churning out sadistic torturers.

Covert operations in Iraq have been raised to a new and more heinous level in Iraq. In April of 2005, the then British Defense Minister announced the formation of a new regiment, *Special Reconnaissance Regiment (SRR)* to provide surveillance for the SAS and the Special Boat Service in their operations in Iraq.

For those who are ignorant of the British military campaign in Northern Ireland, these fascist military thugs are the most sadistic that you can find in the British army. In Northern Ireland, the unit was called *Force Research Unit (FRU)* and it was led by Lt. Colonel Gordon Kerr. It is the British Death Squads. He has since been promoted to Brigadier and assigned to Iraq to carry out the dirty work. He will be heading the SRR. He was previously the military attaché in Beijing. Neil Mackay of *The Sunday Herald* has this to say about him:

There is a phrase set aside in the British army for men like Brigadier Gordon Kerr and its "Green Slime." Soldiers don't mince words, and to regular squaddies and military brass, Kerr and his Intelligence Corps are on roughly the same level as pond life. Highly effective, immensely powerful and very dangerous pond life, but pond life nevertheless.

The Green Slime tag is partly down to the distinctive emerald beret worn by Int. Corps, but let's be frank, it's more a nod to Int. Corps' back-stabbing, double-dealing and underhand tactics and morals. And Kerr is, after all, the archetypal spy; a spook's spook and a master of dirty tricks and dirty wars.

Kerr's role in the secret Cold War against his own side was a sign of his warped sense of duty and led to the most shameful chapter of Britain's dirty war in Ulster. As the Sunday Herald revealed last week, under Kerr's command, the Force Research Unit (FRU)—the most secretive and dangerous of all the covert British military intelligence groups—regularly passed documents on Catholics and nationalists to loyalist terrorists who they were running as agents.

These loyalist double agents, including the Ulster Defense Association's chief of intelligence, Brian Nelson, were handed packages of photographs and military reports detailing the movements and addresses of potential targets, which in turn were passed to loyalist murder gangs. In total, an estimated 15 civilians died as a result of FRU collusion with loyalist terrorists. One victim of this collusion was the Catholic solicitor, Pat Finucane, who counted a number of prominent republicans among his clients. Other victims included known Provos and high ranking republicans; but a handful—perhaps five—were so-called innocents, people who had no other reason to die other than the fact they were Catholic.

In army terms, Kerr has what's termed "protezione"—a mafia term meaning protection. Kerr has connections going right to the heart of the British establishment and his former position as military attaché to Beijing makes him effective joint number two in Britain's entire military intelligence operations.[10]

Given the above history of British *Green Slimes,* we can only expect more suicide bombings, assassinations of Iraqi Resistance leaders and terror tactics. We have been focusing too much on the American military while the British murderers slip in quietly, killing

10 Neil Mackay, The Sunday Herald, November 26, 2000.

silently. But the Americans get all the bad publicity. We must put the spotlight on the Brits as well.

I believe that after reading the above exposés, you are mentally and emotionally prepared to examine in detail torture techniques which I know will spoil your dinner. I promised at the beginning of the Chapter that I will be brutally frank. "Why?" Simple! Tortures follow wars, as surely as night follows day. Reading the quotes on the positive effects of war on society and individuals, one can even be persuaded to accept the arguments of these respectable Megadeath Intellectuals, until we stumble on the dark side of wars—the tortures, beatings, rapes, molestations, humiliation and senseless killings of men, women and children.

To the do-gooders in the so called peace movements, the victims of torture, rape and murder do not want your fanciful definition of peace, slick slogans to adorn conferences and seminars, and sophisticated discourses on how to achieve peace. They want meaningful action!

For a start, stop the wars in Palestine, Iraq and Afghanistan.

Stop the tortures, rapes and beatings.

Stop the killing of the innocents.

Expose the pain and sufferings, and the humiliations.

ACCOUNTABILITY! JUSTICE!

Now read on and don't you squirm.

TORTURE TECHNIQUES OF THE PAIN MERCHANTS

1) **Bastinado:** is a form of torture which consist of beating the soles of the victims' bare feet with a hard object, e.g. a cane, a rod, a whip, a piece of wood. The victim is then forced to walk around on his/her damaged feet, sometimes carrying weights to add to the pressure and the pain and suffering.

2) **Shabach Technique:** This torture technique is very popular with the Zionist Israeli government (especially the Shin Bet, also known as General Security Services or SHABAK, after which the method is named) on Palestinian suspects. It involves the subject sit-

ting on a chair tilting forward, with the arms and legs tied firmly to the chair. The suspect is hooded and subjected to intense noise or music for an extended period of time.

3) **Strappado:** is a form of torture in which the victim is suspended in the air by a rope tied to the hands behind his back, with weights added to increase the pressure and pain. A variant to this method is called the "Reverse Hanging" or the "Palestinian Hanging" This is commonly used by the Zionists as well as in Turkey. And now in Iraq. The first variation has the victim's arms tied behind his back and a rope is tied to his wrists and passed over a beam or a hook on the ceiling. The victim is then pulled up with the arms stretched backwards and upwards thereby exerting tremendous pressure and inflicting excruciating pain on the arms resulting quite often in dislocation of the arms and shoulder sockets.

In the second variation, the victim's hands are tied to the front and he is also hung from the ceiling or beam. The ankles are also tied with weights attached to them. Extreme pain is experienced at the wrists, arms, legs and hips. This method is also known as "squassation."

4) **Water-Boarding:** The victim is strapped to a board and lowered into a tub of water until she or he believes that drowning is imminent. The subject is revived and the process is repeated until the victim relents and confesses to whatever crimes he is alleged to have committed. This method is being used in Guantanamo Bay and in Abu Ghraib prison.

5) **Thumbscrew:** It is an instrument of torture. It is a simple vice, with protruding studs. The victim's thumbs and fingers are placed in the vice and slowly crushed. Sometimes the fingernails are pulled out. The vice can also be applied to the toes. Larger vices are applied to the knees and elbows.

6) **Tucker Telephone:** The device is fashioned out of the old crank phones. The electric generator of the phone is wired in sequence to batteries to administer electric shocks to the victim. It was invented by the resident physician at the Tucker State Prison Farm in the 1960s.

7) **Wire Jacket:** It is a jacket made of wires and placed around the victim's body. The wires are connected to wheels on each side to tighten the jacket when needed. When the wires are tightened, they cut into the victim's flesh.

169

8) **Mock Execution:** The victim is blindfolded and made to believe that he is being led to an execution. He is asked to make his last wishes; other times, the victim is made to dig his own grave; the mock execution can also take the form of firing blanks at the back of the subject's head. The subject suffers severe psychological trauma and complete breakdown.

9) **Rape and Sexual Torture:** It is employed to "soften" the subject for interrogation. In feudal society like Iraq, to be so treated is a dishonor to family and tribe. It can be used as a means of control when the subject is threatened that her/his rape will be exposed. To avoid such a shame, he or she surrenders to the wishes of the torturer.

10) **Sensory Deprivation:** Hooding is a common form of sensory deprivation. The hood is sometimes covered with a nauseating substance which aggravates breathing and disorientation. Sleep deprivation is effected by subjecting the victim to continuous noise or music at high decibels. Food deprivation serves the same purpose.

11) **Boiling:** The victims are literally boiled in a vat of water. The result is often death.

Since September 11, 2001, the Pain Merchants have adopted a new approach to torture. In recent years, we have seen U.S. corporations, multi-national corporations etc., outsourcing some of their operations to third world countries to reduce costs. Outsourcing has also caught up with the torture business. It is called *Rendition.*

Jeffrey St. Clair of *Counterpunch* has this interesting story to tell.

A sleek Gulfstream V jet with the tail number N379P has racked up more international miles than most passenger jets. Since October 2001, this plane has been spotted in some of the world's most exotic and forbidding airports: Tashkent, Uzbekistan; Karachi, Pakistan, Baku, Azerbaijan, Baghdad, Iraq, and Rabat, Morocco. It has also frequently landed at Dulles International, outside Washington, DC and enjoys clearance to land at U.S. military air bases in Scotland, Cyprus and Frankfurt, Germany. Observers around the world have noticed men in hoods and chains being taken on and off the jet. The plane is owned by a company called Bayard Marketing, based in Portland, Oregon. According to FAA records, Bayard's lone corporate officer is a man called, Leonard T. Bayard. There is no contact information available for Bayard. Indeed, there's no public record of Bayard at all. No residential address. No telephone numbers. Nothing!

In fact, Bayard Marketing is a dummy corporation and Leonard Bayard is a false identity. They were both created by the CIA to conceal an operation launched after the attacks of September 11, 2001 to kidnap suspected terrorists and transport them to foreign governments where they could be interrogated using methods outlawed in the United States...Bayard Marketing is one of five or six different front companies the CIA has used to hide its role in the clandestine "rendition" (the term of art for this process) of suspected terrorists. In this case, the CIA's desire to keep the program a secret doesn't spring from a need to protect it from al-Qaeda or other hostile forces, but from public exposure. The rendition of captives for the purpose of torture violates international and U.S. law.

I hope that this chapter has given you another perspective to wars, one which we seldom address i.e., torture, mainly out of ignorance. Even with the exposure of the tortures at Abu Ghraib and Gauntanamo Bay, and in other places, somehow it doesn't really sink in. We find it hard to accept the fact that wars and tortures go hand in hand and it's part of the overall policy and strategy of waging wars.

Torture is terrorism and the culprits are mainly state players, because only states can provide the total system in which it can be implemented. And states get away with torture because the state controls the mass media; any exposure can be easily covered up and excused as a mere aberration, the acts of a few ill-disciplined soldiers.

Torture follows war as night follows day. It is said that bystanders resent the tortures because they make them feel guilty and ashamed for turning a blind eye and not doing anything to prevent it. If you can confront and expose torture, you have taken a positive step to overcome the brainwashing by the Megadeath Intellectuals.

Turn away from torture and all your talk about peace is hypocrisy!

14

The Brainwashed Mind Part 1:
New Technologies for Political Control

> The principal secret of secret intelligence is how to get some-one to do your bidding. Money, sex, fear, and the desire for revenge all work, but none perfectly or dependably. Ideological conviction is probably the best of all, but it is also the rarest. Holding on to spies once they've been recruited is just as diffi-cult ... One way or another, they slipped away. When old hands in the game talk about intelligence trade craft... they talk about two things—how to conduct operations... and how to recruit and manage agents.
>
> **— Thomas Powers**[1]

I want you to read the above quotation at least five times, and on the fifth, read the sentence, *"Ideological conviction is probably the best of all, but it is also the rarest"* three times. Pause and think, and apply the quotation, in particular the sentence that I had singled out, to the present situation in the Middle East.

It is a tough business running spies and it is not even every day that they have to sacrifice their lives for king and country. Agencies are even compelled to outsource some of their operations to mercenaries, but they prefer to be called "contractors."

The way the mass media and military sources attribute the bombings in Iraq and elsewhere to suicide bombers, it is fair to say that by their own reckoning we would have approximately 100 sui-cide bombers killing themselves in the name of Allah in the past year or so. Pause and think again. Each such operation (if it involves a suicide bomber) requires months of preparation—selection of can-

---

1   Thomas Powers, in his Introduction to John Marks' *The Search for the Manchurian Candidate*, (1991, Norton Paperback).

didate, psychological conditioning to commit suicide, specific train-ing in the handling of explosives, reconnaissance, selection of tar-gets, trial runs, security, sourcing of materials, finances, cut-outs, back-ups, safe houses and the whole gamut of logistics that goes into such planning. Not to mention that the handlers must be mind-control experts. And they don't come by the dozen. It is just not pos-sible to have so many willing martyrs, notwithstanding the promise of a ticket to heaven.

Much easier to pick a patsy from a road block or check-point, a random raid on houses; incarcerate him for a day or two to prepare the necessary profile, confiscate his license and wire his car with explosives, to be blown up by remote control or triggered by a cell-phone. After some not too heavy interrogation (to work up some anger), have the patsy released and directed to collect his papers at some police station. When the patsy drives to the station, he gets the one way ticket to meet his maker. All hell breaks loose and Aljazeera and the Western media breaks the news with such headlines—"Suicide bomber in a fit of rage destroys Iraqi police station, kills 50 and wounds hundreds." This is followed by another news story within an hour, "Al Qaeda chief in Iraq, Al Zarqawi claims responsibility and declares another victory for Islam." Two lines are devoted to the bomber—"The identification reveals that he is from Najaf, is married, have two kids. His name is Ali Hassan and a copy of the Quran was found at the scene of the explosion."

Sounds familiar? You bet!

Sure there are suicide bombers, but they are few and definitely not in the numbers churned out by the PSYOPS manipulators. The discussions on false flag operations by the British SAS, CIA etc., in the previous chapters have exposed the real culprits and the rationale behind them. There is no need to go over the same ground here again. Suffice it to say that the Global War on Terrorism is a bogus war, a mere cover for colonial plunder and oppression.

However, many were and still are hoodwinked into supporting the war effort. The line given and accepted is that the boys cannot come home as yet, because the Iraqis cannot be trusted to look after themselves. Civil war would erupt and there would be a bloodbath between the Sunnis and the Kurds and Shiites! If you believe that, then you must believe that the Earth is flat!

We must make an effort to understand how people are brainwashed to support the Zionist warmongers' wars of aggression, and this is what I intend to do in this chapter.

Brainwashing techniques has a long history and the subject covers a wide area, from individual mind-conditioning to mass indoctrination via the mass media etc. The term brainwashing made its début in print in an article published by *The Miami News* in September 1950. The author, Edward Hunter, coined the word as a rather down market translation of the Chinese *hsi-nao,* which meant "to cleanse the mind."[2] Edward Hunter was a CIA employee. He was in fact a propaganda specialist and had served as a "psychological warfare specialist" in the Pentagon.

The concept was used to explain the high number of U.S. soldiers captured by the Chinese forces in the Korean War who "went over" to the other side—"brainwashed" to renounce their allegiance to the United States. It was an emotional concept and was widely disseminated by the media at the time.

Be that as it may, we must approach the subject objectively and pragmatically. And there is no better way to start the discussion, in my view, than to ask the question, "Is there a difference between brainwashing on the one hand, and political indoctrination, the subtle (and not so subtle) influence of advertising and the way we are educated on the other?" I agree with Denise Winn that Robert Lifton got it right when he wrote:

> Behind this web of semantic (and more than semantic) confusion lies an image of "brainwashing" as an all powerful, irresistible, unfathomable and magical method of achieving total control over the human mind. It is of course none of these things and this loose usage makes a rallying point for fear, resentment, urges towards submission, justification for failures, irresponsible accusation and for a wide gamut of emotional extremism. One may justly conclude that the term has a far more precise and questionable usefulness; one may even be tempted to forget about the whole subject....
>
> Yet, to do so would be to overlook one of the major problems of our era—that of the psychology and ethics of directed attempts at changing human beings. **For despite the vicissitudes of brainwashing, the process which gave rise to the name is very much a reality.**[3] (Emphasis added)

2   Denise Winn, *The Manipulated Mind: Brainwashing, Conditioning and Indoctrination,* (1983, Malor Books).

I came in touch with *that reality* in the 1980s, when I began my research into torture techniques. To torture is essentially to control the victim. The filth that came out of the Vietnam War needed to be understood and over the years, I accumulated materials in the hope that one day I would write about it. Events took a dramatic change when I came across an article in 2000 by Dr. Rauni-Leena Kilde, formerly the Chief Medical Officer of Lapland (Northern Finland) on mind control entitled *Microwave Mind: Modern Torture and Control Mechanism Eliminating Human Rights and Privacy*.[4] The information disclosed was scary. The title alone just blew me away. I was on turbo-charge mode. There and then I decided that I must devote more effort in this area of research.

So important is this article to the understanding of mind control, that I am reproducing substantial parts for your benefit.

This is what Dr. Kilde wrote:

> Helsingin Sanomat, the largest newspaper in Scandinavia, wrote in the September 9, 1999 issue that Scientific American magazine estimates that after the Millennium perhaps ALL people will be implanted with a "DNA microchip."
>
> How many people realize what it actually means? Total loss of privacy and total outside control of the person's physical body functions, mental, emotional and thought processes, including the implanted person's subconscious and dreams! For the rest of his life!
>
> It sounds like science fiction but it is secret military and intelligence agencies' mind control technology, which has been experimented with for almost half a century, totally without the knowledge of the general public and even the general academic population.
>
> Supercomputers in Maryland, Israel and elsewhere with a speed of over 20 BILLION bits/sec can monitor millions of people simultaneously. In fact, the whole world population can be totally controlled by these secret brain-computer interactions, however unbelievable it sounds for the uninformed.
>
> Human thought has a speed of 5,000 bits/sec and everyone understands that our brain cannot compete with supercomput-

---

3   Robert Lifton, *Thought Reform and the Psychology of Totalism*, (Victor Gollancz, London).

4   Source: www.raven1.net/kilde1.htm

ers acting via satellites, implants, local facilities, scalar or other forms of biotelemetry.

Each brain has a unique set of bioelectric resonance/entrainment characteristics. Remote neural monitoring systems with supercomputers can send messages through an implanted person's nervous system and affect their performance in any way desired. They can of course be tracked and identified anywhere.

Neuro-electromagnetic involuntary human experimentation has been going on with the so-called "vulnerable population" for about 50 years, in the name of "science" or "national security" in the worst Nazi-type testing, contrary to all human rights. Physical and psychological torture of mind control victims today is like the worst horror movies. Only, unlike the horror movies, it is true. It happens today in the USA, Japan, and Europe. With few exceptions, the mass media suppresses all information about the entire topic.

Mind control technology in the USA is classified under "nonlethal" weaponry. The name is totally misleading because the technology used IS lethal, but death comes slowly in the form of "normal" illnesses, like cancer, leukemia, heart attacks, Alzheimer's disease with loss of short term memory first. No wonder these illnesses have increased all over the world.

Who is behind a sinister plan to microchip and control and torture the general population?

People who have been implanted, involuntarily or through deception voluntarily have become biological robots and guinea pigs for this activity under the guise of national security. The real consequences of microchip implantation (or with today's advanced hidden technology, using only microwave radiation for mind control,) are totally hidden from the public. How many know the real dangers of microwaves through mobile phones? How many believe the disinformation that microwave radiation is not causing health problems? The economic issues in the mobile phone industry are enormous. Therefore health issues are deliberately brushed aside. However, the same thing is inevitable in the future as with the tobacco industry. When economic compensation for health damages becomes big enough, as in the tobacco industry, health hazards will be admitted and users are then responsible for their tobacco-related illnesses.

Mobile phone used in mind control was a brilliant idea. Military and police agencies can follow every user, influence their thoughts through microwaves, cause healthy people to hear voices in their heads and if needed burn their brains in a second by increasing the current 20,000 times. That probably happened to Chechnyan leader General Dudayev who died talking to a mobile phone. Heating effect of tissues with the speed of light is a known effect of High power microwave and electromagnetic pulse weapons.

According to Navy studies they also cause fatigue states, depression, insomnia, aggressiveness, long and especially short term memory loss, short catatonic states, cataracts, leukemia, cancer, heart attacks, brain tumors and so forth. Alteration of behavior and attitudes has been demonstrated as well.

Who are the targets? Experimentation with soldiers and prisoners may continue, as well as handicapped children, mental patients, homosexuals and single women. They are still experimental guinea pigs for electronic and chemical warfare. But today ANYONE can become a target, even those who invented the system. Researchers who find out about this secret radiation of the population become targets themselves.

The U.S. Senate discussed the issue on January 22, 1997. The U.S. Air Force's "Commando Solo" aircraft have been used to send subliminal radio frequency messages to manipulate even the minds of foreign nations in their elections. Haiti and Bosnia are a couple of recent examples.

In July 1994 the U.S. Department of Defense proposed the use of "non- lethal" weapons against anyone engaged in activities the DoD opposes. Thus opposing political views, economic competitors, counterculture individuals and so forth can be beamed to sickness or death.

The Psychiatric Diagnostic Statistical Manual (DSM) for mental disorders has been a brilliant cover up operation in 18 languages to hide the atrocities of military and intelligence agencies' actions towards their targets. THE MANUAL LISTS ALL MIND CONTROL ACTIONS AS SIGNS OF PARANOID SCHIZOPHRENIA.

If a target is under surveillance with modern technology via TV, radio, telephone, loudspeakers, lasers, microwaves, poisoned with mind altering drugs via airducts, giving familiar smells which cause headache, nausea and so forth, if he claims his clothes are poisoned, his food or tap water as well—all medical schools teach their students that the person is paranoid, ESPECIALLY if he believes intelligence agencies are behind it all.

Never is the medical profession told that these are routine actions all over the world by intelligence agencies against their targets. Thus, victims of mind control are falsely considered mentally ill and get no help since they are not believed and their suffering is doubled by ignorant health professionals. The unethical abuses of power by individuals in charge of biomedical telemetry are incomprehensible to normal people.

The goal of mind control is to program an individual to carry out any mission of espionage or assassination even against their will and self-preservation instinct and to control the absolute behavior and thought patterns of the individual. The purpose of mind control is to disrupt memory, discredit people through aberrant behavior, to make them insane or to commit suicide or murder.

How is it possible that this technology is not stopped by top political authorities? They themselves will also be targets someday, a fact they have not always realized. How much are they involved? This year the 1999 European Parliament in "Resolution on Environment, Security, and Foreign Policy," in paragraphs 23, 24, and 27 calls for "non-lethal" weapons technology and development of new arms strategies to be covered and regulated by international conventions.

Also, it calls for an international convention introducing a GLOBAL BAN on all developments and deployments of weapons which might enable ANY FORM OF MANIPULATION OF HUMAN BEINGS.

Project HAARP in Alaska is a global concern, and calls for its legal, ecological, and ethical implications to be examined by an international independent body before any further research and testing. It is possible that the USA will ignore those resolutions. The dangers of non-lethal mind control weapons were already revealed in an expert meeting of the International Committee of the Red Cross in Geneva, in July 1994.

Only increased public awareness of the microchip implants, their frightful consequences to privacy by influencing of individuals' thoughts and actions, causing people to become biological robots with physical and emotional pain whenever the supercomputer technician so wishes, is enough reason to refuse to take the chip into your body for whatever reason. It is the biggest threat to humanity and the most sinister plan to enslave the human race forever.

MICROWAVE MIND CONTROL WITH "NON-LETHAL" WEAPONS IS THE BIGGEST CRIME IN THE HISTORY OF MANKIND AGAINST THE POPULATION OF PLANET EARTH. IT MUST BE STOPPED BY ALL PEOPLES OF THIS GLOBE. (Emphases as in the original)

Those of you, who had never before read any of this, will find it hard to believe that any of the above can be true. This is understandable. If the above is hocus pocus, please ask yourself why the European Commission organized in 2003, February 24 to 26, in Luxembourg a scientific gathering of international experts to discuss the "Application of the Precautionary Principle to EMF." EMF stands for "exposure to electromagnetic fields." The meeting was, as stated in the official circulars, a response to "the need to provide a framework and test it in a case study," and requested by the World Health Organization, the European Commission and the National Institute of Environmental Health Science. The mind controllers are messing around and their activities have aroused the attention of the scientific community. This is serious. The aforesaid meeting was preceded by the publication of a very important report in 1999.

To further allay your reservations, I will now introduce this very⤪ important document, entitled *An Appraisal of Technologies for Political Control* [5] published by the European Parliament, Directorate General of Research (the STOA Program) in 1999. This should get your attention!

The objectives of this report are fourfold: (i) to provide Members of the European Parliament with a guide to recent advances in the *technology of political control*; (ii) to identify, analyze and describe the current state of the art of the most salient developments; (iii) to present members with an account of current trends, both in Europe and Worldwide; and (iv) to develop policy recommendations covering regulatory strategies for their management and future control. [6]

The report contains seven substantive sections which cover respectively:

(i)   The role and function of the technology of political control;

---

5   Report written by Steve Wright, Omega Foundation, for the European Parliament. Edited by Mr. Dick Holdswork, Head of STOA Unit.

6   Ibid.

(ii) Recent trends and innovations (including the implications of globalization, militarization of police equipment, convergence of control systems deployed worldwide and the implications of increasing technology and decision drift);

(iii) Developments in surveillance technology (including the emergence of new forms of local, national and international communication interception networks and the creation of human recognition and tracking devices);

(iv) Innovations in crowd control weapons (including the evolution of a second generation of so-called "less-lethal" weapons' from nuclear labs in the USA);

(v) The emergence of prisoner control as a privatized industry, whilst state prisons face increasing pressure to substitute technology for staff in cost cutting exercises and the social and political implications of replacing policies of rehabilitation with strategies of human warehousing;

(vi) The use of science and technology to devise new efficient mark-free interrogation and torture technologies and their proliferation from the U.S. & Europe;

(vii) The implications of vertical and horizontal proliferation of this technology and the need for an adequate political response by the EU, to ensure it neither threatens civil liberties in Europe, nor reaches the hands of tyrants.[7]

A brief look at the historical development of this concept is instructive. Twenty years ago, the British Society for Social Responsibility of Scientists (BSSRS) warned about the dangers of a new technology of political control. BSSRS defined this technology as "a new type of weaponry... It is the product of the application of science and technology to the problem of *neutralizing the state's internal enemies*. It is mainly directed at civilian populations, and is not intended to kill (and only rarely does). It is aimed as much at hearts and minds as at bodies." For these scientists, "This new weaponry ranges from means of monitoring internal dissent to devices for controlling demonstrations; from new techniques of interrogation to methods of prisoner control. The intended and actual effects of these new technological aids are both broader and more complex than the more

7   Ibid.

180

lethal weaponry they complement." **BSSRS recognized that the weapons and systems developed and tested by the USA in Vietnam, and by the UK in its former colonies, were about to be used on the home front and that the military industrial complex would in the future, rapidly modify its military systems for police and internal security use. In other words, a new technology of repression was being spawned which would find a political niche in Western liberal democracies.** The role of this technology was to provide a technical fix which might effectively crush dissent whilst being designed to mask the level of coercion being deployed. With the advent of the Northern Irish conflict, the genie was out of the bottle and a new laboratory for field testing these technologies had emerged.[8]

There have been quite awesome changes in the technologies available to states for internal control since the first BSSRS publication. **Some of these technologies are highly sensitive politically and without proper regulation can threaten or undermine many of the human rights enshrined in international law, such as the rights of assembly, privacy, due process, freedom of political and cultural expression and protection from torture, arbitrary arrest, cruel and inhumane punishments and extrajudicial execution.**[9]

When the CIA mind-control programs were shut down, most people thought that such abuse would never be allowed again. In fact what has emerged is a more systematic and better funded program involving many governments and security services. We were warned by President Eisenhower to be vigilant against the power of the "military-Industrial Complex." The report states that there is another parallel corrupt power structure called "the Police-Industrial Complex." The growing trend because of the incredible pace of the advances in computer and information technologies is to "increase the power and reliability of the policing process, either enhancing the individual power of police operatives, replacing personnel with less expensive machines to monitor activity or to automate certain police monitoring, detection and communication facilities completely." The report warns that this is a massive industry and the overall trend is toward globalization of these technologies.

8   Ibid.
9   Ibid.

Some social scientists have warned that the above development will result in the militarization of the police and the deployment of the military in civilian affairs as the roles demanded of them by the security state will increasingly overlap. The events after September 11, 2001 constitute conclusive evidence of this trend in the United States and Britain. The deployment of the U.S. marines in the aftermath of the Hurricanes Katrina and Rita in New Orleans and surrounding states is an ominous development.

Already President George W. Bush[10] asked Congress to consider giving him powers to use the military to enforce quarantines in case of an avian influenza epidemic.

He said the military, and perhaps the National Guard, might be needed to take such a role if the feared H5N1 bird flu virus changes enough to cause widespread human infection.

"If we had an outbreak somewhere in the United States, do we not then quarantine that part of the country? And how do you, then, enforce quarantine?" Bush asked at a news conference.

"It's one thing to shut down airplanes. It's another thing to prevent people from coming in to get exposed to the avian flu. And who best to be able to effect a quarantine?" Bush added.

"One option is the use of a military that's able to plan and move. So that's why I put it on the table. I think it's an important debate for Congress to have."

In the United States, active duty military is currently forbidden from undertaking law enforcement duties by the federal Posse Comitatus Act. That law, passed in 1878 after the U.S. Civil War, does not prohibit National Guard troops under state control from doing police work. But, unless the law is changed, it would keep them from doing so if they were activated by Washington under federal control. While the law allows the president to order the military to take control and do police work in an extreme emergency, the White House has been traditionally reluctant to usurp state powers.

But it should be noted that after Hurricanes Katrina and Rita devastated the Gulf region, Bush had asked Congress to consider giving the military control over initial response in dealing with major natural or other domestic disasters. Let us have no illusion. This is the begin-

10   Source: Reuters, October 4, 2005.

ning of the transformation of the United States into a full fledged military security state—a fascist state. Study the history of Germany and Italy prior to World War II and the parallels are there. Ignore this development at your peril!

And when the security state is established, the scenario based on current technologies as stated in the report will become a reality.

> A chilling picture of social and political control... semi-intelligent zone-denial systems using neural networks which can identify and potentially punish unsanctioned behavior ; the advent of global telecommunications surveillance systems using voice recognition and other biometric techniques to facilitate human tracking; data surveillance systems which can match computer held data to visual recognition systems or identify friendship maps simply by analyzing the telephone and e-mail links between who calls whom; new sub-lethal incapacitating weapons used for prison and riot control as well as in sub-state conflict operations other than war; new target acquisition aids, lethal weapons and expanding dum-dum like ammunition which although banned by the Geneva Conventions for use against other state's soldiers, is finding increasing popularity amongst SWAT and special forces teams....

The report goes on to state that:

> The technology of political control produces a continuum of flexible options which stretch from modern law enforcement to advanced state suppression. It is multi-functional and has led to a rapid extension of the scope, efficiency and growth of policing power, creating policing revolutions both within Europe, the U.S. and the rest of the world. The key difference being the level of democratic accountability in the manner in which the technology is applied. Yet because of a process of technological and decision drift these instruments of control, once deployed quickly become "normalized." Their secondary and unanticipated effects often lead to a paramilitarization of the security forces and a militarization of the police—often because the companies which produce them service both markets.

There is another development that is giving me nightmares and may be the explanation for the phenomenon of the "suicide bombers," one of the most efficient programmed killers in recent years. I wonder how many of you have heard of the term "Cybernetics"?

"Cybernetics" is derived from the Greek word "Kubernites" meaning steersman, governor or rudder. It is a theory of communication and control of regulatory feedback. It is the discipline that studies communication and control in living beings or machines. The term "Cybernetics" was coined by the brilliant American mathematician Norbert Wiener and popularized through his book, *Cybernetics, or Control and Communication in the Animal and Machine.* Since then cybernetic technology has been transformed and entails the linking of the brains of people by means of implanted microchips to satellites controlled by supercomputers.

In the follow-up to her ground-breaking article *The Microwave Mind,* Dr. Rauni-Leena Kilde wrote in December 6, 2000 *Microchip Implants, Mind Control and Cybernetics.*[11] The doctor revealed that the first brain implant was done in 1974 in Ohio, USA and also in Stockholm, Sweden. But as far back as 1946, in the United States, innocent babies, without the knowledge of their parents had their skulls inserted with "Brain Electrodes" for research in behavior modification and body functioning. This was an important goal of the CIA and military intelligence after World War II and which I had referred to earlier in this chapter.

It is now technically possible for every newborn to be injected with a microchip and this would serve as a monitoring tool. If this sounds far-fetched, you need only to read *The Washington Post* which carried a story in 1995 that Prince William of Britain was implanted at age 12 so that in the event of a kidnap, the security services can trace the whereabouts of the British heir to the throne immediately, as he would be monitored. The chip's signal would be transmitted through a satellite to the computers at the security services headquarters.

In the 1970s, the size of such implants was about one centimeter. Subsequent developments reduced them to a size no bigger than a grain of rice and made of silicon, and later gallium arsenide. Today, it can be inserted into the back of the neck or intravenously in different parts of the body during surgical operations. Technological innovations have made what we have recently seen in the movie "The Matrix" primitive by comparison. Interestingly, Dr. Kilde revealed that the murdered Prime Minister of Sweden in 1973 authorized the implanting of chips in prisoners and in the 1980s, nursing home

---

11 The article was originally published in the 36th Edition of SPEKULA, the Finnish language journal of Oulu University OLK.

patients were likewise implanted as disclosed in the *Statens Officiella Utraninger,* the Swiss official report.

The military applications of this technology have already been used as far back as the Vietnam War. During the war, soldiers were injected with the "Rambo" chip designed to increase adrenaline flow into the bloodstream. More advanced technology was introduced during the Gulf war according to Dr. Carl Sanders, the inventor of the intelligence-manned interface (IMI) biotic. This allowed the supercomputers at the National Security Agency (NSA) to "see" and "hear" what the soldiers experienced in the battlefield via remote controlling system. The NSA electronic surveillance system can simultaneously track millions of people all over the world. This is because each of us has a unique bio-electrical resonance frequency in the brain, much like our unique fingerprints. With electro-magnetic frequency (EMF) brain stimulation coded, retrieved and stored, signals can be sent to the brain for the desired effect and outcome in the behavior modification agenda. This is no science fiction as U.S. astronauts are implanted before they are sent into space so that their thoughts, emotions etc., can be monitored at all times.

Recall what I wrote about the U.S. Joint Chiefs' Vision 2010 and 2020 blueprints for the U.S. military and the use of the latest technology to transform warfare. The use of cybernetic technologies is but one aspect of that transformation. The NSA's Signals Intelligence Group can even remotely monitor information from a human brain by decoding the evoked potentials (3.50HZ, 5 milliwatt) emitted by the brain. This insidious war against our privacy has already started and is prevalent in the U.S. and Britain and I am sure other hot spots of the world that poses a challenge to the Zionist Anglo-American war cabal's hegemony.

The matter has reached to such a stage that former U.S. Senator John Glenn initiated a discussion about the danger of "radiating" the civilian population, which can be and is carried out by targeting brain functions with electromagnetic fields and beams from helicopters, airplanes, satellites, parked vans, telephone poles, electrical appliances, mobile phones, TV, radios etc.

It is very odd that despite the amount of technical information available, the mass media have remained eerily silent about this danger to people, our society and our way of life. According to Dr. Kilde, one of the reasons why the mass media and the general public have not taken the issue seriously is that whosoever mentions about this subject is invariably labeled as "paranoid" or suffering from "schizophrenia." This coming from an internationally renowned doctor, we must pay serious attention. She further revealed that the American Psychiatric Association's (APA) *Diagnostic Statistical Manual IV* printed in 18 languages is responsible for the cover up by misleading and labeling the effects of mind-control technologies as symptoms of "paranoid schizophrenia." Medical students in psychiatry are taught to adopt this approach, so much so that whenever a victim complains of such effects, they are routinely diagnosed as being mentally ill and "sentenced" to a psychiatric hospital to languish in ignominy and neglect—the mental gulag.

By any measure this is a frightening scenario. But we the people are none the wiser. The key questions we have to ask are:

Why, the development of these technologies in the last twenty years?

Why the need for such intense social and political control?

Why, without exception, are all states adopting, researching and expanding the use of such technologies?

Is such control needed because of the impending economic collapse of Empire Capitalism and the inevitable social upheavals that must follow?

I don't have all the answers. But there is one I know for sure. We are being brainwashed, mind-controlled and programmed. And I, for one, am not going to stand pat, that's for sure!

15

The Brainwashed Mind Part 2:
The Secrets of Mind Control

> And it seems to be perfectly in the cards that there will be within the next generation or so a pharmacological method of making people love their servitude, and producing... a kind of painless concentration camp for entire societies, so that people will in fact have their liberties taken away from them but will rather enjoy it, because they will be distracted from any desire to rebel by propaganda, brainwashing, or brainwashing enhanced by pharmacological methods. And this seems to be the final revolution.
>
> — **Aldous Huxley, 1959**[1]

Some of you may or may not be familiar with Aldous Huxley. He wrote the book *The Brave New World* and is one of the most revered British authors. Read the above quotation again. So, am I still a conspiracy theorist, an alarmist? While most people would react with distaste, the use of the expressions such as, "brainwashed," "mind-controlled" etc, this icon of English literature has no qualms in advocating the need for society to be brainwashed, better still by enhanced pharmacological methods.

Although people are generally aware of the CIA's mind control programs, for some strange reason, no one ever bothers to investigate the real masters of mind control, the British Intelligence Service and its multifarious front organizations. This is the ingenuity of the British Zionists—divert the attention away and point it at the CIA. I hate to say it, but the British elites have always considered their American cousins as the equivalent of the "Bouncers," the muscle

---

1 Cited by John Marks, *The Search for the Manchurian Candidate: The CIA and Mind Control*, (1979, Norton Paperbacks).

power. Someone has got to do the dirty work and it's best to leave it to the GIs. That way, the Brits are never in the limelight, the way of the true puppet masters. The British are the ultimate mind controllers and *High Priests of War*.[2] Underestimate them at your peril. No one in modern history can come near them for their organizational skills, depth of experience, clinical brutality and imperial craftsmanship. They are so very subtle and disarming and often times only when you are at your last gasp of breath that you realize that it was the Brits who did you in, and never a moment too soon. Always bear this in mind.

One of the most effective ways to brainwash people is the planting of ideas via the reading of *specially engineered best sellers.* If you know the *real* history of Aldous Huxley, you cannot but question the motives behind the British Zionist establishment's adulation of this fascist author. Let us examine his pedigree.

He is the grandson of Thomas Huxley, who was involved in the Rhodes Round Table group and a close collaborator of the historian Arnold Toynbee. Toynbee was the Director of Studies of the Royal Institute of International Affairs (RIIA) from 1925-1955 and was the head of Research Division of British Intelligence during World War II. He studied at Oxford under the watchful eye of H.G. Wells, who was the head of British foreign intelligence in the First World War. Huxley was introduced by H.G. Wells to Aleister Crowley, the infamous occultist who established the Isis-Urania Temple of Hermetic Students of the Golden Dawn. In 1937, Huxley went to the United States and worked for a while as a script writer for MGM and Warner Bros. While there, he experimented in the use of the drug LSD with Dr. Humphreys Osmond and Robert Hutchins of University of Chicago. Osmond was involved in CIA's mind-control program MKULTRA and experimented with mescaline, a derivative of the mescal cactus as a cure for mental disorder.

Huxley is therefore very much a product of the intelligence services and the drug lords. You will find this common linkage in anything that has to do with mind-control.

Huxley wrote *The Doors of Perception* which extolled the use of hallucinogenic drugs. Together with Alan Watts, Dr. Gregory

---

2 The expression "High Priests of War" is used as the title to the brilliant book by a courageous American patriot, Michael Collins Piper and is published by the *American Free Press*. A must read that can be purchased online at www.americanfreepress.net.

Bateson (the husband of Dame Margaret Mead), Timothy Leary and Richard Alpert, he was responsible for the drug counter-culture in the United States in the 1960s—the hippies! Another establishment drug pusher was Alan Ginsberg who appeared on national television promoting the use of LSD and marijuana. We became the "flower children."

So now we can appreciate why Aldous Huxley advocated brainwashing by enhanced pharmacological methods. When the youths are in that state of mind, "they will be distracted from any desire to rebel" against the fascist military security state. And that is why the "War on Drugs" like the War on Terrorism is a bogus war. It is no coincidence that the hippie counter-culture was at its height during the Vietnam War and when the youths were fiercely opposing the war, culminating in the massacre of the Kent State University students by the Ohio State National Guard. It was a turning point in the American public opinion, from one of support to outright opposition to the Vietnam War. It comes as no surprise therefore that drug addiction is so rampant amongst youths all over the world. It is one of the most effective weapons of the state to distract rebellious youths from reality into the memory hole. Getting high is a form of mind control and an effective tool for political control by the state.

But who is behind Aldous Huxley, Timothy Leary, Allan Watts, etc., and the insidious counter-culture and the new-age occultism?

It is the British mind-control octopus called the Tavistock Institute. Its tentacles reach far and wide. The institute was responsible in the establishment of the leading think tanks in the United States. Its humble beginnings began with a bequest from the Duke of Bedford, of a building to establish the *Tavistock Clinic* in Tavistock Square in London. The Tavistock Institute founded in 1946 was originally called the *Tavistock Institute of Human Relations*. It engages in research and consultancy work in the social sciences and applied psychology for the European Union, the British government and private institutions and organizations and publishes the journal, *Human Relations*. This is a must read journal, being the mouthpiece of the Mind Controllers.

The Tavistock Clinic was founded by the psychiatrist Hugh Crichton-Miller. The Clinic was commissioned to study the effects of shellshock on British soldiers in the First World War and to determine the "breaking point" of the men under stress. The project was under the direction of John Rawlings-Reese of the British Army

Bureau of Psychological Warfare assisted by Henry Dicks, Ronald Hargreaves, Tommy Wilson and Wilfred Bion. Their focus was on the new *Dynamic Psychologies*. Its early beginning and expertise was therefore in applied psychology—the critical discipline for mind control.

⸙   In 1941, the group of psychiatrists at the Clinic was invited to join the Directorate of Army Psychiatry. These early pioneers recognized that neurotic disabilities were endemic in modern societies and not just confined to soldiers subject to stress in a war environment. The Psychiatrists played a very important role during World War II and the army was greatly influenced by the psychoanalyst Wilfred Bion and psychiatrist Ronald Hargreaves who was working closely with Sir Ronald Adam, the Army Commander in Northern Command. On attaining the rank of Adjutant General, the No. 2 in the army, Tavistock ideas were implemented. A radical method for selecting officers was introduced, based on multi-disciplinary approach as the team were from various disciplines—from psychiatry and clinical psychology to social psychology, sociology and anthropology. They called themselves the "Composite Work Group."

They introduced the following innovation in psychiatry:[3]

- Command psychiatry as a reconnaissance activity leading to the identification of critical problems.

- Social psychiatry as a policy science permitting preventive intervention in large scale problems.

- The co-operation with the military of new institutions to implement these policies.

- The therapeutic community as a new mode of treatment.

- Cultural psychiatry for the analysis of the enemy mentality.

After the war, these valuable lessons were applied to address social problems and the war programs were adapted accordingly. The outcome—*the social engagement of social science.*

A new group had to be formed to spearhead these innovations. The project was called "Operation Phoenix." Again, John Rawlings-

3   Eric Trist and Hugh Murray, A Tavistock Anthology: The Foundation and Development of the Tavistock Institute to 1989. Source:www.moderntimesworkplace.com

Reese[4] was elected and he was joined by Leonard Browne,[5] Henry Dicks who founded the Cultural Psychiatry, Ronald Hargreaves,[6] Mary Luff, Tommy Wilson who became Chairman of the Institute. Two other members were co-opted, namely, Jock Sutherland, who became the Director of the post-war Clinic and Eric Trist who later succeeded Wilson as Chairman of the Institute. One of the first things they did was to incorporate an Institute of Human Relations to study the wider social problems not associated with mental health.

The development of the institute became a reality with generous funding by the Rockefeller Foundation. The institute spearheaded numerous ground breaking studies in social psychology and group dynamics based on studies of self-regulating groups in a coal mine. This is indeed interesting as coal-miners have a history of labor activism and have always been fighting for workers' rights. Motivational research led to the development of new concepts in marketing that ushered in a new era of advertising. These new concepts brought together Lewinian and psychoanalytic thinking which was very effective in the promotion of "pleasure foods"—products of no or little nutritional value but that provided oral satisfaction which helped to reduce anxiety and stress.

The institute has come a long way since then. Its mind-control hidden research network extends from the University of Sussex in Britain to the Stanford Research Institute, Esalen, MIT, the Heritage Foundation, Center of Strategic and International Studies at Georgetown, U.S. Air Force Intelligence, the Rand Corporation and the Mitre Corporation. Another network covers the Mont Pelerin Society, Trilateral Commission, the Ditchley Foundation and the Club of Rome. The website obviously does not mention these institutions. Even those that are mentioned are no doubt involved in one way or another mind control programs.

I know that the above is heavy stuff, but be patient for I have just introduced to you how psychiatry can be applied in a number of ways, even in the consumption of non-nutritional foods. This is the ABC of mind control. Tavistock Institute pioneered this area of research and till today they have no equals. Stay focused and read on.

In due course, the power elites realized that that the techniques spearheaded by the Tavistock Institute could be effectively applied for social and political control objectives. Many of you will find it difficult to

---

4   He founded the World Federation of Mental Health.
5   He became a prominent Alderman in the London County Council.
6   He was later made the Deputy Director of the World Health Organization.

comprehend that there are such people with such grandiose ideas. And once again, I will stand accused as a conspiracy theorist. But I seek your indulgence. Before furnishing you with irrefutable evidence of this scheme for total political control, I would like you to perform a simple exercise.

Take a note pad and write down some of the more common conventional wisdom regarding what constitutes "correct political conduct" which once contravened would land us in detention and/or being ostracized by society. Then ask yourself, "Is this right and fair?" Additionally, you should ask who decided on this particular rule and how was it propagated and enforced.

E.g. when crude price goes up, petrol price is always increased almost immediately, notwithstanding the huge time lag between extraction, refining and delivery to the petrol station. The price increase is also arbitrarily decided. No explanation whatsoever. But you accept it without even a whimper of protest. Invariably everyone else must justify their increase in price because of increased costs. The mantra is, "we must control inflation, and protect the small business and the poor!" But inflation does not apply to oil companies who always report record profits after each price increase. It never even occurs to you that there could be huge payoffs to corrupt officials.

When we don't think, we can be brainwashed and manipulated.

So when I say we are being brainwashed and manipulated, you should ask the simple question, each time something odd happens: "Who benefits from this manipulation?" I shall now provide the answer and thereafter I hope you will be wiser and less gullible.

In his book, *The Impact of Science on Society,*[7] Lord Bertrand Russell wrote:

> **I think the subject which will be of most importance politically is mass psychology. Its importance has been enormously increased by the growth of modern methods of propaganda. Of these the most influential is what is called "education."** Religion plays a part, though a diminishing one; the press, the cinema, and the radio play an increasing part.... It is hoped that in time anybody will be able to persuade anybody of anything if he can catch the patient young and is provided by the State with money and equipment.

7   Lord Bertrand Russell, *The Impact of Science on Society*, (1953, Ams Press)

The subject will make great strides when it is taken up by scientists under a scientific dictatorship. The social psychologists of the future will have a number of classes of school children on whom they will try different methods of producing an unshakable conviction that snow is black....

Although this science will be diligently studied, it will be rigidly confined to the governing class. The populace will not be allowed to know how its convictions were generated. When the technique is perfected, every government that has been in charge of education for a generation will be able to control its subjects securely without the need of armies or policemen. (Emphases added)

The following passages will shake your confidence in the entire edifice of public education.

The scientific rulers will provide one kind of education for ordinary men and women, and another for those who are holders of scientific power. Ordinary men and women will be expected to be docile, industrious, punctual, thoughtless, and contented. Of these qualities probably contentment will be considered the most important. In order to produce it, all researches of psychoanalysis, behaviorism, and biochemistry will be brought into play. All the boys and girls will learn from an early age to be what is called "cooperative," i.e. to do exactly what everybody is doing. Initiative will be discouraged in these children, and insubordination without being punished will be scientifically trained out of them.

On those rare occasions when a boy or girl who has passed the age at which it is usual to determine social status shows such marked ability as to seem the intellectual equal to the rulers, a difficult situation will arise, requiring serious consideration. If the youth is content to abandon his previous associates and to throw in his lot whole-heartedly with the rulers, he may, after suitable tests, be promoted, but if he shows any regrettable solidarity with his previous associates, the rulers will reluctantly conclude that there is nothing to be done with him except to send him to the lethal chamber before his ill-disciplined intelligence has had time to spread revolt. This will be a painful duty to the rulers, but I think they will not shrink from performing it.

There you have it. Nothing can be clearer that this declaration of intent, that the majority of the people will suffer mediocrity and forced "contentment" while the rulers will ensure their dominance and superiority. Mass psychology and brainwashing techniques serve this higher purpose. So get off your butts and get real for once. This is not conspiracy theory. This is reality coming straight from Lord Bertrand Russell. I challenge anyone to prove me wrong on this point!

Now that I got your attention, we shall proceed at a quicker pace.

I had mentioned earlier that one method of mind control was through the use of drugs like LSD. Today, scientists have even gone one step further. Some of you may recall the film, *Eternal Sunshine of the Spotless Mind* which tells a story of a man who had his nasty experience and memories of a screwed-up relationship erased from his brain. What was once a science-fiction is about to be realized and very soon too! Eric Kandel, a Nobel Prize-winning memory researcher[8] at Columbia University in Manhattan, has stated that memory-improving and memory-deleting machines and drugs may be available within five to ten years.[9]

Already there are more than 40 such drugs going through clinical trials with the U.S. Food and Drug Administration. Just imagine: they can delete our memories like pressing the "Delete" function key in our computer keyboard to erase stored data and memories.

So let me warn parents, Muslim parents in particular, especially in this period of total war, when you send your children to public schools in Britain (most likely under scholarships) have you prepared them adequately? Under the present scheme of things, they will be brainwashed to serve "Mother England's" interest first before they will serve you and your country. Think about that.

Why do you think the Zionist Anglo-American establishment is so confident of their ability to manipulate our minds and that of your children? Every foreign student from resource rich countries and/or countries in strategic locations is profiled and identified for future recall—the future collaborators in the civil service, in the military, specially formed political organizations and religious organizations. They have already entered our children's heads, screwed them up properly when they were at the British, American and Australian

8   I bet that most people have not heard of such a science or profession called Memory
    Researcher!

9   Source: Brenda O'Neill, The Mystery of Mind Control. May 4, 2004, BBC News.
    www.bbc.co.uk

schools and universities and we are none the wiser. The next generation propaganda wars have already been lost before the present one is concluded.

In the next few pages I am going to launch a mental assault on your senses, not unlike the situation where a child has been brainwashed by a religious cult and has been rescued and is undergoing treatment and counselling to overcome the intense indoctrination. I offer no apologies for my methods. There is no other way to confront this evil. The truth is often ugly. Face it head on or prepare to sacrifice your children to the mind controllers and the awful fate already decided by people like Lord Bertrand Russell.

I am going to start with a dose of reality. Dr. Jose Delgado, who demonstrated a radio-controlled bull on CNN in 1985, the Director of Neuropsychiatry, Yale University Medical School and author of *Physical Control of the Mind*[10] has openly admitted the agenda whether you like it or not, and whether you accept it or not. This is what he said:

> **We need a program of psychosurgery and political control of our society. The purpose is physical control of the mind.** Everyone who deviates from the given norm can be surgically mutilated. The individual may think that the most important reality is his own existence, but this is only his personal point of view. This lacks historical perspective. Man does not have the right to develop his own mind. This kind of liberal orientation has great appeal. We must electrically control the brain. **Someday armies and generals will be controlled by electrical stimulation of the brain.**[11] (Emphases added)

Today, we already have the *Objective Force Warrior,*[12] the future fighting soldier that incorporates nanotechnology and state of the art weapons and communication systems, with worn power source, enhanced performance mental and visual aids and networked to supercomputers! This is but another step in the direction of Dr. Delgado's agenda in "physical control of the mind."

While some readers may still want to debate the veracity of this exposé, what was conceived 30 years ago is now a reality. And frankly at this point in time, it does not matter whether one agrees or not, but

10 Dr. Jose Delgado, *Physical Control of the Mind*, (1969, Harper & Row, New York).

11 Source" Congressional Record No 26, Vol. 118, February 24, 1974.

12 For more details, see Chapter 5.

those who are prepared to face the consequences will have a better chance of survival!

⚡ Whenever my critics label me a "conspiracy theorist," I always use an easy method to shut them up for good and expose them for what they are—apologists for the Zionist Anglo-American war cabal. I want you to do the same. Don't be afraid. I always draw them into a public debate. That way, when I expose them they have nowhere to hide and they do look so very stupid (once their intellectual garbage is stripped bare), and although they may wear the respectability of an honored gentleman by virtue of some social and academic titles being conferred on them (e.g. Lordship, Knighthood, a "Tan Sri," a "Dato,"[13] Professorship, etc.) or the chairmanship of some corporations, the Enron type "revolving door" appointments.

The method is getting their own kind to expose their hypocrisy and falsehood. So here we go.

In 1994, The U.S. Senate published the Rockefeller Report[14]—*Is Military Research Hazardous to Veterans Health? Lessons Spanning Half a Century.* The title itself is revealing, as the report exposes half a century of secret military programs. In the Foreword to the report, the Chairman said:

> During the last few years, the public has become aware of several examples where U.S. Government researchers **intentionally** exposed Americans to potentially dangerous substances without their knowledge or consent. The Senate Committee in Veterans Affairs... has conducted a comprehensive analysis of the extent to which **veterans participated in such research while serving in the U.S. military.** (Emphases added)

In the Introduction to the report, the Committee stated:

> During the last fifty years, hundreds of thousands of military personnel have been involved in experimentation and other intentional exposures conducted by the Department of Defense (DoD), **often without a service member's knowledge or consent.** In some cases, soldiers who consented to serve as human subjects found themselves participating in experiments quite different from those described at the time they volunteered.... Additionally, soldiers were sometimes ordered by

13 The last two are "Honors" conferred by Malaysian Federal and State Authorities.

14 Source: 103rd Congress, 2nd Session—Committee Print—S.Prt. 103-97. This is a Staff Report Prepared for the Committee on Veterans' Affairs, December 8, 1994. Chairman, John D. Rockefeller IV.

commanding officers to "volunteer" to participate in research or face dire consequences. For example, several Persian Gulf War veterans interviewed by the Committee staff reported that they were **ordered to take experimental vaccines during Operation Desert Shield or face prison....**

Similarly, hundreds of soldiers were subjected to hallucinogens in experimental programs conducted by the DoD in participation with, or sponsored by the CIA. **These service members often unwittingly participated as human subjects in tests for drugs intended for mind-control or behavior modification, often without their knowledge or consent.** (Emphases added)

On June 18, 1997, CNN broadcast an interview with Dr. Steven Aftergood of the Federation of American Scientists relating to government research efforts in mind control. While admitting such efforts, he attempted to excuse the U.S. government, thereby putting his credibility at stake, more so after the Rockefeller Report of 1994, which he seems to be ignorant of, and that of President Clinton's Human Subjects Memo of 1997. I shall come to the latter in a moment. But let us see what Dr. Steven Aftergood has to say in the CNN interview.

Interviewer: What do we know of right now, in relation to government experimentation with mind control?

Steven: The first thing I think needs to be said is that it would be irresponsible to accuse the government of performing secret mind control test on unsuspecting citizens without any evidence. **I do not personally know of any such evidence.** (Emphasis added)

His last sentence is classic propaganda—to put you off. Just because he does not know of any such evidence, and relying on his status as a doctor, he is attempting to influence you to accept that such secret experiments are all hocus-pocus. Remember, earlier, I told you about such persons trying to cover up for the fascist mind controllers—those respectable do-gooders? Well Dr. Steven Aftergood is just one of them. We just caught ourselves a big fish. The last sentence of the quoted report of Senator John D. Rockefeller really nailed him good and contradicts precisely his propaganda ploy. Doesn't he look stupid, when the Rockefeller Report mentions specifically the clandestine experiments using the military as guinea pigs? This is what I mean, when I say we need to catch them in the open.

He continued, but on another issue, tried to minimize the damage. Judge for yourself:

> Steven: Having said that, there is a record of decades of research into technologies of mind control and behavior modification dating back at least into the 1960s if not before. The state of the art has reached astonishing levels of accomplishment. For example, it is now possible to remotely raise a person's body temperature by bathing them in microwave radiation, to the point that they are incapacitated. It is possible to induce auditory hallucinations, in other words to make a person hear things, by means of certain frequencies of electro-magnetic radiation. **And these are things that sound like science fiction or fantasy but they have been demonstrated at least in the laboratory.** (Emphasis added)

It is apparent that the second paragraph of his interview is self contradictory of his earlier statement that he has no personal knowledge of such experiments. Well this is part of the mind game. And in the last sentence of the recorded interview, he tries to belittle the efforts as confined to the laboratory. He denies that there were secret experiments and the government was and is transparent in such matters.

Well, we caught him again big time. This is because in 1997, President Bill Clinton issued the Presidential Human Subjects Memo,[15] excerpts of which are reproduced below. My comments are in bold within brackets.

> I have worked hard to restore trust and ensure openness in government. **[Dr. Steven, please read this sentence again and again. If there were no secret experiments, there would not be a need to restore trust.]** This memorandum will further our progress toward these goals by strengthening the Federal Government's protection of human subjects of classified research. In January 1994, I established the Advisory Committee on Human Radiation Experiments to examine reports that government had funded and conducted unethical human radiation experiments during the Cold War. **[Dr. Steven, please read this sentence again and again. Human radiation experiments were extensive during the Cold War and not confined to laboratory as you tried to suggest.]** I directed the Advisory Committee to uncover the truth, recommend steps to right past wrongs and propose ways to prevent unethical human subjects research from occurring in the future.

15 Source: Federal Register Vol. 62, No. 92—Presidential Documents, March 27, 1997

But let us not be naïve. Notwithstanding President Clinton's directive, the intelligence services will continue with secret experiments for they serve a different interest and answer to another "master."

To hide their hideous experiments and research, the Mind Controllers are using new terminologies. According to Dr. Margaret Singer, Professor Emeritus at the University of California at Berkeley, who is the world's authority on mind control and cults, the academia and government scientists are re-labeling mind control and brainwashing techniques as "Coercive Persuasion," "Coercive Psychological Systems" or "Coercive Influence." Though of minor consolation, they got at least one word right, "coercive." No matter how we sugarcoat the terminology, in essence, mind control and brainwashing techniques is another form of coercion. There is no way one can get away from this fact!

And in the Education Appendix on Coercive Psychological Systems presented to the U.S. Supreme Court in the case of *Wollesheim v Church of Scientology* 89-1367 and 89-1361,[16] Dr. Singer explains:

> Coercion is defined as, "to restrain or constrain by force...." Legally it often implies the use of PHYSICAL FORCE or physical or legal threat. This traditional concept of coercion is far better understood than the technological concepts of "Coercive Persuasion **which are effective restraining, impairing, or compelling through the gradual application of PSYCHOLOGICAL FORCES.** (Emphasis added)

Therefore, from the experts' point of view, coercions are of two types. While we are familiar with the first, **PHYSICAL COERCION**, we have difficulty understanding the second, **PSYCHOLOGICAL COERCION**. This is because there are no physical scars as such in this type of coercion. If a subject exhibits trauma or strange behaviors, resulting from such coercion, the manifestations can be easily covered up as *paranoid schizophrenia*. The victim is then slam-dunked into the memory-hole of a psychiatric institution, for further unrestrained and unprotected hideous experiments. One bird less that "can fly over the cuckoo's nest," if I may borrow the expression.[17]

---

16 Source: www.factnet.org

17 Jack Nichols' incredible performance in the film, *One Flew Over the Cuckoo's Nest*, which tells a story of abused inmates in a psychiatric hospital.

The Education Appendix[18] presented to the U.S. Supreme Court explains that a coercive persuasion program is a *behavioral change technology* applied to cause the "learning" and "adoption" of a set of behaviors or an ideology under certain conditions. It is distinguished from other forms of benign social learning or peaceful persuasion by the conditions under which it is conducted and by the techniques of environmental and interpersonal manipulation employed to suppress particular behaviors and to train others.

Over time, coercive persuasion, a psychological force akin in some ways to our legal concepts of undue influence, can be even MORE effective than pain, torture, drugs, and use of physical force and legal threats. This revelation is mind boggling and shows that the torturers in Abu Ghraib and Guantanamo Bay are still using the crude methods of mind control, and that is why they have been so ineffective.

The Korean War "Manchurian Candidate" misconception of the need for suggestibility-increasing drugs, and physical pain and torture, to effect thought reform, is generally associated with the old concepts and models of brainwashing. *Today, they are not necessary for a coercive persuasion program to be effective.* With drugs, physical pain, torture, or even a physically coercive threat, you can often temporarily make someone do something against their will. You can even make them do something they hate or they really did not like or want to do at the time. They do it, but *their attitude is not changed.* This is much different and far less devastating than that which you are able to achieve with the improvements of coercive persuasion.

With coercive persuasion you can change people's attitudes without their knowledge and volition. You can create new "attitudes" where they will do things willingly which they formerly may have detested, things which previously only torture, physical pain, or drugs could have coerced them to do.

This is a very important point to grasp. Changing behavior is no guarantee that the victim will conform. Attitudes, basically the mindset is far more important. The slave mentality, the submission to Imperial authority and the acknowledgement that the occupiers are intellectually far superior will give rise to a state of affairs whereby the warmongers can exercise total control without any resistance.

18 This explanation is adapted from the Education Appendix @ www.factnet.org

The advances in the extreme anxiety and emotional stress production technologies found in coercive persuasion supersede old style coercion that focuses on pain, torture, drugs, or threat in that these older systems do not change attitude so that subjects follow orders "willingly." Coercive persuasion changes both attitude AND behavior, not JUST BEHAVIOR.

Coercive persuasion or thought reform as it is sometimes known, is best understood as a coordinated system of graduated coercive influence and behavior control designed to deceptively and surreptitiously manipulate and influence individuals, usually in a group setting, in order for the originators of the program to *profit in some way, normally financially or politically.*

The essential strategy used by those operating such programs is to systematically select, sequence and coordinate numerous coercive persuasion tactics over CONTINUOUS PERIODS OF TIME. There are seven main tactic types found in various combinations in a coercive persuasion program. A coercive persuasion program can still be quite effective without the presence of ALL seven of these tactic types.

Tactic 1: The individual is prepared for thought reform through increased suggestibility and/or "softening up," specifically through hypnotic or other suggestibility-increasing techniques such as: A) Extended audio, visual, verbal, or tactile fixation drills; B) Excessive exact repetition of routine activities; C) Decreased sleep; D) Nutritional restriction.

Tactic 2: Using rewards and punishments, efforts are made to establish considerable control over a person's social environment, time, and sources of social support. Social isolation is promoted. Contacts with family and friends are abridged, as are contacts with persons who do not share group-approved attitudes. Economic and other dependence on the group is fostered. In the forerunner to coercive persuasion, brainwashing, this was rather easy to achieve through simple imprisonment.

Tactic 3: Disconfirming information and non-supporting opinions are prohibited in group communication. Rules exist about permissible topics to discuss with outsiders. Communication is highly controlled. An "in-group" language is usually constructed.

Tactic 4: Frequent and intense attempts are made to cause a person to re-evaluate the most central aspects of his or her experience of self and prior conduct in negative ways. Efforts are designed to destabilize and undermine the subject's basic consciousness, reality awareness, world view, emotional control, and defense mechanisms as well as getting them to reinterpret their life's history, and adopt a new version of causality.

Tactic 5: Intense and frequent attempts are made to undermine a person's confidence in himself and his judgment, creating a sense of powerlessness.

Tactic 6: Non-physical punishments are used such as intense humiliation, loss of privilege, social isolation, social status changes, intense guilt, anxiety, manipulation and other techniques for creating strong aversive emotional arousals, etc.

Tactic 7: Certain secular psychological threats [force] are used or are present—the failure to adopt the approved attitude, belief, or consequent behavior will lead to severe punishment or dire consequence, (e.g. physical or mental illness, the reappearance of a prior physical illness, drug dependence, economic collapse, social failure, divorce, disintegration, failure to find a mate, etc.).

Another set of criteria has to do with defining other common elements of mind control systems. If most of Robert Jay Lifton's eight point model of thought reform is being used in a cultic organization, it is most likely a dangerous and destructive cult. These eight points follow:

Robert Jay Lifton's Eight-Point Model of Thought Reform

1. **Environment Control:** Limitation of many/all forms of communication with those outside the group. Books, magazines, letters and visits with friends and family are taboo. "Come out and be separate!"

2. **Mystical Manipulation:** The potential convert to the group becomes convinced of the higher purpose and special calling of the group through a profound encounter / experience, for example, through an alleged miracle or prophetic word of those in the group.

3. **Demand for Purity:** An explicit goal of the group is to bring about some kind of change, whether it be on a global, social, or personal level. "Perfection is possible if one stays with the group and is committed."

4. **Cult of Confession:** The unhealthy practice of self disclosure to members in the group. Often in the context of a public gathering in the group, admitting past sins and imperfections, even doubts about the group and critical thoughts about the integrity of the leaders.

5. **Sacred Science:** The group's perspective is absolutely true and completely adequate to explain EVERYTHING. The doctrine is not subject to amendments or question. ABSOLUTE conformity to the doctrine is required.

6. **Loaded language:** A new vocabulary emerges within the context of the group. Group members "think" within the very abstract and narrow parameters of the group's doctrine. The terminology sufficiently stops members from thinking critically by reinforcing a "black and white" mentality. Loaded terms and clichés prejudice thinking.

7. **Doctrine Over Person:** Pre-group experience and group experience are narrowly and decisively interpreted through the absolute doctrine, even when experience contradicts the doctrine.

8. **Dispensing of Existence:** Salvation is possible only in the group. Those who leave the group are doomed.

The above are the basic tools which we must learn and understand so as to resist future mind control campaigns which would be waged by the Zionist warmongers against us. Study them so that you can better prepare your family for the mental onslaughts. I can only advise—be prepared. Knowledge and understanding is the first step. The rest is up to you.

16

The Mind Rapists:
Inside the Dark Labyrinth

They were naked, half-starved and abused…. Being awakened in the middle of the night, being beaten, lied to, and insulted, was all part of the 'unfreezing process' through which psychological defenses were broken down, and terror and humiliation were induced. Hence, the photographing in the nude, being forced to urinate while running, the sadism and abuse. The aim of the treatment was to cause temporary insanity, a severe psychological injury liable to have lasting consequences….

— **Prof. Robert Daly**[1]

We have no answer to the moral issue….

— **Richard Helms**[2]

The above quotation by Prof. Robert Daly describes the torture conducted by the British military against Irish detainees in Northern Ireland. When we mention about mental torture and mind control, we invariably associate it with the CIA. Let me share something with you. The Brits are still the best, and they are real mean bastards. It was the British that taught the Americans and other military and intelligence services. Mr. F.H. Larkin of the Army Operational Research Establishment was one of the first to travel over to the United States to train his counterparts at Fort Bragg on his experience in British Psychological Warfare Techniques in Malaya from 1952-55. He was in charge of a nine-man research team reporting to AORE and the

---

1 The Professor is an expert in sensory deprivation and was an instructor in psychiatry at the University of North Carolina. Later a lecturer at the Edinburgh University and subsequently at University College, Cork, Rep. of Ireland. Source: "After Effects of Irish Prisoners Subjected to Ill-Treatment and Torture," New Scientist, August 5, 1976.

2 CIA Director. Source: Church Committee Report, Book 1, p. 402.

Director General of the Information Services of the then Federation of Malaya. Forming part of his research team were two men from the Operational Research Office of Johns Hopkins University and a psychologist from Australia. In the first NATO symposium of Defense Psychology held in Paris in 1960, Britain played a leading role. It was only in 1963, that the U.S. Department of Defense (DoD) held its first worldwide Psy-Ops Conference, with Britain, yet again playing a leading role.[3]

The British are very clever in covering up their dirty deeds and in portraying a positive image. It is the courteous and friendly policeman (the English Bobby), ever so kind as to assist a tourist that registers in our minds whenever we think of the British security establishment. The recent cold blooded murder of an innocent Brazilian commuter, shot seven times in the head, while attempting to board an underground train in London by the armed policemen of the Metropolitan Police Force should dispel any illusions as to how dangerous they can be. They have a "shoot-to-kill-first" policy.

When the Irish torture scandal broke out, Lord Parker who was tasked with the investigation into the abuse in Northern Ireland matter-of-factly admitted that sensory derivation (SD) methods used on the Irish detainees were "techniques developed since the war to deal with a number of situations involving internal security." Some or all have played an important part in counter-insurgency operations in Palestine, Malaya, Kenya, Cyprus, British Cameroon, Brunei, British Guyana, Aden and the Persian Gulf.[4]

Amnesty International in its memorandum to the Parker Committee states: "It is because we regard the deliberate destruction of a man's ability to control his own mind with revulsion that we reserve a special place in our catalogue of moral crimes for techniques of thought control and brainwashing. Any interrogation procedure which has the purpose or effect of causing a malfunction or breakdown of a man's mental processes constitutes as grave an assault on the inherent dignity of the human person as more traditional techniques of physical torture."[5]

3   Dr. Armen Victorian, "United States, Canada, Britain: Partners in Mind Control Operations," @ www.WantToKnow.info
4   Source: Parker Report, Cmnd 4901 (HMSO, para 10.
5   Amnesty International, Report of an Enquiry into Allegation of Ill-Treatment in Northern Ireland.

The main centers for the teaching of Psychological Warfare and Torture Methods in Britain are at Ashford in Kent, Caterrick in Yorkshire, Bradbury Lines and Old Sarum in Wiltshire. The infamous Frank Kitson was one of the architects of these courses. There are also the SAS training courses in Bracon Beacons.

Equally sinister were the "Control Units" in British prisons and their activities were at one time "Top Secret." The two most notorious Control Units operated from the Wakefield and the Wormwood Scrubs prisons, where the Sleep Deprivation (SD) method was practiced extensively. The mental torture technique used to break down prisoners was designed for a period of six months or longer. In the first six months, the prisoner is kept in strict solitary confinement where there is no communication at all, not even with the guards except by way of gestures. If the prisoner is stubborn and does not break, the routine is repeated for another six months.

In 1974, Roy Jenkins the then Home Secretary without any remorse or shame declared that "I am satisfied that the safeguards and procedures are such that the trained staff of Wakefield are able to maintain careful and caring watch on the progress and condition of prisoners in the control unit."[6] But why should prisoners be tortured in the first place? And it is to be noted that he was a Labor Party big wig. It is total erroneous to think that Labourites are generally progressives and the Conservatives, reactionary. In Britain, they are but the two sides of a fascist coin. Given this "Labour" pedigree, should we be really surprised by the reactionary policies of Tony Blair? Remember what Lord Bertrand Russell said about the "Rulers." The Blairites and Thatcherites all belong to the "ruling class" and they have never lost a night's sleep when torturing or killing the innocents. Recall the fervent support of Margaret Thatcher for General Pinochet when he was arrested in Britain for War Crimes. And now we have the genocide of the Iraqis by the Bush-Blair coalition forces.

I will now attempt to trace the general history of mind control experiments and programs conducted by the Intelligence Services of the United States and Britain. They collaborated extensively and were frequently joined by the Canadian secret service. The information revealed here is taken from *The Search for the Manchurian Candidate,*[7] *Bluebird: Deliberate Creation of Multiple Personality by Psychi-*

6   House of Commons, November 1974. Hansard

7   John Marks, (1979 Norton Paperback).

atrists,[8] *Mind Controllers*[9] and *A Nation Betrayed*.[10] These are three "must read" books and I do recommend that you go out and buy them immediately.

The systematic development of mind control programs started in earnest at the end of World War II when over 1,000 Nazi doctors and scientists experienced in this field were secretly transferred to the United States in an operation called PAPERCLIP. The French, Russian and British secret services were likewise engaged in such recruitments. The medical establishment in all of these countries connived and collaborated in these programs. Besides mind control programs, there were other equally heinous experiments conducted on unsuspecting human subjects. I would like to touch on this area briefly before focusing on mind control experiments.

The Tuskeegee Syphilis Study will make you want to vomit. The study started in Alabama in 1932 was conducted by the Public Health Service. 399 illiterate and poor black men with syphilis were recruited as test subjects together with 201 black men without syphilis. The idea was not to treat those with syphilis even though the cure for it, penicillin, was available. The families and the subjects were not told about the syphilis and were informed that they merely had "bad blood." The treatment was withheld for 30 years. In the period of the study, doctors made observations and in the final report concluded that the group that had syphilis died younger and were sick more often than the control group. The study was shut down in 1972, following exposure by an investigative journalist. No one knows how many women were ultimately infected and how many children were born infected with syphilis. Can you imagine that at the time, this so-called medical study was praised and supported by the then Surgeon General, the American Heart Association and the Center for Disease Control? The results were published in prestigious peer-reviewed medical journals![11]

The Tuskeegee scandal was followed by the bombshell revelation that unsuspecting humans were subjected to radiation experiments as part of an operation called the MANHATTAN PROJECT (the

8   Collin A. Ross, (2000, Manitou Communications Inc.)
9   Dr. Armen Victorian, Source: www.WantToKnow.info
10 Carol Rutz, @ www.WantToKnow.info
11 E.g. Journal of the American Medical Association, 1936, "Untreated Syphilis in a Male Negro." See also the Archives of Internal Medicine, 1964, "The Tuskeegee Study of Untreated Syphilis."

Atomic Bomb Project). Patients were injected with plutonium without their consent. In another experiment, prisoners in Washington and Oregon state prisons were paid to have their testicles irradiated and were exposed to 600 roentgen of radiation, which is 100 times above the recommended dose. All they got was a miserable U.S. $5 a month.

At the Massachusetts General Hospital, Dr. William Sweet and his team injected terminally ill patients with uranium-235. Pregnant women were also given "cocktails" of radioactive material in order to study their effects on the foetus. In another major study, the Department of Health fed more than 800 women with a "cocktail"-laced with radioactive iron isotope.

What comes next might very well come out of Stephen King's thrillers, but it is not a fiction but a documented crime beyond imagination. Harvard University researchers, sponsored by the U.S. Public Health Service, fed radioactive iodide to 760 mentally retarded children at the Wrentham State School. Some were only one year old. Other prestigious institutions involved in this sordid and inhumane practice were Johns Hopkins, the University of Minnesota and the Massachusetts Institute of Technology. To induce the parents to give their consent, the form stated that the purpose of the experiment was "helping to improve the nutrition of our children."

The Advisory Committee[12] set up by President Clinton following the public outcry, in its report rejected the nutritional claim as without basis.

When legal suits were filed against the Federal government for compensation by victims of radiation experiments, the U.S. Supreme Court held, "We would be creating a potentially enormous financial burden for the Federal Government."

The foregoing exposé and evidence show a pattern of collaboration and connivance by the most respectable scientific and medical institutions with the intelligence services, without which the experiments could not possibly be carried out and shielded from the public for so long.

Now that I've got your attention, it should not come as a surprise anymore that when hideous mind control programs were carried out

12 Faden R.R. Final Report: The Advisory Committee on Human Radiation Experiments. Government Printing Office 1995. Report is available at www.eh.doe.gov/ohre/roadmap/achre/index.html

on unsuspecting human subjects, the best scientific and medical institutions and establishments were likewise involved. The legal profession gets a bad name because of the few bad apples fleecing their clients. But when compared to the crimes of the scientists and the medical profession, lawyers' misconduct are mere "Mary Poppins misdemeanor"!

The CIA initiated its first mind control program on April 20, 1950 under the code name, BLUEBIRD when it was approved by its Director, Roscoe Hillenkoetter. In 1951, when the British and Canadian intelligence services collaborated in the project, it was renamed ARTICHOKE. In a CIA memo dated 1951[13] [CIA MORI ID140401], it was stated that research should focus on the following areas:

- Whether the agency can create by post hypnotic control an action contrary to the subject's morals and principles;

- Whether the agency can induce a subject, through hypnotic control, to perform acts for the agency's benefit;

- Whether the agency can induce, through hypnotic control, a subject's willingness to crash a plane or wreck a train;

- Whether the agency can induce total amnesia;

- Whether the agency can "alter" a subject's personality;

- Whether a system can be devised to make an unwilling subject into a compliant agent to be controlled by an untrained field agent by use of codes and other signs and signals; and

- To devise a variety of ways to conceal sleep inducing agents in common items, such as cigarettes, coffee, tea, liquor and medicine.

Case Study: A CIA document [CIA MORI ID 190684] in 1953 revealed that two 19-year-old girls were brainwashed to the extent that they "could demonstrate that they could pass from a fully awake state to a deep hypnotic controlled state by telephone, by receiving written matter, or by the use of a code, signal or words and that con-

13 CIA MORI ID 140401, pp. 6–7. This is a declassified document. You may order this and other documents referred to in this chapter from www.foia.cia.gov/foia_request.asp. All subsequent references in the page itself or in the footnotes will only identify the document number. Refer to the given website for verification.

trol of those hypnotized can be passed from one individual to another without great difficulty. It has also been shown by experimentation with these girls that they can act as unwilling couriers for information purposes, and that they can be conditioned to a point where they believe a change in identity on their part even on the polygraph."

❦ **Case Study:** Another CIA document [CIA MORI ID19069] in 1954 referred to an experiment where a person could be transformed into an unsuspecting assassin. A woman who had a fear for firearms was brainwashed, and was told to awaken another woman in deep hypnotic sleep. She was instructed that if the other woman would not get up, she should pick up a gun and fire at her. And she did exactly that and on cue went to deep sleep again. In the experiment, the gun was armed with blanks. When the ladies woke up, they could not recall the "shooting" event. On being handed the gun, the subject refused to handle it and denied that she ever participated in the event.

Case Study: The document entitled "SI and H Experimentation"[14] [CIA MORI ID 190527] dated September 25, 1951 describes an exercise by brainwashed subjects to plant a bomb. "[ ][15] was instructed that upon awakening, she would proceed to [ ] room where she would wait at the desk for a telephone call. Upon receiving the call, a person known as "Jim" would engage her in normal conversation. During the course of this conversation, this individual would mention a code word. When she heard this code word, she would pass into a SI trance state, but would not close her eyes and remain perfectly normal and continue the telephone conversation. She was told that upon conclusion of the telephone conversation, she would carry out instructions: [ ] was shown an electric timing device. She was informed that this device was a bomb, and was then instructed on how to attach and set the device. After [ ] learned how to set and attach the device, she was told to take the timing device which was in a briefcase, and proceed to the ladies room. In the ladies room, she would be met by a girl whom she had never seen who would identify herself by the code word "New York." [ ] was then to show this individual how to attach and set the timing device and further instructions would be

---

14 "H" in the declassified CIA documents refers severally to "Hypnotism," "Hypnotized" and "Hypnotist(s)," and "SI" refers to Special Interrogation.

15 Empty braces within a quotation are CIA "white-outs" of the name of the subject for security reasons. These are as per the original document.

given that the timing device was to be carried in the briefcase to [ ] room, placed in the nearest empty electric-light plug and concealed in the bottom, left-hand drawer of [ ] desk, with the device set for 82 seconds and turned on.... [ ] was further instructed that after completion of instructing the other girl and the transferring to the other girl of the incendiary bomb, she was to return at once to the operations room, sit on the sofa, and go into a deep sleep state."

In 1953, the mind control operation was renamed MKULTRA[16] and it continued until early 1960s. Parallel to this operation was another operation called MKDELTA which was into chemical and biological warfare (CBW) products. Another outfit of the CIA, the Technical Services Staff (TSS)[17] in collaboration with the Special Operations Division (SOD) of the Army's biological research center at Fort Detrick, Maryland got into germ warfare under the code name MKNAOMI.

The Church Committee Report, Book 1, revealed that one of the functions of the SOD was to conduct "biological research for the CIA." The Report further states that "SOD agreed to assist the CIA in developing, testing, and maintaining biological agents delivery systems. By this agreement, the CIA acquired the knowledge, skills, and facilities of the Army to develop biological weapons suited for CIA use."[18]

Operation MKULTRA was divided into 140 subprojects most which focus on the mind control drugs. These drugs were used to assist in interrogations and in the creation of amnesia. It was under this project that the drug LSD was widely promoted.[19] Pharmaceutical giants like Eli Lilly were complicit in the production of LSD for the CIA.

LSD, the common name for lysergic acid diethylamide, was discovered by Albert Hoffmann when he was working for the giant Swiss

16 Pronounced as M-K ULTRA. The initials MK identify it as a TSS project. ULTRA has its roots to the World War II intelligence program ULTRA which cracked the German military codes.

17 This is a brainy outfit, consisting of many Ph.D.s with operational experience and they came out with incredible gadgets such as secret writing, invisible ink, forgeries, disguises, and weapons for the spy trade. The character "Q" and his outfit in the James Bond films is a rough equivalent to this outfit.

18 Source: www.gwu.edu/~nsarchive/news/20000817

19 We had earlier discussed the spread of LSD in Chapter 15 by such literary icons as Aldous Huxley and the creation of the hippie movement to divert the anti-war movement in the 1960s and early 1970 at the height of the Vietnam conflict.

pharmaceutical firm, Sandoz. Initial interest in the drug in the United States was spurred by Milton Greenblatt, the research director of the Harvard Medical School who thought that if it can induce psychosis, an antidote may be found to cure schizophrenia.

However, the intelligence services had different ideas, to use the drug to break the will of enemy agents and unlock the secrets in their minds. And if they could do this, the CIA concluded that they could also modify and manipulate human behavior. LSD and mind control took on a new meaning when the project came under the control of Sidney Gottlieb and protected by Richard Helms, who at the material time was head of the Directorate of Operations, commonly referred to as the "Dirty Tricks" department.

The Intelligence Services began pouring money into academia to create a new field of research and the money-for-hire scientists responded enthusiastically. The leading lights were: Bob Hyde at the Boston Psychopathic, Harold Abramson at Mt. Sinai Hospital and Columbia University in New York, Carl Pfeiffer at the University of Illinois Medical School, Harris Isabel of the NIMH sponsored Addiction Research in Lexington, Kentucky, Louis Jolyon West at the University of Oklahoma, and Harold Hodge's group at the University of Rochester.[20]

A plan entitled "Material Testing Program EA 1279" which involved the use of LSD was conducted on groups of volunteers to evaluate their ability to lie whilst under the influence of LSD. There were also memory impairment tests to assess the impact of LSD on memory. A vicious aspect of some of these experiments was the work of Dr. Harris Isabel who had a tendency to target black and gay inmates for experimentation.

In 1964, MKULTRA was renamed yet again as MKSEARCH. Following public outcry against such experiments, the Director of the CIA, Richard Helms ordered that the MKULTRA documents be destroyed.

A discussion on this mind boggling subject would not be complete without highlighting some of the "luminaries of mind control programs." I prefer to call them "Mind Rapists." The common rapist is generally perceived as one who violates the physical body and the privacy of his victim without the victim's consent. A mind rapist is no

20 John Marks, *The Search for the Manchurian Candidate.*

different and could be worse because the mind rapist seeks to destroy the personality of the victim and substitute in its place, such other personality as the rapist desires. And while the common rapists when caught by the law would be punished severely with imprisonment or death, the mind rapists never have to ANSWER for their crimes.

The most notorious mind rapist must be Dr. Ewen Cameron. He began conducting inhumane mind control experiments even before MKULTRA was initiated, at the Brandon Mental Hospital. And that could be the reason for his primary role in CIA sponsored programs. Some of his experiments with patients consist of forcing them to lie naked in red light for eight hours a day for eight months. In another experiment, the doctor would force patients to lie inside an electric cage until their body temperatures reached 102 degrees. A more hideous "treatment" was the use of "coma therapy" whereby patients are induced to a state of coma for 2 to 5 hours per day for up to 50 days!

And while he was performing his evil deeds, he was feted and adulated as the President of the Quebec, Canadian, American and World Psychiatric Associations, of which he was a co-founder. Colin Ross, MD and author of *Bluebird* [21] wrote about a hellish therapy created by the sadistic doctor called PSYCHIC DRIVING:

> In a paper published in the American Journal of Psychiatry entitled "Psychic driving" Dr. Cameron describes his brainwashing techniques and says, "Analogous to this is the breakdown of the individual under continuous interrogation."
>
> Psychic Driving was a procedure carried out in two stages: in the first stage, patients were *"Depatterned,"* which meant they were reduced to a vegetable state through a combination of massive amounts electroconvulsive shock, drug induced sleep and sensory isolation and deprivation. When fully depatterned, patients were incontinent of urine and feces, unable to feed themselves, and unable to state their name, age, location, or the current date.
>
> In the second stage, Psychic Driving was introduced. This consists of hundreds of hours of tape loops being played to the patient through earphones, special helmets or speakers in the sensory isolation room. The tape loop repeated statements of

21 On p. 129 of said book.

supposed psychological significance. If such procedures were carried out under third world dictators, they would be denounced as human rights violations by American and Canadian psychiatry and would be called brainwashing.

So even in brainwashing, we have double standards—whatever the Zionist Anglo-American elite scientific establishment pursues, it is science of the highest standards and their "discovery" peer-reviewed in leading international scientific journals. Anyone else who dare replicate such experiments would be denounced as evil, inhumane, human rights violators etc. Don't get me wrong. I am not saying that I condone such experiments be it by Zionist controlled establishments or third world tyrants. All I am saying is that even evil is perceived differently if it suits the ultimate objective of the global agenda.

It is the same logic with weapons of mass destruction. It is right for the superpower to have it and to use and threaten its use against all and sundry. But if anyone dares to challenge that monopoly, be prepared to be reduced to the stone age.

But the world is changing and the worldwide resistance to hegemony is gaining ground and justice will prevail.

Another mind rapist that needs mention is Dr. G. H. Estabrooks who wrote *Spiritism* [22] and *Hypnotism*.[23] He gave detailed accounts of the experiments to create multiple personality by Dr. P.L. Harriman, a military psychiatrist, and wrote that "the hand of the military must not be tied by any silly prejudices in the minds of the general public. War is the end of all law. In the last analysis any device is justifiable which enables us to protect ourselves from defeat."

In May 1968, an article[24] described him as a consultant to the CIA and quoted him as having said that, "[The] key to creating an effective spy or assassin rests in splitting a man's personality, or creating a multi-personality, with the aid of hypnotism. This is not science fiction. This has and is being done. I have done it."[25]

In *The Military Application of Hypnotism,* a proposal to the CIA, Dr. Estabrooks wrote:

22 G. H. Estabrooks, *Spiritism* (1947, E.P. Dutton, New York)
23 (1943, E.P. Dutton, New York)
24 Providence Evening Bulletin.
25 See also Science Digest, 1971 p 44-50, "Hypnosis Comes of Age."

In deep hypnosis the subject, military or civilian can be given a message to be delivered to say Colonel X in Berlin. The message will be perfectly safe and delivered to the proper person because the subject will have no memory whatsoever in the waking state as to the message. It can be arranged that the subject will have no knowledge of ever having been hypnotized. It can be arranged that no one beside Colonel X in Berlin can hypnotize the subject and recover the message.... I will take a number of men and will establish in them through the use of hypnotism the condition of split personality. Consciously they are ardent Communists, fanatical adherents to the party line. Unconsciously, they will be loyal Americans determined to thwart the communists at every turn.... Consciously they will associate with the communists and learn all their plans. Once every month they, as loyal Americans, will tell what they know. This sounds unbelievable, but I assure you, it will work.

That was back then. Since then the techniques have been developed to a more advanced stage. The so-called "Muslim Fanatics" and "Suicide Bombers" in their taped interviews all exhibit such characteristics. Their messages are scripted to the very T, and after the bombings, family members and friends would testify that their personalities were such they could not have been bombers.

I am not surprised by all this. Hopefully when you have completed reading this book, you will be wiser and better informed about the evil deeds that are been concocted within the **DARK LABYRINTH**.

I would like to conclude by quoting from Carol Rutz, a survivor of the abovementioned experiments, who was sold by her grandfather to the CIA when she was four years old. For 12 years, she was tested, trained and used in various ways. Electric shocks, drugs, hypnosis, sensory deprivation and other types of trauma were used to make her compliant and to split her personality. She was a "Manchurian Candidate" programmed to do the bidding of the CIA. She explains why she wrote the book, *A Nation Betrayed:*

My goal in writing this book is to expose the misuse of power that took place in this country.... Thousands of innocent children who have now grown into adults are silently suffering from the effects of experiments that were done to them by their own government. Many have been diagnosed incorrectly and institutionalized. Some died because they knew too much. Others, like myself were able to obtain competent medical help, and are struggling to heal from the physical and mental ravages upon our beings.

215

For skeptics, no proof will be enough. For others, like myself, unravelling the bizarre nature of my memories has allowed me to regain control of my life. My greatest gift of healing has been to no longer operate out of fear, but from a rational, logical based reality. Will we let this story lay in shadows forever, or do we have the courage to address these wrongs and give survivors back their voices. You be the judge.

My response to this was to write this book and to inform as many as I could about the evil of the Mind Rapists. I pray that you too will do what is necessary to put right the wrong that has been perpetrated against the innocents. I have said earlier, that torture follows wars as surely as night follows day.

Put a stop to wars and we will be able to end such tortures.

17

War Propaganda Part 1:
PsyOps in the 21st Century

> The mind of the enemy and the will of its leaders is a target
> of far more importance than the bodies of its troops.
> — **Brig-Gen S.B. Griffith II, USMC,**
> **Introduction to Mao Tse Tung on Guerrilla Warfare**

> It is your attitude, and the suspicion that you are maturing
> the boldest designs against him, that imposes on your enemy.
> — **Frederick the Great,**
> **Instructions to his Generals, 1747**

What we have learned in the last few chapters on mind control when adapted and applied to warfare is called "PSYOPS" (Psychological Operations). The above quotations were chosen to illustrate how much more important it is to win the battles of the minds of the enemy, in particularly at the Command Levels, than the physical elimination of enemy troops. It is significant that Brig-Gen Griffith II, USMC wrote an introduction to Mao Tse Tung's treatise on Guerrilla Warfare when training U.S. Marines. Third world countries cannot resist imperialist aggressions by conventional warfare as they do not have the means and the capabilities. Resistance has to be by way of guerrilla warfare. This is clearly understood by the general, and therefore the need to study the strategies and tactics of guerrilla warfare.

Likewise the resistance must understand how the imperialist armies think and fight. And psychological warfare is fundamental to any successful prosecution of wars and/or the mounting of the defense to repel such aggressions.

The essence of PSYOPS is winning the mind warfare.

In the earlier chapters of this book, I have adduced sufficient evidence to establish that the Zionist Anglo-American war cabal had in their own words launched World War IV, with the war in Afghanistan and the invasion of Iraq. It does not really matter to me whether you accept the fact that World War IV has started.

But given the declared intentions of the Bush and Blair regimes that they would extend the current conflicts to Syria and Iran and thereafter to dismember the remaining states in the Middle East, it would be utterly foolish and irresponsible not to prepare for war.

Working for peace does not mean that we neglect the need to prepare for self-defense against colonial wars of aggression. I would go so far as saying that the surest way to prevent further wars is to prepare for a solid defense against Zionist wars of aggression. For when the warmongers and the Megadeath Intellectuals are confronted with a determined worldwide resistance, they may have no choice but to desist in the face of overwhelming odds and the adverse global tide of public opinion.

Therefore, it is important we understand the PSYOPS strategies and tactics of our enemy, the Zionist Anglo-American war cabal. The approach in writing this chapter, a difficult one to start with, is to go to the current "bible" of the enemy's PSYOPS. Just like the Holy Bible which consists of several key documents (the Old and New Testaments), the "PSYOPS Bible" is made up of several key documents.

In my view, the starting point should be the study of the U.S. Joint Chiefs of Staff's *Doctrine for Joint Psychological Operation.*[1] This publication sets forth the doctrine to govern the joint activities and performance of the Armed Forces of the United States in joint operations and provides the doctrinal basis for U.S. military involvement in multinational and interagency operations. It is authoritative and specifically provides that if conflict arises between the contents of this publication and the contents of Service publications, this publication will take precedence for the activities of the joint forces unless the Chairman of the Joint Chiefs of Staff, normally in coordination with the other members of the Joint Chiefs of Staff, has provided more current and specific guidance.

Let us now proceed to study this PSYOPS manual.[2]

1   See Appendix 12.
2   The following discussion is adapted from the Manual.

The first principle we must grasp is that PSYOPS are operations planned to convey selected information and indicators to foreign audiences to influence their emotions, motives, objective reasoning, and ultimately *the behavior of foreign governments, organizations, groups, and individuals.* It forms a vital part of the political, military, economic, and informational activities.

A well executed PSYOPS can lower morale and reduce the efficiency of enemy forces and could create dissidence and disaffection within their ranks. There are four categories of PSYOPS:

1. **Strategic:** These programs are conducted predominantly outside the military arena but can be utilized by DoD assets and be supported by military PSYOPS.

2. **Operational:** They are conducted prior to, during war or conflict and at the conclusion of open hostilities in a defined geographic area to promote the effectiveness of the Area Commander's campaigns and strategies.

3. **Tactical:** Conducted in an area assigned to a tactical commander during a time of war or conflict in support of tactical missions.

4. **Consolidation:** These are operations in foreign areas that are inhabited by the enemy or potentially hostile forces and occupied by U.S. forces or in which U.S. forces are based to promote support for U.S. forces' objectives in the area.

All these four categories of operations are intended to establish and reinforce foreign perceptions of U.S. military, political, and economic power and resolve.

It should be emphasized that organizational responsibilities for PSYOPS involve all levels of the chain of command, i.e. from the DoD, including the Secretary of Defense, the Under-Secretary of Defense for Policy or his designee, the DoD General Counsel, and the Chairman of the Joint Chiefs of Staff, and they are tasked with the responsibility of establishing national objectives, policies and strategic plans. The geographic combatant commanders and subordinate joint force commanders are responsible for designing specific staff responsibilities.

Just before the Iraq war, there were criticisms from the anti-war movement against Donald Rumsfeld and Douglas Feith for setting up a special unit to churn out war propaganda, not appreciating that that was and is one of their precise roles as senior officials of the DoD.

Few understand the crucial role of the office of the Under-Secretary of Defense for Policy in PSYOPS.

It is the nerve center for the U.S. PSYOPS and Israel was and is able to control this nerve center because the Neo-Cons have a strangle hold in this critical area and are beholden to Israel. Richard Perle, former Chairman of the Defense Policy Board, Paul Wolfowitz, the former number two at Pentagon and Douglas Feith (No 3 at Pentagon) and Larry Franklin,[3] his aide are all Israeli assets. The manual states that the role of the Under-Secretary for Policy is as follows:

• Acts as principal adviser to the Secretary of Defense on PSYOPS matters.

• Develops PSYOPS policy.

• Coordinates PSYOPS policies, plans, and programs with the NSC and other USG agencies.

• Evaluates the effectiveness of DoD PSYOPS programs.

• Reviews and approves all PSYOPS programs to be conducted during peace or in a war.

Instead of mounting a PSYOPS campaign to counter the DoD PSYOPS, the anti-war movement went off on a tangent. We failed to expose how Israel was directing the U.S. war propaganda.[4] That is why, 50% or more of the American people believed that Saddam Hussein was linked to 9/11 and had weapons of mass destruction even though all the evidence pointed to the contrary.

The anti-war movement did not know how to expose the lies and use it as a PSYOPS weapon.

This is only expected as the anti-war movement does not have the resources of a state and a centralized authority. Given this inherent weakness, we must devise new and innovative methods to mount counter PSYOPS, but more of that later.

The most numerous and generally useful means to conduct PSYOPS are open sources of information. These sources of information should be accessible to or be activities observable by target groups.

---

3   Recently indicted for spying for Israel together with two senior members of AIPAC.

4   In my book, Future FastForward, pp.121–126, 195, and 207–222 I had given details of Israel's propaganda warfare strategies.

In simple terms, this means the mass media, newspapers, television, radio, internet and even mobile phones.

The psychological dimensions as emphasized by the manual, affect those fighting in battle, their military leaders and staffs, the political leaders and the civilian population. If the PSYOPS are successful, we will have an opposing force that is unsure about its cause and capabilities and sure about its impending defeat—an enemy who, even if unwilling to surrender, has little will to engage in combat. This truism is reflected in the famous quotation of Flavius Vegetius Renatus:[5]

To seduce the enemy's soldiers from their allegiance and encourage them to surrender is of especial service, for an adversary is more hurt by desertion then by slaughter.

Another critical area of PSYOPS which we must master is intelligence gathering. Effective PSYOPS actions depend upon current and accurate intelligence information provided through application of the Intelligence Cycle and an effective support system. The support requirements are:

Intelligence:

Current and accurate intelligence information provided through the application of the Intelligence Cycle.

Counterintelligence:

Detects, deters, or neutralizes foreign intelligence targeting.

Command, Control, Communications & Computer Systems:

C4 System Support provides interoperable, rapid, reliable, and secure exchange of information.

Logistics:

Ensures continuous sustenance and support for the psychological operations plan.

---

5   *The Military Institutions of the Romans, ca. 378 AD.*, Translated by John Clarke. Ed. Thomas R. Philips (1985, Greenwood Press).

THE INTELLIGENCE CYCLE

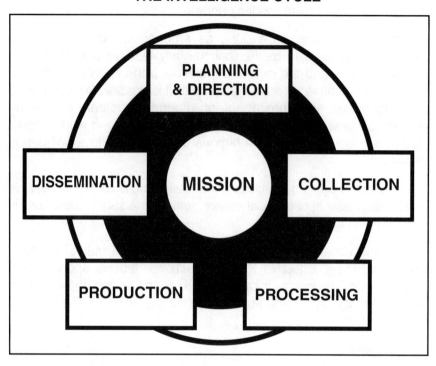

PLANNING & DIRECTION

DISSEMINATION   MISSION   COLLECTION

PRODUCTION   PROCESSING

In the present environment of almost instantaneous communication, one of the challenges faced by a planner of PSYOPS is how to compete with the numerous independent media. Whichever side is most able to manage and control information and thereby the perceptions of the target audience will have a decided advantage in any propaganda war, for *information, and its denial* is power! In the circumstances the report recommended the establishment of the Joint PSYOPS Headquarters which will bring, for the first time, all the military PSYOPS assets under one organization. Commanded by a Flag Officer, the Joint PSYOPS Headquarters will maintain open contacts with civilian advertising and marketing firms to assist in PSYOPS product development and links with academia studying the potential impact of information on the attitudes and behaviors of target audiences. Such collaboration with the civilian sector and academia will enable the war cabal, a near monopoly in the dissemination of information and disinformation. The worldwide resistance must find new ways to overcome this overwhelming propaganda onslaught. This is the greatest challenge for the anti-war movement.

Absent a coordinated and coherent counter PSYOPS against the Zionist war cabal's propaganda offensive the anti-war movement cannot hope to win this mind warfare.

The Manual ALSO stresses the importance of the distinction between planning for joint operations and planning for *overt peacetime PSYOPS programs.* The latter is planned in consonance with the respective U.S. Ambassador's country plan and support national objectives and policy. Military Operations Other Than War (MOOTW) to be effective require interagency coordination at the national level. Typical MOOTW operations not involving the use or threat of force that can be supported by PSYOPS are humanitarian assistance, disaster relief, security assistance, counter-drug operations and peace support operations. During such operations crucial intelligence is gathered and used subsequently. Aid organizations are invariably intelligence gathering fronts for PSYOPS and as such they should be monitored closely. Not enough is done to understand and to evolve a strategy to counter such peacetime PSYOPS. Subversion operations that result in *Behavior Change* and *Regime Change* are key objectives and are reflected in the financing of U.S. preferred candidates in elections of target countries. Most NGOs are front organizations for U.S. PSYOPS during peacetime and hostile fifth columns during open hostilities. It is critical that the resistance follow the money trail, for that is the surest way of unravelling their hidden agenda.

The second document concerning PSYOPS which deserves our attention is the *Report of the Defense Science Board Task Force on the Creation and Dissemination of all Forms of Information in Support of Psychological Operations in Time of Military Conflict* [The Report].[6] The Report has three key objectives:

1.   Assess the capability of the United States Armed Forces to develop programming and to broadcast factual information to a large segment of the general public.

2.   Assess the potential of various airborne and land-based mechanisms to deliver such information, and

3.   Assess other issues in the creation and dissemination of all forms of information in times of conflict, including satellite broadcast

---

6   Issued by the Office of the Under Secretary of Defense For Acquisition, Technology and Logistics in May 2000.

and the use of emerging mobile communication technologies.

The table below illustrates the integrated approach of U.S. PSY-OPS and shows that though in the past there were clear distinction between the three levels of PSYOPS,—Strategic, Operational and Tactical—they have merged post Cold War.

MILITARY PSYOPS "TOOLS OF THE TRADE"[7]		
TELEVISION		
RADIO		
NEWSPAPER		
LEAFLETS		
POSTER, HANDBILLS, ETC.		
LOUDSPEAKERS		
FACE TO FACE		
TACTICAL (LIMITED SCOPE)	OPERATIONAL (THEATER IMPLICATIONS)	STRATEGIC (INTERNATIONAL)

As stated earlier, the office of the Under Secretary of Defense for Policy is the nerve center for U.S. PSYOPS. So when in 2000, the Defense Science Board was tasked with such a major review, it was an irrefutable evidence that way back then, the United States was already preparing for war. And this was even before 9/11. That is why in all my writings, I have always emphasized the need to track and monitor all the relevant nerve centers of the Zionist Anglo-American war cabal. Unfortunately, the anti-war movement did not catch on to such war plans until it was too late.

The Report is unequivocal in re-affirming that military PSYOPS offer a potentially unique and powerful asset in military operations, both in peacetime and in war. It states further that PSYOP products have often been hampered by outdated equipment and organizational issues and this needed to be rectified. Given the broad array

7   Reproduced from the Report, p.12

of complex missions conducted by the U.S. military forces, understanding the culture and preparation of the "soft" battle space is imperative to the conduct of successful operations. It calls for a robust and flexible PSYOP capability without which there cannot be any successful military operations.

It is interesting to note that the Task Force and its Terms of Reference (TOR) were motivated by the congressional language in Pubic Law 106-65, section 1061 of the National Defense Authorization Act for Fiscal Year 2000 which requested the Secretary of Defense to establish a Task Force to examine (1) the use of radio and television broadcasting as a propaganda tool in times of military conflict and (2) the adequacy of the capabilities of the U.S. Armed Forces to make such uses of radio and television during conflicts such as the one in the Federal Republic of Yugoslavia in the Spring of 1999. In essence, the Task Force was not too happy with the effectiveness of PSYOPS during the Balkan wars.

Given the above, should we be at all surprised that Fox News, CNN, CNBC, etc., have been hijacked to serve the war cabal's propaganda objectives? Congress mandated it, funded the study and ensured its effective implementation. Yet, the anti-war movement placed its confidence in the U.S. Congress to stop the war!

I read with much satisfaction that, "in recent past, PSYOP campaigns were utilized by both sides in World War II, the Cold War, Vietnam and the Gulf War. During these large scale conflicts, the PSYOP campaigns were predominantly effective from a United States and coalition partner perspective, except *in Vietnam, where PSYOP was more effectively used by the adversary.*" In my book, *Future FastForward,*[8] I had urged the anti-war movement and the Muslim Ummah to learn from the Vietnamese, but unfortunately, they have not heeded my advice to the detriment of their struggles.

The Report states that from the outset, the Task Force concluded that the "dissemination of information via television (TV) and radio must be viewed as part of a comprehensive PSYOP campaign covering strategic, operational, and tactical military operations." The Task Force spent considerable time and effort in assessing and addressing modern trends in information dissemination and *media content creation.*

---

8   See Chapter 20, specifically page 320.

One such trend is the convergence of transmission networks, as can be seen in a simple example of a broadcast from a radio channel. This can be sent worldwide by the internet and it need not rely on the geographically constrained RF channel. The Task Force identified three major themes:

1.   Conventional terrestrial TV and radio are rapidly being rendered obsolete by novel, digital and "converged" types of media.

2.   A complex and confusing array of incompatible new technologies is currently being fielded and it is extremely difficult to predict which of these will be successful.

3.   Broadcasting to mass audiences is quickly being replaced by narrow-casting to much smaller, more targeted audiences, and even by tailoring media streams for individuals.

It is interesting to note that the Task Force specifically identified AsiaSat as a competitor to *Commando Solo*[9] in current and future PSYOPS. The satellite systems pose several technical challenges for a mobile PSYOP dissemination platform such as Commando Solo. First the media encodings are digital and sometimes proprietary and often encrypted. Thus they cannot be serviced by Commando Solo's current transmission suite. Second, the receivers employ satellite dishes pointed to specific slots in geosynchronous orbits. Commando Solo cannot transmit in such a way that it can be received in these dishes. Thirdly, the satellite systems operate on a variety of bands (L, C, KU) which are not supported by Commando Solo.

Though the above pose certain problems, the Task Force is optimistic that in the near future when the satellite systems become highly subscribed in one or more regions of the world they offer an appealing medium for PSYOPS dissemination since a single system generally offers full continental coverage at relatively low cost. The insertions of "PSYOPS commercials and specials into existing branded channels could prove a highly effective means for disseminating PSYOP contents. To this end, the DoD would strive to be "Anchor Tenant" within such systems in order to ensure that such channels exist and are available to DoD use.

That means in the near future, it would be almost impossible to

---

9   EC-130E Commando Solo is U.S. PSYOPS airborne fleet which has the capability to broadcast AM and FM radio and VHF and UHF TV signals from an Altitude of 18,000 feet.

distinguish what are PSYOP contents and what is genuine commercial content, as in many cases, they would be merged. This is the frightening world of global mind warfare of unprecedented scale. We are going to be more brainwashed than before and we will be none the wiser.

Additionally, the Report has identified the Internet as another strategic medium for PSYOPS, specifically the use of websites and e-mails, and chat rooms and messaging. Wireless telephony is another target for PSYOPS as a medium to deliver content.

The following are some of the recommendations that should be of immediate concern to the anti-war movement:

• PSYOP Force should be adequately resourced and trained to engage a stable of commercial media content providers who can deliver these quality products.

• The Defense Intelligence Agency (DIA) is to be tasked by the Assistant Secretary of Defense for Command, Control, Communications and Intelligence (ASD C31) to establish a Psychological Warfare Intelligence element and to that end implement a robust organic program of open source acquisition.

• That the Office of the Secretary of Defense (OSD) work with the State Department to fund, position, exercise, and maintain suitable distribution channels and brand identities, insofar as these can be reasonably anticipated for future PSYOPS requirements. Liberal reliance on recognized professionals and generous use of highly qualified commercial entities are highly recommended. Buying good content of which the "messages will ride" is a necessary and desirable expenditure.

• The DoD should provide the resources to acquire (rent or purchase) emerging media content and dissemination channels from commercial organizations, and this can be done cheaply by means of being an "anchor tenant."

The Report concludes that if PSYOP is to be a useful tool in the future, it must be a nimble asset capable of delivering the right information quickly, and in a manner that is technologically as sophisticated as any possible competitor within the region. In the future, the value of PSYOP will be clearly seen as best utilized before and after the conflict. PSYOP used before the conflict will help shape military context in a favorable fashion for the U.S. forces. PSYOP after the conflict will shape the way U.S. military actions are perceived by people in the region and help to achieve the end state desired by Theatre CINC and the National Command Authorities (NCA). In the future, bombs and missiles will still determine who militarily wins or loses a conflict at tactical level. PSYOP, though, will determine how long a conflict lasts and the impact of a military struggle on long term U.S. strategic interests.

Space does not allow me to go deeper into this subject though interesting and fascinating it may be. However, I would like to recommend to those professionals who are keen to delve deeper into this subject to read (1) Gary L. Whitley's excellent paper, *PSYOP Operations in the 21st Century*[10] whose views are reflected in the above report by the Defense Science Board and (2) Major Angela Maria Lungu's *WAR.COM: The Internet and Psychological Operations.*[11] Both papers have excellent end notes and a gold mine of selected bibliography. These are *must read documents.*

Gary Whitley is of the view that the internet will revolutionize PSYOP and improve the capabilities of PSYOP to achieve the objectives stated in the National Security Strategy (NSS). Major Angela Maria Lungu echoes the views of Gary Whitley and calls for existing policies and laws to be changed to allow PSYOPS to exploit the medium of the internet.

There are but two powers in the world, the sword and the mind. In the long run, the sword is always beaten by the mind.

— **Napoleon Bonaparte**

One need not destroy one's enemy. One need only destroy his willingness to engage.

— **Sun Tzu**

Killing the enemy's courage is as vital as killing his troops.

— **Karl von Clausevitz**

10 A Strategy Research Project and published by the U.S. Army War College. April 2000.
11 This was a Paper submitted to the Faculty of the Naval War College, for the Department of Joint Military Operations, February 5, 2001.

18

War Propaganda Part 2:
Half-Truths, Limited Truths and Lies

> Most people are easy prey for propaganda because of their firm but entirely erroneous conviction that it is composed only of lies and 'tall stories' and that, conversely, what is true cannot be propaganda. But modern propaganda has long disdained the ridiculous lies of past and outmoded forms of propaganda. It operates instead with many different kinds of truths—half truth, limited truth, truth out of context....
>
> — **Jacques Ellul**[1]

For years I have studied the propaganda techniques of Nazi Germany, especially the writings of the brilliant Joseph Goebbels. Before you make any objections, let me explain. How can we understand the minds of the fascists if we do not learn about the fascists and their ways of executing their plans? The fact that Goebbels was a fascist does not mean that he did not possess a brilliant intellect. We make the greatest mistakes when we are contemptuous of our enemies. That is the surest path to defeat.

Let me share something with you straight away. The propaganda strategies of Douglas Feith, Michael Ledeen, Karl Rove and the rest of the Neo-Cons are carbon copies of the Nazi propaganda machine. They share a similar world view—a fascist militaristic world view. The fact that the U.S. propaganda machine is controlled by Zionist Israel does not detract from the fact that the modus operandi is fascist. Ariel Sharon, Benjamin Netanyahu, Ehud Barak, etc., are Zionist fascists, notwithstanding that Jews were killed by Nazi Germany. It is preposterous to assert that just because Jews were

---

1 Cited by Konrad Kellen in his Introduction to *Propaganda: The Formation of Men's Attitudes*, by Jacques Ellul, (1973, Vintage Books).

killed in the Second World War, they cannot become fascist. The creation of Israel is a fascist enterprise.

Make no mistake about this.

We must therefore understand the fascist world view. There is one more thing you must know. Joseph Goebbels, by his own admission learned the art of propaganda from the British spin masters. Goebbels attributed the defeat of Germany in World War I to Germany's failure to appreciate the importance of propaganda warfare. Germany was defenseless against the British propaganda onslaught. It was only when British propaganda had nearly won over the greater part of the neutral states that the German government appreciated the enormous power of propaganda.

In a speech at Nuremberg in 1934,[2] Goebbels said, "Just as we were militarily and economically unprepared for the war, so too with propaganda. We lost the war in this area more than any other. The cleverest trick used in propaganda against Germany during the war was to accuse Germany of what our enemies themselves were doing."

This was exactly what Bush and Blair were doing in the run up to the Iraq invasion—accusing President Saddam Hussein of killing the innocent, having weapons of mass destruction, threatening neighboring countries etc. Bush and Blair have killed more innocent people than Saddam ever did, unleashed a war of terror across the entire Middle East and threatened to use nuclear weapons. Yet they are perceived as honorable leaders and not as war criminals.

We must not forget that Britain has been an Imperial Power for centuries. Britain had mastered the techniques in the suppression of her colonial subjects by military and psychological means. Without the latter, it would not have been possible for a small army (relatively speaking) to dominate an empire with over a billion population and so extensive that the sun never sets! Lawrence James calls the British "a Warrior Race."[3]

He wrote:

2   Source: www.calvin.edu/academic/cas/gpa/goeb59.htm. Speech given at the rally, Triumph des Willens.

3   Lawrence James, *Warrior Race: A History of the British at War from Roman Times to the Present*, (2002, Abacus Books, London). The author is an Englishman. He studied history and English at York University and a research degree at Merton College, Oxford.

There can hardly be a family in Britain that has not had at least one member who served with the forces in the First and Second World Wars or undertook war work in factories or on farms. This participation still matters.

War has placed its stamp on the development of British society in ways that have either been taken for granted or overlooked. The warrior elite which secured political paramountcy in England, Scotland and Ireland between the Roman evacuation and the Middle Ages evolved into a ruling class that derived political and territorial power from its skills in arms.... Their outlook and values made them natural leaders, which was why victory at Waterloo was allegedly won on the playing fields of Eaton.... What mattered, as the system's defenders always claimed, was that it worked.

The ultimate fascists are the British Zionist establishment elites. / They come in all disguises, but in essence, their world view is imperial and fascist.

How did they rise to such pre-eminence and control?

Remember what Bertrand Russell said about education which I quoted in Chapter 15? Let me repeat here for your benefit.

I think the subject which will be of most importance politically is mass psychology. Its importance has been enormously increased by the growth of modern methods of propaganda. Of these the most influential is what is called education. Religion plays a part, though a diminishing one; the press, the cinema, and the radio play an increasing part.... It is hoped that in time anybody will be able to persuade anybody of anything if he can catch the patient young and is provided by the State with money and equipment.

Although this science will be diligently studied, it will be rigidly confined to the governing class. The populace will not be allowed to know how its convictions were generated. When the technique is perfected, every government that has been in charge of education for a generation will be able to control its subjects securely without the need of armies or policemen.

If you should insist on wearing blinkers and ignore the above quotation, there is not much that I can do. As far as I am concerned, the above represents a fascist world view. Period!

4   Jacques Ellul, *Propaganda: The Formation of Men's Attitude*, (1973, Vintage Books)

According to Konrad Kellen, Ellul's[4] central thesis on propaganda, which corroborates Bertrand Russell's ideas on propaganda, is that "modern propaganda cannot work without 'education'; he thus reverses the widespread notion that education is the best prophylactic against propaganda. On the contrary he says, education, or what usually goes by that word in the modern world, is the absolute prerequisite for propaganda. In fact, education is largely identical with what Ellul calls 'pre-propaganda'—conditioning of minds with vast amounts of incoherent information, already dispensed for ulterior purposes and posing as 'facts' and as 'education'...."[5]

The British intelligence services are the undisputed masters in propaganda warfare. And we need not look further than the Iraq War.

Till today nearly everyone attributes the failure to discover any WMD in Iraq because of *intelligence failures* on the part of the Intelligence Services of the U.S. and Britain. Paul Wolfowitz[6] has already admitted that the WMD was used as a pretext for war. He said, "for reasons that have a lot to do with U.S. government bureaucracy, we settled on the one issue that everyone could agree on: weapons of mass destruction... Look, the primary difference—to put it a little too simply—between North Korea and Iraq is that we have virtually no option with Iraq because the country floats on a sea of oil." The Zionist Anglo-American war cabal knew that there were no WMD in Iraq. But they needed a cogent reason for the illegal invasion. **There was no intelligence failure.**

The fear that Iraq could launch a nuclear or chemical weapon was the propaganda master stroke that would ensure the majority support for a war against Iraq and Saddam Hussein. The demonization of Saddam Hussein is an integral part of this campaign as it would arouse hatred and anger against him. Therefore to get the message across to the public, the intelligence services had to launch a PSYOP by planting false evidence. They got away with it in so far as getting support for the war. But now, the lies have come back to haunt them.

And the masterminds behind this audacious scam were the British Spin doctors. But the Americans took all the blame. There were hardly any serious criticisms against the British warmongers, because from early on, the British succeeded in portraying Blair as

5   Ibid., Introduction by Konrad Kellen.
6   Speech given at the 2003 Asian Security Conference in Singapore.

the moderating influence on Bush and that they were keen to secure international support for the war. The British even conducted the far-cical Hutton and Butler Inquiries to determine whether "intelligence was sexed up." Both the reports exonerated the Government and the intelligence services.

But the truth of the matter was that MI6 was responsible for planting stories about Iraq's WMD. The PSYOP was called "Operation Mass Appeal" and it was conceived and managed by MI6. This operation started way back in the late 1990s. MI6 planted information all over the place, first to convince their counter-parts in Europe that Saddam was developing nerve agents and other chemical/biological weapons. This was even before 9/11. Scott Ritter, the former weapons inspector confessed that he was recruited by MI6 in 1997 for the specific purpose of planting false evidence. According to Ritter, "the aim was to convince the public that Iraq was a far greater threat than it actually was. What MI6 was determined to do by the selective use of intelligence was to give the impression that Saddam still had WMDs or was making them and thereby legitimize sanctions and military action against Iraq."[7]

A key figure in this British PSYOP was Sir Derek Plumby, then Director of the Middle East Department at the Foreign Office and now Ambassador to Egypt. He worked closely with MI6. MI6 passed on false evidence to several countries and Poland, India and South Africa was targeted to receive them because they were part of the Nonaligned Movement who opposed sanctions against Iraq. But of course, Poland later supported the U.S.[8] Planting false evidence overseas is the standard procedure to create what is referred to in the spy trade as "feedback" i.e. to create the illusion that the evidence came from an outside source, thus creating credibility to the story. Such stories are usually planted in local newspapers, which are then picked up by certain foreign correspondents who would report them in key mass media in the U.S. and Britain. Next thing you know the whole world is talking about this planted story as gospel truth.

It is interesting to note that Scott Ritter had exposed this fraud in 2003, but the British Media continues to cover up for Blair and MI6. So all along, Mr. Andrew Gilligan of the BBC was correct in stating that the Intelligence Dossier was "sexed up" but nevertheless, both official

7   Nicholas Rufford, "Revealed: How MI6 Sold the War," December 28, 2003, The Times.
8   Ibid.

inquiries cleared the intelligence services and the Blair regime of any wrongdoing. But the brave journalist was sacked and vilified.

In contrast, the Bush regime's Niger uranium (Yellow Cake story) allegation against Saddam was a classic PSYOP that went wrong and the cover-up was an amateurish attempt to put right what was already broken. While the Blair regime has moved on over the issue of "fixed" intelligence, Bush and the Neo-Cons are deep in this bullshit and it is certain that Mr. Fitzgerald, the Special Prosecutor will hand down indictments against key members of the Bush regime for the fiasco.

Many political pundits hold to the view that Douglas Feith created a unnamed intelligence gathering unit in the Pentagon which was subsequently called the "Office of Special Plans." They got it wrong precisely because they have not read the Joint Chiefs of Staff's *Doctrine for Joint Psychological Operations.*[9] If they had they would have realized immediately that Douglas Feith by virtue of his designation as Under Secretary of Defense for Policy was in charge of PSYOPS. The OSP is a PSYOP unit, not an intelligence gathering unit. There were two parallel PSYOP campaigns, one ran by MI6 (discussed below) and one ran by OSP under Douglas Feith. The objective of both operations was to hoodwink the public that the imminent threat was that Saddam Hussein could and would unleash nuclear and chemical and biological weapons of mass destruction against the United States and Britain.

Lying to induce the nation to support war is nothing new. In fact it is the standard operating procedure for the warmongers. The Gulf of Tonkin incident was a lie which hoodwinked the American people to support the war in Vietnam. The threat of Soviet WMD was exaggerated to enable the Military-Industrial-Financial Complex to launch the Cold War and justify the gigantic military spending. As I had so often stated, a war economy can only be sustained by wars.

Now that we have cleared up this preliminary issue, let us get back to Goebbels and the art of war propaganda.

Have you ever asked yourself, why people who opposed wars before open hostilities broke out, would become ardent supporters when war commences? Take the recent case of the Iraq war. The

9   This doctrine is reviewed extensively in Chapter 17.

British Liberal Party and some of their counterparts in the Labor Party were totally opposed to the Iraqi invasion. But when hostilities commenced, they called on the British people to support the troops.

Have you ever asked yourself why people who opposed wars, never called for the closure of those companies in their own countries which produce bombs, missiles, tanks, fighter aircraft and other armaments to cease operations?

Again take the case of Iraq. Both the United States and Britain were suppliers of all sorts of armaments to Iraq, including biological and chemical weapons. The value of the trade is worth billions of pounds! Maybe that is why these corporations are allowed to continue to do their business. They provide employment and massive trade for Britain.

It is only when the war takes a turn for the worse, as when more and more of their soldiers get killed and there is no end in sight to the killings, and the costs of the war bite into the economy that these people would come out again to protest against the war. Even then, the call is to bring the troops home. But the mess created by the war is not being addressed.

Let me share something with you. In all the above scenarios, the war cabal is in absolute control. The warmongers know that in any build up to a war, there will always be opposition from some quarters or other to the war. They can live with that, because no such opposition has ever stopped a war. They have so conditioned the public mind that when war starts, the public would for the sake of their loved ones in the frontline, rally around the flag. They are told that when war starts, it is not the time to quarrel about the morality of the war, but to see that the war is won and the troops returned home as heroes. The focus is then shifted to the troops, the danger they are facing and the support that must be given to grieving families when one of their own returns in a body bag. But no thought or hardly any thought is given to the civilian victims of the target country. They are mere collateral damage.

In the event of victory, all is forgiven, for the spoils of victory far outweigh the previous anxieties. The war-profiteers have made a killing and some of the war profits would be reinvested in the post war economy. But when the war takes a turn for the worse, there is a need for an "honorable exit strategy," and so the anti-war movement is re-activated to end the war and bring the troops home. It bothers not the warmongers and profiteers that the enterprise has turned into a misadventure. They have made their billions in war profits and it's time to cut and run.

⚑   That is why it is so important to understand how we have been and continue to be brainwashed for war, and programmed to kill for the Zionist Anglo-American war cabal. If we make an effort to study and understand war propaganda and brainwashing techniques, we may just be able to stop future wars.

In his brilliant book, *The Psychology of War*,[10] Lawrence LeShan explains that there are two key factors which can be exploited by the warmongers, namely the psychological needs of the individual and the role of government. In the case of the former, the following quotations cited by the author sum up very well the public mindset for war.

> The human heart is the starting point of all matters pertaining to war.
>
> — **Marechal de Saxe,** *Reveries on the Art of War*, 1731

> Son, when you are trying to stop wars, psychology is the only business you are in.
>
> — **Philip Wylie,** *Opus 21*

> The people on Fieldstone Road in Wellesley, Massachusetts, celebrated the bombing of Pearl Harbor with an enormous party. Of course the families were well aware that war is a terrible thing and they kept saying that to each other, but they were excited, even exalted because hate for a common enemy who is a long way away can make people feel almost ennobled. The radio did not make anything clear, except that the United States had been wantonly attacked and was going to war. 'We are off!' Mark Kettel said, as though the war was a horse race or a long-awaited trip. The first thing most people on Fieldstone Road did was to telephone all their relatives. Families gathered. Neighbors came in, drinks were mixed, and within a few hours the street looked as though a wedding, not a war was being celebrated in every house.
>
> — **Sloan Wilson,** *Ice Brothers*

We cannot simply dismiss this psychological element. It is impor-

---

10 Lawrence LeShan, The Psychology of War (2002, Helios Press)

tant and that is why people are so easily manipulated for war. According to Adlai Stevenson, in the twenty years following World War II there were more than 20 wars in which national armies actively engaged in hostilities with each other. In 1970, a relatively peaceful year, the world had over 16 million people under arms.[11] LeShan further explains that there are four human motivations for war, namely:

1. Displacement of aggression.

2. Projection of self doubts and self-hatred.

3. Lack of meaning and purpose in life.

4. A need for greater belonging to a group.

There is truth in the above, as when one examines the recruitment techniques of any armed forces, they zero in on these vulnerabilities, especially those marginalized in our society. That is why the warmongers will always have a ready pool of youths to be brainwashed for war and programmed to kill. And as Arthur Koestler astutely pointed out that, "the continuous disasters in man's history are mainly due to his excessive capacity and urge to become identified with a tribe, nation, church or cause, and to espouse its credo uncritically and enthusiastically, even if its tenets are contrary to reason, devoid of self-interest and detrimental to claims of self-preservation."[12]

With regard to the role of government in wars, LeShan concludes that the present structures of government descended from those of the ancient world, modified through centuries of experience and thought during which war was still regarded as the central role of government. This long period of development in government shaped its form further until the function of effective war-making potential was built into our present forms of government.[13] Hence, the timely warning of President Eisenhower, all but ignored the menace of the "Military-Industrial Complex."

Given the above circumstances, should we be surprised that wars have been waged so often and seemingly so easily even in the face of fierce opposition? If we are, it is because we failed to appreciate the power of war propaganda.

---

11 Ibid., p. 72.
12 Ibid., cited on p. 83.
13 Ibid., p. 103.

According to Goebbels, propaganda is a means to an end. Its purpose is to lead people to an understanding that will allow them to *willingly and without internal resistance devote themselves to the tasks and goals of a superior leadership.* If propaganda is to succeed, it must know what it wants. It must keep a clear and firm goal in mind, and seek the appropriate means and methods to reach that goal. Propaganda as such is neither good nor evil. Its moral value is determined by the goals it seeks.[14]

As explained by Ellul, because we have a misconception of propaganda as being crude, and made up of lies, we fail to detect the more subtle forms of propaganda. To Goebbels, propaganda must be creative. It is by no means a matter for the bureaucracy or official administration, rather it is a matter of productive fantasy. The genuine propagandist must be a true artist. He must be a master of popular soul, using it as an instrument to express the majesty of a genuine political will. He must be a master of the art of speech, of writing, of journalism, of the poster and of the leaflet, and be able to use the major methods of influencing public opinion such as the press, film and radio to serve his ideas and goals, above all in an age of advancing technology. Propaganda can be pro or con. In neither case does it have to be negative. The only thing that is important is whether or not its words are true and genuine expressions of the people.[15]

Political propaganda, the art of anchoring the things of the state in the broad masses so that the whole nation will feel part of them, cannot therefore remain merely a means to the goal of winning power. It must become a means of building and keeping power. Good propaganda does not need to lie, indeed it may not lie. It has no reason to fear the truth. It is a mistake to believe that people cannot take the truth. It is only a matter of presenting the truth to people in a way that they will be able to understand. A propaganda that lies proves that it has a bad cause. It cannot be successful in the long run. A good propaganda will always come along that serves a good cause. But propaganda is still necessary if a good cause is to succeed. A good cause will lose to a bad one if it depends only on its rightness, while the other side uses the methods of influencing the masses.[16]

14 Speech at Nuremberg 1934, @ www.calvin.edu

15 Ibid.

16 Ibid.

Take the Iraq war. The Bush propaganda machine was brilliant in its execution but its propaganda was grounded on lies. They have even contravened the teachings of their own fascist propaganda master. However, the anti-war movement in spite of having a good cause lost out in the propaganda war because it failed to mount a proper propaganda campaign to influence the masses. While it was able to organize its own constituency, it failed to win over the people like those who live in Fieldstone Road and similar neighborhoods. That was why 50% of Americans believed in the propaganda lies of the Bush and Blair regimes. This is a good example of a good cause losing out to a bad one. The war could have been stopped.

Even though the Bush /Blair propaganda lies have blown back, it is no consolation to the hundreds of thousands of killed and injured and the survivors. The horrific devastation has left a country in ruins and reconstruction and rebuilding will take decades. The troops will return home in the near future, but who will clean up the bloody mess?

It has come to light that the neo-cons were planning for the 2nd Iraq war since 1991. What does this tells us? In time of relative calm and peace, while the peace loving people of the world were complacent and content, the warmongers were making their plans so much so that when they were ready to launch their adventure, we were caught with our pants down! It is during times of relative calm and peace that we should be most vigilant and monitor the activities of the warmongers, the arms industry, and their representatives in government, media and academia. At the slightest hint of war preparation, such as articles, op-eds, research studies by think tanks, and the demand for more military spending, the anti-war movement must come out in full force to identify, isolate and hunt down these warmongers.

The elected officials who dare for a silver dollar to whip up war hysteria, they should be hounded out of office. There will be a money trail. These officials are invariably corrupt. Trashing them before the criminal courts will be an object lesson for the rest to cease their warmongering.

Although we failed to stop the invasion of Iraq, we have in the last few years gained invaluable experience. The Bush and Blair regimes are hell bent to attack Iran and Syria in the near future and are already laying the ground work for war. We must prepare our propaganda offensive now.

The Bush regime has already established the Bureau of Reconstruction and Stabilization, a State Department subgroup tasked in the preparation for future wars. William Pfaff[17] revealed in *The International Herald Tribune* that the bureau has "25 countries under surveillance as possible candidates for Defense Department deconstruction and State Department reconstruction. The bureau's director is recruiting 'rapid reaction forces' of official, non-governmental, and corporate business specialists. He hopes to develop the capacity for three full scale, simultaneous reconstruction operations in different countries."

In plain language what this means is that the Pentagon will send in the army to destroy and "deconstruct" the target countries' key industries and infrastructure, occupy them and then the State Department will send in their financial goons to rape and plunder the countries and give U.S. corporations billion-dollar contracts to reconstruct the target countries.

This agenda was first promoted by Michael Ledeen in his 2002 book, *The War Against the Terror Masters,*[18] calling it "Creative Destruction." He wrote:

> Creative destruction is our middle name, both within our society and abroad. We tear down the old order every day, from business to science, literature, art, architecture, and cinema to politics and the law. Our enemies have always hated this whirlwind of energy and creativity, which menaces their traditions (whatever they may be) and shames them for their inability to keep pace ... They must attack us in order to survive, just as we must destroy them to advance our historic mission.

In the previous chapter I mentioned that the Defense Science Board has recommended the engagement of civilian experts in PSYOPS. This is already a reality. It was reported in June, 2005,[19] that the U.S. Special Operations Command has hired three firms to produce newspaper stories, television broadcast and websites to spread American propaganda overseas. The Tampa-based military headquarters which oversees psychological warfare has a budget of U.S. $100 million for the media campaign. The three companies

---

17 Cited by Chris Moore, "The Politics of 'Creative Destruction'," July 14, 2005. Source: www.antiwar.com

18 Michael Ledeen, *The War Against the Terror Masters*, (2002, Truman Talley Books).

19 James Crawley, "Psychological Warfare Effort to be Outsourced," June 10, 2005. Source: www.timesdespatch.com

identified were Science Applications International Corp. (SAIC), SYColeman Inc. and Lincoln Group Corp. The SAIC ran the U.S. sponsored Iraqi Media Network, a print, radio and television operation, after the fall of Baghdad.

When the Bush regime is turbo-charging PSYOPS, this is a clear indication that more wars are in the pipeline. That there are doubters out there really amazes me, and there are times when I wonder what needs to be done to wake people up to the inevitable slaughter of innocents again. As recent as October 2005, Vice President Cheney in a speech to military personnel declared that the war could go on for decades![20] I reproduce below key excerpts from Cheney's speech which I hope will settle the issue. The speech is classic war propaganda.[21]

> American soldiers are currently serving in 120 countries, and the army remains active, visible sign of America's commitments—defending our interests, standing by our friends, keeping patient vigil against possible danger, and, above all, directly engaging the enemies of the United States.
>
> For many in this generation of soldiers, service to the country has involved accepting some extremely perilous missions. The war on terror is a new kind of war against the most ruthless of enemies, and the fight we are waging is every bit as urgent as it is dangerous. Those who attacked America have proven their eagerness to kill innocent men, women, and children by the thousands. They are looking to obtain weapons of mass destruction by any means they can find, and would not hesitate to use such weapons at the first opportunity. After 9/11 this nation made a decision: Having been attacked by stealth inside our own country, we will not sit back and wait to be hit again. We will prevent attacks by taking the fight to the enemy.

Commentary: War propaganda requires constant repetition. This speech is no exception, repeating the lies that have been exposed. There has been no evidence of any connection between Saddam Hussein, Iraq and 9/11. There were no WMDs found in Iraq. The "Yellow Cake" allegation was a lie created by Dick Cheney's office and the exposure of that lie prompted Cheney's underlings to

---

20　Michael Chossudovsky, "War Without Borders: Continuous Warfare for Decades to Come." Source: www.globalresearch.ca/

21　Please find time to read Joseph Goebbels's speech "Total War" and you will see the similarities. Speech can be downloaded at www.calvin.edu. See excerpts in the next page.

out Ambassador Wilson's wife as a CIA covert agent, to serve as a warning to others not to be a whistle blower and as punishment for Wilson's indiscretion. This is the logic of a warmonger.

> There is still difficult work ahead, because the terrorists regard Iraq as the Central Front in their war against the civilized world. We are dealing with enemies that recognize no rule of warfare and accept no standard of morality, and they are determined to continue waging a campaign of terror against coalition forces, Iraqi security personnel, and other innocents.

Commentary: This is really remarkable. The U.S. rejects the Geneva Conventions and the Conventions on Torture. The U.S. has been exposed as mass torturers in Abu Ghraib and Guantanamo Bay prisons. They waged an illegal war, without the sanction of the UN Security Council and according to the medical journal *Lancet*, killed over 100,000 Iraqis, innocent men, women and children.

> Like other great duties in history, it will require decades of patient effort, and it will be resisted by those whose only hope for power is through the spread of violence.

This is fascist logic. Cheney and his goons arrogate to themselves the power to decide for other people thousands of miles away from the United States what they should have, allegedly for democracy to thrive. But such hypocrites and liars always trip themselves. He let the cat out of the bag when he inadvertently admitted that the reason was and will be "defending our interest."

Since when did we, the people in the third world and our resources became "security interests" of the United States which they arrogate to themselves the right to claim and protect? We welcome trade with any country, and just because we can supply certain commodities and/or goods to the United States, she cannot demand that the continuance of that supply constitutes a "security interest of the United States." It is only an imperialist power that has such a mindset.

Cheney's speech reminds me very much of Goebbels's rallying call to the German people following the defeat at the Battle of Stalingrad, the strategic turning point in World War II.[22] The similari-

---

22 British Imperialist propaganda promotes the idea that it was the invasion of Normandy, D-Day that led to the defeat of Germany. This is one of the biggest lies to come out of World War II. Germany was already defeated when the entire Eastern Front collapsed after the Soviet counterattack, and the British and U.S. forces opened the Western Front to prevent the Soviet Army sweeping across the entire Europe.

ties lie in the call for a sustained effort to continue the war, in the face of defeat. Judge for yourself whether Cheney and Goebbels share the same mindset.

> We face a serious military challenge in the East. The crisis is at the moment a broad one... When the Fûhrer ordered the army to attack the East on June 22 1941, we all knew that this would be the decisive battle of this great struggle. We knew the dangers and difficulties. But we also knew that dangers and difficulties always grow over time, they never diminish. It was two minutes before midnight. Waiting any longer could easily have led to the destruction of the Reich and the total Bolshevization of the European continent.
>
> That is why the battle our soldiers face in the East exceeds in its hardness, dangers and difficulties all human imagining. It demands our full national strength. This is a threat to the Reich and to the European continent that casts all previous dangers into the shadows. If we fail, we will have failed our historic mission.
>
> I speak first to the world, and proclaim three theses regarding our fight against Bolshevist danger in the East.
>
> The first thesis: Were the German Army not in a position to break the danger from the East, the Reich would fall to Bolshevism, and all Europe shortly afterwards.
>
> Second: The German Army, the German people and their allies alone have the strength to save Europe from this threat.
>
> Third: Danger faces us. We must act quickly and decisively, or it will be too late.

Substitute Bolshevism with Islam, East with Middle East, we can see a similar thread running through both speeches. Hitler wants to save Europe from communism. Bush and Blair want to save the world from Islamic extremists and terrorists. At each turn they needed an enemy to mobilize the people for war—in World War II, the United States had to fight Nazism; during the Cold War, the enemy was communism; and now militant Islam is the evil that must be defeated. And as spelt out by Richard Perle, it is going to be a long war.[23] This is how we are being brainwashed for wars.

The speech by Cheney to the Association of U.S. Army on October 5, 2005, quoted above, was preceded by the rabid war-

23 Richard Perle & David Frum, *An End to Evil.*

mongering of Brig-General David Fastaband, the Deputy Director of the Army Training and Doctrine Command's Futures Center. It was part of the brainwashing of U.S. soldiers who have been stirring lately against the rationale of continued occupation of Iraq. Echoing President Bush, the general said:

> The Muslim world is violently opposed to our ideas. We have ideas about freedom ... ideas about democracy, ideas about freedom of commerce, pluralism, rule of law. Our opponents do not share these ideas and a significant percentage of the Muslim world is violently, irreconcilably opposed... People in the CIA tell you, "Hey, it's only 2-3% of the Muslim world that is irreconcilably, violently opposed," but if you do the math, you have 30-50 million irreconcilably, violently opposed combatants. The ideas are incredibly contradictory. So, we are going to have a long war.

However, the anti-war movement can take some comfort that the warmongers are not getting everything their way. There have been some strategic setbacks and this we must exploit in our counter-psyop campaigns. Take for example the much vaunted technological superiority of the U.S. army, in particular "information dominance" from airborne and satellite systems. This is all hogwash. Let me share the insight of a combatant commander, retired British Army Maj. General Jonathan Bailey. This is how he puts it:

> The problem we've got is that we saddle ourselves with all kinds of wonderful concepts and doctrine which are absolute delusions such as information dominance and "transparent battlefields." In Iraq, today, our forces do not have information superiority. This damaging assertion of information superiority, dominance, is absolutely nonsense and it really does misguide our actions.[24]

The reality is that the "Coalition Forces" know nearly nothing about the enemy because they are using guerrilla warfare strategies and tactics and can easily disappear into the terrain of the Iraqi society. In contrast, U.S. and British forces walk around in distinctive uniforms, operate from large, fixed bases, and drive around in distinctive vehicles on known routes, and their military intentions are not in any way unknown to the resistance. The General commented further, "the war we thought we were getting into was a war of choice, but history isn't kind and very often people end up in operations

24 Source: Carl Osgood, "Army Dives Into Cheney's Permanent War Scenario," October 21, 2005, EIR.

which are not of the nature they originally thought."

It is a frightening scenario. To learn from a combatant commander that they have also been brainwashed to believe that they are almost invincible, armed with the most advanced weapon systems, information dominance, air power etc., and to discover in the heat of battle, that it was all nonsense, bullshit and horseshit!

It used to be said that there was honor in war. There were rules of engagement, and the dead were buried with full honors. By the looks of it, the modern warmongers don't give two hoots about honor. What matters is how much can be plundered. They have even banned the publication in the mass media of body bags returning for burial. Brainwashed for war, programmed to kill—expendable!

Herein is our strength. While our enemy is brainwashed for war and deluded into believing that the war is a cakewalk, but soon find themselves in a sea of hostilities, fighting an unjust cause, the resistance on the other hand is fighting a just cause, the liberation of their people and country from illegal occupation. This ideological weapon is more powerful and superior than any weapon systems of the warmongers. Our final victory is assured. Look no further than the heroic struggle of the Vietnamese people against foreign aggression.

Part 4

Endgame:
The Manchurian Candidate
vs The Awakened Mind

Naturally the common people don't want war; neither in Russia, nor in England, nor in America, nor in Germany. That is understood. But after all, it is the leaders of the country who determine policy, and it is always a simple matter to drag the people along, whether it is a democracy, or a fascist dictatorship, or a parliament, or a communist dictatorship. Voice or no voice, the people can always be brought to the bidding of the leaders. That is easy. All you have to do is to tell them they are being attacked, and denounce the pacifists for lack of patriotism and exposing the country to danger. It works the same in any country.

— Hermann Goering

Ours is a world of nuclear giants and ethical infants. We know more about war than we know about peace, more about killing than we know about living. We have grasped the mystery of the atom and rejected the Sermon on the Mount.

— General Omar N. Bradley

I prefer the most unfair peace to the most righteous war.

— Cicero

Peace is not merely a distant goal that we seek, but a means by which we arrive at that goal.

— Dr. Martin Luther King, Jr.

Peace is not the absence of war; it is a virtue; a state of mind; a disposition for benevolence, confidence, and justice.

— Spinoza

19

Packaging War Part 1:
The "Truth" Peddlers

> When truth is a casualty, democracy receives collateral damage.
>
> — Col. (Rtd.) Sam Gardiner

> I think if you say you're going to do something and don't do it, that's trustworthiness.
>
> — George W. Bush[1]

When Andrew Gilligan of the BBC revealed that the Blair regime's intelligence dossier was "sexed up," his reward was an unceremonious sacking by his employers. Instead of defending the courage and integrity of Andrew Gilligan, the sycophant, Richard Sambrook, the BBC's director of news testified at the Hutton Inquiry that one of the failings of Gilligan was his inability to appreciate the "nuances and subtleties" of broadcast journalism. Gilligan was also accused of coloring his stories in "primary colors" rather than shades of grey.[2] A journalist cannot call a lie, a lie but should employ nuances such as Ellul's "limited truth," "half-truth" and anything else but the truth.[3]

Killing innocent children and the elderly is not murder but collateral damage. Dropping cluster bombs in civilian neighborhoods is not terrorism but surgical strikes that minimize collateral damage. Warmongers such as Thomas Friedman need not be subtle and nuanced in their language but should in fact be plain and brutally frank, as when he wrote: "We need to go to the heart of their world

---

1   August, 2000 interview with CNN.
2   The Guardian, September 18, 2003, "Gilligan Left Out in the Cold by BBC."
3   Jacques Ellul, *Propaganda: The Formation of Men's Attitude.*

and beat their brains out…"[4] Making bogus claims, such as Saddam Hussein being capable of launching a WMD attack within 45 minutes need not be subtle and nuanced, notwithstanding experts' testimony that the allegation does not reflect reality.[5] There was no imminent threat. "The whole thing was a fraud," says Senator Edward Kennedy.[6]

Truth comes with a price. The whistleblower at the Ministry of Defense, Dr. David Kelly was ousted by the Blair regime and it was alleged that the pressure of having to face a public inquiry drove him to commit suicide. How very convenient. The truth that he knew and wanted to tell lies buried with him. Blair the war criminal is lauded by Andrew Marr who slavishly says that Blair "stands as a larger man and a stronger Prime Minister as a result."[7] This broadcast journalist confessed upon his appointment as political editor of the BBC, that "When I joined the BBC, my organs of opinion were formally removed."[8]

Across the Atlantic, the mass media was in top gear, trumpeting the crusade to liberate Iraq, code-named *Operation Iraqi Freedom*. It was time for bloodletting. When Ambassador Wilson exposed the lies of the Bush regime for invading Iraq, his wife, a covert CIA agent involved in WMDs was deliberately, and contrary to U.S. laws exposed as an agent by Dick Cheney and his goons to punish Mr. Wilson and to serve as a warning to all future whistleblowers to expect similar treatment should they breach discipline and scuttle the war agenda. When a covert agent is exposed, there is a real danger of physical liquidation by foreign secret services. But then agents are "expendables!"

I believe most people are familiar with the above two stories and how the media assist in government propaganda. But I am not so confident that many are aware that movies and television have always been subject to tight government control, especially if it relates to the military. I am fortunate to come across a recent book that exposes the hidden hand of the military in film and television

---

4   Cited by Anthony Loewenstein in The Truth Tramplers: Media War Spin on Trial, October 1, 2003 Sydney Morning Herald. Quotation taken from Tim Russert Show, CNBC, September 13, 2003.

5   Dimitris Perricos, September 1, 2003 Associated Press.

6   Steve Le Blanc, Kennedy Says War Case a Fraud, Associated Press, September 18, 2003.

7   See note 4 above, quoting BBC 1, News at Ten, April 9, 2003.

8   Ibid., quoting The Independent, January 13, 2000.

production. Written by David L. Robb, *Operation Hollywood: How the Pentagon Shapes and Censors the Movies*[9] is a "must read" book. Although the exposé was timely, the fact remains that the U.S. government, and for that matter many other governments have always manipulated movies in one way or another to serve their political agenda. For more than fifty years, the Department of Defense has been examining and altering movie scripts prior to production. One of the earliest movies that came under the military supervision was the 1927 film *Wings* which won an Oscar.[10]

The pressure exerted by the military establishment, i.e. the Pentagon is often subtle. War films need tanks, aircraft, ships, troops etc., and the principal source is the military. When producer Jerry Bruckheimer wanted to produce and film *Black Hawk Down,* he had to agree to delete any reference to Ranger Specialist John Stebbins who was awarded a Silver Star for bravery, but was convicted and imprisoned for 30 years for raping a 12-year-old boy. The character appeared in the movie but was given another name.[11] To the Pentagon it was a fair deal—good publicity in exchange for access to Black Hawk helicopters in the production of the movie.

David Robb gives an interesting account on how film producers and directors were and are still being pressured to do the bidding of the Pentagon. He reserved praises for Kevin Costner, Oliver Stone, Robert Aldridge, Douglas Day Stewart and Taylor Hackford for not capitulating to the DoD. The author revealed that soon after the U.S. entered World War I, the Committee of Public Information was established to provide guidelines for all media to promote support for the war effort. This collaboration continued through World War II and in 1948, the Special Movie Liaison office was set up, as part of the office of the Assistant Secretary of Defense for Public Affairs.

One of the main objectives for this control was to enable the Pentagon to boost recruitment and retention of personnel in the armed forces. As explained by Major David Georgi, the military adviser to the blockbuster, *Clear and Present Danger,* "always, somewhere in the mind of the producers, they'd try and turn the picture in the direction that they had originally presented to us ... It

9   David L. *Robb, Operation Hollywood: How the Pentagon Shapes and Censors the Movies,* (2004, Prometheus Books)

10 Steven G. Kellman, "Winning the Next War at the Multiplex," The Texas Observer, February 4, 2005. Source: www.texasobserver.org

11 Ibid.

would be my job as technical advisor to make sure that the movie did not stray substantially from the original approved version."[12]

Some of the more recent movies that were subjected to Pentagon's pressure tactics were *The Last Detail* (1973), *Apocalypse Now* (1979), *An Officer and a Gentleman* (1982), *Born on the Fourth of July* (1989) and *Forrest Gump* (1994) but the producers refused to succumb to Pentagon's dictates.

More recent examples mentioned in the book of Mr. Robb were *Thirteen Days* (2000) which was about the Cuban Missile crisis and the debate between the Joint Chiefs and President Kennedy. The Pentagon did not like the portrayal of General Curtis E. LeMay who was a hawk and advocated an attack on Cuba. They wanted a less belligerent general on the movie screen. When the producers refused to compromise, as it was against the historical record, all assistance from Pentagon was denied and parts of the film had to be shot in the Philippines.

Another film, the *Windtalkers,* (2002) directed by the famous action movie director John Woo from Hong Kong was given similar treatment. The story was about "Code Talkers" who were Navajo Indians in the Second World War. Their language was used as a code to send messages which the Japanese were unable to decipher. It was on record, that Code Talkers were each assigned a soldier for protection, but in the event of capture (which would most likely end in torture which may result in the secret being revealed), the soldiers had orders to kill the Code Talkers. The Pentagon wanted a cover-up and demanded changes in the script. Unfortunately, the producers caved in and agreed to the cover-up.

Some films in video format have advertising space available for the military, as it was found that when young kids view them, they were easier to recruit into the Armed Forces. The quid pro quo would be special assistance in the provision of military hardware or in the case of Paramount's *Hunt for Red October* and *Flight of the Intruder,* monies owed to the U.S. Navy were waived. Following the film *Top Gun,* featuring Tom Cruise, recruitment of navy fighter pilots jumped a staggering 500%. That is why just before a major war and during open hostilities, Hollywood would release a spate of new war films, produced in tandem with the war agenda.

12   David L. Robb, op. cit.

The Air Force Liaison Office has its own website, *Wings Over Hollywood*. The CIA in 2001 has its own film industry liaison officer and his responsibility is to "give advice and guidance" to authors, screenwriters, directors and producers and encourage "better understanding of and appreciation for the agency."[13]

Television is not spared. Already we can detect a trend in major channels to focus more on war and war related issues.[14] Three cable channels are devoted exclusively to military matters. A new drama series, produced by Steven Bochco, "Over There" about an army unit in Iraq was released in the summer of 2005. The theme of these dramas is the American war heroes and the noble cause of freedom and democracy for which they are fighting to establish throughout the world. According to Phil Strub, who heads the Pentagon film liaison office, "These days, there is an unwillingness to criticize individual servicemen and women, which was quite common in the Vietnam era. Americans are very disinclined to do that now, and we are very glad this attitude tends to pervade all entertainment."

It is not just war films that interest the military. Such television series as *Star Trek IV, Mars Attack* and even children's entertainment programs such as *Lassie* and *Mickey Mouse Club TV shows* seek Pentagon assistance. Brainwashing for war starts when they are young and most impressionable.

This is but a glimpse into the powerful influence of the Military-Industrial-Financial Complex. Propaganda and brainwashing pervades at every level of society and in all media.

Xinhuanet reported recently[15] that the U.S. Homeland Security Department, following the Pentagon, the CIA, the FBI and other government agencies has hired a Hollywood liaison, Bobbie Faye Ferguson to work with movie makers and scriptwriters. She was a once an actress and now has been tasked to review 14 movies, TV and documentary projects. It was also reported that if she approves a script or idea, the Department of Homeland Security would offer advice and technical assistance to portray in a positive light "Homeland Defenders."

---

13 Cesar G. Soriano and Ann Oldenburg, "With America at War, Hollywood Follows," USA Today, February 8, 2005.

14 Ibid.

15 March 11, 2005.

One such film that came under their review was *Terminal,* starring Tom Hanks, about an immigrant stranded at the John F. Kennedy airport. The TV show *CSI: Miami* was likewise given the same treatment.

ꜜ What is new and frightening is the use of computer games to promote the war culture and mindset. Age is no barrier, as the war games are adapted to various age groups. The video game industry is a U.S. $10 billion a year industry and war games are always high in the charts of best sellers. To name a few:

- Full Spectrum Warrior—a game about a mission in a fictional Middle East urban war zone.

- Mercenaries—covert action in North Korea.

- Battlefield 1942; Call of Duty: Finest Hour—World War II war games.

- Men of Valour—a game relating to the war in Vietnam.

Last year, a company, Kuma Reality Games offered downloadable games based on actual U.S. military operations in Iraq. Such is the popularity of war games, that the U.S. army own computer game, "America's Army" was downloaded more than 17 million times. Microsoft Xbox has a version of the game.

In countries relatively at peace throughout the world, war culture and mindset is being promoted via computer games for the very young to the very old. According to Douglas Gentile, assistant professor of psychology at the Iowa State University and the director of research for the National Institute for Media and Family, such games have "increased in realism dramatically and militarily ... and they have a profound effect ... for a generation now growing up under the threat of terrorism and at war."[16]

In my book, *Future FastForward,*[17] I wrote:

> A survey conducted by Steve Rendall and Tara Broughel during the first three weeks of the war (Iraq) revealed that the sources for the major evening news shows (ABC, CBS, NBC, CNN, FOX and PBS) were predominantly pro-war, from the military, and a majority of former and current government employees. Anti-war sources constituted 10%, academia, think tanks and NGOs made up 4% and government officials

16 Cesar Soriano and Ann Oldenburg, co. cit.

17 *Future FastForward,* p. 34.

who were anti-war numbered 4 as compared to 840 pro-war officials. What was truly astounding was the attitude of some of the leading journalists concerning the lies and deceptions perpetrated by Bush's regime. Thomas Friedman of the New York Times comes to mind. He wrote:

"As far as I'm concerned, we do not need to find any weapons of mass destruction to justify this war. Mr. Bush doesn't owe the world any explanations for missing chemical weapons (even if it turns out that the White House hyped this issue). It is clear that in ending Saddam's tyranny, a huge human engine for mass destruction has been broken."

And we are told that the press is free and honest. Paul Wardman, however, sums up well the state of affairs: "The unfortunate truth is this: George W. Bush is a fraud."

At present, six corporations are in control of the major U.S. mass media. Rupert Murdoch's News Corporation manipulates FOX, HarperCollins, *New York Post*, DirecTV and 34 other stations; Time-Warner controls AOL, CNN, Warner Bros., *Time* and over 100 other magazines; Disney pulls strings at ABC, Disney Channel, ESPN, 10 TV and 29 radio stations; Viacom controls CBS, MTV, Nickelodeon, Paramount Pictures, Simon & Schuster, and 1285 radio stations; General Electric sits on NBC, CNBC, MSNBC, Telemundo, Bravo, and 13 TV stations, and Bertelsmann controls Random House and 80 maga-zines. One company that is closely connected to the Bush regime and unashamedly acts as his mouthpiece is Clear Channel Communications. With 1,200 radio stations, 36 TV stations nationwide and 776,000 dis-plays in 66 countries, it is a media power at its awesome best.[18]

We are led to believe that mainstream media is for the benefit of the ordinary people, you and me. However, a close examination of the "mainstream media" as discussed above tells a different story. They don't really publish news for our benefit, but rather act as instruments of propaganda for big business and other vested inter-ests. We must have no illusions. Most news is "packaged" by editors to serve vested interests.

Prof. Peter Philips[19] drew our attention in an article that a research team at Sonoma State University has recently completed

---

18 *Future FastForward*, p. 34.

19 Prof. Peter Philips, "Big Media Interlocks with Corporate America," July 4, 2005. Source: globalresearch.ca. Prof. Philips is the Prof. of sociology at the Sonoma University and director of Project Censored. Visit Project Censored @ www.projectcensored.org.

a network analysis of the *boards of directors* of the abovementioned top ten media organizations in the US. The shocking conclusion is that *only 118 people comprise the membership on the boards of directors of the top ten media giants.* But their tentacles reach far and wide, for these 118 individuals in turn are members of and/or control corporate boards of 288 national and multinational corporations. The top ten media giants' board members share common membership on each other's boards. Just take a look at the corporate shareholders:

New York Times
Carlyle group, Elli Lily, Ford, Johnson and Johnson, Hallmark, Lehman Bros, Staples, Pepsi.

Washington Post
Lockheed-Martin, Coca Cola, Dun & Bradstreet, Gillette, G.E. Investments, J.P. Morgan, Moody's.

Knight Ridder
Adobe Systems, Echelon, H & R Block, Kimberly-Clark, Starwood Hotels.

The Tribune (Chicago & LA Times)
3M, Allstate, Caterpillar, Conoco Philips, Kraft, McDonalds, Pepsi, Quaker Oats, Shering Plough, Wells Fargo.

News Corp (FOX)
British Airways, Rothschild Investments.

G.E. (NBC)
Anheuser-Busch, Avon, Bechtel, Chevron/Texaco, Coca Cola, Dell, GM, Home Depot, Kellogg, J.P. Morgan, Microsoft, Motorola, Procter & Gamble.

Disney (ABC)
Boeing, Northwest Airlines, Clorox, Estee Lauder, FedEx, Gillette, Halliburton, Kmart, McKesson, Staples, Yahoo.

Viacom (CBS)
American Express, Consolidated Edison, Oracle, Lafarge North America.

Garnett
AP, Lockheed-Martin, Continental Airlines, Goldman Sachs, Prudential, Target, Pepsi.

AOL-Time Warner
Citigroup, Estee Lauder, Colgate-Palmolive, Hilton.

In the circumstances, can we the ordinary people expect unbiased views and news? In the event of corporate corruption such as Enron etc, would these corporate controlled media protect their own kind or perform their civic duties?

Judith Miller of *The New York Times* spewed lie after lie in support of Bush's mad rush to invade Iraq. But after all the devastation and massacre, and having being put into prison for obstruction of justice, she now admits that she was wrong, the media was wrong etc., and puts on a show of contrition. **No one got it wrong.** They lied about WMDs, they lied that Iraq was in some way responsible for 9/11, they lied that there were links between Iraq and Al Qaeda, they forged documents and continue to repeat these lies until today.

Prof. Philips correctly pointed out that we can no longer call such media, mainstream or refer to it as plural. Corporate media according to the good professor is corporate America and he urged people to look at alternative independent sources for news and information.

But there is a larger issue that we should address. Are journalists who knowingly lie and participate in the manufacture of lies to justify or support a war of aggression accomplices to these war crimes and be held accountable? I take the view that they are accomplices and should be tried as accomplices. In the case of Judith Miller of *The New York Times*, and the likes of her, they should be charged for war crimes as much as Bush and Blair. I shall now proceed to explain some relevant principles of the law relating to this issue, beginning with the Nuremberg Charter.

The Charter of the Nuremberg Tribunal is unambiguous as by article 6, it expressly provides:

> The following acts, or any of them, are crimes coming within the jurisdiction of the Tribunal for which there shall be *individual responsibility:*
>
> a) Crimes against peace: namely, planning, preparation, initiation or waging of a war of aggression, or a war in violation of international treaties, agreements or assurances, or participation in a Common Plan, or Conspiracy for the accomplishment of any of the foregoing.

Commentary: Anyone who is part of the war propaganda effort must come within the definition of planning, preparation etc. War propaganda is an essential effort in waging wars. This we have discussed extensively in the previous chapters. Therefore journalists like Judith Miller can and should be indicted for war crimes.

> b) War crimes: namely, violations of the laws or customs of war. Such violations shall include, but not limited to murder, ill-treatment or deportation to slave labor or for any other purpose of civilian population of or in occupied territory, murder or ill-treatment of prisoners of war or persons on the seas, killing of hostages, plunder of public and private property, wanton destruction of cities, towns, or villages, or devastation not justified by military necessity.

Commentary: I would say that embedded journalists who were witnesses to these crimes and failed to report and/or covered up such crimes are at the least accomplices. Their silence allows the perpetuation of such crimes and their failure to turn in photographic evidence in my view constitutes obstruction of justice.

> c) Crimes against Humanity: namely, murder, extermination, enslavement, deportation, and other inhumane acts committed against any civilian population, before or during the war, or persecutions on political, racial, or religious grounds in execution of or in connection with any crime within the jurisdiction of the Tribunal, whether or not in violation of domestic law of any country where perpetrated.

> Leaders, organizers, instigators, and accomplices participating in the formulation or execution of a Common Plan or Conspiracy to commit any of the foregoing crimes are responsible for all acts performed by any persons in execution of such plans.

Commentary: Obviously, journalists can come under the definition of "leaders, organizers, instigators, and accomplices" and should be held accountable for instigating wars.

The Bush and Blair regimes would not have been able to wage such a war but for the connivance and active participation of journalists who spew the lies and propaganda for war.

UNESCO International Principles of Professional Ethics in Journalism likewise impose a heavy burden and duty on journalists to report the truth and not to spew lies and propaganda. Information in journalism is understood as a social good and not a commodity, which means that the journalist shares responsibility for the information transmitted and is thus accountable ultimately to the public at large. The UNESCO principles also call for the ethical commitment to the universal values of humanism and impose a burden and duty on the journalist to abstain from any justification for, or incitement to wars of aggression.[20]

For too long, journalists and the owners of mass media have got away with murder. No longer! They must be held accountable and indicted for war crimes, crimes against humanity and crimes against peace if evidence supports such a charge against them. Journalists acting in the above roles are in fact foot soldiers in the propaganda warfare for imperialist wars of aggression.

In the address to the War Crimes Tribunal in Istanbul, Jayan Nayar[21] asked a critical question of the media, "How do we understand media responsibility in times of war?" The media plays a significant role in constructing the public debate and as such is regarded as bearers of truth-information, the so called "fourth estate" and a vital component in a democracy. "Truth telling" is intrinsically a social function, for from it is enabled informed understanding of the realities of the world and deliberations on the political choices we might collectively make as we engage in the world.[22] With regard to the Iraq War, the media has failed to discharge that duty and to perform that crucial social function of "truth telling." The root cause for this failure, according to Nayar is the parroting of government claims, and their silences and the silencing of the following substantive issues:

- The real reasons for the claim to war, and the implications of the claim to the unilateral right to so-called "preventive" and "pre-emptive" violence without question or challenge.

- The celebration of "Coalition" goodness and the silence of the realities of suffering caused by human and socio-economic destruction.

- The silence on the prevalent spirit of resistance within Iraq.

- The impact of the so-called "anti-terror" and other "security-based" laws which create structures and processes of state terror across the global political landscape.

- The human, social and economic consequences of the spiralling militarization of politics in the name of security.

- The realities of human insecurity, the role of institutions of power in inflicting such conditions of impoverishment and

20 Principle IX, UNESCO International Principles of Professional Ethics in Journalism.
21 Jayan Nayar, "Media Wrong against Truth and Humanity." Source: www.truthout.org
22 Ibid.

insecurity and the vitality of peoples' other visions against war and for peace.

In collaborating with the war cabal, the media has surrendered its hard earned right to be called "truth tellers" in exchange for short term corporate profits and monopoly of access to those who wield political power. More significant, by such connivance the media has misconceived its role as having the right to impose on the world citizenry their values and world view, and the power to determine who should be invaded and who should be spared of violence. The War on Terrorism justifies their new found role. But no matter how they like to dress their warmongerings, the plain simple fact is that they are war criminals within the definition of the Charter of the Nuremberg Tribunal. They must be held accountable.

While it is almost impossible to bring war crimes indictment when the war is ongoing, and the powers that be can and will obstruct such proceedings, it is a different matter for domestic jurisdictions to legislate laws where there are none, and if there are such laws, to prosecute journalists complicit in such crimes. Information has no boundaries and the harm done by journalists in the planning and incitement for war has global dimensions. War cannot be stopped, and peace cannot prevail when the first frontlines are not being fought adequately and/or with sufficient resilience. No government can succeed in forcing the people to go to war without the active participation of the media. This is one area all anti-war and peace movements have neglected to the detriment of our just cause.

It is imperative therefore to expose these war criminals and haul them before a War Crimes Tribunal if we are ever to succeed in preventing future wars. Warmongering can and will stop, if the warmongers are denied their mouthpieces!

20

Packaging War Part 2:
The "Truth" Forgers

> How do Neo-cons bring democracy to Iraq? You invade, you threaten and pressure, you evangelize. This was said to be part of the war on terror, but Iraq feeds terrorism.
>
> — **Brent Scowcroft**[1]

> The propagandist's purpose is to make one set of people forget that certain other sets of people are human.
>
> — **Aldous Huxley**[2]

Since the investigation by the Special Prosecutor into the outing of Valerie Plame, a covert CIA agent, and the wife of former U.S. Ambassador Joseph Wilson by the Bush regime, I have been scouring the local news media for some decent analysis on the implications of the brewing scandal, but unfortunately found none. The forging of documents by the Bush regime to establish a case for war against Iraq did not merit any serious editorials or strategic analysis from the so-called experts. The one critical weapon in our propaganda counter-offensive against the unwarranted demonization of Islam and the Muslim world lay buried in some memory hole.

The evidence is there for the world to see. The Bush regime's key officials are blatant forgers. Watergate was a bungled petty theft; Monica Lewinsky and Bill Clinton's indiscretion is but a reflection of a President's sexual appetite, although both cases involved elements of dishonesty. But for Bush and his war cabal to commit for-

---

1 Brent Scowcroft, interview with Jeffrey Goldberg, The New Yorker, October 31, 2005 issue. "Breaking Ranks: What Turned Brent Scowcroft Against the Bush Administration?"

2 Quoted by John Pilger in his article, "We Need To Be Told," October 13, 2005 ICH. Source: www.informationclearinghouse.info/article10615.htm

gery to justify a barbaric pre-emptive war, this criminal conduct must rank as the front runner for the crime of the century. But we seem to lack the moral strength and courage to criticize the fascist Bush and Blair regimes. Rather the Europeans and the American people do the work of burying such corrupt regimes, notwithstanding that our brothers and sisters are the victims of this forgery and we may be the target in the near future.

The intellectual impotence and/or fatigue are truly astonishing. Yet these same opinion makers never cease to moan and groan that not enough is being done to expose the duplicity of the Neo-cons and teflon Blair. But when some inconsequential corrupt officials are being prosecuted, they warrant a front-page coverage and more gossip on page 3 of the tabloids. Such is our priorities that jockeying for a better standing in Transparency International's subjective ladder of integrity by such show trials is far more important than fighting for justice for the victims of aggression.

I do seek your indulgence, but I have been advised that it is good to let off steam once in a while. Let us move on. The cast of administration officials with known connections to the outing of an undercover agent in order to cover up the forgery seems to involve almost the entire staff of the White House. Judge for yourself!

Karl Rove	John Hannah
Lewis "Scooter" Libby	Scott McClellan
Condoleezza Rice	Dan Barlett
Stephen Hadley	Claire Buchan
Andrew Card	Catherine Martin
Alberto Gonzales	Colin Powell
Mary Matalin	Karen Hughes
Ari Fleischer	Adam Levine
Susan Ralston	Bob Joseph
Israel Hernandez	Vice-President Dick Cheney
President George W. Bush[3]	

What is this forgery we have been referring to? If you can recall, President Bush in his State of Union Speech in January 28, 2003, alleged that Saddam Hussein bought uranium ("Yellow Cake") from Niger for his nuclear weapons program. The President alleged that there were documents from the government of Niger to support this allegation. The sentence in the speech that gave away the fraud is the key:

3   List taken October 6, 2005, from www.ThinkProgress.org

The British Government has learned that Saddam Hussein recently sought significant quantities of uranium from Africa.

Bush attributes the source to the British government. Therefore there is an open declaration that the Blair regime was the source of this intelligence. How this intelligence came to the British hands is a different matter, which will be discussed below. But for now, remember this sentence. The Blair regime has not denied that they were the source for this intelligence and as such can be construed as admitting to the fact.

Therefore, the Blair regime is guilty of this crime as well. It is in fact an open and shut case if there ever was one. After all you don't get a President of the most powerful state in the world to declare how grateful he was for the intelligence which "proved" that he was "telling the truth" in the State of the Union Speech. But there it is for the world to see.

Condoleezza Rice added to the fear of a nuclear war when she said that on September 8, 2002, "We don't want this smoking gun to be a mushroom cloud." But it was all a lie. The documents were in fact forgeries. But who forged these documents? The more important question is why did Bush knowingly use these forgeries to buttress his case for war against Iraq?

However, what has escaped our attention was that way back in 2002, Dick Cheney was already on the air accusing Iraq of having nuclear weapons. This was even before the "yellow cake" story. What was the basis of his allegations? There was no intelligence to support this accusation. I would submit here that Cheney's declaration was in fact a trial balloon to "fix intelligence" around the policy of attacking Iraq, come what may. On March 24, 2002, Cheney appeared on three major Sunday public-affairs programs and declared:

> CNN Late Edition: "This is a man of great evil, as the President said. And he is pursuing nuclear weapons at this time."

> NBC Meet The Press: "There is good reason to believe that he continues to aggressively pursue the development of a nuclear weapon. Now will he have one in a year, five years? I can't be that precise."

> CBS Face The Nation: "The notion of a Saddam Hussein with his great oil wealth, with his inventory that he already has of biological and chemical weapons, that he might actually

acquire a nuclear weapon is, I think, a frightening proposition for anybody who thinks about it. And part of my task out there was to go out and begin the dialogue with our friends to make sure they were thinking about it."

Thereafter the war cabal set in motion a chain of events that gave rise to the forgeries.

ʲ According to the Italian government's investigation, there was a break-in of the Niger Embassy in Rome sometime in early 2002, and the only things that were stolen were letterheads and stationeries. The letterheads were used to show that Saddam Hussein entered into a deal to buy uranium from Niger. These faked documents turned up after a meeting in December 2001, in Rome involving Neo-con Michael Ledeen, Larry Franklin, Harold Rhodes, and Nicolo Pollari, the head of Italy's intelligence agency SISMI, and Antonio Martino, the Italian Defense Minister. The investigation report named four men as likely forgers of the documents, Michael Ledeen, Dewey Clarridge, Ahmed Chalabi and Francis Brookes.

Michael Ledeen had long ties with Italian intelligence and Italian fascists, and was connected to the infamous P2 Freemason Lodge in Italy. He was recruited by Douglas Feith to start up the Office of Special Plans (OSP). This was the man who arranged for Jonathan Pollard to work at the U.S. Navy, which led to nuclear deterrent secrets being passed to Israel. Larry Franklin was recently indicted for leaking classified information to the American Israel Public Affairs Committee (AIPAC). Harold Rhodes worked for the OSP, a PSYOP unit at the Department of Defense which was tasked with fixing intelligence to support the allegation that Saddam Hussein had WMDs.

It has now transpired that Nicolo Pollari brought the story directly to the White House.[4] On September 9, 2002, the head of Italy's intelligence services met with the then Deputy National Security Adviser Stephen Hadley. Soon after the meeting, *Panorama* a weekly magazine owned by the Italian Prime Minister, Mr. Silvio Berlusconi, a staunch ally of Bush, published a story on September 12, 2002 that the Iraqi Intelligence agency, the Mukhabarat had acquired 500 tons of uranium from Niger. Following the story the forged documents were cabled from the U.S. Embassy in Rome to Washington after being delivered to embassy officials by Elisabetta Burba, a

---

4   Laura Rozen, "Le Republica's Scoop Confirmed," October 25, 2005. Source: www.prospect.org

reporter from Panorama. She had received the papers from an Italian middleman named Rocco Martino. Burba did not write the story about the Niger documents but was ordered by her editor, Carlo Rossellia to bring them to the U.S. Embassy.[5] For the moment, please take note the circuitous route in which these documents came to the White House. This is standard operating procedure for such intelligence operations and I will explain in due course some historical precedents.

In February 19, 2002, when the "Yellow Cake" story surfaced, the CIA dispatched former Ambassador Joseph Wilson to Niger to investigate. Without much difficulty, he discovered the story to be false and reported his findings. Mr. Wilson thought that that was the end of the matter. In early March 2002, Dick Cheney requested an update on the Niger uranium issue. After debriefing Mr. Wilson, the CIA wrote a report and disseminated the report on March 8, 2002. By fall of 2002, most of the key players were made aware of the issue. And in October 6, 2002 the Director of CIA Tenet warned that the Niger "Yellow Cake" story should not be used in a presidential speech the next day.[6]

However, as stated earlier, President Bush in his State of the Union speech in January 2003 made reference to the allegation that Iraq sought to acquire uranium from Africa. If that was not bad enough, it was Cheney's office that pushed dubious intelligence data into Colin Powell's speech delivered at the UN in February of 2003. It was Cheney's chief of staff, Lewis "Scooter" Libby, who wrote those particular passages.[7]

Sparks flew a couple months later in March when the IAEA announced that the Niger documents were obvious and clumsy forgeries, full of tell-tale inaccuracies that betrayed the fact that whoever created them didn't know jack about Niger.[8] However, Dick Cheney refused to accept the findings of the IAEA and said that the IAEA was "frankly, wrong."[9]

---

5   Ibid.

6   Senate Intelligence Committee's "Report on the U.S. Intelligence Community's Pre-War Intelligence Assessment on Iraq," July 4, 2004 (The Report) p.56

7   Murray Waas, "Cheney, Libby Blocked Papers To Senate Intelligence Panel," October 27, 2005. The National Journal.

8   Christopher Scheer, Robert Sheer and Lakshmi Chaudhry, *The 5 Biggest Lies Bush Told Us About Iraq*, (2003, Seven Stories Press) p.91

9   Ibid.

Peeved by the falsity of the allegation and the continued reliance on the forgeries by Cheney for the war against Iraq, Ambassador Wilson wrote a column in *The New York Times* on July 6, 2003 exposing the lie. He wrote: "Based on my experience with the administration in the months leading up to the war, I have little choice but to conclude that some of the intelligence related to Iraq's nuclear weapons program was twisted to exaggerate the Iraqi threat."

The White House, with the participation of Karl Rove and Lewis Libby (and according to one recent report, of the President and Vice-President themselves) conceived and then executed a plan to discredit former Ambassador Wilson. Libby has now been indicted for obstruction in the investigation of this scandal by the Special Prosecutor. It is a good bet that eventually Karl Rove might also be indicted. A variety of reports from journalists and others show that as early as the end of May, 2003 White House officials were trying to dig up dirt on Mr. Wilson. And the State Department drafted a top-secret memorandum that identified Valerie Plame (Mrs. Wilson) by her maiden name and made the connection.

On July 13, 2003, Robert Novak, citing two administration sources, identified Valerie Plame by name as a CIA operative, who was still under cover. The exposé compromised not only Plame, but the agents she recruited.[10] Her entire intelligence network was exposed. From intelligence services point of view, this was a massive setback. To destroy an intelligence network for a political vendetta is madness and unheard of in the annals of intelligence services.

There is only one conclusion. The forgery went to the very center of political power in the United States—the Bush White House. A serious crime was committed, forging evidence to wage a war. This had to be covered up. Short of physical liquidation, everyone must have their lips sealed for good! This is the dimension of the scandal. It is worse than Watergate!

What was astonishing was that Valerie Plame and her network were working under-cover to investigate into the proliferation of WMDs, which according to the Bush regime was their number one priority. Thus, the deliberate outing of an invaluable under-cover agent, even when it concerns priority one intelligence, serves as a warning to all that the Bush regime will not shrink from exposing such sources,

---

10 Larry Johnson, a former CIA Intelligence Analyst and State Department Counter-terrorism official, "A Case of Treason," October 6, 2005. Source: www.TomPaine.com

if any attempt is made to undermine the rationale for war. To Larry Johnson, such conduct is despicable and one word describes it— *treason!* [11] James Moore, the Emmy award winning writer considers the case, "the most important criminal case in American history."[12]

Political pundits got it wrong that it was intelligence failures that led to the over estimation of Saddam Hussein WMD capabilities. The entire operation, from picking the issue of WMD as a basis for war, to the forging of documents in support thereof, and the subsequent publication of intelligence estimates was a classic black propaganda operation. And Tony Blair and the British intelligence were in the same shit hole wallowing up to their ears. Remember what Bush said? They were the source!

Such were the lies that the Senate Intelligence Chairman, Pat Roberts, R-Kan., and Vice Chairman Jay Rockefeller, D-W.Va., said that they doubted that the Senate would have authorized the President to go to war if the senators had been given accurate information regarding Iraq's programs on weapons of mass destruction. "I doubt if the votes would have been there," Roberts said. Rockefeller asserted, "We in Congress would not have authorized that war in 75 votes, if we knew what we now know."[13]

This is also a lie by Congress. If the millions who marched to oppose the war knew that the allegations against Iraq were all lies, it is hard to believe that the U.S. Congress was ignorant. The Congress was beholden to Israel and did its bidding and it is much too late to express contrition when so many have died and a country laid waste.

The ultimate truth may never be known as to how the operation was set up, but I have no doubts that the British intelligence and Zionist elements in the U.K. were the masterminds. To many this assertion is ludicrous, when Britain is no longer an imperial power and the U.S. is the sole superpower. It is precisely because, Britain has declined that she needs to adopt new methods and new approaches to maintain and sustain her global ambitions and agenda. If I may use an analogy—the U.S. may be sitting on the throne of power, but it is Britain who is the High Priest, wielding power behind the throne. We shall now examine some British dirty tricks.

11 Ibid.
12 Huffington Post, October 21, 2005.
13 Quoted by Murray Waas, National Journal October 27, 2005

The British, who invented modern war propaganda and inspired Joseph Goebbels, are specialists in the field.[14] At the height of the slaughter, known as the First World War, the Prime Minister, David Lloyd George, confided to C.P. Scott, editor of *The Manchester Guardian*: "If people really knew the truth, the war would be stopped tomorrow. But of course they don't know, and can't know."[15]

The forgeries were exposed and out in the open. The IAEA in the Security Council warned the powers that be, that there were no nuclear-weapons programs in Iraq. Mohammed Elbaradei said:

> Iraq has provided a comprehensive explanation of its relation to Niger. The IAEA was able to review correspondence from the government of Niger and compare full format contents and signature of that correspondence with those of the alleged procurement related documentation. Based on thorough analysis, the IAEA has concluded with concurrence from outside experts, that these documents which formed the basis for the reports of recent uranium transactions between Iraq and Niger are, in fact, not authentic.

Had the mainstream mass media throughout the world, performed their role as "truth tellers," the lies spewn by British and American mass media would have been exposed and their black propaganda would have been ineffective in conning their countries into invading Iraq. If the front page headlines were to drum into their countrymen and women—day in, day out—that the warmongers have forged documents to support their allegations and dared call Bush and Blair and their cabal, liars, forgers and warmongers, the outcome would have been different. We allowed the forgers to commit the crime of the century and get away with it, even as I write.

But this is not the first time that journalists have betrayed their profession. History is replete with examples of such connivance with forgers and liars. In October, 1965 General Suharto seized power from Indonesia's founding father, President Sukarno and unleashed a brutal massacre across the country that the CIA described as "the worst mass murders of the second half of the 20th century." This crime was hardly reported by Western media and the truth remains known to only a few. While there has been extensive reports on the recent "terrorist bombings" in Bali, none mentioned that at the very site of the carnage were the mass graves of an estimated 80,000

14   John Pilger, op. cit.
15   Ibid.

people slaughtered by mobs orchestrated by Suharto and supported by the American and British governments.[16] When bloodletting
starts, it is time for celebration for the "warrior race" and its cousins
in crime. Killing is indeed a blood sport.[17] This is how John Pilger
describes it:

> The American Embassy furnished General Suharto with
> roughly 5,000 names. These were people for assassination,
> and a senior American diplomat checked off the names as
> they were killed or captured. Most were members of the PKI,
> the Indonesian Communist Party. Having already armed and
> equipped Suharto's army, Washington secretly flew in state-
> of-the-art communications equipment whose high frequencies
> were known to the CIA and the National Security Council
> advising the President, Lyndon B. Johnson. Not only did this
> allow Suharto's generals to co-ordinate the massacres, it
> meant that the highest echelons of the U.S. administration
> were listening in.
>
> The Americans worked closely with the British. The British
> Ambassador in Jakarta, Sir Andrew Gilchrist, cabled the for-
> eign office, "I have never concealed from you my belief that a
> little shooting in Indonesia would be an essential preliminary
> to effective change." The "little shooting" saw off between half
> a million and a million people.

Very few know of the British Foreign Service dirty tricks unit
called the "Information Research Department" (IRD) which had a
branch in Singapore and was the nerve center for Cold War
Propaganda. It was "created" by the Labor peer Christopher Mayhew. However, a closer examination of its history reveals that it was
a continuation of the wartime (World War II) "Political Warfare
Executive" (PWE). Although its role was no longer relevant post-
World War II, more farsighted propaganda warriors felt differently,
such as the director of Special Operations Executive (SOE) Collin
Gubbins who urged Robert Bruce Lockhart, the former head of PWE
"to revive the black propaganda organization both in Europe and the
Far East."

There was resistance, but not for long. The climate of the Cold

---

16 Ibid.

17 The British people have been called "The Warrior Race" by British author Lawrence
James in his book of the same title. It is indeed common for the British and American families to have a celebration and a grand send-off for their son marching off to war and brutal killings.

War changed the perspective. The initiators for the project realized that they needed to instill fear within the corridors of power at Whitehall of the Soviet threat. "Protocol M" was released to serve the purpose. The document purports to be a blueprint for communist subversion and sabotage in Germany, in the Ruhr region. It was perceived as a plot to wreck the Marshall Plan. Simon Ollivant who made a study of the "Protocol M" controversy takes the view that the operation was not the work of Mayhew's new unit which at the time was not yet operational, but it was the work of those who were setting up the unit. They needed an enemy to justify the unit's continued existence and funding!

It was in fact a forgery. However, notwithstanding its dubious authenticity, officials continued to rely on it, "not so much a matter of error of judgment, but a deliberate act of policy."[18]

I hope that you can see the parallel with my earlier discussions on the forgery of the Niger "Yellow Cake" documents. Using forged documents is standard operating procedure in black propaganda operations. "Protocol M" was a forgery to instill fear.

The black operation succeeded in convincing the powers that be of the urgency in the establishment of the PSYOP unit. The name given to the unit was "Northern Information Department (NID).[19] But the name was soon changed to "Information Research Department" to avoid confusion with the "Naval Intelligence Department (NID)." One of the early recruits was Guy Burgess, who subsequently defected to the then Soviet Union. Norman Reddaway, Mayhew's private secretary played a critical role in the activities of the unit. He was the mastermind in the art of Black Propaganda.

The most important regional office of the IRD was in Singapore and the unit had an additional office in Hong Kong. One of its earliest missions was to counter nationalist movements fighting for independence in Africa and Asia. The IRD maintained a strong working relationship with the BBC. It supplied material to the BBC provided "it was neither quoted directly nor attributed to the government as being official policy." The corporation was regarded as semi-independent and an authoritative source of factual information which, of course made the insertion of material from IRD "briefing papers" so

18 Stephen Dorril, *MI6: Inside The Covert World of Her Majesty's Secret Intelligence Service*, (2000, Touchstone Books). P.77

19 Ibid., p.74

much more effective and productive in terms of propaganda.[20]

In the ground breaking book, *Britain's Secret Propaganda War*[21] the authors give a chilling account of the black propaganda operations of the IRD. The book revealed that 92 British journalists were on IRD's distribution list. Also revealed was the insidious black operation in Indonesia where the IRD planted *forged documents* suggesting that the PKI committed atrocities and that China intervened in the country in support of the PKI. This was the much needed pretext for General Suharto to unleash a bloody massacre against the Chinese community who were accused of being communist sympathizers.

In an article, following the publication of the book, the authors wrote in the *Independent*[22] that:

> The world's press was systematically manipulated by British intelligence as part of a plot to overthrow Indonesia's President Sukarno in the 1960s, according to Foreign Office documents. The BBC, the Observer and Reuter's news agency were all duped into carrying stories manufactured by agents working for the Foreign Service. Now a Foreign Office document obtained by the Independent on Sunday reveals the full extent of the "dirty tricks" campaign orchestrated from London, and how the world's journalist were manipulated.
>
> A letter marked "secret and personal" from propaganda expert Norman Reddaway to Britain's Ambassador in Jakarta, Sir Andrew Gilchrist, brags about the campaign which aimed to destabilize Mr. Sukarno by suggesting his rule would lead to a communist takeover. One story "went all over the world and back again," writes Reddaway, while information from Gilchrist was "put almost instantly back into Indonesia via the BBC. This included an allegation, with no apparent basis in reality that Indonesian communists were planning to slaughter the citizens of Jakarta.
>
> Last night, Lord Healey owned up to the Foreign Office misinformation campaign. Lord Healey said: "Norman Reddaway had an office in Singapore. They began to put out false information and I think that, to my horror on one occasion, they put forged documents on the bodies of Indonesian soldiers we

20 Ibid., p. 78
21 Lashmar P. and Oliver J., (1998, Sutton Publishing)
22 Paul Lashmar and James Oliver, "They Lied To Put a Killer in Power," April 16, 2000.

had taken. I confronted Reddaway over this.

According to one of the country's leading commentators on security matters—Richard Aldrich, a professor at Nottingham University—the episode shows Britain's post war operations at their most effective. "It represents one of the supreme achievements of the British clandestine services," he said. "In contrast with the American CIA, they remained politically accountable and low-key. Britain has a preference for bribing people rather than blowing them up."

Most of us, one time or another (and some still do) have a positive image of President Kennedy and Prime Minister Macmillan. But they are no different from blood-thirsty Bush and Blair. They have blood on their hands, as a CIA memorandum of 1962 reveals. Both leaders agreed and authorized a plan to "liquidate President Sukarno depending on the situation and available opportunities." According to Reddaway, the overthrow of Sukarno was one of the Foreign Office's "most successful" coups, which they have kept secret until now.

Yet we give credit to the CIA for the bloody coup. The operation was monitored from Phoenix Park, in Singapore which was the British headquarters in the region. IRD was also based there. MI6 kept close links with elements of the Indonesian army through the British embassy. One of these was Ali Murtopo who was later appointed by General Suharto as his Intelligence Chief.

Foreign Office documents revealed that the intelligence services and the IRD learning from their experience in Malaya in the fifties *emphasized the Chinese nature of the communist threat.* According to Roland Challis, the BBC correspondent, the operation to demonize the Chinese community was "one of the more successful things which the West wished on the non-communist politicians in Indonesia—to *transfer the whole idea of communism onto the Chinese minority in Indonesia. It turned into an ethnic thing.* It is a terrible thing to have done to incite the Indonesians to rise and slaughter the Chinese."[23] What the British did in the then Malaya, was replicated in Indonesia. This is the official record. So don't go and accuse me of being a conspiracy theorist. Check your history again. The Chinese were made scapegoats to further British interests in Indonesia.

23 Paul Lashmar and James Oliver, "How We Destroyed Sukarno," December 1, 1998, The Independent.

There at last is the unambiguous admission that ethnic hatred and racial conflicts in the past were generated by the British clandestine service to further their colonial interests in the region. It is so sad to see that there are people in Malaysia today, who have yet to realize that the under-current of racial tension is a leftover of the British "divide and rule" policies and the demonization of the Chinese community when they turned against the British after World War II.

Another example of British black operations is the plan for regime change in Syria fifty years ago. Newly discovered documents[24] show how in 1957, Harold Macmillan and President Dwight Eisenhower approved a CIA-MI6 plan to stage *fake border incidents* as an excuse for an invasion by Syria's pro western neighbors, and then eliminate the rulers in Damascus.[25] Part of the plan states:

> In order to facilitate the action of liberative forces, reduce the capabilities of the Syrian regime to organize and direct its military actions, to hold losses and destruction to a minimum, and to bring about desired results in the shortest possible time, a special effort should be made to eliminate certain key individuals. Their removal should be accomplished early in the course of the uprising and intervention and in the light of circumstances existing at the time.[26]

Also included in the plan was to make Syria "appear as sponsors of plots, sabotage and violence directed at neighboring governments." The plan called for the "CIA and SIS… to use their capabilities in both psychological and action fields to augment tension."

Fortunately, the plan could not be implemented as the Arab States were not willing to attack Syria.

Such is the cunning and duplicity of the British intelligence services, and we would be naïve and stupid to view them as "has beens." They are still the ultimate masters in the black arts. Planting false evidence, forgeries, creating racial tensions and fomenting civil wars are second nature to them. They are more dangerous than the Americans because they are so quiet in their execution and so sub-

---

24 Discovered in the private papers of Duncan Sandys, Macmillan's Defense Minister, by Matthew Jones, a reader in international history at Royal Holloway, University of London.

25 Ben Fenton, "Macmillan Backed Syrian Assassination Plot," September 23, 2003, The Guardian.

26 Ibid.

tle in their dissemination of disinformation. They are indeed the Warrior Race!

This British disease has infected the American political culture. It does not matter who gets killed so long as the Empire's interests are being served. Recall the Iran-Contra scandal. Although, Iraq was supposed to be the client state of the United States and was obtaining support in her war against Iran, the U.S. sold weapons to Iran so that the proceeds could be used to finance the Contras in their war against the Sandinistas in Nicaragua. As I have said in the beginning of this book, war is big business, and the war profiteers will arm both sides to get their blood money. There is no logic in wars from the perspective of the ordinary people. It is senseless killing. But to the warmongers and profiteers, wars are good for business. The key manipulators always get away with their crimes.

The Assistant Secretary of State for Inter-American Affairs, Elliott Abrams pleaded to a charge of withholding information from Congress but was subsequently pardoned by President George H.W. Bush in 1992. He is now re-engaged by junior Bush. Likewise, CIA Central American Task Force Chief, Alan D. Fiers was pardoned for his crimes. CIA Covert Operations Chief, Clair George was convicted for perjury but was pardoned before sentencing.

National Security Adviser Robert McFarlane pleaded guilty to withholding information and was also pardoned. The National Security Council's Oliver North was convicted of several crimes, but his conviction was overturned on appeal on a technicality. The mastermind, John M. Poindexter, National Security Adviser was convicted for conspiracy, making false statements and obstruction of Congress, but his conviction was overturned.

What has happened in Iraq and in the near future, Iran, Syria and elsewhere is but a re-run of the old imperialist policy of plunder and rape of a defenseless country and its people. How many must die before we have the courage to say enough is enough? How many more must die, before we remove the blinkers and stare reality in the face and say, enough is enough?

The next round of bloodletting and celebrations could very well be our turn. What then?

21

The War Criminals—
They Hang Them, Don't They?

It is my conviction that killing under the cloak of war is nothing but an act of murder.

— **Albert Einstein**

Liberty and democracy become unholy when their hands are dyed red with innocent blood.

— **Mohandas Gandhi**

The time has come for everyone to stand up and be counted. The victors hanged the war criminals after World War II was over, but it was no consolation to the millions who were massacred by the fascists in that brutal world war. Today, the Zionist Anglo-American war cabal has called the war on terrorism, World War IV. It has started and will continue for many decades to come. But this time around we cannot wait for the war to be over before we hang them from the gallows. We must bring Bush and Blair and their cohorts to justice now and hang them for their crimes. Justice and the law demand it. The Nuremberg Principles apply to these mass murderers as much as the Nazi war criminals.

It is expressly provided by article 6 of the Nuremberg Principles that leaders, organizers, instigators, and accomplices participating in the formulation or execution of a Common Plan or Conspiracy to commit crimes against peace, war crimes and crimes against humanity are responsible for all acts performed by any persons in execution of such plans.[1] Bush and Blair are personally responsible for all the war crimes committed in Afghanistan and Iraq and must give an account of their actions in a properly constituted war crimes tri-

1   See Chapter 19 for a detailed commentary on the Nuremberg Principles.

bunal. If we fail to do this, we will have failed our children and our children's children. They have slaughtered the innocents in Afghanistan and in Iraq and will continue the mindless killing as they have targeted Syria, Iran and North Korea for starters. The next round, after their adventure in the Middle East may very well be here in South-East Asia. The victims could be your wife, mother, sister, husband, father or brother. What then? I am much reminded by what Pastor Martin Niemoeller said about his inaction in the face of fascism. I hope that you would not have to echo his words, when your family has been slaughtered. He said:

> They first came for the Communists and I didn't speak up because I wasn't a Communist. Then they came for the Jews and I didn't speak up because I wasn't a Jew. Then they came for the trade unionists and I didn't speak up because I wasn't a trade unionist. Then they came for the Catholics and I didn't speak up because I was a Protestant. Then they came for me, and by that time no one else was left to speak up.

Now is the time to speak up and be counted. Get out of your comfort zone and confront the real world, and stop this barbarity and senseless slaughter!

I know it is difficult to make sacrifices. But I am not asking much of you. All each one of you need to do is to disseminate the truth revealed in this book. We must unmask the global agenda of the Zionist Anglo-American war cabal as the starting point. The history of this war cabal is a history of bloodletting over centuries and across the entire world. Consider the following confessions of the leading ideologues of the Zionist war cabal.[2]

Cecil Rhodes:

> I was in the West End of London yesterday and attended a meeting of the unemployed. I listened to the wild speeches, which were just a cry for "bread!" and on the way home I pondered over the scene and I became more than ever convinced of the importance of Imperialism. My cherished idea is a solution for the social problem, i.e. in order to save the 40,000,000 inhabitants of the United Kingdom from a bloody civil war, we colonial statesmen must acquire new lands to settle the surplus population, to provide new markets for the goods produced in the factories and the mines. The Empire, as I have

---

2   All quotations not specifically attributed were sourced from and downloaded from the Z Magazine's Znet website @ www.zmag.org/weluser.htm

always said, is a bread and butter question. If you want to avoid civil war, you must become imperialists.

Let us have no illusions. The British did not come to the then Malaya or anywhere else to give us freedom and independence. Colonial rule and post independence neo-colonial rule has always been and always will be a bread and butter issue for the British people.

President William McKinley—On the takeover of the Philippines:

I don't know how it was, but it came 1) that we could not give them back to Spain—that would be cowardly and dishonorable; 2) that we could not turn them over to France and Germany— our commercial rivals in the Orient—that would be bad business and discreditable; 3) that we could not leave them to themselves—they were unfit for self-government—and they would soon have anarchy and misrule over there worse than Spain's was; and 4) that there was nothing left for us to do but to take them all, and to educate the Filipinos, and uplift and civilize and Christianize them, and by God's grace do the very best we could by them, as our fellowmen for whom Christ also died. And then I went to bed, and went to sleep and slept soundly.

How persuasive and deluding. But as Mark Twain pointed out, statesmen will "invent cheap lies, putting blame upon the nation that is attacked, and every man will be glad of these conscience soothing falsities, and will diligently study them, and refuse to examine any refutations of them." Thus they will by and by convince themselves that the war is just, and will thank God for the better sleep they enjoy after this process of self deception. Was this not how Bush and Blair justify their war of aggression against Iraq?

President Woodrow Wilson:

Since trade ignores national boundaries and the manufacturer insists on having the world as a market, the flag of his nation must follow him, and the doors of the nations which are closed against him must be battered down. Concessions obtained by financiers must be safeguarded by ministers of state, even if sovereignty of unwilling nations be outraged in the process. Colonies must be obtained or planted, in order that no useful corner of the world may be overlooked or left unused.

Today, CEOs sing praises for the globalization agenda, the WTO rules and free trade, not realizing that these global trade rules serve only the interests of the imperialists. Nothing has changed since Cecil Rhodes declared Britain's global agenda. Today, waving the flag for imperial plunder is being described in more colorful terms. Thomas Friedman unashamedly said, "The hidden hand of the market will never work without a hidden fist—McDonalds cannot flourish without McDonnell Douglas, the builder of the F-15. And the hidden fist that keeps the world safe for Silicon Valley's technologies is called the United States Army, Air Force, Navy and Marine Corps."[3]

How has this hidden fist being applied in recent history? One word describes it all—slaughter, brutal mass slaughter. The Zionist Anglo-American war cabal has never been squeamish about unleashing terror and mass murder. Consider the following confessions, statements and opinions.

Winston Churchill:

I do not understand this squeamishness about the use of gas. We have definitely adopted the position at the Peace Conference of arguing in favor of the retention of gas as a permanent method of warfare. It is sheer affectation to lacerate a man with a poisonous fragment of a bursting shell and to boggle at making his eyes water by means of lachrymatory gas. I am strongly in favor of using poisoned gas against uncivilized tribes. The moral effect should be so good that loss of life would be reduced to a minimum. It is not necessary to use only the most deadly gasses: gasses can be used which caused great inconvenience and would spread a lively terror and they would leave no serious permanent effects on most of those affected.[4]

Today, the United States and Britain have the largest cache of biological and chemical weapons in the world, and have threatened to use these weapons against defenseless states. Yet, an illegal war was launched supposedly to rid Iraq of such weapons, but it turned out to be a lie. When Bush and Blair lied, hundreds of thousands died!

Fred Branfman: The Vietnam War

The United States dropped 6,727,084 tons of bombs on Indochina, more than triple what was dropped on all of Europe and the entire Pacific Theatre in World War II. We will never

3   Thomas Friedman, A Manifesto for the Fast World, The New York Times magazine, March 28, 1999.

4   This was Winston Churchill's justification for gassing Iraqis in the early 1920s when the Iraqi people opposed British colonial rule.

know how many innocent Indochinese peasants died from these illegal bombings, but former U.S. Secretary of Defense Robert McNamara has estimated that 3.4 million Indochinese died during the war. Since the vast majority of these perished from U.S. firepower, estimates of the innocents who died must begin in the hundreds of thousands.[5]

Little has changed since the 1970s. Indiscriminate killings are the order of the day and the culprits are once again the Zionist Anglo-American war cabal. The First Gulf War is almost as barbaric as the Vietnam War, notwithstanding that it was over in months.

Ramsay Clark:[6]

Let me tell you what happened briefly. There were 114,000 separate aerial sorties in 42 days—one every 30 seconds. Eighty-eight thousand tons of bombs were dropped. Only seven per cent were guided. Ninety-three per cent were free falling bombs that hit where chance, necessity and no free will took them. There were 38 aircraft lost by the U.S. in the slaughter. That number is less than the accidental losses in war games where no live ammunition is even used. It wasn't even a battle. It was a slaughter. General Kelly said when troops finally moved forward there were not many of them left alive to fight. We killed at least 125,000 soldiers and to date 130,000 civilians. We killed as many as we dared.

Tony Benn:

We used to have a War Office, but now we have a Ministry of Defense, nuclear bombs are now described as deterrents, innocent civilians killed in war are now described as collateral damage and military incompetence leading to U.S. bombs killing British soldiers is cozily described as friendly fire. Those who are in favor of peace are described as mavericks and troublemakers, whereas the real militants are those who want the war.

The 20th century has been described as the most violent century by many political analysts. We had the "Hot Wars," followed by the "Cold War" and several smaller proxy wars. Millions died but the slaughter continues. Eric Hobsbawn observed that the burden of war

5 Fred Branfman, "US War Crimes in Indochina and Our Duty to Truth," Z Magazine, August 26, 2004. @ www.zmag.org/content/showarticle.cfm?SectionID=44&ItemID= 6105
6 Ramsay Clark, former U.S. Attorney General, Final Hearings of the Commission of Inquiry into U.S. Conduct in the Gulf War, February 1992, New York.

has shifted increasingly and dramatically from the armed forces to civilians who were not only its victims, but increasingly the object of military or military-political operations. The contrast between the First World War and the second is dramatic: only 5% of those who died in the first were civilians; in the second, the figure increased to 66%. It is generally supposed that 80 to 90% of those affected by war today are civilians. The proportion has increased since the end of the Cold War because most military operations since then have been conducted not by conscript armies, but by small bodies of regular or irregular troops, in many cases operating high-technology weapons. The Iraq War bears testimony that it is the civilians that are the main victims of war.

In my book, *Future FastForward,* I had described the United States and Britain as "serial war criminal states" and I am more convinced than ever, that I am right in doing so. The reports of barbaric killings by journalists and returning soldiers from Iraq are no different from the reports of killings in the past.

Senator John Kerry, when he returned from Vietnam, in an interview on "Meet the Press" in April 1971 admitted that he committed "the same kind of atrocities as thousand of others" in that he shot in "free fire zones, fired 50 calibre machine gun bullets, used harass-and-interdiction fire, joined in search-and-destroy missions, and burned villages." He agreed that all the acts were contrary to the laws of the Geneva Conventions, and all were in response to orders, written established policies from the top down, and those who gave the orders were war criminals.

Since the British Parliament and the U.S. Congress have failed in their duties to impeach Blair and Bush respectively for war crimes, it is now up to the people of the world to relentlessly pursue these criminals until justice is done.

The War Crimes Act of 1996, a Federal Statute[7] makes it a federal crime for any U.S. national, whether military or civilian to violate the Geneva Conventions by engaging in murder, torture, or inhuman treatment. The law applies to everyone, without exception and not only to those who carry out the acts but those who order the commission of these crimes. There is no time-bar or limitations, which means that President Bush can be indicted even after he leaves office. And the punishment is either life imprisonment or if a *single prisoner dies,* death. Recently, the general in charge of the Abu

---

7   18 U.S.C. s. 2441

Ghraib prison in Iraq admitted in an interview[8] that she broke the Geneva Conventions and said that the orders/instructions were given by Defense Secretary Donald Rumsfeld. She has since been demoted to the rank of Colonel.

Section 2441 provides:

(a) Offense—whoever, whether inside or outside the United States, commits a war crime, in any of the circumstances described in subsection (b) shall be fined under this title or imprisoned for life or any term of years, or both, and if death results to the victim, shall also be subject to the penalty of death.

(b) Circumstances—The circumstances referred to in subsection (a) are that the person committing such war crime or the victim of such war crime is a member of the Armed Forces of the United States or a national of the United States (as defined in section 101 of the Immigration and Nationality Act).

(c) Definition—As used in this section the term "war crime" means any conduct—

(1) defined as a grave breach in any of the international conventions signed at Geneva 12th August 1949, or any protocol to such convention to which the United States is a party;

(2) prohibited by article 23,25, 27, or 28 of the Annex to the Hague Convention IV, Respecting the Laws and Customs of War on Land, signed 18 October 1907;

(3) which constitutes a violation of common article 3 of the international conventions signed at Geneva, 12 August 1949 or any protocol to such convention to which the United States is a party and which deals with non-international armed conflict; or

(4) of a person who, in relation to an armed conflict and contrary to the provisions of the Protocol on the Prohibitions or Restrictions on the Use of Mines, Booby-Traps and other Devices as amended at Geneva on 3 May 1996 (Protocol II as amended on 3 May 1996), when the United States is a party to such Protocol, wilfully kills or causes serious injury to civilians.

8   Interview with Amy Goodman, Democracy Now, October 27, 2005.

There can be no doubt that President Bush, Vice-President Cheney, former Secretary of State, Colin Powell, Secretary of Defense, Donald Rumsfeld, Deputy Secretary of Defense, Paul Wolfowitz, former National Security Adviser and now Secretary of State, Condoleezza Rice, the Joint Chiefs of Staff, previous Commander and current Commander of Central Command are all guilty of war crimes by the above provisions of the War Crimes Act of 1996. And for whatever its worth, the UN Secretary General Kofi Annan has declared that the U.S. led invasion of Iraq was an illegal act that contravened the UN Charter.[9]

A more credible figure to comment on this issue must be Denis Halliday, the former Assistant Secretary General and the former head of UN Humanitarian Mission in Iraq who resigned his post rather than be a party to the genocide of Iraqi children under the UN "Oil for Food" program. In his testimony to the World Tribunal on Iraq, he said that "without the authority that resides in Article 42 of the Charter, and a Security Council Resolution authorizing specific use of force, the Bush/Blair invasion of Iraq is in complete breach of international law. The war crimes committed in that blatant military aggression—the most serious of international crimes—must be charged to Bush as the Commander-in-Chief, and to Blair as Prime Minister who abused war powers. Bush should be charged with use of state terrorism for the opening salvo of the 'Shock and Awe' bombing strikes on Baghdad designed to terrorize by physically and mentally attacking a civilian population. This is a kind of state terrorism that provides a tragic reminder of the U.S. nuclear crime of bombing Hiroshima and Nagasaki. It is the kind of state terrorism beside which small scale 'terrorist' resistance pales in comparison. However, both forms of terrorism are internationally unlawful and unacceptable."

The brilliant lawyer, Professor Francis Boyle, Professor of Law, University of Illinois, a courageous human rights defender and pursuer of war criminals laid down the law succinctly in his article, *Iraq and the Laws of War*.[10] This is a must read article. In summary he said that the Bush-Blair illegal invasion violated the customary international laws of war set forth in the 1907 Hague Convention on the Opening of Hostilities to which the United States and Britain are contracting parties. In the case of the United States, this is evidenced by

9   BBC News, September 16, 2004.

10 Source: www.informationclearinghouse.info. October 14, 2005.

paragraphs 20, 21, 22 and 23 of U.S. Army Field Manual 27-10 (1956). The illegal invasion in also a crime against peace by the Nuremberg Charter (1945), the Nuremberg Judgement (1946), and the Nuremberg Principles (1950) as well as by paragraph 498 of U.S. Army Field Manual 27-10 (1956).

Donald Rumsfeld "Shock and Awe" campaign was a blatant contravention of the 1945 Nuremberg Charter which expressly prohibited "wanton destruction of cities, towns or villages, or devastation not justified by military necessity." It was terror bombing and this could not be denied, as the authors of this strategy stated emphatically that this was the objective—to terrorize the people into submission.

When on May 1, 2003, President Bush declared the end of hostilities on board the U.S. aircraft carrier off the coast of San Diego, the United States became an occupying power in Iraq. The United States and Britain have expressly admitted that status by their letter of May 8, 2003 to the President of the Security Council (S/2003/538). In the circumstances, the U.S. and Britain were and are obliged to recognize and uphold the responsibilities and obligations under applicable international laws as occupying powers under unified command. The letter states:

> The States participating in the Coalition will strictly abide by their obligations under international law, including those relating to the essential humanitarian needs of the people of Iraq.

Therefore the U.S. and Britain are subject to the four Geneva Conventions of 1949, the 1907 Hague Regulations on Land Warfare, U.S. Army Field Manual 27-10 (1956), the British equivalent, the Humanitarian provisions of Additional Protocol One of 1977 to the Four Geneva Conventions of 1949, and the customary international laws of war. The wanton destruction of Iraq and the killing and torture of Iraqis are blatant contraventions of the aforesaid international laws and are war crimes.

According to Prof. Boyle, the installation of the puppet regime during the summer of 2004 does not alter the legal situation and status that the unified command is the occupying authority. As a belligerent occupier, the U.S. and Britain are free to install a puppet government, but are ultimately responsible for the act of their puppets. This is not political rhetoric but the established international law principles under the various conventions cited above. Paragraph 366 of the U.S. Army Field Manual 27-10 (1956), the heading of which states: "Local Government Under Duress and Puppet Governments" stipulates that the U.S. is under an obligation to ensure that its puppet government respect all the abovementioned international conventions and customary international laws of war. This it has failed to do. It has committed further war crimes.

There can never be a transfer of sovereignty from a belligerent occupying power to a puppet government as it is expressly provided by paragraph 353 of the U.S. Army Field Manual 27-10 (1956) which provides:

> Belligerent occupation in a foreign war, being based upon the possession of enemy territory, necessarily implies that the sovereignty of the occupied territory is not vested in the occupying power. Occupation is essentially provisional.

Additionally, paragraph 258 of the U.S. Army Field Manual 27-10 (1956) provides:

Occupation Does Not Transfer Sovereignty

> Being an incident of war, military occupation confers upon the invading force the means of exercising control for the period of occupation. It does not transfer the sovereignty to the occupant, but simply the authority or power to exercise some of the rights of sovereignty. The exercise of these rights results from established power of the occupant and from the necessity of maintaining law and order, indispensable both to the inhabitants and the occupying force.

Therefore sovereignty still resides with the heroic Iraqi people. The United States never had any sovereignty in Iraq and/or the power to transfer sovereignty to any puppet regime.

I am eternally grateful to the good professor for pointing out one very important fact, the UN Resolution 1546 of June 8, 2004 and its implications. I shall quote him in extenso:

> Even the UN Security Council Resolution 1546 of 8 June 2004 "Welcoming" the installation of the puppet Interim Government of Iraq recognized this undeniable fact of international law. Preambular language in this resolution referred to "the letter of 5 June 2004 from the United States Secretary of state to the President of the Council, which is annexed to this resolution." In other words, that annexed letter is a legally binding part of the resolution 1546 (2004). Therein U.S. Secretary of State Colin Powell pledged to the UN Security Council with respect

to the so-called Multinational Force (MNF) in Iraq: "In addition, the forces that make up the MNF are and will remain committed at all times to act consistently with their obligations under the law of armed conflict, including the Geneva Conventions."

Therefore, notwithstanding the rabid ravings of Bush that the Geneva Conventions do not apply, resolution 1546 is clear that the U.S. has unequivocally committed to abide by all relevant international laws on war etc.

The so-called "Constitution" drafted by the puppet government and assisted by the occupying power has no legal basis whatsoever, as by international law, article 43 of the 1907 Hague Regulations rejects and prohibits any change in the basic law of an occupied country. It provides that: "The authority of the legitimate power having in fact passed into the hands of the occupant, the latter shall take all measures in his power to restore, and ensure as far as possible, public order and safety, while *respecting, unless absolutely prevented, the laws in force in the country.* This prohibition is replicated in paragraph 363 of the U.S. Army Field Manual 27-10 (1956).

And any subsequent UN Security Council resolutions by the members thereto that purport to grant the U.S. and Britain any other rights etc., in consistence with the abovementioned conventions are ultra-vires, null and void and tantamount to abetting in the commission of war crimes, and those member countries who have voted for any such resolutions have committed war crimes as aiders and abettors.

The above arguments relating to international laws and the respective equivalents of the U.S. Army Field Manual 27-10 (1956) apply equally to Britain and the other countries of the Coalition. I urge readers to read the excellent joint opinion of Michael Ratner, President, Center on Constitutional Rights, Jules Lobel, Professor of Law, University of Pittsburgh School of Law, Lawyers' Committee on Nuclear Policy and Western States Legal Foundation issued on October 2, 2002.[11] In summary, they said that the so-called "Coalition of the Willing" have contravened the UN Charter relating to wars and have thereby committed war crimes.

In addition, as far as Britain is concerned, we are fortunate to have the "Downing Street Memos" which are irrefutable evidence that Britain under the Blair regime committed war crimes and planned to commit such crimes as far back as 2002. *The Times*

11 Source: http://www.lcnp.org/global/iraqstatement3.htm

newspaper[12] has reported that ministers were warned in July 2002 that Britain was committed to taking part in an American led invasion of Iraq *and they had no choice but to find a way of making it legal.*

This is the smoking gun against war criminal Tony Blair. There was no basis for war, but he had to create a legal basis for war. The "excuse" was to accuse Iraq of not complying with UN Resolution 1441 to declare its WMDs.

An elaborate charade was put up to get the UN Security Council to adopt a resolution (resolution 1441) demanding compliance from Iraq to surrender all WMDs, when all along the warmongers knew that Iraq had no WMDs. Resolution 1441 was part of the charade. The "Yellow Cake" allegation was another part; and so was the speech by Colin Powell at the UN Security Council.

Notwithstanding that Iraq had no WMDs, any denial by Iraq, according to this perverse logic is deemed non-compliance. Thus the "legal basis" was created for war. Even a first year law student would be able to advise that such a basis founded on lies is no basis at all. But we have to bear in mind that imperialist logic is perverse logic.

The briefing paper for the meeting with Blair's inner circle on July 23, 2002 said that since regime change was illegal, it was "necessary to create the conditions" which would make it legal. It went on to say that even if ministers decided that Britain should not take part in an invasion, the American military would request and use British bases for the invasion. This would automatically make Britain complicit in any illegal U.S. action.[13] Present at the meeting were Blair, Geoff Hoon, Jack Straw and Sir Richard Dearlove, Head of MI6. They are war criminals as much as Hitler, Goering, Hess and Speer were condemned as such.

It is therefore a lie to say that Britain went to the United Nations to prevent a war and to give Saddam Hussein an opportunity to comply, when all along, the attempted resolution by the UN Security Council was a charade, to create in fact a trigger mechanism for war! In another document, a Cabinet Office paper, entitled "Conditions for Military Action" dated July 21, 2002 it is interesting to note that ministers were invited to consider inter-alia, the establishment of an ad

12 Michael Smith, "Ministers Were Told of Need for Gulf War 'Excuse'," *The Times*, June 12, 2005.

13 Ibid.

hoc group of officials under Cabinet Office Chairmanship to *consider the development of an information campaign to be agreed with the U.S.*

In short, this means a propaganda campaign for war against Iraq. The government of the United States and Britain from the very beginning realized the need for a propaganda campaign to convince their people to support an illegal war. The people need to be brainwashed for war, and the young volunteers, to be prepared and programmed to kill.

What is incomprehensible for most people is that a government would forge documents and lie to their people to wage a war of aggression for an imperialist agenda. I hope that the evidence presented in this chapter as well as in the previous chapters has shown that nothing, absolutely nothing will deter these war criminals from achieving their global agenda.

The law of Karma has wrought its own retribution—we reap what we sow. And Blair has now to reap the retribution and be hanged for the lies, deceit, forgeries and the war crimes against Iraq. We must relentlessly pursue this war criminal until he is brought before a war crimes tribunal and hanged for his crimes. Nothing short of that punishment will suffice. Only by bringing these murderers to justice will there be hope for peace. The victors of World War II have got away with murders, genocide and other crimes for the last fifty years, camouflaging under the guise of "liberators of fascism" when they are in fact the other side of the same coin. For as long as such leaders are not accountable and do not have to answer for their crimes, they will be emboldened to continue with their global agenda.

And unless they are stopped, the next casualty may very well be a member of your family.

22

The Empire Mindset—
The Geographical Combatant Commander

Our scientific power has outrun our spiritual power. We have guided missiles and misguided men.

— Dr. Martin Luther King Jr.

If they turn on their radars we're going to blow up their goddamn SAMs [surface-to-air missiles]. They know we own their country. We own their airspace. We dictate the way they live and talk. And that's what's great about America right now. It's a good thing, especially when there's a lot of oil out there we need.

— U.S. Brig. General William Looney[1]

Whenever I mention about the Zionist *global* agenda, the general reaction from main street Malaysians is one of disbelief. It is so hard for ordinary people to *think globally.* Yet, we are living in a world of "globalization." This word has been trashed around so much, that it has virtually lost its *real* meaning. And that is good as far as the Zionist war cabal is concerned. To the policy makers, their thinking cap is still about world trade and, would you believe, *fair trade* and the need to fit into the World Trade Organization's (WTO) agenda.

I keep asking myself what must I do or show to my fellow countrymen and others in the third world, that the Zionist Anglo-American Empire's global mindset is not what we think it is. It is said that a picture paints a thousand words. I searched and searched as much as I can from various picture books in bookshops and libraries but came out empty. I almost gave up when by chance I came across a book, *Code Names*,[2] in an obscure bookshelf. I flipped through the pages

---

1 The general who directed the bombing of Iraq in the late 1990s. Source: William Blum, *Rogue State*, (2000, Common Courage).

2 William M. Arkin, *Code Names*, (2005, Steerforth Press)

and told myself that in my next budget, I would get it and walked away. A strange thing happened as I was leaving the bookshop and going for my lunch. "Go and buy that book or you will regret it" boomed right into my ears, and before I could count ten, I was at the cashier counter, paying for it. Instinctively, I flipped the pages again, and the words in Part I of the book nearly floored me. I knew I hit the jackpot. It was exactly what I was looking for. I then googled the DoD website to get the map referred to in the book. There are times when what is obvious and right before your eyes is overlooked. Once again, a guardian angel helped me.

William Arkin is an independent journalist and had served as an intelligence analyst in the U.S. army and what he wrote is what each one of you should know and what I have been trying to convey—*the global agenda* from a military perspective. He explains that the U.S. military divides the world into several Geographical Areas of Command, and where the designated Commander in each area, assumes total responsibility. That there are sovereign countries within these areas is irrelevant to the military doctrine of imposing full spectrum dominance.[3] In brief, the Zionist Anglo-American war cabal divided the world into the following military command zones:

1) Northern Command (NORTHCOM) covering continental USA, Canada, Alaska and parts of Iceland and all the way to the north pole. HQ—Peterson Air Force Base, Colorado.

2) Southern Command (SOUTHCOM) covering the entire Central and South American continent, down to Antarctica. HQ—Miami, Florida.

3) European Command (EUROCOM) covering the entire continent of Europe, the eastern side of Iceland, the vast expanse of Russia, the rest of Africa not within the zone of Central Command and the remaining areas of the Antarctica not within the zone of Southern Command. HQ—Stuttgart-Vaihingen, Germany.

4) Central Command (CENTCOM) covering the entire Middle East, extending eastwards to the Central Asian Republics, Afghanistan, Pakistan and that part of Africa which encompasses Egypt, Sudan, Ethiopia, Somalia and the Horn of Africa. HQ—MacDill AFB, Florida.

3   See Appendix 13 for the Military Map of the World and the executive summary for the rationale behind these geographical areas of command.

5) Pacific Command (PACOM) covering the entire Asian Continent, Southeast Asia, Australia, New Zealand and all the real estate in the Pacific Ocean and Indian Ocean and the Antarctica and that part of Russia known as Siberia. HQ—Honolulu, Hawaii.

I know what you are thinking—"How can the U.S. military treat our countries as part of their military command?" Precisely! That is what I have been saying, that "globalization," "Global Security Interests," "World Trade" etc have different meanings to the war cabal than what we perceive and understand. In the previous chapter, I drew your attention to the views expressed by Cecil Rhodes, President William McKinley, and President Woodrow Wilson to illustrate their peculiar world view—an imperialist's world view. I hope you will agree that those views read in the context of the Zionist Anglo-American Military's division of the world into geographical areas of command have provided a new dimension and understanding of the Zionist Anglo-American Empire's world view. I would like to quote once again Thomas Friedman[4] who wrote in 1999:

> The hidden hand of the market will never work without a hidden fist—McDonalds cannot flourish without McDonnell Douglas, the builder of F-15. And the hidden fist that keeps the world safe for Silicon Valley's technologies is called the United States Army, Air Force, Navy and Marine Corps.

In my recent book, *Future FastForward,* I drew the reader's attention to the Grand Military Strategy propounded by Prof. Thomas Barnett in his book, *The Pentagon's New Map: War and Peace in the 21st Century*[5] which has since been adopted by Donald Rumsfeld. The Grand Military Strategy requires the war cabal to protect their economic interest in the zone called the "Integrated Core" from the enemies in the "Non-integrating Gap," those poor countries which harbor terrorists and failed states; the countries in between called the "Seam States" will act as buffers to prevent any negative spill over from the Gap. The Professor reserves for the war cabal the right to launch any military attacks against the seam states and countries within the Gap.

The professor has recently published a sequel, *The Pentagon's*

4   "A Manifesto for a Fast World," New York Times Magazine, March 28, 1999.

5   Thomas Barnett, *The Pentagon's New Map: War and Peace in the 21st Century*, (2004, Putnam & Sons, New York).

New Map: Blueprint for Action,[6] his road map for Zionist Anglo-American Empire's total domination in the 21st Century.

If the 20th century was considered a violent century, the historians have seen nothing yet of the wars to come. A glimpse of what is to come was given by Michael Ledeen,[7] the fascist ideologue of the Neo-con war cabal. He wrote:

> The awesome power of a free society committed to a single mission is something our enemies cannot imagine... Our unexpectedly quick and impressive victory in Afghanistan is a prelude to a much broader war, which will in all likelihood transform the Middle East for at least a generation, and reshape the politics of many older countries around the world.

When we have two such ideologues advising the war cabal, this is a recipe for disaster and God only knows how many innocents have to die before sanity prevails.

In the circumstances, it is imperative that we pay close attention to what these ideologues are saying. Such is the influence of Prof. Barnett's previous book, that he was confident enough to say that "Long-range planners at various regional commands,[8] as well as at the Pentagon, have embraced its global perspective and the strategic requirements for change that it portends ..." My point here is that the war cabal is already past the point of no return, they have crossed the Rubicon, but the world's peace loving peoples have yet to appreciate the danger that confronts them.

Let's recap what the professor wrote:

> This vision propels a strategy for the United States, one that makes the audacious demand that America equate its national security with that of globalization's continued survival and success... America forgot the connection across the 1990s, enamored as we were with the notion that globalization's unstoppable march around the planet would solve all security problems lying in its path. We learned differently on September 11, 2001. We learned that globalization, and all the freedom it fosters through connectivity, requires a body-

6   Thomas Barnett, *The Pentagon's New Map: Blueprint for Action*, (2005, Putnam & Sons, New York).

7   Michael Ledeen, *War Against the Terror Masters*, (2002, St. Martin's Press, New York).

8   Note the reference to "regional commands," which I had just explained. The convergence of policy and action plan is complete. A totally new kind of warfare awaits us.

guard, because there are still numerous forces throughout the Gap and even inside the Core working against it.

Minus the rhetoric about freedom, this passage when pasted over the quotations by Cecil Rhodes, President McKinley and President Woodrow Wilson, reflects the same imperialist world view—the global network must serve the economic and security interests of the empire! The Professor's good intentions for the world ring hollow, when he let slip the ulterior motive of his grand design when in the Preface to his latest book, he wrote:

> Those ideals exist only to the extent that we make them real in our words, deeds and legacy. This blueprint is not about **them** but **us**—what we stand for and what we believe in. (Emphases added)

He further explained that his grand strategy is not about war in the context of war, but "one that seeks to place our thinking on *war in the context of everything else,* which today goes by the shorthand, globalization."

We should have no illusions. It is "them" and "us" and we do not come within his definition of "us" and so as part of his "them," we must prepare for the coming brutality and slaughter. The peace that the professor hopes for is not the world peace that we yearned for, but the "peace for the empire"—when the world is subjugated and in total submission, then and then only will there be peace for the empire. History is replete with examples that when colonialists and imperialists speak most often of peace, they are in fact waging wars to secure the peace.

Only just recently, Lawrence B. Wilkerson[9] warned that some of the most important decisions about U.S. national security were decided by a secretive little-known cabal led by Dick Cheney and Donald Rumsfeld.[10] In a speech to the New America Foundation he said, "The case that I saw for four-plus years was a case that I have never seen in my studies of aberrations, bastardizations, perturbations, and changes to the national security decision-making process. What I saw was a cabal between the Vice-President of the United States, Richard Cheney, and the Secretary of Defense, Donald Rumsfeld, on critical issues that made decisions that the bureaucra-

9   He served as Chief of Staff to Secretary of State Colin Powell from 2001 to 2005.

10 Lawrence B. Wilkerson, "The White House Cabal," October 25, 2005, Los Angeles Times.

cy did not know were being made."[11]

I hope my critics who objected to my use of such terms as "cabal," "warmongers" etc., will finally acknowledge that these are indeed appropriate terms, especially coming from an insider such as Mr. Wilkerson. He further described the workings of this cabal as "efficient and swift—not unlike the decision-making one would associate more with a dictatorship than a democracy... The decisions of this cabal were sometimes made with the full and witting support of the President and sometimes with something less. More often than not, then National Security Adviser, Condoleezza Rice was simply steamrolled by this cabal."

However, I do not share the notion of Mr. Wilkerson that Ms Rice is a two-bit player. As far as I am concerned, she and Madeline Albright are as much cold blooded killers as Al Capone and his goons. As recent as October 19, 2005 Ms Rice appeared before the Senate Foreign Relations Committee, and when asked whether the Bush regime was planning military strikes against Syria, she replied, "I don't think the President ever takes any of his options off the table concerning anything to do with military force." As far as she is concerned war is always an option, and notwithstanding the fact that as the Secretary of State, she is the No.1 U.S. diplomat. On being challenged by Senator Chafee that only Congress has and retains the authority to declare war, she held her ground and retorted, "Senator, I don't want to try and circumscribe presidential war powers. And I think you'll understand fully that the President retains those powers in the war on terrorism and in the war on Iraq."

The following exchange at the Senate hearing merits repeated reading.

Sen. Richard G. Lugar:[12]

Even if withdrawal timelines are deemed unwise because they might provide a strategic advantage to the insurgency, the American people need to more fully understand the basis upon which our troops are likely to come home.

Condoleezza Rice:

Unless we commit to changing the nature of the Middle East, and if we tire and decide that we are going to withdraw and

11 Bob Herbert, "How Scary Is This?," October 24, 2005, New York Times, quoting Lawrence Wilkerson.

12 Indiana Republican and Chairman of the Senate Foreign Relations Committee.

leave the people of the Middle East to despair, I can assure you that the people of the United States are going to live in insecurity and fear for many, many decades to come.

Sen. Barbara Boxer:

Now, in an unbelievable rewriting of history, you talk about this bolder mission we undertook in response to 9/11 to transform the Middle East with Iraq as an anchor. The administration did-n't tell the American people that at the time. [The original rea-son was Saddam Hussein's WMDs]

Sen. Barack Obama:

This broadening of the mission is disturbing and difficult for us in the Senate to deal with as it requires a leap of faith on our part that a mission of that breadth can be accomplished in a reasonable time frame.

Condoleezza Rice:

We had to make a decision that we are going to go after the root cause of what caused September 11. So what I am describing to you Senator is not what you voted for in the war resolution, but the broader strategy of the administration.

The above exchange during the Senate hearings, incredible as it was, has by the testimony of Ms Rice revealed that the original rea-son for war (which in any event was based on lies) has now been broadened. Like the blood-thirsty vampires, once they have tasted blood, the warmongers will never let up.

Yet, we have political pundits opining that given the situation in Iraq, the war cabal can ill afford another military adventure. To but-tress their position they cite the former Director of NSC under President Ronald Reagan, Lt. General William Odom's recent state-ment that the Iraq war is the "greatest strategic disaster in United States history."[13]

But these political pundits miss the point. The empire's war cabal has a different mindset. It arrogates to itself the power to decide who shall live, who shall die, who is fit to govern and where there should be a regime change. Recall what Brig. General Looney said about Iraq: "They know we own their country. We dictate the way they live and talk."

This madness has been given a nuclear dimension with the

---

13 Cited by Jeremy Brecher and Brendan Smith, "Attack Syria? Invade Iran?," October 20, 2005, Counterpunch.

publication in March 15, 2005 of the Joint Chiefs of Staff's Doctrine for Joint Nuclear Operations.[14] In a public seminar in April 2005, soon after the publication of my book, *Future FastForward,* I drew attention to this new nuclear doctrine. In attendance were my former colleagues and they were stunned by the role given to the Combatant Commanders in the coming nuclear wars. In the past, where the use of nuclear weapons, was as a matter of policy, a strategic weapon of last resort, under the new doctrine, it is to be applied in theatre operations. The Joint Chiefs have declared:

> The guidance in this publication is authoritative; as such, this doctrine will be followed except when, in the judgment of the commander, exceptional circumstances dictate otherwise. If conflicts arise between the contents of this publication and the contents of Service publications, this publication will take precedence unless the Chairman of the Joint Chiefs of Staff, normally in coordination with the other members of the Joint Chiefs, has provided more current and specific guidance.

The Doctrine provides for and allows the use of nuclear weapons in theatre operations in the following scenario:

1. To **counter** potentially overwhelming **adversary conventional forces,** including mobile and area targets troops [troop concentration].

2. For rapid and favorable **war termination** on U.S. terms.

3. To **ensure success** of U.S. and multinational operations.

4. To **demonstrate U.S. intent** and capability to use nuclear weapons to deter adversary use of WMD.

What have changed dramatically from the previous practice are two factors. Firstly, the role assigned to the Combatant Commanders. It is expressly provided that U.S. forces must prepare to use nuclear weapons effectively and that U.S. forces are determined to employ nuclear weapons if necessary to prevent or retaliate against WMD use. The Geographical Commanders, i.e. the respective Commanders of NORTHCOM, SOUTHCOM, EUCOM, CENTCOM and PACOM have the responsibility for "defining theatre objectives, selecting specific targets and targeting objectives, and developing the plans required to support these objectives."

Secondly, and very ominous is the enhanced role of the geo-

14 See Executive Summary in Appendix 10.

graphical Combatant Commander who is now empowered to launch nuclear attacks *to demonstrate U.S. intent and capability to use nuclear weapons to deter an adversary use of WMD.*

This is why I said in my book, *Future FastForward,* and I am repeating here again, that nuclear wars are inevitable in the very near future. In fact I would say, for certain, it would be used in any wars with Iran. Why this certainty?

The U.S. war cabal's military planners have put themselves in a fix in that having declared that they are willing to employ nuclear weapons to *demonstrate U.S. intent* they cannot back down from this stance in any future confrontation. I would go even as far as saying that the U.S. will unilaterally and pre-emptively find an excuse to use nuclear weapons against any state *just to demonstrate this intent.*

There is the historical precedent of Hiroshima and Nagasaki. The bombing of the two cities was not to hasten the conclusion of the Pacific war and to reduce U.S. casualties, as touted by imperialist historians, but as an experiment and more importantly to *demonstrate U.S. intent and willingness to use the nuclear bomb.*

The target for intimidation at the material time was the Soviet Union, as is apparent from the memoirs of the great Soviet Marshall Zhukov who masterminded the defeat of Hitler's once invincible army. He wrote:[15]

> I do not recall the exact date, but after the close of one of the formal meetings Truman informed Stalin that the United States now possessed a bomb of exceptional power, without, however, naming it the atomic bomb.
>
> As was later written abroad at that moment Churchill fixed his gaze on Stalin's face, closely observing his reaction. However, Stalin did not betray his feelings and pretended he saw nothing special in what Truman had imparted to him. Both Churchill and many other Anglo-American authors subsequently assumed that Stalin had really failed to fathom the significance of what he had heard.
>
> In actual fact, on returning to his quarters after the meeting Stalin, in my presence, told Molotov about his conversation with Truman. The latter reacted almost immediately. "Let them. We'll have to talk it over with Kurchatov and get him to speed

15 Georgi Konstantinovich Zhukov, *The Memoirs of Marshall Zhukov,* (1971, Delacorte Press)

things up."

I realized that they were talking about research on the atomic bomb.

It was clear already then that the U.S. government intended to use the atomic weapon for the purpose of achieving its imperialist goals from a position of strength in "the Cold War." This was amply corroborated on August 6 and 8. Without any military need whatsoever, the Americans dropped two atomic bombs on the peaceful and densely populated cities of Hiroshima and Nagasaki.

The reason for employing nuclear weapons as stated in the new doctrine, is the same rationale for the bombings of Hiroshima and Nagasaki. The war cabal got away with this war crime and they are confident that they will get off again in the coming wars. But we must not let them get away with it again!

The most likely candidate would be Iran for a number of reasons. Having demonized Islam and portrayed Iran as a rogue state, part of the Axis of Evil, the Zionist Anglo-American war cabal has prepared the propaganda basis for war. Additionally, such an attack would serve both Israel's and Anglo-American interests in the Middle East and elsewhere. Retaliation, if any by Iran, would be limited in scope and the costs acceptable from any point of view. As far as the war cabal is concerned, such a nuclear war would end the debate once and for all, as to the strategy needed to eliminate the Islamic threat.

I take the view that the 21st century will witness the last great empire wars. No empires have ever whithered away quietly. In their last throes of death, they have no choice but to lash out in a desperate attempt to retain power. And because it is the last grasp for power, the empire will use everything at its disposal. This is the insidious meaning of the oft quoted words of President Bush, "This notion that the United States is getting ready to attack Iran is simply ridiculous…. And having said that, all options are on the table!"[16]

The American Conservative, in July 22, 2005 reported that the Pentagon acting under the instructions from Vice-President Dick Cheney, has tasked the United States Strategic Command (STRATCOM) with drawing up a contingency plan to be employed in **response to another 9/11 type attack on the United States.** The plan includes a large scale air assault on Iran employing both con-

16 Statement by Bush, February 22, 2005, Brussels.

ventional and tactical nuclear weapons.

We must have no illusions. We must be vigilant, for people are easily deluded by the clarion call to ring the bell of freedom and to plant the seeds of democracy. And often in the name of democracy we have waged wars. The words of Mark Twain, when he opposed America's colonization of Philippines are worth repeating and should serve as a timely reminder as to the nature of American imperialism. He wrote:

> I used to be a red hot imperialist. I wanted the American eagle to go screaming into the Pacific. Why not spread its wings over the Philippines, I asked myself? I said to myself. "Here are people who have suffered for three centuries. We can make them as free as ourselves, give them a government and country of their own, put a miniature of the American constitution afloat in the Pacific, and start a brand new republic to take its place among the free nations of the world.

> But I have thought some more, since then, and I have read carefully the Treaty of Paris, and I have seen we do not intend to free, but to subjugate the people of the Philippines. We have gone there to conquer, not to redeem.

> It should, it seems to me, be our pleasure and duty to make those people free, and let them deal with their own domestic questions in their own way. And so I am an anti-imperialist. I am opposed to having the eagle put its talons into any other land.

We must also unmask the fiction of the War on Terror. If there is terrorism, it is the Zionist Anglo-American war cabal's terrorism throughout the world. Look again at the U.S. Military's map of the world in Appendix 13, and ask yourself, "Who seeks to dominate the world by military force?" Ask yourself again, "Since World War II, which country other than the United States and Britain has attacked another country, conducted coups, massacred thousands of innocent civilians and tortured people?"

Mike Whitney in his article, *The Globalization of State Terror*,[17] warned that the war on terror is predicated on two basic theories, pre-emption and enemy combatants. The former overturns the conclusions of the Nuremberg Tribunals and Principles that "war is the supreme crime." And when it is constituted as an essential element of foreign policy, it seeks to legitimize the use of force to assert one

---

17 Source: www.globalresearch.ca. July 27, 2005.

state's superiority over another. The latter, a sinister classification, is being promoted to enable the war criminal to circumvent the rigors of the Geneva Conventions and to treat this category of combatants as undeserving of any human rights. The result is all too clear for everyone to see, the torture of civilians in Guantanamo Bay and Abu Ghraib prisons.

On October 26, 2005, it was reported in *The Washington Post*, that Vice-President Cheney is aggressively pursuing an initiative that is unprecedented for an elected official of the executive branch: he is proposing that Congress legalize torture by Americans. This is not surprising as Cheney's legal counsel (recently promoted as Chief of Staff, following the indictment of Lewis "Scooter" Libby) David Addington was one of the principal authors of the legal memo justifying the torture of suspects.

There is emerging a trend in Malaysia, especially among the businessmen, who have vested interests to kow-tow to the Zionist Anglo-American war cabal and to spread the unfounded fear that opposing the imperialist agenda is detrimental to the interests of Malaysia. These businessmen and CEOs must be exposed as compradors and collaborators and confronted at every turn. They are still a small group, but we should not allow them to multiply and undermine Malaysia's independence and sovereignty. They are also traitors to the UMMAH and must be treated as such, especially when so many Muslims have been brutally murdered. Let this book be a warning to them. There is time yet for them to redeem themselves, but they must be sincere. Otherwise, they must be told that the wrath of the world's people will visit them.

This internal danger facing Malaysia and many other countries is very real. Make no mistake about it. Before any open hostilities, the war cabal always embarks on a campaign of internal subversion and their key allies are such businessmen, carefully nurtured NGOs and religious front organizations. The Zionist war cabal has already started funding such campaigns so that when the appropriate time comes, their puppets and cronies would be installed. We saw this happening in Georgia, and this was quickly followed by the "Orange Revolution" in Ukraine, where a U.S. and British puppet was installed as the President. Then we had the "Cedar Revolution" in Lebanon. Massive amounts of funds were channeled to obscure organizations and overnight they had a "mass following." To give credence to their leaders, these traitors are invited to the United States and Britain and bestowed with awards and titles. Having been properly brainwashed, they are dispatched back to their countries to do their dirty subversion.

These "franchised revolutions" are engineered by the right wing National Endowment for Democracy (NED), the Eurasia Foundation, the Renaissance Foundation, the National Democratic Institute and the International Republican Institute (IRI). Even Muslim organizations are targets as can be seen in Iraq where the Dawa Party and the Supreme Council for the Islamic Revolution have been funded by the occupation authorities. The IRI was behind the coup against President Chávez of Venezuela, as well as the violent overthrow of President Jean Bertrand Aristide of Haiti. The NED is supported by the right wing think tank, Heritage Foundation and receives generous funding from the big oil companies like Exxon, Mobil, Texaco and Chevron. Mark Almond, the Cold War bagman revealed in an article[18] how he financed and organized such coups and elections in the 1980s.

He wrote:

> Throughout the 1980s, in the build-up to the 1989's velvet revolution, a small army of volunteers—and, let's be frank, spies—cooperated to promote what became People's Power. A network of inter-locking foundations and charities mushroomed to organize the logistics of transferring millions of dollars to dissidents. The money came overwhelmingly from NATO states and covert allies such as "neutral" Sweden.

The recent release of *The National Intelligence Strategy of the United States* in October 2005,[19] has added an urgency to the need to address the issue of subversion by such abovementioned organizations in Malaysia and other countries. Prepared under the supervision of the Director of National Intelligence, Mr. John Negroponte, who bloodied his hands in Honduras, El Salvador and Nicaragua in conniving with death squads, the document is the blueprint as well as the road map for the entire U.S. intelligence network to meet the challenges of the 21st century.

Mr. Larry Chin shares my anxiety[20] and warns that it will con-

18 Mark Almond, "The Price of People Power," December 7, 2004, The Guardian.
19 See Appendix 14.
20 Larry Chin, "The New National Intelligence Strategy of the United States: Towards an even more dangerous international security apparatus," October 29, 2005. Source: www.globalresearch.ca

tribute to an "even more dangerous international security apparatus." In his Foreword, Mr. Negroponte calls upon the Intelligence services to "support the spread of freedom, human rights, economic growth and financial stability and the rule of law. We must identify these opportunities for democratic transformation because autocratic and failed states are breeding grounds of international instability, violence and misery."

The emphasis on bolstering democracies in foreign countries is but a euphemism for subversion and regime change through methods outlined above. In the short space of a year, we have seen the introduction of a Grand Military Strategy,[21] a New Doctrine for Joint Nuclear Operations[22] and the National Intelligence Strategy of the United States. This is unprecedented and portends that the war cabal has in place all the elements for waging a global war in the decades to come.

This is the Empire's mindset. It is a real and pressing danger. We must study and prepare to defeat it. Failure means enslavement. We must also resist being brainwashed for war. We must seek the truth and thus be armed and prepared to resist and defeat the warmongers.

21 Propounded by Prof. Thomas Barnett.
22 By the Joint Chiefs of Staff.

Postscript

When writing this book I had some extraordinary experiences, many unexpected things happened and crucial information turned up just in time, and always for the better. From the short experience in writing my previous book, *Future FastForward,* and my speaking engagements soon after, I found that telling the truth is a lot harder than spreading lies. I am therefore not surprised that spin doctors are always so successful in brainwashing people. To disprove a lie, we must dig deep to uncover the story behind the lies and the players who invent those lies. It takes time, money for research and a lot of hard work, which your average Mr. Joe Blow is just not willing to do. If a story is prima facie credible, who is to say that it is propaganda? There is no urgency to examine and refute as his immediate interest is not affairs of the world, but the more mundane issues of bread and butter and the next paycheck.

But I have been blessed in more ways than one. There seems to be a guardian angel ever so willing to point to the right direction and the "chance" of coming across an invaluable piece of intelligence, time after time in my effort to expose the lies and propaganda.

For starters, when I chose the title for this book, some of my friends reeled back in horror, exclaiming, "No one believes in such things! For God's sake, change it. It is too controversial. You will never be taken seriously!"

The fact my friends reacted the way they did reflects how successfully the spin doctors have brainwashed the masses. The word "brainwashed" is indeed frightening. But truth must be confronted. Therefore it is very comforting that there are many establishment insiders who because of the impending danger of nuclear wars and the militarization of the American and British societies have broken ranks and spoken out. One such person is Paul Craig Roberts[1], and in an interview with Steve Watson and Alex Jones of the Infowars Network, on September 6, 2005, Roberts warned:

"Americans are being brainwashed!"

He even called for the impeachment of President Bush so as to prevent more young Americans getting killed in the illegal war in Iraq. So when an American of some standing does not hesitate to use terms such as "brainwashed" why are Malaysians so squeamish about such terms? I venture to guess that when we were under British rule, we were so brainwashed, that we no longer have critical minds. This legacy has since been handed down to our children now studying in our universities—taught by brainwashed lecturers. The refrain "Mother England, land of the free, how shall we extol thee?" seems to echo within the walls of the Ivory Towers! The historians are the worst. There are still a handful left, trained by the British intelligence to cover up the brainwashing and the truth. They have spawned a small network consisting of history and political science graduates, mainly females, to do the dirty work. Track them when they go for their annual pilgrimage to Britain for "refresher" courses and you will know what I mean. But I am getting ahead of myself.

Mr. Roberts has more to share with us, regarding the state of affairs in the United States. Commenting on the devastation wrought by Hurricane Katrina, he said that the Bush regime had used the opportunity to militarize the American society. He accuses the Bush regime of aggravating the crisis. and that the shoot-to-kill order was part of the overall operations in order to set an awful precedent and to aid the Military-Industrial Complex takeover of America. This is a very serious allegation and one cannot simply dismiss it, coming from an establishment figure. In short he is warning that America is turning into a fascist state. I quote:

> The power of the Federal Government is now greater than at any time, it'll never go back and the Posse Comitatus Act[2] has been eroding ever since it was passed in 1878.... Your worst enemy is always your government... never confuse Patriotism with support for the government. You can't let the military take over policing.

1   Paul Craig Roberts was the former Assistant Secretary of the Treasury in the Reagan Administration and has held a number of academic appointments.

2   This Act prevents the U.S. military from usurping the powers and responsibility of civilian authorities and the police in any disaster situation and/or civil commotion, thereby reducing the risk of a military coup in America.

Mr. Roberts went on to describe the prevailing mentality as that of "brown shirts that followed Hitler." Describing the Katrina fiasco as worse than 9/11, because it was announced days ahead of the event, and citing testimony of officials at the scene that there was hardly any response from the Federal authorities, he concluded that the government did nothing **on purpose** in order to provoke the resulting chaos and anarchy so that they could say "look how out of control everything is—we have to have limits on freedom and troops on the streets."

Sure enough on September 15, 2005, President Bush[3] declared that "It is now clear that a challenge on this scale requires greater federal authority and a broader role for the armed forces—the institution of our government most capable of massive logistical operations on a moment's notice." Senator John Warner (R-Va) went further by suggesting that the Posse Comitatus Act be weakened. The military was quick to take the cue and its spokesman, Lawrence Di Rita called the Posse Comitatus a "very archaic" law that hampers the military's ability to respond to a crisis.[4] This is utter rubbish as the Act is a safeguard against the use of the military in a policing role, which is one step away from establishing military rule.

In Britain, a similar trend toward a fascist state is discernible. Tony Blair's terror laws have been subjected to a damning critique by Amnesty International, calling them dangerous, ill-conceived and an assault on human rights.[5]

The terror laws were also criticized for being a blatant attack on the independence of the judiciary and the rule of law. The proposed law contains "sweeping and vague provisions that undermine the rights to freedom, expression and association, the right to liberty, the prohibition of arbitrary detention, the rights to the presumption of innocence and fair trial."

There is even an offense for the "glorification of terrorism" what-

---

3   Gene Healy, "Domestic Militarization: A Disaster in the Making." This article was first published in the Miami Herald, September 24, 2005. Mr. Healy is a senior editor at the Cato Institute and author of the Cato study "Deployed in the U.S.A.: The Creeping Militarization of the Home Front." Source: http://www.cato.org/pub_display.php? pub_id=5043

4   Ibid.

5   Ben Russell and Nigel Morris, "Amnesty International on Terror Laws," November 2, 2005, The Independent.

ever that means. Amnesty further condemned Blair's 12 points anti-terror plan as further assaults on human rights, particularly for those identified as Muslims, foreign nationals and asylum seekers. It said that government statements linking terrorist threat with foreigners were "encouraging xenophobia, racism and faith-hate crimes."

When law lords, a very conservative lot, are up in arms against such draconian laws, take it from me as a barrister of 30 years standing, they are sounding the alarm that the terror laws are a prelude to a fascist state being hoisted upon the British people. Lord Carlile of Berriew, the government's terror watchdog, warned that the 90 days detention without trial could be a breach of human rights law. Lord Steyn, one of the longest serving Law Lords in Britain's top court, the House of Lords, accused the Blair regime of whipping up public fear of terrorism and of being determined "to bend established international law to their will and to undermine its essential structures." He was forced to step down by Blair, from the court hearing a challenge to the legality of detention without trial for foreign terrorist suspects because of his views on human rights.

In a keynote address to a distinguished audience at the annual meeting of the British Institute of International and Comparative Law, including Lord Bingham (senior Law Lord), Lord Brown (another Law Lord), Judge Luzius Wildhaber, President of the European Court of Human Rights in Strasbourg, Sir Franklin Berman QC, former Legal Adviser to the Foreign Office and Elizabeth Wilmhurst, the former Deputy Foreign Office Legal Adviser who resigned over the Attorney-General's incredible advice that the invasion of Iraq was legal, Lord Steyn thundered:

> Nobody doubts in any way the very real risk of international terrorism. But the Belmarsh decision[6] came against the public fear whipped up by the governments of the United States and the United Kingdom since September 11, 2001 and their determination to bend established international law to their will and to undermine its essential structures.

Lord Steyn also noted that as far as he could ascertain, the Belmarsh case was the first in which a *government had sought, and managed, to change the composition of the panel of law lords* due

---

6   The decision of the House of Lords in 2004, by 8–1 ruled that detention without trial of foreign nationals in Belmarsh and Woodhill prisons and the Broadmoor high security hospital breached human rights laws.

to hear a particular case. The Attorney-General on instructions from Blair, demanded that Lord Steyn should recuse himself from the case on account of a lecture he gave in 2002, where he said, "In my view the suspension of article 5 of the European Convention on human rights—which prevents arbitrary detention—so that people can be locked up without trial when there is no evidence on which they could be prosecuted is not in the circumstances justified."

This fascist Attorney-General (Lord Goldsmith) who advised the Blair regime that it was legal to invade Iraq argued before the Judicial Committee of the House of Lords, that unelected judges had no democratic right or mandate, and should defer in the sphere of national security to politicians who had been elected by the people. Fortunately, Lord Bingham, giving the majority opinion resoundingly rebuked the arrogant and intellectually bankrupt Attorney-General by reminding the fascist lawyer that the "wholly democratic mandate" given to judges by parliament in the Human Rights Act, was sufficient to repudiate his ridiculous notion that the executive has absolute unfettered powers in matters of security.[7]

What we have seen in recent years in Britain is the gradual transformation of the Labour Party under the leadership of Tony Blair into a fascist organization. Make no mistake—Blair is a hardcore right wing fascist in the guise of a left wing Labourite.

More recently, on the BBC's Panorama,[8] two eminent former Law Lords took to task Blair's anti-terror laws and plans. Lord Steyn and Lord Lloyd of Berwick were both of the view that the new laws are unlawful and incompatible with the European Convention on Human Rights. Lord Steyn said:

> Experience shows that governments frequently ask for more powers than they need and when they get those powers they abuse them from time to time.

Lord Lloyd remarked, "It begins to look a little like internment. And it would certainly be seen that way by some of the ethnic minorities. Fancy being kept for three months without being charged. Being questioned notionally and not being charged. I think that is intolerable."[9]

7   The Guardian, June 11, 2005.
8   October 7, 2005 and as reported by the Press Association.
9   Ibid.

Tony Benn recently[10] described the British Parliament under the dictatorial glare of fascist Blair as the "British equivalent of the Green Zone in Baghdad: heavily fortified and patrolled by police with submachine guns, with bullet proof glass separating electors in the gallery from those who they elected. But the press gallery has no such glass barrier, for there sit the embedded correspondents, as in Iraq, who are briefed every morning in Downing Street and emerge to tell us what they have been told, repeating the process under Big Ben after their afternoon briefing."

What Tony Benn has to say about the current situation bears critical examination and I would like to quote him *in extenso*:

> What we are witnessing is nothing less than an erosion of parliamentary democracy and its substitution by a near dictatorship, as in the House of Lords forever being topped up by the Prime Minister's nominees—some of whom, we are told, have contributed to New Labour's campaign funds. Lloyd George must be laughing in his grave. A parliamentary chamber chosen by patronage may even be a model of democracy that George Bush and Blair would like to enforce in the Middle East.

> Even Blair's ministerial colleagues have been sidestepped— as they were when Rupert Murdoch demanded a referendum on the European constitution, something which Blair had rejected. However, he reversed his position, announcing it without even consulting the cabinet. It is almost as if democracy has been thrust aside in order to fight the war on terror and preserve our values—values that now include detaining people for months without trial.

> Walter Wolfgang, a refugee from Nazi Germany, was interrogated under the Terrorism Act after he was ejected from the Labor Party conference for heckling the Foreign Secretary. His name—and offense—will be recorded for ever on his identity card and on the security services' database, to which the American authorities have permanent access.

This is indeed a wake up call. The Zionist Anglo-American war cabal has fast forwarded its agenda and by their actions thus far, has indicated that they will brook no interference from anyone who stands in their way.

This dramatic turn of events has the markings of the Zionist modus operandi for the creation of a state of tension. Recall that

10 "It's No Good Blaming Blair," November 2, 2005, The Guardian.

soon after the London bombings on July 7, 2005, Efraim Halevi the former Mossad Chief called for a world war.[11] He wrote:

> We are in the throes of a world war, raging over the entire globe and characterized by the absence of lines of conflict and an easily identifiable enemy. There sometimes long pauses between one attack and another, consequently creating the wrong impression that the battle is all over or at least in the process of being won.
>
> We are in for the long haul and we must brace ourselves for more that will follow. The "Great Wars" of the 20th century lasted less than this war has already lasted and the end is nowhere in sight. The rules of combat must be rapidly adjusted to cater to the necessities of this new and unprecedented situation, and international law must be rewritten in such a way as to permit civilization to defend itself. Anything short of this invites disaster and must not be allowed to happen.

For those who still doubt that a world war has started, I would invite them to read the above passage again, coming from the former chief of the Israel's secret service, the Mossad. Given the above statement, we can safely say that the foreign policies of the United States have merged with those of Israel. I have in fact, as you may recall from the earlier chapters and in my previous book, asserted that Israel has hijacked the U.S. military to serve its interests in the Middle East to the consternation of my critics.

I have been vindicated in more ways than one when Reuters reported that Stephen Hadley[12] the National Security Adviser warned that a hasty withdrawal from Iraq would embolden extremists who seek the destruction of Israel. In remarks prepared for delivery to the annual American Israel Public Affairs Committee (AIPAC) summit, Mr. Hadley declared:

> If freedom prevails in Iraq, others in the region—including Syria and Iran—will be under great pressure to open up their repressive political systems. And that is good news for Israel. The spread of democracy will make the Middle East a safer neighborhood for Israel. An American retreat from Iraq, on the other hand, would only strengthen the terrorists who seek enslavement of Iraq and the eventual destruction of Israel.

11 "Rules of Conflict for a World War," The Jerusalem Post, July 7, 2005. He is now head of the Center for Strategic and Policy Studies at the Hebrew University in Jerusalem.

12 "Stephen Hadley says Iraq Pullout Bad for Israel," November 2, 2005, Reuters.

Another bone of contention I had with my critics is my contention that the Zionist Anglo-American Empire is in a meltdown and in the coming decades, we will witness the end of empire capitalism. I am delighted to say that an internationally renowned historian has come to my rescue on this issue in some sort of way, not that I needed it. The historian, Eric J. Hobsbawn in a lecture given at the Lowell Lecture Hall asserted that "the American Empire will almost certainly fail." The lecture was the second of the three "William E. Massey Lectures" sponsored by Harvard University's Program in the History of American Civilization. The theme for this year's lectures, chosen by Professor of History Sven Beckert is "American Empire in Global Perspective." The other lecturers were Jayati Ghosh from India and Carlos Monsivais from Mexico.

Mr. Hobsbawn challenged his audience to consider critically whether the "U.S. will learn the lesson of the British Empire or will it try to maintain an eroding global position by relying on a failing political force and a military force which is insufficient for the present purposes for which the current American government claims it is designed?" Although the historian did not provide an answer, we can safely say that the answer is embedded in the question itself.

But a more cogent and persuasive evaluation of the state of the empire was provided by Zbigniew Brzezinski in his recent article, *The American Debacle.* The same article entitled *George Bush's Suicidal Statecraft* appeared in the Tribune Media Services International.[13] Referring to the monumental work of the British historian Arnold Toynbee, *Study of History* wherein it was posited that the ultimate cause of imperial collapse was "suicidal statecraft," Brzezinski did not mince his words when he said that the adroit phrase applies appropriately to the policies pursued by the United States since 9/11.

The folly of the war against Iraq has turned out to be more costly in blood and money than anticipated and has aroused worldwide criticisms. Brzezinski was honest enough to admit that in the Middle East, the perception that the U.S. is the imperialistic successor to Britain and a partner of Israel in the military repression of the Arabs is widespread as well as in other parts of the Muslim world. Complicating this sorry foreign policy record are war related eco-

13 The former published in the Los Angeles Times, October 9, 2005 and the latter in Tribune Media Services International, October 13, 2005. Zbigniew Brzezinski was the National Security Adviser to President Jimmy Carter.

nomic trends. He pointed out that the budgets for the DoD and Homeland Security are now larger than the total budget of any nation, and they are likely to continue escalating as budget and trade deficits transform America into the world's No. 1 debtor nation.

In *Future FastForward,* I forecasted that the trend in the future would be away from globalization towards *regionalization.*[14] It is satisfying to know that he shares my concerns but for different reasons. He wrote:

> It should be a source of special concern for thoughtful Americans that even nations known for their traditional affection for America have become openly critical of U.S. policy. As a result, large swathes of the world—including nations in East Asia, Europe and Latin America—have been quietly exploring ways of shaping regional associations tied less to the notions of transpacific, or transatlantic, or hemispheric cooperation with the United States. Geopolitical alienation from America could become a lasting and menacing reality.

> In a very real sense, during the last four years the Bush team has dangerously undercut America's seemingly secure perch on top of the global totem pole by transforming a manageable, though serious, challenge largely of regional origin into an international debacle. Because America is extraordinarily powerful and rich, it can afford, for a while longer, a policy articulated with rhetorical excess and pursued with historical blindness. But in the process, America is likely to become isolated in a hostile world, increasingly vulnerable to terrorist acts and less and less able to exercise constructive global influence. Flailing away with a stick at a hornets' nest while loudly proclaiming "I will stay the course" is an exercise in catastrophic leadership.

To this painful self-criticism I say, Amen!

It is said that "empires are made of blood."[15] The cross which now symbolizes Christianity and its ideals of mercy and tolerance was for centuries the sign of power and of the most atrocious death the Roman Empire could devise—to be crucified on the cross, as was Jesus Christ. Lines of crosses holding thousands of people were erected on the sides of roads leading to Rome warning the foreign traveller and reassuring the Roman citizen of the pitiless power

14 See Chapter 21 for my discussion on this issue.
15 Francesco Sisci, "The American Empire," October 16, 2002, Asia Times.

of Rome. Rome was a cruel empire and it knew it so well that Cato, speaking of the many enemies of Rome, would say, "Let them hate us as long as they fear us."[16] But Rome eventually fell because Christians by the thousands died fearlessly. Painful death was not to be feared, and they embraced martyrdom willingly for the love of Jesus Christ.

The Bush-Blair fascist cabal has forgotten this lesson of the fall of the Roman Empire. The demonization of Islam is not unlike the demonization of Christianity by the Romans; and the rule by fear of atrocious death is no different from the present "Shock and Awe" campaigns and the brutal slaughter of the innocents by cluster bombs and depleted uranium munitions. But the oppressed fear not the painful death and soon this Zionist Anglo-American Empire will also collapse.

The trend is inescapable and inevitable, notwithstanding attempts by such historians as Neill Ferguson who in his recent book, *Colossus: The Price of America's Empire*,[17] called for a benevolent imperial rule—a "liberal empire." What a misnomer if ever there was one—since when has there ever been a "benevolent empire"? Mr. Ferguson has come out with a new spin. The term "empire" should only apply to the old empires. In the context of the present times, empire should be synonymous with "global leadership." Other historians, like Prof. William Hay, explain that America's hegemony was not one that she sought but rather a consequence of the decline of the British Empire and the need to fill the vacuum.[18]

Joseph S. Nye,[19] a former Assistant Secretary of Defense, critiques those who call the United States an empire as being confused, not able to distinguished between *primacy* and *imperial political power*. The basis of his argument is that the U.S. global political influence is different from that of the British who exercised *direct* political control.

The distinction, if any is artificial as the United States throughout the 20th century has never hesitated to use direct military inter-

16 Ibid.
17 Neill Ferguson, *Colossus: The Price of American Power*, (2004, Penguin)
18 Prof. William Anthony Hay, "An American Empire?," April 25, 2004, Washington Times.
19 Joseph Nye is also the Dean of Harvard's Kennedy School of Government and is the author of *The Paradox of American Power: Why the World's Only Superpower Can't Go It Alone*, (New Ed Edition, 2003, Oxford University Press) His views cited here are based on his article, "Is America an Empire?," January 2004, Project Syndicate.

vention, as in Korea, Vietnam, Panama, Grenada and through sub-versions and coups as in Latin America imposed her imperial dictates.

If the United States by mobilizing her entire military might to invade a third rate country for failing to toe her line is not exercising *direct* political control, what is? To intellectuals such as Joseph Nye, the word, "empire" is merely a metaphor! It is interesting how apologists for the Zionist Anglo-American Empire indulge in linguistic contortion exercises to camouflage their true intentions and expect to get away with it.

Two more issues that I need to address—firstly the threat of nuclear wars. In a recent seminar I gave a power-point presentation on the Joint Chiefs of Staff's Doctrine for Joint Nuclear Operations. The reaction was one of disbelief. The mindset seems to be that only rogue states would threaten other states with WMDs. The demonization of Muslim states has been so effective, that many have now equated extremism with Islam, and WMDs with rogue states. And this is notwithstanding that the only country that has unleashed atomic bombs and threatened to use them in future wars is the United States.

It is my hope that the recent petition by 470 physicists including seven Nobel Laureates to oppose the intention of the U.S. to use nuclear weapons against non-nuclear states will put to rest the debate as to who is the real terrorist and who has threatened to use nuclear weapons. The petition calls upon the U.S. to stop threatening non-nuclear weapon states and reminds the world that "humanity has gone more than half a century without using nuclear weapons, in large part because of the success of the Nuclear Non-Proliferation Treaty (NPT). The U.S. use of nuclear weapons against non-nuclear states will destroy the NPT and give strong incentive for other countries to develop and use nuclear weapons.

Those of us who are better informed owe a duty and responsibility to inform the rest of the impending danger. It is only by collective action that we can hope to defeat the warmongers and prevent further wars. The threat of nuclear war is a real and pressing danger. We must join hands with the American people as well as other peace loving people to oppose war and lay the groundwork for a lasting peace.

Secondly, there is an urgent need to bridge the Christian-Muslim divide. A giant step has already been taken by Christians in this regard. Since the publication of my previous book I have been calling for all Christians to continue the struggle by Pope John Paul II to oppose the Bush-Blair regimes and to reach out to the Muslims. It is indeed heartening to note that the bishops of the Church of England have for the first time as a body called upon Western Christians to apologize for the Iraq war as an "act of truth and reconciliation." This is an incredible initiative to build a bridge to link the divide between Muslims and Christians both of whom have been brainwashed to treat each other as enemies. We can and must prevent the "clash of civilizations" and foil the global agenda of the Zionist Anglo-American war cabal.

The Committee of Bishops, chaired by the Bishop of Oxford, Richard Harries also linked U.S. imperialism to the influence of U.S. evangelicals who seemingly pose the real threat to world peace. The report by the Bishop admonished America that "no country should see itself as the redeemer nation, singled out by God as part of his providential plan."[20]

We must build on this momentum and forge a solid world-wide network to oppose the current war agenda of the Bush-Blair regimes. In response to that call, the United Methodist Church Board of Church and Society—the social action committee that both President Bush and Vice-President Cheney belong to—resoundingly passed a resolution calling for the withdrawal of U.S. troops from Iraq with only two "no" votes and one abstention.[21]

The statement from the church read as follows:

> As people of faith, we raise our voice in protest against the tragedy of the unjust war in Iraq. Thousands of lives have been lost and hundreds of billions of dollars wasted in a war the United States initiated and should never have fought. We grieve for all those whose lives have been lost or destroyed in this needless and avoidable tragedy. Military families have suffered undue hardship from prolonged troop rotations in Iraq and loss of loved ones. It is time to bring them home.

> It is our hope and prayer that our statement against the war in Iraq will be heard loud and clear by our fellow United Methodists, President Bush and Vice-President Cheney.

20 Source: The Weekly Standard, October 13, 2005.
21 Source: The Nation, October, 2005.

To this I once again say, Amen!

Christians and Muslims—as well as other peace loving people—are demanding an end to the war.

President Bush, are you listening? Repent, and you may yet be redeemed!

Appendices

Political language… is designed to make lies sound truthful and murder respectable, and to give an appearance of solidity to pure wind.

— **George Orwell, *Shooting an Elephant***

Today the world is the victim of propaganda, because people are not intellectually competent.

— **William Mather Lewis**

And always we had wars, and more wars, and still other wars—all over Europe, all over the world. Sometimes in the private interest of royal families… sometimes to crush a weak nation; but never a war started by the aggressor for any clean purpose—there is no such war in the history of the race.

— **Mark Twain**

The de facto role of the U.S. armed forces will be to keep the world safe for our economy and open to our cultural assault.

— **Major Ralph Peters, U.S. Military**

It is the habit of every aggressor nation to claim that it is acting on the defensive.

— **Jawaharlal Nehru**

Mankind must put an end to war before war puts an end to mankind.

— **John F. Kennedy**

Appendix 1

George Kennan's Long Telegram

George Kennan, *charge d'affaires* at the U.S. Embassy in Moscow, drafted his "long telegram" in February 1946 in response to an urgent request by the U.S. State Department for clarification of Soviet conduct. This complete document is available for download from the George Washington University's web portal @ www.gwu.edu/~nsarchiv/coldwar/documents/episode-1/kennan.htm

861.00/2 - 2246: Telegram
The Charge in the Soviet Union to the Secretary of State
SECRET
Moscow, Feb 22, 1946—9 p.m. [Received Feb 22—3:52 p.m.]

511. Answer to Dept's 284, Feb 3 involves questions so intricate, so delicate, so strange to our form of thought, and so important to analysis of our international environment that I cannot compress answers into single brief message without yielding to what I feel would be dangerous degree of over-simplification. I hope, therefore, Dept will bear with me if I submit in answer to this question five parts, subjects of which will be roughly as follows:

(1) Basic features of post-war Soviet outlook.

(2) Background of this outlook

(3) Its projection in practical policy on official level.

(4) Its projection on unofficial level.

(5) Practical deductions from standpoint of U.S. policy.

I apologize in advance for this burdening of telegraphic channel; but questions involved are of such urgent importance, particularly in view of recent events, that our answers to them, if they deserve attention at all, seem to me to deserve it at once. There follows

Part 1: Basic Features of Post War Soviet Outlook, as Put Forward by Official Propaganda Machine

Are as Follows:

(a) USSR still lives in antagonistic "capitalist encirclement" with which in the long run there can be no permanent peaceful coexistence. As stated by Stalin in 1927 to a delegation of American workers:

"In course of further development of international revolution there will emerge two centers of world significance: a socialist center, drawing to itself the countries which tend toward socialism, and a capitalist center, drawing to itself the countries that incline toward capitalism. Battle between these two centers for command of world economy will decide fate of capitalism and of communism in entire world."

(b) Capitalist world is beset with internal conflicts, inherent in nature of capitalist society. These conflicts are insoluble by means of peaceful compromise. Greatest of them is that between England and U.S.

(c) Internal conflicts of capitalism inevitably generate wars. Wars thus generated may be of two kinds: intra-capitalist wars between two capitalist states, and wars of intervention against socialist world. Smart capitalists, vainly seeking escape from inner conflicts of capitalism, incline toward latter.

(d) Intervention against USSR, while it would be disastrous to those who undertook it, would cause renewed delay in progress of Soviet socialism and must therefore be forestalled at all costs.

(e) Conflicts between capitalist states, though likewise fraught with danger for USSR, nevertheless hold out great possibilities for advancement of socialist cause, particularly if USSR remains militarily powerful, ideologically monolithic and faithful to its present brilliant leadership.

(f) It must be borne in mind that capitalist world is not all bad. In addition to hopelessly reactionary and bourgeois elements, it includes (1) certain wholly enlightened and positive elements united in acceptable communistic parties and (2) certain other elements (now described for tactical reasons as progressive or democratic)

318

whose reactions, aspirations and activities happen to be "objective-ly" favorable to interests of USSR. These last must be encouraged and utilized for Soviet purposes.

(g) Among negative elements of bourgeois-capitalist society, most dangerous of all are those whom Lenin called false friends of the people, namely moderate-socialist or social-democratic leaders (in other words, non-Communist left-wing). These are more dangerous than out-and-out reactionaries, for the latter at least march under their true colors, whereas moderate left-wing leaders confuse people by employing devices of socialism to seine interests of reactionary capital.

So much for premises. To what deductions do they lead from standpoint of Soviet policy? To following:

(a) Everything must be done to advance relative strength of USSR as factor in international society. Conversely, no opportunity most be missed to reduce strength and influence, collectively as well as individually, of capitalist powers.

(b) Soviet efforts, and those of Russia's friends abroad, must be directed toward deepening and exploiting of differences and conflicts between capitalist powers. If these eventually deepen into an "imperialist" war, this war must be turned into revolutionary upheavals within the various capitalist countries.

(c) "Democratic-progressive" elements abroad are to be utilized to maximum to bring pressure to bear on capitalist governments along lines agreeable to Soviet interests.

(d) Relentless battle must be waged against socialist and social-democratic leaders abroad.

Part 2: Background of Outlook

Before examining ramifications of this party line in practice there are certain aspects of it to which I wish to draw attention.

First, it does not represent natural outlook of Russian people. Latter are, by and large, friendly to outside world, eager for experience of it, eager to measure against it talents they are conscious of possessing, eager above all to live in peace and enjoy fruits of their own labor. Party line only represents thesis which official propaganda machine puts forward with great skill and persistence to a public often remarkably resistant in the stronghold of its innermost thoughts. But party line is binding for outlook and conduct of people who make up apparatus of power—party, secret police and Government—and it is exclusively with these that we have to deal.

Second, please note that premises on which this party line is based are for most part simply not true. Experience has shown that peaceful and mutually profitable coexistence of capitalist and socialist states is entirely possible. Basic internal conflicts in advanced countries are no longer primarily those arising out of capitalist ownership of means of production, but are ones arising from advanced urbanism and industrialism as such, which Russia has thus far been spared not by socialism but only by her own backwardness. Internal rivalries of capitalism do not always generate wars; and not all wars are attributable to this cause. To speak of possibility of intervention against USSR today, after elimination of Germany and Japan and after example of recent war, is sheerest nonsense. If not provoked by forces of intolerance and subversion "capitalist" world of today is quite capable of living at peace with itself and with Russia. Finally, no sane person has reason to doubt sincerity of moderate socialist leaders in Western countries. Nor is it fair to deny success of their efforts to improve conditions for working population whenever, as in Scandinavia, they have been given chance to show what they could do.

Falseness of those premises, every one of which predates recent war, was amply demonstrated by that conflict itself Anglo-American differences did not turn out to be major differences of Western World. Capitalist countries, other than those of Axis, showed no disposition to solve their differences by joining in crusade against USSR. Instead of imperialist war turning into civil wars and revolution, USSR found itself obliged to fight side by side with capitalist powers for an avowed community of aim.

Nevertheless, all these theses, however baseless and disproven, are being boldly put forward again today. What does this indicate? It indicates that Soviet party line is not based on any objective analysis of situation beyond Russia's borders; that it has, indeed, little to do with conditions outside of Russia; that it arises mainly from basic inner-Russian necessities which existed before recent war and exist today.

At bottom of Kremlin's neurotic view of world affairs is traditional and instinctive Russian sense of insecurity. Originally, this was insecurity of a peaceful agricultural people trying to live on vast exposed plain in neighborhood of fierce nomadic peoples. To this was added, as Russia came into contact with economically advanced West, fear of more competent, more powerful, more highly organized societies in that area. But this latter type of insecurity was one which afflicted rather Russian rulers than Russian people; for Russian rulers have invariably sensed that their rule was relatively archaic in form fragile and artificial in its psychological foundation, unable to stand comparison or contact with political systems of Western countries. For this reason they have always feared foreign penetration, feared direct contact between Western world and their own, feared what would happen if Russians learned truth about world without or if foreigners learned truth about world within. And they have learned to seek security only in patient but deadly struggle for total destruction of rival power, never in compacts and compromises with it.

It was no coincidence that Marxism, which had smoldered ineffectively for half a century in Western Europe, caught hold and blazed for first time in Russia. Only in this land which had never known a friendly neighbor or indeed any tolerant equilibrium of separate powers, either internal or international, could a doctrine thrive which viewed economic conflicts of society as insoluble by peaceful means. After establishment of Bolshevist regime, Marxist dogma, rendered even more truculent and intolerant by Lenin's interpretation, became a perfect vehicle for sense of insecurity with which Bolsheviks, even more than previous Russian rulers, were afflicted. In this dogma, with its basic altruism of purpose, they found justification for their instinctive fear of outside world, for the dictatorship without which they did not know how to rule, for cruelties they did not dare not to inflict, for sacrifice they felt bound to demand. In the name of Marxism they sacrificed every single ethical value in their methods and tactics. Today they cannot dispense with it. It is fig leaf of their moral and intellectual respectability. Without it they would stand before history, at best, as only the last of that long succession of cruel and wasteful Russian rulers who have relentlessly forced country on to ever new heights of military power in order to guarantee external security of their internally weak regimes. This is why Soviet purposes most always be solemnly clothed in trappings of Marxism, and why no one should underrate importance of dogma in Soviet affairs. Thus Soviet leaders are driven [by?] necessities of their own past and present position to put forward which [apparent omission] outside world as evil, hostile and menacing, but as bearing within itself germs of creeping disease and destined to be wracked with growing internal convulsions until it is given final *Coup de grace* by rising power of socialism and yields to new and better world. This thesis provides justification for that increase of military and police power of Russian state, for that isolation of Russian population from outside world, and for that fluid and constant pressure to extend limits of Russian police power which are together the natural and instinctive urges of Russian rulers. Basically this is only the steady advance of uneasy Russian nationalism, a centuries old movement in which conceptions of offense and defense are inextricably confused. But in new guise of international Marxism, with its honeyed promises to a desperate and war torn outside world, it is more dangerous and insidious than ever before.

It should not be thought from above that Soviet party line is necessarily disingenuous and insincere on part of all those who put it forward. Many of them are too ignorant of outside world and mentally too dependent to question [. . .] self-hypnotism, and who have no difficulty making themselves believe what they find it comforting and convenient to believe. Finally we have the unsolved mystery as to who, if anyone, in this great land actually receives accurate and unbiased information about outside world. In atmosphere of oriental secretiveness and conspiracy which pervades this Government, possibilities for distorting or poisoning sources and currents of information are infinite. The very disrespect of Russians for objective truth—indeed, their disbelief in its existence—leads them to view all stated facts as instruments for furtherance of one ulterior purpose or another. There is good reason to suspect that this Government is actually a conspiracy within a conspiracy; and I for one am reluctant to believe that Stalin himself receives anything like an objective picture of outside world. Here there is ample scope for the type of subtle intrigue at which Russians are past masters. Inability of foreign governments to place their case squarely before Russian policy makers—extent to which they are delivered up in their relations with Russia to good graces of obscure and unknown advisors whom they never see and cannot influence—this to my mind is most disquieting feature of diplomacy in Moscow, and one which Western statesmen would do well to keep in mind if they would understand nature of difficulties encountered here.

Part 3: Projection of Soviet Outlook in Practical Policy on Official Level

We have now seen nature and background of Soviet program. What may we expect by way of its practical implementation?

Soviet policy, as Department implies in its query under reference, is conducted on two planes: (1) official plane represented by actions undertaken officially in name of Soviet Government; and (2) subterranean plane of actions undertaken by agencies for which Soviet Government does not admit responsibility.

Policy promulgated on both planes will be calculated to serve basic policies (a) to (d) outlined in part 1. Actions taken on different planes will differ considerably, but will dovetail into each other in purpose, timing and effect.

On official plane we must look for following:

(a) Internal policy devoted to increasing in every way strength and prestige of Soviet state: intensive military-industrialization; maximum development of armed forces; great displays to impress outsiders; continued secretiveness about internal matters, designed to conceal weaknesses and to keep opponents in dark.

(b) Wherever it is considered timely and promising, efforts will be made to advance official limits of Soviet power. For the moment, these efforts are restricted to certain neighboring points conceived of here as being of immediate strategic necessity, such as Northern Iran, Turkey, possibly Bornholm. However, other points may at any time come into question, if and as concealed Soviet political power is extended to new areas. Thus a "friendly Persian Government might be asked to grant Russia a port on Persian Gulf. Should Spain fall under Communist control, question of Soviet base at Gibraltar Strait might be activated. But such claims will appear on official level only when unofficial preparation is complete.

(c) Russians will participate officially in international organizations where they see opportunity of extending Soviet power or of inhibiting or diluting power of others. Moscow sees in UNO not the mechanism for a permanent and stable world society founded on mutual interest and aims of all nations, but an arena in which aims just mentioned can be favorably pursued. As long as UNO is considered here to serve this purpose, Soviets will remain with it. But if at any time they come to conclusion that it is serving to embarrass or frustrate their aims for power expansion and if they see better prospects for pursuit of these aims along other lines, they will not hesitate to abandon UNO. This would imply, however, that they felt themselves strong enough to split unity of other nations by their withdrawal to render UNO ineffective as a threat to their aims or security, replace it with an international weapon more effective from their viewpoint. Thus Soviet attitude toward UNO will depend largely on loyalty of other nations to it, and on degree of vigor, decisiveness and cohesion with which those nations defend in UNO the peaceful and hopeful concept of international life, which that organization represents to our way of thinking. I reiterate, Moscow has no abstract devotion to UNO ideals. Its attitude to that organization will remain essentially pragmatic and tactical.

(d) Toward colonial areas and backward or dependent peoples, Soviet policy, even on official plane, will be directed toward weakening of power and influence and contacts of advanced Western nations, on theory that in so far as this policy is successful, there will be created a vacuum which will favor Communist-Soviet penetration. Soviet pressure for participation in trusteeship arrangements thus represents, in my opinion, a desire to be in a position to complicate and inhibit exertion of Western influence at such points rather than to provide major channel for exerting of Soviet power. Latter motive is not lacking, but for this Soviets prefer to rely on other channels than official trusteeship arrangements. Thus we may expect to find Soviets asking for admission everywhere to trusteeship or similar arrangements and using levers thus acquired to weaken Western influence among such peoples.

(e) Russians will strive energetically to develop Soviet representation in, and official ties with, countries in which they sense strong possibilities of opposition to Western centers of power. This applies to such widely separated points as Germany, Argentina, Middle Eastern countries, etc.

(f) In international economic matters, Soviet policy will really be dominated by pursuit of autarchy for Soviet Union and Soviet-dominated adjacent areas taken together. That, however, will be underlying policy. As far as official line is concerned, position is not yet clear. Soviet Government has shown strange reticence since termination hostilities on subject foreign trade. If large scale long term credits should be forthcoming, I believe Soviet Government may eventually again do lip service, as it did in 1930's to desirability of building up international economic exchanges in general. Otherwise I think it possible Soviet foreign trade may be restricted largely to Soviet's own security sphere, including occupied areas in Germany, and that a cold official shoulder may be turned to principle of general economic collaboration among nations.

(g) With respect to cultural collaboration, lip service will likewise be rendered to desirability of deepening cultural contacts between peoples, but this will not in practice be interpreted in any way which could weaken security position of Soviet peoples. Actual manifestations of Soviet policy in this respect will be restricted to arid channels of closely shepherded official visits and functions, with superabundance of vodka and speeches and dearth of permanent effects.

(h) Beyond this, Soviet official relations will take what might be called "correct" course with individual foreign governments, with great stress being laid on prestige of Soviet Union and its representatives and with punctilious attention to protocol as distinct from good manners.

Part 4: Following May Be Said as to What We May Expect by Way of Implementation of Basic Soviet Policies on Unofficial, or Subterranean Plane, i.e. on Plane for Which Soviet Government Accepts no Responsibility

Agencies utilized for promulgation of policies on this plane are following:

1.   Inner central core of Communist Parties in other countries. While many of persons who compose this category may also appear and act in unrelated public capacities, they are in reality working closely together as an underground operating directorate of world communism, a concealed Comintern tightly coordinated and directed by Moscow. It is important to remember that this inner core is actually working on underground lines, despite legality of parties with which it is associated.

2.   Rank and file of Communist Parties. Note distinction is drawn between those and persons defined in paragraph 1. This distinction has become much sharper in recent years. Whereas formerly foreign Communist Parties represented a curious (and from Moscow's standpoint often inconvenient) mixture of conspiracy and legitimate activity, now the conspiratorial element has been neatly concentrated in inner circle and ordered underground, while rank and file—no longer even

taken into confidence about realities of movement—are thrust forward as bona fide internal partisans of certain political tendencies within their respective countries, genuinely innocent of conspiratorial connection with foreign states. Only in certain countries where communists are numerically strong do they now regularly appear and act as a body. As a rule they are used to penetrate, and to influence or dominate, as case may be, other organizations less likely to be suspected of being tools of Soviet Government, with a view to accomplishing their purposes through [apparent omission] organizations, rather than by direct action as a separate political party.

3.   A wide variety of national associations or bodies which can be dominated or influenced by such penetration. These include: labor unions, youth leagues, women's organizations, racial societies, religious societies, social organizations, cultural groups, liberal magazines, publishing houses, etc.

4.   International organizations which can be similarly penetrated through influence over various national components. Labor, youth and women's organizations are prominent among them. Particular, almost vital importance is attached in this connection to international labor movement. In this, Moscow sees possibility of sidetracking western governments in world affairs and building up international lobby capable of compelling governments to take actions favorable to Soviet interests in various countries and of paralyzing actions disagreeable to USSR

5.   Russian Orthodox Church, with its foreign branches, and through it the Eastern Orthodox Church in general.

6.   Pan-Slav movement and other movements (Azerbaijan, Armenian, Turcoman, etc.) based on racial groups within Soviet Union.

7.   Governments or governing groups willing to lend themselves to Soviet purposes in one degree or another, such as present Bulgarian and Yugoslav Governments, North Persian regime, Chinese Communists, etc. Not only propaganda machines but actual policies of these regimes can be placed extensively at disposal of USSR.

It may be expected that component parts of this far-flung apparatus will be utilized in accordance with their individual suitability, as follows:

(a) To undermine general political and strategic potential of major western powers. Efforts will be made in such countries to disrupt national self confidence, to hamstring measures of national defense, to increase social and industrial unrest, to stimulate all forms of disunity. All persons with grievances, whether economic or racial, will be urged to spelt (sic) redress not in mediation and compromise, but in defiant violent struggle for destruction of other elements of society. Here poor will be set against rich, black against white, young against old, newcomers against established residents, etc.

(b) On unofficial plane particularly violent efforts will be made to weaken power and influence of Western Powers of [on] colonial backward, or dependent peoples. On this level, no holds will be barred. Mistakes and weaknesses of western colonial administration will be mercilessly exposed and exploited. Liberal opinion in Western countries will be mobilized to weaken colonial policies. Resentment among dependent peoples will be stimulated. And while latter are being encouraged to seek independence of Western Powers, Soviet dominated puppet political machines will be undergoing preparation to take over domestic power in respective colonial areas when independence is achieved.

(c) Where individual governments stand in path of Soviet purposes pressure will be brought for their removal from office. This can happen where governments directly oppose Soviet foreign policy aims (Turkey, Iran), where they seal their territories off against Communist penetration (Switzerland, Portugal), or where they compete too strongly, like Labor Government in England, for moral domination among elements which it is important for Communists to dominate. (Sometimes, two of these elements are present in a single case. Then Communist opposition becomes particularly shrill and savage.

(d) In foreign countries Communists will, as a rule, work toward destruction of all forms of personal independence, economic, political or moral. Their system can handle only individuals who have been brought into complete dependence on higher power. Thus, persons who are financially independent—such as individual businessmen, estate owners, successful farmers, artisans and all those who exercise local leadership or have local prestige, such as popular local clergymen or political figures, are anathema. It is not by chance that even in USSR local officials are kept constantly on move from one job to another, to prevent their taking root.

(e) Everything possible will be done to set major Western Powers against each other. Anti-British talk will be plugged among Americans, anti-American talk among British. Continentals, including Germans, will be taught to abhor both Anglo-Saxon powers. Where suspicions exist, they will be fanned; where not, ignited. No effort will be spared to discredit and combat all efforts which threaten to lead to any sort of unity or cohesion among other [apparent omission] from which Russia might be excluded. Thus, all forms of international organization not amenable to Communist penetration and control, whether it be the Catholic [Church] international economic concerns, or the international fraternity of royalty and aristocracy, must expect to find themselves under fire from many, and often [apparent omission].

(f)   In general, all Soviet efforts on unofficial international plane will be negative and destructive in character, designed to tear down sources of strength beyond reach of Soviet control. This is only in line with basic Soviet instinct that there can be no compromise with rival power and that constructive work can start only when Communist power is doming. But behind all this will be applied insistent, unceasing pressure for penetration and command of key positions in administration and especially in police apparatus of foreign countries. The Soviet regime is a police regime par excellence, reared in the dim half world of Tsarist police intrigue, accustomed to think primarily in terms of police power. This should never be lost sight of in gauging Soviet motives.

Part 5:   [Practical Deductions From Standpoint of U.S. Policy]

In summary, we have here a political force committed fanatically to the belief that with U.S. there can be no permanent *modus vivendi* that it is desirable and necessary that the internal harmony of our society be disrupted, our traditional way of life be destroyed, the international authority of our state be broken, if Soviet power is to be secure. This political force has complete power of disposition over energies of one of world's greatest peoples and resources of world's richest national territory, and is borne along by deep and powerful currents of Russian nationalism. In addition, it has an elaborate and far flung apparatus for exertion of its influence in other countries, an apparatus of amazing flexibility and versatility, managed by people whose experience and skill in underground methods are presumably without parallel in history. Finally, it is seemingly inaccessible to considerations of reality in its basic reactions. For it, the vast fund of objective fact about human society is not, as with us, the measure against which outlook is constantly being tested and re-formed, but a grab bag from which individual items are selected arbitrarily and tendenciously to bolster an outlook already preconceived. This is admittedly not a pleasant picture. Problem of how to cope with this force in [is] undoubtedly greatest task our diplomacy has ever faced and probably greatest it will ever have to face. It should be point of departure from which our political general staff work at present juncture should proceed. It should be approached with same thoroughness and care as solution of major strategic problem in war, and if necessary, with no smaller outlay in planning effort. I cannot attempt to suggest all answers here. But I would like to record my conviction that problem is within our power to solve—and that without recourse to any general military conflict. And in support of this conviction there are certain observations of a more encouraging nature I should like to make:

(1) Soviet power, unlike that of Hitlerite Germany, is neither schematic nor adventuristic. It does not work by fixed plans. It does not take unnecessary risks. Impervious to logic of reason, and it is highly sensitive to logic of force. For this reason it can easily withdraw—and usually does when strong resistance is encountered at any point. Thus, if the adversary has sufficient force and makes clear his readiness to use it, he rarely has to do so. If situations are properly handled there need be no prestige-engaging showdowns.

(2) Gauged against Western World as a whole, Soviets are still by far the weaker force. Thus, their success will really depend on degree of cohesion, firmness and vigor which Western World can muster. And this is factor which it is within our power to influence.

(3) Success of Soviet system, as form of internal power, is not yet finally proven. It has yet to be demonstrated that it can survive supreme test of successive transfer of power from one individual or group to another. Lenin's death was first such transfer, and its effects wracked Soviet state for 15 years. After Stalin's death or retirement will be second. But even this will not be final test. Soviet internal system will now be subjected, by virtue of recent territorial expansions, to series of additional strains which once proved severe tax on Tsardom. We here are convinced that never since termination of civil war have mass of Russian people been emotionally farther removed from doctrines of Communist Party than they are today. In Russia, party has now become a great and—for the moment—highly suc-

cessful apparatus of dictatorial administration, but it has ceased to be a source of emotional inspiration. Thus, internal soundness and permanence of movement need not yet be regarded as assured.

(4) All Soviet propaganda beyond Soviet security sphere is basically negative and destructive. It should therefore be relatively easy to combat it by any intelligent and really constructive program.

For those reasons I think we may approach calmly and with good heart problem of how to deal with Russia. As to how this approach should be made, I only wish to advance, by way of conclusion, following comments:

(1) Our first step must be to apprehend, and recognize for what it is, the nature of the movement with which we are dealing. We must study it with same courage, detachment, objectivity, and same determination not to be emotionally provoked or unseated by it, with which doctor studies unruly and unreasonable individual.

(2) We must see that our public is educated to realities of Russian situation. I cannot over-emphasize importance of this. Press cannot do this alone. It must be done mainly by Government, which is necessarily more experienced and better informed on practical problems involved. In this we need not be deterred by [ugliness?] of picture. I am convinced that there would be far less hysterical anti-Sovietism in our country today if realities of this situation were better understood by our people. There is nothing as dangerous or as terrifying as the unknown. It may also be argued that to reveal more information on our difficulties with Russia would reflect unfavorably on Russian-American relations. I feel that if there is any real risk here involved, it is one which we should have courage to face, and sooner the better. But I cannot see what we would be risking. Our stake in this country, even coming on heels of tremendous demonstrations of our friendship for Russian people, is remarkably small. We have here no investments to guard, no actual trade to lose, virtually no citizens to protect, few cultural contacts to preserve. Our only stake lies in what we hope rather than what we have; and I am convinced we have better chance of realizing those hopes if our public is enlightened and if our dealings with Russians are placed entirely on realistic and matter-of-fact basis.

(3) Much depends on health and vigor of our own society. World communism is like malignant parasite which feeds only on diseased tissue. This is point at which domestic and foreign policies meet.

Every courageous and incisive measure to solve internal problems of our own society, to improve self-confidence, discipline, morale and community spirit of our own people, is a diplomatic victory over Moscow worth a thousand diplomatic notes and joint communiqués. If we cannot abandon fatalism and indifference in face of deficiencies of our own society, Moscow will profit—Moscow cannot help profiting by them in its foreign policies.

(4) We must formulate and put forward for other nations a much more positive and constructive picture of sort of world we would like to see than we have put forward in past. It is not enough to urge people to develop political processes similar to our own. Many foreign peoples, in Europe at least, are tired and frightened by experiences of past, and are less interested in abstract freedom than in security. They are seeking guidance rather than responsibilities. We should be better able than Russians to give them this. And unless we do, Russians certainly will.

(5) Finally we must have courage and self-confidence to cling to our own methods and conceptions of human society. After all, the greatest danger that can befall us in coping with this problem of Soviet communism, is that we shall allow ourselves to become like those with whom we are coping.

KENNAN

800.00B International Red Day/2 - 2546: Airgram

Appendix 2

The Sources of Soviet Conduct
by X (George Kennan)

"The Sources of Soviet Conduct" was published in *Foreign Affairs* in 1947 and was widely circulated upon publication, Although the article was signed by "X," everyone in the know knew that authorship was Kennan's. This complete document is available for download @ www.historyguide.org/europe/kennan.html

Part I

The political personality of Soviet power as we know it today is the product of ideology and circumstances: ideology inherited by the present Soviet leaders from the movement in which they had their political origin, and circumstances of the power which they now have exercised for nearly three decades in Russia. There can be few tasks of psychological analysis more difficult than to try to trace the interaction of these two forces and the relative role of each in the determination of official Soviet conduct, yet the attempt must be made if that conduct is to be understood and effectively countered.

It is difficult to summarize the set of ideological concepts with which the Soviet leaders came into power. Marxian ideology, in its Russian-Communist projection, has always been in process of subtle evolution. The materials on which it bases itself are extensive and complex. But the outstanding features of Communist thought as it existed in 1916 may perhaps be summarized as follows: (a) that the central factor in the life of man, the factor which determines the character of public life and the "physiognomy of society," is the system by which material goods are produced and exchanged; (b) that the capitalist system of production is a nefarious one which inevitably leads to the exploitation of the working class by the capital-owning class and is incapable of developing adequately the economic resources of society or of distributing fairly the material goods produced by human labor; (c) that capitalism contains the seeds of its own destruction and must, in view of the inability of the capital-owning class to adjust itself to economic change, result eventually and inescapably in a revolutionary transfer of power to the working class; and (d) that imperialism, the final phase of capitalism, leads directly to war and revolution.

The rest may be outlined in Lenin's own words: "Unevenness of economic and political development is the inflexible law of capitalism. It follows from this that the victory of Socialism may come originally in a few capitalist countries or even in a single capitalist country. The victorious proletariat of that country, having expropriated the capitalists and having organized Socialist production at home, would rise against the remaining capitalist world, drawing to itself in the process the oppressed classes of other countries." It must be noted that there was no assumption that capitalism would perish without proletarian revolution. A final push was needed from a revolutionary proletariat movement in order to tip over the tottering structure. But it was regarded as inevitable that sooner or later that push be given.

For 50 years prior to the outbreak of the Revolution, this pattern of thought had exercised great fascination for the members of the Russian revolutionary movement. Frustrated, discontented, hopeless of finding self-expression—or too impatient to seek it—in the confining limits of the Tsarist political system, yet lacking wide popular support or their choice of bloody revolution as a means of social betterment, these revolutionists found in Marxist theory a highly convenient rationalization for their own instinctive desires. It afforded pseudo-scientific justification for their impatience, for their categoric denial of all value in the Tsarist system, for their yearning for power and revenge and for their inclination to cut corners in the pursuit of it. It is therefore no wonder that they had come to believe implicitly in the truth and soundness of the Marxist-Leninist teachings, so congenial to their own impulses and emotions. Their sincerity need not be impugned. This is a phenomenon as old as human nature itself. It has never been more aptly described than by Edward Gibbon, who wrote in *The Decline and Fall of the Roman Empire*: "From enthusiasm to imposture the step is perilous and slippery; the demon of Socrates affords a memorable instance of how a wise man may deceive himself, how a good man may deceive others, how the conscience may slumber in a mixed and middle state between self-illusion and voluntary fraud." And it was with this set of conceptions that the members of the Bolshevik Party entered into power.

Now it must be noted that through all the years of preparation for revolution, the attention of these men, as indeed of Marx himself, had been centered less on the future form which Socialism would take than on the necessary overthrow of rival power which, in their view, had to precede the introduction of Socialism. Their views, therefore, on the positive program to be put into effect, once power was attained, were for the most part nebulous, visionary and impractical, beyond the nationalization of industry and the expropriation of large private capital holdings there was no agreed program. The treatment of the peasantry, which, according to the Marxist formulation was not of the proletariat, had always been a vague spot in the pattern of Communist thought: and it remained an object of controversy and vacillation for the first ten years of Communist power.

The circumstances of the immediate post-revolution period—the existence in Russia of civil war and foreign intervention, together with the obvious fact that the Communists represented only a tiny minority of the Russian people—made the establishment of dictatorial power a necessity. The experiment with "war Communism" and the abrupt attempt to eliminate private production and trade had unfortunate economic consequences and caused further bitterness against the new revolutionary regime. While the temporary relaxation of the effort to communize Russia, represented by the New Economic Policy, alleviated some of this economic distress and thereby served its purpose, it also made it evident that the "capitalistic sector of society" was still prepared to profit at once from any relaxation of governmental pressure, and would, if permitted to continue to exist, always constitute a powerful opposing element to the Soviet regime and a serious rival for influence in the country. Somewhat the same situation prevailed with respect to the individual peasant who, in his own small way, was also a private producer.

Lenin, had he lived, might have proved a great enough man to reconcile these conflicting forces to the ultimate benefit of Russian society, though this is questionable. But be that as it may, Stalin, and those whom he led in the struggle for succession to Lenin's position of leadership, were not the men to tolerate rival political forces in the sphere of power which they coveted. Their sense of insecurity was too great. Their particular brand of fanaticism, unmodified by any of the Anglo-Saxon traditions of compromise, was too fierce and too jealous to envisage any permanent sharing of power. From the Russian-Asiatic world out of which they had emerged they carried with them a skepticism as to the possibilities of permanent and peaceful coexistence of rival forces. Easily persuaded of their own doctrinaire "rightness," they insisted on the submission or destruction of all competing power. Outside the Communist Party, Russian society was to have no rigidity. There were to be no forms of collective human activity or association which would not be dominated by the Party. No other force in Russian society was to be permitted to achieve vitality or integrity. Only the Party was to have structure. All else was to be an amorphous mass.

And within the Party the same principle was to apply. The mass of Party members might go through the motions of election, deliberation, decision and action; but in these motions they were to be animated not by their own individual wills but by the awesome breath of the Party leadership and the overbrooding presence of "the word."

Let it be stressed again that subjectively these men probably did not seek absolutism for its own sake. They doubtless believed—and found it easy to believe—that they alone knew what was good for society and that they would accomplish that good once their power was secure and unchallengeable. But in seeking that security of their own rule they were prepared to recognize no restrictions, either of God or man, on the character of their methods. And until such time as that security might be achieved, they placed far down on their scale of operational priorities the comforts and happiness of the peoples entrusted to their care.

Now the outstanding circumstance concerning the Soviet regime is that down to the present day this process of political consolidation has never been completed and the men in the Kremlin have continued to be predominantly absorbed with the struggle to secure and make absolute the power which they seized in November 1917. They have endeavored to secure it primarily against forces at home, within Soviet society itself. But they have also endeavored to secure it against the outside world. For ideology, as we have seen, taught them that the outside world was hostile and that it was their duty eventually to overthrow the political forces beyond their borders. Then powerful hands of Russian history and tradition reached up to sustain them in this feeling. Finally, their own aggressive intransigence with respect to the outside world began to find its own reaction; and they were soon

335

forced, to use another Gibbonesque phrase, "to chastise the contumacy" which they themselves had provoked. It is an undeniable privilege of every man to prove himself right in the thesis that the world is his enemy; for if he reiterates it frequently enough and makes it the background of his conduct he is bound eventually to be right.

Now it lies in the nature of the mental world of the Soviet leaders, as well as in the character of their ideology, that no opposition to them can be officially recognized as having any merit or justification whatsoever. Such opposition can flow, in theory, only from the hostile and incorrigible forces of dying capitalism. As long as remnants of capitalism were officially recognized as existing in Russia, it was possible to place on them, as an internal element, part of the blame for the maintenance of a dictatorial form of society. But as these remnants were liquidated, little by little, this justification fell away, and when it was indicated officially that they had been finally destroyed, it disappeared altogether. And this fact created one of the most basic of the compulsions which came to act upon the Soviet regime: since capitalism no longer existed in Russia and since it could not be admitted that there could be serious or widespread opposition to the Kremlin springing spontaneously from the liberated masses under its authority, it became necessary to justify the retention of the dictatorship by stressing the menace of capitalism abroad.

This began at an early date. In 1924 Stalin specifically defended the retention of the "organs of suppression," meaning, among others, the army and the secret police, on the ground that "as long as there is a capitalistic encirclement there will be danger of intervention with all the consequences that flow from that danger." In accordance with that theory, and from that time on, all internal opposition forces in Russia have consistently been portrayed as the agents of foreign forces of reaction antagonistic to Soviet power.

By the same token, tremendous emphasis has been placed on the original Communist thesis of a basic antagonism between the capitalist and Socialist worlds. It is clear, from many indications, that this emphasis is not founded in reality. The real facts concerning it have been confused by the existence abroad of genuine resentment provoked by Soviet philosophy and tactics and occasionally by the existence of great centers of military power, notably the Nazi regime in Germany and the Japanese Government of the late 1930s, which indeed have aggressive designs against the Soviet Union. But there is ample evidence that the stress laid in Moscow on the menace confronting Soviet society from the world outside its borders is founded not in the realities of foreign antagonism but in the necessity of explaining away the maintenance of dictatorial authority at home.

Now the maintenance of this pattern of Soviet power, namely, the pursuit of unlimited authority domestically, accompanied by the cultivation of the semi-myth of implacable foreign hostility, has gone far to shape the actual machinery of Soviet power as we know it today. Internal organs of administration which did not serve this purpose withered on the vine. Organs which did serve this purpose became vastly swollen. The security of Soviet power came to rest on the iron discipline of the Party, on the severity and ubiquity of the secret police, and on the uncompromising economic monopolism of the state. The "organs of suppression," in which the Soviet leaders had sought security from rival forces, became in large measure the masters of those whom they were designed to serve. Today the major part of the structure of Soviet power is committed to the perfection of the dictatorship and to the maintenance of the concept of Russia as in a state of siege, with the enemy lowering beyond the walls. And the millions of human beings who form that part of the structure of power must defend at all costs this concept of Russia's position, for without it they are themselves superfluous.

As things stand today, the rulers can no longer dream of parting with these organs of suppression. The quest for absolute power, pursued now for nearly three decades with a ruthlessness unparalleled (in scope at least) in modern times, has again produced internally, as it did externally, its own reaction. The excesses of the police apparatus have fanned the potential opposition to the regime into something far greater and more dangerous than it could have been before those excesses began.

But least of all can the rulers dispense with the fiction by which the maintenance of dictatorial power has been defended. For this fiction has been canonized in Soviet philosophy by the excesses already committed in its name; and it is now anchored in the Soviet structure of thought by bonds far greater than those of mere ideology.

Part II

So much for the historical background. What does it spell in terms of the political personality of Soviet power as we know it today?

Of the original ideology, nothing has been officially junked. Belief is maintained in the basic badness of capitalism, in the inevitability of its destruction, in the obligation of the proletariat to assist in that destruction and to take power into its own hands. But stress has come to be laid primarily on those concepts which relate most specifically to the Soviet regime itself: to its position as the sole truly Socialist regime in a dark and misguided world, and to the relationships of power within it.

The first of these concepts is that of the innate antagonism between Capitalism and Socialism. We have seen how deeply that concept has become embedded in foundations of Soviet power. It has profound implications for Russia's conduct as a member of international society. It means that there can never be on Moscow's side a sincere assumption of a community of aims between the Soviet Union and powers which are regarded as capitalist. It must inevitably be assumed in Moscow that the aims of the capitalist world are antagonistic to the Soviet regime, and therefore to the interests of the peoples it controls. If the Soviet government occasionally sets its signature to documents which would indicate the contrary, this is to be regarded as a tactical maneuver permissible in dealing with the enemy (who is without honor) and should be taken in the spirit of *caveat emptor*. Basically, the antagonism remains. It is postulated. And from it flow many of the phenomena which we find disturbing in the Kremlin's conduct of foreign policy: the secretiveness, the lack of frankness, the duplicity, the wary suspiciousness, and the basic unfriendliness of purpose. These phenomena are there to stay, for the foreseeable future. There can be variations of degree and of emphasis. When there is something the Russians want from us, one or the other of these features of their policy may be thrust temporarily into the background; and when that happens there will always be Americans who will leap forward with gleeful announcements that "the Russians have changed," and some who will even try to take credit for having brought about such "changes." But we should not be misled by tactical maneuvers. These characteristics of Soviet policy, like the postulate from which they flow, are basic to the internal nature of Soviet power, and will be with us, whether in the foreground or the background, until the internal nature of Soviet power is changed.

This means we are going to continue for long time to find the Russians difficult to deal with. It does not mean that they should be considered as embarked upon a do-or-die program to overthrow our society by a given date. The theory of the inevitability of the eventual fall of capitalism has the fortunate connotation that there is no hurry about it. The forces of progress can take their time in preparing the final *coup de grâce*. meanwhile, what is vital is that the "Socialist fatherland"—that oasis of power which has already been won for Socialism in the person of the Soviet Union—should be cherished and defended by all good Communists at home and abroad, its fortunes promoted, its enemies badgered and confounded. The promotion of premature, "adventuristic" revolutionary projects abroad which might embarrass Soviet power in any way would be an inexcusable, even a counter-revolutionary act. The cause of Socialism is the support and promotion of Soviet power, as defined in Moscow.

This brings us to the second of the concepts important to contemporary Soviet outlook. That is the infallibility of the Kremlin. The Soviet concept of power, which permits no focal points of organization outside the Party itself, requires that the Party leadership remain in theory the sole repository of truth. For if truth were to be found elsewhere, there would be justification for its expression in organized activity. But it is precisely that which the Kremlin cannot and will not permit.

The leadership of the Communist Party is therefore always right, and has been always right ever since in 1929 Stalin formalized his personal power by announcing that decisions of the Politburo were being taken unanimously.

On the principle of infallibility there rests the iron discipline of the Communist Party. In fact, the two concepts are mutually self-supporting. Perfect discipline requires recognition of infallibility. Infallibility requires the observance of discipline. And the two go far to determine the behaviorism of the entire Soviet apparatus of power. But their effect cannot be understood unless a third factor be taken into account: namely, the fact that the leadership is at liberty to put forward for tactical purposes any particular thesis which it finds useful to the cause at any particular moment and to require the faithful and unquestioning acceptance of that thesis by the members of the movement as a whole. This means that truth is not a constant but is actually created, for all intents and purposes, by the Soviet leaders themselves. It may vary from week to week, from month to month. It is nothing absolute and immutable—nothing which flows from objective reality. It is only the most recent manifestation of the wisdom of those in whom the ultimate wisdom is supposed to reside, because they represent the logic of history. The accumulative effect of these factors is to give to the whole subordinate apparatus of Soviet power an unshakable stubbornness and steadfastness in its orientation. This orientation can be changed at will by the Kremlin but by no other power. Once a given party line has been laid down on a given issue of current policy, the whole Soviet governmental machine, including the mechanism of diplomacy, moves inexorably along the prescribed path, like a persistent toy automobile wound up and headed in a given direction, stopping only when it meets with some unanswerable force. The individuals who are the components of this machine are unamenable to argument or reason, which comes to them from outside sources. Their whole training has taught them to mistrust and discount the glib persuasiveness of the outside world. Like the white dog before the phonograph, they hear only the "master's voice." And if they are to be called off from the purposes last dictated to them, it is the master who must call them off. Thus the foreign representative cannot hope that his words will make any impression on them. The most that he can hope is that they will be transmitted to those at the top, who are capable of changing the party line. But even those are not likely to be swayed by any normal logic in the words of the bourgeois representative. Since there can be no appeal to common purposes, there can be no appeal to common mental approaches. For this reason, facts speak louder than words to the ears of the Kremlin; and words carry the greatest weight when they have the ring of reflecting, or being backed up by, facts of unchallengeable validity.

But we have seen that the Kremlin is under no ideological compulsion to accomplish its purposes in a hurry. Like the Church, it is dealing in ideological concepts which are of long-term validity, and it can afford to be patient. It has no right to risk the existing achievements of the revolution for the sake of vain baubles of the future. The very teachings of Lenin himself require great caution and flexibility in the pursuit of Communist purposes. Again, these precepts are fortified by the lessons of Russian history: of centuries of obscure battles between nomadic forces over the stretches of a vast unfortified plain. Here caution, circumspection, flexibility and deception are the valuable qualities; and their value finds a natural appreciation in the Russian or the oriental mind. Thus the Kremlin has no compunction about retreating in the face of superior forces. And being under the compulsion of no timetable, it does not get panicky under the necessity for such retreat. Its political action is a fluid stream which moves constantly, wherever it is permitted to move, toward a given goal. Its main concern is to make sure that it has filled every nook and cranny available to it in the basin of world power. But if it finds unassailable barriers in its path, it accepts these philosophically and accommodates itself to them. The main thing is that there should always be pressure, unceasing constant pressure, toward the desired goal. There is no trace of any feeling in Soviet psychology that that goal must be reached at any given time.

These considerations make Soviet diplomacy at once easier and more difficult to deal with than the diplomacy of individual aggressive leaders like Napoleon and Hitler. On the one hand it is more sensitive to contrary force, more ready to yield on individual sectors of the diplomatic front when that force is felt to be too strong, and thus more rational in the logic and rhetoric of power. On the other hand it cannot be easily defeated or discouraged by a single victory on the part of its opponents. And the patient persistence by which it is animated means that it can be effectively countered not by sporadic acts which represent the momentary whims of democratic opinion but only by intelligent long-range policies on the part of Russia's adversaries— policies no less steady in their purpose, and no less variegated and resourceful in their application, than those of the Soviet Union itself.

In these circumstances it is clear that the main element of any United States policy toward the Soviet Union must be that of long-term, patient but firm and vigilant containment of Russian expansive tendencies. It is important to note, however, that such a policy has nothing to do with outward histrionics: with threats or blustering or superfluous gestures of outward "toughness." While the Kremlin is basically flexible in its reaction to political realities, it is by no means unamenable to considerations of prestige. Like almost any other government, it can be placed by tactless and threatening gestures in a position where it cannot afford to yield even though this might be dictated by its sense of realism. The Russian leaders are keen judges of human psychology, and as such they are highly conscious that loss of temper and of self-control is never a source of strength in political affairs. They are quick to exploit such evidences of weakness. For these reasons it is a *sine qua non* of successful dealing with Russia that the foreign government in question should remain at all times cool and collected and that its demands on Russian policy should be put forward in such a manner as to leave the way open for a compliance not too detrimental to Russian prestige.

> **Part III**

In the light of the above, it will be clearly seen that the Soviet pressure against the free institutions of the western world is something that can be contained by the adroit and vigilant application of counter-force at a series of constantly shifting geographical and political points, corresponding to the shifts and maneuvers of Soviet policy, but which cannot be charmed or talked out of existence. The Russians look forward to a duel of infinite duration, and they see that already they have scored great successes. It must be borne in mind that there was a time when the Communist Party represented far more of a minority in the sphere of Russian national life than Soviet power today represents in the world community.

But if the ideology convinces the rulers of Russia that truth is on their side and they can therefore afford to wait, those of us on whom that ideology has no claim are free to examine objectively the validity of that premise. The Soviet thesis not only implies complete lack of control by the west over its own economic destiny, it likewise assumes Russian unity, discipline and patience over an infinite period. Let us bring this apocalyptic vision down to earth, and suppose that the western world finds the strength and resourcefulness to contain Soviet power over a period of ten to fifteen years. What does that spell for Russia itself?

The Soviet leaders, taking advantage of the contributions of modern techniques to the arts of despotism, have solved the question of obedience within the confines of their power. Few challenge their authority; and even those who do are unable to make that challenge valid as against the organs of suppression of the state.

The Kremlin has also proved able to accomplish its purpose of building up Russia, regardless of the interests of the inhabitants, and industrial foundation of heavy metallurgy, which is, to be sure, not yet complete but which is nevertheless continuing to grow and is approaching those of the other major industrial countries. All of this, however, both the maintenance of internal political security and the building of heavy industry, has been carried out at a terrible cost in human life and in human hopes and energies. It has necessitated the use of forced labor on a scale unprecedented in modern times under conditions of peace. It has involved the neglect or abuse of other phases of Soviet economic life, particularly agriculture, consumers' goods production, housing and transportation.

To all that, the war has added its tremendous toll of destruction, death and human exhaustion. In consequence of this, we have in Russia today a population which is physically and spiritually tired. The mass of the people are disillusioned, skeptical and no longer as accessible as they once were to the magical attraction which Soviet power still radiates to its followers abroad. The avidity with which people seized upon the slight respite accorded to the Church for tactical reasons during the war was eloquent testimony to the fact that their capacity for faith and devotion found little expression in the purposes of the regime.

In these circumstances, there are limits to the physical and nervous strength of people themselves. These limits are absolute ones, and are binding even for the cruelest dictatorship, because beyond them people cannot be driven. The forced labor camps and the other agencies of constraint provide temporary means of compelling people to work longer hours than their own volition or mere economic pressure would dictate; but if people survive them at all they become old before their time and must be considered as human casualties to the demands of dictatorship. In either case their best powers are no longer available to society and can no longer be enlisted in the service of the state.

Here only the younger generations can help. The younger generation, despite all vicissitudes and sufferings, is numerous and vigorous; and the Russians are a talented people. But it still remains to be seen what will be the effects on mature performance of the abnormal emotional strains of childhood which Soviet dictatorship created and which were enormously increased by the war. Such things as normal security and placidity of home environment have practically ceased to exist in the Soviet Union outside of the most remote farms and villages. And observers are not yet sure whether that is not going to leave its mark on the over-all capacity of the generation now coming into maturity.

In addition to this, we have the fact that Soviet economic development, while it can list certain formidable achievements, has been precariously spotty and uneven. Russian Communists who speak of the "uneven development of capitalism" should blush at the contemplation of their own national economy. Here certain branches of economic life, such as the metallurgical and machine industries, have been pushed out of all proportion to other sectors of economy. Here is a nation striving to become in a short period one of the great industrial nations of the world while it still has no highway network worthy of the name and only a relatively primitive network of railways. Much has been done to increase efficiency of labor and to teach primitive peasants something about the operation of machines. But maintenance is still a crying deficiency of all Soviet economy. Construction is hasty and poor in quality. Depreciation must be enormous. And in vast sectors of economic life it has not yet been possible to instill into labor anything like that general culture of production and technical self-respect which characterizes the skilled worker of the west.

It is difficult to see how these deficiencies can be corrected at an early date by a tired and dispirited population working largely under the shadow of fear and compulsion. And as long as they are not overcome, Russia will remain economically as vulnerable, and in a certain sense an impotent, nation, capable of exporting its enthusiasms and of radiating the strange charm of its primitive political vitality but unable to back up those articles of export by the real evidences of material power and prosperity.

Meanwhile, a great uncertainty hangs over the political life of the Soviet Union. That is the uncertainty involved in the transfer of power from one individual or group of individuals to others.

This is, of course, outstandingly the problem of the personal position of Stalin. We must remember that his succession to Lenin's pinnacle of pre-eminence in the Communist movement was the only such transfer of individual authority which the Soviet Union has experienced. That transfer took 12 years to consolidate. It cost the lives of millions of people and shook the state to its foundations. The attendant tremors were felt all through the international revolutionary movement, to the disadvantage of the Kremlin itself.

It is always possible that another transfer of pre-eminent power may take place quietly and inconspicuously, with no repercussions anywhere. But again, it is possible that the questions involved may unleash, to use some of Lenin's words, one of those "incredibly swift transitions" from "delicate deceit" to "wild violence" which characterize Russian history, and may shake Soviet power to its foundations.

But this is not only a question of Stalin himself. There has been, since 1938, a dangerous congealment of political life in the higher circles of Soviet power. The All-Union Congress of Soviets, in theory the supreme body of the Party, is supposed to meet not less often than once in three years. It will soon be eight full years since its last meeting. During this period membership in the Party has numerically doubled. Party mortality during the war was enormous; and today well over half of the Party members are persons who have entered since the last Party congress was held. meanwhile, the same small group of men has carried on at the top through an amazing series of national vicissitudes. Surely there is some reason why the experiences of the war brought basic political changes to every one of the great governments of the west. Surely the causes of that phenomenon are basic enough to be present somewhere in the obscurity of Soviet political life, as well. And yet no recognition has been given to these causes in Russia.

It must be surmised from this that even within so highly disciplined an organization as the Communist Party there must be a growing divergence in age, outlook and interest between the great mass of Party members, only so recently recruited into the movement, and the little self-perpetuating clique of men at the top, whom most of these Party members have never met, with whom they have never conversed, and with whom they can have no political intimacy.

Who can say whether, in these circumstances, the eventual rejuvenation of the higher spheres of authority (which can only be a matter of time) can take place smoothly and peacefully, or whether rivals in the quest for higher power will not eventually reach down into these politically immature and inexperienced masses in order to find support for their respective claims? If this were ever to happen, strange consequences could flow for the Communist Party: for the membership at large has been exercised only in the practices of iron discipline and obedience and not in the arts of compromise and accommodation. And if disunity were ever to seize and paralyze the Party, the chaos and weakness of Russian society would be revealed in forms beyond description. For we have seen that Soviet power is only concealing an amorphous mass of human beings among whom no independent organizational structure is tolerated. In Russia there is not even such a thing as local government. The present generation of Russians have never known spontaneity of collective action. If, consequently, anything were ever to occur to dis-

345

rupt the unity and efficacy of the Party as a political instrument, Soviet Russia might be changed overnight from one of the strongest to one of the weakest and most pitiable of national societies.

Thus the future of Soviet power may not be by any means as secure as Russian capacity for self-delusion would make it appear to the men of the Kremlin. That they can quietly and easily turn it over to others remains to be proved. Meanwhile, the hardships of their rule and the vicissitudes of international life have taken a heavy toll of the strength and hopes of the great people on whom their power rests. It is curious to note that the ideological power of Soviet authority is strongest today in areas beyond the frontiers of Russia, beyond the reach of its police power. This phenomenon brings to mind a comparison used by Thomas Mann in his great novel *Buddenbrooks*. Observing that human institutions often show the greatest outward brilliance at a moment when inner decay is in reality farthest advanced, he compared one of those stars whose light shines most brightly on this world when in reality it has long since ceased to exist. And who can say with assurance that the strong light still cast by the Kremlin on the dissatisfied peoples of the western world is not the powerful afterglow of a constellation which is in actuality on the wane? This cannot be proved. And it cannot be disproved. But the possibility remains (and in the opinion of this writer it is a strong one) that Soviet power, like the capitalist world of its conception, bears within it the seeds of its own decay, and that the sprouting of these seeds is well advanced.

Part IV

It is clear that the United States cannot expect in the foreseeable future to enjoy political intimacy with the Soviet regime. It must continue to regard the Soviet Union as a rival, not a partner, in the political arena. It must continue to expect that Soviet policies will reflect no abstract love of peace and stability, no real faith in the possibility of a permanent happy coexistence of the Socialist and capitalist worlds, but rather a cautious, persistent pressure toward the disruption and, weakening of all rival influence and rival power.

Balanced against this are the facts that Russia, as opposed to the western world in general, is still by far the weaker party, that Soviet policy is highly flexible, and that Soviet society may well contain deficiencies which will eventually weaken its own total potential. This would of itself warrant the United States entering with reasonable confidence upon a policy of firm containment, designed to confront the Russians with unalterable counter-force at every point where they show signs of encroaching upon he interests of a peaceful and stable world.

But in actuality the possibilities for American policy are by no means limited to holding the line and hoping for the best. It is entirely possible for the United States to influence by its actions the internal developments, both within Russia and throughout the international Communist movement, by which Russian policy is largely determined. This is not only a question of the modest measure of informational activity which this government can conduct in the Soviet Union and elsewhere, although that, too, is important. It is rather a question of the degree to which the United States can create among the peoples of the world generally the impression of a country which knows what it wants, which is coping successfully with the problem of its internal life and with the responsibilities of a World Power, and which has a spiritual vitality capable of holding its own among the major ideological currents of the time. To the extent that such an impression can be created and maintained, the aims of Russian Communism must appear sterile and quixotic, the hopes and enthusiasm of Moscow's supporters must wane, and added strain must be imposed on the Kremlin's foreign policies. For the palsied decrepitude of the capitalist world is the keystone of Communist philosophy. Even the failure of the United States to experience the early economic depression which the ravens of the Red Square have been predicting with such complacent confidence since hostilities ceased would have deep and important repercussions throughout the Communist world.

By the same token, exhibitions of indecision, disunity and internal disintegration within this country have an exhilarating effect on the whole Communist movement. At each evidence of these tendencies, a thrill of hope and excitement goes through the Communist world; a new jauntiness can be noted in the Moscow tread; new groups of foreign supporters climb on to what they can only view as the band wagon of international politics; and Russian pressure increases all along the line in international affairs.

It would be an exaggeration to say that American behavior unassisted and alone could exercise a power of life and death over the Communist movement and bring about the early fall of Soviet power in Russia. But the United States has it in its power to increase enormously the strains under which Soviet policy must operate, to force upon the Kremlin a far greater degree of moderation and circumspection than it has had to observe in recent years, and in this way to promote tendencies which must eventually find their outlet in either the breakup or the gradual mellowing of Soviet power. For no mystical, Messianic movement—and particularly not that of the Kremlin—can face frustration indefinitely without eventually adjusting itself in one way or another to the logic of that state of affairs.

Thus the decision will really fall in large measure in this country itself. The issue of Soviet-American relations is in essence a test of the overall worth of the United States as a nation among nations. To avoid destruction the United States need only measure up to its own best traditions and prove itself worthy of preservation as a great nation.

Surely, there was never a fairer test of national quality than this. In the light of these circumstances, the thoughtful observer of Russian-American relations will find no cause for complaint in the Kremlin's challenge to American society. He will rather experience a certain gratitude to a Providence which, by providing the American people with this implacable challenge, has made their entire security as a nation dependent on their pulling themselves together and accepting the responsibilities of moral and political leadership that history plainly intended them to bear.

Appendix 3

NSC 68: United States Objectives and Programs for National Security

NSC 68 is a declassified top secret National Security Department document. Dated April 7, 1950, it is a report to the President pursuant to the Presidents Directive of January 31, 1950. The complete document is available to the public at www.fas.org/irp/offdocs/nsc-hst/nsc-68.htm.

ANALYSIS

I. Background of the Present Crisis

Within the past thirty-five years the world has experienced two global wars of tremendous violence. It has witnessed two revolutions—the Russian and the Chinese—of extreme scope and intensity. It has also seen the collapse of five empires—the Ottoman, the Austro-Hungarian, German, Italian, and Japanese—and the drastic decline of two major imperial systems, the British and the French. During the span of one generation, the international distribution of power has been fundamentally altered. For several centuries it had proved impossible for any one nation to gain such preponderant strength that a coalition of other nations could not in time face it with greater strength. The international scene was marked by recurring periods of violence and war, but a system of sovereign and independent states was maintained, over which no state was able to achieve hegemony.

Two complex sets of factors have now basically altered this historic distribution of power. First, the defeat of Germany and Japan and the decline of the British and French Empires have interacted with the development of the United States and the Soviet Union in such a way that power increasingly gravitated to these two centers. Second, the Soviet Union, unlike previous aspirants to hegemony, is animated by a new fanatic faith, anti-thetical to our own, and seeks to impose its absolute authority over the rest of the world. Conflict has, therefore, become endemic and is waged, on the part of the Soviet Union, by violent or non-violent methods in accordance with the dictates of expediency. With the development of increasingly terrifying weapons of mass destruction, every individual faces the ever-present possibility of annihilation should the conflict enter the phase of total war.

On the one hand, the people of the world yearn for relief from the anxiety arising from the risk of atomic war. On the other hand, any substantial further extension of the area under the domination of the Kremlin would raise the possibility that no coalition adequate to confront the Kremlin with greater strength could be assembled. It is in this context that this Republic and its citizens in the ascendancy of their strength stand in their deepest peril.

The issues that face us are momentous, involving the fulfillment or destruction not only of this Republic but of civilization itself. They are issues which will not await our deliberations. With conscience and resolution this Government and the people it represents must now take new and fateful decisions.

II. Fundamental Purpose of the United States

The fundamental purpose of the United States is laid down in the Preamble to the Constitution: ". . . to form a more perfect Union, establish justice, insure domestic Tranquility, provide for the common defense, promote the general Welfare, and secure the Blessings of Liberty to ourselves and our Posterity." In essence, the fundamental purpose is to ensure the integrity and vitality of our free society, which is founded upon the dignity and worth of the individual.

Three realities emerge as a consequence of this purpose: Our determination to maintain the essential elements of individual freedom, as set forth in the Constitution and Bill of Rights; our determination to create conditions under which our free and democratic system can live and prosper; and our determination to fight if necessary to defend our way of life, for which as in the Declaration of Independence, "with a firm reliance on the protection of Divine Providence, we mutually pledge to each other our lives, our Fortunes, and our sacred Honor."

III. Fundamental Design of the Kremlin

The fundamental design of those who control the Soviet Union and the international communist movement is to retain and solidify their

350

absolute power, first in the Soviet Union and second in the areas now under their control. In the minds of the Soviet leaders, however, achievement of this design requires the dynamic extension of their authority and the ultimate elimination of any effective opposition to their authority.

The design, therefore, calls for the complete subversion or forcible destruction of the machinery of government and structure of society in the countries of the non-Soviet world and their replacement by an apparatus and structure subservient to and controlled from the Kremlin. To that end Soviet efforts are now directed toward the domination of the Eurasian land mass.

The United States, as the principal center of power in the non-Soviet world and the bulwark of opposition to Soviet expansion, is the principal enemy whose integrity and vitality must be subverted or destroyed by one means or another if the Kremlin is to achieve its fundamental design.

IV. The Underlying Conflict in the Realm of ideas and Values between the U.S. Purpose and the Kremlin Design

A. NATURE OF CONFLICT

The Kremlin regards the United States as the only major threat to the conflict between idea of slavery under the grim oligarchy of the Kremlin, which has come to a crisis with the polarization of power described in Section I, and the exclusive possession of atomic weapons by the two protagonists. The idea of freedom, moreover, is peculiarly and intolerably subversive of the idea of slavery. But the converse is not true. The implacable purpose of the slave state to eliminate the challenge of freedom has placed the two great powers at opposite poles. It is this fact which gives the present polarization of power the quality of crisis.

The free society values the individual as an end in himself, requiring of him only that measure of self-discipline and self-restraint which make the rights of each individual compatible with the rights of every other individual. The freedom of the individual has as its counterpart, therefore, the negative responsibility of the individual not to exercise his freedom in ways inconsistent with the freedom of other individuals and the positive responsibility to make constructive use of his freedom in the building of a just society.

From this idea of freedom with responsibility derives the marvelous

351

diversity, the deep tolerance, the lawfulness of the free society. This is the explanation of the strength of free men. It constitutes the integrity and the vitality of a free and democratic system. The free society attempts to create and maintain an environment in which every individual has the opportunity to realize his creative powers. It also explains why the free society tolerates those within it who would use their freedom to destroy it. By the same token, in relations between nations, the prime reliance of the free society is on the strength and appeal of its idea, and it feels no compulsion sooner or later to bring all societies into conformity with it.

For the free society does not fear, it welcomes, diversity. It derives its strength from its hospitality even to antipathetic ideas. It is a market for free trade in ideas, secure in its faith that free men will take the best wares, and grow to a fuller and better realization of their powers in exercising their choice.

The idea of freedom is the most contagious idea in history, more contagious than the idea of submission to authority. For the breadth of freedom cannot be tolerated in a society which has come under the domination of an individual or group of individuals with a will to absolute power. Where the despot holds absolute power—the absolute power of the absolutely powerful will—all other wills must be subjugated in an act of willing submission, a degradation willed by the individual upon himself under the compulsion of a perverted faith. It is the first article of this faith that he finds and can only find the meaning of his existence in serving the ends of the system. The system becomes God, and submission to the will of God becomes submission to the will of the system. It is not enough to yield outwardly to the system—even Gandhian non-violence is not acceptable—for the spirit of resistance and the devotion to a higher authority might then remain, and the individual would not be wholly submissive.

The same compulsion which demands total power over all men within the Soviet state without a single exception, demands total power over all Communist Parties and all states under Soviet domination. Thus Stalin has said that the theory and tactics of Leninism as expounded by the Bolshevik party are mandatory for the proletarian parties of all countries. A true internationalist is defined as one who unhesitatingly upholds the position of the Soviet Union and in the satellite states true patriotism is love of the Soviet Union. By the same token the "peace policy" of the Soviet Union, described at a Party Congress as "a more advantageous form of fighting capitalism," is a device to divide and immobilize the non-Communist world, and the peace the Soviet Union seeks is the peace of total conformity to Soviet policy.

The antipathy of slavery to freedom explains the Iron Curtain, the isolation, the autarchy of the society whose end is absolute power. The existence and persistence of the idea of freedom is a permanent and continuous threat to the foundation of the slave society; and it therefore regards as intolerable the long continued existence of freedom in the world. What is new, what makes the continuing crisis, is the polarization of power which now inescapably confronts the slave society with the free.

The assault on free institutions is world-wide now, and in the context of the present polarization of power a defeat of free institutions anywhere is a defeat everywhere. The shock we sustained in the destruction of Czechoslovakia was not in the measure of Czechoslovakia's material importance to us. In a material sense, her capabilities were already at Soviet disposal. But when the integrity of Czechoslovak institutions was destroyed, it was in the intangible scale of values that we registered a loss more damaging than the material loss we had already suffered.

Thus unwillingly our free society finds itself mortally challenged by the Soviet system. No other value system is so wholly irreconcilable with ours, so implacable in its purpose to destroy ours, so capable of turning to its own uses the most dangerous and divisive trends in our own society, no other so skillfully and powerfully evokes the elements of irrationality in human nature everywhere, and no other has the support of a great and growing center of military power.

B. OBJECTIVES

The objectives of a free society are determined by its fundamental values and by the necessity for maintaining the material environment in which they flourish. Logically and in fact, therefore, the Kremlin's challenge to the United States is directed not only to our values but to our physical capacity to protect their environment. It is a challenge which encompasses both peace and war and our objectives in peace and war must take account of it.

Thus we must make ourselves strong, both in the way in which we affirm our values in the conduct of our national life, and in the development of our military and economic strength.

We must lead in building a successfully functioning political and economic system in the free world. It is only by practical affirmation, abroad as well as at home, of our essential values, that we can preserve our own integrity, in which lies the real frustration of the Kremlin design.

But beyond thus affirming our values our policy and actions must be such as to foster a fundamental change in the nature of the Soviet system, a change toward which the frustration of the design is the first and perhaps the most important step. Clearly it will not only be less costly but more effective if this change occurs to a maximum extent as a result of internal forces in Soviet society.

In a shrinking world, which now faces the threat of atomic warfare, it is not an adequate objective merely to seek to check the Kremlin design, for the absence of order among nations is becoming less and less tolerable. This fact imposes on us, in our own interests, the responsibility of world leadership. It demands that we make the attempt, and accept the risks inherent in it, to bring about order and justice by means consistent with the principles of freedom and democracy. We should limit our requirement of the Soviet Union to its participation with other nations on the basis of equality and respect for the rights of others. Subject to this requirement, we must with our allies and the former subject peoples seek to create a world society based on the principle of consent. Its framework cannot be inflexible. It will consist of many national communities of great and varying abilities and resources, and hence of war potential. The seeds of conflicts will inevitably exist or will come into being. To acknowledge this is only to acknowledge the impossibility of a final solution. Not to acknowledge it can be fatally dangerous in a world in which there are no final solutions.

All these objectives of a free society are equally valid and necessary in peace and war. But every consideration of devotion to our fundamental values and to our national security demands that we seek to achieve them by the strategy of the Cold War. It is only by developing the moral and material strength of the free world that the Soviet regime will become convinced of the falsity of its assumptions and that the pre-conditions for workable agreements can be created. By practically demonstrating the integrity and vitality of our system the free world widens the area of possible agreement and thus can hope gradually to bring about a Soviet acknowledgement of realities which in sum will eventually constitute a frustration of the Soviet design. Short of this, however, it might be possible to create a situation which will induce the Soviet Union to accommodate itself, with or without

354

the conscious abandonment of its design, to coexistence on tolerable terms with the non-Soviet world. Such a development would be a triumph for the idea of freedom and democracy. It must be an immediate objective of United States policy.

There is no reason, in the event of war, for us to alter our overall objectives. They do not include unconditional surrender, the subjugation of the Russian peoples or a Russia shorn of its economic potential. Such a course would irrevocably unite the Russian people behind the regime which enslaves them. Rather these objectives contemplate Soviet acceptance of the specific and limited conditions requisite to an international environment in which free institutions can flourish, and in which the Russian peoples will have a new chance to work out their own destiny. If we can make the Russian people our allies in the enterprise we will obviously have made our task easier and victory more certain.

The objectives outlined in NSC 20/4 (November 23, 1948) ... are fully consistent with the objectives stated in this paper, and they remain valid. The growing intensity of the conflict which has been imposed upon us, however, requires the changes of emphasis and the additions that are apparent. Coupled with the probable fission bomb capability and possible thermonuclear bomb capability of the Soviet Union, the intensifying struggle requires us to face the fact that we can expect no lasting abatement of the crisis unless and until a change occurs in the nature of the Soviet system.

C. MEANS

The free society is limited in its choice of means to achieve its ends.

Compulsion is the negation of freedom, except when it is used to enforce the rights common to all. The resort to force, internally or externally, is therefore a last resort for a free society. The act is permissible only when one individual or groups of individuals within it threaten the basic rights of other individuals or when another society seeks to impose its will upon it. The free society cherishes and protects as fundamental the rights of the minority against the will of a majority, because these rights are the inalienable rights of each and every individual.

The resort to force, to compulsion, to the imposition of its will is therefore a difficult and dangerous act for a free society, which is warranted only in the face of even greater dangers. The necessity of the act must be clear and compelling; the act must commend itself to the overwhelming majority as an inescapable exception to the basic idea of freedom; or the regenerative capacity of free men after the act has been performed will be endangered.

The Kremlin is able to select whatever means are expedient in seeking to carry out its fundamental design. Thus it can make the best of several possible worlds, conducting the struggle on those levels where it considers it profitable and enjoying the benefits of a pseudo-peace on those levels where it is not ready for a contest. At the ideological or psychological level, in the struggle for men's minds, the conflict is worldwide. At the political and economic level, within states and in the relations between states, the struggle for power is being intensified. And at the military level, the Kremlin has thus far been careful not to commit a technical breach of the peace, although using its vast forces to intimidate its neighbors, and to support an aggressive foreign policy, and not hesitating through its agents to resort to arms in favorable circumstances. The attempt to carry out its fundamental design is being pressed, therefore, with all means which are believed expedient in the present situation, and the Kremlin has inextricably engaged us in the conflict between its design and our purpose.

We have no such freedom of choice, and least of all in the use of force. Resort to war is not only a last resort for a free society, but it is also an act which cannot definitively end the fundamental conflict in the realm of ideas. The idea of slavery can only be overcome by the timely and persistent demonstration of the superiority of the idea of freedom. Military victory alone would only partially and perhaps only temporarily affect the fundamental conflict, for although the ability of the Kremlin to threaten our security might be for a time destroyed, the resurgence of totalitarian forces and the re-establishment of the Soviet system or its equivalent would not be long delayed unless great progress were made in the fundamental conflict.

Practical and ideological considerations therefore both impel us to the conclusion that we have no choice but to demonstrate the superiority of the idea of freedom by its constructive application, and to attempt to change the world situation by means short of war in such a way as to frustrate the Kremlin design and hasten the decay of the Soviet system.

For us the role of military power is to serve the national purpose by deterring an attack upon us while we seek by other means to create an environment in which our free society can flourish, and by fighting, if necessary, to defend the integrity and vitality of our free society and to defeat any aggressor. The Kremlin uses Soviet military power to back up and serve the Kremlin design. It does not hesitate to use military force aggressively if that course is expedient in the achievement of its design. The differences between our fundamental purpose and the Kremlin design, therefore, are reflected in our respective attitudes toward and use of military force.

Our free society, confronted by a threat to its basic values, naturally will take such action, including the use of military force, as may be required to protect those values. The integrity of our system will not be jeopardized by any measures, covert or overt, violent or non-violent, which serve the purposes of frustrating the Kremlin design, nor does the necessity for conducting ourselves so as to affirm our values in actions as well as words forbid such measures, provided only they are appropriately calculated to that end and are not so excessive or misdirected as to make us enemies of the people instead of the evil men who have enslaved them.

But if war comes, what is the role of force? Unless we so use it that the Russian people can perceive that our effort is directed against the regime and its power for aggression, and not against their own interests, we will unite the regime and the people in the kind of last ditch fight in which no underlying problems are solved, new ones are created, and where our basic principles are obscured and compromised. If we do not in the application of force demonstrate the nature of our objectives we will, in fact, have compromised from the outset our fundamental purpose. In the words of the *Federalist* (No. 28) "The means to be employed must be proportioned to the extent of the mischief." The mischief may be a global war or it may be a Soviet campaign for limited objectives. In either case we should take no avoidable initiative which would cause it to become a war of annihilation, and if we have the forces to defeat a Soviet drive for limited objectives it may well be to our interest not to let it become a global war. Our aim in applying force must be to compel the acceptance of terms consistent with our objectives, and our capabilities for the application of force should, therefore, within the limits of what we can sustain over the long pull, be congruent to the range of tasks which we may encounter.

V. Soviet Intentions and Capabilities

A. POLITICAL AND PSYCHOLOGICAL

The Kremlin's design for world domination begins at home. The first concern of a despotic oligarchy is that the local base of its power and authority be secure. The massive fact of the Iron Curtain isolating the Soviet peoples from the outside world, the repeated political purges within the USSR and the institutionalized crimes of the MVD [the Soviet Ministry of Internal Affairs] are evidence that the Kremlin does not feel secure at home and that "the entire coercive force of the socialist state" is more than ever one of seeking to impose its absolute authority over "the economy, manner of life, and conscious-ness of people" (Vyshinski, *The Law of the Soviet State,* p. 74). Similar evidence in the satellite states of Eastern Europe leads to the conclusion that this same policy, in less advanced phases, is being applied to the Kremlin's colonial areas.

Being a totalitarian dictatorship, the Kremlin's objective in these poli-cies is the total subjective submission of the peoples now under its control. The concentration camp is the prototype of the society which these policies are designed to achieve, a society in which the per-sonality of the individual is so broken and perverted that he partici-pates affirmatively in his own degradation.

The Kremlin's policy toward areas not under its control is the elimi-nation of resistance to its will and the extension of its influence and control. It is driven to follow this policy because it cannot, for the rea-sons set forth in Chapter IV, tolerate the existence of free societies; to the Kremlin the most mild and inoffensive free society is an affront, a challenge and a subversive influence. Given the nature of the Kremlin, and the evidence at hand, it seems clear that the ends toward which this policy is directed are the same as those where its control has already been established.

The means employed by the Kremlin in pursuit of this policy are limited only by considerations of expediency. Doctrine is not a lim-iting factor; rather it dictates the employment of violence, subver-sion, and deceit, and rejects moral considerations. In any event, the Kremlin's conviction of its own infallibility has made its devo-tion to theory so subjective that past or present pronouncements as to doctrine offer no reliable guide to future actions. The only apparent restraints on resort to war are, therefore, calculations of practicality.

With particular reference to the United States, the Kremlin's strate-gic and tactical policy is affected by its estimate that we are not only the greatest immediate obstacle which stands between it and world domination, we are also the only power which could release forces in the free and Soviet worlds which could destroy it. The Kremlin's policy toward us is consequently animated by a peculiarly virulent blend of hatred and fear. Its strategy has been one of attempting to undermine the complex of forces, in this country and in the rest of the free world, on which our power is based. In this it has both adhered to doctrine and followed the sound principle of seeking maximum results with minimum risks and commitments. The present application of this strategy is a new form of expression for traditional Russian caution. However, there is no justification in Soviet theory or practice for predicting that, should the Kremlin become convinced that it could cause our downfall by one conclusive blow, it would not seek that solution.

In considering the capabilities of the Soviet world, it is of prime importance to remember that, in contrast to ours, they are being drawn upon at close to the maximum possible extent. Also in contrast to us, the Soviet world can do more with less—it has a lower standard of living, its economy requires less to keep it functioning, and its military machine operates effectively with less elaborate equipment and organization.

The capabilities of the Soviet world are being exploited to the full because the Kremlin is inescapably militant. It is inescapably militant because it possesses and is possessed by a world-wide revolutionary movement, because it is the inheritor of Russian imperialism, and because it is a totalitarian dictatorship. Persistent crisis, conflict, and expansion are the essence of the Kremlin's militancy. This dynamism serves to intensify all Soviet capabilities.

Two enormous organizations, the Communist Party and the secret police, are an outstanding source of strength to the Kremlin. In the Party, it has an apparatus designed to impose at home an ideological uniformity among its people and to act abroad as an instrument of propaganda, subversion and espionage. In its police apparatus, it has a domestic repressive instrument guaranteeing under present circumstances the continued security of the Kremlin.

The demonstrated capabilities of these two basic organizations, operating openly or in disguise, in mass or through single agents, is unparalleled in history. The party, the police and the conspicuous might of the Soviet military machine together tend to create an overall impression of irresistible Soviet power among many peoples of the free world.

The ideological pretensions of the Kremlin are another great source of strength. Its identification of the Soviet system with communism, its peace campaigns and its championing of colonial peoples may be viewed with apathy, if not cynicism, by the oppressed totalitariat of the Soviet world, but in the free world these ideas find favorable responses in vulnerable segments of society. They have found a particularly receptive audience in Asia, especially as the Asiatics have been impressed by what has been plausibly portrayed to them as the rapid advance of the USSR from a backward society to a position of great world power. Thus, in its pretensions to being (a) the source of a new universal faith and (b) the model "scientific" society, the Kremlin cynically identifies itself with the genuine aspirations of large numbers of people, and places itself at the head of an international crusade with all of the benefits which derive therefrom.

Finally, there is a category of capabilities, strictly speaking neither institutional nor ideological, which should be taken into consideration. The extraordinary flexibility of Soviet tactics is certainly a strength. It derives from the utterly amoral and opportunistic conduct of Soviet policy. Combining this quality with the elements of secrecy, the Kremlin possesses a formidable capacity to act with the widest tactical latitude, with stealth, and with speed.

The greatest vulnerability of the Kremlin lies in the basic nature of its relations with the Soviet people.

That relationship is characterized by universal suspicion, fear, and denunciation. It is a relationship in which the Kremlin relies, not only for its power but its very survival, on intricately devised mechanisms of coercion. The Soviet monolith is held together by the Iron Curtain around it and the iron bars within it, not by any force of natural cohesion. These artificial mechanisms of unity have never been intelligently challenged by a strong outside force. The full measure of their vulnerability is therefore not yet evident.

The Kremlin's relations with its satellites and their peoples is likewise a vulnerability. Nationalism still remains the most potent emotional-political force. The well-known ills of colonialism are compounded, however, by the excessive demands of the Kremlin that its satellites accept not only the imperial authority of Moscow but that they believe in and proclaim the ideological primacy and infallibility of the Kremlin. These excessive requirements can be made good only through extreme coercion. The result is that if a satellite feels able to effect its independence of the Kremlin, as Tito was able to do, it is likely to break away.

In short, Soviet ideas and practices run counter to the best and potentially the strongest instincts of men, and deny their most fundamental aspirations. Against an adversary which effectively affirmed the constructive and hopeful instincts of men and was capable of fulfilling their fundamental aspirations, the Soviet system might prove to be fatally weak.

The problem of succession to Stalin is also a Kremlin vulnerability. In a system where supreme power is acquired and held through violence and intimidation, the transfer of that power may well produce a period of instability.

In a very real sense, the Kremlin is a victim of, its own dynamism. This dynamism can become a weakness if it is frustrated, if in its forward thrusts it encounters a superior force which halts the expansion and exerts a superior counterpressure. Yet the Kremlin cannot relax the condition of crisis and mobilization, for to do so would be to lose its dynamism, whereas the seeds of decay within the Soviet system would begin to flourish and fructify.

The Kremlin is, of course, aware of these weaknesses. It must know that in the present world situation they are of secondary significance. So long as the Kremlin retains the initiative, so long as it can keep on the offensive unchallenged by clearly superior counter-force—spiritual as well as material—its vulnerabilities are largely inoperative and even concealed by its successes. The Kremlin has not yet been given real reason to fear and be diverted by the rot within its system.

B. ECONOMIC

The Kremlin has no economic intentions unrelated to its overall policies. Economics in the Soviet world is not an end in itself The Kremlin's policy, in so far as it has to do with economics, is to utilize economic processes to contribute to the overall strength, particularly the war-making capacity of the Soviet system. The material welfare of the totalitariat is severely subordinated to the interest of the system.

As for capabilities, even granting optimistic Soviet reports of production, the total economic strength of the U.S.S.R. compares with that of the U.S. as roughly one to four. This is reflected not only in gross national product (1949: USSR $65 billion; U.S. $250 billion), but in production of key commodities in 1949:

	US	USSR	USSR and EUROPEAN ORBIT COMBINED
Ingot Steel (million met. tons)	80.4	21.5	28.0
Primary aluminum (thousand met. tons)	617.6	130-135	140-145
Electric power (billion kwh)	410	72	112
Crude oil (million met. tons)	276.5	33.0	38.9

Assuming the maintenance of present policies, while a large U.S. advantage is likely to remain, the Soviet Union will be steadily reducing the discrepancy between its overall economic strength and that of the U.S. by continuing to devote proportionately more to capital investment than the U.S.

But a full-scale effort by the U.S. would be capable of precipitately altering this trend. The USSR today is on a near maximum production basis. No matter what efforts Moscow might make, only a relatively slight change in the rate of increase in overall production could be brought about. In the U.S., on the other hand, a very rapid absolute expansion could be realized. The fact remains, however, that so long as the Soviet Union is virtually mobilized, and the United States has scarcely begun to summon up its forces, the greater capabilities of the U.S. are to that extent inoperative in the struggle for power. Moreover, as the Soviet attainment of an atomic capability has demonstrated, the totalitarian state, at least in time of peace, can focus its efforts on any given project far more readily than the democratic state.

In other fields—general technological competence, skilled labor resources, productivity of labor force, etc.—the gap between the USSR and the U.S. roughly corresponds to the gap in production. In the field of scientific research, however, the margin of United States superiority is unclear, especially if the Kremlin can utilize European talents.

C. MILITARY

The Soviet Union is developing the military capacity to support its design for world domination. The Soviet Union actually possesses armed forces far in excess of those necessary to defend its national territory. These armed forces are probably not yet considered by the Soviet Union to be sufficient to initiate a war which would involve the United States. This excessive strength, coupled now with an atomic capability, provides the Soviet Union with great coercive power for use in time of peace in furtherance of its objectives and serves as a deterrent to the victims of its aggression from taking any action in opposition to its tactics which would risk war.

Should a major war occur in 1950 the Soviet Union and its satellites are considered by the Joint Chiefs of Staff to be in a sufficiently advanced state of preparation immediately to undertake and carry out the following campaigns.

    a. To overrun Western Europe, with the possible exception of the Iberian and Scandinavian Peninsulas; to drive toward the oil-bearing areas of the Near and Middle East; and to consolidate Communist gains in the Far East;

    b. To launch air attacks against the British Isles and air and sea attacks against the lines of communications of the Western Powers in the Atlantic and the Pacific;

    c. To attack selected targets with atomic weapons, now including the likelihood of such attacks against targets in Alaska, Canada, and the United States. Alternatively, this capability, coupled with other actions open to the Soviet Union, might deny the United Kingdom as an effective base of operations for allied forces. It also should be possible for the Soviet Union to prevent any allied "Normandy" type amphibious operations intended to force a reentry into the continent of Europe.

After the Soviet Union completed its initial campaigns and consolidated its positions in the Western European area, it could simultaneously conduct:

    a. Full-scale air and limited sea operations against the British Isles;

    b. Invasions of the Iberian and Scandinavian Peninsulas;

    c. Further operations in the Near and Middle East, continued air operations against the North American continent, and air and sea operations against Atlantic and Pacific lines of communication; and

   d.   Diversionary attacks in other areas.

During the course of the offensive operations listed in the second and third paragraphs above, the Soviet Union will have an air defense capability with respect to the vital areas of its own and its satellites' territories which can oppose but cannot prevent allied air operations against these areas.

It is not known whether the Soviet Union possesses war reserves and arsenal capabilities sufficient to supply its satellite armies or even its own forces throughout a long war. It might not be in the interest of the Soviet Union to equip fully its satellite armies, since the possibility of defections would exist.

It is not possible at this time to assess accurately the finite disadvantages to the Soviet Union which may accrue through the implementation of the Economic Cooperation Act of 1948, as amended, and the Mutual Defense Assistance Act of 1949. It should be expected that, as this implementation progresses, the internal security situation of the recipient nations should improve concurrently. In addition, a strong United States military position, plus increases in the armaments of the nations of Western Europe, should strengthen the determination of the recipient nations to counter Soviet moves and in event of war could be considered as likely to delay operations and increase the time required for the Soviet Union to overrun Western Europe. In all probability, although United States backing will stiffen their determination, the armaments increase under the present aid programs will not be of any major consequence prior to 1952. Unless the military strength of the Western European nations is increased on a much larger scale than under current programs and at an accelerated rate, it is more than likely that those nations will not be able to oppose even by 1960 the Soviet armed forces in war with any degree of effectiveness. Considering the Soviet Union military capability, the long-range allied military objective in Western Europe must envisage an increased military strength in that area sufficient possibly to deter the Soviet Union from a major war or, in any event, to delay materially the overrunning of Western Europe and, if feasible, to hold a bridgehead on the continent against Soviet Union offensives.

We do not know accurately what the Soviet atomic capability is but the Central Intelligence Agency intelligence estimates, concurred in by State, Army, Navy, Air Force, and Atomic Energy Commission, assign to the Soviet Union a production capability giving it a fission bomb stockpile within the following ranges:

By mid-1950	10-20
By mid-1951	25-45
By mid-1952	45-90
By mid-1953	70-135
By mid-1954	200

This estimate is admittedly based on incomplete coverage of Soviet activities and represents the production capabilities of known or deducible Soviet plants. If others exist, as is possible, this estimate could lead us into a feeling of superiority in our atomic stockpile that might be dangerously misleading, particularly with regard to the timing of a possible Soviet offensive. On the other hand, if the Soviet Union experiences operating difficulties, this estimate would be reduced. There is some evidence that the Soviet Union is acquiring certain materials essential to research on and development of thermonuclear weapons.

The Soviet Union now has aircraft able to deliver the atomic bomb. Our Intelligence estimates assign to the Soviet Union an atomic bomber capability already in excess of that needed to deliver available bombs. We have at present no evaluated estimate regarding the Soviet accuracy of delivery on target. It is believed that the Soviets cannot deliver their bombs on target with a degree of accuracy comparable to ours, but a planning estimate might well place it at 40-60 percent of bombs sorted. For planning purposes, therefore, the date the Soviets possess an atomic stockpile of 200 bombs would be a critical date for the United States, for the delivery of 100 atomic bombs on targets in the United States would seriously damage this country.

At the time the Soviet Union has a substantial atomic stockpile and if it is assumed that it will strike a strong surprise blow and if it is assumed further that its atomic attacks will be met with no more effective defense opposition than the United States and its allies have programmed, results of those attacks could include:

a. Laying waste to the British Isles and thus depriving the Western Powers of their use as a base;

b. Destruction of the vital centers and of the communications of Western Europe, thus precluding effective defense by the Western Powers; and

c. Delivering devastating attacks on certain vital centers of the United States and Canada.

The possession by the Soviet Union of a thermonuclear capability in addition to this substantial atomic stockpile would result in tremendously increased damage.

During this decade, the defensive capabilities of the Soviet Union will probably be strengthened, particularly by the development and use of modem aircraft, aircraft warning and communications devices, and defensive guided missiles.

VI. US Intentions and Capabilities—Actual and Potential

A. POLITICAL AND PSYCHOLOGICAL

Our overall policy at the present time may be described as one designed to foster a world environment in which the American system can survive and flourish. It therefore rejects the concept of isolation and affirms the necessity of our positive participation in the world community.

This broad intention embraces two subsidiary policies. One is a policy which we would probably pursue even if there were no Soviet threat. It is a policy of attempting to develop a healthy international community. The other is the policy of "containing" the Soviet system. These two policies are closely interrelated and interact on one another. Nevertheless, the distinction between them is basically valid and contributes to a clearer understanding of what we are trying to do.

The policy of striving to develop a healthy international community is the long-term constructive effort which we are engaged in. It was this policy which gave rise to our vigorous sponsorship of the United Nations. It is of course the principal reason for our long continuing endeavors to create and now develop the Inter-American system. It, as much as containment, underlay our efforts to rehabilitate Western Europe. Most of our international economic activities can likewise be explained in terms of this policy.

In a world of polarized power, the policies designed to develop a healthy international community are more than ever necessary to our own strength.

As for the policy of "containment," it is one which seeks by all means short of war to (1) block further expansion of Soviet power, (2) expose the falsities of Soviet pretensions, (3) induce a retraction of the Kremlin's control and influence, and (4) in general, so foster the seeds of destruction within the Soviet system that the Kremlin is brought at least to the point of modifying its behavior to conform to generally accepted international standards.

It was and continues to be cardinal in this policy that we possess superior overall power in ourselves or in dependable combination with other likeminded nations. One of the most important ingredients of power is military strength. In the concept of "containment," the maintenance of a strong military posture is deemed to be essential for two reasons: (1) as an ultimate guarantee of our national security and (2) as an indispensable backdrop to the conduct of the policy of "containment." Without superior aggregate military strength, in being and readily mobilizable, a policy of "containment"—which is in effect a policy of calculated and gradual coercion—is no more than a policy of bluff.

At the same time, it is essential to the successful conduct of a policy of "containment" that we always leave open the possibility of negotiation with the USSR. A diplomatic freeze—and we are in one now—tends to defeat the very purposes of "containment" because it raises tensions at the same time that it makes Soviet retractions and adjustments in the direction of moderated behavior more difficult. It also tends to inhibit our initiative and deprives us of opportunities for maintaining a moral ascendancy in our struggle with the Soviet system.

In "containment" it is desirable to exert pressure in a fashion which will avoid so far as possible directly challenging Soviet prestige, to keep open the possibility for the USSR to retreat before pressure with a minimum loss of face and to secure political advantage from the failure of the Kremlin to yield or take advantage of the openings we leave it.

We have failed to implement adequately these two fundamental aspects of "containment." In the face of obviously mounting Soviet military strength ours has declined relatively. Partly as a byproduct of this, but also for other reasons, we now find ourselves at a diplomatic impasse with the Soviet Union, with the Kremlin growing bolder, with both of us holding on grimly to what we have, and with ourselves facing difficult decisions.

In examining our capabilities it is relevant to ask at the outset—capabilities for what? The answer cannot be stated solely in the negative terms of resisting the Kremlin design. It includes also our capabilities to attain the fundamental purpose of the United States, and to foster a world environment in which our free society can survive and flourish.

Potentially we have these capabilities. We know we have them in the economic and military fields. Potentially we also have them in the political and psychological fields. The vast majority of Americans are confident that the system of values which animates our society—the principles of freedom, tolerance, the importance of the individual, and the supremacy of reason over will—are valid and more vital than the ideology which is the fuel of Soviet dynamism. Translated into terms relevant to the lives of other peoples—our system of values can become perhaps a powerful appeal to millions who now seek or find in authoritarianism a refuge from anxieties, bafflement, and insecurity.

Essentially, our democracy also possesses a unique degree of unity. Our society is fundamentally more cohesive than the Soviet system, the solidarity of which is artificially created through force, fear, and favor. This means that expressions of national consensus in our society are soundly and solidly based. It means that the possibility of revolution in this country is fundamentally less than that in the Soviet system.

These capabilities within us constitute a great potential force in our international relations. The potential within us of bearing witness to the values by which we live holds promise for a dynamic manifestation to the rest of the world of the vitality of our system. The essential tolerance of our world outlook, our generous and constructive impulses, and the absence of covetousness in our international relations are assets of potentially enormous influence.

These then are our potential capabilities. Between them and our capabilities currently being utilized is a wide gap of unactualized power. In sharp contrast is the situation of the Soviet world. Its capabilities are inferior to those of our allies and to our own. But they are mobilized close to the maximum possible extent.

The full power which resides within the American people will be evoked only through the traditional democratic process: This process requires, firstly, that sufficient information regarding the basic political, economic, and military elements of the present situation be made publicly available so that an intelligent popular opinion may be formed.

Having achieved a comprehension of the issues now confronting this Republic, it will then be possible for the American people and the American Government to arrive at a consensus. Out of this common view will develop a determination of the national will and a solid resolute expression of that will. The initiative in this process lies with the Government.

The democratic way is harder than the authoritarian way because, in seeking to protect and fulfill the individual, it demands of him understanding, judgment, and positive participation in the increasingly complex and exacting problems of the modern world. It demands that he exercise discrimination: that while pursuing through free inquiry the search for truth he knows when he should commit an act of faith; that he distinguish between the necessity for tolerance and the necessity for just suppression. A free society is vulnerable in that it is easy for people to lapse into excesses—the excesses of a permanently open mind wishfully waiting for evidence that evil design may become noble purpose, the excess of faith becoming prejudice, the excess of tolerance degenerating into indulgence of conspiracy and the excess of resorting to suppression when more moderate measures are not only more appropriate but more effective.

In coping with dictatorial governments acting in secrecy and with speed, we are also vulnerable in that the democratic process necessarily operates in the open and at a deliberate tempo. Weaknesses in our situation are readily apparent and subject to immediate exploitation. This Government therefore cannot afford in the face of the totalitarian challenge to operate on a narrow margin of strength. A democracy can compensate for its natural vulnerability only if it maintains clearly superior overall power in its most inclusive sense.

The very virtues of our system likewise handicap us in certain respects in our relations with our allies. While it is a general source of strength to us that our relations with our allies are conducted on a basis of persuasion and consent rather than compulsion and capitulation, it is also evident that dissent among us can become a vulnerability. Sometimes the dissent has its principal roots abroad in situations about which we can do nothing. Sometimes it arises largely out of certain weaknesses within ourselves, about which we can do something—our native impetuosity and a tendency to expect too much from people widely divergent from us.

The full capabilities of the rest of the free world are a potential increment to our own capabilities. It may even be said that the capabilities of the Soviet world, specifically the capabilities of the masses who have nothing to lose but their Soviet chains, are a potential which can be enlisted on our side.

Like our own capabilities, those of the rest of the free world exceed the capabilities of the Soviet system. Like our own they are far from being effectively mobilized and employed in the struggle against the Kremlin design. This is so because the rest of the free world lacks a sense of unity, confidence, and common purpose. This is true in even the most homogeneous and advanced segment of the free world—Western Europe.

As we ourselves demonstrate power, confidence, and a sense of moral and political direction, so those same qualities will be evoked in Western Europe. In such a situation, we may also anticipate a general improvement in the political tone in Latin America, Asia, and Africa and the real beginnings of awakening among the Soviet totalitariat.

In the absence of affirmative decision on our part, the rest of the free world is almost certain to become demoralized. Our friends will become more than a liability to us; they can eventually become a positive increment to Soviet power.

In sum, the capabilities of our allies are, in an important sense, a function of our own. An affirmative decision to summon up the potential within ourselves would evoke the potential strength within others and add it to our own.

B. ECONOMIC

1. Capabilities. In contrast to the war economy of the Soviet world (cf. Ch. V-B), the American economy (and the economy of the free world as a whole) is at present directed to the provision of rising standards of living. The military budget of the United States represents 6 to 7 percent of its gross national product (as against 13.8 percent for the Soviet Union). Our North Atlantic Treaty [NAT] allies devoted 4.8 percent of their national product to military purposes in 1949.

This difference in emphasis between the two economies means that the readiness of the free world to support a war effort is tending to decline relative to that of the Soviet Union. There is little direct investment in production facilities for military end-products and in dispersal. There are relatively few men receiving military training and a relatively low rate of production of weapons. However, given time to convert to a war effort, the capabilities of the United States economy and also of the Western European economy would be tremendous. In the light of Soviet military capabilities, a question which may be of decisive importance in the event of war is the question whether there will be time to mobilize our superior human and material resources for a war effort (cf. Chs. VIII and IX).

The capability of the American economy to support a build-up of economic and military strength at home and to assist a build-up abroad is limited not, as in the case of the Soviet Union, so much by the ability to produce as by the decision on the proper allocation of resources to this and other purposes. Even Western Europe could afford to assign a substantially larger proportion of its resources to defense, if the necessary foundation in public understanding and will could be laid, and if the assistance needed to meet its dollar deficit were provided.

A few statistics will help to clarify this point [Table 1].

The Soviet Union is now allocating nearly 40 percent of its gross available resources to military purposes and investment, much of which is in war-supporting industries. It is estimated that even in an emergency the Soviet Union could not increase this proportion to much more than 50 percent, or by one-fourth. The United States, on the other hand, is allocating only about 20 percent of its resources to defense and investment (or 22 percent including foreign assistance), and little of its investment outlays are directed to war-supporting industries. In an emergency the United States could allocate more than 50 percent of its resources to military purposes and foreign assistance, or five to six times as much as at present.

The same point can be brought out by statistics on the use of important products. The Soviet Union is using 14 percent of its ingot steel, 47 percent of its primary aluminum, and 18.5 percent of its crude oil for military purposes, while the corresponding percentages for the United States are 1.7, 8.6, and 5.6. Despite the tremendously larger production of these goods in the United States than the Soviet Union, the latter is actually using, for military purposes, nearly twice as much steel as the United States and 8 to 26 percent more aluminum.

Table 1. Percentage of Gross Available Resources Allocated to Investment, National Defense, and Consumption in East and West, 1949 (in percent of total)

COUNTRY	GROSS INVESTMENT	DEFENSE	CONSUMPTION
USSR	25.4	13.8	60.8
Soviet Orbit	22.0 (a)	4.0 (b)	74.0 (a)
U.S.	13.6	6.5	79.9
European NAT countries	20.4	4.8	74.8

(a) crude estimate. [Footnote in the source text.]

371

(b) Includes Soviet Zone of Germany; otherwise 5 percent. [Footnote in the source text.]

Perhaps the most impressive indication of the economic superiority of the free world over the Soviet world which can be made on the basis of available data is provided in comparisons (based mainly on the *Economic Survey of Europe, 1948)* [Table 2].

Table 2. Comparative Statistics on Economic Capabilities of East and West

	U.S. 1948-49	EUROPEAN NAT COUNTRIES	TOTAL	USSR (1950 PLAN)	SATELLITES 1948-49	TOTAL
Population (millions)	149	173	322	198 (a)	75	273
Employment in non-agricultural establishments (millions)	45	-	-	31 (a)	-	-
Gross National Production (billion dollars)	250	84	334	65 (a)	21	86
National income per capita (current dollars	1700	480	1040	330	280	315
Production data (b):						
Coal (million tons)	582	306	888	250	88	338
Electric power (billion kwh)	356	124	480	82	15	97
Crude petroleum (million tons)	277	1	278	35	5	40
Pig iron (million tons)	55	24	79	19.5	3.2	22.7
Steel (million tons)	80	32	112	25	6	31
Cement (million tons)	35	21	56	10.5	2.1	12.6
Motor vehicles (thousands)	5273	580	5853	500	25	525

(a) 1949 data.

(b) for the European NAT countries and for the satellites, the data include output by major producers.

It should be noted that these comparisons understate the relative position of the NAT countries for several reasons: (1) Canada is excluded because comparable data were not available; (2) the data for the USSR are the 1950 targets (as stated in the fourth five-year plan) rather than actual rates of production and are believed to exceed in many cases the production actually achieved; (3) the data for the European NAT countries are actual data for 1948, and production has generally increased since that time.

Furthermore, the United States could achieve a substantial absolute increase in output and could thereby increase the allocation of resources to a build-up of the economic and military strength of itself and its allies without suffering a decline in its real standard of living. Industrial production declined by 10 percent between the first quarter of 1948 and the last quarter of 1949, and by approximately one-fourth between 1944 and 1949. In March 1950 there were approximately 4,750,000 unemployed, as compared to 1,070,000 in 1943 and 670,000 in 1944. The gross national product declined slowly in 1949 from the peak reached in 1948 ($262 billion in 1948 to an annual rate of $256 billion in the last six months of 1949), and in terms of constant prices declined by about 20 percent between 1944 and 1948.

With a high level of economic activity, the United States could soon attain a gross national product of $300 billion per year, as was pointed out in the President's Economic Report (January 1950). Progress in this direction would permit, and might itself be aided by, a buildup of the economic and military strength of the United States and the free world; furthermore, if a dynamic expansion of the economy were achieved, the necessary build-up could be accomplished without a decrease in the national standard of living because the required resources could be obtained by siphoning off a part of the annual increment in the gross national product. These are facts of fundamental importance in considering the courses of action open to the United States (cf. Ch. IX).

2. *Intentions.* Foreign economic policy is a major instrument in the conduct of United States foreign relations. It is an instrument which can powerfully influence the world environment in ways favorable to the security and welfare of this country. It is also an instrument which, if unwisely formulated and employed, can do actual harm to our national interests. It is an instrument uniquely suited to our capa-

bilities, provided we have the tenacity of purpose and the understanding requisite to a realization of its potentials. Finally, it is an instrument peculiarly appropriate to the Cold War.

The preceding analysis has indicated that an essential element in a program to frustrate the Kremlin design is the development of a successfully functioning system among the free nations. It is clear that economic conditions are among the fundamental determinants of the will and the strength to resist subversion and aggression.

United States foreign economic policy has been designed to assist in the building of such a system and such conditions in the free world. The principal features of this policy can be summarized as follows:

1. assistance to Western Europe in recovery and the creation of a viable economy (the European Recovery Program);

2. assistance to other countries because of their special needs arising out of the war or the Cold War and our special interests in or responsibility for meeting them (grant assistance to Japan, the Philippines, and Korea, loans and credits by the Export-Import Bank, the International Monetary Fund, and the International Bank to Indonesia, Yugoslavia, Iran, etc.);

3. assistance in the development of underdeveloped areas (the Point IV program and loans and credits to various countries, overlapping to some extent with those mentioned under 2);

4. military assistance to the North Atlantic Treaty countries, Greece, Turkey, etc.;

5. restriction of East-West trade in items of military importance to the East;

6. purchase and stockpiling of strategic materials; and

7. efforts to reestablish an international economy based on multilateral trade, declining trade barriers, and convertible currencies (the GATT-ITO program, the Reciprocal Trade Agreements program, the IMF-IBRD program, and the program now being developed to solve the problem of the United States balance of payments).

In both their short and long term aspects, these policies and programs are directed to the strengthening of the free world and therefore to the frustration of the Kremlin design. Despite certain inadequacies and inconsistencies, which are now being studied in connection with the problem of the United States balance of payments, the United States has generally pursued a foreign economic policy which has powerfully supported its overall objectives. The question must nevertheless be asked whether current and currently projected programs will adequately support this policy in the future, in terms both of need and urgency.

The last year has been indecisive in the economic field. The Soviet Union has made considerable progress in integrating the satellite economies of Eastern Europe into the Soviet economy, but still faces very large problems, especially with China. The free nations have important accomplishments to record, but also have tremendous problems still ahead. On balance, neither side can claim any great advantage in this field over its relative position a year ago. The important question therefore becomes: what are the trends?

Several conclusions seem to emerge. First, the Soviet Union is widening the gap between its preparedness for war and the unpreparedness of the free world for war. It is devoting a far greater *proportion* of its resources to military purposes than are the free nations and, in significant components of military power, a greater *absolute* quantity of resources. Second, the Communist success in China, taken with the politico-economic situation in the rest of South and South-East Asia, provides a springboard for a further incursion in this troubled area. Although Communist China faces serious economic problems which may impose some strains on the Soviet economy, it is probable that the social and economic problems faced by the free nations in this area present more than offsetting opportunities for Communist expansion. Third, the Soviet Union holds positions in Europe which, if it maneuvers skillfully, could be used to do great damage to the Western European economy and to the maintenance of the Western orientation of certain countries, particularly Germany and Austria. Fourth, despite (and in part because of) the Titoist' defection, the Soviet Union has accelerated its efforts to integrate satellite economy with its own and to increase the degree of autarchy within the areas under its control.

Fifth, meanwhile, Western Europe, with American (and Canadian) assistance, has achieved a record level of production. However, it faces the prospect of a rapid tapering off of American assistance without the possibility of achieving, by its own efforts, a satisfactory equilibrium with the dollar area. It has also made very little progress toward "economic integration," which would in the long run tend to improve its productivity and to provide an economic environment

375

conducive to political stability. In particular, the movement toward economic integration does not appear to be rapid enough to provide Western Germany with adequate economic opportunities in the West. The United Kingdom still faces economic problems which may require a moderate but politically difficult decline in the British standard of living or more American assistance than is contemplated. At the same time, a strengthening of the British position is needed if the stability of the Commonwealth is not to be impaired and if it is to be a focus of resistance to Communist expansion in South and South-East Asia. Improvement of the British position is also vital in building up the defensive capabilities of Western Europe.

Sixth, throughout Asia the stability of the present moderate governments, which are more in sympathy with our purposes than any probable successor regimes would be, is doubtful. The problem is only in part an economic one. Assistance in economic development is important as a means of holding out to the peoples of Asia some prospect of improvement in standards of living under their present governments. But probably more important are a strengthening of central institutions, an improvement in administration, and generally a development of an economic and social structure within which the peoples of Asia can make more effective use of their great human and material resources.

Seventh, and perhaps most important, there are indications of a letdown of United States efforts under the pressure of the domestic budgetary situation, disillusion resulting from excessively optimistic expectations about the duration and results of our assistance programs, and doubts about the wisdom of continuing to strengthen the free nations as against preparedness measures in light of the intensity of the Cold War.

Eighth, there are grounds for predicting that the United States and other free nations will within a period of a few years at most experience a decline in economic activity of serious proportions unless more positive governmental programs are developed than are now available.

In short, as we look into the future, the programs now planned will not meet the requirements of the free nations. The difficulty does not lie so much in the inadequacy or misdirection of policy as in the inadequacy of planned programs, in terms of timing or impact, to achieve our objectives. The risks inherent in this situation are set forth in the following chapter and a course of action designed to reinvigorate our efforts in order to reverse the present trends and to achieve our fundamental purpose is outlined in Chapter IX.

C. MILITARY

The United States now possesses the greatest military potential of any single nation in the world. The military weaknesses of the United States vis-à-vis the Soviet Union, however, include its numerical inferiority in forces in being and in total manpower. Coupled with the inferiority of forces in being, the United States also lacks tenable positions from which to employ its forces in event of war and munitions power in being and readily available.

It is true that the United States armed forces are now stronger than ever before in other times of apparent peace; it is also true that there exists a sharp disparity between our actual military strength and our commitments. The relationship of our strength to our present commitments, however, is not alone the governing factor. The world situation, as well as commitments, should govern; hence, our military strength more properly should be related to the world situation confronting us. When our military strength is related to the world situation and balanced against the likely exigencies of such a situation, it is clear that our military strength is becoming dangerously inadequate.

If war should begin in 1950, the United States and its allies will have the military capability of conducting defensive operations to provide a reasonable measure of protection to the Western Hemisphere, bases in the Western Pacific, and essential military lines of communication; and an inadequate measure of protection to vital military bases in the United Kingdom and in the Near and Middle East. We will have the capability of conducting powerful offensive air operations against vital elements of the Soviet war-making capacity.

The scale of the operations listed in the preceding paragraph is limited by the effective forces and material in being of the United States and its allies vis-à-vis the Soviet Union. Consistent with the aggressive threat facing us and in consonance with overall strategic plans, the United States must provide to its allies on a continuing basis as large amounts of military assistance as possible without serious detriment to the United States operational requirements.

If the potential military capabilities of the United States and its allies were rapidly and effectively developed, sufficient forces could be produced probably to deter war, or if the Soviet Union chooses war, to withstand the initial Soviet attacks, to stabilize supporting attacks, and to retaliate in turn with even greater impact on the Soviet capabilities. From the military point of view alone, however, this would require not only the generation of the necessary military forces but also the development and stockpiling of improved weapons of all types.

Under existing peacetime conditions, a period of from two to three years is required to produce a material increase in military power. Such increased power could be provided in a somewhat shorter period in a declared period of emergency or in wartime through a full-out national effort. Any increase in military power in peacetime, however, should be related both to its probable military role in war, to the implementation of immediate and long-term United States foreign policy vis-à-vis the Soviet Union, and to the realities of the existing situation. If such a course of increasing our military power is adopted now, the United States would have the capability of eliminating the disparity between its military strength and the exigencies of the situation we face; eventually of gaining the initiative in the "cold" war and of materially delaying if not stopping the Soviet offensives in war itself.

VII. Present Risks

A. GENERAL

It is apparent from the preceding sections that the integrity and vitality of our system is in greater jeopardy than ever before in our history. Even if there were no Soviet Union we would face the great problem of the free society, accentuated manifold in this industrial age, of reconciling order, security, the need for participation, with the requirement of freedom. We would face the fact that in a shrinking world the absence of order among nations is becoming less and less tolerable. The Kremlin design seeks to impose order among nations by means which would destroy our free and democratic system. The Kremlin's possession of atomic weapons puts new power behind its design, and increases the jeopardy to our system. It adds new strains to the uneasy equilibrium-without-order which exists in the world and raises new doubts in men's minds whether the world will long tolerate this tension without moving toward some kind of order, on somebody's terms.

The risks we face are of a new order of magnitude, commensurate with the total struggle in which we are engaged. For a free society there is never total victory, since freedom and democracy are never wholly attained, are always in the process of being attained. But defeat at the hands of the totalitarian is total defeat. These risks crowd in on us, in a shrinking world of polarized power, so as to give us no choice, ultimately, between meeting them effectively or being overcome by them.

B. SPECIFIC

It is quite clear from Soviet theory and practice that the Kremlin seeks to bring the free world under its dominion by the methods of the Cold War. The preferred technique is to subvert by infiltration and intimidation. Every institution of our society is an instrument which it is sought to stultify and turn against our purposes. Those that touch most closely our material and moral strength are obviously the prime targets, labor unions, civic enterprises, schools, churches, and all media for influencing opinion. The effort is not so much to make them serve obvious Soviet ends as to prevent them from serving our ends, and thus to make them sources of confusion in our economy, our culture, and our body politic. The doubts and diversities that in terms of our values are part of the merit of a free system, the weaknesses and the problems that are peculiar to it, the rights and privileges that free men enjoy, and the disorganization and destruction left in the wake of the last attack on our freedoms, all are but opportunities for the Kremlin to do its evil work. Every advantage is taken of the fact that our means of prevention and retaliation are limited by those principles and scruples which are precisely the ones that give our freedom and democracy its meaning for us. None of our scruples deter those whose only code is "morality is that which serves the revolution."

Since everything that gives us or others respect for our institutions is a suitable object for attack, it also fits the Kremlin's design that where, with impunity, we can be insulted and made to suffer indignity the opportunity shall not be missed, particularly in any context which can be used to cast dishonor on our country, our system, our motives, or our methods. Thus the means by which we sought to restore our own economic health in the '30's, and now seek to restore that of the free world, come equally under attack. The military aid by which we sought to help the free world was frantically denounced by the Communists in the early days of the last war, and of course our present efforts to develop adequate military strength for ourselves and our allies are equally denounced.

At the same time the Soviet Union is seeking to create overwhelming military force, in order to back up infiltration with intimidation. In the only terms in which it understands strength, it is seeking to demonstrate to the free world that force and the will to use it are on the side of the Kremlin, that those who lack it are decadent and doomed. In local incidents it threatens and encroaches both for the sake of local gains and to increase anxiety and defeatism in all the free world.

The possession of atomic weapons at each of the opposite poles of power, and the inability (for different reasons) of either side to place any trust in the other, puts a premium on a surprise attack against us. It equally puts a premium on a more violent and ruthless prosecution of its design by Cold War, especially if the Kremlin is sufficiently objective to realize the improbability of our prosecuting a preventive war. It also puts a premium on piecemeal aggression against others, counting on our unwillingness to engage in atomic war unless we are directly attacked. We run all these risks and the added risk of being confused and immobilized by our inability to weigh and choose, and pursue a firm course based on a rational assessment of each.

The risk that we may thereby be prevented or too long delayed in taking all needful measures to maintain the integrity and vitality of our system is great. The risk that our allies will lose their determination is greater. And the risk that in this manner a descending spiral of too little and too late, of doubt and recrimination, may present us with ever narrower and more desperate alternatives, is the greatest risk of all. For example, it is clear that our present weakness would prevent us from offering effective resistance at any of several vital pressure points. The only deterrent we can present to the Kremlin is the evidence we give that we may make any of the critical points which we cannot hold the occasion for a global war of annihilation.

The risk of having no better choice than to capitulate or precipitate a global war at any of a number of pressure points is bad enough in itself, but it is multiplied by the weakness it imparts to our position in the Cold War. Instead of appearing strong and resolute we are continually at the verge of appearing and being alternately irresolute and desperate; yet it is the Cold War which we must win, because both the Kremlin design, and our fundamental purpose give it the first priority.

The frustration of the Kremlin design, however, cannot be accomplished by us alone, as will appear from the analysis in Chapter IX, B. Strength at the center, in the United States, is only the first of two

380

essential elements. The second is that our allies and potential allies do not as a result of a sense of frustration or of Soviet intimidation drift into a course of neutrality eventually leading to Soviet domination. If this were to happen in Germany the effect upon Western Europe and eventually upon us might be catastrophic.

But there are risks in making ourselves strong. A large measure of sacrifice and discipline will be demanded of the American people. They will be asked to give up some of the benefits which they have come to associate with their freedoms. Nothing could be more important than that they fully understand the reasons for this. The risks of a superficial understanding or of an inadequate appreciation of the issues are obvious and might lead to the adoption of measures which in themselves would jeopardize the integrity of our system. At any point in the process of demonstrating our will to make good our fundamental purpose, the Kremlin may decide to precipitate a general war, or in testing us, may go too far. These are risks we will invite by making ourselves strong, but they are lesser risks than those we seek to avoid. Our fundamental purpose is more likely to be defeated from lack of the will to maintain it, than from any mistakes we may make or assault we may undergo because of asserting that will. No people in history have preserved their freedom who thought that by not being strong enough to protect themselves they might prove inoffensive to their enemies.

VIII. Atomic Armaments

A. MILITARY EVALUATION OF U.S. AND USSR ATOMIC CAPA-⁑ BILITIES

1. The United States now has an atomic capability, including both numbers and deliverability, estimated to be adequate, if effectively utilized, to deliver a serious blow against the war-making capacity of the USSR. It is doubted whether such a blow, even if it resulted in the complete destruction of the contemplated target systems, would cause the USSR to sue for terms or prevent Soviet forces from occupying Western Europe against such ground resistance as could presently be mobilized. A very serious initial blow could, however, so reduce the capabilities of the USSR to supply and equip its military organization and its civilian population as to give the United States the prospect of developing a general military superiority in a war of long duration.

2. As the atomic capability of the USSR increases, it will have an

increased ability to hit at our atomic bases and installations and thus seriously hamper the ability of the United States to carry out an attack such as that outlined above. It is quite possible that in the near future the USSR will have a sufficient number of atomic bombs and a sufficient deliverability to raise a question whether Britain with its present inadequate air defense could be relied upon as an advance base from which a major portion of the U.S. attack could be launched.

It is estimated that, within the next four years, the USSR will attain the capability of seriously damaging vital centers of the United States, provided it strikes a surprise blow and provided further that the blow is opposed by no more effective opposition than we now have programmed. Such a blow could so seriously damage the United States as to greatly reduce its superiority in economic potential.

Effective opposition to this Soviet capability will require among other measures greatly increased air warning systems, air defenses, and vigorous development and implementation of a civilian defense program which has been thoroughly integrated with the military defense systems.

In time the atomic capability of the USSR can be expected to grow to a point where, given surprise and no more effective opposition than we now have programmed, the possibility of a decisive initial attack cannot be excluded.

3. In the initial phases of an atomic war, the advantages of initiative and surprise would be very great. A police state living behind an Iron Curtain has an enormous advantage in maintaining the necessary security and centralization of decision required to capitalize on this advantage.

4. For the moment our atomic retaliatory capability is probably adequate to deter the Kremlin from a deliberate direct military attack against ourselves or other free peoples. However, when it calculates that it has a sufficient atomic capability to make a surprise attack on us, nullifying our atomic superiority and creating a military situation decisively in its favor, the Kremlin might be tempted to strike swiftly and with stealth. The existence of two large atomic capabilities in such a relationship might well act, therefore, not as a deterrent, but as an incitement to war.

5. A further increase in the number and power of our atomic

weapons is necessary in order to assure the effectiveness of any U.S. retaliatory blow, but would not of itself seem to change the basic logic of the above points. Greatly increased general air, ground, and sea strength, and increased air defense and civilian defense programs would also be necessary to provide reasonable assurance that the free world could survive an initial surprise atomic attack of the weight which it is estimated the USSR will be capable of delivering by 1954 and still permit the free world to go on to the eventual attainment of its objectives. Furthermore, such a build-up of strength could safeguard and increase our retaliatory power, and thus might put off for some time the date when the Soviet Union could calculate that a surprise blow would be advantageous. This would provide additional time for the effects of our policies to produce a modification of the Soviet system.

6. If the USSR develops a thermonuclear weapon ahead of the US, the risks of greatly increased Soviet pressure against all the free world, or an attack against the US, will be greatly increased.

7. If the U.S. develops a thermonuclear weapon ahead of the USSR, the U.S. should for the time being be able to bring increased pressure on the USSR.

B. STOCKPILING AND USE OF ATOMIC WEAPONS

1. From the foregoing analysis it appears that it would be to the long-term advantage of the United States if atomic weapons were to be effectively eliminated from national peacetime armaments; the additional objectives which must be secured if there is to be a reasonable prospect of such effective elimination of atomic weapons are discussed in Chapter IX. In the absence of such elimination and the securing of these objectives, it would appear that we have no alternative but to increase our atomic capability as rapidly as other considerations make appropriate. In either case, it appears to be imperative to increase as rapidly as possible our general air, ground, and sea strength and that of our allies to a point where we are militarily not so heavily dependent on atomic weapons.

2. As is indicated in Chapter IV, it is important that the United States employ military force only if the necessity for its use is clear and compelling and commends itself to the overwhelming majority of our people. The United States cannot therefore engage in war except as a reaction to aggression of so clear and compelling a nature as to bring the overwhelming majority of our people to accept the use of military force. In the event war comes, our use of force

must be to compel the acceptance of our objectives and must be congruent to the range of tasks which we may encounter.

In the event of a general war with the USSR, it must be anticipated that atomic weapons will be used by each side in the manner it deems best suited to accomplish its objectives. In view of our vulnerability to Soviet atomic attack, it has been argued that we might wish to hold our atomic weapons only for retaliation against prior use by the USSR. To be able to do so and still have hope of achieving our objectives, the non-atomic military capabilities of ourselves and our allies would have to be fully developed and the political weaknesses of the Soviet Union fully exploited. In the event of war, however, we could not be sure that we could move toward the attainment of these objectives without the USSR's resorting sooner or later to the use of its atomic weapons. Only if we had overwhelming atomic superiority and obtained command of the air might the USSR be deterred from employing its atomic weapons as we progressed toward the attainment of our objectives.

In the event the USSR develops by 1954 the atomic capability which we now anticipate, it is hardly conceivable that, if war comes, the Soviet leaders would refrain from the use of atomic weapons unless they felt fully confident of attaining their objectives by other means.

In the event we use atomic weapons either in retaliation for their prior use by the USSR or because there is no alternative method by which we can attain our objectives, it is imperative that the strategic and tactical targets against which they are used be appropriate and the manner in which they are used be consistent with those objectives.

It appears to follow from the above that we should produce and stockpile thermonuclear weapons in the event they prove feasible and would add significantly to our net capability. Not enough is yet known of their potentialities to warrant a judgment at this time regarding their use in war to attain our objectives.

3. It has been suggested that we announce that we will not use atomic weapons except in retaliation against the prior use of such weapons by an aggressor. It has been argued that such a declaration would decrease the danger of an atomic attack against the United States and its allies.

In our present situation of relative unpreparedness in conventional weapons, such a declaration would be interpreted by the USSR as an admission of great weakness and by our allies as a clear indication that we intended to abandon them. Furthermore, it is doubtful whether such a declaration would be taken sufficiently seriously by the Kremlin to constitute an important factor in determining whether or not to attack the United States. It is to be anticipated that the Kremlin would weigh the facts of our capability far more heavily than a declaration of what we proposed to do with that capability.

Unless we are prepared to abandon our objectives, we cannot make such a declaration in good faith until we are confident that we will be in a position to attain our objectives without war, or, in the event of war, without recourse to the use of atomic weapons for strategic or tactical purposes.

C. INTERNATIONAL CONTROL OF ATOMIC ENERGY

1. A discussion of certain of the basic considerations involved in securing effective international control is necessary to make clear why the additional objectives discussed in Chapter IX must be secured.

2. No system of international control could prevent the production and use of atomic weapons in the event of a prolonged war. Even the most effective system of international control could, of itself, only provide (a) assurance that atomic weapons had been eliminated from national peacetime armaments and (b) immediate notice of a violation. In essence, an effective international control system would be expected to assure a certain amount of time after notice of violation before atomic weapons could be used in war.

3. The time period between notice of violation and possible use of atomic weapons in war which a control system could be expected to assure depends upon a number of factors.

The dismantling of existing stockpiles of bombs and the destruction of casings and firing mechanisms could by themselves give little assurance of securing time. Casings and firing mechanisms are presumably easy to produce, even surreptitiously, and the assembly of weapons does not take much time.

If existing stocks of fissionable materials were in some way eliminated and the future production of fissionable materials effectively controlled, war could not start with a surprise atomic attack.

In order to assure an appreciable time lag between notice of violation and the time when atomic weapons might be available in quantity, it would be necessary to destroy all plants capable of making large amounts of fissionable material. Such action would, however, require a moratorium on those possible peacetime uses which call for large quantities of fissionable materials.

Effective control over the production and stockpiling of raw materials might further extend the time period which effective international control would assure. Now that the Russians have learned the technique of producing atomic weapons, the time between violation of an international control agreement and production of atomic weapons will be shorter than was estimated in 1946, except possibly in the field of thermonuclear or other new types of weapons.

4. The certainty of notice of violation also depends upon a number of factors. In the absence of good faith, it is to be doubted whether any system can be designed which will give certainty of notice of violation. International ownership of raw materials and fissionable materials and international ownership and operation of dangerous facilities, coupled with inspection based on continuous unlimited freedom of access to all parts of the Soviet Union (as well as to all parts of the territory of other signatories to the control agreement) appear to be necessary to give the requisite degree of assurance against secret violations. As the Soviet stockpile of fissionable materials grows, the amount which the USSR might secretly withhold and not declare to the inspection agency grows. In this sense, the earlier an agreement is consummated the greater the security it would offer. The possibility of successful secret production operations also increases with developments which may reduce the size and power consumption of individual reactors. The development of a thermonuclear bomb would increase manifold the damage a given amount of fissionable material could do and would, therefore, vastly increase the danger that a decisive advantage could be gained through secret operations.

5. The relative sacrifices which would be involved in international control need also to be considered. If it were possible to negotiate an effective system of international control the United States would presumably sacrifice a much larger stockpile of atomic weapons and a much larger production capacity than would the USSR. The opening up of national territory to international inspection involved in an adequate control and inspection system would have a far greater impact on the USSR than on the United States. If the control system involves the destruction of all large reactors and thus a moratorium on certain possible peacetime uses, the USSR can be expected to argue that it,

because of greater need for new sources of energy, would be making a greater sacrifice in this regard than the United States.

6. The United States and the peoples of the world as a whole desire a respite from the dangers of atomic warfare. The chief difficulty lies in the danger that the respite would be short and that we might not have adequate notice of its pending termination. For such an arrangement to be in the interest of the United States, it is essential that the agreement be entered into in good faith by both sides and the probability against its violation high.

7. The most substantial contribution to security of an effective international control system would, of course, be the opening up of the Soviet Union, as required under the UN plan. Such opening up is not, however, compatible with the maintenance of the Soviet system in its present rigor. This is a major reason for the Soviet refusal to accept the UN plan.

The studies which began with the Acheson-Lilienthal committee and culminated in the present UN plan made it clear that inspection of atomic facilities would not alone give the assurance of control; but that ownership and operation by an international authority of the world's atomic energy activities from the mine to the last use of fissionable materials was also essential. The delegation of sovereignty which this implies is necessary for effective control and, therefore, is as necessary for the United States and the rest of the free world as it is presently unacceptable to the Soviet Union.

It is also clear that a control authority not susceptible directly or indirectly to Soviet domination is equally essential. As the Soviet Union would regard any country not under its domination as under the potential if not the actual domination of the United States, it is clear that what the United States and the non-Soviet world must insist on, the Soviet Union at present rejects.

The principal immediate benefit of international control would be to make a surprise atomic attack impossible, assuming the elimination of large reactors and the effective disposal of stockpiles of fissionable materials. But it is almost certain that the Soviet Union would not agree to the elimination of large reactors, unless the impracticability of producing atomic power for peaceful purposes had been demonstrated beyond a doubt. By the same token, it would not now agree to elimination of its stockpile of fissionable materials.

Finally, the absence of good faith on the part of the USSR must be assumed until there is concrete evidence that there has been a decisive change in Soviet policies. It is to be doubted whether such a change can take place without a change in the nature of the Soviet system itself.

The above considerations make it clear that at least a major change in the relative power positions of the United States and the Soviet Union would have to take place before an effective system of international control could be negotiated. The Soviet Union would have had to have moved a substantial distance down the path of accommodation and compromise before such an arrangement would be conceivable. This conclusion is supported by the Third Report of the United Nations Atomic Energy Commission to the Security Council, May 17, 1948, in which it is stated that ". . . the majority of the Commission has been unable to secure . . . their acceptance of the nature and extent of participation in the world community required of all nations in this field.... As a result, the Commission has been forced to recognize that agreement on effective measures for the control of atomic energy is itself dependent on cooperation in broader fields of policy."

In short, it is impossible to hope that an effective plan for international control can be negotiated unless and until the Kremlin design has been frustrated to a point at which a genuine and drastic change in Soviet policies has taken place.

IX. Possible Courses of Action

Introduction. Four possible courses of action by the United States in the present situation can be distinguished. They are:

a.   Continuation of current policies, with current and currently projected programs for carrying out these policies;
b.   Isolation;
c.   War; and
d.   A more rapid building up of the political, economic, and military strength of the free world than provided under a, with the purpose of reaching, if possible, a tolerable state of order among nations without war and of preparing to defend ourselves in the event that the free world is attacked.

The role of negotiation. Negotiation must be considered in relation to these courses of action. A negotiator always attempts to achieve an agreement which is somewhat better than the realities of his fundamental position would justify and which is, in any case, not worse than his fundamental position requires. This is as true in relations among sovereign states as in relations between individuals. The Soviet Union possesses several advantages over the free world in negotiations on any issue:

a. It can and does enforce secrecy on all significant facts about conditions within the Soviet Union, so that it can be expected to know more about the realities of the free world's position than the free world knows about its position;

b. It does not have to be responsive in any important sense to public opinion;

c. It does not have to consult and agree with any other countries on the terms it will offer and accept; and

d. It can influence public opinion in other countries while insulating the peoples under its control.

These are important advantages. Together with the unfavorable trend of our power position, they militate, as is shown in Section A below, against successful negotiation of a general settlement at this time. For although the United States probably now possesses, principally in atomic weapons, a force adequate to deliver a powerful blow upon the Soviet Union and to open the road to victory in a long war, it is not sufficient by itself to advance the position of the United States in the Cold War.

The problem is to create such political and economic conditions in the free world, backed by force sufficient to inhibit Soviet attack, that the Kremlin will accommodate itself to these conditions, gradually withdraw, and eventually change its policies drastically. It has been shown in Chapter VIII that truly effective control of atomic energy would require such an opening up of the Soviet Union and such evidence in other ways of its good faith and its intent to co-exist in peace as to reflect or at least initiate a change in the Soviet system.

Clearly under present circumstances we will not be able to negotiate a settlement which calls for a change in the Soviet system. What, then, is the role of negotiation?

In the first place, the public in the United States and in other free countries will require, as a condition to firm policies and adequate programs directed to the frustration of the Kremlin design, that the free world be continuously prepared to negotiate agreements with the Soviet Union on equitable terms. It is still argued by many people here

389

and abroad that equitable agreements with the Soviet Union are pos-sible, and this view will gain force if the Soviet Union begins to show signs of accommodation, even on unimportant issues.

The free countries must always, therefore, be prepared to negotiate and must be ready to take the initiative at times in seeking negotiation. They must develop a negotiating position which defines the issues and the terms on which they would be prepared—and at what stages—to accept agreements with the Soviet Union. The terms must be fair in the view of popular opinion in the free world. This means that they must be consistent with a positive program for peace—in har-mony with the United Nations' Charter and providing, at a minimum, for the effective control of all armaments by the United Nations or a successor organization. The terms must not require more of the Soviet Union than such behavior and such participation in a world organization. The fact that such conduct by the Soviet Union is impos-sible without such a radical change in Soviet policies as to constitute a change in the Soviet system would then emerge as a result of the Kremlin's unwillingness to accept such terms or of its bad faith in observing them.

A sound negotiating position is, therefore, an essential element in the ideological conflict. For some time after a decision to build up strength, any offer of, or attempt at, negotiation of a general settle-ment along the lines of the Berkeley speech by the Secretary of State could be only a tactic.

Nevertheless, concurrently with a decision and a start on building up the strength of the free world, it may be desirable to pursue this tac-tic both to gain public support for the program and to minimize the immediate risks of war. It is urgently necessary for the United States to determine its negotiating position and to obtain agreement with its major allies on the purposes and terms of negotiation.

In the second place, assuming that the United States in cooperation with other free countries decides and acts to increase the strength of the free world and assuming that the Kremlin chooses the path of accommodation, it will from time to time be necessary and desirable to negotiate on various specific issues with the Kremlin as the area of possible agreement widens.

The Kremlin will have three major objectives in negotiations with the United States. The first is to eliminate the atomic capabilities of the United States; the second is to prevent the effective mobilization of

390

the superior potential of the free world in human and material resources; and the third is to secure a withdrawal of United States forces from, and commitments to, Europe and Japan. Depending on its evaluation of its own strengths and weaknesses as against the West's (particularly the ability and will of the West to sustain its efforts), it will or will not be prepared to make important concessions to achieve these major objectives. It is unlikely that the Kremlin's evaluation is such that it would now be prepared to make significant concessions.

The objectives of the United States and other free countries in negotiations with the Soviet Union (apart from the ideological objectives discussed above) are to record, in a formal fashion which will facilitate the consolidation and further advance of our position, the process of Soviet accommodation to the new political, psychological, and economic conditions in the world which will result from adoption of the fourth course of action and which will be supported by the increasing military strength developed as an integral part of that course of action. In short, our objectives are to record, where desirable, the gradual withdrawal of the Soviet Union and to facilitate that process by making negotiation, if possible, always more expedient than resort to force.

It must be presumed that for some time the Kremlin will accept agreements only if it is convinced that by acting in bad faith whenever and wherever there is an opportunity to do so with impunity, it can derive greater advantage from the agreements than the free world. For this reason, we must take care that any agreements are enforceable or that they are not susceptible of violation without detection and the possibility of effective countermeasures.

This further suggests that we will have to consider carefully the order in which agreements can be concluded. Agreement on the control of atomic energy would result in a relatively greater disarmament of the United States than of the Soviet Union, even assuming considerable progress in building up the strength of the free world in conventional forces and weapons. It might be accepted by the Soviet Union as part of a deliberate design to move against Western Europe and other areas of strategic importance with conventional forces and weapons. In this event, the United States would find itself at war, having previously disarmed itself in its most important weapon, and would be engaged in a race to redevelop atomic weapons.

This seems to indicate that for the time being the United States and other free countries would have to insist on concurrent agreement on the control of nonatomic forces and weapons and perhaps on the other elements of a general settlement, notably peace treaties with Germany, Austria, and Japan and the withdrawal of Soviet influence from the satellites. If, contrary to our expectations, the Soviet Union should accept agreements promising effective control of atomic energy and conventional armaments, without any other changes in Soviet policies, we would have to consider very carefully whether we could accept such agreements. It is unlikely that this problem will arise.

To the extent that the United States and the rest of the free world succeed in so building up their strength in conventional forces and weapons that a Soviet attack with similar forces could be thwarted or held, we will gain increased flexibility and can seek agreements on the various issues in any order, as they become negotiable.

In the third place, negotiation will play a part in the building up of the strength of the free world, apart from the ideological strength discussed above. This is most evident in the problems of Germany, Austria, and Japan. In the process of building up strength, it may be desirable for the free nations, without the Soviet Union, to conclude separate arrangements with Japan, Western Germany, and Austria which would enlist the energies and resources of these countries in support of the free world. This will be difficult unless it has been demonstrated by attempted negotiation with the Soviet Union that the Soviet Union is not prepared to accept treaties of peace which would leave these countries free, under adequate safeguards, to participate in the United Nations and in regional or broader associations of states consistent with the United Nations' Charter and providing security and adequate opportunities for the peaceful development of their political and economic life.

This demonstrates the importance, from the point of view of negotiation as well as for its relationship to the building up of the strength of the free world (see Section D below), of the problem of closer association—on a regional or a broader basis—among the free countries.

In conclusion, negotiation is not a possible separate course of action but rather a means of gaining support for a program of building strength, of recording, where necessary and desirable, progress in the Cold War, and of facilitating further progress while helping to minimize the risks of war. Ultimately, it is our objective to negotiate a settlement with the Soviet Union (or a successor state or states) on which the world can place reliance as an enforceable instrument of peace. But it is important to emphasize that such a settlement can only record the progress which the free world will have made in creating a political and economic system in the world so successful that the frustration of the Kremlin's design for world domination will be complete. The analysis in the following sections indicates that the building of such a system requires expanded and accelerated programs for the carrying out of current policies.

A. THE FIRST COURSE—CONTINUATION OF CURRENT POLICIES, WITH CURRENT AND CURRENTLY PROJECTED PROGRAMS FOR CARRYING OUT THESE POLICIES

1. Military aspects. On the basis of current programs, the United States has a large potential military capability but an actual capability which, though improving, is declining relative to the USSR, particularly in light of its probable fission bomb capability and possible thermonuclear bomb capability. The same holds true for the free world as a whole relative to the Soviet world as a whole. If war breaks out in 1950 or in the next few years, the United States and its allies, apart from a powerful atomic blow, will be compelled to conduct delaying actions, while building up their strength for a general offensive. A frank evaluation of the requirements, to defend the United States and its vital interests and to support a vigorous initiative in the Cold War, on the one hand, and of present capabilities, on the other, indicates that there is a sharp and growing disparity between them.

A review of Soviet policy shows that the military capabilities, actual and potential, of the United States and the rest of the free world, together with the apparent determination of the free world to resist further Soviet expansion, have not induced the Kremlin to relax its pressures generally or to give up the initiative in the Cold War. On the contrary, the Soviet Union has consistently pursued a bold foreign policy, modified only when its probing revealed a determination and an ability of the free world to resist encroachment upon it. The relative military capabilities of the free world are declining, with the result that its determination to resist may also decline and that the security of the United States and the free world as a whole will be jeopardized.

From the military point of view, the actual and potential capabilities of the United States, given a continuation of current and projected programs, will become less and less effective as a war deterrent. Improvement of the state of readiness will become more and more important not only to inhibit the launching of war by the Soviet Union but also to support a national policy designed to reverse the present ominous trends in international relations. A building up of the military capabilities of the United States and the free world is a pre-condition to the achievement of the objectives outlined in this report and to the protection of the United States against disaster.

Fortunately, the United States military establishment has been developed into a unified and effective force as a result of the policies laid down by the Congress and the vigorous carrying out of these policies by the Administration in the fields of both organization and economy. It is, therefore, a base upon which increased strength can be rapidly built with maximum efficiency and economy.

2. *Political aspects.* The Soviet Union is pursuing the initiative in the conflict with the free world. Its atomic capabilities, together with its successes in the Far East, have led to an increasing confidence on its part and to an increasing nervousness in Western Europe and the rest of the free world. We cannot be sure, of course, how vigorously the Soviet Union will pursue its initiative, nor can we be sure of the strength or weakness of the other free countries in reacting to it. There are, however, ominous signs of further deterioration in the Far East. There are also some indications that a decline in morale and confidence in Western Europe may be expected. In particular, the situation in Germany is unsettled. Should the belief or suspicion spread that the free nations are not now able to prevent the Soviet Union from taking, if it chooses, the military actions outlined in Chapter V, the determination of the free countries to resist probably would lessen and there would be an increasing temptation for them to seek a position of neutrality.

Politically, recognition of the military implications of a continuation of present trends will mean that the United States and especially other free countries will tend to shift to the defensive, or to follow a dangerous policy of bluff, because the maintenance of a firm initiative in the Cold War is closely related to aggregate strength in being and readily available.

This is largely a problem of the incongruity of the current actual capabilities of the free world and the threat to it, for the free world has an economic and military potential far superior to the potential of the Soviet Union and its satellites. The shadow of Soviet force falls darkly on Western Europe and Asia and supports a policy of encroachment. The free world lacks adequate means—in the form of forces in being—to thwart such expansion locally. The United States will therefore be confronted more frequently with the dilemma of reacting totally to a limited extension of Soviet control or of not reacting at all (except with ineffectual protests and half measures). Continuation of present trends is likely to lead, therefore, to a gradual withdrawal under the direct or indirect pressure of the Soviet Union, until we discover one day that we have sacrificed positions of vital interest. In other words, the United States would have chosen, by lack of the necessary decisions and actions, to fall back to isolation in the Western Hemisphere. This course would at best result in only a relatively brief truce and would be ended either by our capitulation or by a defensive war—on unfavorable terms from unfavorable positions—against a Soviet Empire compromising all or most of Eurasia. (See Section B.)

3. Economic and social aspects. As was pointed out in Chapter VI, the present foreign economic policies and programs of the United States will not produce a solution to the problem of international economic equilibrium, notably the problem of the dollar gap, and will not create an economic base conducive to political stability in many important free countries.

The European Recovery Program has been successful in assisting the restoration and expansion of production in Western Europe and has been a major factor in checking the dry rot of Communism in Western Europe. However, little progress has been made toward the resumption by Western Europe of a position of influence in world affairs commensurate with its potential strength. Progress in this direction will require integrated political, economic, and military policies and programs, which are supported by the United States and the Western European countries and which will probably require a deeper participation by the United States than has been contemplated.

The Point IV Program and other assistance programs will not adequately supplement, as now projected, the efforts of other important countries to develop effective institutions, to improve the administration of their affairs, and to achieve a sufficient measure of economic development. The moderate regimes now in power in many countries, like India, Indonesia, Pakistan, and the Philippines, will probably be unable to restore or retain their popular support and authority unless they are assisted in bringing about a more rapid improvement of the economic and social structure than present programs will make possible.

The Executive Branch is now undertaking a study of the problem of the United States balance of payments and of the measures which might be taken by the United States to assist in establishing international economic equilibrium. This is a very important project and work on it should have a high priority. However, unless such an economic program is matched and supplemented by an equally far-sighted and vigorous political and military program, we will not be successful in checking and rolling back the Kremlin's drive.

4. Negotiation. In short, by continuing along its present course the free world will not succeed in making effective use of its vastly superior political, economic, and military potential to build a tolerable state of order among nations. On the contrary, the political, economic, and military situation of the free world is already unsatisfactory and will become less favorable unless we act to reverse present trends.

This situation is one which militates against successful negotiations with the Kremlin—for the terms of agreements on important pending issues would reflect present realities and would therefore be unacceptable, if not disastrous, to the United States and the rest of the free world. Unless a decision had been made and action undertaken to build up the strength, in the broadest sense, of the United States and the free world, an attempt to negotiate a general settlement on terms acceptable to us would be ineffective and probably long drawn out, and might thereby seriously delay the necessary measures to build up our strength.

This is true despite the fact that the United States now has the capability of delivering a powerful blow against the Soviet Union in the event of war, for one of the present realities is that the United States is not prepared to threaten the use of our present atomic superiority to coerce the Soviet Union into acceptable agreements. In light of present trends, the Soviet Union will not withdraw and the only conceivable basis for a general settlement would be spheres of influence and of no influenced "settlement" which the Kremlin could readily exploit to its great advantage. The idea that Germany or Japan or other important areas can exist as islands of neutrality in a divided world is unreal, given the Kremlin design for world domination.

B. THE SECOND COURSE—ISOLATION

Continuation of present trends, it has been shown above, will lead progressively to the withdrawal of the United States from most of its present commitments in Europe and Asia and to our isolation in the

Western Hemisphere and its approaches. This would result not from a conscious decision but from a failure to take the actions necessary to bring our capabilities into line with our commitments and thus to a withdrawal under pressure. This pressure might come from our present Allies, who will tend to seek other "solutions" unless they have confidence in our determination to accelerate our efforts to build a successfully functioning political and economic system in the free world.

There are some who advocate a deliberate decision to isolate ourselves. Superficially, this has some attractiveness as a course of action, for it appears to bring our commitments and capabilities into harmony by reducing the former and by concentrating our present, or perhaps even reduced, military expenditures on the defense of the United States.

This argument overlooks the relativity of capabilities. With the United States in an isolated position, we would have to face the probability that the Soviet Union would quickly dominate most of Eurasia, probably without meeting armed resistance. It would thus acquire a potential far superior to our own, and would promptly proceed to develop this potential with the purpose of eliminating our power, which would, even in isolation, remain as a challenge to it and as an obstacle to the imposition of its kind of order in the world. There is no way to make ourselves inoffensive to the Kremlin except by complete submission to its will. Therefore isolation would in the end condemn us to capitulate or to fight alone and on the defensive, with drastically limited offensive and retaliatory capabilities in comparison with the Soviet Union. (These are the only possibilities, unless we are prepared to risk the future on the hazard that the Soviet Empire, because of over-extension or other reasons, will spontaneously destroy itself from within.)

The argument also overlooks the imponderable, but nevertheless drastic, effects on our belief in ourselves and in our way of life of a deliberate decision to isolate ourselves. As the Soviet Union came to dominate free countries, it is clear that many Americans would feel a deep sense of responsibility and guilt for having abandoned their former friends and allies. As the Soviet Union mobilized the resources of Eurasia, increased its relative military capabilities, and heightened its threat to our security, some would be tempted to accept "peace" on its terms, while many would seek to defend the United States by creating a regimented system which would permit the assignment of a tremendous part of our resources to defense.

Under such a state of affairs our national morale would be corrupted and the integrity and vitality of our system subverted.

Under this course of action, there would be no negotiation, unless on the Kremlin's terms, for we would have given up everything of importance.

It is possible that at some point in the course of isolation, many Americans would come to favor a surprise attack on the Soviet Union and the area under its control, in a desperate attempt to alter decisively the balance of power by an overwhelming blow with modern weapons of mass destruction. It appears unlikely that the Soviet Union would wait for such an attack before launching one of its own. But even if it did and even if our attack were successful, it is clear that the United States would face appalling tasks in establishing a tolerable state of order among nations after such a war and after Soviet occupation of all or most of Eurasia for some years. These tasks appear so enormous and success so unlikely that reason dictates an attempt to achieve our objectives by other means.

C. THE THIRD COURSE—WAR

Some Americans favor a deliberate decision to go to war against the Soviet Union in the near future. It goes without saying that the idea of "preventive" war—in the sense of a military attack not provoked by a military attack upon us or our allies—is generally unacceptable to Americans. Its supporters argue that since the Soviet Union is in fact at war with the free world now and that since the failure of the Soviet Union to use all-out military force is explainable on grounds of expediency, we are at war and should conduct ourselves accordingly. Some further argue that the free world is probably unable, except under the crisis of war, to mobilize and direct its resources to the checking and rolling back of the Kremlin's drive for world dominion. This is a powerful argument in the light of history, but the considerations against war are so compelling that the free world must demonstrate that this argument is wrong. The case for war is premised on the assumption that the United States could launch and sustain an attack of sufficient impact to gain a decisive advantage for the free world in a long war and perhaps to win an early decision.

The ability of the United States to launch effective offensive operations is now limited to attack with atomic weapons. A powerful blow could be delivered upon the Soviet Union, but it is estimated that these operations alone would not force or induce the Kremlin to capitulate and that the Kremlin would still be able to use the forces under its control to dominate most or all of Eurasia. This would probably mean a long and difficult struggle during which the free institutions of Western Europe and many freedom-loving people would be destroyed and the regenerative capacity of Western Europe dealt a crippling blow.

Apart from this, however, a surprise attack upon the Soviet Union, despite the provocativeness of recent Soviet behavior, would be repugnant to many Americans. Although the American people would probably rally in support of the war effort, the shock of responsibility for a surprise attack would be morally corrosive. Many would doubt that it was a "just war" and that all reasonable possibilities for a peaceful settlement had been explored in good faith. Many more, proportionately, would hold such views in other countries, particularly in Western Europe and particularly after Soviet occupation, if only because the Soviet Union would liquidate articulate opponents. It would, therefore, be difficult after such a war to create a satisfactory international order among nations. Victory in such a war would have brought us little if at all closer to victory in the fundamental ideological conflict.

These considerations are no less weighty because they are imponderable, and they rule out an attack unless it is demonstrably in the nature of a counter-attack to a blow which is on its way or about to be delivered. (The military advantages of landing the first blow become increasingly important with modem weapons, and this is a fact which requires us to be on the alert in order to strike with our full weight as soon as we are attacked, and, if possible, before the Soviet blow is actually delivered.) If the argument of Chapter IV is accepted, it follows that there is no "easy" solution and that the only sure victory lies in the frustration of the Kremlin design by the steady development of the moral and material strength of the free world and its projection into the Soviet world in such a way as to bring about an internal change in the Soviet system.

D. THE REMAINING COURSE OF ACTION—A RAPID BUILD-UP OF POLITICAL, ECONOMIC, AND MILITARY STRENGTH IN THE FREE WORLD

A more rapid build-up of political, economic, and military strength and thereby of confidence in the free world than is now contemplated is the only course which is consistent with progress toward achieving our fundamental purpose. The frustration of the Kremlin design requires the free world to develop a successfully functioning political and economic system and a vigorous political offensive against the Soviet Union. These, in turn, require an adequate military shield under which they can develop. It is necessary to have the military power to deter, if possible, Soviet expansion, and to defeat, if necessary, aggressive Soviet or Soviet-directed actions of a limited or total character. The potential strength of the free world is great; its ability to develop these military capabilities and its will to resist Soviet expansion will be determined by the wisdom and will with which it undertakes to meet its political and economic problems.

1. Military aspects. It has been indicated in Chapter VI that U.S. military capabilities are strategically more defensive in nature than offensive and are more potential than actual. It is evident, from an analysis of the past and of the trend of weapon development, that there is now and will be in the future no absolute defense. The history of war also indicates that a favorable decision can only be achieved through offensive action. Even a defensive strategy, if it is to be successful, calls not only for defensive forces to hold vital positions while mobilizing and preparing for the offensive, but also for offensive forces to attack the enemy and keep him off balance.

The two fundamental requirements which must be met by forces in being or readily available are support of foreign policy and protection against disaster. To meet the second requirement, the forces in being or readily available must be able, at a minimum, to perform certain basic tasks:

a. To defend the Western Hemisphere and essential allied areas in order that their war-making capabilities can be developed;
b. To provide and protect a mobilization base while the offensive forces required for victory are being built up;
c. To conduct offensive operations to destroy vital elements of the Soviet war-making capacity, and to keep the enemy off balance until the full offensive strength of the United States and its allies can be brought to bear;
d. To defend and maintain the lines of communication and base areas necessary to the execution of the above tasks; and
e. To provide such aid to allies as is essential to the execution of their role in the above tasks.

In the broadest terms, the ability to perform these tasks requires a build-up of military strength by the United States and its allies to a point at which the combined strength will be superior for at least

400

these tasks, both initially and throughout a war, to the forces that can be brought to bear by the Soviet Union and its satellites. In specific terms, it is not essential to match item for item with the Soviet Union, but to provide an adequate defense against air attack on the United States and Canada and an adequate defense against air and sur-face attack on the United Kingdom and Western Europe, Alaska, the Western Pacific, Africa, and the Near and Middle East, and on the long lines of communication to these areas. Furthermore, it is mandatory that in building up our strength, we enlarge upon our technical superiority by an accelerated exploitation of the scientific potential of the United States and our allies.

Forces of this size and character are necessary not only for protec-tion against disaster but also to support our foreign policy. In fact, it can be argued that larger forces in being and readily available are necessary to inhibit a would-be aggressor than to provide the nucle-us of strength and the mobilization base on which the tremendous forces required for victory can be built. For example, in both World Wars I and II the ultimate victors had the strength, in the end, to win though they had not had the strength in being or readily available to prevent the outbreak of war. In part, at least, this was because they had not had the military strength on which to base a strong foreign policy. At any rate, it is clear that a substantial and rapid building up of strength in the free world is necessary to support a firm policy intended to check and to roll back the Kremlin's drive for world dom-ination.

Moreover, the United States and the other free countries do not now have the forces in being and readily available to defeat local Soviet moves with local action, but must accept reverses or make these local moves the occasion for war—for which we are not prepared. This situation makes for great uneasiness among our allies, particu-larly in Western Europe, for whom total war means, initially, Soviet occupation. Thus, unless our combined strength is rapidly increased, our allies will tend to become increasingly reluctant to support a firm foreign policy on our part and increasingly anxious to seek other solutions, even though they are aware that appeasement means defeat. An important advantage in adopting the fourth course of action lies in its psychological impact—the revival of confidence and hope in the future. It is recognized, of course, that any announce-ment of the recommended course of action could be exploited by the Soviet Union in its peace campaign and would have adverse psy-chological effects in certain parts of the free world until the neces-

401

sary increase in strength has been achieved. Therefore, in any announcement of policy and in the character of the measures adopted, emphasis should be given to the essentially defensive character and care should be taken to minimize, so far as possible, unfavorable domestic and foreign reactions.

2. Political and economic aspects. The immediate objectives—to the achievement of which such a build-up of strength is a necessary though not a sufficient condition—are a renewed initiative in the Cold War and a situation to which the Kremlin would find it expedient to accommodate itself, first by relaxing tensions and pressures and then by gradual withdrawal. The United States cannot alone provide the resources required for such a build-up of strength. The other free countries must carry their part of the burden, but their ability and determination to do it will depend on the action the United States takes to develop its own strength and on the adequacy of its foreign political and economic policies. Improvement in political and economic conditions in the free world, as has been emphasized above, is necessary as a basis for building up the will and the means to resist and for dynamically affirming the integrity and vitality of our free and democratic way of life on which our ultimate victory depends.

At the same time, we should take dynamic steps to reduce the power and influence of the Kremlin inside the Soviet Union and other areas under its control. The objective would be the establishment of friendly regimes not under Kremlin domination. Such action is essential to engage the Kremlin's attention, keep it off balance, and force an increased expenditure of Soviet resources in counteraction. In other words, it would be the current Soviet Cold War technique used against the Soviet Union.

A program for rapidly building up strength and improving political and economic conditions will place heavy demands on our courage and intelligence; it will be costly; it will be dangerous. But half-measures will be more costly and more dangerous, for they will be inadequate to prevent and may actually invite war. Budgetary considerations will need to be subordinated to the stark fact that our very independence as a nation may be at stake.

A comprehensive and decisive program to win the peace and frustrate the Kremlin design should be so designed that it can be sustained for as long as necessary to achieve our national objectives. It would probably involve:

402

1. The development of an adequate political and economic framework for the achievement of our long-range objectives.

2. A substantial increase in expenditures for military purposes adequate to meet the requirements for the tasks listed in Section D-1.

3. A substantial increase in military assistance programs, designed to foster cooperative efforts, which will adequately and efficiently meet the requirements of our allies for the tasks referred to in Section D-1e.

4. Some increase in economic assistance programs and recognition of the need to continue these programs until their purposes have been accomplished.

5. A concerted attack on the problem of the United States balance of payments, along the lines already approved by the President.

6. Development of programs designed to build and maintain confidence among other peoples in our strength and resolution, and to wage overt psychological warfare calculated to encourage mass defections from Soviet allegiance and to frustrate the Kremlin design in other ways.

7. Intensification of affirmative and timely measures and operations by covert means in the fields of economic warfare and political and psychological warfare with a view to fomenting and supporting unrest and revolt in selected strategic satellite countries.

8. Development of internal security and civilian defense programs.

9. Improvement and intensification of intelligence activities.

10. Reduction of Federal expenditures for purposes other than defense and foreign assistance, if necessary by the deferment of certain desirable programs.

11. Increased taxes.

Essential as prerequisites to the success of this program would be (a) consultations with Congressional leaders designed to make the program the object of non-partisan legislative support, and (b) a presentation to the public of a full explanation of the facts and implications of present international trends.

The program will be costly, but it is relevant to recall the dispropor-tion between the potential capabilities of the Soviet and non-Soviet worlds (cf. Chapters V and VI). The Soviet Union is currently devot-ing about 40 percent of available resources (gross national product plus reparations, equal in 1949 to about $65 billion) to military expenditures (14 percent) and to investment (26 percent), much of which is in war-supporting industries. In an emergency the Soviet Union could increase the allocation of resources to these purposes to about 50 percent, or by one-fourth.

The United States is currently devoting about 22 percent of its gross national product ($255 billion in 1949) to military expenditures (6 percent), foreign assistance (2 percent), and investment (14 per-cent), little of which is in war-supporting industries. (As was pointed out in Chapter V, the "fighting value" obtained per dollar of expendi-ture by the Soviet Union considerably exceeds that obtained by the United States, primarily because of the extremely low military and civilian living standards in the Soviet Union.) In an emergency the United States could devote upward of 50 percent of its gross nation-al product to these purposes (as it did during the last war), an increase of several times present expenditures for direct and indirect military purposes and foreign assistance.

From the point of view of the economy as a whole, the program might not result in a real decrease in the standard of living, for the economic effects of the program might be to increase the gross national product by more than the amount being absorbed for addi-tional military and foreign assistance purposes. One of the most sig-nificant lessons of our World War II experience was that the American economy, when it operates at a level approaching full effi-ciency, can provide enormous resources for purposes other than civilian consumption while simultaneously providing a high standard of living. After allowing for price changes, personal consumption expenditures rose by about one-fifth between 1939 and 1944, even though the economy had in the meantime increased the amount of resources going into Government use by $60 $65 billion (in 1939 prices).

This comparison between the potentials of the Soviet Union and the United States also holds true for the Soviet world and the free world and is of fundamental importance in considering the courses of action open to the United States.

404

The comparison gives renewed emphasis to the fact that the problems faced by the free countries in their efforts to build a successfully functioning system lie not so much in the field of economics as in the field of politics. The building of such a system may require more rapid progress toward the closer association of the free countries in harmony with the concept of the United Nations. It is clear that our long-range objectives require a strengthened United Nations, or a successor organization, to which the world can look for the maintenance of peace and order in a system based on freedom and justice. It also seems clear that a unifying ideal of this kind might awaken and arouse the latent spiritual energies of free men everywhere and obtain their enthusiastic support for a positive program for peace going far beyond the frustration of the Kremlin design and opening vistas to the future that would outweigh short-run sacrifices.

The threat to the free world involved in the development of the Soviet Union's atomic and other capabilities will rise steadily and rather rapidly. For the time being, the United States possesses a marked atomic superiority over the Soviet Union which, together with the potential capabilities of the United States and other free countries in other forces and weapons, inhibits aggressive Soviet action. This provides an opportunity for the United States, in cooperation with other free countries, to launch a build-up of strength which will support a firm policy directed to the frustration of the Kremlin design. The immediate goal of our efforts to build a successfully functioning political and economic system in the free world backed by adequate military strength is to postpone and avert the disastrous situation which, in light of the Soviet Union's probable fission bomb capability and possible thermonuclear bomb capability, might arise in 1954 on a continuation of our present programs. By acting promptly and vigorously in such a way that this date is, so to speak, pushed into the future, we would permit time for the process of accommodation, withdrawal and frustration to produce the necessary changes in the Soviet system. Time is short, however, and the risks of war attendant upon a decision to build up strength will steadily increase the longer we defer it.

Appendix 4

Winston Churchill's Iron Curtain Speech

Winston Churchill's *Sinews of Peace* speech was given at Westminster College, in Fulton, Missouri, after he received an honorary degree there. It became famous as the *Iron Curtain Speech* for the phrase "... an Iron Curtain has descended across the Continent." Incidentally, the speech also marked the onset of the Cold War. A complete transcript of the speech can be found @ www.nationalcenter.org/ChurchillIronCurtain.html.

President McCluer, ladies and gentlemen, and last, but certainly not least, the President of the United States of America:

I am very glad indeed to come to Westminster College this afternoon, and I am complimented that you should give me a degree from an institution whose reputation has been so solidly established. The name "Westminster" somehow or other seems familiar to me. I feel as if I have heard of it before. Indeed now that I come to think of it, it was at Westminster that I received a very large part of my education in politics, dialectic, rhetoric, and one or two other things. In fact we have both been educated at the same, or similar, or, at any rate, kindred establishments.

It is also an honor, ladies and gentlemen, perhaps almost unique, for a private visitor to be introduced to an academic audience by the President of the United States. Amid his heavy burdens, duties, and responsibilities—unsought but not recoiled from—the President has traveled a thousand miles to dignify and magnify our meeting here today and to give me an opportunity of addressing this kindred nation, as well as my own countrymen across the ocean, and perhaps some other countries too. The President has told you that it is his wish, as I am sure it is yours, that I should have full liberty to give my true and faithful counsel in these anxious and baffling times. I shall certainly avail myself of this freedom, and feel the more right to do so because any private ambitions I may have cherished in my younger days have been satisfied beyond my wildest dreams. Let me however make it clear that I have no official mission or status of any kind, and that I speak only for myself. There is nothing here but what you see.

I can therefore allow my mind, with the experience of a lifetime, to play over the problems which beset us on the morrow of our absolute victory in arms, and to try to make sure with what strength I have that what has gained with so much sacrifice and suffering shall be preserved for the future glory and safety of mankind.

Ladies and gentlemen, the United States stands at this time at the pinnacle of world power. It is a solemn moment for the American Democracy. For with primacy in power is also joined an awe-inspiring accountability to the future. If you look around you, you must feel not only the sense of duty done but also you must feel anxiety lest you fall below the level of achievement. Opportunity is here and now, clear and shining for both our countries. To reject it or ignore it or fritter it away will bring upon us all the long reproaches of the after-time. It is necessary that the constancy of mind, persistency of purpose, and the grand simplicity of decision shall rule and guide the conduct of the English-speaking peoples in peace as they did in war. We must, and I believe we shall, prove ourselves equal to this severe requirement.

President McCluer, when American military men approach some serious situation they are wont to write at the head of their directive the words "over-all strategic concept." There is wisdom in this, as it leads to clarity of thought. What then is the over-all strategic concept which we should inscribe to-day? It is nothing less than the safety and welfare, the freedom and progress, of all the homes and families of all the men and women in all the lands. And here I speak particularly of the myriad cottage or apartment homes where the wage-earner strives amid the accidents and difficulties of life to guard his wife and children from privation and bring the family up the fear of the Lord, or upon ethical conceptions which often play their potent part.

To give security to these countless homes, they must be shielded from two gaunt marauders, war and tyranny. We all know the frightful disturbance in which the ordinary family is plunged when the curse of war swoops down upon the bread-winner and those for whom he works and contrives. The awful ruin of Europe, with all its vanished glories, and of large parts of Asia glares us in the eyes.

407

When the designs of wicked men or the aggressive urge of mighty States dissolve over large areas the frame of civilized society, humble folk are confronted with difficulties with which they cannot cope. For them is all distorted, all is broken, all is even ground to pulp.

When I stand here this quiet afternoon I shudder to visualize what is actually happening to millions now and what is going to happen in this period when famine stalks the Earth. None can compute what has been called "the unestimated sum of human pain." Our supreme task and duty is to guard the homes of the common people from the horrors and miseries of another war. We are all agreed on that.

Our American military colleagues, after having proclaimed their "over-all strategic concept" and computed available resources, always proceed to the next step—namely, the method. Here again there is widespread agreement. A world organization has already been erected for the prime purpose of preventing war. UNO, the successor of the League of Nations, with the decisive addition of the United States and all that that means, is already at work. We must make sure that its work is fruitful, that it is a reality and not a sham, that it is a force for action, and not merely a frothing of words, that it is a true temple of peace in which the shields of many nations can some day be hung up, and not merely a cockpit in a Tower of Babel. Before we cast away the solid assurances of national armaments for self-preservation we must be certain that our temple is built, not upon shifting sands or quagmires, but upon a rock. Anyone can see with his eyes open that our path will be difficult and also long, but if we persevere together as we did in the two world wars—though not, alas, in the interval between them—I cannot doubt that we shall achieve our common purpose in the end.

I have, however, a definite and practical proposal to make for action. Courts and magistrates may be set up but they cannot function without sheriffs and constables. The United Nations Organization must immediately begin to be equipped with an international armed force. In such a matter we can only go step by step, but we must begin now. I propose that each of the Powers and States should be invited to dedicate a certain number of air squadrons to the service of the world organization. These squadrons would be trained and prepared in their own countries, but would move around in rotation from one country to another. They would wear the uniforms of their own countries but with different badges. They would not be required to act against their own nation, but in other respects they would be direct-

408

ed by the world organization. This might be started on a modest scale and it would grow as confidence grew. I wished to see this done after the First World War, and I devoutly trust that it may be done forthwith.

It would nevertheless, ladies and gentlemen, be wrong and imprudent to entrust the secret knowledge or experience of the atomic bomb, which the United States, great Britain, and Canada now share, to the world organization, while still in its infancy. It would be criminal madness to cast it adrift in this still agitated and un-united world. No one country has slept less well in their beds because this knowledge and the method and the raw materials to apply it, are present largely retained in American hands. I do not believe we should all have slept so soundly had the positions been reversed and some Communist or neo-Fascist State monopolized for the time being these dread agencies. The fear of them alone might easily have been used to enforce totalitarian systems upon the free democratic world, with consequences appalling to human imagination. God has willed that this shall not be and we have at least a breathing space to set our world house in order before this peril has to be encountered: and even then, if no effort is spared, we should still possess so formidable a superiority as to impose effective deterrents upon its employment, or threat of employment, by others. Ultimately, when the essential brotherhood of man is truly embodied and expressed in a world organization with all the necessary practical safeguards to make it effective, these powers would naturally be confided to that world organizations.

Now I come to the second of the two marauders, to the second danger which threatens the cottage homes, and the ordinary people— namely, tyranny. We cannot be blind to the fact that the liberties enjoyed by individual citizens throughout the United States and throughout the British Empire are not valid in a considerable number of countries, some of which are very powerful. In these States control is enforced upon the common people by various kinds of all-embracing police governments to a degree which is overwhelming and contrary to every principle of democracy. The power of the State is exercised without restraint, either by dictators or by compact oligarchies operating through a privileged party and a political police. It is not our duty at this time when difficulties are so numerous to interfere forcibly in the internal affairs of countries which we have not conquered in war, but we must never cease to proclaim in fearless

409

tones the great principles of freedom and the rights of man which are the joint inheritance of the English-speaking world and which through Magna Carta, the Bill of rights, the Habeas Corpus, trial by jury, and the English common law find their most famous expression in the American Declaration of Independence.

All this means that the people of any country have the right, and should have the power by constitutional action, by free unfettered elections, with secret ballot, to choose or change the character or form of government under which they dwell; that freedom of speech and thought should reign; that courts of justice, independent of the executive, unbiased by any party, should administer laws which have received the broad assent of large majorities or are consecrated by time and custom. Here are the title deeds of freedom which should lie in every cottage home. Here is the message of the British and American peoples to mankind. Let us preach what we practice—let us practice what we preach.

Though I have now stated the two great dangers which menace the home of the people, War and Tyranny, I have not yet spoken of poverty and privation which are in many cases the prevailing anxiety. But if the dangers of war and tyranny are removed, there is no doubt that science and cooperation can bring in the next few years, certainly in the next few decades, to the world, newly taught in the sharpening school of war, an expansion of material well-being beyond anything that has yet occurred in human experience.

Now, at this sad and breathless moment, we are plunged in the hunger and distress which are the aftermath of our stupendous struggle; but this will pass and may pass quickly, and there is no reason except human folly or sub-human crime which should deny to all the nations the inauguration and enjoyment of an age of plenty. I have often used words which I learn fifty years ago from a great Irish-American orator, a friend of mine, Mr. Bourke Cockran, "There is enough for all. The Earth is a generous mother; she will provide in plentiful abundance food for all her children if they will but cultivate her soil in justice and peace." So far I feel that we are in full agreement.

Now, while still pursing the method—the method of realizing our over-all strategic concept, I come to the crux of what I have traveled here to say. Neither the sure prevention of war, nor the continuous rise of world organization will be gained without what I have called the fraternal association of the English-speaking peoples. This means a special relationship between the British Commonwealth and Empire and the United States of America. Ladies and gentlemen, this is no time for generality, and I will venture to the precise. Fraternal association requires not only the growing friendship and mutual understanding between our two vast but kindred systems of society, but the continuance of the intimate relations between our military advisers, leading to common study of potential dangers, the similarity of weapons and manuals of instructions, and to the interchange of officers and cadets at technical colleges. It should carry with it the continuance of the present facilities for mutual security by the joint use of all Naval and Air Force bases in the possession of either country all over the world. This would perhaps double the mobility of the American Navy and Air Force. It would greatly expand that of the British Empire forces and it might well lead, if and as the world calms down, to important financial savings. Already we use together a large number of islands; more may well be entrusted to our joint care in the near future.

the United States has already a Permanent Defense Agreement with the Dominion of Canada, which is so devotedly attached to the British Commonwealth and the Empire. This Agreement is more effective than many of those which have been made under formal alliances. This principle should be extended to all the British Commonwealths with full reciprocity. Thus, whatever happens, and thus only, shall we be secure ourselves and able to work together for the high and simple causes that are dear to us and bode no ill to any. Eventually there may come—I feel eventually there will come—the principle of common citizenship, but that we may be content to leave to destiny, whose outstretched arm many of us can already clearly see.

There is however an important question we must ask ourselves. Would a special relationship between the United States and the British Commonwealth be inconsistent with our over-riding loyalties to the World Organization? I reply that, on the contrary, it is probably the only means by which that organization will achieve its full stature and strength. There are already the special United States relations with Canada that I have just mentioned, and there are the relations between the United States and the South American Republics. We British have also our twenty years Treaty of Collaboration and Mutual Assistance with Soviet Russia. I agree with Mr. Bevin, the Foreign Secretary of Great Britain, that it might well be a fifty years treaty so far as we are concerned. We aim at nothing but mutual assistance

411

and collaboration with Russia. The British have an alliance with Portugal unbroken since the year 1384, and which produced fruitful results at a critical moment in the recent war. None of these clashes with the general interest of a world agreement, or a world organization; on the contrary, they help it. "In my father's house are many mansions." Special associations between members of the United Nations which have no aggressive point against any other country, which harbor no design incompatible with the Charter of the United Nations, far from being harmful, are beneficial and, as I believe, indispensable.

I spoke earlier, ladies and gentlemen, of the Temple of Peace. Workmen from all countries must build that temple. If two of the workmen know each other particularly well and are old friends, if their families are intermingled, if they have "faith in each other's purpose, hope in each other's future and charity towards each other's shortcomings"—to quote some good words I read here the other day—why cannot they work together at the common task as friends and partners? Why can they not share their tools and thus increase each other's working powers? Indeed they must do so or else the temple may not be built, or, being built, it may collapse, and we should all be proved again unteachable and have to go and try to learn again for a third time in a school of war incomparably more rigorous than that from which we have just been released. The dark ages may return, the Stone Age may return on the gleaming wings of science, and what might now shower immeasurable material blessings upon mankind, may even bring about its total destruction. Beware, I say; time may be short. Do not let us take the course of allowing events to drift along until it is too late. If there is to be a fraternal association of the kind of I have described, with all the strength and security which both our countries can derive from it, let us make sure that that great fact is known to the world, and that it plays its part in steadying and stabilizing the foundations of peace. There is the path of wisdom. Prevention is better than the cure.

A shadow has fallen upon the scenes so lately light by the Allied victory. Nobody knows what Soviet Russia and its Communist international organization intends to do in the immediate future, or what are the limits, if any, to their expansive and proselytizing tendencies. I have a strong admiration and regard for the valiant Russian people and for my wartime comrade, Marshall Stalin. There is deep sympathy and goodwill in Britain—and I doubt not here also—towards the peoples of all the Russias and a resolve to persevere through many differences and rebuffs in establishing lasting friendships. We understand the Russian need to be secure on her western frontiers by the removal of all possibility of German aggression. We welcome Russia to her rightful place among the leading nations of the world. We welcome her flag upon the seas. Above all, we welcome, or should welcome, constant, frequent and growing contacts between the Russian people and our own people on both sides of the Atlantic. It is my duty however, for I am sure you would wish me to state the facts as I see them to you. It is my duty to place before you certain facts about the present position in Europe.

From Stettin in the Baltic to Trieste in the Adriatic an *Iron Curtain* has descended across the Continent. Behind that line lie all the capitals of the ancient states of Central and Eastern Europe. Warsaw, Berlin, Prague, Vienna, Budapest, Belgrade, Bucharest and Sofia, all these famous cities and the populations around them lie in what I must call the Soviet sphere, and all are subject in one form or another, not only to Soviet influence but to a very high and, in some cases, increasing measure of control from Moscow. Athens alone—Greece with its immortal glories—is free to decide its future at an election under British, American and French observation. The Russian-dominated Polish Government has been encouraged to make enormous and wrongful inroads upon Germany, and mass expulsions of millions of Germans on a scale grievous and undreamed-of are now taking place. The Communist parties, which were very small in all these Eastern States of Europe, have been raised to pre-eminence and power far beyond their numbers and are seeking everywhere to obtain totalitarian control. Police governments are prevailing in nearly every case, and so far, except in Czechoslovakia, there is no true democracy.

Turkey and Persia are both profoundly alarmed and disturbed at the claims which are being made upon them and at the pressure being exerted by the Moscow Government. An attempt is being made by the Russians in Berlin to build up a quasi-Communist party in their zone of occupied Germany by showing special favors to groups of left-wing German leaders. At the end of the fighting last June, the American and British Armies withdrew westward, in accordance with an earlier agreement, to a depth at some points of 150 miles upon a front of nearly four hundred miles, in order to allow our Russian allies to occupy this vast expanse of territory which the Western

Democracies had conquered.

If now the Soviet Government tries, by separate action, to build up a pro-Communist Germany in their areas, this will cause new serious difficulties in the American and British zones, and will give the defeated Germans the power of putting themselves up to auction between the Soviets and the Western Democracies. Whatever conclusions may be drawn from these facts—and facts they are—this is certainly not the Liberated Europe we fought to build up. Nor is it one which contains the essentials of permanent peace.

The safety of the world, ladies and gentlemen, requires a new unity in Europe, from which no nation should be permanently outcast. It is from the quarrels of the strong parent races in Europe that the world wars we have witnessed, or which occurred in former times, have sprung. Twice in our own lifetime we have seen the United States, against their wishes and their traditions, against arguments, the force of which it is impossible not to comprehend, twice we have seen them drawn by irresistible forces, into these wars in time to secure the victory of the good cause, but only after frightful slaughter and devastation have occurred. Twice the United States has had to send several millions of its young men across the Atlantic to find the war; but now war can find any nation, wherever it may dwell between dusk and dawn. Surely we should work with conscious purpose for a grand pacification of Europe, within the structure of the United Nations and in accordance with our Charter. That I feel opens a course of policy of very great importance.

In front of the *Iron Curtain* which lies across Europe are other causes for anxiety. In Italy the Communist Party is seriously hampered by having to support the Communist-trained Marshal Tito's claims to former Italian territory at the head of the Adriatic. Nevertheless the future of Italy hangs in the balance. Again one cannot imagine a regenerated Europe without a strong France. All my public life I never last faith in her destiny, even in the darkest hours. I will not lose faith now. However, in a great number of countries, far from the Russian frontiers and throughout the world, Communist fifth columns are established and work in complete unity and absolute obedience to the directions they receive from the Communist center. Except in the British Commonwealth and in the United States where Communism is in its infancy, the Communist parties or fifth columns constitute a growing challenge and peril to Christian civilization. These are somber facts for anyone to have to recite on the morrow of a victory

414

gained by so much splendid comradeship in arms and in the cause of freedom and democracy; but we should be most unwise not to face them squarely while time remains.

The outlook is also anxious in the Far East and especially in Manchuria. The Agreement which was made at Yalta, to which I was a party, was extremely favorable to Soviet Russia, but it was made at a time when no one could say that the German war might not extend all through the summer and autumn of 1945 and when the Japanese war was expected by the best judges to last for a further 18 months from the end of the German war. In this country you all so well-informed about the Far East, and such devoted friends of China, that I do not need to expatiate on the situation there.

I have, however, felt bound to portray the shadow which, alike in the west and in the east, falls upon the world. I was a minister at the time of the Versailles treaty and a close friend of Mr. Lloyd George, who was the head of the British delegation at Versailles. I did not myself agree with many things that were done, but I have a very strong impression in my mind of that situation, and I find it painful to contrast it with that which prevails now. In those days there were high hopes and unbounded confidence that the wars were over and that the League of Nations would become all-powerful. I do not see or feel that same confidence or even the same hopes in the haggard world at the present time.

On the other hand, ladies and gentlemen, I repulse the idea that a new war is inevitable; still more that it is imminent. It is because I am sure that our fortunes are still in our own hands and that we hold the power to save the future, that I feel the duty to speak out now that I have the occasion and the opportunity to do so. I do not believe that Soviet Russia desires war. What they desire is the fruits of war and the indefinite expansion of their power and doctrines. But what we have to consider here today while time remains, is the permanent prevention of war and the establishment of conditions of freedom and democracy as rapidly as possible in all countries. Our difficulties and dangers will not be removed by closing our eyes to them. They will not be removed by mere waiting to see what happens; nor will they be removed by a policy of appeasement. What is needed is a settlement, and the longer this is delayed, the more difficult it will be and the greater our dangers will become.

From what I have seen of our Russian friends and Allies during the war, I am convinced that there is nothing for which they have less respect than for weakness, especially military weakness. For that reason the old doctrine of a balance of power is unsound. We cannot afford, if we can help it, to work on narrow margins, offering temptations to a trial of strength. If the Western Democracies stand together in strict adherence to the principles will be immense and no one is likely to molest them. If however they become divided of falter in their duty and if these all-important years are allowed to slip away then indeed catastrophe may overwhelm us all.

Last time I saw it all coming and I cried aloud to my own fellow-countrymen and to the world, but no one paid any attention. Up till the year 1933 or even 1935, Germany might have been saved from the awful fate which has overtaken here and we might all have been spared the miseries Hitler let loose upon mankind. There never was a war in history easier to prevent by timely action than the one which has just desolated such great areas of the globe. It could have been prevented in my belief without the firing of a single shot, and Germany might be powerful, prosperous and honored today; but no one would listen and one by one we were all sucked into the awful whirlpool. We surely, ladies and gentlemen, I put it to you, surely, we must not let it happen again. This can only be achieved by reaching now, in 1946, by reaching a good understanding on all points with Russia under the general authority of the United Nations Organization and by the maintenance of that good understanding through many peaceful years, by the whole strength of the English-speaking world and all its connections. There is the solution which I respectfully offer to you in this Address to which I have given the title, "The Sinews of Peace."

Let no man underrate the abiding power of the British Empire and Commonwealth. Because you see the 46 millions in our island harassed about their food supply, of which they only grow one half, even in war-time, or because we have difficulty in restarting our industries and export trade after six years of passionate war effort, do not suppose we shall not come through these dark years of privation as we have come through the glorious years of agony. Do not suppose that half a century from now you will not see 70 or 80 millions of Britons spread about the world united in defense of our traditions, and our way of life, and of the world causes which you and we espouse. If the population of the English-speaking Commonwealths be added to that of the United States with all that such cooperation implies in the air, on the sea, all over the globe and in science and in industry, and in moral force, there will be no quivering, precarious balance of power to offer its temptation to ambition or adventure. On the contrary there will be an overwhelming assurance of security. If we adhere faithfully to the Charter of the United Nations and walk forward in sedate and sober strength seeking no one's land/or treasure, seeking to lay no arbitrary control upon the thoughts of men; if all British moral and material forces and convictions are joined with your own in fraternal association, the highroads of the future will be clear, not only for our time, but for a century to come.

Appendix 5

Project for the New American Century: Letter to President Clinton of January 26, 1998

The following letter was written to President William (Bill) Clinton by members of the Project for the New American Century (PNAC). The letter can be found at the PNAC website @ www.newamericancentury.org/iraqclintonletter.htm.

January 26, 1998

The Honorable William J. Clinton
President of the United States
Washington, DC

Dear Mr. President:

We are writing you because we are convinced that current American policy toward Iraq is not succeeding, and that we may soon face a threat in the Middle East more serious than any we have known since the end of the Cold War. In your upcoming State of the Union Address, you have an opportunity to chart a clear and determined course for meeting this threat. We urge you to seize that opportunity, and to enunciate a new strategy that would secure the interests of the U.S. and our friends and allies around the world. That strategy should aim, above all, at the removal of Saddam Hussein's regime from power. We stand ready to offer our full support in this difficult but necessary endeavor.

The policy of "containment" of Saddam Hussein has been steadily eroding over the past several months. As recent events have demonstrated, we can no longer depend on our partners in the Gulf War coalition to continue to uphold the sanctions or to punish Saddam when he blocks or evades UN inspections. Our ability to ensure that Saddam Hussein is not producing weapons of mass destruction, therefore, has substantially diminished. Even if full inspections were eventually to resume, which now seems highly unlikely, experience has shown that it is difficult if not impossible to monitor Iraq's chemical and biological weapons production. The lengthy period during which the inspectors will have been unable to enter many Iraqi facilities has made it even less likely that they will be able to uncover all of Saddam's secrets. As a result, in the not-too-distant future we will be unable to determine with any reasonable level of confidence whether Iraq does or does not possess such weapons.

Such uncertainty will, by itself, have a seriously destabilizing effect on the entire Middle East. It hardly needs to be added that if Saddam does acquire the capability to deliver weapons of mass destruction, as he is almost certain to do if we continue along the present course, the safety of American troops in the region, of our friends and allies like Israel and the moderate Arab states, and a significant portion of the world's supply of oil will all be put at hazard. As you have rightly declared, Mr. President, the security of the world in the first part of the 21st century will be determined largely by how we handle this threat.

Given the magnitude of the threat, the current policy, which depends for its success upon the steadfastness of our coalition partners and upon the cooperation of Saddam Hussein, is dangerously inade-quate. The only acceptable strategy is one that eliminates the possi-bility that Iraq will be able to use or threaten to use weapons of mass destruction. In the near term, this means a willingness to undertake military action as diplomacy is clearly failing. In the long term, it means removing Saddam Hussein and his regime from power. That now needs to become the aim of American foreign policy.

We urge you to articulate this aim, and to turn your Administration's attention to implementing a strategy for removing Saddam's regime from power. This will require a full complement of diplomatic, politi-cal and military efforts. Although we are fully aware of the dangers and difficulties in implementing this policy, we believe the dangers of failing to do so are far greater. We believe the U.S. has the authority under existing UN resolutions to take the necessary steps, including military steps, to protect our vital interests in the Gulf. In any case, American policy cannot continue to be crippled by a misguided insis-tence on unanimity in the UN Security Council.

419

We urge you to act decisively. If you act now to end the threat of weapons of mass destruction against the U.S. or its allies, you will be acting in the most fundamental national security interests of the country. If we accept a course of weakness and drift, we put our interests and our future at risk.

Sincerely,

Elliott Abrams	Richard L. Armitage	William J. Bennett
Jeffrey Bergner	John Bolton	Paula Dobriansky
Francis Fukuyama	Robert Kagan	Zalmay Khalilzad
William Kristol	Richard Perle	Peter W. Rodman
Donald Rumsfeld	William Schneider, Jr.	Vin Weber
Paul Wolfowitz	R. James Woolsey	Robert B. Zoellick

Appendix 6

Project for the New American Century: Letter to President Bush of September 20, 2001

> This letter was written to President George W. Bush by the PNAC some days after the WTC attacks. It is on the PNAC website @ www.newamericancentury.org/Bushletter.htm.

September 20, 2001

The Honorable George W. Bush
President of the United States
Washington, DC

Dear Mr. President,

We write to endorse your admirable commitment to "lead the world to victory" in the war against terrorism. We fully support your call for "a broad and sustained campaign" against the "terrorist organizations and those who harbor and support them." We agree with Secretary of State Powell that the United States must find and punish the perpetrators of the horrific attack of September 11, and we must, as he said, "go after terrorism wherever we find it in the world" and "get it by its branch and root." We agree with the Secretary of State that U.S. policy must aim not only at finding the people responsible for this incident, but must also target those "other groups out there that mean us no good" and "that have conducted attacks previously against U.S. personnel, U.S. interests and our allies."

In order to carry out this "first war of the 21st century" successfully, and in order, as you have said, to do future "generations a favor by coming together and whipping terrorism," we believe the following steps are necessary parts of a comprehensive strategy.

Osama bin Laden

We agree that a key goal, but by no means the only goal, of the current war on terrorism should be to capture or kill Osama bin Laden, and to destroy his network of associates. To this end, we support the necessary military action in Afghanistan and the provision of substantial financial and military assistance to the anti-Taliban forces in that country.

Iraq

We agree with Secretary of State Powell's recent statement that Saddam Hussein "is one of the leading terrorists on the face of the Earth...." It may be that the Iraqi government provided assistance in some form to the recent attack on the United States. But even if evidence does not link Iraq directly to the attack, any strategy aiming at the eradication of terrorism and its sponsors must include a determined effort to remove Saddam Hussein from power in Iraq. Failure to undertake such an effort will constitute an early and perhaps decisive surrender in the war on international terrorism. The United States must therefore provide full military and financial support to the Iraqi opposition. American military force should be used to provide a "safe zone" in Iraq from which the opposition can operate. And American forces must be prepared to back up our commitment to the Iraqi opposition by all necessary means.

Hezbollah

Hezbollah is one of the leading terrorist organizations in the world. It is suspected of having been involved in the 1998 bombings of the American embassies in Africa, and implicated in the bombing of the U.S. Marine barracks in Beirut in 1983. Hezbollah clearly falls in the category cited by Secretary Powell of groups "that mean us no good" and "that have conducted attacks previously against U.S. personnel, U.S. interests and our allies." Therefore, any war against terrorism must target Hezbollah. We believe the administration should demand that Iran and Syria immediately cease all military, financial, and political support for Hezbollah and its operations. Should Iran and Syria refuse to comply, the administration should consider appropriate measures of retaliation against these known state sponsors of terrorism.

Israel and the Palestinian Authority

Israel has been and remains America's staunchest ally against international terrorism, especially in the Middle East. The United States should fully support our fellow democracy in its fight against terrorism. We should insist that the Palestinian Authority put a stop to terrorism emanating from territories under its control and imprison those planning terrorist attacks against Israel. Until the Palestinian Authority moves against terror, the United States should provide it no further assistance.

U.S. Defense Budget

A serious and victorious war on terrorism will require a large increase in defense spending. Fighting this war may well require the United States to engage a well-armed foe, and will also require that we remain capable of defending our interests elsewhere in the world. We urge that there be no hesitation in requesting whatever funds for defense are needed to allow us to win this war.

There is, of course, much more that will have to be done. Diplomatic efforts will be required to enlist other nations' aid in this war on terrorism. Economic and financial tools at our disposal will have to be used. There are other actions of a military nature that may well be needed. However, in our judgement the steps outlined above constitute the minimum necessary if this war is to be fought effectively and brought to a successful conclusion. Our purpose in writing is to assure you of our support as you do what must be done to lead the nation to victory in this fight.

Sincerely,

William Kristol	Richard V. Allen	Gary Bauer
Jeffrey Bell	William J. Bennett	Rudy Boshwitz
Jeffrey Bergner	Eliot Cohen	Seth Cropsey
Midge Decter	Thomas Donnelly	Nicholas Eberstadt
Hillel Fradkin	Aaron Friedberg	Francis Fukuyama
Frank Gaffney	Jeffrey Gedmin	Reuel Marc Gerecht
Charles Hill	Bruce P. Jackson	Eli S. Jacobs
Michael Joyce	Donald Kagan	Robert Kagan
Jeane Kirkpatrick	John Lehman	Clifford May
Martin Peretz	Richard Perle	Norman Podhoretz
Stephen P. Rosen	Gary Schmitt	William Schneider, Jr.
Richard H. Shultz	Henry Sokolski	Stephen J. Solarz
Vin Weber	Leon Wieseltier	Marshall Wittmann

Charles Krauthammer   Randy Scheunemann

Appendix 7

Project for the New American Century: Letter to President Bush of April 3, 2002

This PNAC letter of endorsement of the President's support of Israel's "fight against terrorism" is a must read. The letter can be downloaded from www.newamericancentury.org/Bushletter-040302.htm.

April 3, 2002

The Honorable George W. Bush
President of the United States
Washington, DC

Dear Mr. President,

We write to thank you for your courageous leadership in the war on terrorism and to offer our full support as you continue to protect the security and well-being of Americans and all freedom-loving peoples around the world.

In particular, we want to commend you for your strong stance in support of the Israeli government as it engages in the present campaign to fight terrorism. As a liberal democracy under repeated attack by murderers who target civilians, Israel now needs and deserves steadfast support. This support, moreover, is essential to Israel's continued survival as a free and democratic nation, for only the United States has the power and influence to provide meaningful assistance to our besieged ally. And with the memory of the terrorist attack of September 11 still seared in our minds and hearts, we Americans ought to be especially eager to show our solidarity in word and deed with a fellow victim of terrorist violence.

No one should doubt that the United States and Israel share a common enemy. We are both targets of what you have correctly called an "Axis of Evil." Israel is targeted in part because it is our friend, and in part because it is an island of liberal, democratic principles—American principles—in a sea of tyranny, intolerance, and hatred. As Secretary of Defense Rumsfeld has pointed out, Iran, Iraq, and Syria are all engaged in "inspiring and financing a culture of political murder and suicide bombing" against Israel, just as they have aided campaigns of terrorism against the United States over the past two decades. You have declared war on international terrorism, Mr. President. Israel is fighting the same war.

This central truth has important implications for any Middle East peace process. For one spoke of the terrorist network consists of Yasser Arafat and the leadership of the Palestinian Authority. Although your critics in the United States, Europe and the Arab world suggest that you and your administration bear some responsibility for the lack of political progress between Israel and the Palestinians, they are mistaken. As Secretary of State Powell recently stated, the present crisis stems not from "the absence of a political way forward" but from "terrorism…, terrorism in its rawest form." That terrorism has been aided, abetted, harbored, and in many instances directed by Mr. Arafat and his top lieutenants. Mr. Arafat has demonstrated time and again that he cannot be part of the peaceful solution of the Israeli-Palestinian conflict. He demonstrated it in July 2000, when he rejected the most generous Israeli peace offer in history; he demonstrated it in September 2000, when he launched the new intifada against Israel; and he demonstrated it again these past two weeks when, despite the hand you offered him through Vice President Cheney, he gave sanction to some of the worst terrorist violence against Israeli citizens.

It is true that the United States has a leading role to play in the Middle East and, potentially, in resolving the conflict between Israel and the Palestinians. But it is critical that negotiations not be the product of terrorism or conducted under the threat of terrorist attack. This would send a most dangerous signal to our adversaries that civilized states do not have the necessary courage to fight terrorism in all its forms.

Mr. President, it can no longer be the policy of the United States to urge, much less to pressure, Israel to continue negotiating with Arafat, any more than we would be willing to be pressured to negotiate with Osama Bin Laden or Mullah Omar. Nor should the United States provide financial support to a Palestinian Authority that acts as a cog in the machine of Middle East terrorism, any more than we would approve of others providing assistance to Al Qaeda.

Instead, the United States should lend its full support to Israel as it seeks to root out the terrorist network that daily threatens the lives of Israeli citizens. Like our own efforts in Afghanistan and elsewhere, Israel's task will not be easy. It will not be accomplished quickly or painlessly. But with fortitude, on our part as well on the part of the Israeli people, it can succeed in significantly reducing the risk of future terrorist attacks against Israel and against us. And, in so doing, we will give the Palestinian people a chance they have so far not had under Arafat's rule—an opportunity to construct a political culture and government that do not marry their national and religious aspirations with suicide bombers.

Furthermore, Mr. President, we urge you to accelerate plans for removing Saddam Hussein from power in Iraq. As you have said, every day that Saddam Hussein remains in power brings closer the day when terrorists will have not just airplanes with which to attack us, but chemical, biological, or nuclear weapons, as well. It is now common knowledge that Saddam, along with Iran, is a funder and supporter of terrorism against Israel. Iraq has harbored terrorists such as Abu Nidal in the past, and it maintains links to the Al Qaeda network. If we do not move against Saddam Hussein and his regime, the damage our Israeli friends and we have suffered until now may someday appear but a prelude to much greater horrors. Moreover, we believe that the surest path to peace in the Middle East lies not through the appeasement of Saddam and other local tyrants, but through a renewed commitment on our part, as you suggested in your State of the Union address, to the birth of freedom and democratic government in the Islamic world.

Mr. President, in that address, you put forth a most compelling vision of a world at peace, free from the threat of terrorism, where freedom flourishes. The strength of that vision lies in its moral clarity and consistency. In the war on terrorism, we cannot condemn some terrorists while claiming that other terrorists are potential partners for peace. We cannot help some allies under siege, while urging others to compromise their fundamental security. As you eloquently stated: "Our enemies send other people's children on missions of suicide and murder. They embrace tyranny and death as a cause and a creed. We stand for a different choice, made long ago, on the day of our founding. We affirm it again today."

Israel's fight against terrorism is our fight. Israel's victory is an important part of our victory. For reasons both moral and strategic, we need to stand with Israel in its fight against terrorism.

Sincerely,

William Kristol	Ken Adelman	Gary Bauer
Jeffrey Bell	William J. Bennett	Ellen Bork
Linda Chavez	Eliot Cohen	Midge Decter
Thomas Donnelly	Nicholas Eberstadt	Hillel Fradkin
Frank Gaffney	Jeffrey Gedmin	Charles Hill
Bruce P. Jackson	Donald Kagan	Robert Kagan
John Lehman	Tod Lindberg	Rich Lowry
Clifford May	Joshua Muravchik	Martin Peretz
Richard Perle	Daniel Pipes	Gary Schmitt
Marshall Wittmann	R. James Woolsey	Stephen P. Rosen
Norman Podhoretz	William Schneider, Jr.	Randy Scheunemann
Reuel Marc Gerecht		

Appendix 8

Joint Chiefs of Staff Joint Vision 2010
America's Military: Preparing for Tomorrow

JCS Joint Vision 2010 provides an operationally based template for the evolution of the Armed Forces and aims to serve as a benchmark for Service and Unified Command visions. This 38-page book is reproduced here in its entirety, without the pictures and graphics. To those interested in getting an electronic copy of the JV2010, it is available for download in Adobe® Acrobat® PDF format at www.dtic.mil/jv2010/jvpub.htm.

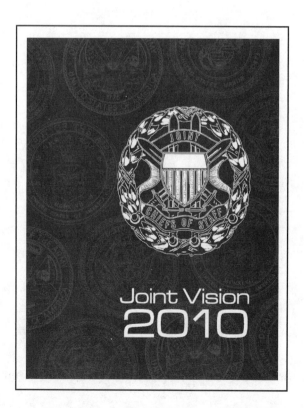

Introduction

Joint Vision 2010 is the conceptual template for how America's Armed Forces will channel the vitality and innovation of our people and leverage technological opportunities to achieve new levels of effectiveness in joint warfighting. Focused on achieving dominance across the range of military operations through the application of new operational concepts, this template provides a common direction for our Services in developing their unique capabilities within a joint framework of doctrine and programs as they prepare to meet an uncertain and challenging future.

JV 2010 begins by addressing the expected continuities and changes in the strategic environment, including technology trends and their implications for our Armed Forces. It recognizes the crucial importance of our current high quality, highly trained forces and provides the basis for their further enhancement by prescribing how we will fight in the early 21st century.

This vision of future warfighting embodies the improved intelligence and command and control available in the information age and goes on to **develop four operational concepts: dominant maneuver, precision engagement, full dimensional protection, and focused logistics.**

Each of the operational concepts incorporates America's core strengths of high quality people and information-age technological advances, builds on proven competencies, and focuses the development of future joint capabilities. Together, the application of these four concepts by robust high quality forces will provide America with the capability to dominate an opponent across the range of military operations. This **Full Spectrum Dominance will be the key characteristic we seek for our Armed Forces in the 21st century.** Joint Vision 2010 then examines the six critical elements required to transform the operational concepts into joint capabilities: people, leadership, doctrine, education and training, organizational structure, and materiel. In its conclusion, JV 2010 assesses the challenges and opportunities in moving toward implementation of the vision.

This vision draws on our most fundamental source of strength—our people. People are the Armed Forces; at the end of the day, our success, in war or in peace, will rest ultimately on the men and women of the Armed Forces.

The skills and vitality of our people will also provide the driving force for shaping change. Channeling our strengths with this vision, **we will move toward a common goal: a joint force—persuasive in peace, decisive in war, preeminent in any form of conflict.**

Threads of Continuity

As we build our forces to this joint vision, there will be strong threads of continuity with the contemporary strategic and operational environment.

Among these threads are American goals and interests, as well as the missions, tasks, strategic concepts, and quality of our Armed Forces.

America's Goals and Interests

America's enduring goals include: protecting the lives and safety of Americans both at home and abroad; maintaining the political freedom and national independence of the U.S. with its values, institutions, and territory intact; and providing for the well-being and prosperity of the nation and its people.

These goals, in turn, generate American interests which must be protected and advanced. Our fundamental interests lie in enhancing U.S. security, promoting prosperity at home, and promoting democracy abroad.

The United States has undertaken foreign and security policies aimed at securing these interests. Ensuring strong relations with our allies, protecting our rights of transit on the high seas, and enlarging the community of free market democracies are examples of policies we are likely to continue to pursue in the years ahead. On the whole, there is likely to be far more continuity than change in these interests and policies.

Missions, Tasks, and Strategic Concepts of the Armed Forces

To protect our vital national interests we will require strong armed forces, which are organized, trained, and equipped to fight and win against any adversary at any level of conflict. Concurrently, we must also be able to employ these forces in operations other than war to assist in the pursuit of other important interests.

The primary task of the Armed Forces will remain to deter conflict—but, should deterrence fail, to fight and win our nation's wars. In addition, we should expect to participate in a broad range of deterrent, conflict prevention, and peacetime activities. Further, our history, strategy, and recent experience suggest that we will usually work in concert with our friends and allies in almost all operations.

America's strategic nuclear deterrent, along with appropriate national level detection and defensive capabilities will likely remain at the core of American national security. However, the bulk of our Armed Forces will be engaged in or training for worldwide military operations. In these operations, we will largely draw upon our conventional warfighting capabilities—we will fight if we must—but will also use these same capabilities to deter, contain conflict, fight and win, or otherwise promote American interests and values.

To ensure we can accomplish these tasks, **power projection, enabled by overseas presence, will likely remain the fundamental strategic concept of our future force.** We will remain largely a force that is based in the continental United States (CONUS). However, our permanently stationed overseas forces, infrastructure and equipment, temporarily deployed forces, and the interaction between U.S. and foreign militaries together demonstrate our commitments, strengthen our military capabilities, and enhance the organization of coalitions and multinational operations to deter or defeat aggression. Power projection from the United States, achieved through rapid strategic mobility, will enable the timely response critical to our deterrent and warfighting capabilities. Our overseas presence and highly mobile forces will both remain essential to future operations.

The Quality of Our Force

Currently, our Armed Forces are the best trained, best equipped, and most ready force in the world. The quality of our people is unequaled at all levels of the chain of command. Leaders in each of our Services are developed through wellconceived, intensive, and long-term programs. Our equipment is first-rate and it is sustainable in all operations. Together, our personnel, leadership, and equipment are molded into exceptionally able forces through stressful training, which closely approximates wartime conditions and requirements.

Since the mid-1980s, this high quality has been the essence of the Armed Forces. Military operations are planned knowing that leaders truly understand the requirements, the equipment is operable and safe, and the men and women at the cutting edge have the skills and character to execute their tasks successfully.

However, this quality force has been achieved only at great expense and effort. It has required the creation of institutions and procedures, sharpened over more than two decades of experience, to develop these Armed Forces in the most effective and efficient manner possible. These institutions and procedures, and the high quality forces they have produced, remain at the very center of Joint Vision 2010.

Attracting people with the intellectual tools, physical skills, and motivation to serve effectively in the military was foremost among the requirements for building a professional, robust, and ready force. In the late 1970s, over 15 percent of our enlistees scored in the lowest category for military qualification examinations. Today, less than 1 percent are in that category and over 90 percent of our enlistees have graduated from high school. The combination of careful targeting of requirements, recruiting incentives, quality of life initiatives, and challenging opportunities has been very effective in attracting the personnel needed to sustain our quality force.

Retention of highly trained Service members in sufficient numbers has also been a key requirement, and we intend to sustain these efforts. Our first-term reenlistment rates have risen by 10 percent over the last fifteen years. Higher retention is the result of a committed effort by top leadership throughout the government toward raising career satisfaction, improving command climates, keeping pay competitive and benefits stable, maintaining time at home and deployed at an acceptable balance, and focusing on quality of life initiatives.

Another element of our success has been effective leadership development. From deliberate and intensive processes involving institutional, on-the-job, and self-study methods, the men and women of our Armed Forces gain the skills, knowledge, and attitudes required to accomplish their required tasks across the range of military operations. These formal development processes are designed to balance timing, costs, and operational requirements, at each level of leadership. We will retain those innovative processes to ensure that we maintain the best possible leadership for our Armed Forces.

Realistic and stressful training has been the primary way to keep readiness high and prepare our men and women to face the challenges of combat. Such training, consisting of carefully balanced programs of individual, crew, and larger organizational training and assessments, is central to training the way we will fight. From individual or crew mission simulators, through full-blown field exercises at home or abroad, realistic, evaluated training is and must remain our best combat multiplier. Joint, coalition, and combined training and exercises have improved our interoperability and understanding of the strengths of each individual Service as well as allies and coalition partners. From the individual warfighter to large multinational forces, this systematic approach has enabled our men and women to hone their skills in practice many times before ever having to perform actual combat missions. These training innovations must be sustained.

Today, our highly trained, quality force has the tools to perform its warfighting tasks. Just 15 years ago, our forces were less well equipped, spare parts inventories were critically short, and sustainability was low. Since then, we have modernized our force and ensured that we procured the parts and provided the training required to take full advantage of this new equipment.

Technologically superior equipment has been critical to the success of our forces in combat. This first-rate equipment, when combined with our top quality forces, has been a key element of our continuing operational successes. We must continue to ensure our soldiers, sailors, airmen, marines are fully capable of fulfilling their required tasks with equipment that is engineered to provide superior mission performance as well as safety and reliability. We must maintain a careful balance between equipping and sustaining our forces and between tooth and tail in our force structure. We must also work to assure an efficient and effective support structure and resources for all of our forces.

Dynamic Changes

Accelerating rates of change will make the future environment more

432

unpredictable and less stable, presenting our Armed Forces with a wide range of plausible futures. Whatever direction global change ultimately takes, it will affect how we think about and conduct joint and multinational operations in the 21st century. How we respond to dynamic changes concerning potential adversaries, technological advances and their implications, and the emerging importance for information superiority will dramatically impact how well our Armed Forces can perform its duties in 2010.

The Imperative of Jointness

America's Armed Forces are smaller than we have been in over 40 years, and we have decreased the percentage of our forces permanently stationed overseas. Faced with flat budgets and increasingly more costly readiness and modernization, we should not expect a return to the larger active forces of the Cold War period.

The American people will continue to expect us to win in any engagement, but they will also expect us to be more efficient in protecting lives and resources while accomplishing the mission successfully. Commanders will be expected to reduce the costs and adverse effects of military operations, from environmental disruption in training to collateral damage in combat. Risks and expenditures will be even more closely scrutinized than they are at present.

Simply to retain our effectiveness with less redundancy, we will need to wring every ounce of capability from every available source. That outcome can only be accomplished through a more seamless integration of Service capabilities. **To achieve this integration while conducting military operations we must be fully joint: institutionally, organizationally, intellectually, and technically.** Future commanders must be able to visualize and create the "best fit" of available forces needed to produce the immediate effects and achieve the desired results.

Multinational Operations

It is not enough just to be joint, **when conducting future operations. We must find the most effective methods for integrating and improving interoperability with allied and coalition partners.** Although our Armed Forces will maintain decisive unilateral strength, we expect to work in concert with allied and coalition forces in nearly all of our future operations, and increasingly, our procedures, programs, and planning must recognize this reality.

Potential Adversaries

There will continue to be states or groups that oppose or threaten American interests and values or those of our friends and allies. Our recognition of these threats and challenges will continue to drive our national security efforts.

433

Greater global interaction will strongly influence the nature of future threats. Wider access to advanced technology along with modern weaponry, including weapons of mass destruction (WMD), and the requisite skills to maintain and employ it, will increase the number of actors with sufficient military potential to upset existing regional balances of power.

Modern systems are sufficiently powerful that smaller numbers can dramatically alter the threats facing us. A number of potential adversaries may acquire the military hardware to make themselves distinctly more dangerous.

Our most vexing future adversary may be one who can use technology to make rapid improvements in its military capabilities that provide asymmetrical counters to U.S. military strengths, including information technologies. Alternatively, the high leverage associated with modern systems means that significant improvements in military capabilities can occur very rapidly, outrunning the pace of compensating political or military countermeasures.

The application of these technologies against us may also prove surprising. Our adversaries will have an independent will, some knowledge of our capabilities, and the desire to avoid our strengths and exploit vulnerabilities. We anticipate the probability of facing technological or operational surprise will increase in the period ahead.

In sum, the U.S. must prepare to face a wider range of threats, emerging unpredictably, employing varying combinations of technology, and challenging us at varying levels of intensity.

Advancing Technology Trends

This era will be one of accelerating technological change. Critical advances will have enormous impact on all military forces. Successful adaptation of new and improved technologies may provide great increases in specific capabilities. Conversely, failure to understand and adapt could lead today's militaries into premature obsolescence and greatly increase the risks that such forces will be incapable of effective operations against forces with high technology.

Long-range precision capability, combined with a wide range of delivery systems, is emerging as a key factor in future warfare. Technological advances will continue the trend toward improved precision. Global positioning systems, high-energy research, electromagnetic technology, and enhanced stand-off capabilities will provide increased accuracy and a wider range of delivery options. These capabilities will increase the combat power available for use against selected objectives, resulting in enhanced economy of force and a higher tempo of operations.

The **ability to produce a broader range of potential weapons effects**, from less lethal to hard target kill, from sensor-fused to directed energy weapons, will further enhance precision capability. Advances in target effects technologies will be integrated into existing weapons and give commanders greater flexibility. These improvements will result in increasingly discrete and precise capabilities, which can achieve optimum results in both combat and other operations.

Advances in low observable technologies and the ability to mask friendly forces will also continue over the next 15 years. Signature reduction will enhance the ability to engage adversaries anywhere in the battlespace and improve the survivability of forces who employ it.

Stealth will strengthen the ability to accomplish surprise, reduce overall force requirements in many operations, and make forces less visible to an unsophisticated or disoriented adversary. Microminiaturization will also promote signature reduction and greatly increase the capabilities available for individuals and small units. Concurrently, multispectral sensing, automated target recognition, and other advances will enhance the detectability of targets across the battlespace, improving detection ranges, turning night into day for some classes of operations, reducing the risk of fratricide and further accelerating operational tempo.

Improvements in information and systems integration technologies will also significantly impact future military operations by providing decision makers with accurate information in a timely manner. Information technology will improve the ability to see, prioritize, assign, and assess information. The fusion of allsource intelligence with the fluid integration of sensors, platforms, command organizations, and logistic support centers will allow a greater number of operational tasks to be accomplished faster. Advances in computer processing, precise global positioning, and telecommunications will provide the capability to determine accurate locations of friendly and enemy forces, as well as to collect, process, and distribute relevant data to thousands of locations. Forces harnessing the capabilities potentially available from this system of systems will gain dominant battlespace awareness, an interactive "picture" which will yield much more accurate assessments of friendly and enemy operations within the area of interest. Although this will not eliminate the fog of war, dominant battlespace awareness will improve situational awareness, decrease response time, and make the battlespace considerably more transparent to those who achieve it.

Implications of Technological Advances on Our Armed Forces

The combination of these technology trends will provide an order of magnitude improvement in lethality. Commanders will be able to attack targets successfully with fewer platforms and less ordnance while achieving objectives more rapidly and with reduced risk. Individual warfighters will be empowered as never before, with an array of detection, targeting, and communications equipment that will greatly magnify the power of small units. Strategically, this improvement will enable more rapid power projection and reduced logistics tails. Operationally, within the theater, these capabilities will mean a more rapid transition from deployment to full operational capability. As a result, we will improve our capability for rapid, worldwide deployment while becoming even more tactically mobile and lethal.

The implications of this increased lethality for overall force structure requirements are unclear. Given current technology, today's force structure is adequate to meet our full range of global needs, but barely so. While these prospective improvements in lethality clearly offer promise of reducing the number of platforms and the amount of ordnance required to destroy targets, many military missions will require occupation of the ground, and intensive physical presence. For these missions the promises of technology are less certain, especially in environments such as cities or jungles.

During all operations, advanced technology in the hands of an adversary will increase the importance of force protection at all echelons. Any efficiencies garnered by our offensive systems must be underwritten by appropriate redundancies to safeguard against unanticipated technological, strategic, or operational surprise.

Adaptations to this increasingly lethal battlespace will be warranted. These adaptations are likely to take the forms of increased stealth, mobility, dispersion and pursuit of a higher tempo of operations among elements within the battlespace.

To cope with more lethal systems and improved targeting, our forces will require stealth and other means of passive protection, along with mobility superior to the enemy's ability to retarget or react to our forces. Increased stealth will reduce an enemy's ability to target our forces. Increased dispersion and mobility are possible offensively because each platform or each individual warfighter carries higher lethality and has greater reach. Defensively, dispersion and higher tempo complicate enemy targeting and reduce the effectiveness of area attack and area denial weaponry such as weapons of mass destruction (WMD). The capability to control the tempo of operations and, if necessary, sustain a tempo faster than the enemy's will also help enable our forces to seize and maintain the initiative during military operations.

Greater mobility and increased dispersion will, in turn, require additional communications and coordination capabilities since the synchronization of these dispersed elements will become even more important. Fortunately, the technology for this improved systems integration is at hand.

The implications of improved systems integration are both profound and complex. New technologies will allow increased capability at lower echelons to control more lethal forces over larger areas, thus leveraging the skills and initiative of individuals and small units. These capabilities could empower a degree of independent maneuver, planning, and coordination at lower echelons, which were normally exercised by more senior commanders in the past. Concurrently, commanders at higher echelons will use these technologies to reduce the friction of war and to apply precise centralized control when and where appropriate.

Even for higher level commanders, the accelerated operational tempo and greater integration requirements will likely create a more stressful, faster moving decision environment. Realtime information will likely drive parallel, not sequential, planning and real-time, not prearranged, decision making. The optimal balance between centralized and decentralized command and control will have to be carefully developed as systems are brought into the inventories.

Emerging Importance of Information Superiority

Throughout history, gathering, exploiting, and protecting information have been critical in command, control, and intelligence. The unqualified importance of information will not change in 2010. What will differ is the increased access to information and improvements in the speed and accuracy of prioritizing and transferring data brought about by advances in technology. While the friction and the fog of war can never be eliminated, new technology promises to mitigate their impact.

Sustaining the responsive, high quality data processing and information needed for joint military operations will require more than just an edge over an adversary. **We must have information superiority: the capability to collect, process, and disseminate an uninterrupted flow of information while exploiting or denying an adversary's ability to do the same.**

Information superiority will require both offensive and defensive information warfare (IW). Offensive information warfare will degrade or exploit an adversary's collection or use of information. It will include both traditional methods, such as a precision attack to destroy an adversary's command and control capability, as well as nontraditional methods such as electronic intrusion into an information and control network to convince, confuse, or deceive enemy military decision makers.

There should be no misunderstanding that our effort to achieve and maintain information superiority will also invite resourceful enemy attacks on our information systems. **Defensive information warfare** to protect our ability to conduct information operations will be one of our biggest challenges in the period ahead. Traditional defensive IW operations include physical security measures and encryption. Nontraditional actions will range from antivirus protection to innovative methods of secure data transmission. In addition, increased strategic level programs will be required in this critical area.

Conduct of Joint Operations

Our forces have been largely organized, trained, and equipped to defeat military forces of our potential adversaries. Direct combat against an enemy's armed forces is the most demanding and complex set of requirements we have faced. Other operations, from humanitarian assistance in peacetime through peace operations in a near hostile environment, have proved to be possible using forces optimized for wartime effectiveness.

Technological advances will magnify the advantages provided by our high quality force. The promise provided by these technologies is best viewed from an operational perspective. In the past, our capabilities often required us to physically mass forces to neutralize enemy power. The time needed to build up and employ massed combat forces, including the platforms, weapons, and associated logistics, required to achieve success resulted in military operations that were largely sequential in nature and tactics which too often saw ground, maritime, and air forces massed in time and space.

By 2010, we should be able to change how we conduct the most intense joint operations. Instead of relying on massed forces and sequential operations, we will achieve massed effects in other ways. Information superiority and advances in technology will enable us to achieve the desired effects through the tailored application of joint combat power. Higher lethality weapons will allow us to conduct attacks concurrently that formerly required massed assets, applied in a sequential manner. With precision targeting and longer range systems, commanders can achieve the necessary destruction or suppression of enemy forces with fewer systems, thereby reducing the need for time-consuming and risky massing of people and equipment. Improved command and control, based on fused, all-source, real-time intelligence will reduce the need to assemble maneuver formations days and hours in advance of attacks. Providing improved targeting information directly to the most effective weapon system will potentially reduce the traditional force requirements at the point of main effort.

All of this suggests that we will be increasingly able to **accomplish the effects of mass—the necessary concentration of combat power at the decisive time and place—with less need to mass forces physically than in the past.** This will enhance our combat capabilities against opposing military forces. **To be sure, this will not obviate the ultimate need for "boots on the ground" in many operations, nor will it relieve our Service men and women of the need to be physically present** at the decisive points in battle or in other operations, or to be exposed to conditions of great danger and hardship.

However, in all operations technological advances and our use of information

438

will give our warfighters at the individual, crew, and small unit levels major qualitative advantages over potential adversaries. Our forces will be able to sense dangers sooner. They will have increased awareness of the overall operational environment, including the situation of friendly forces, allowing them to make better decisions more rapidly. They will have an enhanced ability to produce a range of desired effects by bringing together the correct mix of assets at the place and time most favorable to success. When tied to a more rapid resupply, reinforcement, and reengagement capability, they will be better able to provide the best response at less risk to themselves, based on the mission objectives and circumstances of the battlespace. Whether operating from dispersed locations or in close proximity to each other, the confidence of each individual warfighter or crew will be bolstered by enhanced connectivity to comrades, supporting elements, and higher commands.

In sum, by 2010 we should be able to enhance the capabilities of our forces through technology. This will, in turn, expand our greatest advantage: the adaptability, initiative, teamwork, and commitment of our people at every level.

To exploit the enormous potential of technology, we must develop in a systematic manner the full range of required enhancements. This process must begin with a new conceptual framework for operations.

The basis for this framework is found in the improved command, control, and intelligence which can be assured by information superiority. These are the most straightforward applications of much of the new technology; however, the full impact of these technologies is more profound. Enhanced command and control, and much improved intelligence, along with other applications of new technology will transform the traditional functions of maneuver, strike, protection, and logistics. These transformations will be so powerful that they become, in effect, new operational concepts: dominant maneuver; precision engagement; full dimensional protection; and focused logistics. These operational concepts will provide our forces with a new conceptual framework.

New Operational Concepts: Dominant Maneuver

Dominant maneuver will be the multidimensional application of information, engagement, and mobility capabilities to position and employ widely dispersed joint air, land, sea, and space forces to accomplish the assigned operational tasks. Dominant maneuver will allow our forces to gain a decisive advantage by controlling the breadth, depth, and height of the battlespace.

Through a combination of asymmetric leverage, achieved by our positional advantages, as well as decisive speed and tempo, dominant maneuver allows us to apply decisive force to attack enemy centers of gravity at all levels and compels an adversary to either react from a position of disadvantage or quit.

Dominant maneuver will require forces that are adept at conducting sustained and synchronized operations from dispersed locations. They must be able to apply overwhelming force in the same medium and create asymmetric advantages by attacking cross-dimensionally, such as air or sea against ground or ground and sea against air defenses. These forces must have the ability to outpace and outmaneuver the enemy. Current systems, enhanced by information superiority, will provide a clearer picture of enemy and friendly locations. Information superiority also will allow joint commanders to coordinate widely dispersed units, receive accurate feedback, and execute more demanding, higher precision requirements. Increasingly lethal direct and indirect fire systems, with longer ranges and more accurate targeting, will increase the punch of these forces as they maneuver.

The tailor-to-task organizational ability will provide the additional advantage of self protection —another key element for successfully achieving dominant maneuver. The combination of seamless operations with reduced "buildup time" and a smaller, more widely dispersed footprint will make it much more difficult for an adversary to find and attack our forces. Other defensive measures, low observable technologies, signature reduction, and enhanced deception capabilities will provide similar advantages for protection and improve our chances for mission success.

Altogether, the organizational concept of dominant maneuver is a prescription for more agile, faster moving joint operations, which will combine air, land, and maritime forces more effectively to deliver decisive combat power.

Precision Engagement

Precision engagement will consist of a system of systems that enables our forces to locate the objective or target, provide responsive command and control, generate the desired effect, assess our level of success, and retain the flexibility to reengage with precision when required. Even from extended ranges, precision engagement will allow us to shape the battlespace, enhancing the protection of our forces.

Information operations will tie together high fidelity target acquisition, prioritized requirements, and command and control of joint forces within the battlespace. This combination will provide a greater assurance of delivering the desired effect, lessen the risk to our forces, and minimize collateral damage.

Precision engagement will build on current U.S. advantages in delivery accuracy and low observable technologies. It will use a wide variety of means, including very accurate aerial deliveries or air drops, discriminate weapon strikes, and precise, allweather stand-off capability. Enhanced jointness will ensure greater commonality between Service precision engagement capabilities and provide future joint force commanders with a wider array of responsive, accurate, and flexible options.

Full-Dimensional Protection

We must also protect our own forces from the very technologies that we are exploiting. Unless we provide an adequate measure of protection for our forces, these new operational concepts will be highly vulnerable to disruption. We will achieve this required level of protection through the concept called full dimensional protection. **The primary prerequisite for full-dimensional protection will be control of the battlespace to ensure our forces can maintain freedom of action during deployment, maneuver and engagement, while providing multi-layered defenses for our forces and facilities at all levels.** Full-dimensional protection will enable the effective employment of our forces while degrading opportunities for the enemy. It will be essential, in most cases, for gaining and maintaining the initiative required to execute decisive operations. The concept will be proactive, incorporating both offensive and defensive actions that may extend well into areas of enemy operations.

Full-dimensional protection will be built upon information superiority which will provide multidimensional awareness and assessment, as well as identification of all forces in the battlespace. Information warfare will support this effort by protecting our information systems and processes, while denying an adversary the similar capabilities. Upon this information base, we will employ a full array of active and passive measures at multiple echelons. Active measures will include battlespace control operations to guarantee the air, sea, space, and information superiority that is needed to gain the degree of control to accomplish the assigned tasks. Active measures will also include an integrated, in-depth theater air and missile defense that will exploit Service-unique capabilities to detect, identify, locate, track, and deny enemy attacks on our joint forces.

Passive measures will include the inherent protection provided by information superiority and dispersal to increase our warning of attacks. Operational dispersion will further reduce risks to our forces. New sensors and information dissemination systems will be deployed to detect chemical or biological attack at great ranges and provide warning to specific units that may be affected. Enhanced deception and camouflage measures, increased individual and collective protection, and a joint restoration capability against the effects of WMD are also key elements for achieving full dimensional protection.

Most importantly, **these active and passive measures will be combined to provide a more seamless joint architecture for force protection, which will leverage the contributions of individual Services, systems, and echelons.** The result will be improved freedom of action for friendly forces, and

441

better protection at all echelons against precision attack, weapons of mass destruction, and other conventional or nonconventional systems.

Focused Logistics

Each of the preceding concepts relies on our ability to project power with the most capable forces, at the decisive time and place. To optimize all three concepts, logistics must be responsive, flexible, and precise. Focused logistics will be **the fusion of information, logistics, and transportation technologies to provide rapid crisis response, to track and shift assets even while en route, and to deliver tailored logistics packages and sustainment directly at the strategic, operational, and tactical level of operations.** It will be fully adaptive to the needs of our increasingly dispersed and mobile forces, providing support in hours or days versus weeks. Focused logistics will enable joint forces of the future to be more mobile, versatile, and projectable from anywhere in the world.

Logistic functions will incorporate information technologies to transition from the rigid vertical organizations of the past. Modular and specifically tailored combat service support packages will evolve in response to wideranging contingency requirements. Service and Defense agencies will work jointly and integrate with the civilian sector, where required, to take advantage of advanced business practices, commercial economies, and global networks. Active and reserve combat service support capabilities, prepared for complete integration into joint operations, will provide logistic support and sustainment as long as necessary.

Information technologies will enhance airlift, sealift, and pre-positioning capabilities to lighten deployment loads, assist pinpoint logistics delivery systems, and extend the reach and longevity of systems currently in the inventory. The combined impact of these improvements will be a smaller, more capable deployed force. It will require less continuous support with a smaller logistics footprint, decreasing the vulnerability of our logistics lines of communication.

Full Spectrum Dominance

Each of these new operational concepts will reinforce the others and will allow us to achieve massed effects in warfare from more dispersed forces. This synergy will greatly enhance our capabilities in high intensity conventional military operations.

However, the synergy of these four concepts transcends intense conventional warfighting. Without overspecialization, the development of these new operational concepts has great potential to fulfill more effectively the full range of tasks assigned to us. That is, taken together **these four new concepts will enable us to dominate the full range of military operations from human-**

itarian assistance, through peace operations, up to and into the highest intensity conflict.

Information superiority will provide a commander with enhanced awareness of his area of responsibility, whether his objective is to close with and engage an adversary or render assistance in a humanitarian operation. Surveillance, reconnaissance and knowledge of the precise location of dispersed friendly forces with the ability to direct effectively their efforts are applicable for all military tasks.

Likewise, the tactical mobility required for dominant maneuver which enables our forces rapidly to move into position to overwhelm an enemy will also allow commanders to place forces in positions of control in counterdrug, counterterrorism, or peacekeeping operations. Precision engagement capabilities designed for warfighting tasks will also enable greater discrimination in the application of force against an emerging threat during peace enforcement operations. Full-dimensional protection will allow freedom of action for our forces and limit their vulnerability during combat and noncombat operations. Focused logistics will ensure delivery of the precise amount and types of supplies required for our joint forces to succeed in combat or noncombat operations.

Although the positive implications for enhancing our capabilities across the range of military operations seem obvious, we cannot assume that all new concepts will be equally valuable in all operations. In intensive combat, target destruction may be essential in the early engagements of an operation, but extensive physical presence may later be necessary to accomplish the assigned mission. This presence may be required to fully neutralize enemy forces, deal with prisoners and potentially hostile populations, or otherwise assure that success in attacking targets is followed through to achieve the overall objectives of the operation. For noncombat operations, physical presence will likely be even more important. Thus, we must ensure that capturing the new technologies does not overspecialize the force; **we must retain balanced and sustainable capabilities.** We recognize that, regardless of how sophisticated technology becomes, the individual warfighter's judgment, creativity, and adaptability in the face of highly dynamic situations will be essential to the success of future joint operations. The human element is especially important in situations where we cannot bring our technological capabilities fully to bear against opponents who seek to nullify our technological superiority by various means. In these cases, our success will depend, as it has historically, upon the physical, intellectual, and moral strengths of the individual soldier, sailor, airman, and marine—especially their adaptability in the face of the unexpected.

Critical Considerations

To sustain the Armed Forces and instill these new operational concepts will require high quality people—the key ingredient for success. The judgment, creativity, and fortitude of our people will remain the key to success in future joint operations. Turning concepts into capabilities requires adapting our leadership, doctrine, education and training, organizations, and materiel to meet the high tempo, high technology demands posed by these new concepts.

Dedicated, High Quality People

Thus, recruiting and retaining dedicated high quality people will remain our first priority. Only a force that has the courage, stamina, and intellectual ability to cope with the complexity and rapid pace of future joint operations will have the capability to achieve full spectrum dominance. We cannot expect risk-free, push-button style operations in the future. Military operations will continue to demand extraordinary dedication and sacrifice under the most adverse conditions. Some military operations will require close combat on the ground, at sea, or in the air. The courage and heart of our soldiers, sailors, airmen, and marines will remain the foundation of all that our Armed Forces must do.

Innovative Leadership

The dynamic nature of joint operations in the 21st century battlespace will **require a continued emphasis on developing strong leadership skills.** While we must do everything possible to leverage the power of advanced technologies, there are inherent limitations. Confronting the inevitable friction and fog of war against a resourceful and strong minded adversary, the human dimension including innovative strategic and operational thinking and strong leadership will be essential to achieve decisive results. Effective leadership provides our greatest hedge against uncertainty.

We will build upon the enduring foundation of functional expertise, core values, and high ethical standards. Our future leaders at all levels of command must understand the interrelationships among military power, diplomacy, and economic pressure, as well as the role of various government agencies and non-governmental actors, in achieving our security objectives. They will require a sophisticated understanding of historical context and communication skills to succeed in the future. The evolution of command structures, increased pace and scope of operations, and the continuing refinement of force structure and organizations will require leaders with a knowledge of the capabilities of all four services. Without sacrificing their basic service competencies, these future leaders must be schooled in joint operations from the beginning of their careers.

This leadership development must begin rigorous selection processes and extend beyond formal education and training. Hands-on experience in a variety of progressive assignments must stress innovation, dealing with ambiguity, and a sophisticated understanding of the military art. **In short, our leaders must demonstrate the very highest levels of skill and versatility in ever more complex joint and multinational operations.**

444

Joint Doctrine

As we change the way we fight, **joint doctrine will remain the foundation that fundamentally shapes the way we think about and train for joint military operations.** Joint doctrine is a critical ingredient for success because the way in which leaders think and organize their forces will be as important as the technology we use to conduct future joint operations. Future joint doctrine must articulate the process required for successful joint planning but must be flexible enough to serve as a broad framework to guide our forces in joint and multinational operations. It is the key to enhanced jointness because it transforms technology, new ideas, and operational concepts into joint capabilities.

We will discover new ways to change the development process for joint doctrine. Thus, we must integrate "topdown" doctrine throughout the development cycle, while continuing to ensure that joint doctrine fully incorporates the strengths that each Service brings to joint warfare.

Joint Education and Training

Our education and training programs must prepare joint warriors to meet the challenges of the future battlespace. These programs must emphasize employment of new technologies and achieving the operational concepts outlined in this vision. It is essential that our Joint Professional Military Education (JPME) programs provide our warfighters with an understanding of strategic concepts in the future environment where military force will be applied, as well as an in-depth understanding of individual Service systems and how the integration of these systems enhance joint operations.

The requirement for high quality, realistic, and stressful training that amplifies education and fully prepares our forces for joint operations is similarly important. We must emphasize integration of joint capabilities and develop skills that increase individual and organizational effectiveness. Our training must reflect emerging threats and include both information saturation and total interruption of information flow.

Enhanced modeling and simulation of the battlespace, when coupled to on the ground evaluation with real soldiers, sailors, airmen, and marines, can improve the realism of training, upgrade the levels of day-to-day readiness, and increase our opportunities to test innovative concepts and new strategies. Simulations must be interconnected globally—creating a near-real-time interactive simulation superhighway between our forces in every theater. Each CINC must be able to tap into this global network and connect forces worldwide that would be available for theater operations. This network will allow selected units in CONUS to train with forces located in an overseas theater without actually deploying there. Similarly, we will pursue improvements in our campaign modeling and analysis to exploit the concepts of this vision. This global simulation network must include our Reserve and National Guard units,

445

as well as selected multinational partners, to increase their readiness and interoperability.

Agile Organizations

In order to make optimum use of the technologies and operational concepts discussed earlier, we must carefully examine the traditional criteria governing span of control and organizational layers for the Services, commands, and Defense agencies. We will need organizations and processes that are agile enough to exploit emerging technologies and respond to diverse threats and enemy capabilities. As we move forward, we may require further reductions in supervision and centralized direction.

All organizations must become more responsive to contingencies, with less "startup" time between deployment and employment. Because we rely on the total force to provide the full range of military capabilities, we also require responsive Reserve components that can rapidly integrate into joint organizations.

Increased organizational flexibility will enhance our responsiveness. We will seek organizations that can support flexible force packaging and work to smooth the process further.

Enhanced Materiel

Since most of the platforms expected to be in service in 2010 are already designed or operational, **we will emphasize high leverage, leading edge technology enhancements to increase our capabilities.** We will also place greater emphasis on common usage between Services and increase interoperability among the Services and multinational partners.

We will need a responsive research, development, and acquisition process to incorporate new technologies. This process must leverage technology and management innovations originating in the private sector through responsive access to commercial developments.

Implementing Joint Vision 2010

We must proceed with implementing Joint Vision 2010 in a way that captures the promise of these new concepts while sustaining our readiness and flexibility through every step of this evolution.

The implementation plan will involve CINCs, Services, and joint organizations. Each element must participate in developing and testing these new concepts and their overall integration. Modeling, demonstrations, simulations, technology wargames, and joint exercises will help assess and validate these concepts, as well as assist in developing new operational procedures and organizations.

446

The implementation process will integrate ongoing initiatives, such as the Joint Requirements Oversight Council, Joint Warfighting Capabilities Assessments, and Advanced Capabilities Technology Demonstrations (ACTD), to promote the integrated development of operational capabilities. Concurrently, joint education and doctrinal development must keep pace.

As we implement this vision, affordability of the technologies envisioned to achieve full spectrum dominance will be an important consideration. While we anticipate that some significant improvements in capability may be gained economically, for example through dual-use technologies for C^4I, others will be more difficult to achieve within the budget realities that exist today and will exist into the next century. We anticipate the need to be selective in the technologies we choose, and thus expect continuing assessment and adjustments for affordability as well as for other lessons learned during the implementation process.

Achieving the full promise of this vision will largely depend on how well we structure our defense program. We will have to make hard choices to achieve the tradeoffs that will bring the best balance, most capability, and greatest interoperability for the least cost. Ultimately, we will have to measure continuously the affordability of achieving full spectrum dominance against our overarching need to maintain the quality of our forces, their readiness, and the force structure needed to execute our operational tasks between now and the year 2010.

As we implement this vision, we must acknowledge that strong leadership, warfighting skill, and innovative thinking will be central to developing the detailed requirements and decision points. Our organizational climate must reward critical thinking, foster the competition of ideas, and reduce structural or cultural barriers to innovation. Both in peace and war, the creative talents of our men and women provide us a critical advantage over those who would consider challenging us or our allies.

Conclusion

Today, America's Armed Forces are the world standard for military excellence and joint warfighting. We will further strengthen our military capabilities by taking advantage of improved technology and the vitality and innovation of our people to prepare our forces for the 21st century.

Joint Vision 2010 creates the template to guide the transformation of these concepts into joint operational capabilities. It serves as the basis for focusing the strengths of each individual Service or component to exploit the full array of available capabilities and allow us to achieve full spectrum dominance. It will also guide the evolution of joint doctrine, education, and training to assure we will be able to achieve more seamless joint operations in the future.

As we pursue this vision, we must remain mindful of our responsibilities: to prevent threats to our interests from emerging, deter those that do, and defeat those threats by military force if deterrence fails. In 2010, we will meet these responsibilities with high quality people and leaders, who are trained and ready for joint operations and able to exploit high technology equipment. **Even during a time of unparalleled technological advances we will always rely on the courage, determination, and strength of America's men and women to ensure we are persuasive in peace, decisive in war, and pre-eminent in any form of conflict.**

Appendix 9

Joint Chiefs of Staff Joint Vision 2020
America's Military: Preparing for Tomorrow

JCS Joint Vision 2020 is built upon and extends the conceptual template established by *Joint Vision 2010*. This 40-page book is reproduced here in its entirety, without the pictures and graphics. To those interested in getting an electronic copy of the JV2020, it is available for download in 2 parts in PDF format at www.dtic.mil/jointvision/jvpub2.htm.

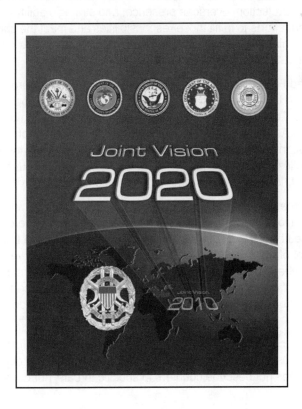

1. INTRODUCTION

The U.S. military today is a force of superbly trained men and women who are ready to deliver victory for our Nation. In support of the objectives of our National Security Strategy, it is routinely employed to shape the international security environment and stands ready to respond across the full range of potential military operations. But the focus of this document is the third element of our strategic approach—the need to prepare now for an uncertain future.

Joint Vision 2020 builds upon and extends the conceptual template established by *Joint Vision 2010* to guide the continuing transformation of America's Armed Forces. The primary purpose of those forces has been and will be to fight and win the Nation's wars. The overall goal of the transformation described in this document is the creation of a force that is dominant across the full spectrum of military operations—persuasive in peace, decisive in war, preeminent in any form of conflict.

In 2020, the nation will face a wide range of interests, opportunities, and challenges and will require a military that can both win wars and contribute to peace. The global interests and responsibilities of the United States will endure, and there is no indication that threats to those interests and responsibilities, or to our allies, will disappear. The strategic concepts of decisive force, power projection, overseas presence, and strategic agility will continue to govern our efforts to fulfill those responsibilities and meet the challenges of the future. This document describes the operational concepts necessary to do so.

If our Armed Forces are to be faster, more lethal, and more precise in 2020 than they are today, we must continue to invest in and develop new military capabilities. This vision describes the ongoing transformation to those new capabilities. As first explained in *JV 2010*, and dependent upon realizing the potential of the information revolution, today's capabilities for maneuver, strike, logistics, and protection will become dominant maneuver, precision engagement, focused logistics, and full dimensional protection.

The joint force, because of its flexibility and responsiveness, will remain the key to operational success in the future. The integration of core competencies provided by the individual Services is essential to the joint team, and the employment of the capabilities of the Total Force (active, reserve, guard, and civilian members) increases the options for the commander and complicates the choices of our opponents. To build the most effective force for 2020, we must be fully joint: intellectually, operationally, organizationally, doctrinally, and technically.

This vision is centered on the joint force in 2020. The date defines a general analytical focus rather than serving as a definitive estimate or deadline. The document does not describe counters to specific threats, nor does it enumerate weapon, communication, or other systems we will develop or purchase. Rather, its purpose is to describe in broad terms the human talent—the professional, well-trained, and ready force—and operational capabilities that will be required for the joint force to succeed across the full range of military operations and accomplish its mission in 2020 and beyond. In describing those capabilities, the vision provides a vector for the wide-ranging program of exercises and experimentation being conducted by the Services and combatant commands and the continuing evolution of the joint force. Based on the joint vision implementation program, many capabilities will be operational well before 2020, while others will continue to be explored and developed through exercises and experimentation.

The overarching focus of this vision is full spectrum dominance—achieved through the interdependent application of dominant maneuver, precision engagement, focused logistics, and full dimensional protection. Attaining that goal requires the steady infusion of new technology and modernization and replacement of equipment. However, material superiority alone is not sufficient. Of greater importance is the development of doctrine, organizations, training and education, leaders, and people that effectively take advantage of the technology.

The evolution of these elements over the next two decades will be strongly influenced by two factors. First, the continued development and proliferation of information technologies will substantially change the conduct of military operations. These changes in the information environment make information superiority a key enabler of the transformation of the operational capabilities of the joint force and the evolution of joint command and control. Second, the U.S. Armed Forces will continue to rely on a capacity for intellectual and technical innovation. The pace of technological change, especially as it fuels changes in the strategic environment, will place a premium on our ability to foster innovation in our people and organizations across the entire range of joint operations. The overall vision of the capabilities we will require in 2020, as introduced above, rests on our assessment of the strategic context in which our forces will operate.

2. STRATEGIC CONTEXT

Three aspects of the world of 2020 have significant implications for the U.S. Armed Forces. First, the United States will continue to have global interests and be engaged with a variety of regional actors. Transportation, communications, and information technology will continue to evolve and foster expanded economic ties and awareness of international events. Our security and economic interests, as well as our political values, will provide the impetus for engagement with international partners. The joint force of 2020 must be prepared to "win" across the full range of military operations in any part of the world, to operate with multinational forces, and to coordinate military opera-

451

tions, as necessary, with government agencies and international organizations.

Second, potential adversaries will have access to the global commercial industrial base and much of the same technology as the U.S. military. We will not necessarily sustain a wide technological advantage over our adversaries in all areas. Increased availability of commercial satellites, digital communications, and the public internet all give adversaries new capabilities at a relatively low cost. We should not expect opponents in 2020 to fight with strictly "industrial age" tools. Our advantage must, therefore, come from leaders, people, doctrine, organizations, and training that enable us to take advantage of technology to achieve superior warfighting effectiveness.

Third, we should expect potential adversaries to adapt as our capabilities evolve. We have superior conventional warfighting capabilities and effective nuclear deterrence today, but this favorable military balance is not static. In the face of such strong capabilities, the appeal of asymmetric approaches and the focus on the development of niche capabilities will increase. By developing and using approaches that avoid U.S. strengths and exploit potential vulnerabilities using significantly different methods of operation, adversaries will attempt to create conditions that effectively delay, deter, or counter the application of U.S. military capabilities.

The potential of such asymmetric approaches is perhaps the most serious danger the United States faces in the immediate future—and this danger includes long-range ballistic missiles and other direct threats to U.S. citizens and territory. The asymmetric methods and objectives of an adversary are often far more important than the relative technological imbalance, and the psychological impact of an attack might far outweigh the actual physical damage inflicted. An adversary may pursue an asymmetric advantage on the tactical, operational, or strategic level by identifying key vulnerabilities and devising asymmetric concepts and capabilities to strike or exploit them. To complicate matters, our adversaries may pursue a combination of asymmetries, or the United States may face a number of adversaries who, in combination, create an asymmetric threat. These asymmetric threats are dynamic and subject to change, and the U.S. Armed Forces must maintain the capabilities necessary to deter, defend against, and defeat any adversary who chooses such an approach. To meet the challenges of the strategic environment in 2020, the joint force must be able to achieve full spectrum dominance.

3. FULL SPECTRUM DOMINANCE

The ultimate goal of our military force is to accomplish the objectives directed by the National Command Authorities. For the joint force of the future, this goal will be achieved through full spectrum dominance—the ability of U.S. forces, operating unilaterally or in combination with multinational and interagency partners, to defeat any adversary and control any situation across the full range of military operations.

The full range of operations includes maintaining a posture of strategic deterrence. It includes theater engagement and presence activities. It includes conflict involving employment of strategic forces and weapons of mass destruction, major theater wars, regional conflicts, and smaller-scale contingencies. It also includes those ambiguous situations residing between peace and war, such as peacekeeping and peace enforcement operations, as well as noncombat humanitarian relief operations and support to domestic authorities.

The label full spectrum dominance implies that U.S. forces are able to conduct prompt, sustained, and synchronized operations with combinations of forces tailored to specific situations and with access to and freedom to operate in all domains—space, sea, land, air, and information. Additionally, given the global nature of our interests and obligations, the United States must maintain its overseas presence forces and the ability to rapidly project power worldwide in order to achieve full spectrum dominance.

Achieving full spectrum dominance means the joint force will fulfill its primary purpose—victory in war, as well as achieving success across the full range of operations, but it does not mean that we will win without cost or difficulty. Conflict results in casualties despite our best efforts to minimize them, and will continue to do so when the force has achieved full spectrum dominance. Additionally, friction is inherent in military operations. The joint force of 2020 will seek to create a "frictional imbalance" in its favor by using the capabilities envisioned in this document, but the fundamental sources of friction cannot be eliminated. We will win—but we should not expect war in the future to be either easy or bloodless.

Sources of Friction

- Effects of danger and exertion
- Existence of uncertainty and chance
- Unpredictable actions of other actors
- Frailties of machines and information
- Humans

The requirement for global operations, the ability to counter adversaries who possess weapons of mass destruction, and the need to shape ambiguous situations at the low end of the range of operations will present special challenges en route to achieving full spectrum dominance. Therefore, the process of creating the joint force of the future must be flexible—to react to changes in the strategic environment and the adaptations of potential enemies, to take advantage of new technologies, and to account for variations in the pace of change. The source of that flexibility is the synergy of the core competencies of the individual Services, integrated into the joint team. These challenges will require a Total Force composed of well-educated, motivated, and competent people who can adapt to the many demands of future joint missions. The transformation of the joint force to reach full spectrum dominance rests upon information superiority as a key enabler and our capacity for innovation.

INFORMATION SUPERIORITY

Information environment—the aggregate of individuals, organizations, and systems that collect, process, or disseminate information, including the information itself. (JP1-02)

Information superiority—the capability to collect, process, and disseminate an uninterrupted flow of information while exploiting or denying an adversary's ability to do the same. (JP1-02) Information superiority is achieved in a noncombat situation or one in which there are no clearly defined adversaries when friendly forces have the information necessary to achieve operational objectives.

Information, information processing, and communications networks are at the core of every military activity. Throughout history, military leaders have regarded information superiority as a key enabler of victory. However, the ongoing "information revolution" is creating not only a quantitative, but a qualitative change in the information environment that by 2020 will result in profound changes in the conduct of military operations. In fact, advances in information capabilities are proceeding so rapidly that there is a risk of outstripping our ability to capture ideas, formulate operational concepts, and develop the capacity to assess results. While the goal of achieving information superiority will not change, the nature, scope, and "rules" of the quest are changing radically.

The qualitative change in the information environment extends the conceptual underpinnings of information superiority beyond the mere accumulation of more, or even better, information. The word "superiority" implies a state or condition of imbalance in one's favor. Information superiority is transitory in nature and must be created and sustained by the joint force through the conduct of information operations. However, the creation of information superiority is not an end in itself.

Information superiority provides the joint force a competitive advantage only when it is effectively translated into superior knowledge and decisions. The joint force must be able to take advantage of superior information converted to superior knowledge to achieve "decision superiority"—better decisions arrived at and implemented faster than an opponent can react, or in a noncombat situation, at a tempo that allows the force to shape the situation or react to changes and accomplish its mission. Decision superiority does not automatically result from information superiority. Organizational and doctrinal adaptation, relevant training and experience, and the proper command and control mechanisms and tools are equally necessary.

The evolution of information technology will increasingly permit us to integrate the traditional forms of information operations with sophisticated all-source intelligence, surveillance, and reconnaissance in a fully synchronized information campaign. The development of a concept labeled the global information grid will provide the network-centric environment required to achieve this goal. The grid will be the globally interconnected, end-to-end set of information capabilities, associated processes, and people to manage and provide information on demand to warfighters, policy makers, and support personnel. It will enhance combat power and contribute to the success of noncombat military operations as well. Realization of the full potential of these changes requires not only technological improvements, but the continued evolution of organizations and doctrine and the development of relevant training to sustain a comparative advantage in the information environment.

We must also remember that information superiority neither equates to perfect information, nor does it mean the elimination of the fog of war. Information systems, processes, and operations add their own sources of friction and fog to the operational environment. Information superiority is fundamental to the transformation of the operational capabilities of the joint force. The joint force of 2020 will use superior information and knowledge to achieve decision superiority, to support advanced command and control capabilities, and to reach the full potential of dominant maneuver, precision engagement, full dimensional protection, and focused logistics. The breadth and pace of this evolution demands flexibility and a readiness to innovate.

INNOVATION

Joint Vision 2010 identified technological innovation as a vital component of the transformation of the joint force. Throughout the industrial age, the United States has relied upon its capacity for technological innovation to succeed in military operations, and the need to do so will continue. It is important, however, to broaden our focus beyond technology and capture the importance of organizational and conceptual innovation as well.

Innovation, in its simplest form, is the combination of new "things" with new "ways" to carry out tasks. In reality, it may result from fielding completely new things, or the imaginative recombination of old things in new ways, or something in between. The ideas in *JV 2010* as carried forward in *JV 2020* are, indeed, innovative and form a vision for integrating doctrine, tactics, training, supporting activities, and technology into new operational capabilities. The innovations that determine joint and Service capabilities will result from a general understanding of what future conflict and military operations will be like, and a view of what the combatant commands and Services must do in order to accomplish assigned missions.

455

An effective innovation process requires continuous learning—a means of interaction and exchange that evaluates goals, operational lessons, exercises, experiments, and simulations—and that must include feedback mechanisms. The Services and combatant commands must allow our highly trained and skilled professionals the opportunity to create new concepts and ideas that may lead to future breakthroughs. We must foster the innovations necessary to create the joint force of the future—not only with decisions regarding future versus present force structure and budgets, but also with a reasonable tolerance for errors and failures in the experimentation process. We must be concerned with efficient use of time and resources and create a process that gives us confidence that our results will produce battlefield success. However, an experimentation process with a low tolerance for error makes it unlikely that the force will identify and nurture the most relevant and productive aspects of new concepts, capabilities, and technology. All individuals and organizations charged with experimentation in support of the evolution of our combat forces must ensure that our natural concern for husbanding resources and ultimately delivering successful results does not prevent us from pursuing innovations with dramatic if uncertain potential.

There is, of course, a high degree of uncertainty inherent in the pursuit of innovation. The key to coping with that uncertainty is bold leadership supported by as much information as possible. Leaders must assess the efficacy of new ideas, the potential drawbacks to new concepts, the capabilities of potential adversaries, the costs versus benefits of new technologies, and the organizational implications of new capabilities. They must make these assessments in the context of an evolving analysis of the economic, political, and technological factors of the anticipated security environment. Each of these assessments will have uncertainty associated with them. But the best innovations have often come from people who made decisions and achieved success despite uncertainties and limited information.

By creating innovation, the combatant commands and Services also create their best opportunities for coping with the increasing pace of change in the overall environment in which they function. Although changing technology is a primary driver of environmental change, it is not the only one. The search for innovation must encompass the entire context of joint operations—which means the Armed Forces must explore changes in doctrine, organization, training, materiel, leadership and education, personnel, and facilities as well as technology. Ultimately, the goal is to develop reasonable approaches with enough flexibility to recover from errors and unforeseen circumstances.

4. Conduct of Joint Operations

The complexities of the future security environment demand that the United States be prepared to face a wide range of threats of varying levels of inten-

456

sity. Success in countering these threats will require the skillful integration of the core competencies of the Services into a joint force tailored to the specific situation and objectives. Commanders must be afforded the opportunity to achieve the level of effectiveness and synergy necessary to conduct decisive operations across the entire range of military operations. When combat operations are required, they must have an overwhelming array of capabilities available to conduct offensive and defensive operations and against which an enemy must defend. Other complex contingencies such as humanitarian relief or peace operations will require a rapid, flexible response to achieve national objectives in the required timeframe. Some situations may require the capabilities of only one Service, but in most cases, a joint force comprised of both Active and Reserve Components will be employed.

The complexity of future operations also requires that, in addition to operating jointly, our forces have the capability to participate effectively as one element of a unified national effort. This integrated approach brings to bear all the tools of statecraft to achieve our national objectives unilaterally when necessary, while making optimum use of the skills and resources provided by multinational military forces, regional and international organizations, nongovernmental organizations, and private voluntary organizations when possible. Participation by the joint force in operations supporting civil authorities will also likely increase in importance due to emerging threats to the U.S. homeland such as terrorism and weapons of mass destruction.

PEOPLE

The core of the joint force of 2020 will continue to be an All Volunteer Force composed of individuals of exceptional dedication and ability. Their quality will matter as never before as our Service members confront a diversity of missions and technological demands that call for adaptability, innovation, precise judgment, forward thinking, and multicultural understanding. The Nation will continue to depend on talented individuals of outstanding character, committed to an ethic of selfless service.

Our people will require a multitude of skills. The Services will play a critical role in perfecting their individual specialties and the core competencies of each organization. In addition, every member of the Total Force must be prepared to apply that expertise to a wide range of missions as a member of the joint team. Our Service members must have the mental agility to transition from preparing for war to enforcing peace to actual combat, when necessary. The joint force commander is thereby provided a powerful, synergistic force capable of dominating across the entire range of operations.

The missions of 2020 will demand Service members who can create and then take advantage of intellectual and technological innovations. Individuals will be challenged by significant responsibilities at tactical levels in the organization and must be capable of making decisions with both operational and strategic

457

implications. Our vision of full spectrum dominance and the transformation of operational capabilities has significant implications for the training and education of our people. The tactics of information operations, the coordination of interagency and multinational operations, as well as the complexity of the modern tools of war all require people who are both talented and trained to exacting standards. Rapid and dispersed operations will require men and women who are part of a cohesive team, yet are capable of operating independently to meet the commander's intent. The evolution of new functional areas, such as space operations and information operations, will require development of appropriate career progression and leadership opportunities for specialists in those fields. The accumulation of training and experience will create a force ready to deploy rapidly to any point on the globe and operate effectively.

The joint force of 2020 will face a number of challenges in recruiting and retaining the outstanding people needed to meet these requirements. First, expanding civilian education and employment opportunities will reduce the number of candidates available for military service. We will continue to focus on our members' standard of living and a competitive compensation strategy to ensure we attract the quality individuals we need. Second, the increasing percentage of members with dependents will require a commitment to family-oriented community support programs and as much stability as possible, as well as close monitoring of the impact of the operations tempo. Finally, our increased dependence on the Reserve Component will require us to address the concerns of our reserve members and their employers regarding the impact on civilian careers. The Department of Defense and Services must meet these challenges head-on.

Military operations will continue to demand extraordinary dedication and sacrifice under the most adverse conditions. Our Total Force, composed of professionals armed with courage, stamina, and intellect, will succeed despite the complexity and pace of future operations.

INTEROPERABILITY

> **Interoperability**—the ability of systems, units, or forces to provide services to and accept services from other systems, units, or forces and to use the services so exchanged to enable them to operate effectively together. (JP1-02)

Interoperability is the foundation of effective joint, multinational, and interagency operations. The joint force has made significant progress toward achieving an optimum level of interoperability, but there must be a concerted effort toward continued improvement. Further improvements will include the refinement of joint doctrine as well as further development of common technologies and processes. Exercises, personnel exchanges, agreement on standardized operating procedures, individual training and education, and planning will further enhance and institutionalize these capabilities. Interoperability is a mandate for the joint force of 2020—especially in terms of

458

communications, common logistics items, and information sharing. Information systems and equipment that enable a common relevant operational picture must work from shared networks that can be accessed by any appropriately cleared participant.

Although technical interoperability is essential, it is not sufficient to ensure effective operations. There must be a suitable focus on procedural and organizational elements, and decision makers at all levels must understand each other's capabilities and constraints. Training and education, experience and exercises, cooperative planning, and skilled liaison at all levels of the joint force will not only overcome the barriers of organizational culture and differing priorities, but will teach members of the joint team to appreciate the full range of Service capabilities available to them.

The future joint force will have the embedded technologies and adaptive organizational structures that will allow trained and experienced people to develop compatible processes and procedures, engage in collaborative planning, and adapt as necessary to specific crisis situations. These features are not only vital to the joint force, but to multinational and interagency operations as well.

i. Multinational Operations

Multinational Operations—a collective term to describe military actions conducted by forces of two or more nations usually undertaken within the structure of a coalition or alliance. (JP1-02)

Since our potential multinational partners will have varying levels of technology, a tailored approach to interoperability that accommodates a wide range of needs and capabilities is necessary. Our more technically advanced allies will have systems and equipment that are essentially compatible, enabling them to interface and share information in order to operate effectively with U.S. forces at all levels. However, we must also be capable of operating with allies and coalition partners who may be technologically incompatible—especially at the tactical level. Additionally, many of our future partners will have significant specialized capabilities that may be integrated into a common operating scheme. At the same time, the existence of these relationships does not imply access to information without constraints. We and our multinational partners will continue to use suitable judgment regarding the protection of sensitive information and information sources.

In all cases, effective command and control is the primary means of successfully extending the joint vision to multinational operations. Technological developments that connect the information systems of partners will provide the links that lead to a common relevant operational picture and improve command and control. However, the sharing of information needed to maintain the tempo of integrated multinational operations also relies heavily on a shared understanding of operational procedures and compatible organizations. The commander must have the ability to evaluate information in its multinational context. That context can only be appreciated if sufficient regional expertise and liaison capability are available on the commander's staff. A deep understanding of the cultural, political, military, and economic characteristics of a region must be established and maintained. Developing this understanding is dependent upon shared training and education, especially with key partners, and may require organizational change as well. The overall effectiveness of multinational operations is, therefore, dependent on interoperability between organizations, processes, and technologies.

ii. Interagency Operations

Interagency Coordination—within the context of Department of Defense involvement, the coordination that occurs between elements of the Department of Defense and engaged U.S. Government agencies, non-governmental organizations, private voluntary organizations, and regional and international organizations for the purpose of accomplishing an objective. (JP1-02)

The primary challenge of interagency operations is to achieve unity of effort despite the diverse cultures, competing interests, and differing priorities of the participating organizations, many of whom guard their relative independence, freedom of action, and impartiality. Additionally, these organizations may lack the structure and resources to support extensive liaison cells or integrative technology. In this environment and in the absence of formal command relationships, the future joint force must be proactive in improving communications, planning, interoperability, and liaison with potential interagency participants. These factors are important in all aspects of interagency operations, but particularly in the context of direct threats to citizens and facilities in the U.S. homeland. Cohesive interagency action is vital to deterring, defending against, and responding to such attacks. The joint force must be prepared to support civilian authorities in a fully integrated effort to meet the needs of U.S. citizens and accomplish the objectives specified by the National Command Authorities.

All organizations have unique information assets that can contribute to the common relevant operational picture and support unified action. They also have unique information requirements. Sharing information with appropriately cleared participants and integration of information from all sources are essential. Understanding each other's requirements and assets is also crucial. More importantly, through training with potential interagency partners, experienced liaisons must be developed to support long-term relationships, collaborative planning in advance of crises, and compatible processes and procedures. As with our multinational partners, interoperability in all areas of interaction is essential to effective interagency operations.

OPERATIONAL CONCEPTS

i. Dominant Maneuver

Dominant Maneuver is the ability of joint forces to gain positional advantage with decisive speed and overwhelming operational tempo in the achievement of assigned military tasks. Widely dispersed joint air, land, sea, amphibious, special operations and space forces, capable of scaling and massing force or forces and the effects of fires as required for either combat or noncombat operations, will secure advantage across the range of military operations through the application of information, deception, engagement, mobility and counter-mobility capabilities.

The joint force capable of dominant maneuver will possess unmatched speed and agility in positioning and repositioning tailored forces from widely dispersed locations to achieve operational objectives quickly and decisively. The employment of dominant maneuver may lead to achieving objectives directly, but can also facilitate employment of the other operational concepts. For example, dominant maneuver may be employed to dislodge enemy forces so they can be destroyed through precision engagement. At times, achieving positional advantage will be a function of operational maneuver over strategic distances. Overseas or US-based units will mass forces or effects directly to the operational theater. Information superiority will support the conduct of dominant maneuver by enabling adaptive and concurrent planning; coordination of widely dispersed units; gathering of timely feedback on the status, location, and activities of subordinate units; and anticipation of the course of events leading to mission accomplishment. The joint force will also be capable of planning and conducting dominant maneuver in cooperation with interagency and multinational partners with varying levels of commitment and capability.

The capability to rapidly mass force or forces and the effects of dispersed forces allows the joint force commander to establish control of the battlespace at the proper time and place. In a conflict, this ability to attain positional advantage allows the commander to employ decisive combat power that will compel an adversary to react from a position of disadvantage, or quit. In other situations, it allows the force to occupy key positions to shape the course of events and minimize hostilities or react decisively if hostilities erupt. And in peacetime, it constitutes a credible capability that influences potential adversaries while reassuring friends and allies.

Beyond the actual physical presence of the force, dominant maneuver creates an impact in the minds of opponents and others in the operational area. That impact is a tool available to the joint force commander across the full

461

range of military operations. In a conflict, for example, the presence or anticipated presence of a decisive force might well cause an enemy to surrender after minimal resistance. During a peacekeeping mission, it may provide motivation for good-faith negotiations or prevent the instigation of civil disturbances. In order to achieve such an impact, the commander will use information operations as a force multiplier by making the available combat power apparent without the need to physically move elements of the force. The joint force commander will be able to take advantage of the potential and actual effects of dominant maneuver to gain the greatest benefit.

ii. Precision Engagement

Precision Engagement is the ability of joint forces to locate, surveil, discern, and track objectives or targets; select, organize, and use the correct systems; generate desired effects; assess results; and reengage with decisive speed and overwhelming operational tempo as required, throughout the full range of military operations.

Simply put, precision engagement is effects-based engagement that is relevant to all types of operations. Its success depends on in-depth analysis to identify and locate critical nodes and targets. The pivotal characteristic of precision engagement is the linking of sensors, delivery systems, and effects. In the joint force of the future, this linkage will take place across Services and will incorporate the applicable capabilities of multinational and interagency partners when appropriate. The resulting system of systems will provide the commander the broadest possible range of capabilities in responding to any situation, including both kinetic and nonkinetic weapons capable of creating the desired lethal or nonlethal effects.

The concept of precision engagement extends beyond precisely striking a target with explosive ordnance. Information superiority will enhance the capability of the joint force commander to understand the situation, determine the effects desired, select a course of action and the forces to execute it, accurately assess the effects of that action, and reengage as necessary while minimizing collateral damage. During conflict, the commander will use precision engagement to obtain lethal and nonlethal effects in support of the objectives of the campaign. This action could include destroying a target using conventional forces, inserting a special operations team, or even the execution of a comprehensive psychological operations mission. In other cases, precision engagement may be used to facilitate dominant maneuver and decisive close combat. The commander may also employ nonkinetic weapons, particularly in the arena of information operations where the targets might be key enemy leaders or troop formations, or the opinion of an adversary population.

In noncombat situations, precision engagement activities will, naturally, focus on nonlethal actions. These actions will be capable of defusing volatile situations, overcoming misinformation campaigns, or directing a flow of refugees to relief stations, for example. Regardless of its application in combat or noncombat operations, the capability to engage precisely allows the commander to shape the situation or battle space in order to achieve the desired effects while minimizing risk to friendly forces and contributing to the most effective use of resources.

iii. Focused Logistics

Focused Logistics is the ability to provide the joint force the right personnel, equipment, and supplies in the right place, at the right time, and in the right quantity, across the full range of military operations. This will be made possible through a real-time, web-based information system providing total asset visibility as part of a common relevant operational picture, effectively linking the operator and logistician across Services and support agencies. Through transformational innovations to organizations and processes, focused logistics will provide the joint warfighter with support for all functions.

Focused logistics will provide military capability by ensuring delivery of the right equipment, supplies, and personnel in the right quantities, to the right place, at the right time to support operational objectives. It will result from revolutionary improvements in information systems, innovation in organizational structures, reengineered processes, and advances in transportation technologies. This transformation has already begun with changes scheduled for the near term (see events highlighted in box at right) facilitating the ultimate realization of the full potential of focused logistics.

Focused Logistics Transformation Path

FY 01, implement systems to assess customer confidence from end to end of the logistics chain using customer wait time metric.

FY 02, implement time definite delivery capabilities using a simplified priority system driven by the customer's required delivery date.

FY 04, implement fixed and deployable automated identification technologies and information systems that provide accurate, actionable total asset visibility.

FY 04, for early deploying forces and **FY 06** for the remaining forces, implement a web-based, shared data environment to ensure the joint warfighters' ability to make timely and confident logistics decisions.

Focused logistics will effectively link all logistics functions and units through advanced information systems that integrate real-time total asset visibility with a common relevant operational picture. These systems will incorporate enhanced decision support tools that will improve analysis, planning, and anticipation of warfighter requirements. They will also provide a more seamless connection to the commercial sector to take advantage of applicable advanced business practices and commercial economies. Combining these capabilities with innovative organizational structures and processes will result in dramatically improved end-to-end management of the entire logistics system and provide precise real-time control of the logistics pipeline to support the joint force commander's priorities. The increased speed, capacity, and efficiency of advanced transportation systems will further improve deployment, distribution, and sustainment. Mutual support relationships and collaborative planning will enable optimum cooperation with multinational and interagency partners.

The result for the joint force of the future will be an improved link between operations and logistics resulting in precise time-definite delivery of assets to the warfighter. This substantially improved operational effectiveness and efficiency, combined with increasing warfighter confidence in these new capabilities, will concurrently reduce sustainment requirements and the vulnerability of logistics lines of communication, while appropriately sizing and potentially reducing the logistics footprint. The capability for focused logistics will effectively support the joint force in combat and provide the primary operational element in the delivery of humanitarian or disaster relief, or other activities across the range of military operations.

iv. **Full Dimensional Protection**

> **Full Dimensional Protection** is the ability of the joint force to protect its personnel and other assets required to decisively execute assigned tasks. Full dimensional protection is achieved through the tailored selection and application of multilayered active and passive measures, within the domains of air, land, sea, space, and information across the range of military operations with an acceptable level of risk.

Our military forces must be capable of conducting decisive operations despite our adversaries' use of a wide range of weapons (including weapons of mass destruction), the conduct of information operations or terrorist attacks, or the presence of asymmetric threats during any phase of these operations. Our people and the other military and nonmilitary assets needed for the successful conduct of operations must be protected wherever they are located—from deployment, to theater combat, to redeployment. Full dimensional protection exists when the joint force can decisively achieve its mission with an acceptable degree of risk in both the physical and information domains.

The capability for full dimensional protection incorporates a complete array of

464

both combat and noncombat actions in offensive and defensive operations, enabled by information superiority. It will be based upon active and passive defensive measures, including theater missile defenses and possibly limited missile defense of the United States; offensive countermeasures; security procedures; antiterrorism measures; enhanced intelligence collection and assessments; emergency preparedness; heightened security awareness; and proactive engagement strategies. Additionally, it will extend beyond the immediate theater of operations to protect our reach-back, logistics, and key capabilities in other locations. There is a critical need for protection of the information content and systems vital for operational success, including increased vigilance in counterintelligence and information security. The joint force of 2020 will integrate protective capabilities from multinational and inter-agency partners when available and will respond to their requirements when possible. Commanders will thoroughly assess and manage risk as they apply protective measures to specific operations, ensuring an appropriate level of safety, compatible with other mission objectives, is provided for all assets.

The joint force commander will thereby be provided an integrated architecture for protection, which will effectively manage risk to the joint force and other assets, and leverage the contributions of all echelons of our forces and those of our multinational and interagency partners. The result will be improved freedom of action for friendly forces and better protection at all echelons.

INFORMATION OPERATIONS

Information operations—those actions taken to affect an adversary's information and information systems while defending one's own information and information systems. (JP1-02) Information operations also include actions taken in a noncombat or ambiguous situation to protect one's own information and information systems as well as those taken to influence target information and information systems.

The Variables of Information Operations

- Multidimensional definition and meaning of "information"—target, weapon, resource, or domain of operations

- Level of action and desired effect—tactical, operational, strategic, or combination

- Objective of operations—providing information, perception management, battlefield dominance, command and control warfare, systemic disruption, or systemic destruction

- Nature of situation—peace, crisis, or conflict

Information operations are essential to achieving full spectrum dominance. The joint force must be capable of conducting information operations, the purpose of which is to facilitate and protect U.S. decision-making processes, and in a conflict, degrade those of an adversary. While activities and capabilities employed to conduct information operations are traditional functions of military forces, the pace of change in the information environment dictates that we expand this view and explore broader information operations strategies and concepts. We must recognize that "nontraditional" adversaries who engage in "nontraditional" conflict are of particular importance in the information domain. The United States itself and U.S. forces around the world are subject to information attacks on a continuous basis regardless of the level and degree of engagement in other domains of operation. The perpetrators of such attacks are not limited to the traditional concept of a uniformed military adversary. Additionally, the actions associated with information operations are wide-ranging—from physical destruction to psychological operations to computer network defense. The task of integrating information operations with other joint force operations is complicated by the need to understand the many variables involved .

Our understanding of the interrelationships of these variables and their impact on military operations will determine the nature of information operations in 2020. The joint force commander will conduct information operations whether facing an adversary during a conflict or engaged in humanitarian relief operations. Such operations will be synchronized with those of multinational and interagency partners as the situation dictates. New offensive capabilities such as computer network attack techniques are evolving. Activities such as information assurance, computer network defense, and counterdeception will defend decision-making processes by neutralizing an adversaries' perception management and intelligence collection efforts, as well as direct attacks on our information systems. Because the ultimate target of information operations is the human decision maker, the joint force commander will have difficulty accurately assessing the effects of those operations. This problem of "battle damage assessment" for information operations is difficult and must be explored through exercises and rigorous experimentation.

The continuing evolution of information operations and the global information environment holds two significant implications. First, operations within the information domain will become as important as those conducted in the domains of sea, land, air, and space. Such operations will be inextricably linked to focused logistics, full dimensional protection, precision engagement, and dominant maneuver, as well as joint command and control. At the same time, information operations may evolve into a separate mission area requiring the Services to maintain appropriately designed organizations and trained specialists. Improvements in doctrine, organization, and technology may lead to decisive outcomes resulting primarily from information operations. As information operations continue to evolve, they, like other military operations, will be conducted consistent with the norms of our society, our alliances with other democratic states, and full respect for the laws of armed conflict. Second, there is significant potential for asymmetric engagements in the information domain. The United States has enjoyed a distinct technological advantage in the information environment and will likely continue to do so. However, as potential adversaries reap the benefits of the information revolution, the comparative advantage for the U.S. and its partners will become more difficult to maintain. Additionally, our ever-increasing dependence on information processes, systems, and technologies adds potential vulnerabilities that must be defended.

JOINT COMMAND AND CONTROL

Command and control—the exercise of authority and direction by a properly designated commander over assigned and attached forces in the accomplishment of the mission. Command and control functions are performed through an arrangement of personnel, equipment, communications, facilities, and procedures employed by a commander in planning, directing, coordinating, and controlling forces and operations in the accomplishment of the mission. (JP1-02)

Command and control is the exercise of authority and direction over the joint force. It is necessary for the integration of the Services' core competencies into effective joint operations. The increasing importance of multinational and interagency aspects of the operations adds complexity and heightens the challenge of doing so. Command and control includes planning, directing, coordinating, and controlling forces and operations, and is focused on the effective execution of the operational plan; but the central function is decision making.

Command and control is most effective when decision superiority exists. Decision superiority results from superior information filtered through the commander's experience, knowledge, training, and judgment; the expertise of supporting staffs and other organizations; and the efficiency of associated processes. While changes in the information environment have led some to focus solely on the contribution of information superiority to command and control, it is equally necessary to understand the complete realm of command and control decision making, the nature of organizational collaboration, and especially, the "human in the loop."

In the joint force of the future, command and control will remain the primary integrating and coordinating function for operational capabilities and Service components. As the nature of military operations evolves, there is a need to evaluate continually the nature of command and control organizations, mechanisms, systems, and tools. There are two major issues to address in this evaluation—command structures and processes, and the information systems and technologies that are best suited to support them. Encompassed within these two issues, examination of the following related ideas and desired capabilities will serve as a catalyst for changes in doctrine, organization, and training.

- Commanders will need a broad understanding of new operational capabilities and new (often highly automated) supporting tools in order to be capable of flexible, adaptive coordination and direction of both forces and sensors.

- The staffs that support commanders must be organized and trained to take advantage of new capabilities. Commanders and staffs must also be capable of command and control in the face of technology failure.

- Commanders will be able to formulate and disseminate intent based upon up-to-date knowledge of the situation existing in the battlespace.

- Joint force headquarters will be dispersed and survivable and capable of coordinating dispersed units and operations. Subordinate headquarters will be small, agile, mobile, dispersed, and networked.

- Faster operations tempos, increased choices among weapons and effects, and greater weapons ranges will require continuous, simultaneous planning and execution at all levels.

- Expanding roles for multinational and interagency partners will require collaborative planning capabilities, technological compatibility/interoperability, and mechanisms for efficient information sharing.

Finally, as these and other changes take place over time, we must carefully examine three aspects of the human element of command and control. First, leaders of the joint force must analyze and understand the meaning of unit cohesion in the context of the small, widely dispersed units that are now envisioned. Second, decision makers at all levels must understand the implications of new technologies that operate continuously in all conditions when human beings are incapable of the same endurance. Third, as new information technologies, systems, and procedures make the same detailed information available at all levels of the chain of command, leaders must understand the implications for decision-making processes, the training of decision makers at all levels, and organizational patterns and procedures. The potential for overcentralization of control and the capacity for relatively junior leaders to make decisions with strategic impact are of particular importance.

It has often been said that command is an art and control is a science—a basic truth that will remain true. Our thinking about command and control must be conceptually based, rather than focused on technology or materiel. Joint command and control is a nexus—a point of connection. It serves as a focal point for humans and technology, our evolving operational capabilities, and the capabilities of the Services. The development of effective joint command and control for the future requires rigorous and wide-ranging experimentation, focused especially on organizational innovation and doctrinal change.

5. IMPLEMENTATION

From Vision to Experimentation

- Joint Vision 2010 (1996)
- Concept for Future Joint Operations (1996-7)
- 21st Century Challenges and Desired Operational Capabilities (1997)
- Joint Warfighting Experimentation Program established, USACOM (JFCOM) as Executive Agent (1998)
- Joint Vision Implementation Master Plan (1998)
- CJCSI 3170, Requirements Generation System (1999)
- JFCOM Joint Experimentation Campaign Plans (1999 and 2000)

Joint Vision 2010 has had a profound impact on the development of U.S. military capabilities. By describing those capabilities necessary to achieve success in 2010, we set in motion three important efforts. First, *JV 2010* established a common framework and language for the Services to develop and explain their unique contributions to the joint force. Second, we created a process for the conduct of joint experimentation and training to test ideas against practice. Finally, we began a process to manage the transformation of doctrine, organization, training, materiel, leadership and education, personnel, and facilities necessary to make the vision a reality. *Joint Vision 2020* builds on this foundation of success and will sustain the momentum of these processes.

The foundation of jointness is the strength of individual Service competencies pulled together. Our objective in implementing the joint vision is the optimal integration of all joint forces and effects. To achieve that goal, the interdependence of the Services requires mutual trust and reliance among all warfighters and a significantly improved level of interoperability—especially in the areas of command and control and sustainment. This interdependence will ultimately result in a whole greater than the sum of its parts, and will contribute to achieving full spectrum dominance through all forces acting in concert. The synergy gained through the interdependence of the Services makes clear that jointness is more than interoperability. The joint force requires capabilities that are beyond the simple combination of Service capabilities, and joint experimentation is the process by which those capabilities will be achieved.

469

To ensure unity of effort and continuity for joint concept development and experimentation, the Secretary of Defense designated the Commander in Chief, Joint Forces Command as the Executive Agent for experimentation design, preparation, execution, and assessment. Annual campaign plans provide focus to this effort and continuity in experimentation. The results of this iterative experimentation cycle are forwarded as comprehensive recommendations for changes in doctrine, organization, training, materiel, leadership and education, personnel, and facilities and lead to the co-evolution of all those elements. The experimentation and implementation process supporting the transformation of the joint force is also dependent upon Service and combatant command exercises and experimentation activities. The Service and combatant command visions support the joint vision by providing guidance for these individual efforts that are congruent with the Chairman's vision. Thus, in their own experimentation venues, the Services may develop recommendations with joint implications and will forward them to the appropriate joint experimentation activity.

To effect transforming and enduring changes to our joint military capabilities, the experimentation and implementation process must include construction of a wide range of scenarios and imaginative conflict simulations to explore the shape of future operations. Such intensive exploration of alternative concepts of operations can help the U.S. military choose innovations that take the greatest advantage of combinations of new ideas and new technologies. The rapid pace of such changes will then drive further development of the experimentation and implementation process to field improved capabilities for the joint force.

The linchpin of progress from vision to experimentation to reality is joint training and education—because they are the keys to intellectual change. Without intellectual change, there is no real change in doctrine, organizations, or leaders. Thus, the implementation process is dependent upon incorporating concepts validated by experimentation into joint professional military education programs and joint exercises. In this way, individual Service members and units become a joint team capable of success across the full range of military operations.

6. Conclusion

This vision is firmly grounded in the view that the U.S. military must be a joint force capable of full spectrum dominance. Its basis is four-fold: the global interests of the United States and the continuing existence of a wide range of potential threats to those interests; the centrality of information technology to the evolution of not only our own military, but also the capabilities of other actors around the globe; the premium a continuing broad range of military operations will place on the successful integration of multinational and interagency partners and the interoperability of processes, organizations, and systems; and our reliance on the joint force as the foundation of future U.S. military operations.

Joint Vision 2020 builds on the foundation and maintains the momentum established with *Joint Vision 2010.* It confirms the direction of the ongoing transformation of operational capabilities, and emphasizes the importance of further experimentation, exercises, analysis, and conceptual thought, especially in the arenas of information operations, joint command and control, and multinational and interagency operations.

This vision recognizes the importance of technology and technical innovation to the U.S. military and its operations. At the same time, it emphasizes that technological innovation must be accompanied by intellectual innovation leading to changes in organization and doctrine. Only then can we reach the full potential of the joint force—decisive capabilities across the full range of military operations. Such a vision depends upon the skill, experience, and training of the people comprising the Total Force and their leaders. The major innovations necessary to operate in the environment depicted herein can only be achieved through the recruitment, development, and retention of men and women with the courage, determination, and strength to ensure we are persuasive in peace, decisive in war, and preeminent in any form of conflict.

Appendix 10

Doctrine for Joint Nuclear Operations

Joint Publication 3-12, *Doctrine for Joint Nuclear Operations*, is a 68-page book issued on 15 March, 2005. Prepared under the direction of the Chairman of the Joint Chiefs of Staff, it provides guidelines for the joint employment of forces in nuclear operations. It provides guidance for the employment of U.S. nuclear forces; command and control relationships; and weapons effect considerations. Another lengthy book, but one considerate enough to come with its own executive summary which is reproduced here. For the keenly interested, the electronic version in PDF format can be downloaded at: www.globalsecurity.org/wmd/library/policy/dod/jp3_12fc2.pdf.

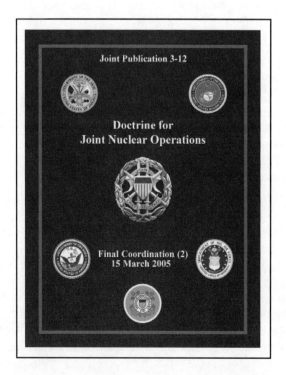

EXECUTIVE SUMMARY

COMMANDER'S OVERVIEW

- Covers Nuclear Force Fundamentals
- Discusses Nuclear Operations
- Covers Theater Nuclear Operations

Nuclear Force Purpose and Principles

The U.S. defense strategy aims to achieve **four key goals** that guide the development of U.S. forces capabilities, their development and use: assuring allies and friends of the U.S. **steadfastness of purpose** and its capability to fulfill its security commitment; **dissuading adversaries** from undertaking programs or operations that could threaten U.S. interests or those of our allies and friends; **deterring aggression and coercion** by deploying forward the capacity to swiftly defeat attacks and imposing sever penalties for aggression on an adversary's military capability and supporting infrastructure; and, **decisively defeating** an adversary if deterrence fails.

The **2001 Nuclear Posture Review** (NPR) constituted the first comprehensive review of nuclear forces since 1994. Because of the critical role played by U.S. nuclear forces in the National Security Strategy of the United States and its allies, the report was broader in scope than required by law. In a significant change to the U.S. approach to offensive nuclear weapons, the 2001 NPR articulated **a new capabilities-based strategy** for U.S. strategic nuclear forces that recognizes the unpredictable security environment and responds to U.S. strategic deterrence objectives and force capability requirements.

The new triad offers a mix of strategic offensive and defensive capabilities that includes nuclear and nonnuclear strike capabilities, active and passive defenses, and a robust research, development, and industrial infrastructure to develop, build, and maintain offensive forces and defensive systems. Enhanced command and control (C2), intelligence, and adaptive planning capabilities support the new triad. The new triad provides a deterrence posture suitable for the emerging threat environment; it incorporates post-Cold War advances in defensive and nonnuclear capabilities; and, it provides additional

473

military options that are credible to adversaries and reassuring to allies.

Fundamental Considerations

Strategic deterrence is defined as the prevention of adversary aggression or coercion that threatens vital interests of the United States and/or our national survival. **Strategic deterrence convinces adversaries not to take grievous courses of action by means of decisive influence over their decision making.**

Deterrence broadly represents the manifestation of a potential adversary's decision to forego actions that he would otherwise attempt. Diplomatically, the central focus of deterrence is for one nation to exert such influence over a potential adversary's decision-making process that the potential adversary makes a deliberate choice to refrain from a course of action. **The focus of U.S. deterrence efforts is therefore to influence potential adversaries to withhold actions intended to harm US' national interests.** Such a decision is based on the adversary's perception of the benefits of various courses of action compared with an estimation of the likelihood and magnitude of the costs or consequences corresponding to these courses of action. It is these adversary perceptions and estimations that U.S. deterrent actions seek to influence. Potential adversary decision making in the face of U.S. deterrent actions is also influenced by their strategic culture, idiosyncrasies of decision mechanisms and the leader's decision style, and leadership risk tolerance.

The U.S. does not make positive statements defining the circumstances under which it would use nuclear weapons.

Maintaining U.S. ambiguity about when it would use nuclear weapons helps create doubt in the minds of potential adversaries, deterring them from taking hostile action. This calculated ambiguity helps reinforce deterrence. If the U.S. clearly defined conditions under which it would use nuclear weapons, others might infer another set of circumstances in which the U.S. would not use nuclear weapons. This perception would increase the chances that hostile leaders might not be deterred from taking actions they perceive as falling below that threshold.

Real force capabilities, U.S. national determination to use them, and a potential adversary's perception of both the capabilities and the will to use them contribute to the effectiveness deterrence. To fulfill this purpose, U.S. military forces are capable of achieving U.S. national objectives throughout the range of military operations. Although the United States may not know with confidence what threats a state, combinations of states, or nonstate actors pose to U.S. interests, it is possible to anticipate the capabilities an adversary might use. Developing and sustaining a modern and diverse portfolio of military capabilities serves the four key defense policy

474

goals, identified earlier, that guide the development, deployment, and use of military forces and capabilities, including nuclear forces.

The decision to employ nuclear weapons at any level requires explicit orders from the President. Senior commanders make recommendations affecting nuclear policy decisions on force structure, weapon and force capabilities, and alternative employment options. The use of nuclear weapons represents a significant escalation from conventional warfare and may be provoked by some action, event, or threat. However, like any military action, **the decision to use nuclear weapons is driven by the political objective sought**. This choice involves many political considerations, all of which impact nuclear weapon use, the types and number of weapons used, and method of employment.

International reaction toward the country or nonstate entity that first employs weapons of mass destruction (WMD) is an important political consideration. The United States and its allies articulated their abhorrence of unrestricted warfare by codifying "laws of war," and turning to definitions of "just war." The tremendous destructive capability of WMD and the consequences of their use resulted in a number of agreements restricting deployment and use. Nevertheless, while the belligerent that initiates nuclear warfare may find itself the target of world condemnation, **no customary or conventional international law prohibits nations from employing nuclear weapons in armed conflict.**

The principle of proportionality requires that the anticipated loss of civilian life and damage to civilian property incidental to attacks must not be excessive in relation to the concrete and direct military advantage expected to be gained. Commanders therefore have the responsibility to attempt to minimize collateral damage to the greatest extent practicable. **The law of armed conflict does not prohibit nuclear weapons use in armed conflict** although they are unique from conventional and even other WMD in the scope of their destructive potential and long-term effects.

Nuclear Operations

The critical elements of strategic and theater nuclear operations include detailed command relationships, command responsibilities, and C2 actions; integrated planning and targeting; employment and force integration; and combat readiness.

National policy requires a single execution and termination authority for the use of nuclear weapons. **The President retains sole authority for the employment and termination of nuclear weapons.** The pace of modern war dictates streamlined and efficient methods of C2. The President and Secretary of Defense must have the most current and available situational information and intelligence and must comprehend all strategic and theater

475

nuclear plans and options. **Top-down communication transmitted over reliable, secure, and survivable communications systems** ensures critical orders are received for execution, increases survivability, and reduces vulnerability of C2 systems across the range of military operations. The

Commander, U.S. Strategic Command, has combatant command (command authority) over selected portions of the nation's strategic nuclear forces and is responsible for the planning and execution of strategic nuclear operations. Circumstantially, geographic combatant commanders may be assigned operational control over U.S. Strategic Command nuclear-capable forces employed for nuclear operations in support of theater conflicts.

Detailed planning is key to the execution of strategic nuclear operations. The President, Secretary of State, and Chairman of the Joint Chiefs of Staff each provide guidance for nuclear weapon planning. An integrated operation plan or series of plans predicated on commonly agreed strategic objectives is an absolute prerequisite to unity of force and strategic nuclear operations execution. This plan or series of plans formalizes the integration of nuclear assets. They clarify command guidance and objectives, effectively assign and prioritize targets, and synchronize execution.

Strategic operational planning must include the ability to respond to new targets and changing priorities before or during the execution of strategic nuclear operations. This **adaptive planning capability** ensures the most efficient use of resources and that strategic forces are fully capable of responding to any new threats that might arise. Strategic planners must also be prepared to conduct **crisis action planning** in those cases where adaptable, deliberate plans do not exist.

Targeting is the process of selecting and prioritizing targets and matching the appropriate response to them, taking into account operational requirements and capabilities. As nonnuclear strike capabilities and nuclear strike are integrated, targets that may have required a nuclear weapon to achieve the needed effects in previous planning may be targeted with conventional weapons, provided the required effects can be achieved.

Whether supporting national strategic goals or geographic combatant commanders, **the nuclear targeting process is cyclical.** The process begins with guidance and priorities issued by the President, Secretary of Defense, and Chairman of the Joint Chiefs of Staff and culminates with the final step of combat assessment. The entire targeting process consists of six phases: commander's objectives, guidance, and intent; target development, validation, nomination, and prioritization; capabilities analysis; commander's decision and force assignment; mission planning and force execution; and, combat assessment.

For many contingencies, existing and emerging conventional capabilities will meet anticipated requirements; however, some contingencies will remain where the most appropriate response may include the use of U.S. nuclear weapons. **Integrating conventional and nuclear attacks** will ensure the most efficient use of force and provide U.S. leaders with a broader range of strike options to address immediate contingencies. Integration of conventional and nuclear forces is therefore crucial to the success of any comprehensive strategy. This integration will ensure optimal targeting, minimal collateral damage, and reduce the probability of escalation.

Basic employment considerations are closely tied to the capabilities of assigned nuclear forces(i.e., weapons, delivery systems, and supporting systems under the combatant command (command authority) of Commander, United States Strategic Command (CDRUSSTRATCOM) and operational control of the geographic combatant commanders). **Each leg of the nuclear triad** offers characteristics that collectively provide a wide range of employment capabilities such as flexibility, effectiveness, survivability, and responsiveness. To maintain their deterrent effect, U.S. nuclear forces must maintain a **strong and visible state of readiness**. Strategic nuclear force readiness levels are categorized as either operationally deployed or as part of the responsive capability. U.S. Operationally Deployed Strategic Nuclear Warheads will be limited to 1,700 to 2,200 by 2012. The remaining U.S. strategic nuclear weapons remain in storage and serve as an augmentation capability should U.S. strategic nuclear force requirements rise above the levels of the Moscow Treaty.

Theater Nuclear Operations

Theater nuclear support may be provided by a geographic combatant commander's assigned forces, United States Strategic Command (USSTRATCOM), or from a supporting combatant commander. **Weapons in the U.S. nuclear arsenal include:** gravity bombs and cruise missiles deliverable by Dual Capable Aircraft and long-range bombers; the Tomahawk Land Attack Missile/Nuclear deliverable by attack submarines; submarine-launched ballistic missiles; and intercontinental ballistic missiles. These systems provide the President and the geographic combatant commander with a wide range of options that can be tailored to meet desired military and political objectives.

The geographic combatant commander is responsible for requesting nuclear support. The commander must ascertain the military situation, assess intelligence inputs, pass information and conclusions to higher levels of command, and upon receipt of execution instructions, control assigned forces to achieve the desired objectives. Subordinate commanders responsible for target nominations submit requests to the geographic combatant commander. **Execution procedures** are flexible and allow for changes in the situation. Commanders will ensure that constraints and release guidance are clearly understood. The commander controlling the nuclear strike package must maintain communications with the delivery unit and establish a chain of succession that maintains connectivity in case of headquarters destruction.

When directed by the President and Secretary of Defense, **joint force commanders (JFCs) plan for nuclear weapon employment in a manner consistent with national policy and strategic guidance.** Geographic combatant commanders are responsible for defining theater objectives and developing nuclear plans required to support those objectives, including selecting targets. When tasked, CDRUSSTRATCOM, as a supporting combatant commander, provides detailed planning support to meet theater planning requirements. All theater nuclear option planning follows prescribed Joint Operation Planning and Execution System procedures to formulate and implement an effective response within the timeframe permitted by the crisis. Since options do not exist for every scenario, combatant commanders must have a capability to perform crisis action planning and execute those plans. Crisis action planning provides the capability to develop new options, or modify existing options, when current limited or major response options are inappropriate. The supported commander defines the desired operational effects, and with USSTRATCOM assistance, develops Theater Nuclear Options to achieve those effects (e.g., disrupt, delay, disable, or destroy).

Nuclear weapons and associated systems may be deployed into theaters, but combatant commanders have no authority to employ them until that authority is specifically granted by the President.

CONCLUSION

This publication outlines military guidance for the exercise of authority by combatant commanders and other JFCs. It prescribes doctrine for joint nuclear planning, operations, and training and serves as a reference to more definitive and classified guidance. U.S. nuclear forces deter potential adversary use of WMD and dissuade against a potential adversary's development of an overwhelming conventional threat. The decision to employ nuclear weapons at any level requires the explicit decision from the President.

Appendix 11

U.S. Space Command Vision for 2020

The U.S. Space Command aims for the domination of space by integrating space forces into warfighting capabilities across the full spectrum of conflict. *Vision for 2020*—embodied in a booklet of 18 pages—serves "as a bridge in the evolution of military space into the 21st century and is the standard by which U.S. Space Command and its Components will measure progress into the future." I have reproduced the length of the booklet here, but you may as well download the e-book version replete with colorful and stunning graphics in PDF format at http://fas.org/spp/military/docops/usspac/visbook.pdf.

A Historic Perspective—the Evolution of Space

Historically, military forces have evolved to protect national interests and investments—both military and economic. During the rise of sea commerce, nations built navies to protect and enhance their commercial interests. During the westward expansion of the continental United States, military outposts and the cavalry emerged to protect our wagon trains, settlements, and railroads.

The emergence of space power follows both of these models. Over the past several decades, space power has primarily supported land, sea, and air operations—strategically and operationally. During the early portion of the 21st century, space power will also evolve into a separate and equal medium of warfare. Likewise, space forces will emerge to protect military and commercial national interests and investment in the space medium due to their increasing importance.

Joint Vision 2010

The medium of space is the fourth medium of warfare— along with land, sea, and air. Space power (systems, capabilities, and forces) will be increasingly leveraged to close the ever-widening gap between diminishing resources and increasing military commitments.

The Joint Vision 2010 operational concepts of **dominant maneuver, precision engagement, full-dimensional protection, and focused logistics** are enabled by information superiority and technological innovation. The end result of these enablers and concepts is **Full Spectrum Dominance.** **Information superiority** relies heavily upon space capabilities to collect, process, and disseminate an uninterrupted flow of information while denying an adversary's ability to fully leverage the same.

The emerging synergy of space superiority with land, sea, and air superiority, will lead to Full Spectrum Dominance. Space forces play an increasingly critical role in providing situational awareness (e.g., global communications; precise navigation; timely and accurate missile warning and weather; and intelligence, surveillance, and reconnaissance [ISR]) to U.S. forces.

Space doctrine, organizations, training, materiel, leadership, and personnel will evolve to fully realize the potential of space power. Space power is a vital element in moving towards the Joint Vision goal of being **persuasive in peace, decisive in war, and preeminent in any form of conflict.**

Future Trends

Although unlikely to be challenged by a global peer competitor, the United States will continue to be challenged regionally. The globalization of the world

480

economy will also continue, with a widening between "haves" and "have-nots." Accelerating rates of technological development will be increasingly driven by the commercial sector—not the military. Increased weapons lethality and precision will lead to new operational doctrine. Information-intensive military force structures will lead to a highly dynamic operations tempo.

Space Trends

Space systems, commercial and military, are proliferating throughout the world. Space commerce is becoming increasingly important to the global economy. Likewise, the importance of space capabilities to military operations is being widely embraced by many nations.

Indeed, so important are space systems to military operations that it is unrealistic to imagine that they will never become targets. Just as land dominance, sea control, and air superiority have become critical elements of current military strategy, space superiority is emerging as an essential element of battlefield success and future warfare.

Implications for U.S. Space Command

The political, economic, technological, and military trends hold significant implications for USSPACECOM. An increased dependence upon space capabilities may lead to increased vulnerabilities. As space systems become lucrative military targets, there will be a critical need to control the space medium to ensure U.S. dominance on future battlefields. Robust capabilities to ensure space superiority must be developed—just as they have been for land, sea, and air.

Our adversaries can be expected to attain ready access to space-derived information through the proliferation of space systems. Turnkey space systems are available to nations with the necessary resources allowing for significant increases in capabilities in a relatively short time. Military use of civil, commercial, and international space systems will continue to increase. However, the military must preserve certain core space capabilities, e.g., missile warning, assured space communications, and large portions of ISR. Other space capabilities, once the domain of the military, can reasonably migrate to the civil and commercial sectors, e.g., weather, GPS, and multi-spectral imagery.

Space operations must be fully integrated with land, sea, and air operations. USSPACECOM must assume a dynamic role in planning and executing joint military operations. Included in that planning should be the prospects for space defense and even space warfare.

Development of ballistic missile defenses using space systems and planning for precision strike from space offers a counter to the worldwide proliferation of WMD.

Vision

Just as land, sea, and air warfare has evolved, USSPACECOM, operating in the space medium, will evolve to perform the missions required by the future environment foreseen in the trends and implications on the preceding pages. This Vision charts a course to purposeful and orderly change.

The two principal themes of the USSPACECOM Vision are **dominating the space medium** and **integrating space power** throughout military operations. Today, the United States is the preeminent military space power. Our Vision is one of maintaining that preeminence—providing a solid foundation for our national security.

Operational Concepts

To move toward the attainment of our Vision, we have adopted four operational concepts:

* **Control of Space**
* **Global Engagement**
* **Full Force Integration**
* **Global Partnerships**

These operational concepts provide the conceptual framework to transform the Vision into capabilities.

Control of Space

Control of Space is the ability to assure access to space, freedom of operations within the space medium, and an ability to deny others the use of space, if required.

The medium of space is recognized as the fourth medium of warfare. Joint operations require the **Control of Space** to achieve overall campaign objectives. The **Control of Space** will encompass protecting U.S. military, civil, and commercial investments in space.

As commercial space systems provide global information and nations tap into this source for military purposes, protecting (as well as negating) these non-military space systems will become more difficult. Due to the importance of commerce and its effects on national security, the United States may evolve into the guardian of space commerce—similar to the historical example of navies protecting sea commerce.

Control of Space is a complex mission that casts USCINCSPACE in a classic warfighter role and mandates an established AOR.

482

Global Engagement

Global Engagement is the application of precision force from, to, and through space. USSPACECOM will have a greatly expanded role as an active warfighter in the years ahead as the combatant command responsible for National Missile Defense (NMD) and space force application. **Global Engagement** combines global surveillance with the potential for a space-based global precision strike capability.

The requirement for **Global Engagement** is based upon the increasing proliferation of missile systems, the requirement for precision strike, and the need for effective forward presence with reduced forward basing.

The proliferation of missiles and weapons of mass destruction (WMD) requires an NMD. NMD will evolve into a mix of ground and space sensors and weapons.

Existing land, sea, and air missions will be enhanced by space systems. Current sea and air strategic attack missions will be augmented by the deployment of space force application systems. Likewise, surface and air surveillance systems (e.g., AWACS and JSTARS) will be augmented by space-based surveillance systems.

Full Force Integration

Full Force Integration is the integration of space forces and space-derived information with land, sea, and air forces and their information. The bottom line is that space power will contribute to getting the right military capability and information to the right people, at the right place, at the right time.

Space forces must be fully integrated in all planning, training, exercises, and operations. **Full Force Integration** includes the merging of information and information systems into a "system of systems" approach. The goal is to achieve the same level of joint operations between space and the other mediums of war-fighting as land, sea, and air currently enjoy today. Innovative organizations, operational concepts, information flows, and people are key elements of **Full Force Integration**. Of these, the dedicated professionals that fill our ranks are our most indispensable assets.

Global Partnerships

Global Partnerships augments military space capabilities through the leveraging of civil, commercial, and international space systems. The growth of non-US military space systems provides the opportunity for the United States to gain increased battlespace awareness and information connectivity in a cost-effective manner. These partnerships provide shared costs, shared risks, and increased opportunities.

Global Partnerships is based upon these factors:

- Dramatic growth in commercial and international space-based capabilities. The development of advanced space systems will be primarily driven by the commercial sector.
- Constrained military spending.
- Growth in multi-national operations and alliances.

The most evident benefit of **Global Partnerships** will be decreased pressure on existing military infrastructure and operations, and reduced maintenance costs by off loading functions to civil and commercial providers. The military can no longer rely solely upon DoD owned and operated capabilities.

Global Partnerships—a fundamental change in providing military space support to the warfighter.

Implementation

The United States Space Command's Space Planning and Requirements System (SPRS) is the established process that will be used to implement this Vision. This end-to-end planning system uses Joint Vision 2010, the National Security Space Master Plan, and the United States Space Command Vision as overarching guidance.

Annually, we assess current and future space requirements, capabilities, and shortfalls in support of all warfighters. With our Vision, we will extend our time horizons from the Future Years Defense Plan to 2020. External organizations (e.g., CINCs, Services, National and Defense organizations) provide valuable input throughout the SPRS process. We fully expect that our Vision and SPRS will drive long-term changes in space doctrine, organizations, training, materiel, leadership, and personnel.

Appendix 12

Doctrine for Joint Psychological Operations

Joint Publication 3-53, *Doctrine for Joint Psychological Operations*, is a 124-page book issued on 5 September, 2003. Prepared under the direction of the Chairman of the Joint Chiefs of Staff, it addresses military psychological operations planning and execution in support of joint, multinational, and interagency efforts across the range of U.S. military operations. As this is quite a lengthy and technical book, I have limited myself to provide an executive summary of its contents (and intents). The complete electronic version of the book is available in PDF format at:

www.iwar.org.uk/psyops/resources/doctrine/psyop-jp-3-53.pdf.

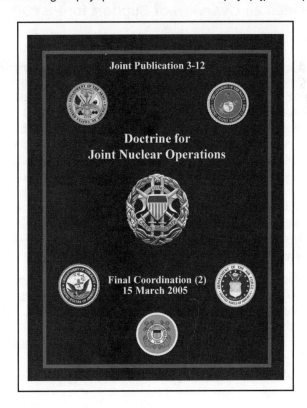

EXECUTIVE SUMMARY

COMMANDER'S OVERVIEW

- Provides an Overview of Psychological Operations (PSYOP)
- Discusses the Organizational Responsibilities for PSYOP
- Covers Command and Control in PSYOP
- Discusses PSYOP Planning
- Covers PSYOP and the Range of Military Operations
- Provides an Overview of Support for PSYOP

General Considerations for Psychological Operations

Psychological Operations (PSYOP) are **operations planned to convey selected information and indicators to foreign audiences to influence their emotions, motives, objective reasoning, and ultimately the behavior of foreign governments, organizations, groups, and individuals.** PSYOP are a vital part of the broad range of U.S. political, military economic, and informational activities. When properly employed, PSYOP can lower the morale and reduce the efficiency of enemy forces and could create dissidence and disaffection within their ranks. There are four categories of military PSYOP; strategic, operational, tactical, and consolidation PSYOP, which are used to establish and reinforce foreign perceptions of U.S. military, political, and economic power and resolve.

The principles of developing PSYOP apply across the range of military operations. Although the complexity of the methodology varies with the target audiences, **basic considerations for development of all PSYOP actions are the same.** Actions essential to successful PSYOP are: a clearly defined mission; analysis of all targets; actions that are evaluated for psychological implications; a reliable medium or media for transmission; rapid exploitation of PSYOP themes; and continual evaluation of the results of

PSYOP for relevance to the mission and goals. Intelligence, counterintelligence, command, control, communications, and computers systems (C4), and logistics support military PSYOP and are invaluable for the success of such actions.

PSYOP techniques are used to plan and execute truth projection activities intended to inform foreign groups and populations persuasively. Public affairs (PA) provide objective reporting, without intent to propagandize. As open sources to foreign countries and the United States, PA channels can be used to disseminate international information. **To maintain the credibility of military PA, steps must be taken to protect against slanting or manipulating such PA channels.** PSYOP messages must be coordinated with counterintelligence planners and operators, with military deception planners, and with operations security planners to ensure that essential secrecy is realized, counterintelligence operations are not compromised, and messages reinforce the desired appreciations of counterintelligence and deception as well as PSYOP plans.

Organizational Responsibilities for PSYOP

The Department of the Defense (DOD), including the Secretary of Defense, the Under Secretary of Defense for Policy or his designee, the DOD General Counsel, and the Chairman of the Joint Chiefs of Staff, are responsible for establishing national objectives, developing policies, and approving strategic plans for PSYOP. **Geographic combatant commanders and subordinate joint force commanders** are responsible for designating specific staff responsibilities, ensuring that plans and programs are coordinated and sufficiently represented, and that PSYOP are monitored and reviewed. **The Commander in Chief, U.S. Special Operations Command** ensures that all PSYOP and support requirements are addressed. **The Military Departments and Services** provide civilian and military personnel with appropriate training and planning skills.

Command and Control During PSYOP

Unless otherwise directed by the National Command Authorities, combatant command exercise combatant command (command authority) over all assigned military PSYOP assets. **Centralizing planning for PSYOP should be focused at the combatant command level.** The combatant commander may place PSYOP forces under operational control of a subordinate joint force or component commander for appropriate mission support; however, it is essential that all PSYOP products (such as leaflets or radio scripts) use the same themes and symbols, necessitating a single product development center.

The organization of forces will vary with the nature of the mission, availability and qualifications of PSYOP personnel, and the supported commander's assessment of the PSYOP force requirement. At first sign of crisis the **PSYOP Assessment Team will assess the situation**, develop objectives and recommend appropriate actions. **A PSYOP Task Force may be required if significant forces will be needed to implement the JFC's PSYOP objectives.** The senior PSYOP officer in the theater will ensure that component staffs are aware of the PSYOP products available and that continuity remains within the psychological objectives.

PSYOP Planning

Planned military PSYOP may affect not only military targets but political, economic, or social structures within the target area. The general objectives of joint PSYOP are: to reduce efficiency of opposing forces; further the U.S. and/or multinational war effort by modifying or manipulating attitudes and behavior of selected audiences; facilitate reorganization and control of occupied or liberated areas in conjunction with civil-military operations; obtain the cooperation of allies or coalition partners and neutrals in any PSYOP effort; and support and enhance humanitarian assistance, foreign internal defense (FID), and/or foreign nation assistance military operations. A thorough knowledge of national and theater military security policies and objectives, joint operations planning skills, and a thorough understanding of the customs, mores, and values of the target audience are required for PSYOP success. **The development of the PSYOP plan requires research and analysis, development of a way to convey or deny information, production requirements, and dissemination plans.**

These sources of information should be accessible to or be activities observable by target groups. **When appropriate, deception means can be used to convey messages to foreign groups having access to foreign intelligence.** Planners must understand both the possibilities and limitations of each means and the factors to consider in their use. **Planners should understand the difference between planning for joint operations and planning for overt peacetime PSYOP programs.** Peacetime programs are planned in consonance with the respective U.S. Ambassador's country plan and support national objectives and policy. Plans for military operations other than war and war also support national objectives and policy but generally have a different focus for PSYOP than peacetime programs.

PSYOP and the Range of Military Operations

The role of PSYOP varies depending on the level of operational activity or environment. Typical military operations other than war (MOOTW) that can be supported by joint PSYOP include humanitarian assistance and disaster relief, nation assistance, security assistance, FID, counterdrug operations, and peace support operations. MOOTW not involving the use or threat of force activities provide training and in-theater access to allow for the facilitation and use of PSYOP during the transition to war. MOOTW involving the use or threat of force require the application of the diplomatic, military economic, and informational instruments of national power. **Nonlethal activities, such as PSYOP, can be decisive In MOOTW involving the use or threat of force.** During war, PSYOP at the strategic, operational, and tactical level may enhance the success of operations at all echelons. **Employment of PSYOP can be equally effective in supporting both offensive and defensive operations conducted by conventional forces.** Special operations are also an integral part of modem warfare which may support conventional military operations or they may be conducted alone. Unconventional warfare, foreign internal defense, direct action, special reconnaissance, counterterrorism, and civil affairs are some of the special operations that may support PSYOP.

Support for PSYOP

PSYOP planners must possess a thorough and current knowledge of these conditions to develop PSYOP targeted at selected foreign groups to influence the objective and emotional reasoning. **Intelligence Support:** This knowledge is obtained through the use of the intelligence cycle which is the process by which intelligence is obtained, produced, and made available to the PSYOP planner. The intelligence cycle has five steps: planning and direction, collection, processing, production, and dissemination. **C4 Systems Support:** Communication between staffs and commands that are planning and executing PSYOP actions are necessary for effective joint use of capabilities. A joint PSYOP communications plan should be prepared to ensure that communications systems are compatible and adequate. **Logistic Support:** PSYOP forces will normally deploy with a 30-day basic load of PSYOP supplies. This is a baseline planning figure and may not be sufficient to meet specific contingency mission requirements. Joint planners must ensure that PSYOP support requirements are taken into account when planning logistic support.

CONCLUSION

Psychological operations are used to convey selected information and indicators to foreign audiences to influence their emotions, objective reasoning, and motives. In order to accomplish this goal, PSYOP must have a clearly defined mission, the ability to analyze and evaluate targets and their effects, a reliable media transmission, and a rapid ability to implement PSYOP. PSYOP depends on communication to ensure proper execution of the mission and objectives. This is carried out by command and control, preplanning and support from all levels.

Appendix 13

The World with Commanders' Areas of Responsibility

"The World with Commanders' Areas of Responsibilities" is the caption atop a world map on the Unified Command Plan (UCP) website of the U.S. Dept. of Defense. The UCP has effectively divvied up the world into five geographical areas among the combatant commanders. Details of the UCP—and a view of the map reproduced below in all its glorious colour— is found at www.defenselink.mil/specials/unifiedcommand/. Further details on the UCP can be found at www.globalsecurity.org/military/agency/dod/intro.htm and other websites. For now, I have provided an executive summary to provide general information on how they have carved up of the world and who got what.

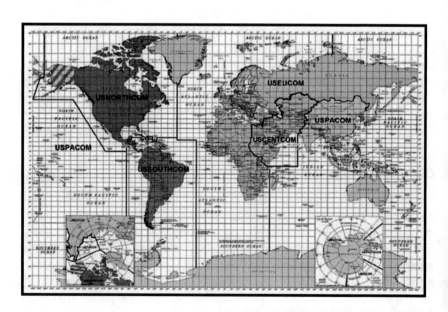

EXECUTIVE SUMMARY

Combatant Commands[1]

Under the Unified Command Plan (UCP) which establishes combatant command missions, responsibilities and force structure, there are five geographical areas of command and four functional commands.

Geographical Area Commands

Central Commands (CENTCOM)

The area covers the Middle East extending east to Pakistan, the Horn of Africa and the Central Asian Republics. It has also responsibility over Syria and Lebanon which prior to 2003 was under EUCOM (European Command) control.

CENTCOM components:

- Armed Forces Command (ARCENT) Third U.S. Army, Fort Mcpherson.
- Central Command Air Forces (CENTAF) 9th Air Force, Shaw Air Force Base
- Marine Forces Central Command (MARCENT), Camp H.M. Smith
- Naval Forces Central Command (NAVCENT), Manama, Bahrain including the Fifth Fleet (Bahrain).
- Special Operations Command Central (SOCCENT), MacDill AFB, with forward Joint Forces Special Operations Component Command in Qatar.

CENTCOM's operation structure for Iraq and Afghanistan includes JTF-7, Iraq and JTF-76 and JTF-180, Afghanistan.

Before 9/11, CENTCOM was responsible for one Operations Plan (OPLAN), seven Operation Plans in Concept Form (CONPLANS) and to Functional Plans. The OPLAN, CENTCOM OPLAN 1003V-03 dated Jan.30 2003, was for the illegal invasion of Iraq codenamed "Operation Iraqi Freedom."

CENTCOM now has CONPLANS for Iran and some areas of the former Soviet Union and more recently, Syria, taking over from EUCOM.

1 Source: William Arkin, *Code Names*. www.codenames.org

European Command (EUCOM)

Area covers 93 nations in Europe, Africa and the Middle East, stretching from Cape of Good Hope to Norway's North Cape and from Iceland to Russia.

EUCOM commander also serves as NATO's senior operational commander, Supreme Allied Commander Operations (formerly SACEUR), and is located in Belgium.

EUCOM components:

• US Force in Europe (USAFE), Ramstein Air Base, Germany consisting of the 3rd Air Force (RAF Mildenhall,UK) and 16th Air Force (Aviano AB, Italy).
• US Army Europe (USAREUR), Heidelberg, Germany
• US Naval Forces Europe (NAVEUR, London UK, consisting of the 6th Fleet (Italy).
• Marine Forces Europe (MARFOREUR), Boebligen, Germany.
• Special Operations Command, Europe (SOCEUR), Stuttgart-Vaihingen, Germany.

EUCOM Sub-unified Commands and JTFs:

• US Forces (USFORAZORES).
• Iceland Defense Force (ICEDEFOR).

Northern Command (NORTHCOM)

Activated in October, 2002 following 9/11 with the primary mission to defend the land, sea and air approaches to the USA assuming missions previously assigned to Joint Forces Command (JFCOM) and the North American Aerospace Defense Command (NORAD), specifically the air, land, sea and space defense of the U.S.

Area covers the continental USA, Alaska, Canada, Mexico and the surrounding waters out to 500 nautical miles. The Commander of NORTHCOM is also commander of NORAD. NORTHCOM provides force protection for domestic military bases and forces and supports the Department of Homeland Security.

NORTHCOM components:

• Standing Joint Force Headquarters North (SJFHQ-North), Colorado.
• JTF—Civil Support (JTF-CS), Fort Monroe
• JTF—6 (JTF-6), Briggs Army Airfield, Fort Bliss.
• JTF National Capital Region, Fort McNair, Washington, DC.

Pacific Command (PACOM)

Area of responsibility covers 43 countries, 20 territories and possessions, and ten U.S. territories making up more than 50% of the Earth's surface and 60% of the world's population. It also supports EUCOM's responsibilities over Russian Far East.

PACOM component:

- Army Pacific (ARPAC), Fort Shafter—I Corps (WA) and 25th Infantry Division (light)
- Marine Forces Pacific (MARFOPAC), Camp H.M. Smith consisting of I Marine Expeditionary Force (CA) and III Marine Expeditionary Force (Japan).
- Pacific Fleet (PACFLT), Pearl Harbor, consisting of the the 3rd Fleet (CA) and 7th Fleet (Japan)
- Pacific Air Forces (PACAF), Hickam AFB consisting of 5th Air Force (Japan), 7th Air Force (South Korea), 11th Air Force (AK) and 13th Air Force (Guam).
- Special Operations Command Pacific (SOCPAC), Camp H.M. Smith. Joint Task Force (JTF) 510 is PACOM's crisis response rapid deployment JTF.

PACOM Sub-unified Commands and JFTs:

- Alaskan Command (ALCOM), Elmendorf AFB, Anchorage, AK
- US Forces Japan (USFJ), Yokota AB, near Tokyo, Japan.
- US Forces Korea (USFK), 8th U.S. Army, Yongsan Army Garrison, Seoul South Korea.
- Joint Interagency task Force West (JIATF-West), Alameda, CA

Southern Command (SOUTHCOM):

The primary responsibility of SOUTHCOM is the development of modern militaries in South and Central American regions for counter-narcotics operations and counter-terrorism. In 2002, Cuba and other Caribbean island nations were transferred to the scope of responsibility of NORTHCOM.

SOUTHCOM components:

- Army South (ARSO), Fort Buchanan, Puerto Rico.
- Southern Air Force (SOUTHAF), Davis-Monthan AFB, AZ
- Naval Forces Southern Command (NAVSO), Mayport, Florida.
- Marine Forces South (MARFORSOUTH), Camp Lejeune, NC.
- Special Operations Command South (SOCSOUTH), Homestead Air Reserve Base, FL.

SOUTHCOM Sub-unified Commands and JFTs:

*   Joint Interagency Task Force—East (JIATF-East), Key West, FL.

*   Counter-Narcotics Task Force that also houses the Joint Southern Surveillance and Reconnaisance Operations Center (JSS-ROC). Coordinates all intelligence operations.

*   Joint Task Force—Bravo (JTF-B), Soto Cano AB, Honduras. Area of responsibility enlarged in 1995 to cover Belize, Costa Rica, El Salvador, Guatemala, Nicaragua and Panama.

*   Joint Task Force—Guantanamo (JTF-GITMO), Cuba. Detainee Operations at Naval Station Guantanamo Bay.

Functional Commands

Joint Forces Command (JFCOM):

Established in October 1, 1999 from the former U.S. Atlantic Command (LANTCOM). Substantially restructured in 2002 when geographic mission in North America was transferred to NORTHCOM and geographic missions in Northern Europe and Atlantic were transferred to EUCOM.

Primary focus is on transformation, joint experimentation, joint training, joint doctrine development, joint force providing, and joint inter-operability. The Commander of JFCOM was also designated NATO's Allied Commander Transformation (ACT) on June 19, 2003.

JFCOM components:

*   Army Forces Command (FORSCOM), Fort McPherson, GA.
*   Air Combat Command (ACC), Langley AFB, VA.
*   Marine Corps Forces, Atlantic (MARFORLANT), Norfolk, VA.
*   Atlantic Fleet, (LANTFLT), Norfolk, VA.
*   Special Operations Command, U.S. Joint Forces Command (SOCJF-COM), Norfolk, VA.
*   The Joint Warfare Analysis Center (JWAC) special access program based at the Naval Surface Warfare Center in Dahlgren, VA coms under JFCOM.

Special Operations Command (SOCOM):

Exercises command authority over all special operations forces (SOF), civil affairs, psychological operations and special counter-terrorism and recon-naissance forces.

There was a major restructure in 2004 when all intelligence, operations and planning functions were consolidated within the Center for Special Operations (CSO), replacing the Center for Intelligence and Information Operations.

The CSO has a subordinate Intelligence Support Group (J-2), Operations Support Group (J-3) and Campaign Support Group (J-5). A Special Operations Joint Interagency Collaboration Center has also been created.

SOCOM components:

- Army Special Operations Command (ARSOC), Fort Bragg, NC.
- Air Force Special Operations Command (AFSOC).
- Naval Special Warfare Command (NAVSPECWARCOM).
- Joint Special Operations Command (JSOC), Fort Bragg, NC.
- Army 75th Ranger Regiment (known internally as Colour Red).
- Naval Special Warfare Development Group (DEVGRU), Virginia Beach, VA. These are the SEAL TEAM 6 (known internally as Colour Blue)
- 24th Special Tactics Squadron, Pope AFB, NC.
- 66th Air Operations Squadron, Fort Bragg, NC.
- JSOC Air Component, The 1st Battalion, 16th Special Operations Air Regiment (SOAR), Fort Campbell, KY.
- Army Tactical Support Team, Fort Belvoir, VA
- Intelligence Support Activity (Gray Fox), Fort Belvoir, VA.
- Joint Communications Unit, MacDill AFB, FL.

Strategic Command (STATCOM):

It was originally formed to merge navy and air force strategic nuclear forces under one unified command. It is now a single U.S. military command responsible for the day-to-day readiness of nuclear forces, prepare nuclear war plans and maintain readiness under the Joint Strategic Capabilities Plan (JSCP).

In 2002, Space Command (SPACECOM) merged with STRATCOM, making it responsible also U.S. military worldwide with space support, intelligence communications, weather information, navigation and ballistic missile attack warnings. It also provides and prepares nuclear options for theatre command war plans to regional commanders specifically CENTCOM, EUCOM and PACOM.

STATCOM components:

- Air Force Space Command
- Army Space and Missile Defense Command
- Marine Forces Strategic Command
- Naval Network Warfare Command

- Task Forces

It is headquartered in three centers:

- Joint Integrated Analysis and Planning Center (JIAPC), Offutt AFB, Bellevue, NE
- Joint Information Operations Center (JIOC), Lackland AFB, San Antonio, TX.
- Joint Task Force—Computer Network Operations (JTF-CNO), Arlington, VA.

Transportation Command (TRANSCOM):

- Based in Scott AFB, Illinois, it provides strategic air, land and sea transportation for the Department of Defense (DoD) through three military commands:
- Air Mobility Command (AMC), Scott AFB, Il. Operation of airlift aircraft and Civil Reserve Air Fleet (CRAF).
- Military Surface Deployment and Distribution Command, Alexandria, VA.
- Military Sealift Command (MSC), Washington, DC.

Appendix 14

The National Intelligence Strategy of The United States of America:
Transformation through Integration and Innovation

The National Intelligence Strategy of the United States of America (NIS) is a 32-page publication released by the Director of National Intelligence, John D. Negroponte, to establish the strategic objectives for the Intelligence Community. The NIS serves both as a mission statement as well as an action document. The complete publication is reproduced here, but those who wish to have an electronic version of the document may download a PDF version at www.dni.gov/NISOctober2005.pdf.

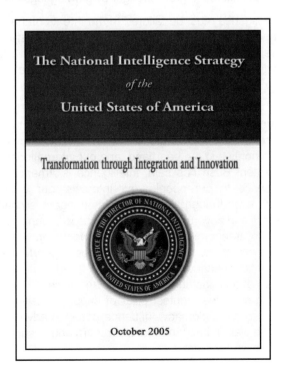

FOREWORD

The new concept of "national intelligence" codified by the Intelligence Reform and Terrorism Prevention Act passed by Congress in 2004 has its origins in the tragedy of September 11, 2001 and President Bush's *National Security Strategy of the United States of America.* The President signed the new law with the expectation that "our vast intelligence enterprise will become more unified, coordinated, and effective." Our charge is clear:

- Integrate the domestic and foreign dimensions of U.S. intelligence so that there are no gaps in our understanding of threats to our national security;

- Bring more depth and accuracy to intelligence analysis; and

- Ensure that U.S. intelligence resources generate future capabilities as well as present results.

Implicit in each of these tasks is the assumption that this new approach to "national intelligence" represents a far-reaching reform of previous intelligence practices and arrangements. National intelligence must be collaborative, penetrating, objective, and farsighted. It must recognize that its various institutional cultures developed as they did for good reasons while accepting the fact that all cultures either evolve or expire, and the time has come for our domestic and foreign intelligence cultures to grow stronger by growing together.

US national intelligence must be tailored to the threats of the 21st century, which seldom conform to the traditional profiles of hostile states and alliances. Adversarial states have learned to mask their intentions and capabilities, while terrorists and other non-state actors use commonplace technologies to boost their striking power and enhance their elusiveness.

The first order of business for U.S. national intelligence, therefore, is to inform and warn the President, the Cabinet, the Congress, the Joint Chiefs of Staff and commanders in the field, domestic law enforcement and homeland security authorities in the heartland, and our international allies. In this sense, as President Bush has said, intelligence is America's first line of defense, in service to our people, our interests, our values, and our Constitution. But even though the future holds dangerous challenges both within our borders and beyond, it also presents us with opportunities to support the spread of freedom, human rights, economic growth and financial stability, and the rule of law. We must identify these opportunities for democratic transformation because autocratic and failed states are breeding grounds of international instability, violence, and misery. For U.S. national security, democracy is the stoutest pillar of support. Intelligence can and should be used to aid diplomacy, influence potential adversaries prior to crises, help make war an instrument of last resort, and ensure victory in the event that conflict is unavoidable.

498

At its core, this National Intelligence Strategy capitalizes on the extraordinary talents and patriotism of America's diverse intelligence professionals,
those serving today and those joining us tomorrow. This strategy also relies
on our nation's tradition of teamwork and technological innovation to integrate the work of our distinct components into collaborative success. It sets
forth two kinds of strategic objectives—mission and enterprise—and calls
for plans that recognize each Intelligence Community member's core
strengths and competencies, and are written in consultation with the relevant departments and agencies. Finally, it states the importance of institut-
ing methods of self-evaluation to ensure that the Intelligence Community
meets decision-makers' needs and upholds the rule of law. The emphasis
placed here on national intelligence reflects a change in the threats we face
as a nation, not a change in our commitment to civil liberties and freedom.

A strategy is a statement of fundamental values, highest priorities, and orientation toward the future, but it is an action document as well. For U.S. national intelligence, the time for change is now. There are no easy answers to the
risks contemplated here, or the risks that might emerge. This strategy therefore accepts risk as intelligence's natural and permanent field of action and is
based on the proposition that to preserve our security in a dangerous century, vigilance is not enough. U.S. national intelligence must do more.

(Signed) John D. Negroponte
Director of National Intelligence

THE NATIONAL INTELLIGENCE STRATEGY OF THE UNITED STATES OF AMERICA

Our Vision—What we will become:

A unified enterprise of innovative intelligence professionals whose common
purpose in defending American lives and interests, and advancing
American values, draws strength from our democratic institutions, diversity,
and intellectual and technological prowess.

Our Mission—What we must do:

*   Collect, analyze, and disseminate accurate, timely, and objective intel-
    ligence, independent of political considerations, to the President and all
    who make and implement U.S. national security policy, fight our wars,
    protect our nation, and enforce our laws.

*   Conduct the U.S. government's national intelligence program and spe-
    cial activities as directed by the President.

*   Transform our capabilities in order to stay ahead of evolving threats to
    the United States, exploiting risk while recognizing the impossibility of

eliminating it.

- Deploy effective counterintelligence measures that enhance and protect our activities to ensure the integrity of the intelligence system, our technology, our armed forces, and our government's decision processes.

- Perform our duties under law in a manner that respects the civil liberties and privacy of all Americans.

Our Strategy—How we will succeed:

The stakes for America in the 21st century demand that we be more agile and resourceful than our adversaries. Our strategy is to integrate, through intelligence policy, doctrine, and technology, the different enterprises of the Intelligence Community. It encompasses current intelligence activities as well as future capabilities to ensure that we are more effective in the years ahead than we are today. The fifteen strategic objectives outlined in this strategy can be differentiated as mission objectives and enterprise objectives.

Mission objectives relate to our efforts to predict, penetrate, and preempt threats to our national security and to assist all who make and implement U.S. national security policy, fight our wars, protect our nation, and enforce our laws in the implementation of national policy goals.

Enterprise objectives relate to our capacity to maintain competitive advantages over states and forces that threaten the security of our nation.

Transformation of the Intelligence Community will be driven by the doctrinal principle of integration. Our transformation will be centered on a high-performing intelligence workforce that is:

- Results-focused
- Bold
- Self-evaluating

- Collaborative
- Future-oriented
- Innovative

These six characteristics are interdependent and mutually reinforcing. They will shape our internal policies, programs, institutions, and technologies.

Strategic Objectives

Mission Objectives: To provide accurate and timely intelligence and conduct intelligence programs and activities directed by the President, we must support the following objectives drawn from the *National Security Strategy:*

1. Defeat terrorists at home and abroad by disarming their operational capabilities and seizing the initiative from them by promoting the growth of freedom and democracy.

2. Prevent and counter the spread of weapons of mass destruction.

3. Bolster the growth of democracy and sustain peaceful democratic states.

4. Develop innovative ways to penetrate and analyze the most difficult targets.

5. Anticipate developments of strategic concern and identify opportunities as well as vulnerabilities for decision-makers.

Enterprise Objectives: To transform our capabilities faster than threats emerge, protect what needs to be protected, and perform our duties according to the law, we must:

1. Build an integrated intelligence capability to address threats to the homeland, consistent with U.S. laws and the protection of privacy and civil liberties.

2. Strengthen analytic expertise, methods, and practices; tap expertise wherever it resides; and explore alternative analytic views.

3. Rebalance, integrate, and optimize collection capabilities to meet current and future customer and analytic priorities.

4. Attract, engage, and unify an innovative and results-focused Intelligence Community workforce.

5. Ensure that Intelligence Community members and customers can access the intelligence they need when they need it.

6. Establish new and strengthen existing foreign intelligence relationships to help us meet global security challenges.

7. Create clear, uniform security practices and rules that allow us to work together, protect our nation's secrets, and enable aggressive counter-intelligence activities.

8. Exploit path-breaking scientific and research advances that will enable us to maintain and extend intelligence advantages against emerging threats.

9. Learn from our successes and mistakes to anticipate and be ready for new challenges.

10. Eliminate redundancy and programs that add little or no value and redirect savings to existing and emerging national security priorities.

STRATEGY GUIDANCE

Mission Objectives

1. Defeat terrorists at home and abroad by disarming their operational capabilities and seizing the initiative from them by promoting the growth of freedom and democracy.

The United States is fighting a war against terror in which our first priority is to identify, disrupt, and destroy terrorist organizations of global reach and attack their leadership, their command, control, and communications, and their material support and finances. Intelligence Community efforts therefore must:

- Integrate and invigorate all U.S. intelligence efforts to identify and disrupt terrorist organizations abroad and within U.S. borders.

- Uncover terrorist plans and intentions, especially those that may involve obtaining or using weapons of mass destruction.

- Deny terrorists operational haven, sanctuary, and political legitimacy by supporting democratization and the rule of law in vulnerable areas.

- Enable those outside the Intelligence Community with valuable counterterrorism information (such as police, corrections officers, and border patrol officers) to contribute to the national counterterrorism effort.

- Create an information sharing environment in which access to terrorism information is matched to the roles, responsibilities, and missions of all organizations engaged in countering terrorism, and is timely, accessible, and relevant to their needs.

The Director of the National Counterterrorism Center will develop a comprehensive national intelligence plan for supporting the nation's war on terror. The plan will identify the roles and responsibilities of each member of the Intelligence Community involved in supporting our national counterterrorism efforts, including their relationships with law enforcement and homeland security authorities. The Program Manager, Information Sharing Environment, will ensure the information needs of federal, state, local, and tribal governments and the private sector are identified and satisfied.

2. Prevent and counter the spread of weapons of mass destruction.

The comprehensive strategy of the U.S. government to combat weapons of mass destruction includes proactive counterproliferation efforts, strengthened nonproliferation efforts to prevent rogue states and terrorists from acquiring these technologies, and effective consequence management to respond to the effects of their use—whether by terrorists or hostile states.

As the WMD Commission stated in its March 2005 report, "There is no single strategy the Intelligence Community can pursue to counter the 'proliferation' menace." Rather, each destructive capability—biological, nuclear, chemical, radiological, or otherwise—will require unique and focused approaches to combating their use. To this end, Intelligence Community efforts must:

- Focus aggressive and innovative collection techniques to close knowledge gaps related to these technologies and associated weapons programs, particularly in the area of bioterrorism, to identify the methods of conveyance, and to prevent them from reaching our shores.

- Reach outside the Intelligence Community for information and expertise relevant to these technologies.

- Integrate the analytic effort within the Intelligence Community, under the leadership of the National Counter-Proliferation Center, by drawing upon the unique expertise and comparative advantages of each Intelligence Community organization.

- Work closely with foreign intelligence services to form a common assessment of threats and develop effective options in response.

- Ensure that weapons of mass destruction intelligence information is coupled with protective countermeasures information and disseminated to all who fight our wars, protect our nation, and enforce our laws.

The Director of the National Counter-Proliferation Center will develop a comprehensive national intelligence plan for supporting the nation's efforts to prevent and counter the development and proliferation of weapons of mass destruction. The plan will identify the roles and responsibilities of each member of the Intelligence Community, including their relationships with law enforcement and homeland security authorities.

3. Bolster the growth of democracy and sustain peaceful democratic states.

We have learned to our peril that the lack of freedom in one state endangers the peace and freedom of others and that failed states are a refuge and breeding ground of extremism. Self-sustaining democratic states are essential to world peace and development.

The Intelligence Community—its collectors, analysts, and operators—therefore must:

- Support diplomatic and military efforts (including pre- and post-conflict) when intervention is necessary.

- Forge relationships with new and incipient democracies that can help them strengthen the rule of law and ward off threats to representative government.

- Provide policymakers with an enhanced analytic framework for identifying both the threats to and opportunities for promoting democracy (including free markets and economic development), as well as warning of state failure.

The Deputy Director of National Intelligence for Customer Outcomes will develop a plan to accomplish these objectives. The Deputy Director of National Intelligence for Analysis will contribute to that plan by surveying the analytic expertise and production on democratization and state failure, and the level of Community support now provided to policymakers, identifying knowledge gaps and ways to address them, and improving support to those responsible for monitoring and assisting political and economic development and reducing the danger of state failure. The Deputy Director of National Intelligence for Collection will draft a collection plan, including the use of open sources, responsive to the information needs of this integrated plan.

4.   Develop innovative ways to penetrate and analyze the most difficult targets.

America's toughest adversaries know a great deal about our intelligence system and are becoming better at hiding their intentions and capabilities. Some are ruled by closed leadership cadres, and protected by disciplined security and intelligence services. Others are amorphous groups or networks that may share common goals, training, and methods, but which operate independently. The Intelligence Community needs capabilities to penetrate the thinking of both sets of leaders by:

*   Making the best use of all-source intelligence, including from open sources, on the most difficult targets.

*   Developing new methodologies, including specialized training and career development, for analyzing the capabilities and intentions of hard targets.

*   Improving human intelligence and corresponding technical intelligence capabilities.

*   Assessing the intelligence capabilities and actions of our adversaries to ensure that an insightful counterintelligence analytic capability helps to penetrate hard targets and understand their leadership cadres.

The Deputy Director of National Intelligence for Collection will develop a plan for improving penetration of hard targets. The Deputy Director of National Intelligence for Analysis will develop a plan to assess the current state of knowledge, identify and close gaps, bolster expertise and research on these targets, and develop new methodologies against them. The National Counterterrorism Center and the National Counterintelligence Executive will devise plans to enhance analysis of terror networks and foreign intelligence establishments and activities. The latter plan will include a means to integrate counterintelligence with other sources to capitalize on opportunities for strategic offensive activities.

5.   Anticipate developments of strategic concern and identify opportunities as well as vulnerabilities for decision-makers.

In a world in which developments anywhere can quickly affect American citizens and interests at home and abroad, the Intelligence Community must alert policymakers to problems before they escalate, and provide insights

504

into their causes and effects. Analysis must do more than just describe what is happening and why; it must identify a range of opportunities for (and likely consequences of) diplomatic, military, law enforcement, or homeland security action.

To support policymakers, the Intelligence Community should develop, sustain, and have access to expertise on every region, every transnational security issue, and every threat to the American people. The Intelligence Community will:

- Identify and analyze possible opportunities as well as warn of potential problems.

- Promote deeper cultural understanding, better language proficiency, and scientific and technological knowledge among personnel at all levels.

- Identify gaps in coverage and work to close them through recruitment, training, and consultation with outside expertise.

- Make attention to long-term and strategic analysis a part of every analyst's assigned responsibilities, train analysts to anticipate developments likely to affect U.S. interests, and ensure they are alert to possibilities for timely action.

The Deputy Director of National Intelligence for Analysis will establish a strategic research and analysis unit in the National Intelligence Council; develop procedures to inventory Intelligence Community analytic capabilities on all regions, specified threats, and transnational issues; develop a plan to improve the language skills, scientific and technological skills, and cultural insight of analysts; and work with the analytic components of all Intelligence Community agencies to close gaps, facilitate collaboration, and achieve appropriate balances between long-term and current analysis.

Enterprise Objectives

1. Build an integrated intelligence capability to address threats to the homeland, consistent with U.S. laws and the protection of privacy and civil liberties.

Ubiquitous communications technology, easy international travel, and extremists with the resources and the intent to harm Americans wherever they may reside force us to rethink the way we conduct intelligence collection at home and its relationship with traditional intelligence gathering methods abroad. Consistent with applicable laws and the protection of civil liberties and privacy, U.S. intelligence elements must focus their capabilities to ensure that:

- Intelligence elements in the Departments of Justice and Homeland Security are properly resourced and closely integrated within the larger Intelligence Community.

505

- All Intelligence Community components assist in facilitating the integration of collection and analysis against terrorists, weapons of mass destruction, and other threats to the homeland.

- State, local, and tribal entities and the private sector are connected to our homeland security and intelligence efforts.

The Deputy Director of National Intelligence for Management will develop a financial, information, and human resource plan for our intelligence capabilities to deal with threats at home that ensures the full and lawful integration of the Intelligence Community elements of the Departments of Justice and Homeland Security with the other Community elements. The Program Manager, Information Sharing Environment, in conjunction with the Chief Information Officer, will develop a plan to facilitate the means for sharing terrorism information among all appropriate federal, state, local, and tribal entities, and the private sector. The Civil Liberties Protection Officer will develop a plan to ensure that improvements to these capabilities are achieved with due regard for the privacy and civil liberties of Americans.

2.   Strengthen analytic expertise, methods, and practices; tap expertise wherever it resides; and explore alternative analytic views.

To avoid intelligence failures, the analytic judgments presented to policymakers must be the product of an enterprise that values differing perspectives, nurtures and rewards expertise, and is agile and innovative in the way it deploys and utilizes that expertise.

To strengthen and sustain Intelligence Community analytic capabilities and to ensure that appropriate expertise is brought to bear efficiently and constructively, the Intelligence Community must:

- Build and sustain the expertise and capacity of the Intelligence Community's analyst "corps," leveraging the unique capabilities of each component, and fostering cross-agency collaboration at all levels.

- Utilize expertise from outside the Intelligence Community to inform judgments and to bolster areas where knowledge is lacking in the Community.

- Improve analytic methods and practices across the Community, ensuring rigor and the exploration of alternative analysis.

The Deputy Director of National Intelligence for Analysis will develop a plan to identify expertise inside and outside government, establish virtual teams of experts and interested analysts from across the Intelligence Community and U.S. government, improve cooperation between analysis and collection, improve analytic methods and practices, and ensure analytic integrity. The plan will also address new processes to allow the Office of the Director of National Intelligence to manage key intelligence issues, including inventorying analytic leads and activities for high priority issues, identifying knowledge gaps, and working with collection managers to close them.

3.   Rebalance, integrate, and optimize collection capabilities to meet current and future customer and analytic priorities.

Our technical means of collecting information must remain unmatched. They allow us to avert conflict, expand peace, and win wars. The nation gains when our technical systems are developed for multiple purposes, but long development schedules and changing requirements undermine our agility and resources. Accordingly, the Intelligence Community must:

*   Expand collection and analysis from open sources, and manage them as integrated intelligence activities.

*   Establish a national clandestine service to integrate all the elements of human source collection in accord with the highest traditions of professionalism and intellectual prowess.

*   Rebalance the technical collection architecture to improve responsiveness to user requirements; enhance flexibility and survivability; and provide new sources and methods for current and emerging targets.

*   Expand the reporting of information of intelligence value from state, local, and tribal law enforcement entities and private sector stakeholders.

The Deputy Director of National Intelligence for Collection will develop a comprehensive plan for achieving a new balance among our various collection methods—open, human, and technical sources—while taking account of the differing legal and policy framework for collection within the United States. The plan will reflect the changed nature of the threats we face, the vast opportunities of the information age, and new non traditional sources of information now available. The Foreign Denial and Deception Committee will complete a plan for countering denial and deception practices deployed against us.

4.   Attract, engage, and unify an innovative and results-focused Intelligence Community workforce.

The complexity of the challenges the United States faces in the 21st century will require those who serve in the Intelligence Community, both military and civilian, to apply expertise against a wide range of threats, and to become more adept and innovative in acquiring, analyzing, and communicating the knowledge that policymakers need.

In order to ensure the Intelligence Community is able to meet these expectations, it must:

*   Recruit exceptional individuals from a diverse talent pool, train and develop them to meet the challenges they will face, and then deploy them in ways that maximize their talents and potential.

- Reward expertise, excellence, and commitment to service; provide opportunities for professional growth and leadership development, and encourage initiative, innovation, resourcefulness, and resilience among the civilian and military members of the Intelligence Community and those who lead them.

- Build an Intelligence Community-wide culture that values the abilities of each of its members and provides them developmental opportunities across the Intelligence Community in accord with their aptitudes and aspirations.

The Chief Human Capital Officer, in partnership with the Chief Training and Education Officer, will develop an Intelligence Community Strategic Human Capital Plan that will enable Community elements to: identify mission-critical human resource requirements; train, develop, and promote Community professionals according to rigorous, competency-based standards; select a senior leadership cadre that promotes high performance, employee engagement, information sharing, and collaboration; and develop evaluation and reward systems that reinforce excellence among professionals and those who lead them.

5. Ensure that Intelligence Community members and customers can access the intelligence they need when they need it.

The Intelligence Reform and Terrorism Prevention Act of 2004 directed the Director of National Intelligence to "ensure maximum availability of and access to intelligence information." We must ensure maximum interoperability inside the Community while creating effective, flexible links to customers. Intelligence Community efforts must:

- Remove impediments to information sharing within the Community, and establish policies that reflect need-to-share (versus need-to-know) for all data, removing the "ownership" by agency of intelligence information.

- Build a user-friendly system that allows customers to find needed intelligence and access it immediately.

- Develop flexible and secure networks adaptable to a rapidly changing environment and capable of getting intelligence in an unclassified form to nontraditional customers such as state, local, and tribal governments and the private sector.

- Create an intelligence "cyber community" where analysts, collectors, and customers can interact swiftly and easily in considering classified information.

The Deputy Director of National Intelligence for Customer Outcomes will oversee the development of plans to provide maximum access to intelligence information among Intelligence Community customers, consistent with applicable laws and the protection of civil liberties and privacy. The

Program Manager, Information Sharing Environment, will create a plan to ensure that the Information Sharing Environment provides the functional equivalent of, or otherwise supports, a decentralized, distributed, and coordinated environment as described in Section 1016(b)(2) of the Intelligence Reform and Terrorism Prevention Act of 2004. The Chief Information Of ricer will develop a plan to ensure that activities and procurements relating to the information technology infrastructure and enterprise architecture of the Intelligence Community meet the need to share information more broadly.

6. Establish new and strengthen existing foreign intelligence relationships to help us meet global security challenges.

Since our most serious national security challenges are transnational, the Community must enlist like-minded nations to extend our reach. As the *National Security Strategy* states, "no nation can build a safer, better world alone." To this end, we must:

- Engage and invigorate friendly foreign intelligence services' efforts that could aid in the identification and disruption of terrorist organizations abroad and within U.S. borders.

- Coordinate closely with foreign intelligence services to inform a common assessment of threats and options in response.

- Ensure that insights gained from our foreign intelligence relationships inform intelligence judgments and develop effective options in response.

The Deputy Director of National Intelligence for Customer Outcomes will direct the development of a strategic plan on foreign intelligence relationships to ensure that the relationships are being adequately coordinated and employed to meet national security threats. This plan will include a process to identify existing gaps as well as to determine if new foreign intelligence relationships need to be established or existing relationships strengthened.

7. Create clear, uniform security practices and rules that allow us to work together, protect our nation's secrets, and enable aggressive counterintelligence activities.

The Intelligence Community must dramatically change the basis of its security and counterintelligence policies in order to remain effective. We must rigorously assess threat, vulnerability, and protection requirements to further overall Community objectives. Intelligence Community efforts must:

- Redefine classification guidelines to allow for a large body of "sensitive" information with flexible use and sharing arrangements, and a smaller body of "restricted" information available to fewer personnel.

- Establish uniform and reciprocal Intelligence Community guidance on security issues of common concern, including access to facilities, and electronic access to systems and databases.

509

BRAINWASHED FOR WAR: PROGRAMMED TO KILL

- Institute new procedures, including innovative security assessment and reliability monitoring, permitting agencies to expeditiously assess personnel with potential vulnerabilities.

- Ensure the various Intelligence Community elements conducting counterintelligence activities act as a cohesive whole to undertake aggressive, unified counterintelligence operations.

The Deputy Director of National Intelligence for Management will develop a plan for changing physical, information, and personnel security policies impeding the Intelligence Community's ability to achieve its mission and enterprise objectives. The National Counterintelligence Executive, in the plan for implementing the National Counterintelligence Strategy, will describe how the Community will undertake aggressive counterintelligence operations with greater unity of effort. The Chief Information Officer will develop a plan for new security policies that promote information sharing across the Intelligence Community.

8. Exploit path-breaking scientific and research advances that will enable us to maintain and extend intelligence advantages against emerging threats.

Globalization and accelerating scientific and technological progress threaten to erode the Intelligence Community's technical collection means, to undermine our ability to identify/access world-class scientific expertise, and to degrade our ability to exploit emerging technological advances.

The Intelligence Community's ability to identify and leverage cutting-edge scientific and technological research depends on our capacity to forecast technological trends, interact with leading researchers, and gain early access to innovative concepts and designs. To this end, Intelligence Community efforts must:

- Establish a centrally led, but de-centrally executed, process for Intelligence Community scientific and technological activities.

- Deepen technical expertise and strengthen advanced research and development programs within the agencies.

- Identify high risk, high reward research for special emphasis by the Office of the Director of National Intelligence, particularly in the "white spaces" between various agency efforts.

- Foster joint development among agency research efforts, where appropriate.

The Associate Director of National Intelligence for Science and Technology will develop a plan for leading the Intelligence Community's science and technology resources and activities. The plan will identify the roles and responsibilities for each member of the Intelligence Community engaged in

510

scientific and technological activities.

9. Learn from our successes and mistakes to anticipate and be ready for new challenges.

The Intelligence Community must continuously improve its ability to record, assess, and learn from its performance, in part by establishing metrics to measure its performance. The process of conducting performance reviews and learning from both successes and failures should help identify systemic shortcomings. In addition to assimilating lessons, the Community must also assess its readiness. Intelligence Community efforts must:

- Create a lessons-learned function to assess the effectiveness of the Community's activities as a "system of systems" in supporting national policy goals.

- Establish a rigorous evaluation process that determines how well individual strategic plans meet their stated goals and how effectively they support the relevant mission and enterprise objectives.

- Incorporate into each agency's strategic plan a readiness component addressing crises and contingencies.

- Create a robust command and control system for the Director of National Intelligence.

The Deputy Director of National Intelligence for Management will develop plans to assess the Community's performance against mission and enterprise objectives, establish a Community wide lessons-learned function, and guide the improvement of readiness within the agencies. The Chief Information Officer will develop a plan to ensure the functioning of the Director of National Intelligence's command and control system in all contingencies.

10. Eliminate redundancy and programs that add little or no value and redirect savings to existing and emerging national security priorities.

The Intelligence Community is a vast enterprise, with areas of overlapping missions and expertise. In some instances, the overlap adds value; in others it consumes resources more appropriately directed to the Intelligence Community member having the mission at its core, or to emerging national security threats.

The Intelligence Community must manage its resources by examining national security priorities, both short and long term, and quickly adapt to changes in them. The Community must also revise its financial procedures and processes; existing budget reports are not providing the level of consistency required for appropriate oversight. To this end, the Intelligence Community must:

- Standardize, synchronize, and coordinate financial reporting in order to provide a comprehensive and auditable record of Community expenditures.

- Assess the current program development process with emphasis on evaluating how program submissions are aligned against objectives.

- Eliminate mission and program redundancy that adds little or no value.

- End programs/projects that no longer meet national security priorities or that do not deliver as promised.

- Consolidate similar programs and missions under one Community lead.

- Redirect resources saved through consolidation and terminated programs to existing and emerging threats.

- Ensure that new systems are developed in compliance with an Intelligence Community Enterprise Architecture.

The Deputy Director of National Intelligence for Management will develop a plan to identify and eliminate unnecessary redundancy and low value programs within the Intelligence Community. The plan will also address how to identify missions and programs where resources should be redirected to meet new and emerging national security threats and to enhance secure intelligence capabilities for organizations that function primarily in the United States. The plan will specify the roles and responsibilities of Intelligence Community members engaged in resource management and program development to continually examine their programs and missions and to collaborate with one another in arriving at recommendations for mission adjustments, program consolidations or terminations, and areas ripe for redirection of resources. It will also describe how to strengthen the Community's financial management systems with the goal of achieving comprehensive audits of the major intelligence programs.

Next Steps

These strategic objectives will guide Intelligence Community policy, planning, collection, analysis, operations, programming, acquisition, budgeting, and execution. They will be overseen by senior officials of the Office of the Director of National Intelligence, but will be implemented through an integrated Intelligence Community effort to capitalize on the comparative advantages of constituent organizations.

- The Deputy Director of National Intelligence for Management will develop a strategic planning and evaluation process for the Intelligence Community.

- The Fiscal Year 2008 planning, programming, and performance guidance will reflect these mission and enterprise objectives. Ongoing program and budget activities for Fiscal Years 2006 and 2007 will adjust to these objectives to the maximum extent possible.

Index

9/11 (or September 11) 1, 9, 54, 58,
69, 71, 72, 73, 74, 75, 95, 130,
150, 152, 170, 171, 182, 220, 224,
233, 241, 257, 291, 294, 297, 304,
305, 309, 421, 424, 491, 492, 498
Abrams, Elliott 274, 420
Abu Ghraib 29, 95, 127, 150, 152,
159, 162, 163, 164, 165, 166, 169,
171, 200, 242, 281, 299
Adam, Sir Ronald 190
Addington, David 299
Afghan War 11
Aftergood, Dr. Steven 197
Agent Orange 43
Al Qaeda 93, 97, 127, 130, 136,
137, 141, 142, 152, 173, 257, 426
Al-Zarqawi 136, 137, 142
Albright, Madeline 29, 293
Almond, Mark 300
Alperovitz, Gar 39
Alsop, Joseph 24
Alterman, Eric 38
American Revolution, the xvi
Amit, Daniel 99
Aristide, Jean Bertrand 300
Arkin, William 289
Atomic Energy Organization of Iran
(AEOI) 107
Bailey, Maj. Gen. Jonathan 244
Bank of England 15, 16, 17
Barak, Ehud xxiv, 229

Barnes, Harry Elmer 36, 45, 48, 54
Barnett, Prof. Thomas P.M. 138,
139, 290, 291
Barrie, Sir James Mathew xv
Baruch Plan, the 43
Bateson, Dr. Gregory 188
Battle of Stalingrad, the 33, 242
Bechtel 7, 256
Becker, Ernest 157
Beckert, Prof. Sven 309
Begin, Menachem 141
Benn, Tony 279, 307
Berlusconi, Silvio 264
Berman, Q.C., Sir Franklin 305
Bernardi, General Friedrich von 158
Bertell, Dr. Rosalie 90
Bible, the Holy 218
Bilmes, Linda 9
Bion, Wilfred 190
Bissell, Richard 24
Blair, Tony ix, xii, 9, 11, 62, 95, 98,
99, 122, 127, 128, 141, 146, 153,
160, 206, 218, 230, 232, 233, 234,
239, 243, 249, 250, 257, 258, 262,
263, 267, 268, 272, 275, 277, 278,
280, 282, 285, 286, 287, 305, 306,
307, 311, 313
Blum, William 43, 44
Bochco, Steven 253
Bohlen, Chip 24
Bohr, Niels 59

Bolton, John R. 104, 420
Bonaparte, Napoleon 228
Boxer, Barbara 294
Boyle, Prof. Francis 282, 283
Bradley, General Omar N. 140, 247
Brainwashing xviii, 49, 53, 83, 171,
174, 187, 189, 193, 199, 200, 201,
205, 213, 214, 236, 244, 253, 302,
303
Branfman, Fred 278
Brookes, Francis 264
Brown, Anthony Cave xxiii
Brown, Walter 31
Browne, Leonard 190
Bruce, David 24
Bruce, Paul 131
Bruckheimer, Jerry 251
Brzezinski, Zbigniew 54, 94, 309
Burba, Elisabetta 265
Burgess, Guy 270
Bush Doctrine, the 73, 97
Bush, George H.W. 70, 146, 274
Bush, George W. ix, xii, xiii, 7, 8, 11,
17, 20, 29, 35, 41, 47, 62, 69, 71,
72, 73, 74, 89, 95, 96, 97, 98, 99,
101, 103, 104, 108, 111, 117, 121,
122, 127, 128, 130, 146, 150, 151,
152, 153, 160, 165, 182, 218, 230,
233, 234, 239, 240, 241, 243, 244,
250, 255, 257, 258, 261, 262, 263,
264, 265, 266, 267, 268, 272, 274,
275, 277, 278, 280, 282, 285, 293,
297, 303, 307, 310, 311, 313, 314,
421, 424, 498
Butler, Eric 15
Butler, Major General Smedley 4, 8
Byrnes, James 31
Caldicott, Dr. Helen 88
Cameron, Dr. Ewen 213
Central Intelligence Agency (CIA)
xiv, 30, 44, 92, 107, 108, 116, 122,
128, 140, 141, 142, 143, 149, 165,
166, 171, 173, 174, 181, 184, 187,
188, 197, 204, 209, 210, 211, 212,
213, 214, 215, 242, 244, 250, 253,
261, 265, 266, 268, 269, 272, 273,
274
Chalabi, Ahmed 115, 264
Challis, Roland 272
Chamberlain, Neville 37
Chávez, Hugo Rafael (Frías) 105,
300
Cheney, Richard Bruce (Dick) 8, 21,
70, 108, 146, 241, 242, 243, 250,
262, 263, 265, 266, 282, 292, 297,
299, 313, 425
Chin, Larry 300
Chossudovsky, Prof. Michel 90, 142
Christianity 62, 63, 310, 311
Churchill, Sir Winston xxi, xxiii, 34,
37, 38, 39, 40, 42, 73, 278, 296,
406
Clark, Ramsay 24, 279
Clarridge, Dewey 264
Clausevitz, Karl von 3, 228
Clifford, Clark 24
Clinton, William (Bill) J. 68, 146,
197, 198, 199, 208, 261, 418
Cohen, Eliot 94, 98, 423, 427
Colbert, James 67
Cold War, the (or World War III or
Third World War 23, 24, 28, 29,
31, 32, 33, 34, 35, 37, 38, 39, 40,
41, 42, 44, 45, 46, 47, 56, 61, 62,
64, 65, 66, 67, 68, 69, 73, 92, 93,
95, 97, 112, 130, 131, 167, 198,
224, 225, 234, 243, 269, 279, 280,
297, 300, 354, 374, 376, 379, 382,
383, 391, 394, 395, 396, 404, 405,
406, 418, 433, 474
Combatant Commanders 85, 219,
295, 476, 477, 478, 487, 490
Cook, Robin 141
Crichton-Miller, Hugh 189
Daly, Prof. Robert 204
de Kock, Colonel Eugene 133
de Saxe, Marechal 236
Dearlove, Sir Richard 286
Declaration of Independence xvi, 22,
350, 410
Defense Policy Guidance 70, 73

Defense Intelligence Agency (DIA) 227

Defense Planning Guidance 66

Delgado, Dr. Jose 195

Department of Defense (DoD) 10, 56, 82, 166, 177, 196, 205, 251, 264, 458, 460, 496

Deterding, Sir Henry 16

Di Rita, Lawrence 304

Dicks, Henry 189, 191

Dien Bien Phu 43

Domino Theory, the 12, 43

Dulles, John Foster 12

Einstein, Albert 275

Eisenhower, Dwight 31, 43, 56, 60, 181, 237, 273

Elbaradei, Mohammed 102, 268

Ellul, Jacques 229, 231, 232, 238, 249

Empire Capitalism 3, 186, 309

Engdahl, William 20, 125

Engelhardt, Tom 11

Estabrooks, Dr. G.H. 214

Estes, General Howell M. III 87

Fairbank, Charles, Jr. 67

Fastaband, Brig-Gen David 244

Federal Reserve System xix, 17

Feith, Douglas 67, 219, 220, 229, 234, 264

Ferguson, Bobbie Faye 253

Ferguson, Neill xix, 311

Fiers, Alan D. 274

First Gulf War 11, 67, 90, 279

FitzGerald, Desmond 24

Force Research Unit, the (FRU) 133, 166, 167

Ford, Gerald 108

Ford, Henry 14

Forrestal, Jim 24

Franklin, Larry 220, 264

Franks, General Tommy 146

Frederick the Great 217

Friedman, Thomas xx, 83, 84, 249, 255, 278, 290

Frum, David 1, 22, 64, 115

Full Spectrum Dominance 75, 85, 144, 289, 429, 442, 444, 447, 451, 452, 453, 454, 457, 466, 469, 470, 480

Fulton, Kevin 132, 133

Future Combat Systems (FCS) 6, 56, 57

Gaddis, John Lewis 24, 73, 74

Galbraith, Prof. James K. 14, 47, 48

Gandhi, Mohandas Karamchand, Mahatma 93, 275

Garcia, General Lucas 144

Gardiner, Col. (Rtd.) Sam 249

Gareau, Frederick 126

General Dynamics 6, 7

Geneva Conventions 127, 150, 152, 160, 164, 183, 242, 280, 281, 283, 285, 299

Gentile, Douglas 254

George, Clair 274

George, David Lloyd 268, 307, 415

Georgi, Major David 251

Gettys, Maj. Gen. Charles 147

Ghosh, Jayati 309

Gilchrist, Sir Andrew 269, 271

Gilligan, Andrew 233, 249

Glen, John 185

Glen, Tom 147

Goebbels, Joseph 229, 230, 234, 238, 242, 243, 268

Goering, Herman 77, 247, 286

Gonzales, Alberto 150, 151, 160, 161, 262

Gottlieb, Sidney 212

Graham, Katherine 24

Greenblatt, Milton 212

Greenspan, Alan 18, 19

Griffith, Brig-Gen S.B. II 217

Guantanamo Bay 29, 127, 150, 165, 169, 200, 242, 299

Gubbins, Collin 269

Gurion, David Ben 141

Hadley, Stephen 262, 264, 308

Halevi, Efraim 308

Halliburton 7, 8, 17, 20, 256

Halliday, Denis 282

Hargreaves, Ronald 190, 191

Harries, Richard (Bishop of Oxford) 313

Harriman, Dr. P.L. 214

Hay, Prof. William Anthony 311

Healey, Lord 271

Helms, Richard 204, 212

Hillenkoetter, Roscoe 209

Hiroshima 24, 27, 31, 35, 37, 282, 296, 297

Hitler, Adolf xv, xxii, xxiii, xxiv, 15, 16, 33, 34, 37, 38, 153, 157, 243, 286, 296, 304, 329, 341, 416

Hobsbawn, Eric J. 279, 309

Hoffmann, Albert 211

Holbrook, Richard 23

Hoon, Geoff 286

Hopkins, Harry 37

Human Rights Watch, the (HRW) 164

Hunter, Duncan 11

Hunter, Edward 174

Hurricane Katrina 47, 182, 303, 304

Hurricane Rita 182

Hussein, Saddam 27, 67, 68, 72, 75, 93, 119, 123, 146, 220, 230, 232, 233, 234, 241, 250, 255, 262, 263, 264, 267, 286, 294, 418, 419, 422, 426

Huxley, Aldous 187, 188, 189

Huxley, Thomas 188

Information Research Department (IRD) 269, 270, 271, 272

International Atomic Energy Agency (IAEA) 102, 103, 109, 113, 265, 268

Iran Freedom Support Act 116

Iran Policy Committee (IPC) 115, 116, 117, 120, 121, 122

Iraq Liberation Act 68, 116

Iron Curtain 34, 37, 42, 47, 73, 353, 358, 360, 382, 406, 413, 414

Islam 28, 35, 62, 63, 64, 65, 94, 97, 98, 125, 137, 173, 243, 261, 297, 311, 312

James, Lawrence 230

Jenkins, Roy 206

Johnson, Chalmers 10

Johnson, Louis 26

Johnson, Lyndon B. 25, 146, 269

Jones, Alex 303

Judaism xxii, 64

Kagan, Donald 74, 423, 427

Kagan, Robert 35, 420, 423, 427

Kandel, Eric 194

Keith, Sir Arthur 157

Kellen, Konrad 231

Kelly, Dr. David 250

Kennan, George 1, 22, 23, 24, 37, 40, 61, 69, 317, 331, 332

Kennedy, Edward 250

Kennedy, John F. 25, 33, 252, 254, 272, 315

Kerr, Brig. Gen. Gordon 166, 167

Kerry, John 280

Kessler, Charles 36

Key, Ellen 126

Khrushchev, Nikita (Sergeevich) 33

Kilde, Dr. Rauni-Leena 175, 184, 185

King, Dr. Martin Luther, Jr. 79, 247, 288

King George III xvi, xvii

King, Stephen 208

Kissinger, Henry Alfred 108, 109, 125, 146

Kitson, General Frank 130, 133, 206

Koestler, Arthur 140, 158, 237

Korean War 9, 25, 36, 174, 200

Kristol, William 22, 35, 68, 420, 423, 427

Kuznick, Peter 31

Kyle, Jon 94

La Botz, Dan 47

La Follette, Robert M. 94

La Rocque, Admiral Gene 4
Laden, Osama bin 61, 130, 141, 142, 421, 422, 425
Larkin, F.H. 204
Leahy, William 31
Leary, Timothy 188, 189
Ledeen, Michael 45, 229, 240, 264, 291
LeMay, General Curtis E. 252
LeShan, Lawrence 236, 237
Levin, Carl 126
Lewinsky, Monica 261
Libby, Lewis "Scooter" 262, 265, 266, 299
Lieberman, Joseph 94
Lifton, Robert Jay 174, 202
Linder, Doug 145
Lobel, Jules 285
Lockhart, Robert Bruce 269
Lockheed-Martin 6, 21, 256
Loewenberg, Robert 67
London Controlling Section (LCS) xxiii
Looney, Brig. Gen. William 288, 294
Luff, Mary 191
Lugar, Richard G. 293
Lungu, Major Angela Maria 228
MacArthur, General Douglas 31
Mackay, Neil 132, 166
Macmillan, Harold 272, 273
Madison, James 94
Magee, John Joe 133
Majors, John 146
Malaysia 71, 98, 102, 123, 129, 138, 139, 145, 151, 273, 299, 300
Manhattan Project 5, 31, 207
Manning, Robert 33
Mao Zedong (or Mao Tse Tung) xviii, 25, 217
Marr, Andrew 250
Marshall Plan 22, 270
Martino, Antonio 264
Martino, Rocco 265

Mayer, Arno J. 61
Mayhew, Christopher 269, 270
McDonalds xx, xxi, 256, 278, 290
McDonnell Douglas xx, xxi, 83, 278, 290
McFarlane, Robert 274
McKinley, William 277, 290, 292
McNamara, Robert 25, 97, 146, 279
Mead, Dame Margaret 188
Megadeath Intellectuals 56, 61, 62, 63, 65, 66, 68, 69, 71, 73, 75, 79, 82, 83, 91, 98, 100, 142, 143, 149, 150, 160, 168, 171, 218
Mendelssohn, Rabbi Felix xxii, 64
Meyers, General Richard B. 89
MI6 (British Intelligence) xiv, 128, 142, 143, 233, 234, 272, 273, 286
Militant Christianity 62
Militant Islam xxi, 1, 27, 62, 64, 65, 69, 71, 72, 74, 75, 96, 243
Military State Capitalism 45, 46, 54
Miller, Judith 257, 258
Milosevic, Slobodan 146
Mind Control xviii, 175, 176, 177, 178, 179, 184, 187, 189, 190, 191, 194, 197, 198, 199, 200, 202, 203, 204, 205, 206, 207,
Mind Control (cont'd) 208, 209, 211, 212, 213, 217
Mind Controllers 179, 188, 189, 195, 197, 199, 207
Monsivais, Carlos 309
Montt, General Rios 144
Moore, James 267
Moret, Leuren 59, 90
Morgan, David R. 31
Mossad (Israeli Intelligence) xiv, 128, 142, 143, 308
Muggeridge, Malcolm xv
Mujahideen-e Khalq (MEK) 116, 117, 118, 122
Murdoch, Rupert 255, 307
Murtopo, Ali 272
Musharraf, Pervez 98
My Lai Massacres 29, 43, 127, 145

Nagasaki 24, 27, 31, 35, 37, 282, 296, 297

Nagin, Ray 47

Nanotechnology 56, 195

National Counterintelligence Executive 504, 510

National Counterintelligence Strategy 510

National Counterterrorism Center 502, 504

National Defense Authorization Act 225

National Security State, the 45, 47, 48, 49, 54, 57, 65, 86, 87

National Security Strategy (NSS) 27, 69, 73, 74, 104, 228, 450, 473, 498, 500, 509

National Space Policy 89

Nayar, Jayan 259

Negroponte, John D. 300, 301, 497, 499

Netanyahu, Benjamin 119, 229

Niemoeller, Pastor Martin 276

Nitze, Paul Henry 22, 23, 24, 25, 26, 35, 40, 61

Nixon, Richard 12, 20, 116, 146

Nonaligned Movement (NAM) 102, 113, 123, 233

Nordhaus, William 9

Norman, Montagu 15, 16

North, Oliver 274

Northrop-Grumman 6, 7, 21

Novak, Robert 266

Nuclear Defense Agency 90

Nuclear Fuel Cycle 108, 111

Nuclear Non-Proliferation Treaty (NPT) 90, 102, 105, 107, 109, 110, 111, 112, 113, 120, 123, 312

Nuremberg Charter 257, 260, 283

Nuremberg Judgment 283

Nuremberg Principles 275, 283, 298

Nuremberg War Crimes Tribunal xxii, xxiii, 77, 153, 230, 260, 298

Nye, Joseph S. 311, 312

Obama, Barack 294

Odom, Lt. Gen. William 294

Offner, Arnold A. 37

Ollivant, Simon 270

Operation Desert Fox 69

Operation Desert Shield 197

Operation Phoenix 43, 190

Operation Vulture 43

Organization of Islamic Conference (OIC) 102, 105, 113, 123

Orwell, George 45, 315

Pain Merchants 148, 149, 152, 165, 168, 170

Pan-Arabism 67

Paper Money 14, 15, 17, 18, 19, 20, 21, 124, 153, 154

Paterson, William 15

Paul, Dr. Ron 18, 19

Pax Americana 10, 70

Peace Dividend 65

Pearl Harbor 58, 71, 73, 95, 236, 493

Pearson, Simon 95, 98

Pentagon, the 10, 11, 21, 56, 71, 138, 150, 152, 174, 220, 234, 240, 251, 252, 253, 290, 291, 297

Perle, Richard 1, 22, 64, 65, 67, 75, 115, 119, 220, 243, 420, 423, 427

Peters, Major Ralph 79, 80, 81, 82, 83, 84, 93, 94, 98, 315

Peterson, Evan Augustine III 10

Pfaff, William 240

Philips, Prof. Peter 255, 257

Pilger, John 269

Pinochet, General Augusto 206

Plame, Valerie 261, 266

Plumby, Sir Derek 233

Podhoretz, Norman 22, 94, 96, 97, 98, 423, 427

Poindexter, John M. 274

Pollard, Jonathan 264

Pope John Paul II 313

Posse Comitatus Act, the 182, 303, 304

Powell, Colin 96, 103, 120, 147, 262, 265, 282, 284, 286, 421, 422, 425

Powers, Thomas 172

Pre-emption 73, 74, 97, 298

Project for a New American Century (PNAC) 68, 72, 109, 115, 116, 119, 418, 421, 424

Propaganda Warfare xvi, xviii, 62, 81, 143, 220, 230, 232, 259

Prophet Muhammad 62

Province Interrogation Centre (PIC) 148, 149

Psychological Operations (PSYOPS) 134, 173, 217, 218, 219, 220, 221, 222, 223, 224, 225, 226, 227, 228, 234, 240, 462, 466, 485, 486, 489, 494

Qur'an, the Holy 63

Raskin, Marcus 56

Ratner, Michael 285

Rawlings-Reese, John 189, 190

Raytheon 6, 7, 21

Reagan, Ronald 12, 25, 129, 146, 294, 303

Reddaway, Norman 270, 271, 272

Regan, Donald 129

Reserve Currency 20, 21, 124

Rhodes, Cecil 276, 278, 290, 292

Rhodes, Harold 264

Rice, Condoleezza 27, 54, 109, 118, 155, 262, 263, 282, 293, 294

Ries, Al 3

Ritter, Scott 121, 233

Robb, David L. 251, 252

Roberts, Pat 267

Roberts, Paul Craig 129, 130, 303, 304

Rockefeller, Jay 267

Rockefeller, John D. 197

Rockefeller Report, the 196, 197

Roosevelt, Franklin Delano xxii, 34, 37, 38, 73

Ros-Lehtinen, Ileana 116

Ross, Collin A. 213

Ross, Dennis 66

Rossellia, Carlo 265

Rostow, Eugene 24

Rothbard, Murray 55

Rove, Karl 229, 262, 266

Rumsfeld, Donald 20, 57, 72, 146, 152, 219, 281, 282, 283, 290, 292, 420, 425

Russell, Lord Bertrand 192, 194, 195, 206, 231, 232

Russian Revolution, the 39

Rutz, Carol 215

Saladin 63

Sambrook, Richard 249

Sanchez, General Ricardo 146

Sanders, Dr. Carl 185

Sanford, Victoria 144

Schultz, George 7

Scowcroft, Brent 261

Selden, Mark 31

Shalikashvili, John M. 84

Shamir, Yitzhak 141

Sharon, Ariel 98, 119, 141, 229

Shawcross, Sir Hartle xxii

Shelton, General Henry H. 85

Sherman, General W. 98

"Shock and Awe" Campaign 41, 96, 115, 282, 283, 311

Singapore xxi, 269, 270, 271, 272

Singer, Dr. Margaret 199

Smith, Ian 133

Snowe, Olympia 10

St. Clair, Jeffrey 170

Stalin, Joseph xxi, 23, 34, 37, 38, 39, 46, 296, 318, 322, 329, 334, 336, 339, 344, 345, 352, 361, 412

State Terrorism 126, 127, 129, 131, 141, 282

Stebbins, John 251

Steinitz, Yuval 122

Stevenson, Adlai 237

Strategic Defense Initiative (SDI) 90

Straw, Jack 286

Strub, Phil 253

Suharto, General 268, 269, 271, 272
Sukarno 268, 271, 272
Sun Tzu 93, 228
Sutherland, Jock 191
Sweet, Dr. William 208
Symington, Stuart 25
Syria Accountability Act 116
Taguba, Major Gen. Antonio 162
Talbot, Strobe 35
Taliban, the 75, 97, 128, 130, 152, 160, 422
Teller, Edward 59
Terrorism xix, 1, 58, 68, 71, 72, 74, 75, 96, 106, 119, 126, 127, 128, 130, 131, 137, 141, 144, 171, 249, 254, 261, 275, 282, 293, 298, 304, 305, 421, 422, 423, 424, 425, 426, 427, 457, 502, 506
Terrorism Prevention Act 498, 508, 509
Thatcher, Margaret 132, 146, 206
Thich Nhat Hanh 101
Thompson, Robert 148, 149
Tiger Force 43, 148
Tilford, Dr. Earl 95, 98
Tornberg, Dr. David 159
Torture Convention 152, 160
Toynbee, Arnold 188, 309
Trist, Eric 191
Troop, Jonathan 67
Trout, Jack 3
Truman Doctrine 22, 39
Truman, Harry S. 26, 31, 38, 43, 69, 296
Twain, Mark 92, 277, 298, 315
UN Charter 282, 285, 390, 392, 412, 414, 417
UN Security Council 66, 109, 110, 113, 120, 123, 242, 268, 269, 282, 283, 284, 285, 286, 388, 419
United Nations (UN) 9, 12, 94, 103, 105, 106, 286, 366, 388, 390, 392, 405, 408, 412, 414, 416, 417

US War Crimes Act 152, 280, 282
Vandenberg, General Hoyt S. 25
Vietnam War 4, 12, 36, 97, 175, 185, 189, 278, 279
War Constitution 22, 61, 68, 73, 75
War on Islam 28
War on Terrorism xxi, 27, 28, 35, 36, 47, 55, 56, 58, 61, 62, 65, 71, 72, 74, 75, 95, 137, 141, 150, 151, 152, 164, 173, 189, 260, 275, 293, 422, 423, 424, 426
Warner, John 304
Washington, George xvi
Watson, Steve 303
Watt, Lt. General James 77
Watts, Allan 188, 189
Weil, Simone xiii, 84
Weizmann, Chaim xxii, 64
Westmoreland, General William C. 146
Whitley, Gary L. 228
Whitney, Mike 298
Wiener, Norbert 184
Wildhaber, Judge Luzius 305
Wilkerson, Lawrence B. 292, 293
Williams, William Appleman 39
Wilmhurst, Elizabeth 305
Wilson, Joseph 242, 250, 261, 265, 266
Wilson, Sloan 236
Wilson, Tommy 190, 191
Wilson, Woodrow 17, 277, 290, 292
Winn, Denise 174
Wisner, Frank 24
Wolfgang 307
Wolfowitz, Paul 20, 35, 57, 59, 65, 67, 73, 80, 94, 108, 123, 220, 232, 282, 420
Woo, John 252
Woolsey, James R. 92, 93, 94, 98, 107, 420, 427
World Bank, the 123
World Jewish Congress xxii, 64

World Trade Organization (WTO)
277, 288
World War I (or First World War) 17,
36, 73, 92, 155, 188, 189, 230,
251, 268, 280, 409
World War II (or Second World War)
xvi, xxii, 9, 23, 25, 26, 31, 33, 36,
37, 38, 40, 42, 43, 62, 64, 73, 75,
97, 153, 183, 184, 188, 190, 207,
211, 225, 230, 231, 237, 242, 243,
251, 252, 254, 269, 273, 275, 278,
287, 298
World War IV (or Fourth World War,
the) 61, 68, 92, 94, 95, 96, 97,
98, 218, 275
Wurmser, David 67
Wurmser, Meyrav 67
Wylie, Philip 236
Yalta Conference 37, 38, 39, 415
Yamani, Sheikh Zaki 125
Yinon, Oded 119
Zapatero, Jose Luis 137
Zhukov, Georgi Konstantinovich 296

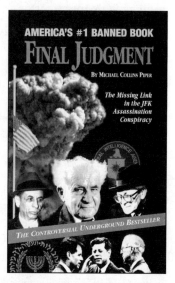

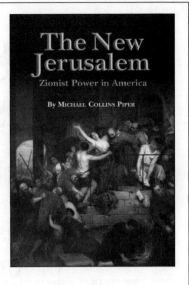

The High Priests of War

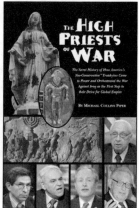

The Secret History of America's Neo-Cons

THE HIGH PRIESTS OF WAR: The Secret History of How America's Neo-Conservative Trotskyites Came to Power and How They Orhestrated the War Against Iraq as the First Step in Their Drive for Global Power—The secret history of how America's "neo-conservative" Trotskyites came to power and orchestrated the war against Iraq as the first step in their drive for Global Empire, the so-called New World Order. This is the only full-length book on the "neo-cons" that tells the entire story—no holds-barred. The book is now being circulated internationally and is being translated into a variety of languages, acclaimed as the one book that explains the "who, what, when, where, why and how" of the tragic involvement of the United States in the Iraq war. This fast-reading, carefully-documented 144-page volume has helped spread the word about the REAL reason for the Iraq war and how it is all part of a grand design that is being suppressed by the Controlled Media.

Softcover, 144 pages, $19.95. No S&H.

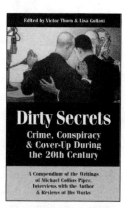

The Judas Goats:
The Enemy Within

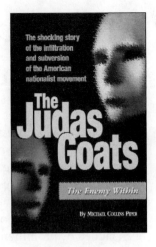

The shocking story of the infiltration and subversion of the American nationalist movement

The Judas Goats

The Enemy Within

By MICHAEL COLLINS PIPER

The Shocking Story of the Infiltration and Subversion of the American Nationalist Movement

THIS 376-PAGE MASTERWORK from the pen of international lecturer, journalist and radio talk show host Michael Collins Piper is more than a cut-and-dried timeline. This is the inside story—never-before-told—of the personalities, motivations and devious plots used to infiltrate and destroy the American Nationalist and Patriot movements in America. From the spy inside the Vatican to FDR's Mass Sedition Trial to Newt Gingrich, The John Birch Society, the operators of COINTELPRO, J. Edgar Hoover, Roy Bullock, the Anti-Defamation League, KGB and Joseph McCarthy, see who the "Judas Goats" were, how they operated and how they failed—or succeeded—in destroying some of the finest men and patriotic institutions America has ever produced. Uniquely designed from cover to cover by the multi-talented author himself, this book is loaded with illustrations, rare photos and a complete subject index. You won't be able to put this book down—44 fast-paced chapters take you on a world tour of some of the best—and least—known "Judas Goats" who have managed to infiltrate and sabotage patriot organizations from within.

Softcover, 376 pages, $25. No S&H.

American Free Press
Special Subscription Deal

There is no other paper in America like *American Free Press* (AFP). Every week the hard-driving journalists at American Free Press dig for the truth,—no matter where the facts may lead. AFP's reporting has been lauded by prominent personalities across the globe, while here at home the controlled media and global power elite try their best to make you believe what you are getting in mainstream publications

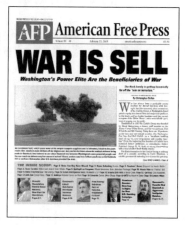

and on the nightly news is "the whole truth." Nothing could be further from the truth!

From the unanswered questions about 9-11, the free trade fiasco, the happenings in our corrupt Congress, uncontrolled immigration, alternative health news and more, AFP tackles the toughest issues of the day with a no-holds-barred reporting style that has earned us a host of devoted followers—and powerful enemies.

Isn't it time you started getting a fresh, honest approach to the news that can make or break the future of you and your family?

You'll find all that in AFP plus lots more. AFP is guaranteed to provide all the "sizzle" we promise or we will refund the unused portion of your subscription—no questions asked!

Special "FREE BOOKS" Offer!

Get a FREE copy of Michael Collins Piper's *The High Priests of War: The Secret History of the Neo-Cons* ($19.95 retail) when you subscribe to AFP for ONE year (52 yearly issues). Get TWO FREE BOOKS— *The High Priests of War* PLUS *The New Jerusalem: Zionist Power in America*—when you subscribe to AFP for TWO years 104 issues) for $99. Send payment to AFP, 645 Pennsylvania Avenue SE, Suite 100, Washington, D.C. 20003 using the coupon in the back.

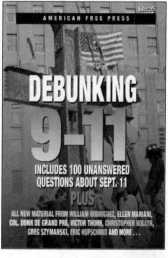

AMERICAN FREE PRESS ORDERING COUPON

Item#	Description/Title	Qty	Cost Ea.	Total
			SUBTOTAL	
Add S&H: No S&H inside U.S. Outside U.S. add $3 per book				
Send a 1-year subscription to AFP for $59 plus 1 free book*				
Send a 2-year subscription to AFP for $99 plus 2 free books**				
			TOTAL	

*NOTE ABOUT FREE BOOKS: For a one-year subscription to *American Free Press* newspaper ($59), we'll send you one free copy of Michael Collins Piper's *The High Priests of War*. For a two-year subscription we'll send you *The High Priests of War* PLUS *The New Jerusalem: Zionist Power in America*—almost $40 in free books!

PAYMENT OPTIONS: ❏ CHECKMO   ❏ VISA   ❏ MASTERCARD

Card # _____

Expiration Date _____ Signature _____

BFW106

CUSTOMER INFORMATION:

NAME _____

ADDRESS _____

CIty/STATE/ZIP _____

RETURN WITH PAYMENT TO: AMERICAN FREE PRESS, 645 Pennsylvania Avenue SE, Suite 100, Washington, D.C. 20003. Call 1-888-699-NEWS (6397) toll free to charge a subscription or books to Visa or MasterCard.

AMERICAN FREE PRESS ORDERING COUPON

Item#	Description/Title	Qty	Cost Ea.	Total
	SUBTOTAL			
Add S&H: No S&H inside U.S. Outside U.S. add $3 per book				
Send a 1-year subscription to AFP for $59 plus 1 free book*				
Send a 2-year subscription to AFP for $99 plus 2 free books**				
	TOTAL			

*NOTE ABOUT FREE BOOKS: For a one-year subscription to *American Free Press* newspaper ($59), we'll send you one free copy of Michael Collins Piper's *The High Priests of War*. For a two-year subscription we'll send you *The High Priests of War* PLUS *The New Jerusalem: Zionist Power in America*—almost $40 in free books!

PAYMENT OPTIONS: ❏ CHECKMO ❏ VISA ❏ MASTERCARD

Card # _____

Expiration Date _____ Signature _____

BFW106

CUSTOMER INFORMATION:

NAME _____

ADDRESS _____

CIty/STATE/ZIP _____

RETURN WITH PAYMENT TO: AMERICAN FREE PRESS, 645 Pennsylvania Avenue SE, Suite 100, Washington, D.C. 20003. Call 1-888-699-NEWS (6397) toll free to charge a subscription or books to Visa or MasterCard.